A HISTORY
OF
AMERICAN EDUCATION

THE MACMILLAN COMPANY
NEW YORK • CHICAGO
DALLAS • ATLANTA • SAN FRANCISCO
LONDON • MANILA

THE MACMILLAN COMPANY
OF CANADA, LIMITED
TORONTO

A HISTORY
OF
AMERICAN
EDUCATION

H. G. Good
THE OHIO STATE UNIVERSITY

The Macmillan Company, *New York*

Library of Congress catalog card number: 56–7303

PREFACE

THE RECENT rather than the remote past, the problems facing us rather than those which have been solved, will receive the greater share of attention in this book. We shall deal at greater length with the past fifty years than with the preceding fifty, with the past century than with the two earlier ones. This distribution of our attention over the three centuries of American educational history is not to be ascribed to the greater number of pupils taught and dollars spent in later times or to the greater mass of documents available to the historian. It is due to the direct bearing of recent trends and present conditions upon future action. The book is to be useful to teachers and citizens.

Anyone who takes a stand at any epoch in history can see a new education growing out of the past. Examples can be given. Public education grew out of private; the high school is the descendant of the academy and the elementary school; the American kindergarten evolved from the German kindergarten; and general education is a modified form of liberal education. This book teaches that progress comes from the wise and skilful use of what we have. It implies that we should heed the admonition of Francis Bacon whose words, slightly edited, were these: "Ask Counsel of both Times: of the Ancient Time, what of it is worth keeping, and of the Latter Time, what is fittest for the new day; but seek as well to create Good Precedents as to follow them."

America has created many good educational precedents. She has opened or will open schools of all levels to all the people of every color and condition and both sexes. She has been a pioneer in the education of women. It is one phase of that vast program to offer to each one the kind of education that he wants rather than to impose upon him what others think he should have.

American education has been brought down from the clouds to deal with the needs of the office, farm, mart, shop, and home, where people work and live. This is a good precedent. But the problems of philosophy, government, and pure science are not therefore to be less studied. The education of the many in the practical affairs of life is no substitute for the cultivation

v

of high genius for mathematics, physics, chemistry; and it is also dangerous to neglect the humanities—for what shall it profit a man to save his life and lose his sense of values?

If the constant recurrence of the words "America" and "American" should displease friendly neighbors, the author can only plead that he has been unable to make a pronounceable adjective from the noun "United States." And then, from Canada and Mexico to Chile and Brazil, the other American nations all have distinctive names with well-sounding adjectives.

The author is grateful for help received. Professors Roscoe H. Eckelberry, Everett Kircher, and Robert Sutton, all of the faculty of The Ohio State University, and Gerald Read of Kent State University read portions of the manuscript and their advice has been of great value. The entire work has been substantially improved by the detailed criticism supplied by Professor William W. Brickman of New York University. My wife, Maude W. Good, has been my constant and indispensable adviser.

Columbus, Ohio   H. G. GOOD

CONTENTS

PART I

Introduction

A SHORT HISTORY

EDUCATION in America has an English heritage that reaches across the three and one-half centuries between the first and the second Elizabeth. Originally an extension of the education of England and Europe, it soon began to acquire characteristics suited to its new home and people. When in the course of human events the thirteen colonies banded themselves together to form a new nation, American education also became independent.

To prevent the history of the following chapters from being lost in the events and to indicate what the whole "adds up to" are the purposes of this preliminary interpretation.

1. EDUCATION AND HISTORY

Family and church provided education in early times, but a tendency which set in more than a century ago in America, and earlier in Europe, has now placed the major phases and most schools under the care of local, state, and national governments. This threefold division in control is not peculiar to the United States. Many private and church schools remain, but their pupils are only a fraction of the whole number.

The history of education is a phase not only of national history but also of the history of mankind and particularly of the history of culture and civilization. "Above all nations," said Goldwin Smith, "is humanity." The arts, sciences, and spiritual possessions which are taught in schools are just what distinguishes civilized life from barbarism. They are the supranational possessions of mankind. Civilization and nationalism are today the impelling motives of education. The question may be raised whether conflict between them can be avoided and how this may be done.

History has two meanings. It may mean the course of events, as when we say that Russia has had a turbulent, or modern Switzerland a tranquil, history; or it may mean the record of the events in a work such as the

3

History of the United States from the Compromise of 1850 by James Ford Rhodes. It will be useful to give brief consideration to the nature of written history.

History in this sense is the record of human experience. It is an account of actions and occurrences and their meanings. Often it is easy to tell what meanings an author sees in his narrative, even though he does not state them. We may be sure that it had a meaning for him. To assume otherwise is to suppose that he was merely exercising his typewriter.

Even the selection of an item to go into the record shows that the recorder considered it somehow memorable and significant. There are no bare facts. We always bring a "mental set" to the materials of history. This makes it impossible to get behind or under actions and occurrences in order to see them as they would be "in themselves." The point of this is that the student of history must come to the record with a critical mind and the determination to evaluate the implicit as well as the expressed opinions of his author.

2. HISTORICAL PERIODS

Not only the selection but also the grouping of historical actions and occurrences is a method of indicating their meaning. Dividing the record into periods is not mainly a typographical device. It is a means of indicating the turning points in the development of a nation, a policy, or a school system. From the first pages of this chapter it will be apparent that the history of American education, as it will be told in the present book, must be divided into two main periods, the colonial and the national.

By adopting the Constitution of 1787, the people established a federal republic and a government of limited powers not including any power over education. For fifty years the states left education to private corporations and local civil units. But this policy was reversed and they have now created state education departments with extensive powers and large funds. Federal aid to education has likewise increased from the original grants of wild land to large annual sums assigned to the states, to veterans, and to universities for research and other purposes. The Supreme Court, the Office of Education, and a number of national schools and research institutions have influence upon education in the states. The state systems are unequally developed but have a family resemblance that is increasing. Every citizen of a state is also a citizen of the United States and may cross state boundaries at will. There is no distinct national school system but instead a composite system made up of local, state, and national components. No merely legalistic treatment could do justice to this combination.

We choose the year 1787 to separate the history of American education into its main periods. For reasons other than those indicated above we should choose another year, perhaps 1865, or 1890. Certainly the educational transformations of the last ninety years have been greater than everything that occurred in the whole of colonial and early national times. But the foundations for these great changes were laid by the Constitution and the federal republic of equal states. The subdivisions of the main periods are shown in the following tabular view.

TABULAR VIEW OF HISTORICAL PERIODS

	1607–1725	TRANSPLANTATION AND DECLINE
The Colonial Period 1607–1787	1725–1787	ADVANCED SCHOOLS AND COLLEGES Rise of urban practical schools and of colleges to serve different classes of people. Low condition of rural schools.
	1787–1837	THE ACADEMY MOVEMENT Adoption of the Constitution; American textbooks; national theory of education; plans for state systems, for normal schools, academy movement.
	1837–1860	THE EDUCATIONAL AWAKENING State systems; rise of school administration; public education propaganda; books and magazines for teachers.
The National Period 1787–	1860–1890	THE NEW EDUCATION Land-grant colleges; introduction of kindergarten, new methods, nature study; specialization of teacher education; new beginning of public education in the South; spread of high school; advance in higher education.
	1890–	SCIENCE AND DEMOCRACY National aid to vocational education; compulsory attendance; Dewey's educational theory and Progressive education; educational research; propaganda; efforts to renew public interest and support.

3. BEGINNINGS

The educational destitution of the colonies was due to inherited tradition and the hard conditions of life in a new country. The class organization of society which had come down from the Middle Ages was introduced into a wilderness. The highest ranks were missing, for dukes do not emigrate; but there were many poor, even some redemptioners and slaves. There were real class distinctions that resisted the leveling influences of the frontier for two centuries but succumbed in many cases to the forces released by the Revolution.

Education was a privilege except for orphan and pauper children who were apprenticed and compelled to acquire a trade; and sometimes the three R's were included. The rudimentary elementary schools were for the common people, although girls attended very little. Latin schools and colleges formed a separate scholastic world.

Children were put to work as soon as infancy was past and their daily labors often extended into the evenings. Homes provided little opportunity for comfortable reading and study. Teachers had no education beyond what they were to impart. The level of secular culture was low. For a century there were hardly any newspapers and no regular postal service.

4. RELIGIOUS INTOLERANCE

From the time of the Reformation the English people had been schooled in intolerance of Catholicism and the fear of Catholic subversion and conquest by a Catholic power. Many of the first settlers in America could recall the chilling panic which the Spanish Armada had inspired. The wars of religion and the established churches had raised religious dissent in Europe to a semblance of treason.

The intolerance of the colonists was embodied in laws which imposed severe disabilities upon Catholics. Even in Maryland, founded as a haven for persecuted English Catholics, the Act of Toleration was soon repealed. They fared better in Rhode Island and in Pennsylvania. Great hostility to the Catholic Church and its members was shown in Massachusetts where the school law of 1647 and the schoolbooks such as the *New England Primer* were explicitly directed against the Catholic religion. Puritanism implied intolerance, and John Cotton declared that "toleration made the world anti-Christian." But in this, Puritans were not different from their adversaries.

The great danger came from the French in Canada and the Ohio-

Mississippi country. The Declaration of Independence claims that the Quebec Act threatened to use Catholic trappers, settlers, and missionaries "to bring on the inhabitants of our frontiers the merciless Indian savages." John Witherspoon, a signer of the Declaration of Independence, declared that it was this fear which united the colonies sufficiently to make the Revolutionary War possible, but this may be a somewhat extravagant view.

The war and the French alliance in 1778 changed the feeling of the people. American Catholics became patriots. The well-known Catholic cleric from Maryland, John Carroll, visiting Boston during the Revolution, was amazed to receive a friendly reception from the patriot leaders. During the latter years of the war, many French fighting men fraternized with Americans, but during the excesses of the French Revolution this love again grew cool.

The Constitutional Convention skirted the divisive religious question, but the First Amendment cut the Gordian knot. It says: "Congress shall make no law respecting an establishment of religion or prohibiting the free exercise thereof." This turned the question over to the states, and nine of these had establishments of religion at that time. When the Fourteenth Amendment came to be applied to public education the religious question was raised again in new forms.

5. RETREAT AND ADVANCE

Education did not prosper in the seventeenth century. It had declined even in eastern Massachusetts where it had enjoyed an auspicious beginning. At times Harvard was not far from extinction. Outside the towns, barbarism was increasing. On the frontier, which in the days of the Revolution was still close to the coast, there were schools only when an itinerant teacher came along to instruct children at low prices. The town schools of New England were splintered into moving and district schools.

There was some advance in the eighteenth century. Practical schools appeared in towns and prepared navigators, surveyors, and bookkeepers, some in day and some in evening schools. There were teachers of languages, ancient and modern; of mathematics, pure and applied; and of handwriting, humble and fancy. These schools offered the "new education" of those times.

Educational opportunity remained very unequal. One-third of the founding fathers had little formal education; the upper fourth had graduated from college. In a more representative group the lower section would have been larger and the proportion of the well educated much smaller.

Vocational conditions and public opinion favored the early entrance upon a lifework with a minimum of schooling, and many considered college education useless for practical men. This was Franklin's opinion. Using Locke and other writers he compiled a theory of utilitarian education which served to support the academy movement. The academies extended educational opportunity, but only to the middle class who could spare the time and pay the fees.

Without independence the separate social classes might have been more strictly maintained and the neglect of elementary schools might have continued longer. A new task also was assigned to schools, the teaching of citizenship in a federal republic. The period was notable for its theories of national education and a national school system.

The origin of government among men was ascribed to an agreement between people living in a state of nature, without law. In theory this agreement, called the social compact, was made between equals and entailed the principle that the civil institutions must preserve this equality. This excluded a nobility and all recognition of social classes in the law. Before the law all citizens were equal. They had exchanged the dangers and isolation of the state of nature and also its unlimited freedom for civil protection and civil freedom. Equal educational opportunity is necessary if all citizens in a republic are to be able to preserve their rights and to serve their country.

The social compact need not be regarded as a historical event. It may be taken as a logical account of the foundations of government. If the foundations are not well-laid and a government becomes tyrannical, the ultimate remedy according to this theory is revolution. In this way the Declaration of Independence justified the American Revolution. And it has been held that the Constitutional Convention carried through another revolution since it did not obey its commission to bring in amendments to the Articles of Confederation but instead prepared a new instrument.

The new Constitution omitted all mention of education; and this was taken to mean that public education is reserved to the states and private education to the people. But the first part of this opinion, repeated by the historians, has proved an illusion. The Supreme Court so frequently invades this supposed freedom of the states that the Court has been called "the National School Board." The designation is not wholly inappropriate, for the Court has handed down many decisions to determine what the states may do and may not do in regard to education.

As the territory of the country increased, the unity of the nation was promoted by the formation, not of colonies, but of self-governing, equal states and a federal judiciary to provide a uniform interpretation of the Constitution and the laws. Unity was also promoted in material ways by internal improvements which annihilated distance and extended communication. Among these unifying factors public education was to have an important place.

The colleges multiplied threefold within a decade after the Revolutionary War, but they remained small and conservative. Equality of educational opportunity did not at once come through the colleges. They were nearly as remote from life as ever and youth largely ignored them. Young women were barred. The young men who matriculated were subjected to textbook recitations and a schoolmaster discipline from which frequent rebellions provided some relief. There was more hope from the academy movement which grew to great proportions.

6. STATE SYSTEMS

Progress came from the bottom and moved upwards. True public education with state control and support developed most rapidly in the age of Jackson. The public schools had to overcome not only public apathy but also a varied positive opposition. They had to conquer the fears of churchmen and the wealthy, the charge of socialism, the resistance of the private school interests, the pauper taint, repugnance to the school tax, and the want of a settled plan. The two mentioned last were perhaps first in importance.

The early state superintendents had to spend themselves in overcoming public apathy and opposition. They were missionaries. The school tax was a new tax, and new taxes are the most unpopular taxes. The first opposing argument was that no one should be compelled to pay to educate another man's children; the second, that the recipients would be paupers and the schools pauper schools; and the third, that the schools should be supported in other ways, as from a state fund, or state appropriations from the general fund and by nuisance taxes, land grants, or fees.

The first public schools, like the private ones, were separate institutions, monads that neither received nor gave out any light. The individual teacher could conduct his ungraded school without regard to any other. Lancaster, who organized a form of monitorial school described in Chapter V, offered some help in organizing large schools, but most schools were small and without a settled curriculum.

State and city school administrators appeared about the same time

(1840). New York State was an early exception. At first superintendents had charge of property and finances, but they soon acquired some control over teachers and education—from every standpoint a significant development. The coming of the administrator indicates that the need for unity and system had become evident. The systems, as they evolved, promised to everyone an opportunity equal to that of others to develop those talents with which nature had endowed him and thereby to make real the political equality which was recognized by the law and which formed the essential character of a republic. These are the wise and generous words of Condorcet.

School systems were firmly established but not fully developed in the Northern states before the Civil War. In most Southern states they existed only on paper, if at all. In that section the planters had a firm hold upon political action; there was a lack of industries, markets, and occupations that required schooling, while the cities drew off those seeking an education. The private schools, church colleges, and conservative economic and religious orientation of the upper classes were not favorable to an education that would have "made real the political equality recognized by the law" of a republic. After reconstruction the South became converted to the public school idea.

There is a certain logic inherent in the evolution of public school systems. The early steps were not wholly due to local circumstances or to chance. State systems were based upon constitutional and legislative provisions, and the early ones were often of a general and even permissive kind. The creation of local school districts, often coterminous with existing civil units such as the township, was an early step. A board with limited powers, especially in regard to finances, was created. The earliest means of support did not depend mainly upon a school tax. Tax laws or rate bills were used to supplement other financial measures; and when the school tax became a major charge, the law placed limitations on the rate, as if the people were likely to pauperize themselves. Tax limitation was a contrivance of real estate and other financial interests. It was not intended to improve schools.

Easy qualifications for teachers, moral and literary at first, were set up. Professional requirements were added later and led to the establishment of normal schools. Curriculum legislation began with the three R's, but in time it was carried to extreme and even absurd lengths. The first supervision was religious, and was carried out by ministers. They were succeeded by *ex officio* civil officers and these by professional supervisors. The early laws stated who was to be allowed to attend the schools, and only after many years did the legislatures venture to enact compulsory attendance laws. A comparative study of state school legislation would be rewarding, but it is to be remembered that much of the later legislation was copied from the older states.

7. IMPROVED METHODS

In the nineteenth century the scope of elementary education was broadened, the schools were graded, the kindergarten and the high school were added, compulsory attendance laws were passed, and real systems were formed. From the time of Horace Mann there was a continuous effort to improve instruction and to overcome the formal and mechanical character of the schools. Early attention centered upon reading and arithmetic. Mann favored the word method in beginning reading, but phonic and other methods were often used in combination. Pestalozzi, the great Swiss educator and reformer of elementary education, practically created primary arithmetic, in contrast to the commercial variety, and he had a strong and good influence upon instruction. His method was based upon the now obvious idea that children should understand number and should not merely learn to manipulate figures. Scientific research has made further improvements in the teaching of these and other subjects.

In a more general way, Pestalozzi favored the encouragement of observation, inquiry, and expression by pupils. And even more important was his kindly spirit and love of children which helped to transform the harsh schools of early days. Many educators continued to accept the view, not peculiar to Pestalozzi, that the transfer of training was easy and almost complete; but objections to this comfortable doctrine began to appear by 1840.

8. NATIVE INSTITUTIONS AND FOREIGN IDEAS

Borrowed plans, practices, and ideas have to be fitted into existing conditions and needs if they are to be useful or are even to survive. Many attempts were made in the nineteenth century by Danish immigrants to introduce their folk schools, which are highly successful in their native land; but they have not grown well in the American soil and climate. Transplantation such as the settlers carried out can hardly succeed except in a new country without a settled social order and institutions.

Even the early settlers made some adaptations; but more fully developed and civilized America made greater ones in her extensive educational importations. The English college grew into the American university topped by a graduate school made in Germany; but this also was changed to serve American needs better. The English academy became the American academy, a very different institution which became the mother of both the high school and the normal school. It will not be denied that the normal school was an academy with reviews of the common branches and a few professional studies and skills added. It would have been purely American if it had not incorporated Pestalozzi's theory and practice into its professional work.

Pestalozzian doctrines were imported from Switzerland but also indirectly and in impure forms from other countries which had obtained them from the source. They were first brought in, after 1800, at the same time as the English Lancasterian system which they ousted and superseded. Such importation, as we have already said, may be of great advantage, "seeing that every nation affords not experience and tradition enough for all kind of learning," as John Milton said. Such importation is practiced in all the arts and sciences of all countries.

Borrowing was comparatively easy in the nineteenth century when there was no tariff on ideas, no fear, no censorship, or secrecy. Distance, poor travel accommodation, and language were the main barriers. Today much of the world is hidden behind political curtains.

Borrowing was always easiest between countries with a similar history and a common language. The educational purposes and systems of the English-speaking countries resemble each other as do those of the Latin, the Scandinavian, and the Arabic countries.

Before the educational awakening there was hardly any American literature on teaching and school administration. Some of this defect was made good by the propaganda for public education, the annual reports of state superintendents, published addresses, and several noteworthy textbooks on teaching. These were concerned with domestic problems. But there were also republications of English books, translations of continental works, and reports on observations of European education. A little later, Henry Barnard became the most prolific translator and publisher of German, Swiss, and other European educational publications.

In the course of these borrowings the United States also became a lender of educational doctrine. Domingo Faustino Sarmiento (1811–1888) of Chile and Argentina and José Pedro Varela (1848–1879) of Uruguay introduced North American practices into their countries. Canada and the United States exchanged ideas. The Dalton Plan had a wide but only temporary vogue abroad. American intelligence testing and the books of John Dewey have gone to most parts of the world. Since World War I, many Americans have served as advisers in organizing or reorganizing the schools of several countries. Foreign students in America return home with their observations. Study of comparative education and the work of UNESCO help to make the education of all free countries a matter of international knowledge.

9. UNITY OUT OF DIVERSITY

State universities which had remained in a coma for decades began to stir when in the latter nineteenth century the states began to provide regular support. At the same time the land-grant colleges attained their adolescence. These are signs that the public which had created the elementary school and high school was undertaking to complete the system. The public colleges were to serve the needs of the people more fully. At the same time business and philanthropic agencies were creating great private engineering schools and universities.

Independent, affiliated, and state colleges for women and also coeducation were promoted. Advanced Negro colleges such as Fisk and Howard were opened immediately after the Civil War; and after the second Morrill Act, seventeen land-grant colleges for Negroes were established. Municipal universities were founded early, but these developed more fully after 1900. In 1876 Johns Hopkins University, which was to serve as a model for graduate schools, was established. Other universities introduced graduate work by 1900.

Strong forces tended to draw this array of higher institutions together. The liberal institutions introduced practical and vocational work, and the engineering and agricultural schools had to provide general education as a basis for technical studies. The universities began to prepare teachers and to accept secondary school graduates on certificate. In 1900 it must have seemed that the system, extending from the kindergarten to the graduate school, was complete.

Actually a series of reorganizations had already begun forming junior high schools, junior colleges, and teachers' colleges. Each of these was a variation from an older form that was considered standard. Each was intended to increase the holding power of the chain of institutions by extending the opportunities of the unit below it and by preparing students for entrance into the unit above it.

The Morrill Act and supplementing laws made for unity. They narrowed the gap between practical and cultural education and that between the laboring and the directing classes. They were intended to improve work and wages rather than to increase culture and learning; but it is to be remembered that these aims are not separable in the way often supposed. The laws were, secondly, a means of federal and state cooperation, and also a device which permitted the federal government to direct education in the states and thereby to exercise a power not granted by the Constitution. No state has refused the funds because it objected to the conditions.

Why this plan could not be extended to include general elementary and secondary schooling is a political question. But some special factors are involved. We name only factors related to Negro schools and private schools, and the persistence of a local and state tradition in school support.

10. SCHOOL AND CHILD

Teacher and child are the leading characters in the educational drama. If the child is to play his part well, the teacher should be well prepared. The formal preparation of elementary teachers began more than a century ago, that of secondary teachers, seventy-five years ago, and that of college teachers has even now made only slight progress.

Teachers in schools of every grade vary in personal qualifications, scholarship, and professional abilities. Many do not have satisfactory academic and professional preparation. In the years after a war or when the country is passing through the upper half of the business cycle, the demand for teachers exceeds the supply of competent ones. At such times many unprepared persons are installed in classrooms by the grace of superintendents and state boards. For the children this is one of the less favorable features of American education.

There is no simple solution of this recurrent problem. Salaries comparable to the wages of bricklayers and highly skilled mechanics would be one step in the right direction. Adult education agencies should provide the people with opportunities to learn the truth about the condition and the needs of the schools. If "war is too important a matter to be left to the generals," as Clemenceau is supposed to have said, education is too important to be left to the superintendents. But if laymen are to be most helpful, they must be deeply interested and well informed, hence the need for adult education in school affairs.

In early schools little attention was given to the special needs of particular children. The blind, deaf, or otherwise seriously handicapped child was excluded. The slow learner was tolerated but was not given much help. Many people held the mistaken belief that better than average retention compensated for slow acquisition. Psychologists showed that this is an

error and that the contrary is the truth. Bright pupils learn faster than dull
ones and retain longer and more accurately what they have acquired.

How great the differences are was not known seventy-five years ago.
Those who first allowed individual pupils to progress as fast as they could go
received an object lesson in individual differences. They found that the
best pupils were able to do five or ten times as much as the slow ones. Here
is one of the sources of Progressive education.

Individual instruction and the elective system were separately developed about 1875. By the former plan all followed the same outline, each
at his own rate. The elective system allowed students to choose among
several subjects and at a given time to carry as many as they were able
to master. Both plans are examples of limited individualism. The extreme
case would be that of self-education, the pupil selecting his own subject-
matter and working with it after his own ideas. Since this would entirely
dispense with teachers, they should not be expected to recommend it.

Teachers found it hard to manage plans of even limited individualism
because their classes were too large. Space and equipment were often lacking. Teachers did not all have the required training or disposition. And
there is also the argument of Progressive educators that the school is a
social and should be a socializing institution.

The promoters of individualist plans advanced both psychological and
administrative reasons for them. They claimed an increased interest, a saving of time, the meeting of the pupil's special needs, and they asserted that
individual and group activities could be fruitfully used in combination.
Several formalized plans such as the Dalton, Winnetka, and Gary Plans,
aroused immediate enthusiasm which, however, did not last. But while individual instruction has not been maintained in its early forms, it has had a
lasting effect upon practice.

Greater effort to appeal to the interest of pupils may have been the
most useful result of the individualist movement. The attempt to enlist the
pupil's interest has affected all schools. It has resulted in the use of activities, problems, and projects, and in the cases of advanced students in original
investigation. This is, again, one of the sources of Progressive education.
As used by F. W. Parker and Dewey the appeal to interest had both individual and social outcomes, including group projects and specialized contributions by members, the organization of a school community carrying on
selected tasks, and the cooperation of school and society. In such sharing,
Dewey saw the root of democracy.

Dewey made growth the object of education and thinking the means
of growth. Most of his illustrative problems were of a scientific character.

But much of the thinking done by intelligent men does not concern material objects and does not follow the systematic forms proposed by Dewey. If we should conclude that Dewey's emphasis upon reflective thinking was an overemphasis, we might call it the philosopher's fallacy. Educators seem to have too uncritically accepted his view about discovery through inductive thinking.

Life demands other qualifications also. Good habits are important, and so are pleasing manners. An educated use of language is acquired by observation, imitation, and endless practice, without much aid from the syllogism. In our laborious lives some vocational skills are necessary, and many of these are learned, like language, by imitative practice. By mixing in society and also from a study of history, literature, and the Bible, one can improve in the understanding of people—a useful acquirement. The search for beauty and sublimity in nature and the arts has its rewards. Finally, to the oracular Doctor Johnson it seemed that varied knowledge and the use of it in conversation is a worthy aim of education. We would not minimize science, thinking, or scientific investigation, but an educational philosophy should be hospitable to other goals for twelve or more years of schooling.

11. SOCIETY AND THE SCHOOL

A scientific movement paralleled the rise of Progressive education, and to a limited extent the two cooperated but their bases were entirely different. One was founded upon measured observations and experiment and the other upon philosophic insight and regard for personality. Many educators conceded that each party had seized upon valuable ideas, but they were different and at times seemed hard to reconcile. It is to be noted in particular that science seeks to discover uniformities that can be used in making comparisons, calculating averages, and setting up standards.

The practical object of applied science is to improve practice by reducing it to uniform rules. As teaching and administration become systematic, two results follow. There will be less need for genius in the teacher and for clairvoyance in the public which employs him. The work of the teacher will become more like that of the engineer who builds a bridge; and the public which pays the bill will have better means of knowing the quality of the performance.

The public has meanwhile become interested in the schools. Such interest has never been wholly lacking. Public schools, at least, have always been publicly criticized. But today newspapers, weekly and monthly magazines, the radio and television, are used by friends and enemies. Public interest has grown with the means of public information. And while it is unfortunate that some have become the avowed enemies of public education and others use the poisoned pen against freedom of teaching, even these clouds reflect the sunlight. Enemies call forth friends and defenders and these have become a multitude. The serious postwar attacks on education have again declined to normal proportions.

Educational measurements and experiments enable school people to give the public a more exact statement of the condition of education than was formerly possible. Real knowledge will cut down the volume of ignorant propaganda. Comparison is a powerful searchlight. The history of education, by comparing the present with the past, can demonstrate progress and show also where further work is needed. Comparison of local with national norms and comparison of present achievement with reasonable ideals will give guidance to society and the schools. These are services made possible by scientific studies of education.

Society demands much more of the schools than ever before. The late-pattern high schools and the present-day universities have greatly expanded their vocational offerings. This public pressure has been increased by the growing enrollments; and the demand for vocational education will become still heavier in the future. In high school and university the new conditions have greatly increased the need for educational and vocational guidance. Parallel with the vocational trend there has come a wholesome emphasis upon general education and the cultivation of the personality and the humanistic qualities of students.

There are also some danger signs. One is the decline in the study of languages, mathematics, and the sciences. For economic development, for defense, for cooperation with our allies and the winning of new friends, these are important studies.

Although enrollments are growing, there is still a lamentable waste of intellectual ability. Many of the prospectively best students do not enroll in college or even in high school; and of those who do enroll many fail to graduate. For these conditions there are many reasons, but the lack of the means to stay in school is a black mark against the social order.

Society does not support the schools adequately. Great business corporations and wealthy foundations seem to have a keener sense of the need than the voters. In times of distress, in wartime, in financial panic, the schools are among the first to have their incomes cut. They are not the first to have the cuts restored when times improve. In times of public excitement, intellectual freedom seems less secure in public than in some private schools. The cure for these difficulties is to be found in fuller information. To doubt this is to doubt that the public is genuinely favorable to good education.

BOOKS AND PAPERS

Two numbers of the *Review of Educational Research,* for October, 1936, and October, 1939, respectively, contain bibliographies in the history of American education. Many books dealing with this subject are also given by William W. Brickman in his *Guide to Research in Educational History* (New York, New York University Bookstore, 1949). This work, as its title indicates, deals with the nature of historical research and gives directions to those who work with materials on education. There is no better way for students to learn from history than by attempting to write some. We list four textbooks and two books of readings in the history of American education.

Butts, R. Freeman, and Lawrence Cremin, *A History of Education in American Culture,* New York, 1953.

Cubberley, Elwood P., *Readings in Public Education in the United States,* Boston, 1934.

Edwards, Newton, and H. G. Richey, *The School in the American Social Order,* Boston, 1947.

Knight, Edgar W., *Education in the United States,* Boston, 1951, third edition.

Knight, Edgar W., and Clifton L. Hall, *Readings in American Educational History,* New York, 1951.

Noble, Stuart G., *A History of American Education,* New York, 1954, second edition.

Chapter I

CHILDREN IN THE
NEW WORLD

THE permanent British settlements in North America began at Jamestown in Virginia in 1607. In 1776 the thirteen separate colonies extended along the Atlantic coast from New Brunswick to Georgia. In that stretch of 1,300 miles, people from many countries and coming from all but the highest social levels had founded their homes. In that period of 170 years great social changes had occurred. In a summary only the most general conditions and changes can be entered. And in a history of education those factors should be selected which were closely related to the schools. Such factors were the growth of towns and, in the towns and on the plantations, the development of a wealthy class; new occupations; new means of transportation and communication; the introduction of the apprenticeship system; and the establishment of schools for the different classes of people in town and country.

1. Town and Country

Some of the first settlers, being farmers, soon spread out along the rivers and through the valleys into the open country. This event took place as soon as the Indians had been driven out, as in Virginia, or placated, as in Pennsylvania. Some of the first settlements remained villages for a long time; but a few, in favorable locations, developed into what were regarded as cities. On the eve of the Revolution about 4 per cent of the people lived in the five largest towns, Philadelphia, New York, Boston, Newport, and Charleston. The combined population of these five centers was only 100,-000. There were also twelve or fifteen smaller towns such as Albany, Salem, Lancaster, Baltimore, and Savannah and many small places with a few score or a few hundred inhabitants. Many families in the villages and even towns had some land or were otherwise employed in rural occupations.

More than 90 per cent of the late colonial people, and still more at an earlier time, lived in mere hamlets or on farms and plantations.

Here there is a fundamental difference between the rural economy of Europe and that of America. In Europe farmers live in villages, and they daily travel back and forth between their homes and their land. Most rural villages have children enough to form a school. But the American farmer lives on his acres, in many cases a half mile or more from his nearest neighbor. Before the invention of the school bus, the one-room school was the chief educational institution for country children.

Schools were less easily accessible in the country and more primitive than in the city, the terms were short, the interest in education less, and during some years there was no school in a given community. Such deficiencies were greatest among the poor, the unskilled, the plantation workers, lumbermen, trappers, and frontiersmen. Both city and country life has been greatly modified since colonial times, but the countryside has undergone the greater transformation. In large sections of the country good roads, electric power, all the means of communication, modern houses, farm machinery, and the consolidated school have tended to equalize the living conditions of town and country. In colonial days there was in all these matters an absolute contrast.

By continued immigration and natural increase, the population of the thirteen colonies reached 1,600,000 by 1760, but nearly one-fourth were slaves. The whole population reached 2,500,000 before the Revolution. They supported themselves by agriculture, fishing, the fur trade, simple manufactures, lumber and ship stores, shipbuilding, and domestic and foreign commerce. Fast Yankee-built ships carried cargoes of tobacco, flour, lumber, and fish to all ports of the world. These were bulky goods, and in the absence of similar products on the homeward voyage the captains often brought immigrants for ballast. Sometimes these were Negroes to be sold into slavery. A portion of the foreign trade formed a nefarious triangle: the carrying of molasses from the West Indies to New England, there to be made into rum to be exchanged in Africa for slaves to work in the West Indian sugar cane plantations.

Besides the common elementary education, some colonial occupations required a knowledge of applied mathematics and other useful subjects. Ship captains needed to understand the science and art of navigation. The surveyor's skill was needed to lay out cities, public subdivisions, and private tracts of land and to build canals and other large "works." There were no typewriters, and penmanship was joined to arithmetic and bookkeeping in the course of studies pursued by young aspirants to business success. Languages were in demand. Numerous teachers of these and other subjects not taught in the regular schools and colleges advertised their schools in the newspapers of all the larger towns.

2. HOME MANUFACTURES

English mercantile policy was partly responsible for the development of hand-industry in the colonies. The mother country thought of the colonies, and too often of the colonists, as existing for the profit and convenience of England and the English. They tried to use the colonies as sources of raw materials to be made into usable products by English labor and manufacturers. Some of the products were to be sold back to the Americans. According to mercantilist doctrine, out of this process England was to get work and wages for her people and precious metal for her hoard.

The policy was not wholly unfavorable to America. Bounties were paid on masts and naval stores, and colonial products were often given favorable terms in the English market. Adam Smith thought British colonial policy not illiberal. But that policy was framed by the English, not by the Americans themselves; and perhaps none will accept imposed restrictions willingly. There was right on both sides. The English justly pointed to their services in building up and defending America. The Americans desired freedom to develop their own economy. England later found ways to resolve such differences; but in the eighteenth century things were allowed to drift, then suddenly checked, and a crisis resulted.

One element of the crisis was the prohibition of manufacturing by the colonists. In all the colonies from Maryland northward, free labor and economic conditions favored handicrafts for local markets and household manufactures for home use. Even on the plantations of the South there were skilled workers, slave and free. It was to the colonial interest to avoid using the expensive English goods and to oppose English mercantilist policy. To dress in homespun became a matter of colonial patriotism.

Virginia began about the same time as Massachusetts to encourage the raising of wool and flax and the practice of spinning and weaving as a policy. In 1646 Virginia provided that two children from each county were to be taught at public cost the arts of carding, knitting, and spinning. Fines against the exportation of wool and laws to encourage textile production in linen, wool, and cotton goods were found in many colonies in the seventeenth century. Bounties were laid on wolves because they killed sheep.

Twice in the eighteenth century, Boston attempted to conduct a public spinning school, but neither effort succeeded well. The first such school was opened about 1720 partly for the children of Irish immigrants then arriving. The town selectmen voted 300 pounds for a school for "the Instruction of the Children of this Town in spinning." The second effort was a feature of the attempt to encourage the patriotic use of homespun during the heated controversies with England before the Revolution. These premature attempts in vocational education did not add much to what the people were doing anyway.

Some colonial manufactures could be carried on in the house or shop, and therefore during the long winter evenings and when the weather was inclement. Much of the work required only simple materials and no great skill. And children could do or help in doing such work using textiles, wood, and leather in making clothes, shoes, casks, hats, and other articles. They could help to boil soap made of animal fat and a lye made from wood ash; to burn charcoal; to make candles by dipping or by pouring tallow into a mold; to boil apple butter; and to work in other occupations.

There were also manufactures that required the skills and strength of men. Chains, anchors, farm implements, and household utensils were made of iron found in most of the colonies. For fuel, charcoal was used and its production was a business in itself. Shipbuilding has been mentioned. There were saw, grist, and flour mills. Flour was an article of export from Philadelphia. That city had the first paper mill in the colonies. It was established on the brawling Wissahickon by William Rittenhouse whose son, David, became an astronomer. Before the Revolution, the colonies had gone some distance on the way toward industrial independence. Political independence followed after. But intellectual independence was delayed.

3. CHILD LIFE AND LABOR

The occupations of the people and their domestic arrangements affect education and culture in every society. Men, women, and children all had to work in colonial society merely to live, and to work hard to live in a civilized manner. Child labor laws were not even thought of, and children began to work at an early age and soon became accustomed to employment and skilful in it. In their teens boys did the work of men, girls of women. They matured early. "With us," Franklin said, "marriages are [consummated] in the morning of life; our children are educated and settled in the world by noon."

Such arrangements left little time for schooling, reading, music and other arts, or any leisure activities. There was little to suggest such activities and diversions in a land which had few libraries, theaters, musical organizations, and no athletics. Some notice must be taken of the various "bees," quilting, husking, singing, barn-raisings, weddings and consequent "bell-ings," housewarmings, hunts, horse races, and other country amusements. There were lecture-days and training-days in New England. Customs and facilities varied with time and place. In the course of the colonial period some deprivations were made good in the cities. Books and libraries and leisure increased and the theater and musical organizations were accepted and established; but few were able to enjoy their productions. Schools and colleges were founded early but developed slowly. A number of men could be named who under unfavorable circumstances created for themselves opportunities for self-education. Such were Franklin, John and William Bartram, and David Rittenhouse.

Poor lighting and lack of privacy and leisure made the evening hours unfavorable for study. Candles were made of tallow, bayberry, or wax, and making them cost time that should have been spent in using them. Windows were small, so that even in daytime the houses were dimly lighted. Heating was another difficulty. To supply the wood and to tend the fire in one of the great open fireplaces added much to the labor of a household. Phosphorus matches were unknown, and the ancient habit of covering up the fire to keep it alive through the night gave us the word "curfew," the sign for children to leave the streets. Because of the cost and labor involved in keeping up a great wood-fire, only one room was heated or even partly heated. Diarists reported that in the cold northern winters the ink sometimes froze on their pens as they wrote within a few feet of the fire. With the whole household gathered around the fireplace, there was no opportunity for quiet and sustained mental work.

In spinning and weaving, mending and cobbling, in making splint-brooms out of soft yellow birchwood and dozens of other useful implements, many carved out with a jackknife, there was a kind of education. Boys and girls learned to be cooperative, to take responsibility, and to be unbelievably industrious. They acquired many skills and learned the uses and possibilities of many kinds of materials. In our day the school tries, not always successfully, to "make work" to develop skilful hands and active brains in the youth. In earlier times the teacher did not need to invent such forms of industrial arts education.

4. TRAVEL AND TRANSPORTATION

With all their inventiveness and mechanical skill, travel and transportation remained slow and costly and laborious for Americans throughout the colonial period. Water-travel with boats, canoes, or the clumsy dugout was the cheapest. Canoes were useful where portages were required. The dugout was made, as the word indicates, by hollowing out a large log and "was fashioned like a trough for Swine." Fishing smacks, sloops, and larger sailing vessels were used on the ocean.

On land, men walked or rode on horseback and used pack-horses or heavy wagons to transport goods. But for wheeled vehicles roads were necessary. The Conestoga wagon was a later invention. It became common in the eighteenth century and continued in use until the settlements had reached the Pacific coast. The deep sag in the bottom of this "covered wagon" kept the freight from sliding back and forth on mountain roads.

Light, four-wheeled vehicles such as coaches were not much used until after the Revolution, because the roads were too bad and too few. In 1767 it still took two days for a fast coach to travel the ninety miles from Philadelphia to New York. An early turnpike extended sixty miles from Philadelphia to Lancaster, and the Mohawk Valley had another. But generally, roads, bridges, and taverns providing lodging for travelers were found in the vicinity of large towns only.

As a result of such conditions, most of the people were rooted in one spot and isolated from the life of the outside world. Men lived an entire lifetime without ever going to the nearest city, although it was only twenty or thirty miles away. It was more difficult to arrange for a trip within the colonies than for one across the ocean. This was one of the reasons why early America faced toward Europe and not toward her own West. News—"intelligence," as it was called—was transmitted mainly by word of mouth. A weekly post was established between Boston and New York in 1692, but there was no public intercolonial postal system until 1707; and then it reached only a few of the larger towns. This topic will be more fully treated in the next section. The few newspapers had a very limited circulation and were small and dull. Most colonial Americans suffered from a lack of intellectual stimuli; and this did not help to dispel ancient error.

The "mental outfit" which the colonists had brought with them was largely drawn from a superstitious past. "If there was much lack of book learning in the generation of English people that sprung up first in American soil, there was some gain in a life in which exigent wants compelled a habit of shrewd observation." So Edward Eggleston wrote, and so it might seem; but let us see. The people after a century of shrewd American observation still believed that a long hair from a horse's tail if left in the water would turn into a snake. It was long held that some birds grew on trees and that some birds wintered at the bottom of ponds or retreated from the cold blasts of earthly winds to the moon. Witchcraft, Indian medicines, ghosts, and the terror inspired by comets and eclipses long survived the most careful observation of the average American.

Children were more useful in colonial than in later times because there was work for them to do; but children valued for the work they can do are likely to be exploited, as were the children in the factories of the industrial revolution. In the colonies children's tasks were not purely routine and did not so easily lead to exploitation. Yet overwork was certainly common. The stern religious views of the parents deprived many New England children of opportunity for play and companionship. Parents of many sections felt that children should be docile and quiet, speaking only when spoken to. Many were frightened by the harsh Puritan theology. Nearly all books were religious works.

5. FREEDOM OF THE PRESS

Even in England the newspaper was in its infancy when the first American settlements were being made; and in the colonies there was no successful paper before 1704 when the Boston *News-Letter* was established. During the remaining seventy years of colonial dependence the newspaper developed into an institution that was to play a great part in the struggle with Great Britain and eventually also in the development of education.

It is evident that the school and the press are interrelated. When the school has taught the elements of reading, the newspaper provides a means of further education not only in reading but in topics and fields of general interest; and it is often brought into the classrooms of even elementary schools. The colonial newspaper performed a special service for education in the private school period. It was through the newspaper advertisements that the private schools were able to present to the public information about their facilities, subjects taught, terms, and dates of opening. Through newspaper reports on school "exhibitions," plays, examinations, and other public events, the schools received a great deal of free advertising. School news is now an important part of the content of the daily paper, and through the "readers' letters" the public can express its views on the conduct of the schools. The newspaper as an instrument in the public relations policy of the school was not so highly developed in colonial times, but it is today one of the most important means of communication between school and people. It is also one of the chief reasons why the school is much concerned with the freedom and fairness of the press.

The early colonial newspapers were not free, but were published "by authority" of the government, or were controlled by a Puritan oligarchy as in Massachusetts, or by the Friends' Monthly Meeting as in Philadelphia. Freedom of speech and the press, essentials in a democracy, had to be won. It was gradually won in a number of dramatic lawsuits, one of the most exciting being that against John Peter Zenger of New York.

Zenger was the publisher of the New York *Weekly Journal,* founded in 1733 with the help of merchants, landowners, and lawyers who were opposed to the governor, William Cosby. Cosby, who had been driven from a government post in Minorca by charges that he had been involved in irregular financial practices, tried some of the same schemes in New York. Zenger's backers used the *Journal* to attack the governor and the court which he controlled; and when the grand jury would not indict Zenger on charge of seditious libel, the governor had him arrested "on information." When the case was tried the governor had the attorneys for the defense disbarred and Zenger was recommitted to jail.

The issue was whether the freedom of the press could be maintained against the opposition of an arbitrary royal governor. The leaders of the popular party sprang a surprise at the second arraignment. They had engaged Andrew Hamilton of Philadelphia to defend Zenger. Hamilton argued, against the actual law at the time, that the jury had the right to determine whether the matter which Zenger had published was libelous. He convinced the jury that "the truth published from a good motive" cannot be considered libelous, and this principle has since been incorporated in law. The jury at some risk to themselves brought in a verdict of acquittal.

Andrew Hamilton's advocacy in the Zenger case has been compared with the speech of James Otis against the writs of assistance. He was not only a highly astute lawyer but also a successful administrator, and he was the architect and selected the site for the old Pennsylvania State House which we know as Independence Hall. But the victory in the Zenger case for the freedom of the press is his highest title to fame.

Although the Zenger case ended auspiciously, freedom of the press, like freedom of speech and teaching, must be continuously guarded and maintained if it is to be safe. In the dispute which preceded the Revolutionary War the royalist authorities attempted to secure an indictment for libel against Isaiah Thomas, famous printer and the publisher of a patriot paper, the *Massachusetts Spy.* As in the Zenger case, the grand jury refused to return a true bill and a suit was lodged on "information." But when it became evident that no jury would convict, the case was dropped.

The newspapers played an important part in the pre-Revolutionary debate. They had increased in number from a single paper in 1704 to about fifty in 1776, and many took the patriot side. One of the mistakes made by the British in their plan to tax the colonists was the choice of a stamp tax with the requirement that newspapers and legal documents such as deeds and contracts had to be stamped. This aroused the opposition of two of the most vocal groups in the colonies, the newspaper proprietors and the lawyers. Only a tax on sermons would have been more ill-advised.

The multiplication of newspapers had another influence with a bearing upon the spread of information and education. It stirred up the demand for a better postal service. The need for such service was felt in the colonies from early times, and various suggestions and practical efforts were made as the population increased and spread. To meet the need was for obvious reasons difficult. Governor Lovelace of New York took an interest in the problem in 1673, and eleven years later it was again taken up by Governor Dongan of the same colony. Both efforts were premature, but in 1692 the British government assigned the monopoly of a weekly postal service between New York and Boston. So bad were the roads that a week was actually required. It was the practice of the post riders to start toward each other from the two termini of the route and to exchange mail bags somewhere near the mid-point.

Early in the eighteenth century regular post routes were established between Philadelphia, New York, and Boston with a few short spurs and some irregular service to New Hampshire and Virginia at the ends of the main route. The early postmasters were almost invariably newspaper publishers and sometimes used their office to distribute their own papers and to prevent the circulation of competing sheets.

The colonial service became a branch of the British postal system in 1707 and American postmasters general were thereafter appointed by the Crown. The need for a means to send official communications to the governors and to receive their reports was a reason for British interest in the matter. Postage on private letters was still collected on delivery and the charges were proportioned to the distance. To carry a single sheet from London to New York cost one shilling and from New York to Charleston the cost was one shilling ninepence. There were no postage stamps. The carriers had a way of defrauding the department by carrying letters in their pockets instead of the sealed post bags and collecting the charges for their own use. No wonder that the government lost money on its postal service.

Benjamin Franklin was appointed Postmaster General in 1753. Contrary to his claim that he never sought an office, he worked hard and used influence to get this one. But he greatly improved the service, extended it to cover the whole coast line, and made it yield a profit to the government. He established a rate for newspapers that was fair to all and required carriers to accept and deliver all papers for which carriage was paid. In 1774 he was removed after years of absentee operation; but the new American government reappointed him. This time he held the office for only one year and then secured it for his son-in-law, Richard Bache.

The circulation of newspapers and the transmission of letters, magazines, books, and all means of communication are educational agencies. There would be little use in learning to read if reading matter were not made available. The publishing business, the post office, and the public library serve and are served by the public school.

6. Apprenticeship

Children did not always have a family to look after them. Some were brought to America in their teens without the parents. These and not only children whose parents had died were known in common speech and in law as orphans. Court records show that some of them were mistreated. Those who were apprenticed were to be educated and put in the way to become useful citizens. Apprenticeship successfully completed brought the young person the rights and privileges of citizenship that were denied to the poor and unskilled youth.

The law and the custom of apprenticeship came from the mother country; but it had been a form of education in the oldest societies from the dawn of history and apparently before there were any records. The essence of apprenticeship consists in a combination of education and skilled industry by which the master of a trade teaches its "mysteries" to a novice. Specific directions, observation, and imitation are the methods. The moral conduct and behavior which an artisan must exhibit are instilled by the way. At the time of the American settlement it was often customary to permit the apprentice to attend school long enough to acquire the arts of reading and writing.

Learning to do by doing has been employed in the oldest arts and sciences from early times. It is not something that our contemporaries have a right to crow over as if it were their discovery. And although it has become the habit to speak of it with bated breath, it has no magical powers. Those who merely imitate, without theorizing and experimenting, learn to do only what has been done before. And this was the usual result of an apprenticeship. But the system had real value, as one would infer from the fact that it lasted so many centuries. The work was concrete, measurable. It was easy to tell whether the craftsman's level of skill and knowledge had been attained. It permitted no bluffing. It produced salable products and transformed boys who had no "influence" into useful men. It helped to solve two social problems by reducing the number of possible vagabonds and by supplying society with necessary goods and services. Unfortunately, girls, who were usually excluded from the schools, were also excluded from apprenticeship.

The colonists were not wholly dependent upon apprenticeship for their supply of skilled workers. Many artisans came from abroad. Edward Johnson in his *Wonder-working Providence* listed about thirty trades that were practiced in Massachusetts in the middle of the seventeenth century. He reported that the coopers and shoemakers had formed guilds. Some of these craftsmen may have learned their craft in America, but many others continued to come from abroad. Some came as redemptioners permitting the ship-captain to sell their skill and time for four years or more to pay for their passage across the ocean. Among them were schoolmasters, bookkeepers, bookbinders, gardeners, carpenters, and blacksmiths.

7. EDUCATION AND LABOR LAWS

In colonial life, apprenticeship served to replenish the skilled labor force, but it was also a police measure to prevent vagrancy, idling, and begging. The Massachusetts Bay Colony law of 1642 mentioned the great neglect of parents and masters in training their children in "learning and labor and other employments which may be profitable to the Commonwealth." To remedy this defect the selectmen of each town were required to attend to the "calling and employment of children" and "especially of their ability to read and understand the principles of religion and the capital laws of the country." Children who were not receiving such an education were to be apprenticed to masters who would teach them. The town was to provide materials and tools for vocational instruction, but books are not mentioned.

This was an educational law that did not mention schools. It required the parent or master to teach his child or apprentice, but permitted this to be done in the home or shop. It required the selectmen to watch over the behavior and habits of the young. And the whole tenor of the act shows that its purpose was to promote not only the welfare of the children but also the general welfare of the colony and people. The tendency for the state to enter the family and to assert a public interest in the upbringing of the children may be thought to have had its beginning in the English-speaking world in this law. Town records show that it was enforced, but we do not know how universally it was enforced.

If the law of 1642 did start a new trend in the relation of the state to education, it will be desirable to fix its antecedents more exactly. The Massachusetts law can be traced to the English Reformation which, by the stress it laid upon the Bible, led many, but the Puritans especially, to insist that children must be taught to read. There were accompanying economic factors. The hard lot of the poor was doubled and their number was increased by the closing of the monasteries, the enclosing of the common lands to make sheepwalks, and the currency inflation from the influx of South American silver and gold. The economic distress in England in the sixteenth and seventeenth centuries was a prime cause of the rapid peopling of the colonies. It was also a cause of the English poor and apprenticeship laws.

Laws for the relief or public support of the poor began before 1540 and were gradually strengthened by successive enactments. It was soon seen that if the poor youth were taught trades they would be less likely to require public alms. The Statute of Artificers of 1562 was in part a compulsory apprenticeship law. This was a beginning. The climax was in the Poor Law of 1601 which was a code on relief, apprenticeship, and punishment for the lazy and recalcitrant. This law was enacted just before the English settlements where the law was duly copied.

The other colonies were slow in following the lead of Massachusetts Bay in adding the teaching of reading, religion, and the colony laws to apprenticeship. An early law of Virginia published the English Statute of Artificers and another in 1642 conferred upon justices of the peace the power to bind out and to apprentice children. But not until 1701 did the law require the teaching of reading and writing. In Pennsylvania the earliest laws required that all children must "be taught some useful trade or skill that the poor may work to live, and the rich, if they become poor, may not want." A Maryland law charged the judges to inquire whether the masters were teaching the apprentices or merely employing them at common labor. The northern colonies approached the example set by Massachusetts Bay, but enforcement was a problem everywhere and especially where the masters were themselves unskilful and illiterate. But such as they were, the apprenticeship laws were the first attempts by American governments to compel the education of children.

8. Spelling Book and Quill Pens

To learn to read was the first and greatest task set the school children of early days. The Protestants who settled in the English colonies set great store by books, especially the Bible. And they valued the school most of all because it taught their children to read the Bible. But this was a goal, not the beginning. The hornbook or battledore was the first instrument put into the hands of the little children when they entered the dame school. The hornbook was a small, wooden, paddle-shaped implement. A sheet of paper, with the alphabet, numerals, Lord's Prayer, and other reading matter, was pasted upon the blade and the whole was covered with sheets of transparent horn, hence the name. The battledore, made of stiff paper, contained similar materials. In the dame school, kept by a woman in her home, the smallest children learned to read.

Schools were dull and often grim. About the middle of the colonial period, John Locke wrote that he "had a fancy that learning might be made a play and recreation to children" so that they would "desire to be taught." Many Americans in the eighteenth century read Locke's *Thoughts,* but there is no record of any who put his "fancy" to the test. To do that they would have had to discard the hornbook and the rod.

The primer came after the hornbook. The primer can be traced from the later Middle Ages. It was, as the name indicates, intended for a first book. There were many different primers in use at different times. But the one that was most commonly used in early American schools was *The New England Primer*. Its history has been written by the historian and bibliographer, Paul Leicester Ford, who estimated that 3,000,000 copies were printed. Although it was in common use for a century and its range extended far beyond New England, this would be a large number to be purchased by the small populations of colonial times. It set the pace for such widely used schoolbooks as Noah Webster's spelling book, Lindley Murray's grammar, Warren Colburn's arithmetic, and William Holmes McGuffey's readers. Crudely printed and illustrated with rough woodcuts, its appearance did not recommend it. Its best-known feature is the rhymed alphabet which began

> In Adam's fall
> We sinnèd all.

There was an outline of Puritan theology including the *Shorter Catechism,* John Cotton's *Spiritual Milk for Babes,* and other pieces. An examination of the book reveals better than many words could do how the philosophy of childhood education has changed since the seventeenth century.

After the primer and catechism it was the old custom to introduce the Psalter or Book of Psalms and then the New Testament and the Bible as a whole. Locke criticised this sequence and advised the use of stories; but excepting the Bible stories of Joseph, which Thomas Mann uses as a text for adults, Locke could remember only two that seemed suitable, *Aesop's Fables* and *Reynard the Fox*. The day for children's literature did not dawn until the latter part of the eighteenth century. Meanwhile, the spelling book came into use.

The spelling book is as indicative of an era and the changed temper of American education as *The New England Primer*. It signifies the growth of secularism or at least of a neutrality in religion which permitted the establishment of common schools without a particular confession of faith. A spelling book was printed on the first American press at Cambridge, Massachusetts, before 1650. The book is thought to have been Edmund Coote's *English Schoolmaster*, but no copy of this imprint remains. It was not a secular book. Besides the alphabet and spelling exercises, it had a short catechism, prayers, psalms, writing copies, and a list of "hard words alphabetically arranged and sensibly explained." This idea of teaching little children "hard words" out of context and before they were needed was an almost universal teaching error of those and later days. In later days "helps" in the study of English print became common, but before 1600 there was not even a dictionary. An early hint of an English dictionary was called a list of "hard usual English words" and came out in London in 1604, just three years before the settlement at Jamestown. And when the great dictionaries of the eighteenth century appeared they were too expensive for schools.

Meanwhile, there was the spelling book. George Fox, Quaker founder, prepared a schoolbook, *Instructions for Right Spelling and Plain Directions for Reading and Writing True English*. It was, like many later spellers, a sort of omnibus book, having spelling-words, catechism, proverbs, scripture selections, and some arithmetic lessons. Thomas Dilworth's *A New Guide to the English Tongue* continued in use in American schools even after the Revolution. William Perry, like Dilworth an Englishman, tried to improve upon the title and contents of the *New Guide*. He called his book *The Only Sure Guide to the English Tongue, or New Pronouncing Spelling-Book*. In America it was issued (1785) by the famous printer and historian of American printing named above, Isaiah Thomas. He reported that in the course of thirty years he had sold about 300,000 copies.

Two years before the appearance of Perry's *Only Sure Guide,* Noah Webster, an American compiler at last, prepared the most famous speller and most widely sold of American schoolbooks, *The American Spelling Book* (1783), in popular speech called "the blue-backed spelling book." It was the first of a three-book series, speller, grammar, and reader. For the series, Webster, who was a pedant as well as a businessman, invented the grand title, *A Grammatical Institute of the English Language.* The spelling book continued in use for more than a century and the numbers reported sold reached an astronomical figure. Not too much dependence should be placed upon such figures, for they are often estimates, and usually not underestimates. It is, however, certain that Webster's spelling book and its competitors put an end to the importation and the reprinting in America of English books of this kind. But we have overstepped the limits of the colonial period.

The extraordinary vogue of spelling in colonial and later schools may have been due, in part, to mistaken notions of the nature of language and of the way by which one learns to spell. The science of language was in its infancy and Americans knew little of what there was to be known. Their great mistake was the failure to understand that speech is the real, the living language, and that writing and print are only its lifeless symbols. A related error was the choice of separate words as the elementary units of language. The true elements are expressed thoughts, that is, statements, questions, or commands, or even ejaculations, for example, "Well, I never!" meaning "I am astonished." This emphasis upon separate words led them in turn to spelling, as if one could not recognize a word without spelling it.

From all this came the mistaken pedagogy of reading, which had for centuries deceived teachers including Pestalozzi. The first step in that old method was to teach the names of the twenty-six letters; then to have the children spell and pronounce several hundred two- and three-letter syllables; and thirdly, to spell words syllable by syllable, as "sat-is-fy" thus: "s-a-t, sat; i-s, is, satis; f-y, fy, satisfy." After this had gone on for many dreary weeks, the child was taught to read. And he learned, by recognizing phrases and words and sentences without spelling, exactly as he would have learned in the first place without knowing the names of the letters. To learn those names in proper order is a very simple matter when the time comes to consult the dictionary. Some training in phonetics is also given. Those who criticise the newer methods of teaching beginning reading do not always take the trouble to understand what the problem is. A little knowledge of the history of education would be useful to them.

Beginning reading was, in colonial times, often taught in the dame school. And the schooldame had no knowledge of pedagogy or the science of language. She invariably followed a dead routine. But better-educated teachers for long years did no better. If in some corners the old methods are still in use even now, that is unprofessional conduct.

Quill pens were used through the colonial period and fifty years beyond. They were cut with a penknife (appropriate word) from goose quills, and had to be mended and repointed from time to time. There were no lead pencils, crayons, chalk, blackboards, or unsanitary and noisy slates and slate pencils. Writing was not taught in the dame school because the little tots could not manage pen and ink. There were no cheap and handy paper tablets, but foolscap could be stitched together at home and used for writing material. Copybooks and ciphering-books were made in this manner. Much of the teacher's time was occupied with the making and mending of pens, the setting of copies, and the supervision of time-consuming writing exercises.

Excepting only arithmetic and handwriting, all subjects were taught through oral recitations. Reading, spelling, grammar, and, when they were later introduced, history and geography were recited orally. This was partly owing, no doubt, to the cost of paper.

The almost exclusive use of the oral method had an unfortunate effect upon the whole curriculum. When pupils had mastered the simplest mechanics of reading, the recitation was conducted by having each one read a paragraph or stanza aloud until the entire lesson had been read. Often there was no attention to the meaning of the passage or even of the new words. Only the pronunciation was important. This was word-calling, not reading. It tended to restrict the amount of material that could be covered and to forestall the development of silent reading. Its bad effect upon the teaching of spelling is evident. Subjects such as grammar or geography were taught by an oral question-and-answer method based upon the words of the book. Nearly everything that was taught in the old school was taught from a book, and taught not by discussion but by question and answer, questions often from the book by the teacher, and answers in the words of the book by the pupils.

9. ARITHMETICS AND GRAMMARS

The Hindu-Arabic numerals were introduced into Europe in 1202 if Leonardo of Pisa was, as is believed, the first to use them in a Latin book. That was four centuries before the English settlements in America, and all that time was required to secure acceptance of this new method of calculating "with the pen." In earlier times a "manual method" of calculating with calculi or pebbles or counters on a counting-board or abacus was used and it continued in use, probably, because so many people were illiterate and unable to use the pen. By the seventeenth century the battle had been won. People continued to count on their fingers and to calculate without calculi, "in their heads," but there is no known case of the use of the abacus and "manual arithmetic" in early American schools. This was an important change. Older European arithmetic books often promised to teach both methods.

Today teachers have gone back to the manual method of using beans or other small objects in teaching beginners to count and to make simple combinations of numbers. This is an example of the principle that the way in which a process was first developed in practical life may be a guide to the intelligent teaching of it to beginners. The teaching of language through use in speaking and writing rather than through grammar is another example of the principle. The idea is suggestive but not universally applicable.

In arithmetic the use of objects was reintroduced after it had long gone out of use. There is a story that Napoleon's soldiers brought back some examples of counting frames or abaci from Russia. Edward Brooks, an American teacher of arithmetic, in his *Normal Methods of Teaching* (1879), strongly recommended the constant use of the abacus in arithmetic. The kindergarten also aided in revolutionizing the beginnings of number work. The colonial school rarely hit upon such enlightened ideas of teaching.

Only the business uses of arithmetic and bookkeeping and the geometry and trigonometry used in surveying and navigation were much valued by early America. And these practical applications were often taught in special schools advertised in the newspapers. Mathematics as an intellectual pursuit had only slight appeal in colonial days. Young Benjamin Franklin wrote a characteristic essay on the usefulness of mathematics. But even scientists or promoters of science as the younger John Winthrop (1714–1779), David Rittenhouse, and Thomas Jefferson cannot be called exceptions. They also considered mathematics as only a useful tool. No original work in mathematics was produced and the colleges taught no courses that would now be considered advanced. The Boston Latin School appears to have taught no mathematics before the Revolution. In the Middle States, Benjamin Rush went through a Latin School and Princeton College without coming into contact with the subject.

In early times skill in even the common measurements and simple calculation was not thought necessary for everyone. Such skill, however, was essential in commercial life and most trades; and it could be acquired in special writing and reckoning schools. In New York and other commercial and seaport towns, private teachers of these subjects were numerous after 1700. Philadelphia had many schools offering instruction in arithmetic and applied mathematics, and the Penn Charter School and the later Academy of that city each had a separate mathematical department. Isaac Greenwood of Boston wrote *Arithmetick Vulgar and Decimal* (1729), the first separate arithmetic text by a native American, but it was too advanced for beginners. The Dutch schools of New Amsterdam gave attention to the arithmetic needed in that trading post, and there Peter Venema prepared an arithmetic text in the Dutch language. But until the Revolution nearly all textbooks were written in England and imported or reprinted in the colonies. After the Revolution a large number of American textbooks appeared. There were several reasons for this, but the adoption of our new decimal monetary system was one.

Arithmetic was an extremely complicated subject in early times. It has been much simplified and the teaching of it has been much improved. In earlier days the books began with abstract definitions. Then followed rules for writing and reading numbers; the four fundamental operations including five or more "cases" of multiplication; common and decimal fractions; and weights and measures in profusion, often to the confusion of the pupil. Under the last-named topic one had to learn what a firkin is, a puncheon, a quintal, and the difference between a Flemish and an English ell. There was also the "rule of three" in several cases and a number of different "rules" for the calculation of interest. This enumeration could be continued, but enough has been given to show that the old arithmetic was composed of many special topics and technical processes. The new arithmetic omits unnecessary topics and attempts to make all processes understandable. In a later chapter we shall come back to this topic.

The study of English grammar which was to occupy so large a portion of school time in the nineteenth century had barely begun in colonial schools. But propaganda for the teaching of grammar had started early. As early as the winter of 1734–1735, a writer in the *American Weekly Mercury* advised parents "to decide early whether their children are to become scholars or clerks and tradesmen, in order that they may receive their Education accordingly." Even if they were to become scholars it seemed to him best to have them begin with the English rather than the Latin grammar. Both the views and the language of the *Mercury* article point to Franklin as the probable author.

In grammar as in arithmetic, English textbooks were used at first. Robert Lowth and Thomas Sheridan were among the authors whose books were reprinted in America. About the time of the Revolution, Anthony Benezet, a teacher of the Penn Charter School, published *The Pennsylvania Spelling-Book* and an "easy introduction" to English grammar. The *Grammatical Institutes* prepared by John Ash was intended to prepare children for the more difficult work by Lowth. The grammar prepared by Noah Webster has been mentioned. As in the case of arithmetic, the Latin schools neglected English grammar and many private masters offered to teach it. Literature, geography, history, and other subjects were rarely taught before 1800 or 1850.

10. TYPES AND SYSTEMS OF SCHOOLS

Colonial school arrangements were casual and the result of mere custom when not specially adapted to local peculiarities. Many schools were not permanent or located in one place or so located that all the children could have access to a school. School terms were short, the most frequent term being three months. The attendance was irregular and there was no established curriculum in the lower or common schools. Teachers had no formal preparation in regard to how or what to teach, and they made the curriculum out of what they knew and what books were at hand.

There was a general lack of system or rather one may discern the faint outlines of several systems. At least two kinds of schools were in the mind of the author who wrote the article on the study of grammar published in the *American Weekly Mercury* in 1735. He spoke of preparing children to become clerks and tradesmen or scholars, thus drawing a line between common school education or, if a little more advanced, what was called "a good English education" and, on the other side of the line, a classical education in Latin school and college for "scholars." On one side were the dame school, elementary school, apprenticeship, and the private schools in the cities which taught practical subjects and advertised their offerings in the newspapers; on the other side stood the preparatory Latin school and the college, ready to prepare future ministers, lawyers, and doctors, or, as the writer of 1735 more briefly and less accurately said, "scholars."

The dame school was held in the narrow and perhaps untidy quarters of a kitchen or bedroom. The teacher, ordinarily a housewife, sometimes a widow, collected a small fee for teaching very young children "their letters," syllables, spelling, and reading. The hornbook and primer were the usual teaching materials.

When the child had learned to read a little and was to learn to write he had to be removed from the dame school, to a district, a neighborhood, a subscription, an "old field," or a parochial school. These are merely different names for the ordinary elementary school under various forms of management. The district school was controlled by an elected board, and the neighborhood school by a committee or trustee informally selected. The subscription school was a private school conducted in accordance with a contract subscribed to by the teacher and patrons; and generally the "old field" school was merely a variety of subscription school. The name was derived from its location on waste or exhausted land. Parochial schools were connected with a church. Literally taken, a parochial school is the school of a parish and the term is most frequently applied to Catholic schools connected with parish churches; but other Christian bodies also established and maintained local schools. Lutherans support many parish schools. The Monthly Meetings of the Friends, which have advisory and to some degree directive functions in relation to local meetings, established schools. The Anglican Society for the Propagation of the Gospel in Foreign Parts, that is, outside of England, established schools in America. All the schools here reviewed were generally elementary schools teaching spelling, reading, writing, arithmetic, religion, and often also sewing to girls. They were ungraded, poorly equipped, and some were unsupervised schools. The nub of this discussion is that there was no fully developed system of elementary schools in the colonies.

A few examples existed in which the beginnings of system may be seen. In its educational management, Holland had devised a form of cooperation between church and state and this was carried into New Netherland. The Dutch West India Company had almost complete control of the government of the colony on the Hudson and they appointed the schoolmaster and paid his salary. He had other income also. The schools were not free, except to the poor. Town rates or compulsory contributions were exacted; and in the village of Bergen, in what is now New Jersey, and apparently in other towns also, these rates became a school tax. A house was provided for the schoolmaster and the school was maintained in the same building. Thus the government, which was exercised by the Dutch West India Company, provided for the "prudentials," that is, the finances and equipment of the schools.

The church looked out for the qualifications including the piety and orthodoxy of the schoolmaster. New Amsterdam had a school in 1638 which became the still functioning School of the Collegiate Dutch Reformed Church. Other schools were opened as needed in a score of near-by villages and in settlements on Long Island and along the Hudson River to Albany and beyond. These schools were modeled upon the parochial schools of Holland. The ruling body of the mother church in Amsterdam selected and certified the schoolmasters for competence, character, and doctrine. They were rated as minor officials of the church and served the church by carrying announcements, ringing the church bell, and, in the minister's absence, taking charge of the services on the Sabbath. This system of state-church cooperation could not become a permanent arrangement in a country that was to reject the state-church principle. But in any case the English came in and established a new government.

There were also private schoolmasters in New Netherland as in other colonies where there were towns. These taught penmanship, arithmetic, bookkeeping, and other useful subjects. Some conducted evening schools for apprentices and others who were employed in the daytime. In the Dutch period even these private schoolmasters were licensed to carry on their occupation.

The Dutch language continued in use in the family, church, and school of the descendants of the original settlers for many generations after the English moved in (1664). For example, Peter Venema's arithmetic was published in 1730. For a long time many communities had to support schools in two languages. And this is merely the first example of such conditions wherever in later years there were large bodies of non-English citizens.

Some of the English governors of New York continued the practice of licensing only those schoolmasters who had been approved in the home country. In this case the home authority was the Church of England working through the agency of the Society for the Propagation of the Gospel in Foreign Parts. This missionary body founded in 1701 at once became active in the settlements and trading posts in the West Indies, throughout the Middle and Southern colonies where there were Anglican churches, and especially in New York. They maintained schools and their missionaries exercised a watchful interest over the teaching of religion. The charity school established by the Society in New York City in 1710 became the School of Trinity Church and still survives. They supplied and directed schoolmasters, set up school and parish libraries, provided textbooks, and attempted to invigorate inactive congregations, to convert Indians, and in every way to promote the growth of the church. The teachers' pay was provided in part by the Society and in part by the community. The schools were mainly elementary charity schools charging fees against those who could pay but admitting poor children free. Sometimes they taught more advanced subjects. This is another example of a tentative system of elementary schools, but the influence of the Society came to an end in the Revolution.

New England was the home of the town as a political unit, the annual town meeting, and the town school. From English custom and for worship and defense, the settlers centered their homes in small villages. Also, nature cut up the surface of the country into valleys and meadows and hills and supplied the land with many small streams that once supplied water power to mills and factories. At first the land about a village was parceled out in strips, in the fashion of the Middle Ages. The region lacked the deep, rich soil of more level sections and had no staple crop such as the tobacco, cotton, and rice of the South or the wheat and flour of Pennsylvania. For all these reasons New England became a land of villages, small farms, family industries, and local governments by town, that is, township units.

The government of New England was as significant for its educational arrangements as were its physical and economic features. And the Massachusetts Bay Colony, not Plymouth, set the pattern for its political and educational development. At first those who had the right of suffrage all voted in Boston. When the distances of Salem, Dorchester, Cambridge, and other towns made voting in the capital inconvenient, a representative system was introduced. This took place in 1634, but Virginia had taken such action before. Then each town sent its representative, or a number if the town was large, to the general court or legislature to make laws for the colony. The general court was also a judicial body at first and gave directions for the enforcement of the laws it had enacted. All civic matters in each town were decided in the annual town meeting of the voters. One of such civic matters was the choice of representatives in the general court; and others were the maintenance of public services, such as roads and schools. Not everyone could vote in a town meeting. For sixty years following the settlement only men who were members of the church and had a certain amount of property were allowed to vote.

The government and the church were closely united in New England. And in harmony with its system of local government by each town was the fact that New England was the land of the Congregational Church in which each congregation was a semi-independent unit. The Calvinist theory also held that the state is the arm of the church. The general court legislated for both town and congregation. Each of these managed its own internal affairs, but the agents were the same people.

In Europe the church and school had been intimately connected for more than a thousand years. And this connection was retained in most of the schools in all the colonies. Apprenticeship and the private schools in the cities were at least partial exceptions tending to develop in a secularist direction. But the usual elementary school, Latin school, and college were religious schools teaching the doctrine approved by the parents of the children. This was not new. From early times when the church had been surrounded by the pagan world and in much of the medieval period while she was set in the midst of barbarians, the school was a natural and necessary ally, or rather instrument, for the church conducted her own schools and frequently there were no others.

The Puritans, even more than most Christians, were convinced of the necessity for Christian schools. They demanded that the children should be taught to read and to know the principles of their faith as stated in the catechism and confession. Unlike some Protestants, the Puritans also demanded an educated minister for every pulpit. This made necessary an elementary school for all, boys and girls alike, and a Latin school and college for the education of leaders in church and state. This was the exact demand of many of the reformers from Luther on. Thus state and church and school were brought into an intimate union. As a result the Bay Colony provided by law for all three in less than twenty years from its founding.

Some Massachusetts towns established schools of their own accord but not all did so; and in 1647 the general court passed the act, which from the language of its preamble is known as "the old deluder Satan" law, and which required all towns of fifty families to maintain an elementary school; and towns of one hundred families to provide a secondary school to fit boys for college. The law set a fine for failure to comply. A single teacher, qualified to teach both English branches and Latin, fully satisfied the terms of the law. Even so, some towns found it cheaper to pay the fine than to maintain the school.

The law was not always obeyed. In many towns the number of pupils preparing for college was often very small and some of this small number were prepared under private tuition by the minister. At a given time a town school might not have a single Latin pupil. Some towns evaded the law quite deliberately and skilfully. Teachers were employed while the general court was in session and dismissed when it adjourned; or a teacher shuttled back and forth between neighboring towns as frequently as was necessary to delude the authorities into believing that each town was maintaining a school. The larger and richer towns maintained the schools more continuously, but even in these the number of Latin pupils was often small. In the seventeenth century the New England colonies except Rhode Island enacted laws similar to the Massachusetts law of 1647.

Gradually the town schools declined. With the removal of the Indians (1675) and the spreading out of the settlers taking up new lands, the homes became more widely and thinly scattered over the townships. Hamlets began to dot the countryside. The people in the outlying parts of a town found the distance from the school too great for their children. To serve the more isolated families the teacher began to move from place to place within the town, teaching a few months in one village and a similar time in another. Sometimes the school was held for short periods in as many as six places in a town. In 1710 in the town of Malden the teacher was required to teach in three places; in 1737 in Lunenburg in four places; and in 1725 in Harwich in six. In this last-cited case the lengths of the terms at each stand varied from four months to almost nine, and three and one-half years were needed to complete one round. Obviously some of the children would attend only a single term in three or four years. But this was an extreme case. This phase in the decline of the New England schools is known as the moving-school phase.

In the next phase the townships were divided into independent school districts, each with a separate board and each maintaining a simple elementary school for a term as short as three months. This was the district school of tradition, the school of the little red schoolhouse celebrated by romantic former pupils, a poor thing indeed but suitable for thinly settled sections. Like the similar neighborhood school of the Appalachian valleys in Pennsylvania and Virginia, the district school grew up without legislation. In Massachusetts it was legalized in 1768 and 1789 and in New Hampshire in 1805. A further description of the district system will be found in Chapter VIII.

Another device of the district system was the provision of two terms in a year, a winter term for the big boys and girls who were released from much of the farm work at that season and a summer term for little children. The winter term was apt to be rough, not in regard to the weather only, and the teacher had to be a strong and resolute man. In the summer terms girls were given an opportunity to teach. As the schools in New England declined, those parents who could afford to do so sent their children to private schools. Even in Boston there were at times more pupils in the private than in the city public schools; and this was true as late as 1820.

The district school and system were important in our history, and the term should be defined. There are several kinds of school districts. Townships, counties, cities with vast populations, special areas formed *ad hoc*, and indeed any bounded areas may become school districts by merely setting up agencies to erect, direct, and maintain schools for the people within its borders. In this most general sense of the term, each of the states is a school district enclosing many subordinate districts. But when the "district system" is mentioned the reference is to a particular size of districts, namely, the smallest possible administrative school units, those with a single one-teacher school and a board to direct it. The essence of it is in the separation of each school and board from all others. Although it is a misuse of words to call these adjoining educational atoms a system, this is historically the sense of the word.

The so-called district system spread from state to state across the country with the frontier settlements. Having been formed to meet the needs of thinly settled regions where only a handful of children could come together in one place, the system was also carried into cities where each ward had its one-teacher school and special trustees. When city school boards were formed they were composed of these ward officials, and on the boards they represented their wards rather than the city as a whole.

As the population in more recent times grew dense, the district system was abandoned and larger units and schools with several or many teachers substituted. The process is not yet completed. An urgent problem in many states is that of creating larger and fewer districts to equalize costs, promote secondary, technical, and special education, place schools in the best locations, facilitate supervision, and enlist capable personnel. This problem is being slowly and painfully solved.

11. COLONIAL TEACHERS

Just as there is no single description that will fit all present-day teachers so there is none for all colonial teachers. Everyone is an individual, and in characterizing a whole class or profession of people much allowance must be made for the variations that will exist in any large group of people. Colonial teachers were of several kinds. This can be demonstrated from the records. There were teachers who absconded, got drunk, were cruel, or committed financial irregularities. But several considerations must be kept in mind in passing judgment. Standards of conduct vary with time and we should not too severely condemn errors that were overlooked when they were committed. We should not judge the innocent by the guilty or the accused who may not have been guilty. To concentrate upon the black sheep alone will not convey the truth about the flock.

Those who appointed teachers in colonial times no doubt tried to secure good men. No doubt they looked for character, education, manners, and whatever other qualities were demanded at the time. Sometimes they were unable to judge the applicant's characteristics, particularly his educational qualifications. Sometimes there was not much choice because of the small number of candidates. Sometimes special qualifications, such as church membership or ability to play the organ were overvalued in comparison with knowledge or teaching ability. Present-day authors sometimes criticize our forefathers because they demanded church membership or conformity in doctrine, but this is a wholly unhistorical position. Of course, Friends' schools were to be taught by teachers who belonged to the Society, and Lutheran schools by Lutheran teachers. And taking an analogous example from the present day, of course, American communities do not want their children taught by Communist teachers.

The teachers of Puritan New England were frequently, in some towns almost always, college graduates. The Society for the Propagation of the Gospel took great care in selecting prudent, learned, politically loyal, and pious teachers who conformed to the doctrine and discipline of the Church of England. The teachers in the Friends' schools were generally of good repute. Some of the teachers of private schools in Boston, Philadelphia, and other towns were honorable and distinguished. Probably the teachers of the district schools and many of the subscription schools did not always meet the highest educational and character standards. Some colonial teachers, even in that day when corporal punishment was approved, were known for their brutality and tyranny. But these were exceptions.

One curious custom of that time was "boarding 'round." The teacher in the district school was lodged and boarded for a week at a time in the family, first of one patron, and then of another. By this device the school money was made to last a little longer than it otherwise would have done. The practice did not enhance the dignity of the profession or make it easier to secure good teachers. The short terms made teaching a part-time employment. The wages were low, about equal to those of a good farm hand. The lack of equipment, the limited curriculum, and the irregularity of attendance further reduced the desirability of the calling. One cannot feel any surprise that few remained in the vocation more than a few years.

Teachers in the Latin schools and tutors in the colleges stood in the highest ranks of the occupation. Two of the famous teachers in the Latin schools of New England were Elijah Corlett of Cambridge and Ezekiel Cheever of New Haven and Boston. Cheever taught for seventy years and has been celebrated in verse and story, not least skilfully by Nathaniel Hawthorne in his *Grandfather's Chair*.

The colonial population grew rapidly, the settlements became denser in the East and spread toward the West, and some wealth was accumulated and comfort attained. The colonial period covers one-half of the time that has elapsed since the settlement of Jamestown; and the changes that occurred during that time must be kept constantly in mind. Only slight intimations of that development can be given in a brief summary. Ninety per cent of the people were still engaged in rural and outdoor occupations and one-fourth of them were slaves at the end of the period. To supply themselves with good schools would have been a very difficult task.

Home manufactures gave employment to many, even the children. Living conditions in the homes were not conducive to the intellectual life. Superstition played a greater role in many minds than science or literature. Children matured early and received only a rudimentary education. Mathematics and its practical applications were taught to young adults in private schools.

The means of communication improved. Roads and an intercolonial postal service to distribute newspapers and letters helped to spread ideas. A great victory for the freedom of the press was won in the Zenger case.

The apprentice system gave vocational training. Skilled artisans from abroad kept coming and trained young workmen, and thus the system was to a degree self-maintaining. There were guilds but they played a minor part. The colonies also had to deal with young vagrants, orphans, and neglected children. Apprenticeship laws were passed partly as police and partly as relief measures. The "learning and labor" law of 1642 in Massachusetts was one of these, but there were also comparable laws in other colonies.

Standards of teaching and learning in colonial schools were low because frontier conditions did not permit or demand anything better. The different school systems varied slightly in administration but hardly in purpose. Subscription, neighborhood, and "old field" schools were adaptations to local conditions. Some of the neighborhood schools had a community or democratic basis but no legal status. The highly lauded town schools were anticipated by similar school legislation and church regulation in several European countries where Lutheran or Calvinist principles prevailed. The town schools of early New England were sectarian, controlled by the church and partly administered by the state as the arm of the church.

The common judgment that this was a period of transplantation is correct; but as schools were multiplied to meet the needs of a growing population, they were not always improved. And indeed some of the changes introduced into American education were changes for the worse. The moving and district schools, the backwoods schools in the log schoolhouses, the custom of "boarding 'round" for three-months' terms, and the multitude of small schools competing with one another in the cities were not improvements.

QUESTIONS

1. Why were the differences between urban and rural schools greater in early times than they are today? The differences between these two groups of schools should be studied for every period. It is a persistent problem.

2. Why did schools and educational attitudes differ in the several sections

of colonial America? These sectional differences are continuing features and should be studied for every period.

↗   3. In the colonies how did the elementary education of boys differ from that of girls? Why?

↗   4. Did the practical education acquired from the ordinary activities in living and working in colonial times provide full development of human capacity and adequate preparation for service to community and colony? This question will require full consideration. A short answer will not do.

↗   5. Consider the suggestion (p. 29) that old things must have merit and compare it with the freely expressed view that the newest idea, invention, or institution is best. What is your statement on the relation between the merit and the persistence of ideas, or other human achievements?

✗   6. How are freedom and ease of communication related to education?

↗   7. What are the merits and defects of an apprenticeship type of education? What part does high skill play in life?

✗   8. What is the definition of education as it was carried out in colonial schools?

BOOKS AND PAPERS

Among the books on children and home life in colonial times there are several written by Mrs. Alice Morse Earle. Of these *Child Life in Colonial Days* is perhaps most pertinent to the present chapter. For bibliographical help one can go to Monica Kiefer's *American Children Through Their Books, 1700–1835* (Philadelphia, 1948). With the description of the books there is much information in this volume on the manners, religion, discipline, and medical treatment of children. Some sources on the childhood of persons who became eminent may be gathered by using the bibliographies in the *Dictionary of American Biography* and from Barnard's *American Journal of Education*.

In this and following chapter-bibliographies, short titles are used; and except in the case of university presses and institutions of learning, the names of publishers are generally omitted.

Anonymous, "Some Thoughts of Education," *American Weekly Mercury*, December 31, January 7, 1735. Also in R. F. Seybolt, *The Private School*, University of Illinois, 1925.

Beverley, Robert, *History and Present State of Virginia*, edited by L. B. Wright, University of North Carolina Press, 1947. Treats of eighteenth century conditions.

Brumbaugh, M. G., *Life and Works of Christopher Dock*, Philadelphia, 1908.

Fleming, Sandford, *Children and Puritanism*, Yale University Press, 1933.

Ford, P. L., *The New England Primer*, New York, 1898.

Jameson, J. F., Editor, *Johnson's Wonder-Working Providence, 1628–1651*, New York, 1910.

Jernegan, M. W., *Laboring and Dependent Classes in Colonial America, 1607–1783,* University of Chicago Press, 1931.

Kilpatrick, W. H., *Dutch Schools of New Netherland and Colonial New York,* Washington, U. S. Government Printing Office, 1912.

Knight, E. W., *Public Education in the South,* Boston, 1922; *A Documentary History of Education in the South before 1860,* Chapel Hill, University of North Carolina Press, 1949–1953, five volumes.

Konwiser, H. M., *Colonial and Revolutionary Posts,* Richmond, Virginia, Dietz, 1931.

Maurer, C. L., *Early Lutheran Education in Pennsylvania,* Philadelphia, 1932.

Rich, W. E., *History of the United States Post Office to 1829,* Harvard University Press, 1924.

Rutherford, Livingston, *John Peter Zenger, His Press, His Trial,* New York, 1904.

Schlesinger, Arthur M., *Learning How to Behave, A Historical Study of American Etiquette Books,* New York, 1946.

Schuyler, L. R., *Liberty of the Press in the Colonies,* New York, 1905.

Tryon, R. M., *Household Manufactures, 1640–1860,* University of Chicago Press, 1917.

Tuer, A. W., *History of the Hornbook,* New York, 1896.

Wickersham, J. P., *History of Education in Pennsylvania,* Lancaster, Pennsylvania, 1886.

Woody, Thomas, *Early Quaker Education in Pennsylvania,* New York, Teachers College, Columbia University, 1920.

Chapter II

UPPER SCHOOLS
AND COLLEGES

CHIEFLY boys and young men attended the upper schools and colleges of the colonies. Private schools taught girls needlework, penmanship, music, and even languages, but these were lower rather than upper schools. Girls did not go to college and therefore did not prepare for college. The Latin grammar school and the college were the uninvaded preserves of the male sex; and the college remained to them inviolate until 1838 when Oberlin opened her regular college course to girls.

The colonial upper schools and colleges were for a select class of youth. Some were the ambitious sons of struggling but sacrificial farmers, for the poor boy in America has always found ways to go to college. What will happen if fees, especially in public institutions, continue to rise is not to be predicted. Others were the sons of the wealthy and professional classes. All hoped to become the ministers, teachers, lawyers, civil servants, doctors, and businessmen of their generation. Some became architects and erected the fine buildings of the larger colonial towns. The numbers of these students were limited, but then so were the suitable positions.

Their teachers, their parents, and they themselves when they thought about it believed that a classical education would help to provide a solid foundation for such elevated careers. That these studies had little to say about the particular problems which they would meet in life was considered a positive merit. Direct and specific preparation for many of the unpredictable and infinitely diverse problems of life being impossible, they had recourse to a general education which would help to solve all problems. This was their belief and decision two centuries ago. Today, and now that the ancient classics have been dislodged from their privileged position, educators with the support of engineers, physicians, and scientists are returning to the theory and practice of general education.

The upper schools of the colonies were of two kinds, the Latin grammar schools and the practical schools in the commercial cities. Only the former prepared pupils for college and were traditionally recognized as

48

secondary schools. The practical schools offered what was then called an English education, that is, not a classical one. This is the kind of education which Franklin valued and tried to promote in Philadelphia. The mathematical and English subjects of such schools formed an upper story based upon the studies which had been begun in the elementary schools. The integration between elementary and practical schools was loose, or rather was lacking, but the two were of the same kind and belonged together.

In the same manner the college formed the upper story of the studies which had been begun in the Latin grammar school. The connection between these two was close, having been formed centuries earlier. They formed a single system. By undertaking the study of Latin, a boy by this beginning announced his choice of a career that would take him away from the shop, the farm, or the accountant's desk to a professional or managerial occupation. Not much time could be spared for preparation. Active life for both the student and the apprentice began at about the same early age; and this age was eighteen years, which was the normal age for graduation from college. Americans, as Franklin said, matured young and married early. But in such matters there are always many exceptions; and in respect to early marriage, Franklin himself was an exception.

1. WHERE THE LATIN SCHOOLS CAME FROM

Like other institutions the Latin grammar school is best explained by its history. Only by examining its origin, nature, and purpose and its role in early times and foreign countries, can an understanding be gained of the American imitation. Our examination must be brief. The speech of ancient Rome was carried through all the Mediterranean countries of three continents, to the shores of the Black Sea and the valley of the Danube, where the name of Roumania still testifies to its ancient use, and in the north and west to the British Isles. It was carried by merchants, government officials, soldiers, and from the first Christian century by the Roman Catholic Church and its indefatigable missionaries.

In all this area in which a score of nations now find room, Latin was the language, not of peasants, but of governors, traders, students, and the church. Hundreds of dialects were used in this area. Many of them were only spoken, having no literature. Many were lacking in the words needed to discuss all general or abstract questions. Because Latin had this vocabulary and was a cultivated language it became the universal language of educated western Europe. It was used by those who had business beyond the narrow limits of a neighborhood or who wished to convey general ideas.

Of the changes which the Latin language suffered in the long centuries of the Middle Ages we shall not speak. There are good reasons for this omission. One reason is that it was not the medieval Latin of business, law, or the church that was studied in the later schools. The schools, from which the colonial teachers borrowed, taught the literary language of the ancient Roman poets, orators, historians, and moralists, the language of Cicero, Virgil, and Livy. These writers and others who resembled them were judged to belong to the highest class of writers and are therefore called classical.

The meaning of the word "classical" is not precise like that of a mathematical term. But it is of such importance in our account that some explanation of its meaning must be set down here. The classical writers dealt with universal topics which concern all men, simply as men. They wrote of travel and adventure, of fate and unseen powers, of war and danger, of love, courage, loyalty, and their opposites, especially when they can be seen embodied in the actions of persons. Cicero, for example, wrote of "traitorous Catiline," eulogized Roman culture, and, among a hundred themes, wrote on friendship, old age, and the education of an orator-statesman. Classical writings are generally marked by restraint, clearness, and regular form in contrast with the formless and exuberant manner of the romantic writers. The language of the classical writers of whom we are thinking was modeled upon the speech of the best-educated Romans of the two centuries following 100 B.C. This definition of the word "classical" will have its uses, but it should be received as only the beginning of wisdom in respect to the topic.

The secondary schools of Europe had become classical before the English settled in America. Their medieval textbooks of grammar, rhetoric, and logic had been put away and the classical writers had been substituted. But as we have indicated, it was the language rather than the mattter of these writers that was studied. They were studied as models of style, construction, and diction, not for their philosophies of life. But usually only selections from their works were read; and therefore the boys frequently failed to get a clear impression of the whole mind and personality of an author. Nor was there much effort to teach the place of a writer in the history of his time, or to consider the problems which he faced and his purpose in writing. Thus authors became the texts for "exercises" in grammar.

In the seventeenth century there was no real understanding of Greek civilization or of its relation to Roman culture. War and politics formed the main content of historical study, and these activities were treated as the work of individuals. Ancient economics and science were unknown, as was the archaeology of the classical civilizations. The Germans were only beginning to study these subjects, and the period of the new humanism was still in the future. The enthusiasm for classical learning which had marked the Renaissance was dead; the interest in the history of civilization was unborn when the settlers transplanted the English type of grammar school to American soil.

From John Locke's *Thoughts* we may learn something, most of it unfavorable, of the English grammar schools. He was a Westminster pupil at the exact time when the Puritans of Massachusetts were enacting the "old deluder Satan" law. His main criticism is directed against the rude manners and bad conduct that impaired the schools; but he also held that the intellectual work was inferior. If so, these conditions were not due to any sparing of the rod, for the school was then under Busby, the floggingest headmaster of them all. We cannot go into it here, but Locke's estimate may not have been entirely just. In any case the American schools could not even come up to their English models.

The English grammar schools of the seventeenth century were day schools. So were the American. The English schools were small, having perhaps fifty to one hundred boys; the American were smaller. The Boston Latin School, however, had 147 pupils in 1767; and between 1744 and the outbreak of the Revolution its numbers never fell below one hundred. It was probably the largest in the colonies. The North Latin School of Boston was only one-third to one-half as large in the same period, and those in smaller towns had very few Latin pupils along with many taking English studies. The curriculum was more extensive and the exercises more numerous in England than in America; but to this important matter we shall return.

2. EARLY LATIN SCHOOLS

Two of the earliest efforts in America to establish schools were made in Virginia and one of these was an endeavor to found a Latin school. About 1620 funds were collected and plans were made to teach a "convenient number" of Indian youth the art of reading, the principles of the Christian religion, and a useful trade. This is a group of ideas resembling those of the Massachusetts Bay Colony law of 1642 and they came from the same general sources, namely, the Reformation and the practice of apprenticeship. About the same time plans were made to erect a building for a Latin school, a master was appointed, and it was proposed to have an usher, that is, an assistant, to teach writing and arithmetic. The Indian massacre of 1622 ended these efforts.

Two Virginia schools that may have taught Latin at an early date were the Symms School endowed by a will of 1634 and the Eaton School by a somewhat later bequest. Very little is known of these institutions, but they were not in operation for any extended time. A connection is claimed to exist between the early foundations and the twentieth century Symms-Eaton School of Hampton. There were private Latin grammar schools in colonial Virginia such as the two conducted by clergymen in which Thomas Jefferson prepared for college. Others are known to have existed, but their history is often hard to trace. A Latin grammar school was connected with William and Mary College. Other colonies in the South had private schools. One of some note that was in existence before 1750 was conducted by Samuel Finley, later president of Princeton College. It was located at Nottingham in Cecil County, Maryland, and an academy at this place, as the custom of schools is, claims a connection with Dr. Finley's old school.

The reasons why the South had difficulty in developing and maintaining large numbers of good schools in colonial times are well known and were known then. The unnamed author of "An Advisive Narrative concerning Virginia" (1662) asserted that from "the sparse population" there has resulted "their almost general want of Schooles for the education of their Children"; and that this lack caused their youth who were "beautiful and comely Persons . . . [to be] unserviceable for any great Employments either in Church or State," as it also obstructed the "Conversion of the Heathen." This "advisive" account declared that towns were a necessity, with funds from England, English workmen to erect buildings and clergymen for the service of the church and the catechizing and teaching not only of children but of parents and masters as well. The author seems to have feared a return to barbarism in the colony. He proposed the creation of "Virginia Fellowships" at the English universities for the aid of those who would prepare themselves for service in the churches of the colony. The "Narrative" was submitted to the Bishop of London but apparently nothing was done to carry out its suggestions.

Many Southern planters' sons were educated abroad, and others in family schools on the plantations, while some were sent to northern schools. But it was not only the planters' sons who attended English and European schools. From all or nearly all of the colonies and from city and plantation, some of those who could afford to do so sent their youth to study and travel in older countries. The "grand tour" was still an institution in Europe where for educational purposes boys of the higher classes were conducted by their tutors through the leading countries. Catholic parents were apt to patronize church establishments in France or Belgium. Other young gentlemen might go to one or another of the classical schools of England, as did Edgar Allan Poe at a later date. Some went to study law at the Inns of Court in London, for in the South especially, as in South America today, a legal education was considered particularly appropriate for a gentleman. Classical learning was also highly favored in the South. And no part of the country sent more students of law and classics to England than Charleston, South Carolina.

Charleston also had classical schools of her own. The Society for the Propagation of the Gospel, private interests, and the state legislature co-operated in erecting a Latin school about 1712. In consideration of grants from the state treasury it was to educate twelve boys free. In Charleston and elsewhere, those who could afford to pay for a foreign education were a small minority. Some important Americans, like the Carrolls and the Pinckneys, were educated abroad, but the total number formed only a small proportion of the youth.

The best account of a mansion-house or family school on a plantation is that of Philip Fithian. He was a Princeton graduate and taught in the Carter family of northern Virginia. He left an account of the social life of the time (1773) and of his work as a teacher. A more modest example is that of John Harrower, an indentured servant, employed as a teacher in the Daingerfield family of Fredericksburg. One of his achievements was the instruction of a deaf boy from a neighboring plantation. In general, the fact is that Latin grammar schools were not numerous in the South; and many which were opened did not continue permanently. Parents could not assume that as their children developed, a secondary school or any school would, as a matter of course, be within easy reach.

In New England the Latin school flourished in a modest sort of way. For fifty years Boston had no other town school than its Latin School which may have taught English also. Doubtless there were private schools. Other towns followed the example set by the capital city, and five—Charlestown, Salem, Dorchester, Cambridge, and Roxbury—did so by 1645. The passing of the law of 1647, noted in the preceding chapter, probably indicates that many of the town fathers in other places were not as fervent in their zeal for schools as the colony fathers desired. Some schools were opened but did not "succeed" or were operated intermittently. Some had difficulty in finding a master. Some employed means of evading the provisions of the law. About one-third of the towns of Massachusetts had schools by 1700. Of the remaining towns, many were too small to fall under the provisions of the hundred-family law.

There is more direct evidence that the Latin school was not popular in all parts of the commonwealth. One example, already mentioned in the preceding chapter, is found in the history of the town of Woburn. While the General Court was in session in a particular year, the teacher of the town of Andover was engaged to teach also at Woburn and his appointment was certified to the General Court. Then this Andover teacher, who bore the doubly famous name of Dudley Bradstreet, took a day off from his regular duties to open the school at Woburn. But, as he no doubt expected, no pupils came and without pupils there were no duties. Yet the town had a master and therefore a school. Collecting his fee for the day's attendance as master he returned to his regular duties in Andover. Thus it appears that absenteeism was not entirely confined to church administration but appeared, if rarely, also in the schools.

Towns sometimes directed the selectmen to hire a teacher at the cheapest rate possible. One town reported that its people favored "common learning" but that few wished to become scholars. The small number of college students in the colonial colleges shows that this distaste was widely shared. During her first sixty years Harvard was the only college in the colonies, and yet the average number of graduates for each of those sixty years was only eight. And most of these students had come from five towns, namely, Boston, Cambridge, Charlestown, Dorchester, and Roxbury, the same five named above except that Boston takes the place of Salem. Some Latin schools in Massachusetts did not prepare a single student for college in ten or even in twenty years. W. H. Small, who was a careful student of the whole subject, came to a radical conclusion on the unpopularity of the Latin grammar school in Massachusetts. He wrote: "The whole [eighteenth] century is marked by indifference to the law [of 1647] or open defiance of it. More and more the conviction is forced upon us that this form of school existed not by popular will but by force of law."

Although Connecticut was "out West" in the early seventeenth century, there are records of several Latin grammar schools in the colony before 1650. It seems probable that there were such schools in New Haven and Hartford in 1639, and the latter town made an appropriation for a town school in 1642 when the noted master, Ezekiel Cheever, was appointed to teach in it. The Connecticut school law of 1650 was an almost exact copy of the Massachusetts law of 1647.

Within a year after his arrival in Philadelphia, William Penn and the council (1683) engaged a teacher of reading, writing, and bookkeeping; and it was proposed, but perhaps not carried out, to open a school of an academic character, teaching the sciences. After years of silence the record was resumed. From this continuation it appears that the Friends' Monthly Meeting established a "Public School" in 1689. By-and-by the city council of Philadelphia claimed the right to pass upon the qualifications of the teacher. Perhaps the friction growing out of this conflict over jurisdiction led the Friends to petition for a charter for "their" school. The Monthly Meeting asked for the right "to choose and admit" and "to remove and displace" the trustees, masters, and pupils in any way they pleased and "as often as said meeting shall see occasion." The request was granted, the charter issued (1701), and thus began the William Penn Charter School.

Among its early teachers before the charter was granted were men educated in German and Scottish universities and therefore capable of teaching the classics. One was the German scholar, Francis Daniel Pastorius (1651–1720), and associated with him was a teacher of writing and arithmetic. At that time (1699) the school seems to have had two departments, one the classical, and another the English and mathematical. Pastorius did not stay long. Probably there were few pupils in the classics and that department may have lapsed for a time. The teaching in other branches was certainly continued. By the methods frequently employed to secure the earliest credible date for the founding of schools, it might be possible to push the origin of the Penn Charter School back to 1683 when a school was first opened in Philadelphia, but the connection is doubtful. The William Penn Charter School became the center of a system of charity schools located in different parts of the city. Support for the school and its pendent charity schools came from rents, gifts, legacies, and fees but, from the first, instruction was free to the poor.

Friends' children were often a minority and this caused concern in the Monthly Meeting over the bad manners and morals of some others, which tended to corrupt those who had been more carefully reared. This has been a problem of Friends' schools in many times and places, for the desire to promote the Friends' way of life is the primary reason for their schools. One method of coping with this problem consisted in the selection of the pupils to be admitted and the employment of teachers who were members of the Society. This practice is, no doubt, the source of the term "select school" used by the Society. The matter has a special pertinence at present when several other religious bodies which have been sending their children to the public schools are deserting them and establishing their own denominational schools.

Several other Latin grammar schools were established in the Middle Colonies before the Revolution. They were usually religious in tone without being controlled or supported by a church. The "Log-College" at Neshaminy (1726–1742) was conducted by Presbyterians but not officially connected with the Presbyterian church, and the same statement applies to four or more other Pennsylvania schools where ministers taught languages and some theology to those who aspired to the same vocation. Lutherans and others also conducted Latin schools. There were some efforts to establish an Episcopal Latin school in Philadelphia before the Revolution, but they did not succeed until 1787 when the Episcopal Academy was incorporated.

3. LATIN SCHOOL CURRICULUM

To prepare boys for college was the task and purpose of the Latin grammar school. An early statement of this assignment is found in the admission requirements of Harvard College in 1642. At that time boys were to be admitted when they were able to read Cicero at sight, speak Latin, make Latin verses, and give the forms, the declensions and conjugations, of the Greek nouns and verbs. The close connection between the Latin school and college is also indicated by some phrases from *New England's First Fruits,* a pamphlet published in London in 1643. It said that a "fair grammar school" had been erected by the side of Harvard College "for the training up of young scholars" in "academical learning" until they were judged ripe enough to be received into the college. The reference is to the Cambridge Latin School.

There are no records for a detailed study of the curricula of the different schools. Perhaps it is a warranted inference that few or no colonial schools had a more complete and extended offering than that of the Boston Latin School. Even this school has no clear record of its curriculum before the year 1712. At that time the first three years were spent upon the elements of Latin, the declensions, conjugations, simple agreements, and vocabulary. In the fourth year Erasmus' *Colloquies* and Ovid were read. In the fifth year these were continued and Cicero's *Epistles* were added. Cicero, Ovid, Lucius Florus, and Virgil were studied in the sixth year. And in the seventh and last year a whole flock of authors, for the first time including Greek writers, were read. They were Cicero, Justin, Virgil, Horace, Juvenal, Persius, the *Greek Testament,* Isocrates, Homer, and even Hesiod. It is to be particularly noted that according to this curriculum, which was written out by Nathaniel Williams, the successor to Ezekiel Cheever, the boys seem not to have begun the study of Greek until the last quarter of the sixth year. And the following year they were expected to read not only the *Greek Testament,* which might be considered possible, but also difficult authors such as Isocrates and Hesiod.

Various required exercises were included in this curriculum of 1712.

Master Williams wrote that in "the fourth year, or sooner if their capacities allow it" they were to translate Erasmus with the help of dictionary and grammar. Each made a copy which was corrected by the master, and after several days they were required to translate it back into the Latin of the author. Other exercises were explained by Williams, but this one is of special interest because it shows that the famous method of double translation recommended by the Spaniard, Juan Luis Vives, and the Englishman, Roger Ascham, was introduced into an American school. This was a true case of transplantation. A plan very similar to this plan of double translation was used by Franklin in the effort to acquire a good English style. He paraphrased passages of good prose and after some time, working from the paraphrase, he tried to write in the manner of the original.

While the young Latin scholars of Boston were something more than mere beginners, they did not accomplish as much as was expected of the contemporary schoolboys of Old England. We may compare the Boston Latin School with England's Westminster. Several of the authors commonly read in England were neglected in Massachusetts. Such authors were Sallust, Livy, Caesar; and of the Greeks, Lucian and Demosthenes. Terence is not named in the Boston curriculum of 1712, but we learn that Cheever had used this author. The authors and subjects taught in both schools appear later in the Boston course than in the Westminster schedule. Thus the *Colloquies* of Erasmus were introduced in the second year at Westminster but not until the fourth year in the American school, and this two-year difference in favor of the English boys is uniformly maintained. The following table shows this uniform difference. The Roman figures indicate years of the course in each case.

WESTMINSTER-BOSTON CURRICULUM TABLE (1712)

Books	Westminster	Boston
Erasmus' *Colloquies* appears in year	II	IV
Cicero's *Epistles* " " "	III	V
Greek *Grammar* " " "	IV	VI
Cicero's *de Officiis* " " "	IV	VI
Justin " " "	V	VII
Isocrates " " "	V	VII

This comparison is incomplete because in many cases the two schools used different books, and the school exercises also differ. But it seems clear that the English schoolboy was expected to cover far more ground than the American. The disparity is only increased when we recall that after making slow progress for six years the Boston school attempted to redress the balance by introducing ten new authors in the last year. For the later curricula of the Boston Latin School the *Tercentenary History* by Pauline Holmes, as listed in the chapter bibliography, may be consulted.

Little is known of the curricula of the other colonial Latin schools. Something can be inferred from the college entrance requirements, but unfortunately we do not know how strictly they were interpreted. The Princeton requirements of 1748 were about the same as those of Harvard in 1642. Except that Yale had recently added arithmetic (1745) to its requirements, college admission studies had remained practically unchanged for a century. Translation from English into Latin and Latin versification were sometimes expected. In some colleges the president and two tutors had to certify the candidate's fitness. Much less emphasis was laid upon Greek than upon Latin in both Latin school and college course.

Few boys acquired such a mastery of Latin as would have enabled them to read and enjoy the ancient authors without the help of lexicon and grammar. Yet there were other benefits. John Adams, Jefferson, Madison, Hamilton, and others had somehow, partly from secondary sources, acquired a knowledge of the politics of the Greek democracies and the Roman republic, knowledge that served them well in the Revolution, in the Constitutional Convention, and in public life in general. Jefferson and perhaps a few others lived with and loved the ancient literatures to the end of their days. Now great literature is functional, in a noble sense of this slippery word, in the life of anyone who has the capacity to respond to it. This is a constant argument for the study of Latin and Greek by such persons. But American conditions did not stimulate enthusiasm for classical studies. The time available for study was short, the need for practical skill was great, and doubtless many college graduates never looked into their Virgil or Homer in later life.

4. THE COLONIAL COLLEGES

The first American colleges were small, unprogressive, widely scattered and isolated, and six of the first nine were less than thirty years old when the colonial period ended. The other three were ancient by comparison. The foundation dates of all are indicated in the table below. Harvard, the oldest, had been founded in 1636, and after a bad beginning graduated its first class in 1642. We have already noted that for sixty years it remained the only college in British America. William and Mary was merely a grammar school at first and conferred its first degrees in 1700. A third college, Yale, was chartered as a collegiate school the year following (1701),

THE COLONIAL COLLEGES

Present and Early Names		First Charter	First Degrees
Harvard University	Harvard College	1636	1642
William and Mary College	William and Mary College	1693	1700
Yale University	Collegiate School, and		
	Yale College	1701	1702
Princeton University	College of New Jersey	1746	1748
Columbia University	King's College	1754	1758
University of Pennsylvania	College of Philadelphia	1755	1757
Brown University	College of Rhode Island	1764	1769
Rutgers University	Queen's College	1766	1774
Dartmouth College	Dartmouth College	1769	1771

but had difficulty in finding a permanent home. Its very existence was endangered by the struggle between three towns each of which wanted the school. It was not finally located at New Haven until 1717. Hartford, one of the contestants, was promised the State House to compensate it for the loss of the college; and for many years Connecticut maintained two capital cities, Hartford and New Haven. The other six foundations had hardly come into full operation when the Revolutionary War broke out and in several cases seriously interrupted the work of the colleges.

Although most of the American colleges were young in 1776, higher education was already hoary with age. Higher education was the daughter of the church, and the oldest universities in Europe are older than any existing institution except the church. In the Middle Ages, as the universities began to take form, residence halls for students were founded. The residents of the halls gradually formed organized bodies, with laws, property, officers, and corporate rights and powers. The Roman word for such a body was *collegium,* whence the English word "college." In the universities, professors, tutors, students, and officials were expected to live a communal or collegiate life, eating at a common table, lodging in college buildings, and conforming to college laws.

Upon such a plan the colleges of Oxford and Cambridge were set up and this was the plan followed also in America. But in England each university included and exercised certain controls over her several colleges, and only the university had the power to confer degrees. An analogy with the American government will be illuminating. The colleges of Oxford, for example, may be taken to correspond to the states and the university to correspond to the federal government. As in the United States, each student is a citizen or member of his college and also of the university. But the English system of congregating a score or more colleges in one place under the control of a university could not be followed in the new world. In early America, owing to the dispersion of the people, each college was chartered as an independent degree-granting institution that in England would have been considered a small university.

The medieval universities had a medieval curriculum. It was composed, on one side, of professional studies, law, medicine, and divinity, and on the other of logic and other so-called liberal arts. The Renaissance brought in a new conception of liberal education based upon a classical curriculum, critical methods, and a modern individualistic spirit. Some religious reformers, such as Eramus, John Colet, Sir Thomas More, and their successors, accepted this outlook and introduced the "new learning" into Oxford and Cambridge. By the seventeenth century, Emmanuel College, Cambridge, whence many of the founders and supporters of Harvard came, had become a center of the Puritan religion. To the classical impulse the reformers added the study of the Scriptures including the Greek New Testament, the Hebrew of the Old Testament, and theology. The American colleges, therefore, began with a curriculum that had been laid down in somewhat separate strata by three great movements, the medieval university movement, the Renaissance, and the Reformation. From the first had come logic, rhetoric, some scraps of ancient mathematics and science, and the constant exercises in academic disputation; from the second, the Latin and Greek classics; and from the Reformation, the Hebrew and other Semitic languages, the Old and New Testament studies, and Protestant theology. Of modern science, history, or literature there was hardly a trace, certainly no more than a trace. Such rigid systems based upon the past are the natural result of strict orthodoxy whether it be in religious, civil, or economic affairs.

As the first European universities were the children of the church so the first American colleges were the children of the Protestant churches. Although some were not legally bound to any denomination, yet all had moral and customary religious bonds. The exception, if there was an exception, was the College of Philadelphia. Its founders ruled out sectarianism, claiming that the trustees were selected "without regard to religious persuasion." They were selected, as the historian Edward Cheyney believes, for their wealth, liberality, and social influence. Nevertheless, three-fourths of them were Episcopalians, the provost was an Episcopal clergyman, and "an Anglican tinge colored the institution during the whole colonial period." But this college did not have the preparation of ministers as its purpose, an important difference.

The education of ministers was the primary purpose at several of the colleges, never the only one. Many things besides divinity were taught in all of them and for several reasons. Ministers were expected to have a general as well as a theological education. And the colleges needed students and did not wish to exclude boys who belonged to other than the ruling denomination or who were preparing for other secular professions. Nor did these have any other choice, for all the colleges except the one in Philadelphia were denominational. Only the medical school of the College of Philadelphia offered professional education outside the ministry and this for only ten years before the Revolutionary War began. In the senses here indicated it is true, as Professor Samuel Eliot Morison is anxious to maintain, that early Harvard was not a divinity school; but it is also true that its primary purpose was the preparation of ministers because the founders dreaded to leave "an illiterate ministry" to the Puritan Congregational churches when those ministers who had come from England "should lie in the dust."

Although the colleges were church institutions, they had to appeal to the state for legal rights and powers, such as the right to receive and hold property and the power to grant degrees. Harvard was founded "to supply the publicke with fit Instruments principally for the work of the Ministry." A new college, Yale, was created in Connecticut partly through the machinations of the Mathers, who had lost their hold upon Harvard, and partly because, for some, that institution was becoming too liberal in its theology. The founders of Yale required the "Westminster Confession to be diligently read in the Latin Tongue and well studyed [sic] by all the Schollars," "for the upholding of the Christian protestant Religion by a succession of Learned and Orthodox men." The State of Connecticut in the Yale Charter of 1701 asserted its desire to support "so necessary and Religious an undertaking."

As indicated above, the colleges did not exclude students because they came from a denomination other than the one controlling the college in question. They never followed the English practice of setting up religious tests in the charters or college laws. But such matters can also be managed by consent and common understanding without legal warrant. In their public statements the denominational attitudes of the later colleges were liberal.

The charter of Brown University (1764) opened all offices except the presidency and all staff positions to Protestants of any denomination. The youth of all denominations were assured of equal advantages. The members of the board were taken from four denominations in fixed proportions, but the Baptists retained a large majority. The Dartmouth charter (1769) had no religious tests for students, president, or trustees, and no person was to be excluded on account of "speculative sentiments in religion." And seven of the eleven trustees were to be laymen. This board was remarkable also on account of its small size.

The charter of Queen's College (1770) was granted in answer to the petition of the ministers and elders of the Reformed churches among the people who had come from the United Provinces, that is, from Holland. The purpose was stated in the most general terms to be "the education of youth in the learned languages, liberal and useful arts and sciences, and especially in divinity, preparing them for the ministry and other good offices." The president was to be a member of the Dutch Reformed Church, but there was no test for the thirty-eight trustees. Although no religious requirement for the professor of divinity was stated, his membership in the Dutch Reformed Church was taken for granted. The most extraordinary requirement of the Queen's College charter was that there was "always to be one professor" whose duty it should be to instruct the students in the use and grammar of the English language. This was necessary because Dutch was the native language of many students. The college had trouble in maintaining itself, and at the turn of the century was closed for several years.

The colonial colleges were small. To discover how incredibly tiny they were in comparison with small-college enrollments in the twentieth century we must go to the records, not the college historians. Harvard had about twenty students in 1642 and sixty in 1670. But a decade later the college enrollments again dropped to very low levels. Better times followed and about 1690 the annual number of graduates over a ten-year period averaged thirteen. The enrollment moved upward until 1725, downward to another low about 1750, and again reached a new high just before the Revolution. In 1775 Harvard graduated forty, Yale thirty-five, Columbia thirteen, Dartmouth eleven, and Pennsylvania eight. At Princeton the graduates numbered twenty-seven in 1776, seven in 1777, and an average of six for the following five years. The war was no doubt responsible for the decline. Most of the colleges maintained preparatory Latin schools or departments, and the enrollments in these were often larger than those in the colleges themselves. The colleges did not issue annual catalogues, but one may estimate that the total enrollment in the nine colleges on the eve of the Revolution was 750 students and had probably never exceeded that figure. This number of college students out of a population of nearly 2,000,000 white persons—for slaves did not go to college—is only one-fiftieth of the numbers that come from a similar population today. It was as though a whole state such as Kansas were sending only 750 students to college.

The colleges were small and correspondingly poor. They did not have the noble architecture, the velvet lawns, the well-stocked libraries, or the abundant leisure that surrounded the university students of England. The buildings were mere shells, and even when the outside was made of stone, the inside—the floors and partitions—was of wood. This helps to explain the frequent college fires. Students normally entered at the age of fourteen and were required to live "in college" in bare, uncomfortable, and un-adorned study-bedrooms and to subsist on the food furnished at the college commons. Bad and insufficient food was one of the chief causes of the numerous college riots carried out by students. Arbitrary government was another, and so was the poor teaching of a barren curriculum. Standards of work doubtless rose as the colleges became better established, but they were not high. In the early years of one now famous university, a student reported that all they did was to "construe poorly" five or six orations of Cicero, five or six books of Virgil, and most of the Greek Testament and to gain "a very superficial knowledge of part of the Hebrew Psalter." Every-where the formal classwork consisted of recitations from a textbook. There were no electives. All students of each year recited from the same books, usually to a tutor who was himself a recent graduate without advanced education.

The English universities were operating upon one of the lowest levels of their whole history when the American colleges were rising. Edward Gibbon, Adam Smith, and others testify to that. The frontier conditions in America depressed still further that low-level education, borrowed from England. Yet great men, the founders of the Republic, came from those poor institutions. It is possible to gain an education under untoward circum-stances. And those poor institutions had the capacity to grow with the country and to become the large and great universities of the present. This development did not begin in colonial times. In that period the realist pri-vate schools gave the best example of educational enterprise.

5. REALIST AND CLASSICAL THEORY

The realist conception of education and the older classical scheme were like oil and water—they would not mix. Not until the nineteenth century did the older Latin schools introduce English, modern languages, and science into the classical course. At the Boston Latin School the change was made gradually between 1814 and 1829. In colonial times and after, some of the Latin schools had a form of "released time" when the boys or some of them were excused for part of the school day to take lessons from another school or a tutor in handwriting, arithmetic, bookkeeping, or English.

The other comparable colonial device was the two-course plan such as the Penn Charter School employed. But this was after all different because the two courses, the classical and realist, were taken by different groups of pupils. It may be compared with the practice of many Latin schools which gave classical instruction to boys who were to go to college and elementary teaching in reading and arithmetic to others who were intended for business or the farm. Such facts reveal the contrast, even the opposition and conflict, between the older form of education and the new.

The conflict grew out of psychological and historical causes. A classical education was the avenue to the old professions and especially the ministry. For the clergy the ancient languages were a necessary instrument. Their pertinence in the study of law and medicine was less evident; but it was easy to assume that what was good for the highest profession was also good for those of somewhat lower degree. And the desire of the professional class to maintain their standing as a class apart was one reason why all regularly educated men insisted upon the pre-eminence of that kind of education.

There was, secondly, the belief in the disciplinary value of classical studies. This belief was hardly even scrutinized in colonial times, but the basis for it has since been severely shaken. It is true that language instruction was better organized, and equipped with better books and aids than English and science instruction; but it is somewhat ironical and yet a fact that the belief in automatic transfer and the dependence upon prepared exercises should have tended to dampen the enthusiasm and to lessen the industry of Latin teachers. In the third place, in education as well as in business, possession is nine parts of the law. The classics held and had long held the field and it was much easier for them to continue in possession than for the new subjects to invade it.

Private schools were the early dispensers of realist education and from these, pulled this way and that by educational and social forces, the hybrid American academy developed. But the realist movement did not originate in America and was no longer new when it was introduced. In the earlier half of the sixteenth century, traces of such ideas were to be found in the works of Luther and Vives. In the following century John Amos Comenius, "that incomparable Moravian," became a missionary for these principles and some of his books were brought to America, but if they had any influence, it cannot be made out now. Nor can we now prove or disprove the belief of Cotton Mather that Comenius was considered for the presidency of Harvard. Bacon and Locke were better known in the new world, and the stimulating effect of their views was acknowledged. There was the Puritan academy of England which one might have expected to find copied in Puritan New England, but clerical and classical influence was too strong. Realism was more acceptable in the Middle Colonies and in busy commercial cities everywhere. It was encouraged by the founder of Pennsylvania, himself a product of classical Oxford.

William Penn recorded his enlightened views in his *Frame of Government* (1682), written in England. He taught that government should actively promote good as well as repress evil. That is a free government where the people make their own laws; and that will be a good one where the people are wise and virtuous. But virtue and wisdom do not come by inheritance; they must, he claimed, be propagated by education.

The *Frame* provided that the governor and council were to establish and direct all public schools and to reward authors and inventors. At the age of twelve, children were to be taught a trade or useful occupation, that "none may be idle, but the poor may work to live, and the rich, if they become poor, may not want." He demanded that the government should look after this because "it is a sort of trustee of the youth," and they in their turn are soon to be the rulers. He would spare no cost for the education of his own children but urged that they should be taught useful knowledge, "consistent with truth and godliness." He recommended mathematics applied to shipbuilding, navigation, surveying, and other crafts; but he especially praised argriculture, "which is an occupation, industrious, healthy, honest, and of good example."

Penn's realism, partly revealed in the preceding sentences, is more fully developed in his *Reflections and Maxims*, a work of his old age. Penn wrote that the physical world is what youth ought to study; children can best understand sensible things; but we fail to include these in their education. Instead "we press their memory too soon." We load them with words, rules of grammar, rhetoric, and a foreign language or two. We are at great pains "to make them scholars but not men."

There is, however, no necessary opposition between scholarship and manhood and Penn's sharp antithesis is false. But many of the more radical Reformation groups, Friends, Moravians, Pietists, Anabaptists, agreed with his main position. And all these sects were well represented in Pennsylvania. Education, they held, should promote piety, practicality, industry, and business success.

For the higher learning they had no high regard; but in the seventeenth and eighteenth centuries some of them did not see how one could get along without Latin. Penn's *Reflections* spread the view of Comenius. He admitted that languages should not be neglected but thought "things are still to be preferred." He pointed out that children love to use their hands in making tools, playthings, and useful objects and thought that this hint should not be overlooked by teachers. But there should be books in Latin for children; and these should deal with nature and mechanical subjects so that at school "they might learn things [together] with words." It is too bad that gardeners, farmers, and artisans so often do not understand the science of their calling. Besides, from nature we may learn to admire the wisdom of the Creator. This may, indeed, be a paraphrase of some passages by Comenius. These views, like the theory of classical education, came from Europe, and they were well suited to the immediate needs of middle-class America.

6. PRIVATE SCHOOLS

Private adventure schools, unsupervised and without any connection with other schools, were numerous in colonial times. They were conducted by individual teachers who earned a living by this means. For support the teachers depended upon fees paid by the pupils whom they were able to attract; for regulations they relied upon custom or invented their own new ones. Such schools were as private as a grocery store, and their success, like that of a store, depended upon their ability to supply and sell a product, namely, instruction in knowledge and skill. Many private schools were found even in the New England towns where there also were town and district schools. Thirty-five years after the close of the Revolution in the city of Boston there still were as many children in the private schools as in the public ones. Everywhere a large proportion of the private schools taught only the rudiments to children. The consideration of these was taken up in Chapter II, but there were also some advanced schools which will be treated here.

By 1700 the larger towns had become important centers of trade. In these towns there was need for those who had acquired a more advanced education, those who could write a good business hand, and were quick and accurate at figures and the various kinds of weights and measures; those who could keep a set of books; and those who could apply the elements of astronomy, geometry, and trigonometry to navigation and surveying. In a new country the work of the surveyor had a special importance. He served as the engineer in road building, laying out towns, erecting public works, and plotting farms and larger tracts of land. The schools taught the mathematics, basic science, and business practice needed in such work, and the other skills were acquired in an informal apprenticeship. There were no developed schools of engineering in America until long after the colonial period had ended; but the private schools laid the foundations of a practical engineering profession and thus of a new class of skilled people performing necessary functions.

The nature of these schools and the quality of their teachers can be more concretely shown by means of a few examples. For comparison we shall also include some teachers of the classics and other subjects. Most of our examples will be drawn from Philadelphia and surroundings because it was the early center of science and realist education. Good examples could be drawn from New York, Boston, and other places. Because Philadelphia was a new city in the first half of the eighteenth century and growing very rapidly, most of the teachers came from other colonies or from England or Germany. And we shall not be able to exhibit many typical teachers. The very fact that these teachers made enough of a mark in the world to get into the historical record stamps them as somewhat unusual.

The teachers of secondary school subjects, and conductors of private schools were men. At the end of the colonial period many women were engaged in teaching elementary schools, but nearly all the teachers of classics, modern languages, mathematics, and English grammar were men. Indeed, there were few places where women could have learned these subjects. We offer brief accounts of some Philadelphia teachers and a few others as evidence of the character of the private schools and schoolteachers of the eighteenth century.

Theophilus Grew (d. 1759) was a teacher of mathematics who first came into notice at Annapolis in 1732 as a successful almanac-maker. Two years later Grew was in Philadelphia offering to teach mathematics from arithmetic to trigonometry with many practical applications; and except for one brief absence he remained in that city and calling. His general repute is indicated by his work as a consultant in the long contest over the boundary-line between Pennsylvania and Maryland. If he was largely self-educated, as seems probable, this fact would be another proof of his ability. In 1750 he was appointed mathematics master in the Philadelphia Academy, but he continued to carry on his evening school as well. This again shows that some of the colonial teachers were men of quality.

There were many private schoolteachers of many subjects in the colonies, especially in the eighteenth century. In his work on *The Private School* in the colonies, Seybolt compiled a list of the private teachers in Philadelphia between the years 1722 and 1783. Most of these names were taken from newspaper advertisements. Seybolt's list, admittedly incomplete, contained ninety-seven names; and to these Professor James Mulhern has added sixty-five others with the statement that the total of 162 names does not yet account for all the private teachers of the city in the period designated above.

One of the names omitted by Seybolt is that of Thomas Godfrey (1704–1749) who advertised for mathematical pupils in 1740. Godfrey was also a maker of mathematical instruments. He was a member of Franklin's club, The Junto, and when he died, Franklin in an obituary notice said he had "an uncommon genius for all kinds of Mathematical Learning, with which he was extremely well acquainted. He invented the new Reflecting Quadrant used in Navigation." So he did, but Edmund Halley had made the same invention independently and the Royal Society divided its prize of about eighty pounds equally between the two men.

We turn now to New England for an illuminating example. For about a decade, Isaac Greenwood was Hollis Professor of Mathematics at Harvard College (1727–1738), and when he was dismissed from that position he went back to his earlier business, the private teaching of mathematics. He offered subjects ranging from the elements to the calculus, and his language shows awareness of both Newtonian and Leibnitzian methods. It is probable that some advanced subjects were occasionally advertised merely as "good business" without the intention or ability to teach them, but this remark does not apply to Greenwood.

All through the eighteenth century Boston, New York, Philadelphia, and other cities had private teachers of mathematics and its applications to dialing, gauging, mensuration, navigation, surveying, and bookkeeping. This tendency to emphasize practical applications is what one should expect in a new and undeveloped country. Andrew Lamb, who taught in Philadelphia for forty years, was one of those who featured the teaching of navigation. He claimed knowledge of both the science and art. In his advertisements he said: "Sailors, take a friend's advice, be not cheated by land-men that pretend to navigation for they know nothing of a sea-journal,

which is the principal thing you want to know, and the use of sea-charts."
He declared that his pupils were qualified to go as mates on the first voyage. He may be compared with Christopher Colles of the same city who
offered to teach "land-men's crafts," especially the building of all kinds of
mills and waterworks, such as dams, canals, docks and bridges, and military branches including gunnery and fortification. Colles' reputation was
good enough so that John Fitch considered asking him for technical assistance in constructing what was to become the most extraordinary "water-
work" of its time, namely the first successful steamboat. In the end, however, Henry Voight became Fitch's assistant.

The most practical, because it is universally needed, branch of mathematics is arithmetic, the first and simplest. With independence, American
arithmetic books began to appear, not slowly and timidly but in great
profusion. One of the first was by Nicholas Pike (1743–1819), his *New
and Complete System of Arithmetic* (1778). He was the master of the
Newburyport, Massachusetts, grammar school and also carried on a private
evening school. His book explained the then new federal money. According to Professor L. C. Karpinski, he made in this and other respects "an
enduring contribution to American education."

Arithmetic and grammar books for the elementary schools were considered in the preceding chapter. English composition, grammar, and
public speaking were not often offered in private schools until late in the
colonial period. Reading and writing were taught in elementary schools,
and German, French, Portuguese, and Spanish as well as the ancient languages in the private day and evening schools; but grammatical and practical instruction in English "as a science and as a language" was rare before
1750. A notable teacher of these branches was David James Dove (c. 1696–
1769), who was installed in 1751 as the English master in the Philadelphia
Academy. His mathematical colleague, Grew, had been in office for a
year at that time. Dove, like Grew, although possibly lacking collegiate
education, was highly competent. He was a native of England and was
fifty-four years old when he arrived in America.

At the Academy he attracted so many pupils that he was given
two assistants. As Franklin was quick to realize, he was a find for the
new institution, but in less than three years he fell out with the board.
After that he taught a private coeducational school and had two boys who
were to be famous, Richard Peters and Alexander Graydon, among his
pupils. From the *Memoir* left by Graydon we learn that it was Dove's
practice in his school to substitute disgrace for corporal punishment. This
took the form of sticking the rod under the collar and part way down the

pupil's back while the other end projected above his head. Thus decorated, the culprit had to stand on a bench for a period supposed to be proportionate to his offense. After a time Dove accepted the position of English teacher in the Germantown Union School, which had been founded to compete with the Philadelphia Academy; but he soon resigned to set up his own school next door to the Union School in order the better to compete with that rival. Dove was also a forceful, sarcastic writer and a skilful etcher, but with all his talents he lacked one talent, that of cooperating with others.

At the close of the colonial period, John Poor (1752–1829), a graduate of Harvard, became the head of "the justly famous Young Ladies' Academy" in Philadelphia where he worked from 1787 to 1809. This school, according to Professor Thomas Woody, drew pupils from several states and foreign countries and received a charter in 1792, "the first encouragement of the sort given to girls' education in the United States." It was at this school in 1787 that Benjamin Rush delivered his address, "Thoughts on Female Education."

While these and other immigrants from England and New England and from the continent of Europe were creating the beginnings of a new education in Philadelphia, a devoted elementary teacher in the country near-by was writing an early book on education, one of the first to be composed in America. This was Christopher Dock (c. 1698–1771), "the pious schoolmaster on the Skippack." He came to Pennsylvania about 1710 or later, from Germany; and sometime in the following decade he opened a school among the Mennonites of Montgomery County. Part of the time he had two schools, teaching three days of each week at Salford and the other three at Skippack. As a device for motivating work in composition he had the pupils of each school write letters to those of the other school. He served as the carrier. His book on education, called *Schulordnung* (1770), deals with manners, morals, piety, and schoolkeeping. He was himself noted for simplicity, piety, and a gentle disposition. In regard to discipline he had the arresting thought that the teacher should find the cause of misconduct and should treat that rather than the symptoms. The early schoolmaster on the Skippack has as secure a place in the educational history of that time as the teachers of applied mathematics and the languages.

The preceding paragraphs on a few teachers of the private school era will be of some help in finding the answer to questions raised in Chapter II about the characters and qualifications of colonial teachers. But not too much weight must be placed upon a few examples; and the collection of all possible information would not provide the data for wide and safe generalizations. It must always be remembered that most teachers were "humble folk," like most farmers, housewives, mechanics, and other people of the lower middle class. They left little information about themselves and attracted little attention from others. Some things, however, we may infer and a few things we may know.

We know that teaching was a highly competitive business without regulating legislation or supervision, and without any great number of endowed or chartered schools to set standards for the emulation of the wise and honest. The first colleges in the four middle colonies of New York, New Jersey, Pennsylvania, and Maryland came into operation in the middle of the eighteenth century. Before that time there were few good grammar schools in these colonies. Neither colleges nor grammar schools had considered any change in method or curricula to meet the needs of the people more adequately. It was the private schools such as those named above which attempted to prepare youth for an active life in a new country. The chief controlling and directing force among these was competition. Teachers in their advertisements exploited their advantages of experience and education; offered a far greater number of subjects than they could teach in any one term; and claimed to be the inventors or the heirs of new methods capable of performing miracles of facile instruction.

Long experience as a teacher and practical experience on Atlantic voyages were reasons advanced by Andrew Lamb why the public should continue to patronize his teaching of navigation. His statement that his pupils "could go as mates on their first voyage" seems questionable. Others made more extravagant claims. At a later period N. G. Dufief claimed to have a method by which he could "teach French" in thirty-six lessons. Others in other subjects reduced the needed hours. The somewhat notorious James G. Bennett advertised as follows: "It is now well-known that a complete knowledge of bookkeeping as applied to the various branches of commercial business can be acquired in twenty private lectures of one hour each. Terms, twenty dollars." Some claimed that they had enjoyed the patronage of famous persons, even that of King George II. Occasionally a letter was written to a newspaper to ridicule the extravagant claims of those who were designated as "quack teachers," or the "48-lesson man."

The usual term in the private schools was about thirteen weeks, or a quarter of a year. Fees were often collected in advance, but occasionally a teacher lost his pay because he did not hold to this rule. Seybolt quoted one man who gave as the reason for strict enforcement of the prepayment rule that he had been committed to debtor's prison because previous pupils neglected to pay their fees. One object of the society of private schoolteachers founded in New York City in 1794 was to aid members in collecting delinquent bills.

Many teachers were to some extent specialists. The largest number taught the rudiments only, reading and perhaps writing and arithmetic. But there were those who taught mainly mathematical subjects, or one or more languages, or the various kinds of spoken and written English, or perhaps only penmanship. The teaching of penmanship was almost a profession in itself. The number of different "hands" was legion. One man offered to teach the Round Text hand, the ledger, the plain or ornamental Italian, the ordinary running hand, and also the Roman, Italic, Old English, German Text, and other hands, as well as embellishing and flourishing. Fancy penmanship was an "accomplishment." The academic subjects and especially mathematics and its applications were divided into many subdivisions. In a single announcement, a teacher might offer to teach as many as twenty-five separate subjects. It is not known how large the classes were, how many classes a teacher undertook to meet in one term, or how many times they met each week. The academy inherited many of the characteristics of the private schools which had prepared the way for it.

7. Franklin's Plans for an Academy

The academy was a transitional institution bridging the differences between the Latin school, the private school of the colonial cities, and the public high school. It shared some of the characteristics of each of these. This transition was to a large extent accomplished by 1876 when the National Centennial was celebrated. A hundred years earlier there had been very few academies. In 1876 there were thousands, but many were yielding to the encroachments of the high school. Meanwhile, the academy had also become a preparatory institution and helped to transmit to the high school its twofold function of preparing pupils for direct entrance upon life or for admission to college. Thus there have been three main types of American secondary schools: the classical or Latin grammar school from the settlements to the Revolution; the academy from the Revolution to the Civil War or somewhat beyond, perhaps to 1876; and the high school to the present. Schools of all of those types are still in operation.

When fully mature, the academy was a middle school that was governed under a state charter by a board of trustees, with a broad realist curriculum loosely held together. But common usage does not always follow this definition. Many schools called academies were never chartered, and many taught Latin and Greek as well as realist subjects. Many preparatory schools attached to colleges were also called academies. One might say that in popular speech any semiprivate or wholly private secondary school is an academy, and in New York and a few other states several public high schools still retain their former title of academy. This is an example of the loose use of terms in education; and for this there seems to be no easy cure. The conclusion is that ideally an academy is the kind of institution defined at the beginning of this paragraph, but that practically it may diverge in various ways from the ideal.

Several new educational opportunities were provided by the private schools and academies. They offered instruction above the elements to girls of the middle classes. This was a real advance and in this America was a pioneer. Elementary home economics was taught in an early girls' academy. Some schools gave instruction in methods of teaching and school management, providing professional preparation for teaching to boys and girls before there were any normal schools. Handwriting, commercial arithmetic, and bookkeeping were taught to young business people. Some academies were established by religious denominations. Some were boarding schools. It is evident that the academy was an experimental institution tending to become an all-purpose school, but developing without over-all planning.

One attempt to provide a reasoned design was made by Benjamin Franklin about the middle of the eighteenth century. His *Proposals Relating to the Education of Youth in Pennsylvania* (1749) came out several years before William Smith's *Mirania* and long before Dock's *Schulordnung*. The *Proposals* was only a pamphlet but it was a significant publication on education as a special subject; and it led to a practical result, the founding of the Philadelphia Academy. This was its object.

Franklin had already founded a reading club, the mother, as he claimed, of those subscription libraries which formed the reading tastes of his countrymen, "and made tradesmen and farmers as intelligent as the gentry of other countries." Out of his junto the American Philosophical Society grew, a learned body on the order of the Royal Society of London. This has shown the vitality of several of Franklin's creations. Some years ago this Society, which was organized by Franklin in 1743 "for the promotion of useful knowledge among the British plantations in America," celebrated the completion of its second century. It is a scientific rather than, in the present sense of the word, a philosophical society. It has always had famous names on its rolls; and among the earliest were Doctor Thomas Bond, who was a pupil of John Kearsley; John Bartram, botanist; and Thomas Godfrey, mathematician and maker of astronomical instruments. In the promotion of his reading club, library, and learned society, Franklin did not meet the opposition which dogged his academy project.

The *Proposals* was not intended to be original in idea, but only in its demand that the idea should be put to work. Franklin's chief purpose was to show that the idea was not new but was reasonable, widely accepted as an idea, and should be acted upon. He named and quoted the great writers who had supported his views, particularly John Locke, no doubt because he was read and approved in America. All this was to show that this idea was not the effect of a chance inspiration, nor the plan of an educational amateur, but was one developed by experienced teachers and educational philosophers. He stated the realist as opposed to the classical position in education, but he could not point to many institutions such as he had in mind. The first German *Realschule* had been opened in Berlin only two years earlier, but of this he was unaware. He did not refer to the Puritan academies in England, perhaps because his plan differed from their practice.

What was to be taught was the main topic of the pamphlet. Twenty or more subjects were proposed. Most of these can be placed under three major heads and their subdivisions, English, mathematics, and history. Franklin's concern with history is the outstanding fact here, for English and mathematics were the leading subjects in the private schools. The proposal to teach history was new; and the history was to be the "new history" of morals, customs, commerce, practical arts and religion, not merely the old history of war and politics. He supported the realist demand for concrete teaching aids. The subjects may be set down in semitabular form as follows:

Physical exercises, running, jumping, wrestling, swimming
Handwriting, drawing with perspective
Arithmetic, accounts, geometry, astronomy (no algebra)
English as a language, grammar, literature
History, ancient, modern, English, the new universal history
Geography with maps
Oratory, debating
Logic
Morality, "benignity of mind, religion, studied historically . . . the excellence of the Christian religion and proofs of Divine Providence"
Natural history, gardening, agriculture, and, according to individual taste and need, languages ancient and modern.

This is a realist curriculum. Franklin meant to provide an educational program suitable for the commercial and productive classes. Bacon had said that knowledge is for delight and power. Franklin attempted to increase the delight and power, especially the latter, of merchants, mechanics, and active men in general. He placed great emphasis upon skill in the use of the English language, a lesson that he had learned in his work as a printer and in his experience in persuading his fellow townsmen to good works.

To administer the program he urged the formation of an academy with a charter and a board of trustees. The *Proposals* dealt with the location of the building, the grounds and lands, and the equipment and apparatus. Not all of his proposals were accepted. The academy did not, as he had intended, become a boarding school, nor did it adopt a school uniform for the pupils. The trustees may not have taken the personal interest in the pupils that Franklin desired. Educational tradition was too strong for him. His associates insisted upon a classical course in the academy parallel to the realist program. After instructor David James Dove left, the English course faltered. The institution became mainly a Latin school to prepare students for the College of Philadelphia which was opened in 1755. Franklin's exposure of the bad faith, as it seemed to him, of the trustees in devitalizing his realist program was one of the last acts of his life, and shows how dear to him that program was.

While the academy was still in the formative stage, Franklin distributed his *Idea of an English School,* a paper of ten or twelve pages. This was an exposition of Franklin's central idea. In it he outlined the work to be done in each of the six years which he proposed for boys eight years old who had already acquired the arts of reading and writing. No place was given to foreign languages. In the *Proposals* they had been named at the end for those who should need them; from the *Idea* they were omitted. In this period Franklin still believed that he could win general support for his English school by making concessions to the Latinists. This was a mistake to be expected of an inexperienced person, and Franklin should have known better.

The *Constitutions* of the Philadelphia Academy provided for both a classical school or department and an English-mathematical one. The classical master was made rector of the entire institution, thus placing the English-mathematical master and his school in subordinate positions; and his salary was set at double the amount paid the English master. The fate of the English school has already been indicated. When the academy became an appendage to the college it was felt by some that an English School was wholly out of place in the collegiate environment.

Just before the college was established, the Reverend William Smith was chosen to teach in the classical school of the academy in May, 1754.

He had been educated at the University of Aberdeen and had been a schoolmaster in Scotland. In America he published a pamphlet called *A General Idea of the College of Mirania.* In this essay he gave considerable support to Franklin's scheme for an academy; but it does not appear that he tried to promote the English school, especially after March, 1755, when he became head of the college with the title of provost. For whatever reasons, the English school became an elementary school for little children. The chief reasons were not the absence of Franklin, the connection with the college, the appointment of the classically trained provost, or the higher salary of the classics master in the academy. The chief reason was one that even Franklin could not overcome. People just did not believe that an education without Latin was real education. An English education might do for shopkeepers and mechanics who, it was thought, were probably not capable of taking a high polish anyway. It required a hundred years to convince the larger public of this error.

Education above the elementary grades was not often open to girls in the colonies. Advanced education was to be broad and liberal. Only the private schools aimed to teach what was directly useful in practical life. Classical education was based upon those ancient literary works which scholars considered the best of their kinds because they deal with universal topics, in a restrained and logical manner, and in elevated language.

Latin schools and colleges, coming out of a long European history, supplied this kind of education. When they were transplanted, the early enthusiasm for the "new learning" had already declined; and the later interest in ancient culture, philosophy, art, and economics had not yet arisen. In the interval these institutions were largely grammatical and stylistic institutes. The Latin schools were most numerous in New England, where they were town schools, but even in New England they were not popular in the more rural parts. In the rest of the colonies the Latin schools were usually private and often temporary. The curriculum everywhere consisted mainly of Latin grammar and authors and the elements of the Greek language.

The colonial colleges continued these studies and added Hebrew, academic disputation, medieval mathematics and science, and theology. Their primary purpose was the preparation of ministers, but a majority of the students followed other vocations. The students lived a meager collegiate life under the close supervision of the college officers. Disorder was common, in reaction to the close surveillance, poor teaching, and unattractive living conditions.

The conflict between the older classical and the rising realist education grew out of various causes. There was social discrimination favoring the classically educated professional classes and against those in the practical vocations. The belief in the superior disciplinary effects of classical studies were met with skepticism. It was pointed out that many college men were impractical theorists and dreamers. The needs of a new country were set against the long and honorable history of classical education. Realism was brought in from abroad in the ideas of Comenius, Locke, and William Penn. Penn in several ways anticipated Franklin who, however, cited other authorities.

Private realistic schools were numerous in the cities in the last colonial century. They taught modern languages, practical knowledge and skills, and the applications of mathematics to navigation and engineering. A few examples illustrate the nature of these schools and also illustrate what is well known, that some of the teachers were both able and eminent. These private schools prepared the way for the American academy; and Franklin's creation must be considered an example of an institution that was too far ahead of the time for success.

QUESTIONS

1. Why did the colonists transplant classical schools instead of creating new upper schools more appropriate to American needs?

2. What kinds of schools should they have established for those able to stay in school to age fourteen? until age eighteen?

3. Why were girls excluded from all education except the most elementary? Consider traditional reasons and taboos, economic factors, notions about family government, health, the distribution of intelligence, and any others.

4. Would you argue that education for women is more important on the frontier than in a developed country?

5. Prepare a report on the teachers of the Boston Latin School. What general conclusions may and what may not be drawn from your report? Use the *History* by Pauline Holmes and other books.

6. Why did American Latin schools fail to reach the standards of those in England?

7. What factors aided and what retarded the development of realist schools? Consider among several others the scientific activity of the Middle Colonies.

8. Compare the early William Penn Charter School with Franklin's academy. Use James Mulhern's *History of Secondary Education in Pennsylvania*, Thomas Woody's *Educational Views of Benjamin Franklin*, Wickersham's *History of Education in Pennsylvania*, the *Dictionary of American Biography*, and other books.

9. What were the salient features of Franklin's plan? How original was his scheme?

BOOKS AND PAPERS

There are many histories of individual colleges but there is no space to list them. Morison on Harvard, Cheyney on the University of Pennsylvania, and, although it is very brief, Wertenbaker on Princeton are examples of good ones. Some college histories are poor because they include much trivial material, are badly written, or are too distended, running to so many volumes in some cases that no one will read them. We have at least one good history of a Latin school, that by Pauline Holmes, listed below.

Bridenbaugh, Carl, *Cities in the Wilderness, 1625–1742*, New York, 1938.

Brown, E. E., *Making of Our Middle Schools*, New York, 1905.

Coon, C. L., *North Carolina Schools and Academies, 1790–1840, A Documentary History*, Raleigh, 1915.

Elsbree, W. S., *The American Teacher*, New York, 1939.

Fithian, Philip Vickers, *Journal and Letters . . . 1773–1774, A Plantation Tutor of the Old Dominion*, edited by H. D. Farish, Williamsburg, Virginia, 1943.

Force, Peter, Editor, *Tracts and Other Papers*, Washington, D. C., 1938. The "Advisive Narrative" is No. 15, Vol. III.

Holmes, Pauline, *History of the Boston Public Latin School, 1635–1935*, Harvard University Press, 1935.

Hornberger, Theodore, *Scientific Thought in the American Colleges, 1638–1800*, University of Texas Press, 1945.

Kraus, Michael, *Intercolonial Aspects of American Culture*, Columbia University Press, 1928.

Potter, David, *Debating in the Colonial Chartered Colleges, 1642–1800*, New York, Teachers College, Columbia University, 1944.

Small, W. H., *Early New England Schools*, Boston, 1914.

Smith, William, *The Works of William Smith, Late Provost, College of Philadelphia*, Philadelphia, 1803, containing "A General Idea of the College of Mirania."

Thwing, C. F., *History of Higher Education in America*, New York, 1906.

Uhl, W. L., *Secondary School Curricula*, New York, 1927.

Wertenbaker, T. J., *The Puritan Oligarchy*, New York, 1947, containing a somewhat more favorable view of Puritan institutions than that expressed in the same author's *The First Americans* (1927).

Woody, Thomas, *History of Women's Education in the United States*, Lancaster, Pennsylvania, 1929; and editor of *Educational Views of Benjamin Franklin* (New York, 1931), which contains the chief educational writings of Franklin, but his paper "On the Usefulness of Mathematics" is reprinted in D. E. Smith and J. Ginsberg, *History of Mathematics in America*, Chicago, 1934.

Young, R. F., *Comenius and the Indians of New England*, London, 1929; and *Comenius in England*, London, 1932, with mention (p. 93) of the use of the *Janua* in New England.

PART II

Chapter III

LIBERTY AND LEARNING

CONTEMPORARIES noted that the American Revolution began before the Revolutionary War and continued after the peace. Some attempted to trace its origins from the Reformation or from the "glorious revolution" of the English Whigs in 1688. Whatever the origins, its effects were felt in Britain, in France, even in Russia, and it promoted freedom for most of Latin America.

The greatest effects of the Revolution were felt in British America where it led to the founding of an independent nation, the United States of America. The adoption of the federal principle was a happy inspiration, for instead of exploiting the territories it gave them the assurance and the method of becoming states equal to the oldest in the Union. The federal court provided for a single system of justice in the entire land. The separation of church and state forestalled all fear of religious wars.

National unity was increased by the free movement of goods and persons from state to state. Jefferson proposed the decimal system of coinage, and Nicholas Pike's *Arithmetic*, "for the use of the citizens of the United States," introduced it into schools and won the praise of Washington. Noah Webster proposed the use of an American language instead of the English, but since the two were nearly identical this had no very momentous results. He did produce *An American Dictionary of the English Language*. The painters began to use American subjects and writers tried to create an American literature.

The educational thinkers of the Revolution and the following years were led by Jefferson, Benjamin Rush, Robert Coram, James Sullivan, Noah Webster, Pierre Samuel Du Pont de Nemours, Samuel Knox, and Samuel Harrison Smith; and many of these and of the founders of the nation saw the problem of education as a political question and treated it as a phase of public policy. Education in their view was a means of preserving liberty, securing unity, promoting good citizenship, and developing the resources of the land and people. Education would help maintain the union of states, a united people, and a republican government.

Not all the writers of the early years were wise and some of their thought was ill-timed. There was abroad a wrong idea that a national system of education under centralized federal control was both feasible and desirable. There was inadequate understanding of the principle that successful school-systems must grow in intimate connection with the societies which they serve. This generalization is illustrated by many contemporary national systems, the English, the French, and even the Russian, each of which has conformed to the social conditions of its country. Recent Russian history does not contradict the principle. It was the liberal education of the early 1920's that conflicted with Russian history; it is the present authoritarian system which agrees best with Russian autocracy, past and present. In the new United States with its individualism, localism, states' rights, and denominationalism, a centralized school system should not have been so much as thought of.

Many new trends revealed themselves and old ones continued in the Revolutionary and early national periods. Numerous colleges were established by the religious denominations. Efforts were made during the war and afterward to change some of the older colleges into state institutions. A new state university movement led to the creation of twenty or more such institutions before the Civil War. But even with the support of George Washington the national university idea could not be realized in an actual institution. The federal government began to make grants of land to the states for state universities and for elementary schools. Local efforts and state constitutions and laws made provision for public elementary education in the early national period; and the public high school began to dispute the ground occupied by the academy. Several of these topics are discussed below and the others will be taken up in the following chapters.

1. Two Theories

For some time after the Revolutionary War, activity in higher education far exceeded that in the development of the common schools. There are several reasons for this. The children of the poor did not have time to attend school for extended periods. The colleges appealed to the well-to-do, they had a fixed curriculum, and they prepared professional people. Workingmen's sons would be workingmen and, it was thought, they needed little schooling. The population was scattered and it was difficult to gather small children into schools. Colleges and academies were often boarding institutions. Finally, those most active in school promotion were college-trained and naturally favored the kind of education which they themselves had enjoyed.

Another phenomenon of the post-Revolutionary and early national periods that needs to be explained is the feverish American borrowing of foreign ideas and practices. This seems to be in conflict with the prevailing nationalism. Before the Civil War the United States introduced French military education at West Point, French methods in civil engineering education, and with British help the new French mathematical methods. French systems of teaching the deaf and the blind were borrowed. England supplied the monitorial schools; but these were shortly superseded by the Pestalozzian doctrines from Switzerland and Germany. Another Swiss, Fellenberg, contributed the manual labor system, which had a brief vogue. The American normal school, largely a native development, was influenced by various European examples. This list could be made longer.

No doubt there are several reasons for this American receptivity. The new nation was educationally underdeveloped and there was need for institutions to cope with growing requirements. With the struggle for independence and its achievement came greater exposure to foreign practices. The alliance with France, a country with a highly developed special and technological education, was a factor. Travel and books contributed. Educationally the mother country was in one of her most unprogressive periods at the time when the colonies revolted. The mere fact of separation may have been a positive influence toward borrowing from Europe rather than Britain.

2. FOUNDING FATHERS AT SCHOOL

One way to build a bridge from the colonial to the national period is to answer the question: What schooling was received by those who lived during the transition? This will be to leave abstractions and to turn to facts. Our bridge will not be a very wide one because the known facts about the individual farmers, frontiersmen, workers, and housewives are not abundant. We do know something about the education of many of those who were leaders in the Revolution and in the framing of the government. But these were not average men. They were all unusual at least in this, that they were in positions of national importance at critical times. We shall examine the schooling of those who signed any one of three political documents, the Declaration of Independence, the Articles of Confederation, and the Constitution of the United States.

Two men, Robert Morris and Roger Sherman, signed all three of these documents and a number signed two of them. There are 117 different names attached to the instruments. All the colonies were, of course, represented. With few exceptions these leaders were born in the first half of the century of decision and none later than 1760. The oldest was Benjamin Franklin, born in 1706, and the youngest was Jonathan Dayton of New Jersey who was only twenty-seven when he served in the Constitutional Convention.

The educational opportunities of the period from about 1712 to 1782 have been considered in a general way in the preceding chapters. The particular information about the education of these signers comes from the *Dictionary of American Biography* and similar sources. Their opportunities ranged from almost none to the best that America and Europe together could offer. It probably is significant that the signers of the earliest document, the Declaration, had received appreciably less schooling than either of the other groups. The movers for independence were not mainly upper-class people. Franklin recorded that he attended school for two years. About one-third of his colleagues in the Congress of 1776 had attended only country schools or had been mainly self-taught. There were some such in each of the other groups but in smaller proportions. Those with little formal education came from every section and had used their opportunities in various ways. Stephen Hopkins of Rhode Island, a farm boy, became a practical surveyor and learned politics as moderator of town meetings. Roger Sherman of Connecticut was apprenticed to a shoemaker and became successively a writer, publisher, and lawyer. John Penn of North Carolina attended a country school and read law in books borrowed from a friend. Others read medical books and helped a doctor in his practice. Mercantile careers, especially when they were not too successful, gave leisure to read.

At the opposite end of the range there were thirty-eight graduates of American colleges, the larger numbers from Harvard, Yale, Princeton, and Pennsylvania. Jefferson graduated from William and Mary and Gouverneur Morris from Columbia. The ages of the whole group at graduation ranged from fifteen to twenty-four years. James Madison stayed at Princeton for a year after graduation to study ethics and theology under Witherspoon. Two of these college graduates went abroad to study medicine, Benjamin Rush at Edinburgh and Hugh Williamson at Utrecht.

Others of the founding fathers had studied in the secondary schools or the ancient universities of England, or had read law in the Middle Temple, which was in effect a law school. Most of these, as noted before, were Southerners, chiefly South Carolinians. Few were given such extended opportunities as came to Charles Cotesworth Pinckney of Charleston. After working at home with the aid of a tutor, he was sent to Westminster School, matriculated at Oxford where he heard Blackstone, entered the Middle Temple, and wound up in France where he studied botany and chemistry under leading scientists, and military science in a royal military academy at Caen. Charles and Daniel Carroll of Maryland, Richard Henry Lee of Virginia, and William H. Drayton of South Carolina also were educated in Europe. Two famous Scotsmen who belong to the signers, John Wither- spoon and James Wilson, were educated in their native land.

Our bridge is narrow and somewhat frail and we must resist the tempta- tion to draw a heavy load of conclusions over it. It is safe to say that many of these 117 signers were exceptional. Such men create opportunities. Schools are useful even to the most gifted, more useful than to the less gifted; but they are not indispensable. One of every three of these statesmen had only a few months of schooling, usually in poor schools; and one in four had a college education.

3. LIBERTY BEGINS IN THE MIND

The principles of liberty and of public education in a free country are complementary. To study the origins of public education in the United States one must examine the American doctrine of liberty. Thomas Jefferson always declared, whenever the subject came up in his later years, that in writing the Declaration of Independence it had been no part of his purpose to aim at originality. That would have defeated his purpose. The sentiment of the document, he said (with considerable exaggeration) to one who had asked, "was the sentiment of all America." Men would certainly not have risked their lives and honor upon that sentiment if it had not been their own.

The Declaration is, therefore, a primary source for the principles of liberty which the Americans of 1776 intended to maintain. The funda- mental principle was this, that governments derive their just powers from the consent of the governed. The patriots considered self-government a natural right, guaranteed by the law of nature. This Jefferson asserted.

Two years before the Declaration, Jefferson had written a *Summary View of the Rights of British America* and its contents may help to explain why he was chosen to write the Declaration of Independence. In the *Sum- mary View* he held that the king was only the chief officer of the people and that he had only those powers which the laws gave him. For the people he claimed the "natural right" to emigrate and to establish a new society with such laws as they believed would conduce to their happiness.

The ruling political theory of the time, as we have noted in the Introduction, was that of the law of nature and the social compact. Early man was thought to have lived in a state of nature without organized society or government or public order. Men maintained themselves by craft and force. They overcame the brutishness of such a condition by a compact in which the many promised cooperation to each other and loyalty to a ruler in exchange for the promise of orderly processes of security and justice. Thus was a political society created in which all were in a sense equal. Rulers governed by consent and, according to John Locke, remained rulers only as long as they kept their part of the compact. If either party failed to keep the compact, mankind, it was held, would revert to a state of nature and a new beginning would be in order. There was discussion both in 1776 and 1787, each a revolutionary era, whether the country was not then in a state of nature.

These ideas were current in the ancient world and some of them may be found in Plato's *Republic;* but they were developed for England and America by John Locke and later in Europe by Jean Jacques Burlamaqui (1694–1748), an Italo-Swiss jurist whose *Principles of Natural Law* was translated into English in the last year of the author's life. A Philadelphia historian, Sidney G. Fisher, wrote, "To this day anyone going to the Philadelphia Library and asking for No. 77 can take into his hands the identical, well-worn volume which delegates to the Congress read with earnest, anxious minds." The reference is to the library of the Philadelphia Library Company, of which Franklin was the leading founder.

These exponents of natural law held that the pursuit of happiness and therefore of self-development is a right inhering in all men; that civil equality, equal standing before the law, and equal treatment by the courts are simple attributes of citizenship; that the people themselves have the right to frame a government and laws that will promote these great ends. And they held that these principles were not invented but were discovered in the nature of man and written on the human heart.

The application of this philosophy to education is not difficult. It declares that social institutions must preserve and not infringe upon the natural equality of human beings. That equality is infringed when the wealthy and the well-born are given opportunities to mature their talents that are denied to poor children, lacking an address and a name. Schools cannot make people alike in attainment; but they must open to all every opportunity for growth and acquirement.

The founders of the United States realized that the liberties of the citizen are jeopardized if he does not early acquire the understanding of those rights and the intelligence to maintain them. They say that it is through education that he must gain this knowledge and training. They understood that unless the rule of the people leads to prosperity, happiness, and justice, that unless they rule wisely they will lose the chance to rule at all. With such a philosophy the nation's stake in a sound and freely accessible education is obvious.

How gradually this political philosophy was transmitted from the leaders to the people and applied to education is a great part of the following story. Only slowly did it become clear that this doctrine not only justifies but requires a complete system of public schools equally open to all. Eventually it was admitted that this places upon the legislature the duty "to provide by law for a general system of education ascending in a regular gradation from township schools to a State University, wherein tuition shall be gratis and equally open to all." This is the language of the first (1816) constitution of Indiana; but its demand was not soon to be achieved and has not yet been achieved everywhere and for all.

The federal Constitution does not deal with education, but its indirect influences upon education have been manifold and profound. Most profound has been the doctrine of reserved powers stated in the Tenth Amendment. This has not only left education to the states as a reserved power but it has served to warn off the federal government from interference with education in the states. It has not served to prevent Congress from distributing aid to education in the states, chiefly aid in vocational fields. This power to distribute educational funds implies the power to withhold them and thus to control education in the states by indirection. The First Amendment, dealing with religion and with freedom of communication; the Fourteenth Amendment with its "due process" clause; the power to maintain a postal system and to promote science and the useful arts; the powers assigned to the Supreme Court or developed by it; the general welfare clause (I, 8) and the taxing power—all and sundry have been used in ways that have influenced education in the states. Attention is to be given also to the provision of the Constitution that "the United States shall guarantee to every State in this Union a republican form of government" (IV, 4). The question arises whether such a form of government can be maintained without a system of public education. This question which may have seemed academic earlier may yet become practical. The racial segregation decision of the Supreme Court of 1954 may make it so. But in the past and in the main, public education has been a state function, based upon state constitutions and laws.

The states have allowed considerable freedom to the local divisions. Communities which desire to go beyond the minimal requirements of the state law have an open road. But there are strict state requirements and controls. On the other hand, the whole system is gradually becoming more uniform over the nation. The trend toward a national school system is persistent. Whether direct federal requirements and controls will eventually be developed cannot be known now.

4. EDUCATION IN THE STATE CONSTITUTIONS

The new state constitutions contained the earliest official statements on education in the evolving nation. Two months before independence was declared the Continental Congress advised the people of the colonies to form their governments. In ten of the colonies, this was done promptly. Connecticut and Rhode Island merely altered their charters; and Massachusetts, delayed by partisan struggles, adopted a new constitution in 1780.

Provisions on education were included in six of the eleven new constitutions. These paragraphs were moderate in their demands; but to have included them at all was an advance upon the thought of earlier times, when the state, which speaks for all the people, was not expected to speak or act in regard to education. Educational provisions in the new constitutions are evidence that the political philosophy analyzed above was at work in this field. They are evidence that the states were beginning to sense the necessity of education for citizenship and public service.

Those beginnings were moderate. Pennsylvania in 1776 adopted one of the most radical of the new constitutions. It provided for a unicameral legislature and assigned to it the power to elect the governor. But the educational clause, Section 44, provided only that "a school or schools shall be established in every county by the legislature, for the convenient instruction of youth with such salaries to the masters, paid by the public, as may enable them to instruct youth at low prices; and all useful learning shall be duly encouraged and promoted in one or more universities."

By adopting this section the state acknowledged a duty to promote education but it did nothing more. One school in each county, the minimal demand, would have served only a minute fraction of the people; and the legislature could choose its own time to act. It did; it chose not to act. The schools were not to be free but the constitution did not say whether the salaries were to be paid by the state, county, or other unit. The last part of the clause may have given warrant for the seizure of the College of Philadelphia, to be described below. This timid educational section was copied by other states. Omitting a few unimportant words, it was incorporated in the North Carolina constitution of 1776; in substance in the constitutions of Vermont and Georgia in 1777; and it may have influenced the Missouri constitution of 1820.

The central idea of all these provisions was that the state should supplement private facilities. There was no thought of universal public schooling. And before the end of the war the people began to grow more conservative, a trend that frequently shows itself in the later phases of a revolutionary movement. As the early constitutions were revised toward the end of the century, provision was made for the education of the poor only. The second constitution of Pennsylvania (1790) asked the legislature to provide free education for the poor, and the constitutions adopted in 1798 by Georgia and Delaware were even less explicit.

The financial stringency and the mounting state debts in the war and afterward made the legislatures even more cautious. There was a tendency for constitutional provisions on education to become long, eloquent, and indefinite. This is notably the case with the constitution adopted in 1780, after a heated struggle, by the state which led all the rest in education, Massachusetts. John Adams wrote the educational sections. He began with a historical introduction celebrating the "wise and pious ancestors" who had founded Harvard, and "divers persons" who had added to its endowment, and he praised the constitution and powers of the corporation and the overseers of the college. The rights and powers of Harvard are duly confirmed. The next section declares that "wisdom and knowledge as well as virtue" are necessary to self-government, and finally it calls upon the legislatures and magistrates to cherish "literature and the sciences and all seminaries of them. . . ." Four years later New Hampshire, which had omitted education from its first constitution in 1776, incorporated in its revised instrument some of the ideas just quoted from the constitution of its southern neighbor.

The flowing periods of Adams have sometimes imposed upon historians of education the belief that these provisions were far "ahead of the general conceptions of the time." This is a mistake. Adams himself in a letter written twenty-five years later said with truth and candor that the words had come from his heart rather than his head. A more compact and eloquent but possibly derivative statement of the same general thought was incorporated into the Northwest Ordinance of 1787, and was admired and copied into legal documents in various states. It read: "Religion, morality, and knowledge being necessary to good government and the happiness of mankind, schools and the means of education shall forever be encouraged" by the legislatures. Few or none would doubt that this is a good sentiment; but as law it leaves out the essential elements.

5. JEFFERSON'S PLAN

The Virginia "bill for the more general diffusion of knowledge" which Jefferson prepared in 1779 provided for a primary school in every "hundred," a unit comparable to a township. These schools were to be publicly controlled and in part publicly supported. Children could attend without charge for three years, and longer by paying tuition. Reading, writing, arithmetic, and the history of Greece, Rome, England, and America were to be the subjects of instruction. The Bible, commonly read in schools at that time, was not mentioned, and Jefferson was against putting the Bible "into the hands of children at an age when their judgments are not sufficiently matured."

Because, in his view, the reasoning powers did not develop much before the age of fifteen, Jefferson considered memory work most appropriate for children. All free children, boys and girls, living within a given hundred were, as we have seen, to receive free instruction in its school for the term of three years and afterwards at private expense as long as might be desired. For every ten schools there was to be an overseer, "eminent for his learning, integrity, and fidelity to the commonwealth." He was to appoint the teachers and supervise the schools. In the bill the space for the teachers' salaries was left blank.

The bill of 1779 provided for twenty secondary schools distributed throughout the state. Bright boys selected from the primary schools were to be given two or more years of free education in the classics, English grammar, geography, and arithmetic through cube root. Capable pupils were to be retained for the full six-year course of secondary schooling. From those who were culled out, teachers for the primary schools were to be chosen. Those who attained the highest distinction in the secondary schools were to be sent to William and Mary College for a complete education, free. This selective scheme was to apply to the scholarship pupils only. Those able to pay could send their sons to school and college at their own cost and without meeting the competitive tests. The secondary schools were to be controlled by public boards of visitors.

Jefferson has been both praised and condemned for this plan of secular and public education. One opening for criticism is provided by the fact that the great Virginia democrat, who was violently anti-Platonist, devised an educational plan that has a resemblance to Plato's own. And then he provided for only three years of free education. On the latter point it is to be kept in mind that Virginia had no system of schools nor any effective public opinion in favor of establishing one. Three years of free schooling was not all that Jefferson might have desired, but as a skilful politician he knew it was unwise to ask for more. Even the selective feature can be defended. In extending educational privileges to new classes, some kind of selection has throughout history been very often used. Too often selection has been based upon wealth or family or influence; Jefferson agreed with Plato in basing it upon merit. This defense does not meet the fundamental objection that the bill proposed class legislation in conflict with the political principles of its author. Doubtless Jefferson meant it to be the first step on the way to a system of universal public education.

It was too long a step for Virginia to take at that time and for many years. The legislature did not consider the bill in 1779; and when it was taken up in 1796 it was passed in an optional and therefore ineffective form. For thirty years after writing the bill Jefferson was engaged in politics and public service, but education became his chief public interest after his retirement. His leadership in forming the University of Virginia was exercised in this later period of his life.

Political, practical, and intellectual motives led him to devote so much attention to education. He held that education while not the only need was, in his words: "essentially necessary" in a republic. Education was useful, he saw, for increasing production, saving labor, preserving health, and especially for the improvement of agriculture, "a science of the very first order." Beyond the ever-present political issues and practical needs, Jefferson was devoted to intellectual interests. He possessed these in greater variety than almost any other American of his time. He knew by experience that learning is good not only for use but also for itself alone, that is, for personal satisfaction.

From Paris in 1786 he wrote to a friend that only an educated people could preserve their freedom and promote their own real happiness. This education, he said, "it is the business of the state to provide and that upon a general plan." To John Adams he once said that his bill of 1779 was intended "to defeat the competition of wealth and birth for public positions."

Because "the people are the best judges of local issues" and "the safest depositories of freedom," Jefferson favored local control of the primary schools. The people themselves, he said, do incomparably better than a central government what they are competent to understand. Of compelling attendance at school there was no question in America then. Once, indeed, he revealed a more urgent temper. He proposed to withhold the ballot from those who, given the opportunity, did not learn to read. John Adams disagreed.

6. Statesmen and Utopians

Many of the statemen in the new republic gave expression to their views upon education, frequently to their views on its political importance. Washington gave personal attention to the schooling of his foster children and grandchildren and even of the children of relatives and friends. He contributed to the support of schools in Alexandria and elsewhere. He urged Congress to aid in the promotion of science and literature; to establish a national military school; and to consider the proposal to create a national university. His fundamental view was stated in his first message to Congress and again in similar language in the Farewell Address in the now familiar words: "Promote, then, as an object of primary importance, institutions for the general diffusion of knowledge. In proportion as the structure of government gives force to public opinion, it is essential that public opinion should be enlightened." These we know were Washington's sentiments even though the words were supplied by Hamilton.

Education as public policy was a frequent topic with John Adams. He had a special distinction among the greater statesmen. He had been a teacher. The small town where Adams was born and where he always lived was noted for the number of students which it sent to Harvard College, of which number he was one. He graduated in 1755. Undecided with regard to a profession, he became the master of a Latin school and taught for three years, but unwillingly. At twenty-three he became a lawyer and began the hard, laborious climb to eminence as an attorney, political scientist, and statesman.

Among his early publications was his study of the canon law and the feudal law, "the two great systems of tyranny" since the beginning of Christianity, so he declared. In this dissertation he asserted the rights of the poor, "for such they have, undoubtedly, antecedent to all earthly government . . . rights derived from the great Legislator of the universe." This is the concept of a higher law to which the provisions of the social compact had to conform if they were to be valid. Now Adams makes the application to education. The great, he said, keep the poor from the knowledge of their rights; and it is knowledge alone, diffused through the whole body of the people, that can preserve them from tyranny. Jefferson would not have disagreed.

The "happy condition" of Massachusetts, Adams ascribed to four institutions, the town meetings, the congregations, the schools, and the militia. In his *Defence of the Constitutions of the American States* he spoke particularly of education, declaring that under a free government it is more indispensable and must be more general than under any other. All the peo-

ple of every rank and class must be educated in a republic; and schools must
be conveniently located and maintained at public expense. If nations ever
become wise no human being will be allowed to grow up in ignorance.

That John Adams thought the educated class should rule will not surprise anyone who knows him; but he also believed that they in fact do rule.
He made a little calculation on the latter point. Massachusetts, he wrote, "has
probably educated as many sons to letters, in proportion to numbers, as any
state in the union, perhaps as any nation ancient or modern." He calculated
that over the whole period of nearly two centuries since the founding of
Harvard, about one in 750 of the whole people had been graduated by the
college. If this calculation is correct the proportion in Massachusetts was
about three times that of all America. And what did these graduates do?
They governed the province and state, they were the ministers, lawyers,
physicians, and teachers, the bankers, scholars, and leaders in all lines. And
they still, he declared, govern and lead. "I hope, then," he wrote to John
Taylor of Caroline, "you will acknowledge that 'abilities' form a distinction
and confer a privilege, in fact, though they give no peculiar rights in society."

Other political leaders expressed their views on education. Samuel
Adams wished to have children in early youth taught the art of self-government and the doctrines of religion. John Jay considered "knowledge to be
the soul of a republic." Madison declared that "knowledge will forever
govern ignorance; and a people who mean to be their own governors must
arm themselves with the power which knowledge gives." Over and over this
theme is repeated. Thus Benjamin Rush: "To conform the principles,
morals, and manners of our citizens to our republican forms of government
it is absolutely necessary that knowledge of every kind should be dissemi-
nated through every part of the United States."

In our time of troubles before the new government was firmly established, many men who had faith in republican government and in the power
of education to fit men to govern themselves became obsessed with the fear
that time was running out. Men of experience in public affairs, lawyers, and
public officials, such men as James Sullivan (1744–1808) of Massachusetts
and Nathaniel Chipman (1752–1843) of Vermont feared that disaster
might overtake the country before citizens were made aware of the dangers.
They feared disunity and insurrection and the loss of public and private
credit because of the general ignorance. The remedy, education, they feared
would not arrive in time. It was, to borrow a twentieth century phrase, a
race between education and catastrophe.

Yet no one had a workable plan. Many plans were proposed by Robert

Coram, Samuel Knox, Samuel Harrison Smith, Du Pont de Nemours, and others. But the planners did not show how the schools could be supported or administered or how the teachers could be secured. Several proposed a national system for this highly decentralized country. Many years of thought and trial were required for the solution of these essential practical problems. Meanwhile the country survived and even prospered.

7. THE NATIONAL UNIVERSITY IDEA

The idea of a national university," wrote Professor Edgar B. Wesley, "has one marked characteristic; it persists." On this it would not be unfair to remark that it is only the idea that persists. The idea is old, but contrary to the opinion of some there is no trustworthy evidence that it was expressed before 1787. And there is no present indication that such an institution will be established.

The *American Museum* for January, 1787, contained an article entitled "Address to the People of the United States," written by Benjamin Rush. He favored a number of political measures that were intended to increase the power of the federal government. And he proposed, as far as known for the first time, the establishment of a "federal university." Rush defined his idea more fully in the same magazine (November, 1788) in an article that was widely copied, "Plan of a Federal University." Between these two appearances of the idea, Madison had moved in the Constitutional Convention to include among the powers of Congress the power to establish a national university; but his motion was lost. Washington took up the idea and urged it upon the attention of Congress. He bequeathed stock in a navigation company for the future endowment of the school, but this property proved valueless. Four of the first six presidents recommended the consideration of the idea to Congress. After John Quincy Adams retired nothing more was heard of it in the national councils for forty years.

Renewed agitation began in Grant's administration and continued for many years. But again the efforts failed of reaching their object. And in the course of the century the Library of Congress, the Smithsonian Institution, the several departments of the government, and other public and private institutions have made the City of Washington a great educational and research center. Independent and state universities, the country over, perform the legitimate functions that Rush and the early leaders assigned to their proposed institution. During the height of the agitation in the latter part of the nineteenth century, several leading presidents of the larger universities were in opposition to the whole idea. Such an institution would not, however, be unique. Many Latin-American countries have national universities. But the Anglo-Saxon countries and the other nations which have influenced American education strongly do not. At present the need for federal aid to primary and secondary schools is far more urgent than the need for a federal or national university.

8. College Enthusiasm

No new colleges were founded in the heat of the Revolutionary struggle, but with the approach of peace many were established as if to make up for lost time. None of the oldest colleges was more than a few miles from salt water, but the people were now moving into Kentucky and Ohio. American distances were great, travel across the mountains was difficult, college expenses in Eastern towns were high, and, not least in importance, the East was becoming too liberal in its theology for the West. If the Western people were to have adequate college opportunities and the Western churches an orthodox ministry, new institutions were needed.

New foundations were created with such speed, one after another, that President Ezra Stiles of Yale, borrowing a word from the religious vocabulary of the time, was led to speak of "college enthusiasm." Counting only the viable institutions, seventeen colleges were founded before the end of the century and twelve more by 1820. And this was only the beginning of what became a race, for, by 1860, 182 of the country's "permanent" colleges had been established. Nine out of every ten had some connection with a religious society.

Not all the forces of that time were favorable to the colleges. On the contrary, these 182 were the survivors of a much larger number. For lack of students or funds, by reason of dissension in the faculties or the constituencies, because of bad management within or competition without, those colleges which had been unwisely established, with more zeal than calculation, died. Perhaps half of the colleges of this middle period did not survive their twentieth year.

There was also another cause. As later in the French Revolution, when the *sans culottes* thought scholars unnecessary, so in our own Revolution and afterward there were some who were against all but the most elementary education. The opposition was in part due to a false notion of equality. Not all people could go to college; and it was held that those who did go obtained an unfair advantage over others. Robert Coram called it "a scandal to civilized society that part only of the citizens should be sent to colleges and universities to learn to cheat the rest of their liberties." John Adams, replying to a letter from a New Jersey correspondent, J. D. Sergeant, admitted that there was everywhere "a spice" of prejudice against liberal education. "But," he said, "liberty has no enemy more dangerous" than this. Some found the reasons for this opposition in the impractical curriculum, in the vanity and pride of collegians, or in the destructive effect of a college education upon the religious faith of the students.

From the standpoint of the objectors there was merit in these objections. Orthodoxy was in particular danger in the late eighteenth century. The views of the Enlightenment were almost universal in some of the older colleges. Deism and materialism were widely affirmed by the students. Yale, which had been founded less than a century before because Harvard was becoming liberal, had hardly any professing Christians among her students. This was, however, a passing fashion; and to its passing the new president inaugurated at Yale in 1795 made a contribution. This president was Timothy Dwight (1752–1817).

The list below contains the names of seventeen colleges, now reduced to sixteen, founded between the close of the Revolutionary War and the end of the century. Most of these were frontier institutions. They were located

COLLEGES OF THE EARLY NATIONAL PERIOD

Earlier Names	Present Names	First Charter	First Degrees
Washington College	Washington College	1782	1783
Liberty Hall Academy	Washington and Lee University	1782	1785
Hampden-Sidney College	Hampden-Sidney College	1783	1786
Transylvania Seminary	Transylvania College	1783	1790
Dickinson College	Dickinson College	1783	1787
St. John's College	St. John's College	1784	1793
University of Georgia (Franklin College)	University of Georgia	1785	1804
Franklin College, 1787 Marshall College, 1836	Franklin and Marshall College	1787	1853
University of North Carolina	University of North Carolina	1789	1798
University of Vermont	University of Vermont	1791	1804
Williams College	Williams College	1793	1795
Bowdoin College	Bowdoin College	1794	1806
Greeneville College	Tusculum College	1794	1808
Blount College	University of Tennessee	1794	1806
Union College	Union College (Schenectady)	1795	1800
Middlebury College	Middlebury College	1800	1802

on the second American frontier beginning in Maine, passing through western Vermont and Massachusetts, touching a few points in central New York and Pennsylvania, and spreading out into a great Appalachian triangle with its base in Georgia and Tennessee. This pressing of the colleges upon new and newer frontiers was to be repeated again and again as the people moved westward. Because the institutions founded in decades before and after 1800 were small and poor in their early years they did not maintain high standards; but instead, in America, "the spontaneous inpulse to general culture was widely diffused" among the people. And this wide diffusion of a moderate culture was both more useful and politically wiser in a new republic than the creation of a small class of savants would have been. The course taken was not due to careful planning, however, but was the natural result of the social and material conditions.

9. The Older Colleges and the States

None of the colonial colleges were state schools, but Harvard and William and Mary were partially endowed and supported by the government. A majority of the Visitors of the latter were publicly appointed. Yale, or a Yale faction, at least, desired to have the state represented on the board and this was achieved in 1792. In other cases the Revolution brought on criticism and attacks from the outside because the colleges were considered insufficiently patriotic. A plan to have the State of New York take control of Columbia failed; but instead a board, the University of the State of New York (1784, 1787), was created and given general powers over all secondary and higher institutions.

The most radical change wrought by the Revolution overtook the College of Philadelphia, which, though a temporary result, is as instructive as the Dartmouth College case, to be considered later. The college operated under charters of 1753 and 1755. In the former year, William Smith was appointed with Franklin's approval to a teaching position and soon became provost or head. By the latter year he was already thick in Pennsylvania politics. He was an Anglican clergyman and, together with some of the trustees, was accused of Tory sentiments. We have seen that the college was considered to be under church influence. By 1756 the incautious provost was writing to a brother clergyman in England that more than half of the trustees were favorable to the church which, he said, "by soft and easy means daily gains ground" in the college. The honored historian of the University of Pennsylvania speaks of the institution's "Anglican tinge," but this looks like pretty full color.

In the Revolution Doctor Smith rejected all part in the movement for independence, while the state of Pennsylvania had become democratic and in 1776 adopted the most liberal of the new constitutions. That instrument, as noted above, proposed the creation of "one or more state universities." The party which had come into power was not favorable to the college with its loyalist and Anglican connections. A legislative committee was appointed to prepare a report. They found in attendance twenty-two college, forty medical, and about eighty preparatory students. The finances were not in a satisfactory condition and, of course, the committee and the legislature did not wish to be pleased. Their minds had been made up to reconstruct the school on patriotic and more modern lines. It will not be necessary to make direct comparisons with recent legislative investigations.

The board of trustees and the faculty were dissolved. Rules conformable to the new state government were laid down. Additional funds were voted. A new board of twenty-four trustees was named. The charters of 1753 and 1755 were retained but, in harmony with the change in academic language that was developing, the institution was rechristened the University of the State of Pennsylvania.

The new trustees and the new faculty were able men and some of them, for example, John Dickinson of the trustees and David Rittenhouse of the faculty, were eminent. The program of studies was expanded and greater attention was given to the sciences. Four parallel courses were set up for the students' choices. There is here a slight anticipation of specialization and the elective system; and this was the year when Jefferson was proposing his new plan of education and modernizing the college of William and Mary. The great difficulty at the new university in Pennsylvania was financial. The depreciation of the Continental money, the commercial debacle, and the difficulty in collecting the rents from the confiscated Tory estates assigned to the university kept the institution poor.

The old College of Philadelphia with the old board and staff had not ceased to operate in the meantime but was carrying on its work in new quarters. Its officers and friends regarded the legislature's action as illegal and as an unjust and vindictive expropriation. After ten years, with the winning of independence and the peace, the cooling of tempers and a shift in the political forces in the state, a majority of the legislature had come to hold similar views. In 1789 the funds, as far as possible, and the powers of the old College were restored to it. Two years later the two institutions were joined to form the present University of Pennsylvania, an independent institution. This curious episode was a rehearsal for the Dartmouth College dispute, forty years later.

The famous lawsuit over the control of Dartmouth College arose out
of the political conflict between the Jeffersonians and Federalists in New
Hampshire. In 1816 the Jeffersonians had control of the legislature while
Federalists still controlled the college, a close parallel to the Pennsylvania
situation of 1779. Personality difficulties were involved in both cases but
these may be neglected here. In New Hampshire the Democratic-Republi-
cans so changed the charter that its original provisions were practically
annulled and then set up a new institution, the University of New Hampshire. The board of the college, in turn, brought suit to retain their rights
and privileges; and this cause eventually reached the United States Supreme Court. The highest court's decision, written by the Federalist jurist,
Chief Justice John Marshall, and handed down in 1819, declared that the
college charter was a contract and that under the Constitution the binding
force of contracts could not be impaired (I, 10). This restored the board
and the college to their earlier status and ended all serious efforts to transform independent colleges into state institutions by legislative expropriation.
This is an example of influence upon education growing out of the Constitution. The present University of New Hampshire is the outgrowth of a
land-grant college established in 1868. It has no connection with the earlier
institution bearing the same name.

Some writers have tried to assess the influence of the Dartmouth College decision upon education. One student found "convincing evidence"
that the decision helped to delay the state university movement by as much
as fifty years. But he did not present the evidence. The state university
movement had begun long before and several such institutions were in
active operation when the Dartmouth case arose. Usually a different view
has been taken of the educational effect of the decision. Charles and Mary
Beard in their *Rise of American Civilization* claimed that the decision
cleared the way for both private and state institutions. It made the church
colleges "secure from popular storms" and notified the states that public
universities would have to be created and could not be fashioned out of
existing colleges against their will. Both of these statements are clearly true.
But *post hoc non ergo propter hoc*. It does not follow that the rapid establishment of both types of institutions which followed the decision was due
to the decision to any important extent.

The political character of the attack upon the charter is one of the facts
which should not be ignored in an attempt to understand American education. That the motive was political is indicated by the message of the governor to the New Hampshire legislature in 1816. He argued that the charter
of 1769 contained monarchical principles, especially the co-optation prin-

ciple by which members of the board were empowered to fill vacancies in their own body. This principle he declared to be "hostile to the spirit and genius of a free government," and advised a change in the "mode of election." All governments, he added, have exercised the right to amend and improve acts of incorporation.

The governor sent a copy of the message to Monticello, and Jefferson replied in a letter of July 21, 1816, which became famous. He wrote that a monarch might have to be restrained from interfering with a trust or charter but such a restriction "against the nation itself" he thought "most absurd." All laws should be alterable, otherwise "the earth belongs to the dead, and not to the living." This letter raises fundamental questions. One such question may be whether the party in power in 1816 in New Hampshire was the state "itself" and was competent to express the state's true and permanent will. All laws and constitutions should be alterable but not for transient causes, as Jefferson himself had said, or in the heat of passion for partisan purposes.

10. EARLY STATE UNIVERSITIES

Forty years separated the attack upon the College of Philadelphia and the verdict in the case of Dartmouth College. In that interval the first nine of the present state universities were begun, two in Ohio, one in Vermont, and six in the South. The University of Virginia, the last of this group of nine, was chartered in 1819 but not opened until 1825. It was the only one that from the first maintained high standards, but even so Jefferson complained that they had accepted "shameful Latinists" at first. It was a collection of academic "schools," very different in plan from the usual American state university; but it aimed to do advanced work at a time when the typical college was conducting textbook recitations.

The first of the nine to be named and chartered was the University of Georgia. It was granted a charter in 1785 and an endowment of 40,000 acres of wild land. It was provided with an academic senate composed of a board of trustees and a board of visitors. The trustees were the active policy-making and governing body and the visitors had power to examine the students and to review and even veto trustee action. The early Americans, possessed of a dread of irremediable tryanny, resorted to such checks and balances; and such a dual government is still operating at Harvard University. The University of Georgia was to be composed of a number of colleges and the first of these, Franklin College, was opened not in 1785 but in 1801 and remained small and mediocre for many years. Georgia, like other states, provided some financial aid in the early years, then completely neglected it, and commenced to supply regular support only in 1875. Thus the University of Georgia, in its financial history, resembles most of the early state universities. It was not till after the Civil War that the states began to see the necessity and to assume the obligation for continuous support of their universities. The University of Georgia now comprises eight senior colleges, nine junior colleges, an extension division, and the experiment stations, all under a Board of Regents and a Chancellor for the whole system.

Although the University of Georgia was the first state university to be chartered, the University of North Carolina was the first to be opened. This means that we must rule out such controlling boards as the University of the State of New York and such temporary institutions as the University of the State of Pennsylvania, both earlier than either Georgia or North Carolina.

The University of North Carolina received its charter in 1789. The proudest feature of its early history is that, like the Mecklenburg Resolutions, it was a result of a people's pursuit of independence and self-government. Otherwise it had a humble origin. The charter of 1789 made the board self-perpetuating by co-optation. Each judicial district was to have one representative on the board, but distances and travel difficulties made this an unwise provision. The framers also provided that there should be no regulations that would interfere with the rights of the students as men and citizens. This was 1789. To the students this meant freedom; to the faculty, police duty. The mandate against unrepublican laws did not prevent the promulgation of the usual rules against profanity, firearms, liquor, absence from chapel and from divine service on Sunday, and others taken from the college books of laws of the period. The university set up a court to try offenders and instituted five degrees of punishment ranging from a reprimand to expulsion; and in the application of these and other laws the administration managed to provoke a first-class riot and rebellion before the school was five years old.

Financially the young university was as poor and as completely neglected by the state as other such institutions. No appropriations were voted. Indeed, the first legislative appropriation for current expenses was secured by the then just elected president of the university, Kemp P. Battle, in 1876. Some funds were realized in the early years from escheats, from unclaimed warrants of Revolutionary soldiers, and from lotteries. Attacks were leveled at the institution because it brought professors from other states, especially Northerners whose politics did not please the South. There were few schools in the state able to prepare students. The university was formally opened on January 15, 1795, but the first student did not arrive until February 12. The cost of board was fixed at thirty dollars a year. The faculty consisted of Dr. David Ker, a classical scholar recently from Ireland.

A simple course of study consisting of common school and secondary school branches was offered. There were forty students by the end of the first term. At the opening of the second term the preparatory classes were separated from those of college rank and a plan projected that required six professors, the president included. Latin and Greek were required for the bachelor of arts degree; but students were also allowed to select any studies for which they were prepared and upon completion of these they were given a certificate stating what they had accomplished. The author of this sensible scheme soon left the university and the new president, who was American-born and educated under President Witherspoon, made the University of North Carolina as nearly as possible into a Southern Princeton. In its small equipment, its primitive surroundings, and its lack of state support, the University of North Carolina was like a great many of the early institutions of its kind. From such origins many justly respected state universities have developed. To understand more fully that present institutions have not always been what they are, that they have grown to their present state from small beginnings by overcoming difficulties, and that success is not accidental are some of the objects of historical study. State universities provide excellent illustrations.

Further examples of early state universities which began as poorly equipped seminaries or preparatory schools are numerous. We may summarize several of the unfavorable conditions. Sometimes the schools were located in small, comparatively inaccessible towns without adequate lodging and board and without foot or street pavements. The people often lacked understanding of the nature and objects of advanced education and tried to compel institutions to meet their uninformed ideas. Interference by unlawful means in the internal affairs of a frontier state university was not unknown. Preparatory schools were often lacking in new states and the university was compelled to establish such a school. We have seen that the University of Virginia, although it had the finest campus of its time, suffered from lack of qualified students. The University of Michigan established "branches" in various towns to provide itself with freshmen able to do college work. At the same time most of the early state universities did not have the library, laboratories, or staff to meet the needs of strong collegians.

Everywhere relations with the state were unsatisfactory. Legislatures chartered institutions under the title of state university but provided them

with co-optative governing boards. There were early so-called state universities that were merely independent colleges. And like other independent
colleges they received no sustaining appropriations or other help from the
state. Many of these schools were under the tacit control of religious denominations, usually the Presbyterians, Congregationalists, or Methodists.
There was no conception of the service functions of a state university or of
its present relations to the public school system. The state university idea
like the institution itself has been a gradual, often painful, growth.

This survey may properly close with a few further examples to accompany that of their leader in time, the University of North Carolina. The
University of Vermont, with a self-perpetuating board, was created in 1791.
Some state universities were formed from previously founded colleges; but
in most of these cases there was no opposition to the action. Blount College
was given a charter by the state of Tennessee in 1794. It was a Presbyterian
school. By a series of legislative changes and recharterings it became the
state university in 1879. The process required eighty-five years. In the
course of a similarly long and bewildering series of changes of name and
purpose, South Carolina College, created in 1805 as a state school, became
the university of the state, for the second time, in 1906. It should be plainly
said that, as already intimated, authorities do not always agree on all these
dates. Colleges usually try to select the earliest defensible foundation date.
Tewksbury's *Founding of American Colleges* has been generally but not
invariably followed in the above account.

Indiana University uses 1820 as its natal year, but Tewksbury dates
the charter of Indiana College in 1828 and of the university in 1838. Before the school became a college it had for some years been known as Indiana Seminary. The first teacher of the school, Baynard Rush Hall, has
himself written a pungent, often humorous account of the primitive conditions surrounding this pioneer college in the woods and of the quarrels
within the school and between it and the townspeople.

Ohio was the first of the states to profit from the new land-grant policy
of Congress. That plan, followed consistently as new western states were
admitted into the Union, assigned two townships of land to each state for
a university. Ohio, however, received three townships and established two
universities. These were Ohio University at Athens (1804) and Miami
University at Oxford (1809). They received their charters and grants of
land and then were completely neglected by the public authorities. For
long periods they were carried on more under denominational than state
care.

The South and West became the state university sections. New England and the Middle States were late in creating similar institutions. New York began to develop her state university after World War II. Only yesterday, Pennsylvania changed the name of her state college to state university but without changing the nature of the institution.

Political and educational ideas generated in the struggle for independence continued to influence Americans for a long time after the peace. A new kind of education suitable for a republican people was seen to be necessary. Some impatient individuals proposed a national system that would have imposed upon society the schools they thought needed. Fortunately, democratic processes were followed even though they were slow. Whether from success in the war or for some other reason, there was greater interest in higher than in primary education. The new era was marked also by great attention to foreign educational developments.

The times clearly called for the expansion and the improvement of education, since it appears that only one-fourth of the Revolutionary statemen had received what was then regarded as a finished schooling and the lowest third had received very little schooling. Equal political privileges in the new nation clearly pointed to a need for equal educational opportunities. Political liberty and citizenship necessitated political education because, so it was declared, men who do not know and value their rights will lose them.

The federal Constitution does not mention education but it has had great educational influence. Its greatest influence in this field comes from its doctrine of reserved powers. Upon this is based the doctrine of state control of education, and this in connection with the doctrine of states' rights has been a determining influence in American education. The early state constitutions made only weak references to education when they made any, showing that even the states were not ready to pursue a vigorous educational policy. Most of the eloquent passages in the early state constitutions were ineffective sentiment.

Realistic criticism of Jefferson's selective plan must be based upon the actual and backward condition of education and educational sentiment in Virginia in 1779. On the other hand, Jefferson's greatest interest was in advanced education and he was, like lesser contemporaries, too much under the influence of the Renaissance tradition. Few or none at that time saw what Pestalozzi was just then developing, namely the liberalizing possibilities of vernacular education in the elementary school.

The national university idea arose in this period but never became embodied in an institution. A host of new church colleges were established, especially in the South. The state university movement was growing and Jefferson regarded the University of Virginia as the crowning achievement of his life; but the true greatness and real function of the state university was a later discovery.

QUESTIONS

1. What conclusions may be drawn from the facts in the second section of
this chapter? And do you agree with the one stated in the chapter summary,
beginning with "Equal political privileges"?

2. Does liberty begin in the mind? How would the application of your
answer affect schools? Why is liberty to be prized?

3. Why was all direct reference to education excluded from the federal
Constitution? How and when has the Constitution affected American education?
This question will be pertinent at many points of the following history.

4. Would strong educational provisions, even mandatory ones, in the early
state constitutions have been (a) possible and (b) useful?

✕ 5. Can the selective features of Jefferson's plan be explained? Justified? Is
not all effective education selective?

6. Was John Adams correct in the claim that the educated class held the
power in society? In this connection consider the facts in the second section of
this chapter.

7. What could a national university do that is not done now and what
could it do better than what is now done by other universities?

8. Why did both hostility to higher education and greatly increased promotion of it show themselves after the Revolution? Was there any relation between
the two? Did its enemies stimulate its friends to greater exertions?

9. What would have been the effect upon college education if the attacks
upon Pennsylvania and Dartmouth had been permanently successful?

BOOKS AND PAPERS

The publication of a definitive edition of the papers of Thomas Jefferson
by the Princeton University Press is proceeding. A complete edition of the papers
of George Washington has been published. And there have long been available
extensive published collections of the works of these and other statesmen. President Eisenhower has endorsed the report of the National Historical Publications
Commission, which recommended, as part of an extensive program of publication, the inclusion of the papers of Mann, Barnard, Emma Willard, and other
educators. Such a program should include the papers of the eighteenth century
writers who urged the promotion of national education as an aid to the national
unity which the new Constitution was to secure.

Cajori, Florian, *Teaching and History of Mathematics in the United States,*
Washington, U. S. Government Printing Office, 1890, Circular of Information, No. 3.
Du Pont de Nemours, Pierre Samuel, *National Education in the United States,*
translated by B. G. Du Pont, University of Delaware, 1923.

Erikson, Erik M., and D. Rowe, *American Constitutional History*, New York, 1933.

Good, H. G., *Benjamin Rush and His Services to American Education*, Berne, Indiana, 1918; and "Who First Proposed a National University?" *School and Society*, March 11, 1916.

Hansen, A. O., *Liberalism and American Education in the Eighteenth Century*, New York, 1926, containing summaries of documents and extensive bibliographies; an important book, half of which (pp. 45–199) is concerned with plans for national education.

Hinsdale, B. A., Compiler, "Documents Illustrative of American Educational History," *Annual Report* of the U. S. Commissioner of Education, 1892–1893, Vol. 2, pp. 1225–1414, Washington, U. S. Government Printing Office, 1895.

Honeywell, Roy J., *Educational Work of Thomas Jefferson*, Harvard University Press, 1931.

Hoyt, John W., *Memorial in Regard to a National University*, Washington, U. S. Government Printing Office, 1892, Miscellaneous Senate Document, No. 222, Fifty-second Congress, First Session.

Lyon, Hastings, *The Constitution and the Men Who Made It*, Boston, 1936.

Schuyler, R. L., *The Constitution of the United States*, New York, 1923.

Tewksbury, D. G., *Founding of American Colleges and Universities before the Civil War*, New York, Teachers College, Columbia University, 1932.

Walsh, James J., *Education of the Founding Fathers*, Fordham University Press, 1935.

Wesley, Edgar B., *Proposed: The University of the United States*, University of Minnesota Press, 1936. This paper does not show how it is known that "the idea of a national university was widely current in 1786," as stated (p. 3n.).

Chapter IV

EXPERIMENTS IN LEARNING

T HE spirit of young America as it spread in the valley of democracy was celebrated by the youthful Emerson. His America was still a country of open frontiers, the land of the pioneers, conquerors of the West. Every person stood alone there, and counted as a unit. Assistance or protection could be secured if there was need, but there were few civil associations or laws to help or to hinder.

In the East, people depended more upon each other and upon government. Industry was flourishing, population was becoming dense, and cities were breeding slums, political and social diseases. People united to instruct the young, aid the weak, and raise the distressed. They tried to reform prisons and asylums, reduce intemperance and poverty, and to teach the deaf and the blind. A movement looking toward the abolition of slavery was arising. Private schools and public education were parts of this many-sided reform effort. To educate the children of everyman was the greatest reform of all.

Private education may be interpreted as either an obstacle or as an aid to the acceptance of public education. In different ways it was both hindrance and help. Without private schools and their teachers and patrons, public education could never have come into being. Temporarily good private schools delayed the transition, but in the end the greater the services they rendered the more they served to increase the desire to extend these advantages to the whole community.

The movement for public education began in the private schools, where the spirit of the pioneer penetrated. Experiments in education were numerous in the period of the academy, the country college, the manual labor schools, seminaries for girls, lyceums, mechanics' institutes, the educational plans of organized labor, and the introduction of phrenology and other crotchets.

We shall see that the people demanded a wider educational opportunity than the private, tuition-supported schools could provide. This demand, although there was serious opposition and conflict, was favored by people of every class and profession. The lyceum and a large part of the newspaper press supported the movement. In this chapter we shall deal chiefly with the private phases of the whole movement and in Chapter VII with the rise of state systems. No one state or section can claim exclusive credit. Emerson was indulging in hyperbole when he said: "Europe extends to the Alleghenies; America lies beyond." In time "the sentiment of all America" favored public education but without proscribing private schools.

1. Possessing the Land

When the new Constitution and the government had come into operation, the next event in the history of the United States was the expansion and settlement of its territory. The passes and valleys of the Appalachian highland were the open gateways into Kentucky, Tennessee, and Georgia, where the new colleges mentioned above were established. This settling of the earliest Southwest was the beginning of the migration that was to span the continent. To occupy the coastal strip and the adjacent valleys had required two centuries. All the remainder of the vast area between the two oceans was acquired, settled, and organized into forty-five states and three territories in one century. With the opening of Oklahoma in 1890 the last physical frontier in the Old West disappeared. Before this, however, still another new frontier, separated from the rest of the country, had been acquired in 1867 through the purchase of Alaska. This increased the continental area to be governed from Washington to about 3,500,000 square miles.

In making the peace of 1783, the Whig government of Great Britain ceded the whole region from the mountains to the Mississippi. If there was any calculation that the western lands would prove a cause of dissension between the states, it was an error. The western lands had already in fact been ceded to the national government; and the public domain tended to unify rather than to divide the country and was one of the chief means to increase the power of the government.

Distances and the snail-pace travel of those times was a matter of great concern. Madison discussed this problem in Numbers 10 and 14 of the *Federalist*. He argued that with such improvements in roads and interior navigation as he could foresee, the territory to the Mississippi River was not too large for a republican government; that the representatives from the most distant parts would be able to reach the seat of government in time to perform their duties. He did not anticipate the steamboat, railroad, or telegraph (1844); but neither did he have any prevision of the territorial expansion that was soon to begin.

The Northwest Ordinance for the government of the territory north of the Ohio was adopted in the year when the Constitution was framed. In the preceding chapters its clause on education was mentioned. Its most celebrated clause, apparently written by Nathan Dane (1752–1835), of Massachusetts, excluded slavery from the territory. This, no doubt, deterred planters, but it did not prevent the entrance of others from the South. Settlers came from all sections, as is shown by the names of such towns as Richmond, New Albany, New Philadelphia, Lancaster, Springfield, Princeton, Akron, and many more. Many came from that earliest Southwest mentioned before. These were up-country people who owned no slaves. They were backwoodsmen who built their log cabins out of sight of any neighbors and who were compelled to move again and again because the settlements were becoming too dense around them. Abraham Lincoln's people in Kentucky were of this type. Others came across the mountains from western Virginia and Pennsylvania into Ohio and Indiana and later to the forests of Wisconsin. Pioneers from New England and New York came to the southern shores of Lake Erie but also to Cincinnati and many other parts of the territory. These were the times and places of the subscription schools and other private enterprises described by Doctor Daniel Drake, and illustrated by the occasional manuscripts of teachers' contracts that have escaped destruction.

2. EAST AND WEST

Two new classes that worried the men of property in the East were the pioneers, woodsmen, and small farmers in the West, and the new labor organizations in the cities, the two groups which contributed most heavily to the election of Jackson in 1828. To the latter group we shall return in a later section. The old colonial antipathy between the seaboard and the back country was repeated in the old Northwest and flared up again and again as in the eighties in Populism, and in 1896 in the free silver campaign under Bryan. By 1820 Ohio was fourth in population among the states, exceeded only by New York, Pennsylvania, and Virginia. In that year Ohio and Kentucky together had well over 1,000,000 people in a nation of less than 10,000,000.

The migration from the East tended to retard the growth of the older states while accelerating that of the new ones. This population shift made it difficult to provide schooling for the children of the pioneers. Frequently they did not get any. As Lincoln has recorded, the people did not take it for granted that those to whom they were talking were able to read and write. The movement toward the West was to continue a long time, while the West itself was growing into a great giant. The country east of the Mississippi had not been fully settled when the area of the United States was more than doubled by the Louisiana Purchase (1803). Soon afterward Florida was added, then Texas, California, the Oregon country, and in 1867, Alaska. The writers of the *Federalist* would have had great difficulty to show that so large a republic was possible. Mechanical invention solved the problem. Incidentally, the air-line distances of Juneau and Seattle to the national capital differ by only 500 miles; and Hawaii is far closer in travel time than Boston was in 1787.

Invention helped to weld the far-flung republic into a unit. Once more we must return to 1787. The successful operation of a steamboat on the Delaware River by John Fitch while the Convention was in session was an event worthy to be chronicled with the stories of the Constitution and the Northwest Ordinance. Twenty years later Robert Fulton renewed the effort to develop steam navigation; and by 1820 river and coastal steamers were numerous. The ocean-crossing steamship was almost ready. The railroad era began in Jackson's administration and led at once to the development of civil engineering courses and departments in academies and colleges.

Along with the political came the industrial revolution. Slater's spinning mill (1791) and Whitney's cotton gin (1793) together with steam power began the transformation of the textile industry. From these mechanical changes important social results flowed. One was the formation of an unskilled urban working class; and another was the growth of the plantation and slavery under the rule of King Cotton. Manufactures stimulated the growth of northern cities. This was due not alone to the industrial development but also to the growth of immigration and the invention of farm machinery, which reduced the number of farm workers needed on a given number of acres.

Industry and the prairies supported each other in soliciting immigrants from the Old World. Between 1820 and 1860, 5,000,000 came through the Atlantic ports to live in the United States; and these numbers were to swell to much greater ones after the Civil War. The illiterate peasants from southern Europe, the freeing of the slaves, and the thin population on the frontier created difficult educational problems.

3. EARLY ACADEMIES

Signs pointed to the growth, in the early nineteenth century, of a new social order with a closer approach to the political equality of man with man. The newer states gave up the custom of requiring property qualifications for voting and the older states lowered theirs and then abandoned them entirely. Various devices were used to prevent small groups of the wealthy and well-born from remaining in power. The caucus with local committees to sound out and to create sentiment was used by the supporters of Jefferson. The two-party system, each party harboring men from all ranks and conditions, was either the finest achievement or the best luck of American politics. The party convention to select national candidates; shorter terms; and rotation in office—these were intended to distribute political power. Like other political devices they had their bad effects and could be perverted to evil uses. By 1824 eighteen of the twenty-four states had provided that the presidential electors were to be chosen by the people, not as formerly by the state legislatures. Educational campaigns for democracy and also attempts to suppress it were contemporary with the rise of the workingmen's organizations and the campaign for the rights of women instituted in 1845 by Lucretia Mott and Elizabeth Cady Stanton. It was noted, especially by foreign visitors, that an extraordinary number of societies, conventions, publications, and platforms poured forth their propaganda. New educational agencies arose. The academy, a private enterprise institution, was such an agency.

The American academy, as noted before, was a transitional institution. In general a private school, it was in some instances at least semipublic. It gave opportunity to that middle class of pupils who could afford the time and cost of some schooling above the elementary but who were in many cases not preparing for college. It was the second of the three American middle schools and formed the bridge from the Latin school to the public high school. Its period of dominance extended from the Revolution through and beyond the Civil War. By the decade of the eighties, educators who noted contemporary trends predicted that the high school would win in the competition. In that period many academies were turned into public high schools under local elected boards.

Another change took place toward the end of the century. As the old academy with its village associations and its local and middle-class patronage declined, a new kind of academy developed. Many of these new institutions were boarding schools. Some were both expensive and socially exclusive, drawing their pupils from widely separated places. Some were military academies, or provided other facilities not found in public schools. Others were church-connected, often Catholic, schools. Not a few catered to pupils who did not do well in public schools. Most of them had this common characteristic that they served those whom the public school system failed

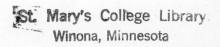

to satisfy. A well-known handbook of private schools, prepared and published by Porter Sargent of Boston, lists several thousand such secondary, or both elementary and secondary, schools. More recently some have added junior-college work.

Some of the early academies were merely modified Latin schools teaching also some modern subjects. This was true of the Governor Dummer Academy incorporated in 1782. One of the early pupils which this school prepared for Harvard was Samuel Phillips of the family which founded and endowed the Phillips Andover (chartered 1780) and Phillips Exeter (1781) Academies to instruct youth not only in academic subjects "but more especially to learn them the great and real business of living." A school founded in Virginia in 1776 was appropriately called Liberty Hall Academy. It has since become Washington and Lee University. Erasmus Hall and Clinton Academy were founded in the state of New York in 1787. Thus it is evident that the academy movement gathered strength in different parts of the country before 1800 and, as the table in the following section shows, schools of this type were endowed in considerable numbers in that early period. They were not always called academies but often seminaries, institutes, halls, lyceums, and by still other titles.

4. Numbers and Distribution of Academies

As the people increased and formed new towns, the academies multiplied without becoming larger or notably better equipped and more efficient. In New York State the average enrollment in the incorporated schools was less than seventy-five in the early period and did not reach two hundred at any time in the nineteenth century. The unchartered academies were at all times far more numerous than the incorporated ones and, in the first half of the century at least, much smaller. While these statements are based upon the known facts concerning New York State academies, it is probable that they have a wider application also.

A somewhat expanded discussion of New York developments may be justified because in that state these institutions were especially strong and numerous. The number, as the following table shows, was nearly one and one-half times as great as that of the next most populous state.

For incorporation by the Regents of New York, the academies had to meet certain standards with regard to the amount of property owned, the number of books in the library, and the number of students in attendance. Here we see the introduction of those quantitative measures of school efficiency later used by the regional associations for standardizing high

NUMBER OF ACADEMIES INCORPORATED IN SEVERAL STATES DURING CERTAIN PERIODS

	Va.	Md.	Pa.	N.Y.	Mass.	O.	Ind.	Totals
1775–1800	20	7	11	19	17	0	0	75
1801–1820	32	31	36	25	19	16	3	162
1821–1840	33	64	34	101	78	97	72	479
1841–1860	40	55	101	139	40	86	84	545
1861–1870	1	3	38	30	10	8	30	120
	126	160	220	314	164	207	189	1381

The above table has been compiled from figures found in Heatwole on Virginia, Slaybaugh on Maryland, Mulhern on Pennsylvania, Miller on New York, Walton on Massachusetts, Burrell on Ohio, and Boone on Indiana. The Maryland and Ohio figures are taken from manuscripts prepared under the sponsorship of respectively Professors James Mulhern of the University of Pennsylvania and R. H. Eckelberry of the Ohio State University. Official records being what they are, it is not likely that the figures are entirely trustworthy. The figures for Ohio, to take one example, do not agree with those given by E. A. Miller in the *School Review* for June, 1920.

schools. The incorporated academies of New York could expect a measure of financial support from the state. Although the amount was never large, there is evidence that it tended to encourage the founding of new schools, perhaps to the disadvantage of existing ones.

No restrictions upon the founding of academies were written into law. On the contrary, the law of 1784 which first created the Board of Regents plainly said that no person or persons should be deprived of the "right to erect such schools or colleges as to him or them shall seem proper." This was clearly meant to keep the field free from state interference and almost asserted that school founding is a natural right. It is a good example of the pioneer attitude. This attitude on the part of government, not by any means obsolete, permits the operation, occasionally, of schools that may endanger the health, waste the time, or possibly pervert the morals of pupils.

In other states where there was no state board of education, charters were granted by special act, or this power was vested in a state officer, usually the secretary of state. In Pennsylvania the county courts had this power from about 1840 and exercised it freely. Some of the Pennsylvania academies—the Bedford Academy is an instance—came close to being public schools in that the charters provided for the annual election of trustees by the voters. But many academies in that state were controlled by private stock companies, another example of free enterprise in education. Land was freely voted by the legislature of Pennsylvania and other states for academy endowment. At the time when the present concept of public education was still cloudy and in process of formation, these schools were associated in the public mind with the public schools if not actually considered as a link in that system.

Massachusetts was one of the states that attempted to control the founding and location of new academies. The report (1797) of a legislative committee, which it is claimed was written by Nathan Dane, recommended a general scheme of state endowment upon three conditions: (1) that each academy must have a constituency of thirty to forty thousand people not already served by a similar school; (2) that all parts of the state must be served equally by state endowments of land; and (3) that no grant should be made to an academy unless it already had in hand permanent funds to maintain its buildings and equipment and pay part of its salaries.

Not many states attempted to regulate the academies founded within their limits; and the institution spread to all or nearly all parts of the country. Late in the eighteenth and in the following century, girls' and coeducational academies began to flourish. Greenfield Hill in Connecticut was a private school for both boys and girls conducted with great success by Timothy Dwight until he was chosen president of Yale College. Sarah Pierce had a well-patronized school for girls at Litchfield where she had Catherine Esther Beecher for a pupil. And Miss Beecher in turn established the Hartford Female Seminary, incorporated in 1827, where her sister Harriet taught some of the English and perhaps also some of the sentiment which helped to make her *Uncle Tom's Cabin* popular. Incorporation, good equipment, and specialist teachers with a departmental organization were among the notable features of the Hartford Female Seminary.

Emma Willard was even better known than Catherine Beecher as the founder of an early school for girls; and her sister, Almira Lincoln Phelps, was a close second. After serving her apprenticeship in her home state of Connecticut and at Middlebury, Vermont, Mrs. Willard moved to New York State. In 1819 she established her seminary at Troy and this school became a permanent institution. Although the preparation of teachers was one of her objects, she did not forget that many of her girls would marry and become homemakers. She taught an elementary form of practical home economics, and this has caused some to consider her as the founder of that field of study. She at least held the conviction that homemaking could be developed into a teachable science and art. Many of her graduates taught in the girls' academies of the Southern states. She also traveled widely, wrote textbooks, and engaged in the promotion of education for peace.

In the older portions of the South, academies had appeared as early as they did anywhere, and they spread rapidly soon after the Revolution. Many were established by the Baptist, Methodist, Presbyterian, and other denominations. In state after state, academies bore such Methodist names as Wesleyan, Cokesbury, or Asbury, and Bible names such as Bethel or Ebenezer. Virginia and the Carolinas were much under the Princeton influence exerted by the graduates of the New Jersey college. Some of the Presbyterian academies in the South were, however, taught by Scotch-Irish teachers from overseas. One example was William McWhir who has a certain distinction from the fact that at Alexandria, Virginia, he had two of George Washington's nephews as pupils. One of the Southern states known for the strength of its academy movement was North Carolina. In his *Public School Education in North Carolina,* Professor Edgar W. Knight gives a list of about 175 academies; and for the year 1840 about 140 with 4,400 pupils were reported in operation. This would indicate an average enrollment of little more than thirty.

The South was the region of the county academies also. Maryland, Georgia, and Louisiana tried the county academy system with land endowments provided by the state. The lands were not very productive and the plan was not often successful. Tennessee may serve as an example. On the same day in one act, on September 13, 1806, the legislature of Tennessee incorporated twenty-seven county academies. Public lands were set aside for their support; and from 1840 to the Civil War the legislature annually appropriated $18,000 to be divided equally among the county academies which had by that time increased to seventy-four. This sum of $250 to a county in addition to student fees made the difference between survival and extinction to many schools. But it had another effect, that of delaying the development of the public high school.

In Iowa, organized as a territory in 1838, high schools were formed before an extensive academy movement had time to develop; and a great many of these schools never got beyond the paper stage. Catherine Beecher as the agent of the Women's Educational Association was active in founding a girls' school at Dubuque. It went into operation in 1855, but four years later it was sold to the public school district of the city. In contrast was Howe's Academy of Mount Pleasant which was aggressively coeducational. The founder asserted that "this is God's plan, in the establishment of families," and insisted that educationally boys and girls must be treated exactly alike. The school lasted until 1916 when, no longer able to compete with the now universal high school, it had to close.

The old academy was succeeded after 1890 by the new. Many are church schools maintained by the Roman Catholic, Lutheran, and other religious bodies to instil their doctrines in the youth. A considerable number are military schools, which put boys into school uniforms and subject them to military discipline. Some are ranch schools, which offer life in the open with horseback riding and outdoor sports. The military and ranch schools are boarding schools. There are, on the other hand, country day schools in the suburbs or in the outskirts of the great cities. Many of these were established after World War I when the Progressive movement was growing. A few are coaching schools for slow learners who are to be prepared for college. The varieties are numerous and the student can gain further information from Porter Sargent's *Handbook of Private Schools* to which reference has already been made.

5 . PROBLEMS, ARGUMENTS, AND DISPUTES

Laissez faire in regard to private schools opened the way to the establishment of many weak institutions. They must have been badly located or inefficient or both because they did not long survive. Up to the year 1870 the New York Regents had incorporated 314 academies, but the largest number reporting in any single year was 190. This was in 1865. What had happened to the rest? One of every twelve incorporated academies died in its first year, half of them survived for fifteen years or less, and only one in eight lived for half a century. The average life span of the schools established in the successive periods, moreover, became progressively shorter. The earliest group lived an average of sixty years before they were closed or were transformed into some other kind of institution. A middle group incorporated between 1800 and 1827 survived forty-eight years. And those founded in the next period ending in 1857 were merged with public high schools, sold, or otherwise eliminated from the list of accepted academies in twenty-five years. The rise of the public high school is one cause of the early demise of many, but other academies were closed before the high school became a factor.

The mortality rate of the private, select, and other unincorporated schools and academies is not known. But the general reason why they were not recognized was that they were weak. They were far more numerous than the Regents' academies, in 1870 at least eleven times as numerous. Many were the purely personal ventures of individual teachers. For all these reasons it is unlikely that they were a dependable source of secondary education of good quality. In these respects New York seems typical. In 1837 the South Reading, Massachusetts, academy building was sold for use as a public school. Two years later the Lexington academy building was used for the first state normal school. After the middle of the century every decade saw several Massachusetts academies turned into public grammar or high schools. Not only one but six Pennsylvania academies became state normal schools; many in this state were sold to pay debts or to save the investment of stockholders; and forty or more were donated to public school boards. The same processes occurred in other states.

Laissez faire and improvisation ruled also in the department of the academy curriculum. Many academies, like their predecessors, the private schools, did not establish orderly sequences of studies but organized instruction in those subjects for which there was a demand and for which teachers were available. When more definite requirements were set forth they often included an English, a scientific, and a college preparatory curriculum. Each school had its own policy in permitting substitutions and in allowing pupils to take extra subjects. Work in methods of teaching was an occasional extra. In girls' academies a special charge was often made for instruction in piano or French. Fees for elementary branches were lower than those for secondary subjects.

One circumstance that strongly affected the offerings of any given school was the enrollment and the consequent number of teachers. Since the academies depended so largely upon fees and therefore desired to attract many pupils, it is understandable that they should have attempted to teach too many subjects. Many classes, heavy schedules, and superficial work would seem to be the probable results. But in one of the few cases where this opinion can be checked it is seemingly incorrect. The case is that of the Moravian school, Nazareth Hall in Pennsylvania. In 1793 six of the regular teachers taught respectively fourteen, fifteen, sixteen, nineteen, twenty and twenty periods a week, assignments that would not be considered excessive by high school teachers today. But this was a large school and it is probable that many academy teachers taught not twenty but thirty periods a week.

The academies, considered all together, offered many subjects. The list of all the branches found in the New York academies contains 154 entries. But in this list the English language is divided into six subdivisions, from spelling to rhetoric, and physics into ten, from acoustics to statics. But however we combine, rearrange, and count them, the number of branches was large. And the range extended from the most elementary branches to advanced studies usually taught in colleges. There were academies that promised to teach analytic and descriptive geometry, Oriental languages, psychology, and metaphysics. They entered the fields of business, theology, engineering, and teaching; and occasionally one offered a counterfeit subject. One such subject was called "phreno-mnemotechny."

Like the fabled horseman riding off in all directions at once, the academy attempted too many services to achieve any of them without lost motion. For this reason it came into conflict with the supporters of more specialized schools. Academies and private schools enrolled far more elementary than secondary pupils, and in their own neighborhoods often seriously weakened the public schools. Public school superintendents were not slow in calling attention to this; and they also denied the claims of the academies that they were better equipped to prepare boys for college. Because the academies prepared teachers, the proponents of normal school education were offended. The rising business colleges claimed superior capacity to prepare bookkeepers because their teachers were specialists. The academies suffered the usual fate of the path-breaker. They had pioneered in many fields, and the specialists whom they had trained now turned to the creation of institutions that would supersede them.

For a time the academies benefited from public hostility to the school tax. It is true that they also received lands and money from the states. Perhaps every state in the first half of the nineteenth century provided endowments and current funds for the use of its academies. But these, although really contributed by all the citizens, were a hidden tax that if noticed was not felt. Such gifts, therefore, aroused little opposition as compared with a tax, however reasonable, that had to be paid out of money in hand.

The private and semipublic status of the academies which had once been a virtue was later considered a vice. George Clinton (wealthy governor of New York but elected by the people, at least by those who had the vote), in his message to the legislature in 1795, declared that the advantages of the academies "are principally confined to the children of the opulent, and that a great proportion of the community is excluded from their immediate advantages." It was the sentiment that the greater proportion of the community should not be excluded from the immediate advantages of education that led America to prefer the high school to the academy. The cities with multiplying jobs for well-educated youth, the laboring classes demanding opportunity, the equalitarian sentiment on the frontier, manhood suffrage, and all that is meant by "the age of Jackson" spelled out the spread of public and the decline of private education; but the change required decades.

6. ORGANIZED LABOR AND THE SCHOOLS

The coming of the factory and the new industrial system led to the development of a wage-earning class of people who did not own the tools they used, or work in their own shops, or need any great skill. Today these people form the great body of the members of the Congress of Industrial Organizations. The older American Federation of Labor (1886) has a larger proportion of craftsmen, highly skilled workers, and it was these who formed the first labor organizations. The comparison is still a good one, even though the two bodies were united in 1955.

The coming of the factory also caused the rise of new classes at the other end of the economic scale. In addition to the rich farmers and planters and the merchants and land speculators, there now developed manufacturers and financiers who provided capital for the industries. In early times farmers, small manufacturers, mechanics, and craftsmen had much in common and formed the economic opposition to the bankers, merchants, importers, and speculators. The former class, joined by the frontiersmen, were supporters of Jefferson and later of Jackson, and opponents of Hamilton and Biddle and their centralizing financial policies.

The boundaries between the common occupations were easy to cross or to erase completely. Farmers were in many cases small manufacturers or skilled workmen, operating grist or saw mills, blacksmith or wheelwright shops. Journeymen craftsmen owned their homes and frequently developed a small business. Laborers acquired land and became farmers. But the factories and the cities disrupted this simple, rural economy. Factory workers became a separate class. Without tools or home ownership they became dependent upon the managers and foremen of large plants and were interchangeable like the parts of the machines which they tended.

Organization, beginning in Washington's administration, developed slowly. At first the unions were local bodies in which the workers in each craft, the tailors, printers, shoemakers, were organized separately. One of the most surprising of these was the Society of Associated Teachers of New York (1794). They united to help the members collect overdue tuition bills, relieve distress among the members and their widows, and promote the interests of their vocation. Their Jeffersonian outlook is proved by a public letter of welcome to Joseph Priestley, chemist, teacher, liberal preacher, and refugee from political persecution. The membership was not large in comparison with the number of teachers in the city and the bargaining power of the society was weak. As public education developed, teachers in public schools organized to secure favorable school laws and also to gain higher pay; but they have generally hesitated to use the strike as a weapon because they regard themselves as public servants and the stoppage of their work as against the interests of the children. In recent times a group affiliated with the American Federation of Labor, the Teachers' Federation, has favored and sometimes employed more aggressive action.

Artisans and factory workers made a different kind of union history. City-wide unions were formed after the depression of 1819, and in the latter twenties they began to take an active part in politics. A Workingmen's party was organized in New York and Philadelphia in 1828. Its tangible demand was for shorter hours, but they supported this demand not upon whim or the mere desire for ease and comfort but upon political grounds and the familiar doctrine of natural rights. They understood Jefferson's declaration that all men are created equal to mean that every man whether employer or laborer was entitled to one vote, to even-handed justice, and to educational opportunity. Only with leisure and through education can a man develop his talents and inform his mind so that he will be able to carry out his duties as a citizen. Some of the early leaders impetuously declared that if the legislators had done their duty these ideals would have been realized in the first years of the Republic.

A minor success along these lines was achieved by the nameless author of a labor pamphlet published in Philadelphia in 1827. He urged the establishment in every larger town of a newspaper not controlled by special interests and a library with reading rooms and a place for lectures and debates to be open every evening and holiday. These things were done. An early labor paper, the *Mechanics' Free Press*, was founded in Philadelphia and proved the forerunner of many such journals established in 1830 and the following years; and the Mechanics' Library Company of Philadelphia was formed in those years.

The Workingmen's party of the same city conducted a campaign for public schools. An 1829 committee report was published, setting forth the lamentable conditions then existing. They rejected the pauper system which provided free instruction only to those who testified that they could not pay the low fees of the elementary schools. They asked for free and universal infant and elementary schools in which the teaching was not to be restricted to "words and figures" but would also attempt to form rational self-governing character. They favored a manual labor school in each county of the state. They proposed the creation of local school boards elected by the people and responsible to them. This was a highly significant demand and an attack upon the current practice of frittering away public money by appropriating it to private school societies.

The report, as one would expect, excited both favorable and hostile comment. It is easy to believe that it had an influence in forming the body of opinion which came to the support of the fundamental school law of Pennsylvania which was enacted a few years later. But in 1834 when that law was passed the Workingmen's Party was no longer active. It is not correct to say, as some writers have said, that organized labor was the chief artificer of public education. This is a point in our history that is sometimes disputed, and influence is hard to measure; but there are solid facts that bear upon the issue. The early unions were small and the movement was destroyed by the financial panic of 1837. Until the middle of the century the suffrage was restricted in several of the most populous states. Public education was favored, and propaganda for it was supported by men and women of many classes including some of the rich, the governors of the states, editors, ministers, doctors, lawyers, and even some of those who taught and many who were taught in private schools. There were also opponents in many classes, but the movement for public education was not a class movement. It is to be remembered that the laboring people had much to gain from public education, but even they were divided upon the issue.

Not all of the early labor leaders were of the same mind; and the Workingmen's party, especially in New York City, developed a socialist wing. These ascribed their distresses to the unequal distribution of the land and of private property. The main body, however, disclaimed such "agrarianism," but opponents accused all workingmen of secret sympathy with it. Among the radical labor editors was Robert Dale Owen, son of the socialist Robert Owen, who had established the New Harmony colony (1825) in Indiana. Absolute equality, the elimination of all class differences, was the younger Owen's object. To reach this object he proposed a system of free, public boarding schools for all children. He was not the first to think of this, or the last.

Owen's plan was explained in six issues of a labor paper which he edited. The essays were copied by several newspapers and also distributed as a pamphlet. His schools were to be supported by taxation at a time (1830) when the school tax was in many states nonexistent. But the main object was not merely free education but uniform education, clothing, food, and lodging for all children in the effort to develop a classless social order. This plan of a socialist pioneer received no support from the individualistic pioneers who then formed so large a part of America.

7. Opposition to Public Education

Workingmen argued that the civil equality which a republican government implies brings with it the necessity for free and universal education. It was this equalitarian principle which roused the opposition of some members of the privileged classes. Their spokesmen ridiculed the idea of education for laboring people. The New York *Morning Herald* said that the long apprenticeship in youth and long hours of labor in manhood made universal education impossible. The Philadelphia *National Gazette* declared that the "peasant" must labor in order that the rich might cultivate his mind. "No government, no statesman, no philanthropist can furnish what is incompatible with the very organization and being of civil society." The editor saw the school tax above the horizon, still small "like a man's hand," in the day of Elijah, but large enough to cause alarm. He wrote that "the scheme of universal Equal Education at the expense of the State is virtually 'agrarianism,' an arbitrary division of the property of the rich with the poor."

Other editors tried to convince their readers that public schools must be inefficient. The *Connecticut Courant* pointed to the decadent system of its own state as evidence. The *Courant* showed that the funds from the sale of the lands in the Western Reserve had kept the state from levying a school tax. The results were low salaries, poorly prepared teachers, ungraded schools, and short terms. "When the money is used up, the school term ends," the editor reported; and this was true. But from these premises he drew the false conclusion that public schools are always poor schools. Henry Barnard was soon to show the people of Connecticut how they could improve their schools and they did so, although they might have done more.

Some newspapers found the idea of advanced education for women highly amusing. Hundreds of academies and a few colleges had proved that it was entirely feasible, but some editors were hard to persuade. They found the dream of grand republican seminaries "ridiculous." Perhaps the reference to the "Roman matrons" that the schools were expected to produce was a sneer at classical studies for young women. The whole series of arguments against opportunities for labor, the poor, and women, against the school tax and against the possibility of efficient public schools was intended to preserve intrenched selfishness and special privilege. The history of public education has shown how erroneous these editorial opinions and arguments were.

8. THE ORGANS OF PUBLIC OPINION

With the ballot came the need to spread knowledge more quickly and widely. The newspapers became means to this end. They numbered about 800 in the nation in 1830 and increased to 1,400 in a decade. Circulations were still small but were increasing; and the distribution was local but growing wider. After the telegraph came into use, the papers were able to report the debates and votes in Congress, the actions of conventions, and the speeches at public meetings. Every city now had its newspapers, and larger cities sometimes supported a dozen. Some of the distinguished papers were the Washington *National Intelligencer* which had been founded at the suggestion of Thomas Jefferson, the Richmond *Enquirer*, and the New Orleans *Picayune*. In New York, Horace Greeley was editor of the *Tribune*, William Cullen Bryant of the *Post*, and Henry J. Raymond of the *Times*. A weekly edition of the *Tribune* which carried stories, poems, book reviews, and travel letters was sent to places as far away as the Midwest. Before the Civil War 400 daily papers, ten times as many weeklies, and several hundred magazines were being published in the United States.

Some magazines were regional in their appeal. The *Knickerbocker* of New York and the *Southern Literary Messenger* of Richmond are examples. The latter was edited for a short time by Edgar Allan Poe as was *Graham's Magazine* of Philadelphia. There is educational significance in the growing circulations of the women's magazines. Most popular in 1830 was Sarah J. Hale's *The Ladies' Magazine;* and Mrs. Hale also edited the highly successful *Godey's Lady's Book. Godey's* developed the permanent formula for magazines of its class when it added the multiple departments of fashions, fiction, housekeeping, recipes, education and child care, with many pictures. Different in kind, intended for both sexes, and national in their circulation were the *North American Review,* founded in 1815 and continuing far into the next century, and *Niles' Register* of Baltimore. The *Review* was a critical journal, and the *Register* a collection of information and opinion in part clipped from other papers, still a popular type.

Specialized journals in law, medicine, religion, and education were also established. The *American Journal of Science,* founded in 1818 and edited by Benjamin Silliman, and other scientific and scholarly journals were published in the period. The *Academician* (1818), an educational magazine, was edited by Albert and John W. Picket, and the *American Journal of Education* (1826) by William Russell. A new editor, William C. Woodbridge, changed the name of the *Journal* to the *American Annals of Education*. Other educators, Horace Mann, Henry Barnard, and J. Orville Taylor, also founded magazines devoted to the improvement of teaching.

Next to the press, the lyceum became the means of developing educational sentiment and opinion. The lyceum was a lecture system of which Josiah Holbrook became the promoter. The *American Journal of Education* in 1826 published an outline of the plan; and the institution spread from city to city and state to state until most of the North and West were well supplied with lyceum centers. In less than a decade from the beginning, 3,000 local lyceums were reported. Lectures were not new. Amos Eaton had been delivering courses of scientific lectures in Massachusetts and New York for many years before 1826. The novelty consisted in setting up permanent local and state organizations to promote lectures, engage lecturers, and administer the programs. The whole system was a voluntary form of adult education without public support or regulation. The speakers brought to the communities, often isolated places, ideas and views on science, history, politics, education, morals, or civic improvement. Committees arranged for the sale of season tickets and the patronage determined the number of the lectures and the fees paid for them.

The lyceum movement was not only a system of adult education but also a means for the advancement of public education. Local lyceums held meetings on school improvement but it was the state lyceum organizations and the national body composed of delegates from the states that made the greatest efforts to secure the passage of good school laws and the establishment of state education departments. The American Lyceum, which was the national body, held nine annual meetings to consider the best means of organizing and supporting public schools. The last meeting was held in 1839. It may have been a casualty of the economic depression.

Other societies to a certain extent paralleled this second function of the lyceum movement. The Pennsylvania Society for the Promotion of Public Schools, the American Institute of Instruction, and the Western Literary Institute were devoted to the improvement of schools and the development of public school systems. The first of these with Roberts Vaux as president was organized in 1827 and the other two soon after.

The Pennsylvania Society had a share in creating the supporting opinion for the general school law of 1834, which became the foundation for the Pennsylvania public school system. The American Institute of Instruction usually met in Boston and was in the main a New England association. But many educators of national reputation appeared on its programs and its annual reports reflect the history of educational opinion for many years. The Western Literary Institute met in Cincinnati and received delegates from most of the Western and Southern states. It was influential in securing the passage of "the great school law of Ohio" in 1838 and in suggesting the report on European education by Calvin E. Stowe. And as the early teachers' society of New York City had given encouragement to the publication of *The Academician* so the Western Literary Institute helped to form a public for *The Western Academician and Journal of Education and Science* (1837–1838).

The transitional character of these three and similar societies is shown by the fact that they were not confined to teachers alone. The membership included men from many walks of life, businessmen, lawyers, ministers, college professors, and physicians. All who were concerned with education as a public service were welcome. After the public schools were established in the form of separate state systems it became advisable for the teachers to form state associations, and these became professional groups without many members from the general public. Much later the parent-teacher associations were devised to bring the two parties together once more.

9. Social Reforms and Reformers

The establishment of free schools for all the children of all the people forms one of the greatest of social reforms, but this was accompanied by many others that gave further substance and character to this experimental age. Sentiment and support for any given kind of reform often worked to the advantage of other kinds. Emerson indicated one of the types when he alleged that every young man was carrying about with him some plan for an ideal society. The socialism of Robert Owen and Fourierism, which for a little while expressed itself in Brook Farm, Oneida, New Harmony, and other community projects, were some of these utopian plans. Successful special efforts in education were made to teach the deaf, the blind, and those of low mentality. Humanitarians tried to secure decent treatment for the insane, the criminal, and the indigent. Societies were formed to reduce the lessening but still widespread evils of intemperance.

Slavery, however, produced the most violent public agitation of the years between Jackson and Lincoln. It was in 1831 that Garrison founded *The Liberator*. A leading abolition center and a station on the underground railroad were created two years later when Oberlin College was founded.

For thirty years the South met agitation and argument by counterargument. The Constitution accepted the fact of slavery and it gave Congress no power to interfere with it. Slaves were to enter into the reckoning of the number of representatives that any state was to send to Congress. For twenty years the slave trade was to be protected. By a clever use of language all this was said without once naming slaves or slavery, and this doubtless indicates a certain sensitiveness on the subject as early as 1787. In 1861 the whole debate burst into flame and slavery disappeared in a terrible war. The slaves were freed. But the freeing of 4,000,000 illiterate slaves and the sectional hostility and the destruction caused by the war set for the country some of the most perplexing educational problems of its entire history.

The evil lot of some other unfortunates was partially alleviated about the same time, in one case by a teacher. This was Dorothea Lynde Dix (1802–1887), who taught school for many years. At the age of thirty-three she was the head of a school for girls in Boston and a writer of didactic books for children. One of these, her *Conversations on Common Things* (1824), went through many editions. But her great achievement was the improvement of the treatment of the insane and the change which she produced in the public attitude toward those hapless sick people. Her success was due to her thorough investigation of the conditions and her full reports revealing mistreatment of the insane in prisons, almshouses, and asylums. Her work as a nurse and nursing administrator in the army during the Civil War would have made her famous if that work had not been overmatched by her services as the "apostle to the insane." But even today mental patients are sometimes mistreated or neglected and there is need for care lest practice in some hospitals slip back to the intolerable conditions revealed by Dorothea Dix more than a century ago. The battle against inhumanity, like that against ignorance, is a constant and continuing one.

Another battle was that for prison reform, which began in the work of John Howard and Elizabeth Fry in England. This did not go unnoticed in America, where such reforms were also needed, and where two reform systems competed with each other. One was the Auburn plan providing small cells, complete isolation, and no work, and the other the Pennsylvania plan with larger cells, an exercise space, and work with pay. The latter was more expensive but also more humane. How humane imprisonment should be was a problem. The penology of the time had not fully overcome the notion that the purpose of imprisonment was retribution; but the best thought of the time was that its purpose should be reform, re-education, and the return of the offender to orderly, civil society.

The inclusion here of these examples of social pioneering may be questioned. But they are in each case examples of adult education, of the deliberate promotion of a public opinion that would lead to action. They involved the re-education of public servants, of police officers, prison wardens, turnkeys, guards, nurses, hospital attendants, even physicians. And they posed educational problems, those of educating the freedmen, the mentally ill, and the criminal. But these examples also have a larger relation to educational movements. Like public education movements they illustrate the growth of a social conscience and of a sense of the need to strengthen weak links in the social chain. By social osmosis any one reform tends to suggest others in near-by domains.

10. EDUCATIONAL REFORMS

Early in the nineteenth century, schools were established for the deaf and the blind. Thomas Hopkins Gallaudet, who is otherwise known as the promoter of normal schools, learned the French methods of teaching the deaf by means of the sign language of gestures and the manual alphabet. Under his direction the school at Hartford was opened about 1817 and its methods were widely accepted by later schools of its kind. Nearly all the early schools for the deaf were founded by state action and were residential schools. When Horace Mann and Samuel Gridley Howe on their tour of Europe in the middle forties discovered the lip-reading and voice methods in use in the German schools for the deaf, they jumped to the unwarranted conclusion that manual methods were out-of-date and should be discarded. Present educators of the deaf and deafened use both manual and vocal methods.

About 1832, schools for the blind were opened almost simultaneously in Boston, New York, and Philadelphia. The head of the Boston school for the blind was Samuel Gridley Howe, who made his institution known, by voice and pen, and by touring the country with his best pupils and persuading state legislatures to establish similar schools. He did much to provide books for the blind, but the alphabet which he used has long been discarded for the now almost universal six-point Braille. Laura Bridgman, a blind deaf-mute from New Hampshire, was Howe's most famous pupil and his success with her was his greatest triumph. It was also a great triumph for the art and science of education. We shall return to this topic in Chapter XIV.

Both Gallaudet and Howe established classes for children of low intelligence in their schools—Gallaudet about 1820 but Howe not until much later. It was, however, gradually discovered that the training of mental defectives is a special task requiring teachers with special preparation; and separate schools and classes were established for them. Provision for them and for deaf, blind, and crippled children is now made by many cities; and in some cases the national service clubs provide funds for such education.

Of the numerous communal societies, each proposing to teach mankind how life should be lived, the only one which made much use of the school in that task was New Harmony in Indiana. It was established about 1825 by the British utopian socialist, Robert Owen, the founder of the well-advertised infant schools of New Lanark in Scotland. During its brief period, New Harmony was the home of a remarkable group of scientists. The schools were planned by the geologist, William Maclure, who had brought Joseph Neef from Europe where he had been, in his own words, "a coadjutor of Pestalozzi." Neef was placed in charge of the New Harmony schools. Manual training and instruction in the sciences were given a larger place there than they were to have in the schools of the country for many years. What effect this might have had upon schools in general is unknown, for Owen was soon compelled to withdraw his support and the New Harmony community came to an early end.

Other schools of the period were more successful in teaching manual training, science, agriculture, and engineering. The Gardiner Lyceum in Maine was opened in 1823 and has been called the first school of agriculture in America. It had some success in teaching the practical applications of science to agriculture, but when the state withdrew its support this school also was closed. The Rensselaer School, now the Rensselaer Polytechnic Institute, was likewise founded (1825) to aid the farmer by preparing science lecturers who were to serve the rural schools. In its original conception it was, therefore, a kind of normal school, but many of its graduates found positions in higher educational institutions and in the service of the various state governments. In harmony with its early plan the methods used in the school emphasized skill in teaching as well as investigation.

The techniques of the school were devised by the head teacher, Amos Eaton. On his plan, the students, some of them college graduates, were divided into small groups of five or six persons. Each group took some chemical, physical, or other problem, usually one of technological importance, and made experiments, carried out field studies, read the pertinent literature, and made a report to the rest of the school. The report was not to be merely verbal. The group had to go through the physical processes and demonstrate their methods and results. Many of Eaton's pupils attained high rank in scientific investigation and in teaching. After 1835, with the coming of the railroad, the Rensselaer School developed into a school of civil engineering.

11. An Educational Liberal Speaks Out

Workingmen wanted free public schools; so did farmers, businessmen, and many others. But they were not clear about the kind of schools they desired and therefore could not agree. And even if they had been better prepared to say what kind of schools they desired, they might have been divided over the best way to secure them. The average citizens of 1830 wanted better school buildings but they were not keen to pay for them. They desired to have new subjects introduced, geography, United States history, English grammar, but they were less eager to have a longer school term. They wanted to have their children get on in life. To do that the children needed arithmetic, reading, and writing. Good English was important and also good manners; but about the general aims of education the pioneers had not thought a great deal when Emerson began to write on such matters.

Emerson was a philosopher, not a school founder like Franklin or an administrative leader like Horace Mann. Ideas were his specialty; and confidence in the power of education and faith in the free individual were his basic ideas. Education, he declared, has produced civilization, and civilized man is as far above savage man as the savages are above the wild beasts. The universe exists to produce men. It produces men by answering their questions, and we must believe that it will eventually answer all the questions that men can ask. The perfect man when he appears will be produced by education. It follows, does it not, that the universe is a school and all the men and women merely teachers?

Every person, Emerson said, is a new Will. He is not to repeat the experiences of others—or to obey them. He is an original, not a copy, and men must let him be himself. The secret of right education consists in respecting the pupil. He has the right to say to the State: "You shall educate me, not as you will, but as I will," and not in elementary branches only but extensively in the arts, sciences, languages. Emerson, the individualist, considered this the basic premise of education in a democracy.

In method and content, Emerson's plan resembled those of the realists. Learning should proceed by means of experiment and self-activity. Books were to be used only "when the boy is ready for them." We might with advantage follow the Roman rule, he thought, and teach only what does not require the use of chairs and desks and the equipment for listening, as John Dewey was to say. Emerson, the thinker, writer, and lecturer, was scornful of books and lectures. Our education is an education of words, he cried. After fifteen years spent in classrooms we come out with a bag full of—wind. Thoreau in a canoe is the best pedagogue. The true school is one which collects about a natural teacher like Socrates or Jesus. When we leave the natural method, and adopt a fixed program, and insist upon uniform required subjects, and draw in large numbers of students, then we are tempted to introduce rules, organization, discipline, and bribes. Then education, as was to be said afterward, becomes a ritual, not an adventure.

The tradition to which Emerson's philosophy of education belongs was developed by Rousseau and more recently has been carried forward by John Dewey. Something may, of course, be said in opposition to Emerson's views. It will seem to many that the child is less free, less an individual, and more dependent upon the family, society, and the long past than Emerson thought. Originality and freedom are not absolute any more than obedience and cooperation are. The child may not have a clear idea of the kind of education that he wants now or will later wish for; and the state which collects and dispenses tax money may have a notion of its own regarding the kind of education that it is willing to support. Emerson's confused attitude toward books and direct experience might serve as topics for further homilies.

Emerson, like Milton, was a kind of Platonist and humanist, each of his own kind to be sure. Each took a realist position in education, scorning the philosophy on which they had nourished their souls. Man wills to have what he lacks and thus mankind progresses on a zigzag course that cannot be read unless one studies a long section of it. Hence one of the uses of the history of education. And hence, also, it may be admitted, Emerson's emphasis was needed in the formal, repressive schools of his time. It may be that universal and suitable opportunity, in a sense, does imply that the free individual must be educated as he wills and not as others will.

The people acquired the land west of the Great River and they occupied it, all in the nineteenth century. This was their greatest achievement, one that brought on the Civil War and determined its outcome; and it made the United States a powerful, and for a time a largely self-contained, nation. Invention made possible the extension of representative government to the vast new areas, and the creation of new states on the pattern of the old. The pioneering spirit which marked the physical and political development was active also in education.

Pioneering in education was necessary if provision was to be made for the children of the frontiersmen, of the laboring people in the cities, and of the new immigrants. This part of the story will be told in the chapter which follows this one. The age was also interested in the education of men of technical skill and practical affairs, and in the education of girls. A great number of private and semipublic academies were founded to serve these wants and needs of a middle class which, although not rich, was able to pay for its education. The academies were noted for the diversity of their subject-offerings. In their effort to meet all demands and even to anticipate them, the academies frequently became superficial; and a fierce competition for students led to the closing of many of the weaker schools. The academy was a transitional institution; and when the high school overtook it, the academy became a supplementary institution fitting into niches not well filled by the public schools.

People of all classes worked for the creation of public school systems, but there were also some who were strongly opposed. Some of the large newspapers ridiculed the aspirations of the masses and attacked the efforts of organized labor, of educators, state governors, and other public men to promote school systems. The lecture system known as the lyceum spread rapidly over the country. The American Lyceum was a strong promoter of state school systems; and support was given by educational magazines, teachers' societies, and promotional associations formed by leaders in business and public affairs.

Social reforms were paralleled by new educational efforts and the two kinds of activity reinforced each other. Among the new activities in education were the schools for the deaf, the blind, and the mentally retarded, schools emphasizing science such as Neef's at New Harmony, and schools of agriculture and engineering. Amos Eaton devised a scheme of activity instruction that is in the best educational tradition. Samuel Gridley Howe originated a plan that was effective in teaching a deaf and blind girl, Laura Bridgman, the first such case in history. The same methods, improved by Anne Sullivan, succeeded even more brilliantly with Helen Keller, as we shall see later.

Emerson expressed the spirit of the pioneer. His views on education have the virtues and the defects of the extreme individualist. With increasing tendencies toward social control and the welfare state, his views may become even more challenging in the future than they were in his own time, for the individualist has a part of the truth about human nature.

QUESTIONS

1. Why did the South permit the exclusion of slavery from the Northwest Territory? How may this have affected the development of education in the Territory and in the states carved out of it?

2. Evidently invention was economically and politically important. How, if at all, was it important to education?

3. How would the high school have been different without the academy, that is, if it had directly followed the Latin school?

4. Why were academies numerous in the South where there were few Latin schools and few high schools before 1900?

5. Why do governments which supervise public schools fail to take steps to protect the children in the private schools?

6. Why did organized labor favor and some great newspapers oppose the extension of education?

7. Why did educational and social reforms tend to develop together?

8. Compare Eaton's plan of teaching with other activity methods, such as the seminar, project, problem, and "workshop" plans.

9. Why is it useful to study Emerson's educational philosophy and perhaps most useful for those to do so who tend to disagree with it?

BOOKS AND PAPERS

On the growth of the population, consult E. B. Greene and Virginia Harrington, *American Population Before the Federal Census of 1790* (New York, 1932), and Bureau of the Census, *A Century of Population Growth* (Washington, 1909). Among the books elsewhere mentioned which will be useful for this chapter are one by E. E. Brown, another by James Mulhern on secondary education, and three by Thomas Woody on Quaker education, Franklin as educator, and the education of women.

Abbott, Edith, *Some American Pioneers in Social Welfare,* University of Chicago Press, 1937.

Anonymous, *Historical Sketches of Education in Michigan, Office of the Superintendent of Public Instruction,* 1880, Lansing, 1881.

Carlton, Frank T., *Economic Influences Upon Educational Progress in the United States, 1820–1850,* Madison, Wisconsin, 1908.

Coon, C. L., *North Carolina Schools and Academies, 1790–1840, A Documentary History,* Raleigh, 1915.

Curoe, P. R. V., *Educational Attitudes and Policies of Organized Labor in the United States,* New York, Teachers College, Columbia University, 1926.

Davies, John, *Phrenology, Fad or Science,* Yale University Press, 1955.

Drake, Daniel, *Pioneer Life in Kentucky,* Cincinnati, 1870.

Finegan, T. E., *Teacher Training Agencies, A Historical Review,* Albany, University of the State of New York, 1917. Treats of New York State and has matter on the Society of Teachers of New York City; but for the minutes of this early teachers' association, see the State Superintendent's *Annual Report* for 1891.

Fuess, Claude M., *An Old New England School, Phillips Academy, Andover,* Boston, 1917.

Hayes, C. B., *The American Lyceum,* Washington, U. S. Government Printing Office, Bureau of Education Bulletin, 1932, No. 12, with bibliography.

Hodgen, Margaret T., *Worker's Education in England and the United States,* New York, 1925, with bibliography.

Jackson, Sidney L., *America's Struggle for Free Schools,* Washington, D. C., 1941.

Knight, E. W., *Public Education in the South,* Boston, 1922.

Leopold, R. W., *Robert Dale Owen,* Harvard University Press, 1940.

Lockwood, G. B., *The New Harmony Movement,* New York, 1905; and see a paper by C. A. Browne, "Science at New Harmony," *Scientific Monthly,* June, 1936.

McAllister, Ethel M., *Amos Eaton, Scientist and Educator, 1776–1842,* University of Pennsylvania Press, 1941; and see a paper which deals with Eaton's students, by H. G. Good, "Amos Eaton, Scientist and Teacher of Science," *Scientific Monthly,* November, 1941.

Mansfield, E. D., *Personal Memories, 1803–1843,* Cincinnati, 1879.

Miller, G. F., "Academy System of the State of New York," *Fifteenth Annual Report* of the Education Department, Vol. 2, pp. 76–246, Albany, 1919.

Reichel, L. T., *History of Nazareth Hall,* Philadelphia, 1855.

Ricketts, P. C., *History of the Rensselaer Polytechnic Institute, 1824–1934,* third edition, New York, 1934.

Stevens, Neil E., "America's First Agricultural School," *Scientific Monthly,* December, 1921.

Walton, George A., "Report on Academies," *Fortieth Annual Report* of the Board of Education [of Massachusetts], Boston, 1877.

Chapter V

FROM PRIVATE SCHOOLS
TO STATE SYSTEMS

UNTIL far into the nineteenth century most elementary schools were private schools. Most of them, whether they were public or private, were ungraded and unsupervised; and nowhere did they form a regular system or articulate well with the schools above or below them. The terms were short, frequently lasting only three months. Horace Mann in his boyhood never attended school for more than ten or twelve weeks in any single year. Henry Barnard had slight regard for the dame and district schools which he first attended. Barnard will be noticed in the following chapters.

Country schools were the poorest, often being only makeshift subscription or district schools, teaching little besides reading, writing, and simple calculation, and that little, not well. School buildings were as poor as the schools and often were unfit for use. Many of the well-to-do families sent their children to private schools and thus lost interest in the public schools and weakened their support. Those who were unable to pay were admitted free in public schools as charity pupils. Public schools were widely considered as schools for the poor.

The movement for the improvement of public education developed slowly before 1830 but more rapidly thereafter. New York had created her Board of Regents, and had made a state appropriation for schools before 1800 and established the first American state superintendency of common schools in 1812. Other states followed this example. Pennsylvania (1834), Ohio (1837), Massachusetts (1837), and about the same time Michigan and Kentucky were laying more or less firm foundations for their future systems.

By then the private school tradition was giving ground to the public school movement. The pauper school and the rate bill were becoming odious to the generation which had elected Jackson. The workingmen, frontiersmen, many professional men, and men with political insight demanded a closer approach to equality of educational opportunity. They were resolved to create a common school for rich and poor and they understood that only the states could provide universal, free education.

The Lancasterian schools, which will be more fully considered below, formed a middle term between the ungraded private and the graded public schools. The Lancasterian schools were private, but they showed the way to a school so moderate in cost that the public became willing to assume its support. Also the Lancasterian or monitorial schools were established in cities where a large number of children could be educated together. And the cities became the leaders in developing public education and state systems of support and regulation. For rural people, especially, the state system was the only solution of the problem of universal education.

1. Philanthropic Endeavor

Many cities established public schools under special laws before the state as a whole was ready to take so advanced a step. Philadelphia, Lancaster and other cities of Pennsylvania, Baltimore in Maryland, Cincinnati in Ohio are examples. Many special laws were passed in the several states to permit cities to go ahead of the country districts in their educational provision.

In the cities also there were many philanthropic societies which established schools for special classes of children. There were schools for free Negroes, for the children of particular religious denominations, for poor boys; there were Sunday Schools and evening schools; and in 1806 the Lancasterian schools of England were introduced into New York City. They spread to other cities like a brush fire, but in many places, like such a fire, they soon died out. In New York City they persisted, and to support and promote them there was chartered in 1805 the Society for Establishing a Free School in the City of New York for the Education of Such Poor Children as do not Belong to or are not Provided for by any Religious Society. This title was to prevent opposition from church charity schools by showing that the new society would not trench upon ground already occupied.

The Free School Society was later known as the Public School Society but it was actually a private organization and its schools were private schools. The first school, opened in 1806, was followed by others, and the society remained active until 1853, when it transferred its property to the city Board of Education, which had been created eleven years before. For nearly fifty years the society rendered useful service but it failed, as philanthropic efforts were bound to fail, in the effort to enroll all the unschooled children of a city.

2. WHY THE LANCASTERIAN SCHOOLS FAILED

The Free School Society used the Lancasterian system, more descriptively called the monitorial, or mutual instruction, system. This system had been developed in England by Joseph Lancaster (1778–1838). Although he developed faults of character, he was a good teacher and successful promoter. The essential idea of mutual instruction was not his own. It had apparently been borrowed from Andrew Bell (1753–1832), who had obtained it from schools in India. The Jesuits, Comenius, and others had anticipated Bell and Lancaster. In Lancasterian schools, a part or all of the teaching was done by the more advanced pupils, those who knew a little more instructing those knowing a little less. This was the essential feature. The schools were called mutual instruction schools because the pupils taught each other, or monitorial schools because the pupils appointed to teach or help in other ways were called monitors. There were teaching monitors, monitors of discipline, monitors of this and that, and inevitably a head-monitor in charge of the monitors.

The Lancasterian schools had a more than half-way military organization. Pupils rose, marched, wheeled, sat down, and took up their books at a word of command. They were minutely graded into those who were studying words of one, two, three, or more syllables and so in other subjects. Classes were to be kept very small. Every monitor and every child was to have something to do every minute and a motive for doing it.

Many of the motives that were used were not the best. Extensive use was made of punishments and of rewards and rivalry. For punishment, Lancaster even made use of shackles and of the dunce cap; for rewards, there were badges, offices, and orders of merit. By such means he avoided the use of the strap; but they tended to make the children conceited and priggish and did not increase their love of knowledge or their desire to cooperate with others.

The system was intended to educate the poor and the cheapness of it was its chief recommendation. The cost per pupil was low when the schools were large because they required only one salaried person, the principal. With 500 or more pupils the expense for each might be as low as two or three dollars a year. Many ingenious ways were used of saving expense on books, supplies, and equipment. Writing with the fingers on sand tables, the use of slates, of wallcharts instead of books, and memorizing from dictation were some of these ways.

The curriculum and aims were narrow and mechanical. No such lofty purposes as education for citizenship or the liberal education of the poor entered into Lancaster's plans. These were the ideas of Pestalozzi. Lancaster, aiming chiefly at literacy, began with the alphabet, spelling, reading, the catechism, and Bible verses, and added some arithmetic and geography. Practically all of it was memory work, for that was all that the child monitors were able to conduct.

From the Lancasterian school opened in New York in 1806 as a beginning, the plan spread to the cities and towns of the entire country. In New York funds to the amount of several thousand dollars were collected preparatory to the opening of the first school. But later the city council and the state legislature also appropriated funds in support of the expanding system. The society began to build its own schoolhouses. The first one provided for 500 children in one room, 150 in another, and also living quarters for the head-teacher. Girls were admitted to the schools after 1819.

In 1826 the society began to charge fees for the tuition of those able to pay, although still admitting the poor free. This brought on dissension and loss of patronage and the fee system was abandoned six years later. Meanwhile, various religious groups had demanded a share in the public funds which had been given the Free, or Public, School Society. The educational deficiencies of the method were also becoming clear and the legislature withheld further funds. Through the years the society enrolled more than 500,000 children and expended $3,500,000. When its work was done it turned over to the board of education more than 100 schoolhouses and other property. As in other such cases, the transfer should have been made much earlier.

The transfer occurred in 1853, but the blow which was to destroy the Public School Society was struck in 1842. It came about in the following way. The society's schools used the King James translation of the Bible, a version to which Catholics have always objected. Some of the reading books also were offensive, but at first the Catholics lacked the numbers and leadership to effect a change. State and city school funds were distributed to the Public School Society and sometimes to other teaching bodies. But in 1831 the Common Council made the mistake of assigning some funds to the Protestant Orphan Society and refusing aid to the Catholic Orphan Asylum when equal treatment was requested. From that time there was no peace in New York City school affairs until a genuine public school system was created.

That was a period of strong and mounting nativist sentiment and of particular opposition to the Irish Catholic immigration which was increasing. By 1840 two new personalities, Governor William H. Seward and Bishop John Hughes of the New York diocese, had become active in the controversy. The governor was willing to use public funds to aid parochial schools and the bishop would have accepted this settlement; but the Common Council supported by the Protestant churches and the newspapers rejected the plan. The able secretary of state, John C. Spencer, who also served as the state superintendent of common schools, proposed to extend the state school laws to the city, a simple and logical solution, but one that was not accepted at first.

Speakers who discussed the problem abused the Catholic minority and they in turn broke up the meetings. In the fall of 1841, the bishop and his aides put up a Catholic party ticket in the city and it polled enough votes to give the victory to the Whigs. This taught the Democrats that in the city, at least, the Catholics held the balance of power. The Democratic legislature which assembled in January, 1842, was anxious to regain Catholic support in New York City. On the school question it adopted the solution which had been proposed by Superintendent Spencer, a solution which neither Democrats nor Whigs, neither Catholics nor Protestants in the city, really wanted. It, however, passed the Maclay bill (1842) which simply applied the state educational law to New York City. The law provided for a board of education, its members to be elected by wards, and forbade the payment of public funds to schools which taught or favored any sectarian religious doctrine. The Public School Society did not long survive the loss of public funds. The courts were to be called upon to decide whether the English Bible used by Protestants is a sectarian book, whether it might be studied as literature rather than as religion, and other related questions.

The struggle in New York was peaceful and polite in comparison with the violence that broke out in Philadelphia over the same question. That city had long had a public school system when the Catholic Bishop Francis Patrick Kenrick in 1842 addressed a letter to the Controllers of the Public Schools. He asked that Catholic children might be permitted to read from the Douay Bible instead of the King James, and the board agreed. But Protestant religious papers, speakers, pamphleteers, and secular newspapers so worked upon the people that rioting, the destruction of two Catholic churches, and several fatalities resulted. This happened in May and again in July of 1844 and may have been induced by the rapid influx of Irish mill and railroad workers and the disturbance to the economic, political, and religious life of an old American community with strong nativist convictions.

The most important legal case in this period, which involved the reading of the Bible in schools, was *Donahoe* v. *Richards,* 38 Maine, 376 (1854). The Supreme Court of Maine decided that a board had the legal and constitutional right to expel a child from school for refusing to read the Bible used by the school even though the child or its parents had religious scruples against doing so. This case also led to a great uproar in the small community where it originated. The rule was considered decisive until the Supreme Court of Wisconsin in 1890 reversed it in *Weiss* v. *District Board, City of Edgerton,* 76 Wisc. 177 (1890). The court in this case held that reading the Bible, a sectarian book, is worship, and declared: "It is believed that Wisconsin is the first state whose constitution contains a direct prohibition of sectarian instruction in the public schools." The question of religion in public education will come up again and we must now return to the spread of the Lancasterian system.

A free school begun by a group of Quakers who called themselves the Association of Friends for the Instruction of Poor Children introduced the monitorial system into Philadelphia about 1807. The system was also introduced into some of the charity schools founded earlier. Both New York and Philadelphia established Lancasterian model or teacher-training schools, and when Lancaster came from England to the Quaker City he was employed as head of the model school which then had over 700 pupils. These model schools were among the earliest American institutions to attempt the training of teachers. The one in Philadelphia was opened in 1818. The training consisted merely in teaching young men how to organize and operate a Lancasterian school. Lancaster's *Improvements in Education* (1803), which went through several editions and republications, was a practical manual. He had no new—or old—psychology or philosophy of education.

From New York and Philadelphia the monitorial system spread to Albany, Poughkeepsie, and Schenectady, and to Harrisburg, Lancaster, Erie, and other places. In the West, monitorial schools were established in Cincinnati and Detroit. Lancaster's pupils, and their pupils, spread the schools far and wide. In many cities, the Lancasterian system prepared the way for the establishment of public education. This occurred in New York, Philadelphia, Baltimore, and elsewhere. Newspapers and public men favored the plan. When its defects—superficial teaching, mechanical administration, appeal to wrong motives—became apparent, it was abandoned even more rapidly than it had been introduced. Before Lancaster's death in 1838, his movement had become a lost cause. But significant results had been achieved. Many had been convinced that the cost of universal education would not be prohibitive. Schoolmen had learned lessons in the organization and grading of schools.

Contemporary estimates were, however, sharply divided. William Dunlap, theatrical manager and playwright, was favorably impressed when he heard Lancaster speak, but after a second lecture he called him "a quack." Others thought him a charlatan. But DeWitt Clinton, twice governor of New York, called him a benefactor of the human race, the creator of a new era in education, a blessing sent down from heaven to redeem the poor of this world from the power and dominion of ignorance. There was some truth in every one of these apparently conflicting views. Lancaster was vain, extravagant, a poor manager, and something of a mountebank, as Sir Walter Scott charged; but his system, which was not wholly his own, rendered valuable service in the promotion of education.

3. AN AMERICAN PRINCIPLE

When the Lancasterian schools and the whole philanthropic system were gradually discarded in the early nineteenth century, a new principle was substituted. This was the principle of free education for all in public, common schools. Because the monitorial system had provided schools and some education, however defective, for many, a more complete education was now to be offered to all. But there was a further reason for this expansion in new political conditions that had nothing to do with the whimsies of Joseph Lancaster. The new principle was one that fitted in with the rise of the common man to power. The common man demanded schools that were common in the sense that children were admitted free and without regard to social class.

This was an American idea. Europe with its dual systems did not have it and therefore the United States could not borrow it. This idea was the cornerstone of educational democracy, and it must be emphasized that it was laid in the time of Horace Mann and Henry Barnard, and that later philosophies merely built upon it.

True, it has had to be reinterpreted from time to time. It was gradually recognized that the principle meant that country children shall have as good an education as city children; Negro children, Mexicans, and Nisei as good an education as Anglo-Saxons; children in the South equal opportunity with those in the North; and those with mechanical aptitudes as careful nurture as those who are apt in the use of pen and tongue. The principle has had to be interpreted, and applied. This has been much of the task of education in the last hundred years. Those who accepted the principle a hundred and more years ago were too often satisfied when they had provided equal opportunity in a one-room school, which offered little opportunity at best.

Emerson, who had given vigorous expression to the principle, had a broad and deep conception of education; but he lacked in understanding of the means. He did not understand the function of the state as provider of opportunity. Public educational meetings, even when Horace Mann was the speaker, drew from him only a yawn. His one-sided individualism needed tempering with social responsibility, cooperation, and a dash of conformity. Such individualism had long gone hand-in-hand with philanthropy, offering a full meal to a fortunate few but only crumbs to the many. This is just what was wrong with the philanthropic arrangements that were to be superseded.

And some of Emerson's praise of the old New England plan of education was not deserved. The first schools, it has been shown in earlier chapters, were transplanted. They taught merely the elements of literacy and religion. The chief purpose of the early laws was to provide for the neglected portion of the youth, the poor, orphans, and children of neglectful parents. It is a pertinent comment that the level of education among the dependent classes began to decline soon after the settlements and continued on its downward course for a century. Evasion of the law of 1647 was frequent. Even in New England, the region of so-called state activity in education, the church was far more active than the state in promoting and controlling schools. The principle that boys and girls, all the children of all the people, should be educated in free, public schools, under the direction and with the aid of the state, was a later idea.

4. Defining Public Education

To draw a correct definition of public education from students would be a difficult task for any modern Socrates. The task is made difficult by the qualities that private and public schools have in common, and by the habit of people to use general descriptive words instead of exact, scientific ones. If they are questioned, students will say that public schools are common, free, open to all, supported from taxes, and controlled by elected boards. In the class of private schools there are, it will be replied, church, military, preparatory, and country day schools, while public schools show less variety. But such arrays of casually chosen similarities and differences can hardly be made the basis of a definition.

Even the courts have found it difficult to draw a clear and simple distinction. They have sometimes held that a public school is "a common school, one that is open to all, belonging to the public" Mo. Court of Appeals, *Roach* v. *St. Louis*, 7 Mo. App. 567 (1879). These phrases are neither synonymous nor exact. By "common" the court doubtless meant inclusive rather than inferior. And "open to all" is too broad. Both private and public schools limit attendance in many ways such as by age, ability, preparation, or place of residence. No school is literally open to everyone. We may take the third phrase as the best, although the statement that a public school belongs to the public is not very informative.

When the problem has come before the courts, which has very frequently occurred, they have generally considered only the elementary public schools; and this has been one source of their difficulty, for there are public high schools, universities, and schools for the deaf, to take a few examples. High schools are public and now fairly common in all states, but they were public before they became common. State universities and state schools for the deaf are public but not common. Public schools are not always free, which is probably what the court meant by "open to all." Free, private schools are now rare, while of public schools the reverse is the case. Thus we see that historical changes as well as the various levels of public education make it difficult to frame a simple definition.

The sources of a school's support have been held to determine its public or private character. The courts have generally rejected this criterion. Legislatures have granted lands and funds to private schools as a sort of "protection" of an infant and not lucrative industry; public schools have accepted gifts or bequests; and neither school has been changed in character thereby. But if a school received all or nearly all of its support from public sources, it is a question whether it could resist the pressure to become a part of the public system.

We shall not reach a definition on these inductive lines. A decision in 1869 by the Supreme Court of Massachusetts will be more helpful. The Court declared that to be public, a school must be "under the order and superintendence of the public"; and that this is not the case when the trustees have to be chosen from the membership of certain churches. This decision bears upon the question whether the Massachusetts school laws of the seventeenth century, including that of 1647, formed the beginning of public education in America. By this test it seems that the town schools established under the law of 1647 were not public. But we may ask: Does not the fact that everyone belonged to the same church alter the whole case? And did the coming of many sects into the colony, a historical change in the population, transform public schools into private ones?

We shall briefly recapitulate. It is difficult and may not always be necessary to make a sharp distinction. But when it is necessary, the criterion of control should determine whether a school is to be considered as a public school. In a democracy, at least, a school is public when its control and management are vested in the civil electorate, the body of the voters. But public schools have many characteristics. They are usually tax-supported, relatively free, open to a wide public, often nonsectarian, and integrated into a state system of schools. They have these additional characteristics because they are controlled by the people.

5. State Systems in Outline

Recent state constitutions direct the legislatures to establish systems of public schools. Earlier constitutions often omitted the subject or spoke in vague terms. Later instruments have become more explicit.

The Constitution of Illinois of 1870 provided that the legislature should "provide for a thorough and efficient system of free schools whereby all the children of this State may receive a good common school education." A few years later the state supreme court held that this was a minimal requirement which did not operate against the establishment of high schools. Other state constitutions have demanded the establishment and maintenance of "a general, suitable, and efficient system of free schools" (Arkansas, 1874); "a general uniform, and thorough system of public, free, common schools" (Idaho, 1890); or "a liberal system of public schools throughout the State" (Alabama, 1901). Evidently it is not considered sufficient to order the formation of a public school system; but the language of the constitutions is largely rhetorical, and often it is copied from similar documents in other states.

State systems have evolved slowly and experimentally and are the results of constitutional and legislative provisions. Much of the legislation has been of a piecemeal nature, and in the early laws moral, religious, and eleemosynary purposes are evident. From the first the colonies and later the states were independent and, as a result, so were their educational systems. This is a noteworthy feature of American educational organization. The "reserved powers" clause of the federal Constitution preserved this independence.

The variety of the state systems is increased by the economic and population differences between the states and sections. The greatest difference among the systems has been the segregation of Negro from white pupils in separate schools in the South. Northern cities sometimes separate the races, but this has not been required by state law. There are great differences in the degree of state control of schools. New York, Maryland, and New Hampshire are examples of strict and detailed control, while many of the states on the plains, such as Kansas, Nebraska, or the Dakotas, and some in the South permit the locality to exercise broad powers. It is important to know that the states can control the local schools completely if the legislature so votes. Even the school units, the cities, townships, and districts are creatures of the state and derive all their powers from the state. It is important to know this when men argue for the preservation of local autonomy in school matters and when it is proposed "to give the schools back to the people." Only by permission of the state legislature or power delegated by it can the local school district control its own affairs.

The differences between the state control systems are lessened by the constant migration and free communication between the states and within each one of them. They are also lessened by the influence of the federal Constitution. The Supreme Court in the so-called Oregon case (1925), for example, denied the right of any state to abolish private schools just because they are private, or to require all children to attend public schools. Federal aid to education in the states has done a great deal to promote similar developments in the different states in vocational and higher education. States also copy each other. Almost all states now have a state board of education, although the constitution and powers of these boards differ widely. All states have school systems, elementary, secondary, and higher, that are similar but not equally fully developed or equally well supported. It is readily possible to exaggerate the differences, great as they still are, between the state systems. The outlines of a national pattern are clear.

6. An Early Start in New York

In the remaining sections of this chapter we shall examine the early history of state systems. The educational history of colonial New York did not give promise of the rapid progress that was to take place under the federal Constitution. A law of 1784, revised in 1787, started the movement by creating the Board of Regents to have direction of secondary and collegiate education. A law of 1812 created the first American state superintendency of common schools. In 1834 New York began to support the academic education of teachers. Some of the academies set up classes for the study of educational problems, such as teaching methods or school organization. These events are enough to show that New York began early in developing a state system; but no state has been able to lead in every-thing, or all of the time.

There was no reference to education in the first New York constitution as passed in 1777 or as amended in 1801. The governors and a committee of the Regents urged the importance of universal education and pointed to the progress of neighboring states. But the Regents had no money for ele-mentary education. It is not clear what progress they had observed in neigh-boring states in 1787; and it is perhaps surprising to find a board charged with the care of secondary schools and colleges concerning itself with ele-mentary schools.

We shall trace the beginning of the state system of elementary educa-tion. The first concrete step was not the law of 1812 but the granting of land for school support. About the time when the old Congress in its Survey Ordinance of 1785 set aside Section Sixteen of each western township for schools (see Section 8, this chapter), New York, which did not share in that plan, enacted a corresponding law based upon its own "wild lands." The second step was taken ten years later (1795) through the passage of "An Act for the Encouragement of Schools." The encouragement was in the form of an annual appropriation, to be continued for five years, of $100,000 for schools.

The quotas of this sum for the counties and the formula for the dis-tribution to the towns were stated in the law; and each town was required to raise by property tax one-half as much as it was to receive from the state. This principle of conditional giving has been widely followed by the states, by the national government in its dollar-matching-dollar requirements, and also by private donors. The schools were not made free but the New York law was mandatory. Each town was required to elect school commissioners to certify the teachers and supervise the schools. The attempt to extend the act in 1800 failed, although by only a few votes, and state aid ended for the time.

If the Regents had been charged with the administration of the com-mon schools, New York would have begun with a more complete system. But the contrast between elementary and secondary-higher education which at that time existed in the minds of men forbade this. Unfortunately, the separate administrations built up special interests that were to prevent unification for more than a hundred years.

The administration of the lower schools, separated from that of the Regents, was instituted, as indicated above, by the appointment of a super-intendent of common schools under the law of 1812. The appointee was a young lawyer, Gideon Hawley (1785–1870); and his duties were to be primarily fiscal. After the effort to renew the treasury grants for schools failed in 1800, the legislature laid the foundations of a common school fund that was to produce twice the sum of $100,000 a year. The proceeds from the sale of 500,000 acres of state lands were to be accumulated until the amount of $4,000,000 was attained. Local school units, in order to participate in the proceeds, were to be required to raise a specified tax. For the accomplishment of these purposes an official was needed, and in this way there appeared in the United States the office of state superintendent of schools.

The first duty of the first state superintendent was to digest plans for the management of the common school fund; and the second was to improve the organization of the common schools. He was to supervise the collection of school moneys, to accumulate moneys from the sale of lands in the school fund, to report the expenditure of school funds, and "to give information to the legislature respecting all matters referred to him by either branch thereof, or which will appertain to his office; and generally to perform all such services relative to the welfare of the schools as he shall be directed to perform. . . ."

Americans of those times, still shuddering over the memory of the tyranny of George the Third, feared all executive power whether of the governor or of the lowly school superintendent of the state. Hawley, however, had somewhat more power than the usual state superintendent was to be granted for a century afterward; and he made the most of what he had. In his administration was begun that concentration in his office of judicial influence over education which has made the New York department one of the strongest in the nation. Hawley served as superintendent for nine years, until 1821, when by a political maneuver the office was abolished. His duties were added to those of the secretary of state. The same process was followed in other states. The first superintendent's office in Maryland continued two years (1826–1828), in Ohio three years (1837–1840), in New Hampshire four years (1846–1850). There were shorter or longer interruptions in the continuity of the office in almost half of the states. Hawley, it is pleasant to report, was promptly chosen secretary of the Board of Regents.

New York began to experiment with the public preparation of teachers in 1834. In that year a new law provided aid to one academy in each of the eight judicial districts for the maintenance of a special class for teachers. Ten years later the normal school at Albany was created and others followed after the Civil War. Both plans of teacher-training were maintained for many years. A union free-school system providing for the public support of high schools was begun by a permissive law of 1853. But the rural schools of New York did not become entirely free until 1867 and after a great political fight. Cities had earlier abolished the rate bill, a method of assessing the costs of a school upon the patrons in the proportions of the total number of days attended by all the children sent by each patron. The separate state school office to provide supervision over elementary education was restored in 1854; but the two branches, one dealing with elementary and the other with secondary and higher schools, remained separate until 1904. Then they were combined under a single officer whose dual title is reminiscent of the old division. He is the president of the University of the State of New York and commissioner of education. The first to hold this office was Andrew Sloan Draper (1848–1913), who had for a decade been president of the University of Illinois.

7. Pennsylvania Beginnings

In Pennsylvania, as in other states, the cities secured special legislation giving them permission to form their own school systems. To pass general school laws for a state was more difficult, especially if the laws were to be mandatory. Most states, therefore, started with permissive laws and set up fixed requirements only when favorable sentiment had been formed.

In Pennsylvania as elsewhere there were many arguments against public education. It was new and it was expensive. Radical democrats tended to oppose all grants of executive power and all new offices if they could be avoided. Some thought public schools socialistic. Country people were opposed to schools because the children were needed on the farms. Schooling made them lazy and vain, it was claimed. Many Germans wanted their own language taught in schools. Some Germans were Lutherans, some were Catholics, and both favored parochial schools. Some German sects were opposed to too much schooling as tending to change their views and way of life. Much of the opposition to public education in Pennsylvania came from the German and the mountain counties.

Before the 1830's most states depended upon subscription schools and public schools supported by tuition fees, rate bills, and proceeds from school lands. The school tax was almost unknown. Pennsylvania had done almost nothing. Its constitution of 1790 enjoined the legislature to establish schools in which the poor would receive free instruction. The legislature did not act for almost twenty years; and then it passed the pernicious law of 1809 which established no schools but asked poor parents to confess their poverty to private schoolteachers who would then be reimbursed by the state. There cannot have been many worse forms of school legislation.

For more than forty years after 1790, the state, outside of the towns, was without public schools. This was not wholly owing to lack of effort. A bill providing for a county system of free schools was actually passed by both houses in 1794, but was lost in conference committee through a disagreement over details. A general public school law was passed in 1824. This included the provision that the poor should be given free tuition. But the attack upon even this weak law became so violent that the legislature hastened to repeal it before it came into operation.

Ten years later the public school forces were more determined and successful. George Wolf, a former teacher, was governor; Samuel Breck who had entered politics expressly to work for public education served as chairman of the joint committee of the two houses upon education; and Roberts Vaux led the Pennsylvania Society for the Promotion of Public Schools. The committee in presenting its bill took care to say that they had omitted the word "poor." They said: "Let all fare alike in the primary schools and imbibe the republican spirit." After the long hard campaign, the bill, to the surprise of many, was accepted almost unanimously. The fight came afterward but the campaign to repeal it failed.

The act of 1834 should not have aroused such bitter opposition, for it was an optional law. It made cities, boroughs, counties, and townships the administrative units. Except for a brief period, Pennsylvania escaped the district system. The law instituted the school tax and gave state appropriations to those units in which the tax was collected. This was a means to encourage the acceptance of the law. In all units which accepted the law, the schools were made free; and in 1848 the law became mandatory. Each local unit was governed by six elective directors. The secretary of state was made superintendent of common schools, *ex officio,* until 1857 when a separate office was created. A law of 1854 had established the county superintendency and permitted the grading of the schools. Several other states, Maine, Vermont, New York, and Ohio, established or re-established the state superintendency in the fifties; and several also passed permissive school grading laws at this time.

8. On the Western Frontier

Several states in the old Northwest enacted general school laws and created state systems fairly early. Those states had the benefit of the Congressional school lands; but these proved less valuable than the people had expected. The Survey Ordinance of 1785 reserved Lot. No. 16 of every township "for the maintenance of public schools within said township." In the survey plan each township was a square, six miles on a side, and was divided into thirty-six sections each one mile square and numbered as in the diagram below. As the diagram shows, the sixteenth section was the third from the northern and the third from the western boundaries of the township. The reservation of this square mile of land (640 acres) in every township for the schools did not apply to the older states. Ohio, admitted into the Union in 1803, was the first state to receive the grant. Later states in some cases received two sections and even four sections in each township for school support. The legislature of each state had the duty to conserve and manage the school lands. Some states managed them well, collecting the rents and applying them to the schools. Others sold the lands early,

6	5	4	3	2	1
7	8	9	10	11	12
18	17	16	15	14	13
19	20	21	22	23	24
30	29	28	27	26	25
31	32	33	34	35	36

usually at low prices, and in some cases dissipated the money. Ohio belongs to the latter group.

The Ordinance of 1787 asked the legislatures of the Northwest Territory to encourage schools and the means of education; but the legislature of Ohio did not heed this admonition until the session of 1821, when the first general school law was adopted. It was weak, like most early school laws. It proposed the division of the townships into school districts at the option of the voters and the election of district school committees of three members. Two-thirds of the householders of a district had to consent before a schoolhouse could be built. A tax could be laid to make up the deficiency caused by the inability of some to pay their school fees. Thus was the district system imported from the East to become the basis of public education in Ohio. The next legislature had a majority of both houses opposed to public education, and in the words of an early historian of the state, "They broke up in a row and went home." The first great forward steps were taken in 1837 and 1838.

The office of superintendent of common schools was created in March, 1837, and Samuel Lewis, a successful, self-educated lawyer was chosen to fill it. His duties were to collect information, to promote interest in, and to report on common schools. His first report was a progressive statement. He urged the establishment of school libraries and of high schools. He laid bare the scandalous mismanagement of the school lands; and he showed that even with competent administration the income from these lands would be inadequate to support the schools. He proposed an increase in the state school fund to provide an annual income of $200,000. He recommended laws giving districts power to borrow money for buildings; providing for local school supervision in city and country; and requiring full educational and financial reports. He proposed a state school journal and *The Ohio Common School Director* (1839) was established.

The law of 1838 which followed this report provided for a school census, a common school fund, and a county school tax of two mills. It established county and township supervision, although by *ex officio* personnel. It gave local boards the power to control the curriculum but required that all schools must be taught in the English language. This provision was aimed at the German schools which had been established in Cincinnati. But there were already so many influential Germans in that city that they were able to secure the repeal of this clause. In 1840 the office of state superintendent was abolished, and his duties were assigned to the secretary of state. Some of the ground thus given up was not recovered until 1853, when the state office was re-established, a state tax levied, the rate bill abolished, the schools made free, and a beginning made in the curbing of the district system.

In Michigan, as in many other states, the chief city first developed schools. The trading post of Detroit is said to have had schools in 1755, and there were a number of Catholic missions among the Indians when Father Gabriel Richard arrived in 1798. He established schools for both races and obtained recognition for education from the territorial legislature which passed the general school law of 1809. The town had a newspaper in 1817 and a Lancasterian school a year later. Detroit was a westerly outpost of the Lancasterian movement and about the same time the home of the curious university named Catholepistemiad, or institution of universal knowledge,

FROM PRIVATE SCHOOLS TO STATE SYSTEMS 151

chartered in 1817. The name was based upon the old idea that a university teaches all knowledge, a misconception that probably will never die. Detroit entered upon the main-traveled road of educational progress in 1838 by establishing public schools, making them free in 1842 when the city board of education was instituted.

The first general school law (1809) of the territory provided for the creation of school districts, the conducting of a school census, and the laying of a school tax. This early legislature knew what must be provided first in framing a new school system, but the time was not ripe and the law was stillborn. A second general school law (1829) was modeled after the Massachusetts law of 1789. The kinds of schools, whether elementary or secondary, and the length of the terms were to be based upon the number of people in an area. The voters of a township were permitted to divide the area into districts, each with one teacher and three elected trustees. The law was optional. Support was to come from school lands and taxation but the rate bill was soon substituted, and was used until 1869, longer than in New York.

Michigan was the fourth state carved out of the Northwest Territory and was admitted into the Union, as the twenty-sixth state, in 1837. She profited from the mistakes of her sister states in managing school lands. Michigan, while still a territory, appointed a superintendent of common schools to administer her school lands and managed them as one property; and also applied the proceeds as needed by any part of the state instead of applying the income from a particular section only in the township whence it was derived. The state constitution of 1835 made education a branch of the state government and provided for the establishment of a state school office. The law of 1837 created the office of superintendent of public instruction and gave the officer supervisory power over the schools and the management of the school lands. The law provided for state and local taxation and local boards, but it assigned strong supervisory powers to the superintendent. These were the ideas of the framer of the law, John D. Pierce, who had read Victor Cousin's report on the schools of Prussia. From that document he gathered that centralized power was essential. As a matter of practical politics and as it applied to the formative period of American education, this was an overstatement. If one considers the history of the colonies, the early conditions in the Union, and the people and their manner of life, it is easy to arrive at the opposite conclusion, that the district system and local controls were unavoidable.

Indiana is an excellent example of a state that long suffered from an excess of localism and frontier democracy. The constitution of 1816 required the legislature to establish a general system of free schools equally open to all. This was the voice of enlightened people, but there were too few of them. For many years the state suffered under the most virulent forms of the district system and the rate bill. The school law of 1833 was one of the weakest of such instruments, and the kind of schools which resulted is described in Edward Eggleston's *The Hoosier Schoolmaster*. Millard F. Kennedy in his *Schoolmaster of Yesterday* shows a more recent picture of the Indiana pioneer school and teacher; and Jesse Macy's *Autobiography* paints the vocational versatility of the pioneer. Macy's family, about 1850, had a farm with a tannery and sawmill, and raised wool and flax and made them into cloth and clothes. A sugar-maple "orchard" necessitated a coopering business. Most of the farmers were also carpenters, builders, joiners, and cabinet-makers, or blacksmiths, or shoemakers. Teaching was also such a part-time trade; and the results were equally crude.

The Indiana Constitution of 1851 repeated the mandate of 1816 and the general school law of 1852 was to fulfil its demands. Unfortunately, as it turned out, the new constitution demanded the erection of a "general and uniform system of common schools." The state supreme court thereupon pronounced all local school taxes unconstitutional, since they would vary from district to district and thus destroy the uniformity of the system. The state common school fund was able to provide for public schools for only two months annually at a "uniform" salary of fifty-five dollars for the term. Districts which had a sufficient number of paying pupils used the rate bill to extend the term. Not until 1867 did the schools of Indiana become free for a longer term than two months.

The discovery of gold caused a rapid increase in the population of California at a time when large areas east of the Rockies were unoccupied. There was only one cabin on San Francisco Bay in 1835, but upon the admission of the state into the Union in 1850, California had 90,000 people, most of them in the general region of the Bay. People came from all parts of the East and foreign lands. They continued to come. The census of 1860 showed that the population of the state was more than four times as great as it had been ten years earlier.

The first constitution provided for an elected state superintendent and for the preservation of the school lands, and required the legislature to establish a common school system. At its first session no such action was taken by the legislature; but in 1851 it created a primitive district system similar to those of the preceding century in the East. The elected district trustees were empowered to build schoolhouses but not to levy a tax for this or any other purpose. They were to examine teachers and give certificates good for one year only. The law was based upon the supposition that there was a common school fund, which was contrary to fact, and it provided for the distribution of the nonexistent proceeds, not only to public schools but also to church, orphan, almshouse, and any other private schools according to the number of children in each. The third session of the legislature authorized a small county tax for schools, and made the county treasurer *ex officio* superintendent of schools, as had been done in eastern states earlier. It all sounds as though school systems in their evolution were bound to begin in the same way and to traverse the same inexorable steps in a series comparable to the culture epochs; but in fact the sparse and shifting rural population was the reason for such laws, here as elsewhere.

Nor was religious controversy lacking. In San Francisco at first Bible reading in the schools was a requirement; and over some objections this was carried out. In 1854 the offices of the school trustees and superintendent formerly chosen by the council were made elective. Church and other nonpublic schools were amalgamated with the public schools. To share in the public funds, teachers in Catholic, Methodist, and other schools now had to be examined by the public agency. In this merger the religious controversy again broke out and the discord was promoted by the Know Nothing party of that time. The issue was not settled until many years later when all religious exercises were banned from the city schools and from the public schools of the state.

The city schools were far ahead of those in the rural parts of the state. In California, as in New York or Pennsylvania, the city schools operated under special charters which provided for both funds and freedom. Cities developed graded, free schools, while the ungraded schools in the country limped behind with short terms, maintained by tuition charges and assessments.

In California, as in other newer states, the new day in education came quickly. In the 1860's the state developed a progressive system that deserved and gained the praises of Henry Barnard and other national leaders. In 1862 John Swett, a teacher from New Hampshire and Massachusetts, was elected state superintendent. If he was not the author of the slogan that "the wealth of the state must educate the children of the state," he used it skilfully. He had the touch of a master politician. Calling a state teachers' institute, he had every teacher who attended take back to his district and circulate petitions to the legislature for a state school tax and better schools. The response was universal and effective. He secured legislation providing for a state board with power to set up a curriculum and to select textbooks, a state school tax, increased county and local taxes, free schools (1867), school libraries, a state educational journal, *The California Teacher*, a longer term, and the professional preparation of teachers. Henry Barnard said: "There is nothing so liberal in the way of taxation in any other state in the world." William Russell, founder of the old *American Journal of Education*, who had been one of John Swett's teachers, sent his warm commendation.

Before turning to the New England frontier, it may be noted that in several states the schools did not become free until the 1860's. Such states were California, Indiana, Michigan, New York, and in New England, Connecticut and Rhode Island. In Massachusetts, Delaware, and Pennsylvania (a few districts excepted) the schools became free before 1850. Vermont made its schools free in 1850, Ohio in 1853. There is no apparent regional trend here, nor any clear line between older and newer states.

9. NEW ENGLAND FRONTIER

Education in early New England lacked central guidance and a general plan. Each town was an independent school district. Soon the unity of the town as a school district was impaired by the moving school and shattered by the district system. The extreme decentralizing trend of the section was most evident in the thinly settled portions such as the northern states and the western part of Massachusetts.

Take New Hampshire, for example, which became independent of Massachusetts in 1679. School developments resembled those of rural Massachusetts. The moving school and the district system began to appear about 1700. One town, Londonderry, in 1736 voted that the town schoolmaster should teach for two months in each of five places in the town and for one month in each of two others. According to the last royal governor, nine-tenths of the towns had no school or had one kept by an ignorant and immoral itinerant. The governor's statement may have been prejudiced and it is doubtful that he had any detailed knowledge of the conditions. But we know that in 1805 the district system was made legal, an action that had already been taken in Massachusetts. This system satisfied the law of New Hampshire until 1885, when it was abolished.

Long before 1885 a new age had dawned in much of the country. Of high importance among the changes which affected schools were the rise of industry, the growth of towns, the opening of the West, and the invention of farm implements. The people of New Hampshire moved to the cities or left the state. Many farms were abandoned. The immigrants who moved in settled in the cities and worked in factories. The census of 1870 showed a decline in the population of the state. Fifty years before, in 1820, eighty of every hundred persons in New Hampshire lived on farms; but fifty years after 1870, in 1920, only twenty-five of every hundred remained on farms. In many cases the rural leaders had been the first to leave. The district schools were left with few pupils or none. Nineteen-twenty was the turning point in school administration.

There had been several efforts to create a state school office in New Hampshire. A law of 1846 provided for a state school commissioner to be appointed by the governor with the consent of the council. But his duties were few and his powers negligible. He was merely to visit schools, gather statistics, and make an annual report. As in other states, even this insignificant office was abolished in 1850. After a period of county supervision, in 1867, the office of superintendent of public instruction was created, but again without the powers implied by such a title. This lasted fifty years. And then, in 1919, partly as a result of the revelations produced by World War I, a highly centralized department of state school administration was created.

The new law provided for a state board "with the same powers of management, supervision, and direction over all public schools in this state as the directors of the ordinary business corporation have over the business of the corporation, except as its powers may be limited by law." This means that the board could do anything that was not contrary to common or statute law. New Hampshire at last had a powerful state organization. But the business corporation, engaged in making and marketing consumer goods, is hardly a fit model for a state school board. The law of 1919 has been modified. But we have gone far enough to see how persistent the small pattern organization was in this rural and mountainous state.

Before we turn to the awakening in Massachusetts we shall briefly notice the state school offices of the present day. With all the progress of the last hundred years, there is room for further advancement. All forty-eight states now have a chief school official and all but three states have a state board of education. Ohio became the forty-fifth state (1955) to establish a state board.

The qualifications of the chief officer vary from state to state. In some states he must be a college graduate; in some he must have had educational experience; or the law may demand a special kind of certificate assuring his possession of both education and experience; but in about one-fourth of the states there is no specified qualification. He is elected by popular vote in two-thirds of the states, and in the rest he is appointed by the governor or chosen by the state board. Most states have fixed terms of two to four years, but in one-third the tenure is indefinite and the incumbent may serve for many years. In ten states the term is only two years, and when the two major parties are evenly balanced the chance for re-election is precarious. Although there is a top salary of $20,000 or $25,000 in a few states, some states pay no more than the principal of a high school receives.

Now and then in one state or another the office attracts and holds men of the highest caliber, and not always by paying a high salary. Horace Mann endured the labor and abuse of the office for twelve years at $1,500 a year. There have been other great superintendents of public instruction or commissioners of education, such as John Swett of California, Newton Bateman of Illinois, and Andrew S. Draper of New York, but the average capacity of the holders of the office has not been high.

Early state boards, like the early state superintendents, were given little power. This has been changed in several states, but in many cases they have neither the legal responsibility nor the staff to perform the functions that are or should be devolved upon them. In thirty-one states the members are appointed by the governor or are members *ex officio*. But the worst of the situation is that the qualifications for membership are low, and in one-third of the states there are no special requirements.

With the advice and recommendation of the chief school officer, the state board should formulate the state educational policies, submit the budget, and propose needed legislation. In many states, the state department inspects schools and enforces the laws. In addition to these major duties, many minor ones must be performed. The staffs of the departments are often inadequate, and half of the personnel may be concerned with vocational education. The conclusion is that although the central agencies in the state systems have seen great development since 1850, they have not kept pace in qualifications, members, and delegated powers with the need of the present.

10. MASSACHUSETTS INDICTED

"The newer Western States," wrote Francis Adams, "enjoy one great advantage over the people of Massachusetts. They have been exempted from the immense labor of forever boasting of their ancestors, and so have more time to devote to their posterity." Adams was born and educated in central New York, but by 1875 when he wrote these ill-tempered sentences he had become an expatriate and lived in England. But the reformers of education in Massachusetts actually were in a position of some difficulty.

The schools of that colony had soon begun to decline from the standards set by the early laws. Their defects continued to grow and multiply until they led to the public school movement and controversy in the first half of the nineteenth century. The reformers of this period had to rouse Massachusetts from her educational slumbers; and they tried to do this by praising the educational wisdom and enterprise of the colony fathers while castigating the irresponsibility of their degenerate sons. But apparently such schools as most native-born historians ascribe to early Massachusetts never existed except in the first years and the wealthy eastern towns of the state.

In any event the reformers could not propose a return to the conditions of 1647 and therefore had to explain why the bright prospects of the Bay Colony had been dimmed. There was a sound judgment underneath the Adams sarcasm. Others also noticed that some newer states were more ambitious and less bound by the past than the East, but the West lacked the wealth and concentrated population of parts of New York and Massachusetts.

Three Massachusetts reformers gave comparable accounts of the shortcomings of the contemporary schools: These were: James Gordon Carter (1795–1849), Samuel Read Hall (1795–1877), and Horace Mann (1796–1859). Carter had been a district school teacher before he prepared his two series of influential newspaper articles on education. These were also published in pamphlet form as *Letters . . . on the Free Schools of New England* (1824) and *Essays upon Popular Education* (1826). Elected to the legislature, Carter prepared a bill to establish normal schools, which failed, and one to create a state board of education, which succeeded (1837). Thus he opened the way for the career of Horace Mann, who continued to work on the lines proposed by Carter. Hall published his *Lectures on School-Keeping* and this contained a criticism of contemporary schools.

Although Carter praised the early schools of the colony, he admitted that they had not been free from bigotry and intolerance. He condemned the law of 1789 for its "alarming relaxation" of standards, but conceded that this law merely ratified what had long been common practice, the district organization and the neglect of the Latin schools. He charged that the people in his time were satisfied with short terms, irregular attendance, a narrow curriculum, ungraded schools, and untrained teachers. "Thus," he wrote, "we have departed more and more widely from the principle assumed by our fathers in the establishment of the Free Schools, viz., to provide as good instruction in all elementary and common branches of knowledge for the poorest citizen in the Commonwealth as the richest could buy with all his wealth." But the early elementary schools were not free; the public high school became free in Massachusetts only in 1891;

and Carter's statement tacitly admits that the purpose of colony action in education was to provide for the poor. He also agreed that the Latin schools were "always viewed with prejudice" as "an institution for the accommodation of a few at the expense of the many."

Good schools, said Carter, who was most effective when dealing with the positive side of his subject, will be expensive, for the district system must be abandoned. The schools must be graded, supplied with well-prepared teachers, uniform books, and a broader curriculum which must include physical education. He was not deceived by the Lancasterian schools, which he called "a hollow mockery." His outline of the normal school was almost a blueprint of the institutions later established under Mann. He favored Baconian inductive methods, knowing little of Pestalozzi. Before long the legislature, partly as a result of Carter's agitation, took action, restoring town control, establishing a common school fund, requiring the teaching of advanced subjects in large towns, and eventually creating the state board and a state education office.

The opening lectures in Hall's book on teaching also deal with the defects of the schools of New England and set down eight separate causes of their low condition. Some of these stemmed from scanty support resulting in poor buildings, a lack of teaching aids, low salaries, and teachers with only a district school education. But Hall believed that there were more fundamental causes. The communities were rent by sectarian controversies and the people refused to perform their Christian duties toward the schools. These conditions led to the establishment of private schools and the drawing off of still more support from public education and thus to the forming of a vicious circle.

As critic and reformer, Mann agreed with his contemporaries on the wisdom of the educational plans of the Bay Colony and, in contrast, on the bitterness of their present fruits. But the early laws were not as good as the reformers claimed. The early laws set no standards of support, or of teacher competence, and were silent on other vital matters. The famous law of 1647 merely said that "there shall be schools"; and the fine for noncompliance was so low that it constituted an invitation to evasion. Enforcement of the law depended upon the chance that some citizen would report the delinquent town to the general court.

In his *Tenth Report* as secretary of the Massachusetts Board of Education, Mann declared that it would be easy to write a history of popular education in Massachusetts. The cornerstone of this facile history was to be the declaration that the law of 1647 had made education both universal and free. Mann was mistaken. Girls were not regularly admitted to the common schools until after the Revolution. A school tax was first required by the law of 1827, and the schools were made free by the law of 1834. Education is not universal when one-half of the children are excluded and the other half attend irregularly; and it is not free while rate bills are levied.

At the beginning of his term of office, Mann charged that the towns and visiting committees were not obeying the law. They did not, he declared, select uniform textbooks, employ qualified teachers, make the required reports, or even maintain the schools which the law enjoined. He did not fail to notice the poor support given to the public schools and the large amounts expended for private instruction. Absence from school, up to half the enrollment, was a major evil. The attendance of children was sometimes equally or even more disastrous. Every year from three to four hundred school rebellions resulted in the closing, before the end of the term, of one out of every ten schools in Massachusetts. This information comes from Mann's *Second Report,* not from a school novel. Bad school buildings were a contributing factor to bad conduct.

The teachers were not satisfactory. The solution of this problem was to be found in improved preparation, higher salaries, and better working conditions. And although there has been great improvement in all these areas, this is just what is recommended now, more than a century after Mann. In his time the wages of a male teacher in Massachusetts were

TEACHERS' MONTHLY WAGES, EXCLUSIVE OF BOARD, ABOUT 1847

	Men	Women
Massachusetts	24.51	8.07
Pennsylvania	17.02	10.09
Connecticut	16.00	6.50
Ohio	15.42	8.73
Maine	15.40	4.80
New York	14.96	6.69
New Hampshire	13.50	5.65
Michigan	12.71	5.36
Indiana	12.00	6.00
Vermont	12.00	4.75

From Mann's *Eleventh Report.* The states in the table are arranged in the order of the wages paid men teachers. Note that the rank order for women teachers is not the same.

about equal to those of a farm hand. Women earned less than men by one-half or two-thirds. Board was added to the money wage; but it had to be secured by boarding 'round. This Mann considered an indignity to which no teacher should be subjected.

The curriculum seemed poorly adapted to the needs of farmers, railroad builders, and factory operatives. Mann was a utilitarian and a moralist. Perhaps he was a utilitarian even in his ethics, but he was no professional philosopher and he may not have been clear on this point in his own mind. But he did believe that knowledge should be practically useful and that utility outranks artistic elegance and philosophic wisdom. This set for him the problem of selecting the most useful knowledge, a topic upon which Herbert Spencer also was to write.

In the report for 1839, Mann studied the knowledge needed by engineers, artisans, and machinists, namely, knowledge of materials, of power and its transmission, of mathematics; and for navigation, a knowledge of astronomy also. In citizenship and government, a sound judgment must be based upon knowledge of social organization and social forces. He said that all this applied with force to the manufacturing and commercial state of Massachusetts. He returned to this argument again and again. He urged the teaching of physiology, by which he meant both "the laws of life" and the preservation of health. He ended his curriculum theory with the conclusion that "caprice rather than intelligence has presided" over the selection of subjects.

To show how capricious the selection seemed to him, Mann raised such questions as these which follow: Do the numbers of the pupils who study the several subjects correspond to the relative importance of the studies? Why should algebra, which not one man in a thousand ever uses in the business of life, be studied by twice as many pupils as bookkeeping, which everyone, even the day laborer, needs? Is there a single subject more necessary than physiology? The conclusion was that a sound and practical treatise on the relative value of school studies was much needed. Such a book would show what studies should be taken up and in what order. It would enable students to pursue studies "for periods of time proportional to their respective utility."

We shall see that several writers have attempted to fill this need but without distinguished success. We shall note, for example, that Charles W. Eliot, president of Harvard University, thought bookkeeping, as taught, was a useless subject and algebra of great value; but in another connection he thought all subjects of equal value when seriously pursued for equal periods of time. Herbert Spencer, the English philosopher, and Edward

Brooks, superintendent of the schools of Philadelphia, agreed more or less closely with Mann. That educators are unable to solve this basic curriculum problem is an educational misfortune if not a scandal.

11. MASSACHUSETTS VINDICATED

The vigor of the effort put forth by Massachusetts to improve education corresponded to the greatness of the need. Improvement depended upon the public mind and conscience. To gain the moral and financial support of the public for his proposals was Horace Mann's task in Massachusetts, as it was the problem of other reformers in other states as well. Mann, a lawyer, legislator, and politician, developed into a missionary, a public relations expert, and an educational field general. Against angry opposition on more than one front he won a series of campaigns if not the war. Final victory in this war, with lasting peace, is probably not possible. Men do not agree upon the kind of schools they want. Some do not want public schools at all. Unless the fight is constantly pressed, it will certainly be lost. This was one of Mann's axioms.

Mann was driven by the conviction that education is the certain means to prosperity, security, happiness, and salvation. It was no mere job that he had undertaken. It was a call, his vocation to make a better world. He did not invent but he used the suggestion to "open a school and close a jail." He was not alone in this faith. In 1830 all America hoped for a new social order and many were certain that education was the means to produce it. Much of this heady optimism has given way to a sounder, more moderate estimate of the power of education.

Mann used several means to reach the people. His annual report was his message on the state of public education in Massachusetts. In the reports he also considered large questions of theory and practice. He founded the *Common School Journal* (1839) to deal with issues as they arose and to reach the teachers, members of school boards, and the public. He was tireless in traveling over the state and addressing meetings. He regarded the normal schools as the most effective means to carry the new methods and ideas of good education to young teachers who would apply them. Unfortunately, they enrolled only a small minority of the state's teachers. Although it was no part of his official duty, Mann answered many calls from Southern and Western states for addresses and advice. Late in life, when president of Antioch College, he seems to have been asked to aid in framing a school code for the state of Iowa. He visited Europe and the resulting *Seventh Report* was one of his most famous publications. He entertained visiting educators who came for help, including Domingo Faustino Sarmiento from Chile.

School improvement had begun in Massachusetts before Mann became secretary. Even the law of 1789, which was the radical Samuel Adams' idea of radical democracy in education, had one progressive feature. It provided for the admission of girls to the district schools. A new epoch began in 1818. The primary schools and the high school of Boston may have influenced the enactment of the law of 1827, but this is not stated as a known result. An act of 1826 began to undo the errors of 1789 by partially restoring the control of the towns over the school districts. Each town was required to elect a school committee with the duty to choose the textbooks and to examine the teachers. The districts employed the teachers and managed the school property. Mann charged that two-thirds of the towns did not examine the teachers or did so merely perfunctorily; and he suspected collusion between town and district authorities to enable any district to employ any teachers whom the district wanted even though they could not qualify. One-third of the towns did not select the books and as a result the textbooks were not uniform. In these and other cases, Mann's task was that of inducing local authorities to obey the laws.

A state school fund was established in 1834. Towns were to receive a proportionate share in the proceeds on the condition that they would annually raise one dollar per child and would make the school reports required by the law. Thus the towns were to be remunerated for doing their duty. Mann's first report showed that in 1837 the annual cost of teaching a child in the district schools was three dollars and thirty-five cents and in private schools, twelve dollars.

Everywhere in the nation there were groups of people who were against public education. In Massachusetts there were those who opposed school improvement because it would increase taxes, tend to centralize control, interfere with farm work, family discipline, or religion, and foster socialism. The economic upset of the panic of 1837 raised a tension that was increased by Mann's effort to have the laws obeyed and his success in establishing the state normal schools. The opposition declared the public schools godless, the normal schools useless and expensive, and the state board an example of Prussian centralization. The opposition to Mann is evidence of his influence. It may have been the state board that saved the state school office, which in some other states was at least temporarily abolished.

For one reason or another, Mann was under attack during much of his whole term of office (1837–1848); and some of the shafts were directed against him personally rather than against his policies. We shall not repeat these. But there were three particular controversies which filled most of those years. They were the attack upon the normal schools and board of education which came to a head in the legislature of 1840, the pamphlet war with the teachers of Boston, and the controversy over the teaching of religion in the common schools. The first two of these, Mann may be said to have won in the sense that he had the better of the argument and the opposition was silenced. The third was a running battle which continued for years, and although Mann may have won a tactical victory the question was not finally settled and the last of it has not yet been heard.

Mann and the board, not being satisfied with the condition of the schools, tried to improve them. This was their first offence. In 1839 the legislature passed a law that required every district, including those which maintained schools for only two or three months, to extend the annual school term to six months. In the same year the legislature accepted, from Edmund Dwight, public-spirited citizen and friend of Mann, a donation of $10,000 and added to it an equal amount for state normal schools, the first in America. One was opened at Lexington, the same year, in an academy building that stood facing the town common. Three were established in Mann's term, and two others later.

In the winter of 1840 a well-planned assault was made upon the board of education and its "Prussian" policy of state control of education. Actually the board had no important powers of control. The committee on education in the lower house split over the issues. The majority report was an itemized attack upon the board and also upon the whole idea of professional education. This again is a matter that has not been settled in a hundred years. The hostile majority in the committee addressed themselves to the interests of private teachers and their influential patrons, to the taxpayers still wincing from the effects of the panic of 1837, to religious sectaries, and to the pride of self-made teachers. The weakness of their attack was in its lack of any positive plan to improve the common schools; and the people and legislature had come to believe that the common schools needed improvement. The legislature voted to support the board and to develop the normal schools. But such questions can rarely be settled permanently and today the content and value of the professional education of teachers is again an issue.

The *Seventh Report* of Mann contained his account of his European journey and his conclusions upon what he had observed. He was favorably impressed with much that he saw in German schools, the knowledge, teaching skill and unobtrusive management shown by the teachers, the curriculum, the friendly relations between teachers and taught. Mann's praise of Europe was taken by some Boston teachers as disparagement of their own knowledge, skill, and discipline. Thirty-one principals started a pamphlet attack and Mann replied. The shrill tone of his rejoinders has been criticized. Outsiders joined in the fray, which lasted for a year and a half and attracted the attention of the whole country.

The subject of corporal punishment, against which Mann expressed decided adverse opinions, irritated the masters most of all. Mann did not propose to have physical chastisement completely banned but he wanted all other available means of reform tried first. In the Boston schools it is said to have been administered freely and with great severity. Edward Everett Hale considered the Boston masters "inferior men" and believed that "cowhiding" and "thrashing" were their chief accomplishments. He reported in *A New England Boyhood* that his father would not send him to such schools as the Boston grammar schools were but did send him to the Latin school, "a civilized place." At a somewhat earlier time, however, if not when Hale was a pupil, there was a good deal of flogging even in the Latin school, with all its civilization, and also a robust school rebellion which drove the teacher from his post.

The sequel to this controversy with the Boston masters was a city-wide written examination of the pupils of the grammar schools. This was arranged by Mann and his friend, Samuel Gridley Howe, who had conveniently been elected at the proper time to the Boston school board. As a result, four of the grammar school principals were dismissed from their positions.

The most sustained of the controversies in which Mann was involved grew out of the demand by fundamentalists for doctrinal religious teaching in the schools. This would have been contrary to a law of 1827 which was re-enacted in principle in 1835. Mann was not to be blamed for the law itself, but he had interpreted it and urged compliance with its provisions. And he was a Unitarian at heart, although not a member of any denomination at the time, and his personal religion was brought under attack. Those of the opposition understood that he would make no concession to their demands.

The controversy could have been anticipated. In the circumstances it was almost inevitable. Dogmatic Calvinism had been taught in the schools of Massachusetts from the settlement for almost two centuries. The *New England Primer* and the *Westminster Catechism* had been in daily use. The minister regularly visited the schools to teach religion and to see that it was taught.

Meanwhile, two religious changes were taking place. With the acceptance of a policy of toleration many sects came in; and secondly, orthodoxy was losing ground to a growing liberalism. Within two generations of the settlement of Boston, the liberal religious trend at Harvard became one of the reasons for the founding of Yale. In his youth, John Adams, born in 1735, became aware of the growth of Unitarian sentiment among his friends and neighbors. In a well-known educational clause of the Massachusetts Constitution of 1780, which was written by Adams, the legislature is enjoined to cherish humanity, benevolence, charity, and other virtues, but religion is not mentioned. Before the time of Horace Mann the orthodox Calvinists had become a minority in the state and it had become impossible to find any sectarian creed that everybody, or even a majority, wanted taught.

All this led directly to the prohibition of sectarian teaching by the law of 1827. But there was remaining a large body of Calvinists, both Congregational and Presbyterian, in the state and outside of it, who felt in conscience bound to try to turn back the clock. Mann was caught between two irreconcilable parties.

Mann proposed to have the schools teach what was common to Protestant creeds, to have the Bible read without comment, and to have teachers by word and life illustrate nonsectarian Christianity. Even though Roman Catholics and unbelievers did not enter the fight, Mann did not satisfy his opponents. They called his proposal a "godless scepticism." The Presbyterian Synod of New Jersey in 1845 expressed the fear that it would develop "infidel youth who will not be fit to maintain our free institutions." The editor of a Protestant Episcopal church paper accused him of "watering down" Christianity. The worst result of the controversy was that it led to an attack upon the whole concept of universal, free education. Mann was not to bear the blows unaided. Many papers came to his defense. Many orthodox as well as liberal Christians, including the governor of the state, who was a Baptist, supported him. For many years a solution similar to the one proposed in Mann's time was widely accepted but, as every newspaper reader knows, the question of religion in relation to public education is again a problem today.

In spite of all the opposition and indeed partly because of it and through it, Mann succeeded in powerfully stimulating public education in Massachusetts. The opposition drew to his side many supporters and there were also many who had from the first been his friends and friends of the cause. Such were Edmund Dwight, who gave $10,000 for normal schools, Governor Edward Everett, Josiah Quincy, then president of Harvard College, Charles Brooks, a promoter of normal schools, Senator Charles Sumner, George B. Emerson, author and teacher of note, and numerous others. Mann promoted too many improvements to have all of them named here. He aided in bringing back the town government of schools in place of the district system; in the formation of school libraries with books useful for morals, health, agriculture, and other practical interests; in developing instruction in vocal music and drawing and improved methods in teaching primary reading; in developing a sane discipline; in urging the construction of decent schoolhouses and the introduction of blackboards; in forming teachers' institutes which in Massachusetts were able to enlist the genius of Agassiz; in establishing the payment of school board members for attendance at meetings; and, dearest to his heart of all his improvements, in the creation of the state normal schools. His reputation extended far beyond Massachusetts to all parts of the United States, to South America and Europe. Many people from the Southern and Western states applied to him for help with their school problems. In France and England tribute was paid to his talents and achievements.

He said: "I regard normal schools as a new instrument of progress for the improvement of the human race. I consider that without them the public schools would lose their strength and power for good and become mere charity schools." Much as he disliked to admit it, that is what the public schools were when all the wealthier families patronized private schools and when even in the public schools those able to pay were asked to do so. "Neither the art of printing," he wrote, "nor the freedom of the press, nor free suffrage could long subsist for useful and salutary ends if schools for the education of teachers ceased to exist."

Before the expiration of Mann's period in office (1837–1848) the cause of public education and the development of state systems had made great progress in Massachusetts and the nation. By 1848 twenty-four of the thirty states of the Union had a state school office, although some offices were directed by *ex officio* chiefs. The local school tax and state aid were widely accepted and formed the fulcrum and lever of school improvement.

In Massachusetts during Mann's secretaryship, the annual state appropriation had doubled and local taxation had grown even more rapidly. More than $2,000,000 was expended in improving schoolhouses. Salaries had increased by more than 50 per cent. The average school term had been lengthened. Much of the progress, however, had occurred only in the richer parts of the state. By 1847 Mann had been converted to the principle of compulsory attendance, and in 1852 Massachusetts passed a law requiring children to attend school. As this was the first such law in the nation, it was, as one would expect, a weak one. The state normal schools, also the first in the Union, had become fairly well established, and three states, New York, Connecticut, and Michigan, had established similar institutions.

It would be difficult to assign the proper share of credit for these achievements to the chief movers. Certainly Mann was a powerful force, a great promoter, a devoted servant. But many of the ideas had been proposed before his time. The normal school idea had been urged for fifty years and recently by two great governors of the state, Levi Lincoln and Edward Everett. Finally, the donation of Dwight, the management of Mann, and the teaching skill of Cyrus Peirce brought them into existence and then saved them from threatened destruction. In this and other ways Massachusetts became an educational leader and example in the time of Horace Mann.

The Lancasterian schools prepared the way for the transition from private to public education; and this transition took place in the period preceding the Civil War. The new idea was to provide free education for all children in public schools, open to all classes and to rich and poor alike. This principle was favored by the democratic trends in the country. The early tendency was to interpret the principle to cover only elementary schooling for white children; but a much broader interpretation is now accepted.

Public education is variously defined, but the key fact is this, that it is controlled and administered by those who are appointed by and accountable to the civil electorate, the voters. Public education is developed in state systems that vary from state to state; but there are powerful influences which tend to direct the development of the state systems along parallel paths.

The state which first developed a present-day type of system was New York. In that state a Board of Regents for secondary and higher education was created in 1784 and the first common school superintendency in 1812. New York used the method of stimulating local effort by rewarding units which raised their own contribution, by granting them state appropriations. The state began to aid the preparation of teachers in 1834, established a normal school in 1844, and gave public support to high schools in 1853.

After nine years the state superintendency was abolished and the duties of the office added to those of the secretary of state. This plan was continued until 1853, when the state superintendency was restored. Half a century later the secondary-higher and the primary systems were united into one state school administrative agency (1904).

Because of the diverse nationalities and religions in the state, Pennsylvania found it hard to pass a general school law. Even so she was the next state after

New York to create such a law (1834) but on an optional basis only. It was in 1857 that the state established a separate state superintendency. Until that time the secretary of state had performed the duties of such an office.

Ohio was admitted in 1803 and was the first state to receive the federal land grants for public schools, commonly called Sixteenth Section grants; and additional grants for a university. The other states west of Ohio shared in this distribution of land for schools. In Ohio as in New York the office of state superintendent was abolished and not restored until after the middle of the century. In Michigan and Massachusetts among the early states this office was permanent from the first, although efforts were made to destroy it. Indiana is a good state in which to study the influence of the frontier upon education. The public schools of Indiana, California, and New York did not become free until after the Civil War, but later states provided for free education from the first and in some cases even while they had only territorial status. This is an example of older states influencing the practice of newer ones. California was much influenced by New York.

New England was famous for good schools in its cities, but there were many children not in school even in the cities and many poor schools in the country districts. Excepting Massachusetts, the states in this section were not especially prompt in developing state systems nor were these highly developed at first. Massachusetts was in the van and profited from the promotion work of several governors and from that of James G. Carter, but especially from the leadership of Horace Mann. Many who migrated from Massachusetts to the West helped to develop public education in distant states.

QUESTIONS

1. What part can philanthropy play in a nation served by public education? Consider the individual donors, the campaigns for funds, the wealthy foundations, contributions to colleges by business corporations.

2. Did the Lancasterian method of mutual instruction rest upon a true insight into education and psychological processes? In what ways could the method be usefully employed today?

3. How much of the history of American education could be treated under what is here called "an American principle"?

4. Why is it difficult to define "public education"?

5. Why did many states retrace their steps in the development of their systems of education? Study cases.

6. What are the essential parts of a state system?

7. Why were permissive laws frequently enacted and with what results? What national education acts were permissive? What further use could be made of this strategy?

8. Outline the somewhat conflicting, at least contrasting, effects of the

frontier upon educational development. Do these tend to support the "Turner thesis"?

9. Would it have been better tactics for the Massachusetts reformers to assert that they were proposing a radically different educational program than the one initiated by the founders of the colony? How was it different?

10. What was the "vicious circle" in the fact that both private and public schools existed in large numbers in Massachusetts? What is the probability of a return to this condition in the United States?

11. How does one reconcile the common belief in a century of progress with the fact that the schools are now, as then, suffering from low salaries, uncongenial working conditions, teacher shortages, many partially unqualified teachers, and so on?

12. In Chapter Two of *A New England Boyhood* by Edward Everett Hale, it is said: "It will be hard to make boys and girls of the present day understand how much was then expected from reforms in education." Collect and analyze the evidence; and compare it with the hopes of 1900 and after.

13. Why did Mann become involved in more than one man's share of educational controversy?

14. Why do you judge the controversies to have been favorable (or unfavorable) to the improvement of education?

BOOKS AND PAPERS

A literature of school reminiscences exists in several, perhaps in all civilized, languages. Such memories are frequently worked into novels such as *The Hoosier Schoolmaster,* which is an eminent example of a large class. In his *American Journal of Education,* Barnard prints many reminiscences, and Professor Thomas Woody transmits one such account in the *History of Education Journal* (Winter, 1954). For documents, such as teachers' contracts, see Cubberley's *Readings in Public Education;* Knight and Hall's *Readings in American Educational History* (New York, 1951). The National Education Association is providing reprints of Mann's *Reports* at a modest price.

Adams, Francis, *Free School System of the United States,* London, 1875.

Billington, R. A., *The Protestant Crusade, 1800–1860,* New York, 1938.

Bishop, E. A., *Development of a State School System: New Hampshire,* New York, Teachers College, Columbia University, 1930.

Bourne, W. O., *History of the Public School Society of the City of New York,* New York, 1870.

Brubacher, John S., *Judicial Power of the New York Commissioner of Education,* New York, Teachers College, Columbia University, 1927.

Carter, J. G., *Letters on the Free Schools of New England,* Boston, 1824; *Essays on Popular Education,* Boston, 1826.

Compayré, Gabriel, *Horace Mann and the Public School in the United States,* New York, 1907. The translation from the French is by Mary D. Frost, and the book is evidence of the esteem in which Mann was held abroad.

Culver, R. B., *Horace Mann and Religion in the Massachusetts Public Schools,* Yale University Press, 1925.

Hamilton, O. T., *The Courts and the Curriculum,* New York, Teachers College, Columbia University, 1927.

Hamilton, Robert R., and Paul Mort, *The Law and Education with Cases,* Chicago, 1941.

Hinsdale, B. A., *Horace Mann and the Common School Revival,* New York, 1898.

Jackson, Sidney, *America's Struggle for Free Schools,* Washington, 1941.

Kennedy, M. F., *Schoolmaster of Yesterday,* New York, 1940. Written in collaboration with Alvin F. Harlow.

McCadden, Joseph J., *Education in Pennsylvania, 1801–1835,* University of Pennsylvania Press, 1937, with bibliography.

McVey, F. L., *The Gates Open Slowly, A History of Education in Kentucky,* University of Kentucky Press, 1949.

Mann, Mrs. Mary, Editor, *Life and Works of Horace Mann,* in five volumes, Boston, 1865–1868. There are later editions of the whole or part of this work. The *Life* was written by Mrs. Mann.

Norton, A. O., *The First State Normal School, The Journals of Cyrus Peirce and Mary Swift,* Harvard University Press, 1926.

Reeder, W. G., *Chief State School Official,* Washington, U. S. Government Printing Office, Bureau of Education Bulletin, 1924, No. 5.

Reigart, J. F., *Lancasterian System in New York City,* New York, Teachers College, Columbia University, 1916.

Spaulding, F. E., *One School Administrator's Philosophy,* New York, 1952, containing an account of rural education in New Hampshire about 1875.

Stewart, W., and W. M. French, "The Influence of Horace Mann on Sarmiento," *Hispanic-American Historical Review,* February, 1940.

Swett, John, *Public Education in California,* New York, 1911.

Williams, E. I. F., *Horace Mann, Educational Statesman,* New York, 1937.

Chapter VI

FROM SCHOOLKEEPING
TO TEACHING

THE adoption of the principle of free education for all in a public school common to all led to the adoption of new principles of teaching. These principles were compounded of parts of political equality, democracy, and practicality, with the idealism, scientific method, and child psychology which stemmed from Comenius, Francis Bacon, John Locke, and Rousseau. To assign particular items to individual authors would be difficult.

The great mediator through whom the foreign ideas were transmitted was Pestalozzi who has been called the founder of the modern elementary school. It is modern because it offers a liberal education instead of teaching merely the literary skills to which the old school mainly restricted itself. But Pestalozzi worked in Switzerland, wrote in German, which few Americans could read, and his career closed in 1827. These factors, added to the wide difference between the American and European societies, made an exact translation of his program impossible. But an American version of his principles together with native ideas changed schoolkeeping to teaching.

The ideas of Pestalozzi had their period of greatest influence in the educational awakening. But it was his ideas also which at a later date formed the closest alliance with the kindergarten and child study ideas to form what was called the "new education," and served, still later, as the opening phase of Progressive education. Teachers and textbook writers frequently indicated their debt to Pestalozzi, but not all of them. This was perhaps in the nature of things for, as Horace Mann said, many shared Pestalozzi's views and applied his principles who had never heard his name. Many also must have independently developed views and practices similar to his. It is by no means safe to equate similarity to a source with derivation from it.

1. AN EARLY INTERPRETER

Joseph Neef, who had been one of Pestalozzi's assistants at Burgdorf in Switzerland, was brought to Pennsylvania by William Maclure, a philanthropic Scotch-American who was also a leading geologist. The purpose was to introduce Pestalozzi's methods; and in a few years Neef published his *Sketch of a Plan and Method of Education* (1808) and opened a school near Philadelphia. The school had to meet the competition of the Lancasterian system at the time of its rising popularity; but Neef obtained pupils, some from great distances. One of his pupils was David Farragut, later an admiral but then a young midshipman. The admiral gave a good report of his early schooling, of the useful knowledge gained, the oral instruction, the collections of minerals and plants gathered on long excursions with their hatless teacher, the swimming, climbing, and military drill. This was evidently no Gradgrind's school. Neef also taught at New Harmony, Indiana, in Robert Owen's community and at other places, but he failed to make any deep impression.

The book by Neef is a first-hand account of the Pestalozzian program and the first such account given to Americans. He proposed to have his pupils learn by inquiry and investigation. They would learn old things in a new way. Arithmetic was taught in very short steps, using objects and by having the pupils work out the number combinations. Drawing was to come before writing, and a great deal of oral work before reading. Books were not to be used until after the pupil had made much progress through conversation. In geography the pupils were to measure gardens and fields and draw plans to scale. The book shows Pestalozzi's work in his earlier rather than his Yverdon period.

2. VOICES OF THE PROFESSION

Early educational journals gave educators a chance to discuss the principles of teaching. One such paper, *The Academician* (New York, 1818–1820), published interpretations of the views of Locke, George Jardine, Scottish professor and author of *Outlines of Philosophical Education* (1818), Richard Edgeworth and his daughter, Maria Edgeworth, the authors of *Practical Education* (1798), and Pestalozzi. An anonymous contributor who had collected books on Pestalozzi by French and German authors was convinced that these views, already well known in Europe, should also be published in the United States. He described Pestalozzi's object lessons with their use of observation, description, and drawing; and he devoted space to the Swiss educator's *Mothers' Book*. In the second installment of the series, he wrote as though he were reporting a personal observation of the routine of the Yverdon school, and indeed as though he had taken part in a first lesson of the day. This lesson was a walk before breakfast to study nature and to collect objects for further study. The author identified himself only as "a native of Clinton County." This county occupies the northeastern corner of New York state.

At this time (1818) John Griscom, chemist and teacher, was touring Europe and he visited Pestalozzi; but being unable to speak German he had to depend upon the account given him by J. P. Greaves, an Englishman then living at Yverdon. Griscom attended classes in arithmetic, languages, and drawing, and observed an exercise in which Pestalozzi, as Griscom understood, taught religion. He made some observations on the teacher's earnestness and the pupil's close attention. Griscom reported that there was nothing mechanical in Pestalozzi's school, as there was in Lancaster's, and he professed to believe that the Swiss teacher's life and labors were forming "a most important epoch in the history of education." But this favorable view did not prevent him from shortly establishing a private Lancasterian high school in New York City. Not in this case alone were the practical realities of America more powerful than an ideal. In Emerson's words "Cripple Practice" could not overtake "Winged Theory."

A second teacher's magazine, the *American Journal of Education* (Boston, 1826–1830) was founded by William Russell (1798–1873). Russell was educated at Glasgow, Scotland, under George Jardine. In the first number of the *Journal,* Russell recommended the teaching of history to small children by means of stories told by the teacher, and urged that the stories should deal with local happenings so that the children could be taken to visit the places where they had occurred. He argued for home geography also. He urged the use of supplementary reading material so that the children would not be compelled "to plod their weary way again and again over the same lessons." These ideas, if they were not his own, may have come from the Hill family, which employed such methods at the Hazelwood School near Birmingham, England; or they may have been diffused in the educational atmosphere from the writings of Locke, Rousseau, and the Edgeworths.

The early numbers of Russell's *American Journal* treated American topics and reported American news. In its pages appear the men and measures that were changing education. The abortive effort of 1825 to establish a state school of agriculture in Massachusetts, as recommended by Governor Levi Lincoln, is reported. There were articles on physical education, mutual instruction, the education of girls, and the infant school, the newest thing on the educational horizon. Russell published the "Faculty Report" of 1826 directed to the trustees of Amherst College in which there was proposed "a department of the science of education" for that institution; and the Massachusetts law of March 10, 1827, which provided a legal basis for the public high school in that state. There is a description of the Gardiner Lyceum in Maine, with a particular account of the plan of student self-government followed in that school.

The *Journal* did not print much on Pestalozzi, and this may have been due to lack of information about him. In the July number of 1827 there was a favorable review of *The Pestalozzian Primer* (Harrisburg, 1827). The compiler of this schoolbook was John M. Keagy, a Swiss-American physician who was conducting a Pestalozzian school in Harrisburg. In the November number there is an obituary paragraph on Pestalozzi, then recently deceased. More than a year later Russell compiled from *The Academician* of the preceding decade an article on Pestalozzi's principles of instruction. This came out in 1829 in the March–April number of the *Journal*, which had recently been changed from a monthly to a bimonthly magazine. This is evidence that it was not prospering, and after two more years its place was taken by the *American Annals of Education* with William C. Woodbridge as editor.

In a candid footnote to the article taken from *The Academician*, it is explained that Russell had no knowledge of the earlier paper when he started the *Journal*. Russell declared that he had thought of himself as an absolute pioneer in American educational journalism. Was this error due to the obscurity of *The Academician*, to the lack of libraries and infrequent communication between educators, or to the provincialism of Russell and his associates? We do not know. The fact may be evidence of nothing more than a faulty memory. Twenty years later Russell in an address again erroneously referred to his *Journal* as "the first enterprise of the kind in the English language."

How much of Russell's mature doctrine was due to Pestalozzi also remains in doubt. The content of his *Intellectual Education*, prepared about 1850, has many points of agreement with the Pestalozzian system of ideas. He emphasizes the training of the perceptive faculties. He would encourage the child's curiosity and the kindred element of wonder. He extolled the advantages of novelty and variety in teaching and proposed the study of insects to develop habits of attentive observation. He tried to find an ABC of observation, almost certainly a Pestalozzian idea; and chose color, form, number, weight, and sound for his alphabet. He urged the use of teaching aids. He would not have teachers ask questions prepared in the textbook but proposed instead the use of questions asked by the children themselves. The purpose of all this was the development of the mental powers to compare, classify, and generalize.

EDUCATIONAL JOURNALS OF THE AWAKENING

1. *Academician*	New York	1818–1820
2. *American Journal of Education*	Boston	1826–1830
3. *Teachers' Guide and Parents' Assistant*	Portland, Me.	1826–1828
4. *American Quarterly Register and Journal of the American Education Society*	Andover	1829–1843
5. *American Annals of Education*	Boston	1830–1839
6. *Common School Assistant*	Albany	1836–1840
7. *Common School Advocate*	Cincinnati	1837–1841
8. *Western Academician and Journal of Education and Science*	Cincinnati	1838–1839
9. *Journal of Education*	Detroit, etc.	1838–1840
10. *Connecticut Common School Journal*	Hartford	1838–1842
11. *Common School Journal*	Boston	1839–1852
12. *District School Journal*	Albany	1840–1852
13. *Common School Journal of the State of Pennsylvania*	Philadelphia	1844
14. *Journal of the Rhode Island Institute of Instruction*		1845–1849
15. *Ohio School Journal*	Kirtland and Columbus	1846–1850

Note.—Although none of the above journals was permanent—and only three survived for more than a decade—these were among the most important magazines of the teaching profession during the first quarter century of the awakening.

Pestalozzianism "by association" is indicated by Russell's selection of the faculty of the private normal school which he founded at Lancaster, Massachusetts, in 1853. The group included Lowell Mason, Hermann Krüsi, Jr., Dana P. Colburn, Louis Agassiz, and Arnold Guyot. Of these the first three were avowed disciples of the Swiss master. Agassiz and Guyot paid no attention to pedagogy, but in their teaching methods they fitted in with the others.

The conclusion is that before 1830 little was known of Pestalozzi in New England and not a great deal in the rest of the country. The Fellenberg manual labor system, which had a Pestalozzian origin, was introduced in 1816 and began to spread about 1830. Some of this was due to William

C. Woodbridge, who had traveled in Europe and who continued the work of the *American Journal* in the *American Annals of Education*. He did much more than Russell had done to publish the doctrines of both Fellenberg and Pestalozzi.

A second instrument of publicity was the official report on education in foreign countries. In later times and more academic circles, this type of reporting came to be known as comparative education. Three reports on European, chiefly German, education had a special importance. Victor Cousin made a study, for the French government of Louis Philippe, of the organization of the Prussian schools (1831). At the request of the Ohio legislature, Calvin E. Stowe in 1837 reported on elementary instruction in Europe, and this study was reprinted in the official documents of six states in addition to Ohio, namely Pennsylvania, which provided both an English and a German text, Michigan, Massachusetts, North Carolina, New York, and Virginia. And the third example was by Horace Mann, whose observations of 1843 were included in his *Seventh Report* to the Massachusetts board. It was this which touched off the controversy with the teachers of Boston; but its real importance lay in its account of the teachers, teaching, and spirit of the German schools.

Among the topics treated by Stowe and Mann were many that were new, or new to Americans, at that time. Instead of beginning with the alphabet on the children's first day of school, the German teachers prepared them for instruction in reading by conversation lessons; and when reading was begun it was taught by a combination of word and phonic methods. Mann fought hard for better methods in primary reading, and while his influence prevailed in some schools, the alphabet was still taught first in many schools at the end of the century.

The German schools had an "enriched" curriculum. Object lessons, nature study, home geography, music, and drawing, common subjects where the influence of Pestalozzi was felt, were not often found in America in 1840. Arithmetic taught by analysis instead of by rule aroused Mann's admiration, while Stowe, referring to the books by Warren Colburn or Joseph Ray, thought this method was already in common use in the United States. Stowe was right about the books but may have been mistaken about their wide use and influence.

German teachers were active. They did not sit down, they moved about. They knew their material, needing no book in the hand while teaching. They did not hear lessons, they taught children, taught them knowledge, ideas, skills, and subjects. They held the attention and were kind and considerate. Mann saw no evidence of the use of corporal punishment. It is just possible that he was not shown everything. There is no doubt that these two reports, widely read, made an impression upon the teaching and conduct of schools in favored places. But we must not forget the angry retort of the Boston masters, nor fail to notice that cities farther removed from Mann in space and mental outlook did not bother to reply. In the open country the ideas may have had little immediate effect.

Mann was critical of the autocracy of the German rulers and the submissiveness of their people and he was not, perhaps, unaware that schools can be used to produce slaves. But he waxed enthusiastic over the German schools and their teachers. He came back more than ever convinced that the normal school held the key to the improved education of the future. Massachusetts had opened a state normal school four years earlier, in July, 1839. It followed the programs developed by T. H. Gallaudet and J. G. Carter and was actually provided by equal amounts of private and public money. But it was Mann's persistence and the generous contribution of his friend, Edmund Dwight, that made the school a reality. Two others were added soon after. In 1844 New York also founded one in Albany. A total of about a dozen state normal schools were in operation by 1861.

The early normal schools reviewed the common branches with their teen-age pupils, added a few secondary school studies, taught two or three courses in methods, school management, and elementary psychology, and conducted a primary school for observation and practice teaching. The normal schools formed a third means of turning schoolkeeping into teaching and by far the most effective one in the case of those whom they reached. But they reached so few. For every teacher who had graduated from a normal school, or even attended one for part of a year, the typical state had to employ many with less preparation or none.

Other means were also used to reach more teachers. The teachers' institute, meeting once a year for only a week, and the normal institute with a term of four to six weeks were invented in the forties. High schools introduced a teachers' normal course. County and city normal schools were established. City superintendents conducted Saturday classes for professional study. Teachers' associations, presenting speakers on educational improvement, became active about 1830. That is when the American Institute of Instruction in the East and the Western Literary Institute and College of Professional Teachers of the Midwest were organized. The state teachers' associations followed. All of these brought books, magazines, educational leaders, information, and ideas to the teachers. Of great importance was the summer school, but that developed after the Civil War. Not all teachers heard the call of these voices, or, hearing, caught the vision of a new school; but what they heard and gathered was a gain. No one had even spoken to their predecessors of a better way.

3. A LIGHT-BEARER

Those who prefer to have their history presented in neat, separate periods might find three eras in the nineteenth century. These would be the academy movement, the educational awakening, and the "new education." Mann and Henry Barnard (1811–1900) both began their lifework in the awakening. Mann's career closed early at Antioch College; but Barnard, who lived to the age of almost ninety years, continued on through the new education of William Torrey Harris, William H. Payne, Francis W. Parker, and their contemporaries.

While Mann and Barnard agreed upon many questions, they were very different personalities. No great controversies are associated with Barnard's name. His opponents rarely attacked him and he attacked no one. He had the temperament of the student and it was owing to him that educators had the information to form considered opinions upon the educational questions of his time. Some, at least, of the light which he shed was his own. He was a source as well as a bearer of educational wisdom.

Both Mann and Barnard were drafted for work in education. Neither chose it, but Barnard had unconsciously made some preparation for it. At Yale he had successfully cultivated the art of public speech. He took several trips in the United States and in 1835–1836 he made the first of several extended tours of Europe. On this first European visit he became acquainted with the Pestalozzian movement and met the educational statesman, Henry Brougham, in England. He thought highly of travel as a means of education, and doubtless gained that benefit from his own journeys; but the most useful result for others came from the ideas and knowledge of education which he gathered.

He has been called an interpreter of Pestalozzi, but he was much more. He also interpreted Froebel, the kindergarten, the normal school, and other means for the professional education of teachers. He recognized the favorable effect of the high school upon the lower schools. He had as great an interest in the practical problems as in the theory of education, and he provided full knowledge on many topics in place of the scattered information which alone was available before.

When the Connecticut legislature provided for a state board to promote the common schools, Barnard was chosen its secretary. After four active years he found himself without an office because party politics had caused the repeal of the law of 1838. The same sort of attack had succeeded, as noted above, in Ohio and elsewhere, but had failed in Massachusetts. Until the political wheel in Connecticut turned full circle, Barnard was appointed to the state education office in Rhode Island and then, with the Whigs again in power, he returned to his own state as state superintendent and principal of the new state normal school. Barnard claimed that he made fifteen hundred speeches on education in the course of his life, most of them in his fifteen years as state school officer. He visited schools, advised and encouraged teachers, founded and edited state school journals in the two states in which he served, answered a heavy mail, and made out his annual reports.

In his first annual report, Barnard gave an account of his observations on European education. In 1850 the Connecticut legislature asked him to prepare two books for teachers. He prepared a work on school architecture, the first systematic treatise on the subject. It created a new branch of professional study. The second book was on the professional education of teachers and covered the whole subject as it existed at that time. A few years later he issued a third book, a work on comparative education with the title, *National Education in Europe*.

Barnard's greatest literary achievement was his *American Journal of Education*, the second educational journal to use this title. It was started in 1855 and continued for thirty-one volumes. It has been called an encyclopedia of education, but it lacks organization and is rather a thesaurus or treasury of educational materials. Its value was increased when, after Barnard's time, an index to the *Journal* was prepared.

In practical administration Barnard was not successful. Such was his fame that extraordinary numbers of city superintendencies, state university presidencies, and normal school principalships were offered him. He was for brief periods president of the University of Wisconsin and of St. John's College, and was for three years (1867–1870) the first United States commissioner of education. But he was no politician; his administrative practices were loose; and he expected everyone to be discreet, honest, and loyal, and was, therefore, if for no other reason, a bad judge of men.

The whole range of education received the attention of Barnard. He favored infant schools and was apparently the first native American to notice the kindergarten, an example of which he saw in London when he was a delegate to an international exposition. This was the kindergarten conducted by a sister of the German-American, Mrs. Carl Schurz, who opened a little private kindergarten in her home at Watertown, Wisconsin, in 1855. He was an earnest promoter of high schools and adult education.

And although he had only the briefest experience as a teacher, he turned a bright light into and over all the schools of his time.

4. TRANSCENDENTAL SCHOOLMASTER

A list of home-grown educators of the early national period will include the names of Ralph Waldo Emerson and Bronson Alcott (1799–1888) and will place these men in the same idealist and transcendentalist bracket. As educational philosophers they belonged to the school which regards individual growth as the end, and self-expression and creative activity as the great means, of education. The members of this school differ among themselves at many points, for the group includes Rousseau, Froebel, Tolstoi, and Dewey. In their educational philosophy, Emerson and Alcott were bold and enterprising. But in practice as a young teacher Emerson was timid and conventional. Alcott supported his brave words with deeds and took the unhappy consequences.

In a letter Alcott explained that whatever children themselves do becomes a part of them; and that he did not measure progress by the number of pages covered. He declared that instruction should not be drawn from books alone. It is absurd to believe statements just because they are found in print. How to escape such a silly plight? His answer, worthy of Emerson, was that children should learn to be independent and even eccentric if their reason approves. This was not copied from Emerson but anticipated him. It shows that the author did not mean to be a docile disciple. The course here recommended is a discipline for heroes and martyrs.

Alcott's preparation included the peddling of tinware among the planters' families of the South, who taught him gentility, an initiation in North Carolina into the Quaker doctrine of the inner light which blended with his native mysticism, and the reading of Milton, John Bunyan, William Penn's *No Cross, No Crown,* the *Journals* of George Fox and John Woolman, and many other books, including some about Pestalozzi but none by him. His cousin and friend, William A. Alcott, was acquainted with William C. Woodbridge, and Woodbridge, who made several tours of Europe, was able to tell the Alcotts about education in foreign lands. This was not the usual preparation of country school teachers.

At the age of twenty-four Bronson Alcott began, and for five years continued, to teach in district schools near his home in Connecticut. From his home he went to Boston to teach in an infant school, then to Germantown, Pennsylvania; and finally he conducted the Temple School in Boston (1834–1836) until its sudden debacle permanently ended his career as a teacher of children.

His teaching became progressively freer and more untraditional as he gained in experience and suffered from opposition. Of opposition there was no lack. In his first school he introduced light gymnastics including exercises that to the eyes of his Puritan patrons resembled dancing, and the children dramatized stories. Even these mild innovations disturbed some of the parents, but they did not interfere. There was carping because there was not enough memorizing and because the children were encouraged to express their own ideas on questions they did not understand.

Alcott, like the noted English headmaster, Edward Thring, of Uppingham School, thought the "almighty wall" a great teacher; and he tried to make his walls and his entire schoolroom beautiful, spending his little sum of money somewhat lavishly for works of art and fine furniture. Mystic and neo-Platonist that he was, he considered nature a symbol of the divine reality. Under the influence of Wordsworth's Ode he came to believe that inborn truth, the ideas and sentiments of the children's minds, were proper objects of introspective study by the children.

The curriculum of the Temple School has been published. In the twenty-two lessons which made up the work of a week, two dealt with arithmetic, two with geography, one was a drawing lesson, and the other seventeen were devoted to word study, conversations on soul and body and on the Gospels, and to writing in the pupils' personal journals. The absence of science is to be noted. Not the senses but the "inner sense" was what Alcott was bent upon cultivating.

The final explosion at the Temple School was occasioned by the publication of the Conversations on the Gospels, exercises that he had conducted with the children. There were other causes. Alcott was an abolitionist in an era when Boston was wildly antiabolitionist; his faithful and very capable and sensible wife was Abbie May, the sister of a noted abolitionist, S. J. May; and the Alcotts had made a friendly visit to William Lloyd Garrison when he was confined in city prison. Alcott had admitted a Negro girl as a pupil of his school. But it was the Conversations which started the withdrawal of pupils until only his own children and the young Negro were left.

The offending book, like Alcott, was religious, but its religion was not that of Boston. Its inquiring, Socratic method, based upon the view that all truth is implicit within the soul whence it is to be drawn out by questioning, offended many, including some teachers. W. E. Channing, a liberal, and generally friendly to Alcott, doubted that the mind of a child should be so much turned inward. The book dealt in a very delicate way with sex in an age which allowed no one, not even a physician, to speak publicly of such matters. Alcott had gone too far along these lines—and on borrowed money. The sheriff sold the statuary, the furniture, and the library, all the property that Alcott had in the school; and he could not secure a teaching position elsewhere. The people preferred less transcendental teachers for their children.

5. TEACHING READING

New ways of teaching reading came to be used in the educational awakening. Before 1800 the spelling book had taken the place of the primer as the pupil's first book, and Noah Webster's *Spelling-Book* had been started on its ominous course through the schools. Webster was born in 1758 and he has told us that when he was young the books used in school were "chiefly or wholly, Dilworth's Spelling Books, the Psalter, Testament, and Bible." Others have reported that in the dame school the children were called up one by one; and the teacher with a penknife pointed to the letters of the alphabet, one at a time, and asked, "What's that?" Learning the alphabet might take three to six months and then spelling was begun. Reading came later. Although better ways were known, this incredibly dull and wasteful method was followed in American schools long after 1800. A French professor-politician, Joseph Jacotot (1770–1840), had devised a "universal method" by word recognition, and he was not by any means the first nor was he wholly unknown in the United States.

Samuel Worcester may have been familiar with Jacotot's method when he published his *Primer* in 1828. Bache in his *Report* said the system of Jacotot was well known. Worcester explained in his book that a child may learn to read words by seeing them and hearing them pronounced and explained, without knowing the letters. This idea did not meet with the universal favor which it deserved to obtain. Ten years later, Horace Mann in his *Second Report* attacked the old method with vigor, argument, and examples, and he returned to the subject upon his return from Germany. He based his claim for the word method not upon common sense alone but also upon the good results obtained in Boston where it was in use. In 1842 George B. Emerson proposed for discussion at teachers' meetings this question: "Have you tried the experiment of teaching" children to read before they know the letters and with what result? On a later page of *The School and the Schoolmaster* he described the method in a lesson based upon Worcester's *Primer*. Other teachers and textbook writers continued the campaign, and the new method slowly gained ground over the old custom and against the wishes of many parents. In the last century other methods have been devised; the experiments and the books and articles on the teaching of reading have multiplied and are still increasing.

The content of the reading books was also changing in the educational awakening. Noah Webster's three-book series consisted of a speller, reader, and grammar. Webster's aims were moralistic, patriotic, and linguistic. He tried to unify America by inculcating common sentiments and a uniform language. Others also purposed to foster Americanism, and this sentiment was sometimes fed upon anti-British prejudice. William Russell protested against the use of pictures or words that would tend to arouse animosities against foreign nations. This is a universal problem not confined to America or to schools; but schools have been flagrantly used by many governments to inculcate not merely a necessary patriotism but chauvinism and national hatreds. The United Nations and UNESCO, in trying to control these trends, have to meet the opposition of superpatriots and demagogic politicians.

Closely related to the moral and political purposes of the reading lessons was the emphasis upon oral reading and public speaking. School reading books often had an introductory section giving advice upon accent, phrasing, stress, pauses, stops, and gestures. Even in country schools, Friday was speaking-day. The great fault of this elocution, as it was called, was its affectation of elegance. This is the fault of those who, having little to say, yet feel impelled to speak, perhaps by the hope of applause. Real oratory or serious public speaking is a different matter, and it is surprising to find an artificial elocution in the schools in the great period of American oratory. Careful exposition and serious argument would have been more appropriate.

Republics have been noted for their oratory. We may think of Greece, Rome, France, England, and the United States. The orator, said Quintilian, is a good man speaking; and Emerson said the man behind the speech gives it weight. Perhaps these words imply what should not be forgotten, that the orator speaks on matters of general interest and importance. Politics is the most frequent subject. The deep and powerful stream of American political oratory had its source in the fateful issues of revolution and independence, and was fed by the debates on the Constitution, the tariff, slavery, secession, and reunion. It began with James Otis and John Adams, flowed from the lips of Webster and Clay, and ended for the time with Abraham Lincoln. The period after the Civil War had few great speakers in Congress and none in the Presidency.

The educational awakening was a period of warm political debate, torchlight and log-cabin processions, and great and small orators. In common school and college, bright young people were seeking to become public speakers, and often valued what they gained in their literary societies more highly than the work of the classroom. The lyceum movement was in its more flourishing era. The leaders in the movement for public education were notable public speakers in many cases, and as an orator among the educators Horace Mann was pre-eminent. Today, owing to a change in taste, his reports read much better than his speeches. Living in the time of Daniel Webster and Edward Everett, his long sentences, unusual words, and far-fetched analogies seem not to have attracted any special notice; but before his death in 1859 people had come to prefer the plain style of Lincoln.

Meanwhile those who compiled school reading books began to choose selections that would convey useful knowledge and serve the purposes of practical life. Upon his return from Europe, Horace Mann complained that American reading books were literary when they should have been informative and utilitarian. The reading books which he had examined over there and approved dealt with the phenomena of nature or with food, utensils, the qualities and uses of materials, and with houses and their construction. In the process of learning to read, the child should also gain useful knowledge. This utilitarian aim was gradually added to the patriotic, moralistic, and other earlier tendencies; and there was even a slight trend to encourage supplementary reading and the formation of school libraries.

6. ELEMENTARY SCHOOLBOOKS

New principles of teaching can be spread by means of lectures or by books on educational theory intended for teachers. These are the means used in schools, study classes, and meetings attended by teachers. A more direct way to introduce changes in instruction is followed when the new principles are embodied in textbooks. Both methods, the instruction of teachers and new textbooks, were used to improve elementary education. New or unusual subjects such as geography, nature study, and music were introduced and old ones like arithmetic were transformed.

The older geography textbooks had been summaries of information which the pupils were asked to memorize. This was not worth doing, for it would not be retained; and, outside of schools, such information would be found as needed in a reference book. In some of the older books, rhyme was used to aid the pupil in his distasteful task. For example, one such rhyming geography was written about 1785 by Robert Davidson, a professor in Dickinson College. Sometimes a tune was added and the list of the states, their capital cities, and the rivers on which they were located were repeated in singsong. This was the *reductio ad absurdum* of geography instruction, and evidently needed to be reformed.

The reformed method consisted of the selection of more interesting material, appealing to the children's understanding, and whenever possible, showing them the objects with which they were dealing. The authors of the newer textbooks began with the phenomena of the locality and after some explorations taught pupils to draw plans and maps of the schoolroom, the schoolyard, and the surrounding region. These were steps in the right direction. Among the writers of such books was W. C. Woodbridge, who collaborated on a widely used elementary text with Emma Willard; and another was William B. Fowle. Much more might have been done in developing exercises to be carried out by the children and in connecting geography with studies of weather, the action of wind and water, and with life on the farm; but a beginning was made in developing a rational study of the earth. The Swiss geographer, Arnold Guyot, lectured to teachers and wrote textbooks; and after the Civil War a more pronounced effort was made to improve the teaching of geography.

Music was added to the elementary school course in the educational awakening. Except for literature, which was administered in small snippets in the reading books, music was the first of the fine arts to be taught in the lower schools. Drawing, modeling, dramatics were not added until the latter half of the century. It was not until after his return from Germany, where every teacher was able to read music and to play an instrument, that Mann took occasion to recommend the teaching of music; and he felt that he should apologize for his previous neglect. Boston had added music to its curriculum in 1838 and had engaged a music supervisor. Several cities in New York had introduced the art even earlier, about 1830. Lowell Mason was the music supervisor in Boston and he developed a superior program. He was also engaged by the state of Massachusetts as a lecturer on music education at the annual series of teachers' institutes. His exercise books and musical collections were widely used. His principles of music teaching followed those of Pestalozzi. But Mason did not hesitate to compose and improvise in the middle of a lesson, and he varied the application of his principles so frequently that he can hardly be said to have followed any system strictly. Others may assign him to his rank as a musician, but there is excellent evidence that he was a master teacher.

The principles of Pestalozzi were also applied in the teaching of arithmetic and, in the first instance, by Warren Colburn, whose *First*

Lessons in Arithmetic on the Plan of Pestalozzi, completed in 1821, opened
a new era in the teaching of the subject in the United States. Before publishing the little book, Colburn took the precaution to have it tried out
in the classes of the newly opened high school of Boston, the English Classical School. The principal, George B. Emerson, used it while it was still
in manuscript and gave a highly favorable account of it. He called it "our
only perfect school-book." In a later edition Colburn explained that he had
not seen any work of Pestalozzi "but only a brief outline by another." This
other one may have been Joseph Neef, whose *Sketch of a Plan* contains
twenty pages on the teaching of arithmetic with a plate showing Pestalozzi's Table of Units. Colburn's claim that his problems were his own
must be admitted. He was indebted to Pestalozzi for some indispensable
ideas.

The ideas were such as the following. Beginning with the counting
of objects, the child must be led to understand each step. There must be
no learning by rote, no rules, and no appeal to authority but only to reason,
that is, the child's reason, not the teacher's. Arithmetic is the art of com-
prehending numbers, not the manipulation of figures. In the beginning,
therefore, the numbers must be both small and concrete. The early work
must be done without writing, that is, "in the head." This is the origin
of mental arithmetic, which lasted for almost a century as a distinct branch
of study in the schools. Another principle is that school arithmetic should
be applied in many fields, such as travel, sport, kitchen recipes, population,
sizes of hats or shoes, and not, as formerly, to commercial topics only. Colburn's book had an extraordinary success. In the first quarter century after
publication more than forty editions came from the presses. It was translated into foreign languages and imitated at home.

The new and more inductive geography books, music exercise books,
and mental arithmetics made great changes in the schools where they
were used. The books, in fact, changed not the teaching only but the subjects themselves. Other subjects or activities were beginning to come in—a
little history, physiology, health and physical education—but progress was
slow and unevenly distributed.

7. USEFUL KNOWLEDGE MADE INTERESTING

School terms gradually became a little longer, attendance a little more
regular, and printing much cheaper and faster. As more children learned
to read with ease and pleasure and as families acquired the means to
indulge the taste for reading, schools, teachers, and writers set about the

task of satisfying the demand. This process called into play one of the leading functions of teachers in all times and places, the business of simplifying knowledge and ideas so that more people might be able to acquire and understand them.

The lyceums which began in 1826 were one agency exercising this function. They sprang up, as we have seen, in all parts of the northern and western states where there were enough people with easy access to the meeting places. The task of the lyceum lecturer was that of spreading knowledge and ideas by putting them into the common speech without, as Matthew Arnold advised, debasing either.

There was a great and rising interest in the sciences both as pure knowledge and ideas and as useful applications to practical life. There was a marked interest in the relations between science and religion. Much of this centered upon a comparison of the teachings of geology and Genesis. The evolution controversy was still in the future. There was keen interest in the application of science to agriculture partly because the old lands of the East now had to compete with the black soil of Illinois and Wisconsin. Agricultural geology, chemistry, and botany and economic entomology were developing and were raising the belief that the farmer would gain great help from them. This hope was not to be realized at once but it affected schools and lyceums hardly less because of that.

The naturalistic movement in the schools of Europe was in full swing. It had begun with Basedow and Rousseau and was continued with variations by Pestalozzi and Froebel. The school movement there, as in the United States, was part cause, part effect, of the rise of a children's literature. One model for children's books had been furnished by DeFoe, and everywhere men had written and children had read the extended Robinson literature, mostly imitations that lacked the power of the original; but the tastes—of writers, adults, not children—had now changed and in the United States children's books had become practical, informative, and moralistic.

There is no good reason, some educators of the period said, why elements of useful knowledge should not be acquired in every district school in addition to the present limited course. They argued that good supplementary reading books would accomplish this end and would be interesting besides. This was not wholly new. Even the *New England Primer* began with a natural history alphabet, as in "The Whale's the Monarch of the Main as is the Lion of the Plain." But the rest of the book does not fulfil this early promise.

A change took place about 1800. In 1794, for example, Isaiah Thomas published *The Natural History of Beasts, Which are to be Met With in the*

Four Quarters of the Globe. But most of the beasts, such as the lion and tiger, lived in quarters of the globe with which American children were not familiar. Perhaps the purpose was to arouse the imagination of the children or to stimulate their interest by presenting things new and strange. Other books with comparable titles presented more accessible animals, birds, plants and trees.

Some authors tried to make factual material more appealing by throwing it into a conversational form. *Conversations on Common Things or Guide to Knowledge* was prepared by "a teacher" who furnished questions for other teachers to ask. This book soon reached a second edition, and some books of this sort went through many editions. One of the most popular authors was Mrs. Jane Haldimand Marcet (1769–1858). Beginning early in the new century when she was thirty-two years old, she wrote many books for children and several of them in conversational form. One was her *Conversations on Political Economy,* which won the praise of Jean Baptiste Say and T. B. Macaulay. While her book on economics was praised, her *Conversations on Chemistry* was popular. It appeared in 1806 and in half a century sold 160,000 copies in the United States alone. Also popular was the companion volume, *Conversations in Natural Philosophy* (1819).

Mrs. Marcet's *Natural Philosophy* was revised in 1826 by Thomas P. Jones, a competent scientist who in this same year (1826) founded and long edited the *Journal of the Franklin Institute* of Philadelphia. A reviewer of this edition considered the book suitable for supplementary reading in common schools. He deplored the shortcomings of a system of education which allowed children to go out knowing nothing of the simplest operations of nature. Another reviewer preferred his science full strength, undiluted with conversation. "Leave out," he commanded, "all the twaddle by Caroline and Emily, present the science in plain didactic form, and you will have one of the best textbooks in the language."

There were also early how-to-do books. One was written by Samuel Read Hall, who is known only for his *Lectures on School-Keeping* (1829). Hall may have been the first American to write a how-to-do book for children. His book was called *The Child's Friend; or Things which Every Boy Can Do* (Boston, 1833). Some of the suggestions were exercises in elementary science and were intended to cultivate the child's ingenuity.

Stories which dealt with nature, travel, crafts, and juvenile science were written in great numbers. Two of the writers whose books are still remembered, although no longer read, were Samuel Griswold Goodrich (1793–1879), better known as Peter Parley, and Jacob Abbott (1803–1879). Both were prolific and often wrote on subjects that had to do with nature and with morals and manners.

The Tales of Peter Parley about America (1827) was followed by more than a hundred volumes in which the same fictitious character, a kindly and omniscient old gentleman, answers the curious questions of excessively polite children with an unnatural appetite for knowledge. Literally millions of copies of Peter Parley books were sold. Many were not written by Goodrich but by collaborators including, of all people, Nathaniel Hawthorne. Goodrich was really like the Peter Parley of his books, a kind of stream of consciousness writer, as his *Reminiscences of a Lifetime* (1856), in two garrulous volumes, shows. This book is also a source on the schools of about 1800.

Jacob Abbott was a minister and a teacher. He founded the Mount Vernon School for Girls in Boston and wrote an early book on teaching. But he was best-known as a writer for children. His series of Rollo books ran to twenty-eight volumes; and he also wrote a series on "science for the young," a Lucy series, and others. His characters are very good, not the mischievous rogues of daily experience. Abbott also wrote a large number of biographies for the young and these were still read fifty years later. His subjects were captains and kings, like Alexander and Julius Caesar. This may imply a "great man" view of history, but although he attempted to teach history, geography, and elementary sciences, he was neither a historian nor a scientist. That such didactic, moral, and superficial books as those of Goodrich and Abbott were read by young adolescents of several generations, raises questions about the nature of American education.

8. PESTALOZZIAN PRINCIPLES CRITICIZED

Although some forms of Pestalozzian education gained wide approval in America, there were those who thought they had detected flaws in it. This critical response became more marked in the latter part of the century when the English version of Pestalozzi's system was imported; but it must be recalled that few Americans had direct knowledge of the system at its source. Few Americans saw Pestalozzi or his schools. They came into the movement too late. What Woodbridge, Stowe, Mann, and the rest studied was a series of imitations. This American Pestalozzianism was in great degree an imitation twice removed. Therefore, what was criticized was something attributed to Pestalozzi and was not always true to his principles. Here we shall give some early criticism only, leaving the discussion of the imported English Pestalozzianism to a later chapter.

A critical article appeared in the *American Annals of Education* for January, 1837. It seems to bear the stamp of William A. Alcott's writing, but it is unsigned. The writer claims that in his zeal for the development of the faculties, Pestalozzi tended to undervalue positive knowledge. His pupils were encouraged to investigate and reflect and they sometimes had a surfeit of practice, but they did not obtain a sufficient body of correct information. If for "development of the faculties" we substitute "power of thinking and problem-solving," the criticism of Pestalozzi in 1837 will be similar to what is sometimes said of Progressive education now. One hears it said that Progressives do not teach knowledge except as it helps in thinking and in solving problems. While Pestalozzi sought to develop many faculties—observation, imagination, reasoning, and others—the Progressives reduce all of them to one, the thinking which solves problems. This parallel between early critics of Pestalozzi and late critics of Progressive education suggests that the two movements may be of the same species.

The numerous studies which Pestalozzi really favored, it was said, would not be needed to achieve the objects of his disciplinary theory. Pestalozzi had greatly enriched the curriculum, adding many skills, arts like music, and naturalistic studies like home geography. If one assumes wide and easy transfer of training, as Pestalozzi did, a much simpler curriculum would have been sufficient. There seems to be a conflict in his own principles; or perhaps we should tolerantly say that this practice was better than his principles.

He did not indiscriminately favor all subjects and this provided a foothold for a further criticism. He discounted history and any subjects which depend upon the testimony of witnesses and participants. He is said to have called history "a tissue of lies." One may ask how this can be known if historical truth is unattainable, for it is only by means of true history that false history can be detected. Napoleon, whom Pestalozzi held in abhorrence, declared history to be "a fable agreed upon"; but one suspects that this opinion reflected his fear that it would tell the truth about him. No such suspicion can apply to Pestalozzi, who was the soul of truthfulness; and this is a truth attested by history.

The critics of Pestalozzi's attitude toward history claim that moral education must be based upon the study of man and of moral conduct. The same remark would apply to other social studies, for all these, including psychology and education, are to a great degree historical studies. Whether the principles of Pestalozzi have been generally useful and successful is itself a question that only history can settle.

In the 1830's Pestalozzian influence was effective when it supported existing educational trends, but otherwise it was not, or at least not always. For example, Pestalozzi worked along philanthropic lines and his schools were private schools. In America the demand for universal education in public schools was becoming strong and continued to grow. The introduction of new studies such as geography had preceded Pestalozzi's influence. His example affected textbooks and methods in geography in this early period but more especially after the Civil War. In spite of Pestalozzi's attitude, American history was introduced and gradually became a regular study. In the improvement of elementary reading instruction his methodic work was wholly mistaken and his practice was not helpful. Thus the American response to the Pestalozzian principles was itself a criticism of them.

9. TEACHING AIDS

Great as the Swiss master was, his success was limited by the lack of equipment. In the absence of books, laboratory supplies, well-equipped shops, he somehow got along without them. And this was the state of all schools until the nineteenth century and in fact until late in that century. How bare the American schools were can be seen in the pictures and descriptions that have come down to us.

The general tradition and practice of the schools was against self-activity and investigation by the pupils. In this respect at least, Pestalozzi was on the side of the future. He promoted investigation and he improvised physical means. In America, as long as the spelling book dominated instruction, there was no need for teaching aids, but this situation changed when new studies and methods came in. The Lancasterian movement had done something to supply simple physical materials, such as sand tables, wall-charts, and even blackboards.

About 1817 the blackboard was introduced at West Point, Dartmouth, and other colleges. Twenty years later it was still unusual in the primary schools of Massachusetts, and Horace Mann exerted himself with considerable success to urge its introduction. George B. Emerson in 1842 spoke of the blackboard as if it were standard equipment, but this was not true in the rural schools. A curious article on "Black Tablets" by Gallaudet appeared in the *American Journal of Education* in 1830. He explained that large slate slabs were hard to obtain and proposed a mixture of lime, plaster of Paris, and lampblack to be spread on the wall of the schoolroom. He recommended the use of such a writing surface in teaching handwriting, arithmetic, and map-drawing. Such suggestions for improvising aids are rare in the school publications of that time.

Commercial makers of school equipment were also few. It was fifty years later, in 1884, that the National Education Association, meeting at

Madison, Wisconsin, in its resolutions took especial note of the "excellent displays of school products and appliances." Those who examine the large present-day exhibits of the thousands of "school products and appliances," extending from pencil sharpeners to school buses, have some difficulty in "thinking away" this wealth of aids and "thinking back" to the bare walls and desks of early times.

One of the early suppliers of elementary school equipment was Josiah Holbrook (1788–1854), promoter of the lyceum movement. He offered for sale "an apparatus," that is, a collection composed of geometrical forms, a numeral frame, a globe, two maps, an orrery, instruments to illustrate the seasons, and simple equipment for the teaching of physics and chemistry. A Boston instrument-maker offered air pumps, model steam engines, and machines to demonstrate the simple mechanical powers. He offered to manufacture orreries on commission. Probably few schools had the means to purchase such equipment in the 1830's and '40's, but in time demand and supply increased together. The normal schools were helpful in this improvement by showing young teachers how to use teaching aids. Most of the materials remained quite simple until after laboratories, shops, and kitchens were installed and electric current was supplied. The growth of invention and industry and the larger funds which became available to school boards were corresponding factors in the equipment of the modern school. In the 1830's a school was comparatively fortunate if it had a blackboard.

10. Books for Teachers

The multiplication of educational writings was an element in the general movement known as the educational awakening; and it was especially connected with the rise of teachers' classes and normal schools. There were the reports on education in Europe by Calvin E. Stowe, Alexander Dallas Bache, and Horace Mann, which gave extended consideration to curricula and methods. The Bache report was not the result of a hurried trip. While Stowe and Mann each spent a few weeks or months on the ground, Bache prosecuted his inquiries for two years. The ideas of the time were spread by numerous published addresses also. Such were those issued by the American Institute of Instruction, which usually met in Boston, and by the Western Literary Institute and College of Professional Teachers of Cincinnati. The latter society expired in 1845 but published its annual proceedings until that time. The American Institute of Instruction proved a more permanent body and continued its meetings and publications until 1908. Some thirty educational journals were established by

1840, but only nine continued publication for two years or longer. Reports, proceedings, and addresses of societies, journals, and educational textbooks were the chief printed means for disseminating ideas and information in the awakening.

The early books for teachers attempted to treat the whole field of education, including school management, curriculum, and methods, within the compass of one small volume. Sometimes they also considered the equipment of schools, the preparation of teachers, and the problems of a general educational philosophy.

A list of these early books will include at least the following:

Schulordnung, by Christopher Dock	1770
Sketch of a Plan . . . of Education, by Joseph Neef	1808
Method of Instructing . . . in the Arts of Writing and Reading, by Joseph Neef	1813
Lectures on School-Keeping, by Samuel R. Hall	1829
The Teacher, by Jacob Abbott	1833
The School and the Schoolmaster, by Alonzo Potter and George B. Emerson	1842
Theory and Practice of Teaching, by David P. Page	1847

The first of these books to have any great influence was Hall's *Lectures on School-Keeping*. It deals with discipline, method, and curriculum and includes the natural sciences among common school studies. The teacher should explain the how and why of common natural phenomena. In this field the recommended methods were taken from Bacon and Pestalozzi. The teacher was advised not to take "yes" for an answer when pupils say they understand. It is the teacher's duty to find out for himself whether they do.

The *American Journal of Education,* established after Hall began teaching in the academy at Concord, Vermont, where he wrote his book, is the main source cited by him. As this magazine furnished some of the materials so it may also have been the stimulus which called out the book. The *Academician* is not mentioned. Hall's volume attained a considerable circulation. In the year of publication it was used as a textbook in a teacher's class at Canandaigua Academy, New York, and perhaps at other places. By special arrangement, 10,000 copies of the third edition were printed in 1832 and bound in paper to be distributed to the schools of the State of New York. This distribution gave one of the participants, James Wadsworth, the idea of district school libraries in New York. These, as we shall see, became a reality. The fourth edition of Hall's book came out in 1833 and the fifth about twenty years later. A centennial volume containing a reprint of the first edition is included in the bibliography of the present chapter.

The boys and girls in their late teens who were enrolled in normal schools and normal classes in academies and high schools needed simple textbooks. Hall's was such a book and in 1833 another appeared. This was Abbott's *The Teacher,* "a book full of ingenious devices." It is a book on school management suggesting ways of meeting or forestalling many of the petty but distracting problems that beginning teachers have to solve. By anticipating the pupils' difficulties and making careful assignments, questions about lessons may be anticipated and answered before they are asked. Teaching pupils how to study is one of the teacher's duties. Pupils may help in distributing and collecting papers and may be encouraged to carry on a limited form of self-government, with a court to handle minor offenses. There is an account of the origin and conduct of the system of self-government used in the Gardiner Lyceum, but for common schools Abbott preferred a less elaborate constitution.

Whether the self-government system at the Gardiner Lyceum had an independent origin there, as Abbott seems to have believed, or was borrowed may not be known; but it was not unique. Experimental schools had long used it. Fellenberg had such a scheme operating at Hofwyl and this is a possible source of the Gardiner Lyceum plan. Froebel at Keilhau, the Hazelwood School in England under Thomas Wright Hill and his family, and Thomas Jefferson at the University of Virginia made various efforts to operate school republics. In all ages this has been a natural thought of people who value freedom. As George B. Emerson said, Abbott's *The Teacher* was "a book full of ingenious devices"; and it has excellent advice on the daily tasks of the teacher, along with a good deal of moralizing.

Other early books for teachers were *The Teacher Taught,* by Emerson Davis who was known as a textbook writer; *The Teacher's Manual,* by Thomas H. Palmer; and *Suggestions on Education,* by Catherine Esther Beecher. More important and more comprehensive than these was *The School and the Schoolmaster* (1842), by Potter and Emerson. Alonzo Potter was a teacher who became a bishop of the Episcopal Church, and George B. Emerson was the first principal of the Boston high school of 1821. Their book is in two parts evidently written without sufficient collaboration by the authors. The first part, by Potter, discusses the school as a social agency and insists that public education must be directed toward the public interest. It deals with the duties of school trustees and once again reviews the defects of the common schools and the proposed remedies.

In the second part, Emerson deals with the organization and management of schools and the best modes of instruction. In dealing with instruction he offers some general principles: that the teacher should follow "the order of Nature"; that instruction should be so thorough that the pupils can go through the lesson without hesitation; and that the teacher should help pupils with their difficulties, just enough and not too much. Although vague, as most general principles of teaching are, these call attention to the need at important points for tact and judgment. They also reveal an emphasis upon high standards.

In dealing with special methods, Emerson is much more exact. Although he considers eleven common school branches, he devotes more than half of the whole treatment to three: reading, grammar, and arithmetic. He took a decided stand upon one of the questions then very prominent at teachers' meetings, namely, the use of emulation. He was against all use of prizes, rivalry, and marks of distinction as incentives in school.

In his demand for high academic standards, Emerson makes a statement, almost a proposal, that foreshadows future practice. We may premise that in 1842 college standards were neither high nor fixed and that Emerson had been a tutor in mathematics at Harvard. He wrote that "every college examiner who lowers the standard of requirement does a wrong to all youth who are looking in that direction," that is, who desire a sound education. And he adds that "if all the colleges of the Northern and Middle States could be induced to unite," they could at once raise the standard of all preparatory schools. This idea became a fact fifty years later with the formation of the regional accrediting associations, the Carnegie units, and the College Entrance Examination Board. The question of standards is one of the crucial questions not only in secondary education but in all education; and it spawns many further questions. It is also a question for which there is no generally accepted solution. It may be a "persistent problem," since the answer would depend upon philosophy.

The School and the Schoolmaster was written at the invitation of a man already mentioned, James Wadsworth, wealthy agriculturist and philanthropist of New York. He paid the authors for their work, and paid also for the manufacture of an edition of 15,000 copies, so that one copy might be placed in every school of New York and one given to each school official. The governor of Massachusetts at the time was Martin Brimmer, who was Wadsworth's son-in-law, and he paid for the distribution of a copy to each school district of Massachusetts. When the school journal, *Common School Assistant* (Albany, New York, 1836–1840), was established, nearly 40,000 copies of the paper were distributed each month during the first year through the aid of several "philanthropic gentlemen." All these distributions were sequels to the circulation of Hall's book with which we remember Wadsworth was also concerned.

A somewhat similar sequel was the founding of district school libraries in New York. Wadsworth, who had enough political influence to be a factor in the decision to build the Erie Canal over the opposition of the Hudson River counties, worked upon Governor Marcy and others to secure the passage of a school library law. And a law was enacted in 1835 which permitted the districts to tax themselves for the purchase of books; but few did this. When the surplus revenue deposit was made in 1837, Wadsworth and others secured the allocation of a part of New York's share to the school library project. With this money and a further donation by Wadsworth, books for children were added to the books for the teacher of every district school in the state. The results were not as happy as had been expected, as we shall see in a later chapter.

An early indication of the coming awakening came in the introduction of Pestalozzian ideas through the agency of a private citizen who brought Joseph Neef to Philadelphia. Neef was considered "an odd fellow" and not the best choice as the ambassador for strange new ideas, for which the new world was hardly prepared. The publications which were to make those ideas known were themselves little known. No one can say how much influence Pestalozzi's doctrines exercised in the early United States, but it is clear that they did not spread quickly and that native practices incorporated and adapted them to suit American needs. Apparently there was no direct imitation of Pestalozzi.

Teachers found means of expressing themselves in the newspapers, as J. G. Carter had done, in the new educational magazines, in their reports upon foreign school systems, and in the meetings of the rising educational associations. The normal schools helped teachers to improve their own schools and also made them missionaries of general school improvement. School publicity was essential to the awakening.

A test case of the effect of foreign ideas might be made of the change in Alcott's views and practice. When he began teaching he knew little if anything of European schools, yet the superiority of his school over the old district school was noteworthy. Meanwhile, he learned much of Pestalozzi but became less rather than more like him. At the summit of his teaching career, no one could call him a Pestalozzian unless his appeal to the conscience of children makes him one.

New methods of teaching children to read were developed before 1830, methods whose superiority is unquestioned, but they were not quickly adopted. The content of the reading books became less political or literary and more practical. Great attention was still given to oral reading and public speaking. Schoolbooks in several subjects were changed to appeal to the senses, the active powers, and the reason of children. A considerable children's literature of common and practical knowledge developed; and conversational and story forms were used in the effort to make useful knowledge interesting.

Although new teaching aids were introduced in the period of the awakening, they were few and, except for the blackboard, of minor importance. Such aids were used first in colleges and secondary schools and became available to primary schools only in recent times. Books for teachers multiplied and were greatly improved in this period. But at the end of the period, about 1860, they were still brief and comprehensive summaries, single volumes, that contained what it was considered necessary for every teacher to know.

QUESTIONS

1. Was the growing interest in European schools an effect or a cause of the educational awakening?

2. Why do you agree (or, as the case may be, disagree) with the rather common view that Alcott was "the American Pestalozzi" or an American Pestalozzian?

3. How may the dependence of one person or a group upon another be proved? What specific cases of Pestalozzi's influence upon American education can be proved?

4. How may one account for the slight influence of Joseph Neef? In developing your answer, consider the Lancasterian schools, the War of 1812, the existing views of elementary education, and other factors.

5. Why were the normal schools less effective in improving teachers and teaching than their promoters hoped?

6. Do you agree that textbooks affect teaching more strongly as well as more directly than theories about teaching? Why, or why not, and under what circumstances?

7. What were the values of the teaching of "mental arithmetic" and how can they be preserved, or again introduced?

8. Why have none of the children's books of the period covered in this chapter retained their once great popularity?

9. Apply the analysis used in your answer to No. 8, or a similar one, to the books and journals for teachers.

10. Now, since a book attacking current methods of teaching beginning reading has been a best-seller for many weeks, discuss the paragraph on reading and reading books in the summary of this chapter.

BOOKS AND PAPERS

Professional books, journals, reports on foreign education, and private and public normal schools were among the means which aided in transforming school-keeping into teaching. The book by Joseph Neef, although somewhat erratic, was more progressive than S. R. Hall's *Lectures* which came twenty years later. Albert Picket founded a teachers journal, the *Academician*, which was followed by better ones, edited by William Russell, W. C. Woodbridge, and their successors. Reports by Cousin, Stowe, Bache, and Mann gave Americans some knowledge of European schools; but private and public normal schools were the most effective means to improve teaching. Arthur M. Schlesinger's *Learning to Behave*, which is mentioned in the bibliography of Chapter I, could be appropriately listed in the present bibliography also.

Barnard, Henry, *School Architecture*, Hartford, 1842; and many later revisions, with slightly different titles, the sixth edition 1855; *Normal Schools and other Institutions for the Professional Education of Teachers*, Hartford, 1851, reprinted, Greeley, Colorado, 1929; *National Education in Europe*, Hartford, 1854.

Blair, Anna L., *Henry Barnard*, Minneapolis, 1938.

Brubacher, John S., *Henry Barnard on Education*, New York, 1931.

Davis, S. E., *Educational Periodicals during the Nineteenth Century*, Washington, U. S. Government Printing Office, Bureau of Education Bulletin, 1919, No. 28.

Flueckiger, S. L., *Lowell Mason's Contribution to Music Education*, Columbus, Ohio, 1936, an unpublished dissertation at the Ohio State University.

Hinsdale, B. A., "Notes on the History of Foreign Influence upon Education in the United States," *Annual Report* of the U. S. Commissioner of Education, 1897–1898, Vol. 1, pp. 591–629.

Monroe, Will S., *History of the Pestalozzian Movement in the United States*, Syracuse, New York, 1907, a useful but incomplete treatment, not free from positive errors.

Neef, Joseph, *Sketch of a Plan and Method of Education*, Philadelphia, 1808; and, on Neef as a teacher, see Charles Lewis, *D. G. Farragut, Admiral in the Making*, Annapolis, 1941.

Potter, A., and George B. Emerson, *The School and the Schoolmaster*, New York, 1842. Emerson, who contributed the more important sections of this book, wrote his *Reminiscences*, Boston, 1878. See also Barnard's *Journal*, Vol. V, pp. 389 ff. and 417 ff.

Rich, Arthur L., *Lowell Mason*, University of North Carolina Press, 1946.

Russell, William, "Intellectual Education," in Barnard's *Papers for the Teacher*, First Series, New York, 1860.

Sanborn, F. B., and W. T. Harris, *A. Bronson Alcott, His Life and Philosophy*,

Boston, 1893. There are several recent books on Alcott by Dorothy Mc-Cuskey, Odell Shepard, and others. Elizabeth Peabody prepared the *Record of Mr. Alcott's School,* Boston, 1874.

Sullivan, Mark, *Our Times,* New York, 1932. Vol. 2 contains matter on school elocution.

Sunderman, L. F., "History of Public School Music, 1830–1840," *Educational Record,* April, 1941.

Thursfield, Richard E., *Henry Barnard's American Journal of Education,* Johns Hopkins Press, 1945.

Wright, A. D., and G. E. Gardner, *Hall's Lectures on School-Keeping,* a facsimile reprint, Dartmouth Press, 1929.

PART III

Chapter VII

EXPANDING ELEMENTARY
EDUCATION

A FAMOUS ancient teacher once explained that, in his country, education began with the earliest years of childhood and lasted to the very end of life. We shall appropriate the first part of this explanation by defining elementary education so that it will begin in early childhood. The years which follow after childhood may be left to other forms of education but the whole of childhood belongs to the elementary school.

The teacher of the ancient time continued, saying that as soon as the child was able to understand what was spoken, parents and nurses taught him to say what was true and to do what was right. Later there was instruction in reading and writing, learning songs and playing a stringed instrument, and games and sports. Knowledge can be taught in play according to this writer, who lived more than two thousand years ago. The music, games, and dances, he believed, would mold the manners of the children and would form their character. Altering the plays and songs of a people, he continued, will in time change their customs, laws, and the constitution of the state. In his country, as children increased in years, they trained in the gymnasium and they learned the laws in order to become courageous in war and wise in council. This teacher was Plato (B.C. 427–347) of ancient Athens.

Some of the founders of American education had a less generous conception. Education was not to begin in early childhood and it was not to continue long. Little time could be spared for schooling. That little was to be devoted to the three R's and no time was to be wasted on "fads and frills" such as music, games, and dances were thought to be.

We have seen that a change was taking place in the 1830's. Horace Mann was attempting to introduce practical subjects. Informational books for children were being written. The methods of teaching were undergoing reformation. Buildings and equipment were improving. But there is no accurate information on the extent of these changes, no census of the number of schools that were improved or the exact degree of that improvement. There was a trend and that is all we can say.

Two thousand years earlier the ancient Greeks, of whom Plato spoke, had been much concerned with the activities of children, less with the accumulation of knowledge. It was the kindergarten, music, handwork, nature study, and elementary science that introduced activities into the elementary school. A new period began after the Civil War. This is the time of the so-called "new education." A new institution, the kindergarten, which we shall consider part of elementary education, was introduced. Child study and the normal schools, also, brought new light and a new spirit to elementary education.

1. THE AMERICAN KINDERGARTEN

The term "American kindergarten" has two different connotations. Some kindergartners in the United States, with authentic knowledge of Froebel's doctrine and complete devotion to his purpose, felt free to accuse their American colleagues of ignorance and heresy. They lashed out at those who seemed to promote spurious and degenerate forms of the kindergarten, forms which did not follow the founder's precepts and exercises. They were equally hostile to those who were attempting to make money out of the movement. Both educational malpractice and greed were charged. It will not be profitable to rake over the ashes of these old fires; but it may prove useful to know that the American was sometimes regarded as a spurious version of the true German kindergarten.

The words "American kindergarten" are also used simply to designate the kindergarten as it existed and developed in America. And in this process it slowly but steadily diverged from the Froebelian model. Americans certainly knew less about Froebel than some of the German experts, felt less piety toward him and, for these reasons, were more willing to question his ideas and to take an experimental attitude toward his institution. It is intended here to use the words "American kindergarten" in this neutral sense but without denying that there may have been some bogus kindergartens and mercenary kindergartners.

The child study movement which paralleled the introduction of the kindergarten was not without effect upon the new institution. The kindergarten was one of the reasons for the developing interest in child study, but it was in turn affected by what was learned about child development and behavior. Before 1870 little was heard in America about the kindergarten, but in a decade it became a subject of frequent consideration at educational meetings. In 1884 the National Education Association recognized a separate kindergarten department.

The creator of the kindergarten, Friedrich Froebel (1782–1852), was part religious mystic but also part scientist and lifelong observer of the ways of children. His writing is frequently cloudy but the key idea is clear. It is this: "What one tries to represent or do he begins to understand." We understand what we make, and through making it we also learn to value it. It becomes for us a standard. Therein lies a danger. The small-town banker who wrote a book about his trip around the world confessed that he read his own book more than any others.

The child is characterized by his activities, so Froebel teaches. And as every child is an individual, different from all others, and is self-active, every child's activities are creative. Yet these activities must be called out by suggestion, example, and material facilities. Early in his career, Froebel was a teacher of boys and only afterwards did he teach little children. Thus the activities which he selected and devised for children of different ages range from pat-a-cake to group self-government.

The recognition that creative activity is educative led Froebel to collect a wide range of individual and social plays, games, handwork, projects of building and constructing, collecting, gardening, music and the plastic arts, story-telling, and so on up to the already-mentioned self-government in a school democracy. These activities demand, and therefore develop, skills, and from skills come the enrichment of life and, indeed, civilization. It is to be noted that Froebel was not wholly original, for he had among his books a well-thumbed copy of J. H. Heusinger's *On Using Children's Strong Urge to Activity,* which taught similar doctrine.

The histories of philosophy do not mention him, but Froebel was something of a philosopher. The key to his philosophy may again be found in a sentence. He wrote: "In all things there lives and reigns an Eternal Law, based upon an all-pervading, power-filled, living, self-conscious and hence Eternal Unity which is God." And as God is the Creator so the self-active child is a creator in a small sphere, but in its own right.

No proof of these insights is offered and the relation of creation to law is not explained. But it should be made clear that human creation is of an entirely different order from that of the Biblical conception of the creation. Man "creates" neither the matter nor the laws of nature. He discovers, obeys, and uses them as best he may. Froebel assimilates man's creation to God's. Since Froebel's day this ambiguous use of double-edged words has become all too common in educational discussion. And, in the second place, the introduction of this religious concept had important effects upon the history of the kindergarten and not least in the United States, where the reformers, philanthropists, and the churches became its early promoters.

We have called Froebel something of a philosopher. Perhaps he was rather a poet looking at the stars as compared with the astronomer with his proofs and figures in the lecture room. At least he continued to speak in symbolic terms. The round ball, without separate parts, was to symbolize, even to the little child, the unity of the world. The other "gifts" also had hidden meanings that were supposed to influence even the unconscious or subconscious mind.

The kindergarten itself was one of the symbols of this symbolical thinker. It was a symbol of society, a soul-garden that was also a school for the "education of man." The word signifies that children, whom Froebel correctly considered as organic beings, are to grow as plants grow in a garden. The teacher's work, like the gardener's, is to improve the soil and protect the plants from weeds that might choke them. That is all. The creative activity of the child will do the rest. Froebel interpreted this activity as the unfolding of something that was "preformed" in the child. With respect to preformation, symbolism, and some other ideas, Froebel was the victim of the immature philosophy and science of his day.

Symbolism is, however, a necessary means in all education. Symbols are means of communication. They communicate both ideas and feelings. Words are symbols of ideas, and ideas are symbols of things. Many things such as the flag or the fire bell are symbols. Symbols may suggest or connote as well as denote. The flag stands for the nation and it suggests, and by suggesting may call out, patriotism. Froebel's mistake was that he thought the little child could by himself discover the meaning of an arbitrary symbol. Some things, to be learned, must be taught, by teachers, books, social experience, or otherwise, but certainly taught.

The American kindergarten gradually eliminated Froebel's immature science and much of his mysticism. But this took time. Henry Barnard published an early kindergarten notice. His more extensive publications on this subject came much later. Elizabeth Peabody studied in Germany in the later sixties; but most Americans were taught by Germans in the United States and only gradually did they form their own more critical views of the Froebelian theory. The disciples of the master long tried to hold to the very words, and "gifts" and exercises that had been transmitted to them. Mrs. Matilde Kriege and her daughter established a training school for kindergartners at Boston in 1868. Others soon followed at New

York, Washington, San Francisco, and elsewhere. The California Kindergarten Union (1879) had for one of its purposes the preservation of the "pure doctrines" of Froebel; and the American Froebel Union was formed to protect the name of kindergarten from "ignorant imitations and perversions." The struggle between conservative and liberal views continued for a long time. It was partly for this reason that John Dewey was unwilling to admit the kindergarten, by name, into his experimental school; but he was also opposed to much of Froebel's theory.

One may hope that what was called American ignorance and perversion yielded to study and honest effort. But there were other factors. The attempt to keep the kindergarten unchanged was bound to fail. School supply houses provided new materials. The exercises increased in number and variety. Small movable tables and chairs, not made "merely for listening," were used, and the children helped with the housekeeping. Attention was given to health habits, rest and sleep as well as activity were found useful, and free lunches were supplied. The use of English instead of German made changes in the verbal material, and substitutes were found for the crude early translations of the original songs, stories, and poems. The American took the place of the Froebelian kindergarten. It followed Froebel's spirit rather than his set form.

Many of the early kindergartens were established for the children of the poor. Philanthropists who were interested in developing manual skills, which might later prove useful to mechanics or factory hands, took a long chance in donating funds for kindergarten education. Churches and groups of church and school people established "free" or "charity" kindergartens as missionary institutions. The Young Women's Christian Association took an active part. So did the Society for Ethical Culture in New York under the leadership of Dr. Felix Adler, who also played an active part in introducing the kindergarten in California. Adler stressed the educative value of work which, he said, is not something added to education but is an organic part of it. It cultivates hand and brain, making the hand "wise and cunning" and the brain "clear and vigorous and enlightened." Under his direction the Ethical Culture Schools were developed as a continuous ladder without the clash between the kindergarten and the primary grades which long afflicted some school systems.

The kindergarten was made a part of the public school system of St. Louis in 1873. This was the achievement of a philanthropic kindergartner, Susan Blow, and a capable superintendent of schools, William Torrey Harris. Seven years later there were more than fifty public kindergartens in the city. Other cities followed slowly, but after 1890 progress became more rapid. Until that date there were about as many children in private as in public kindergartens, but by 1900 the latter were forging ahead and the combined enrollment of both had increased from about 30,000 in 1890 to about seven times that number in 1900. Kindergartens have been common only in cities and towns. The growth of cities and the recent increase in the birth rate have raised attendance to new high levels.

Many special problems have interested American kindergartners. Such were handwork and industrial education; and the manual training movement was connected with the kindergarten philosophy. The kindergarten was integrated with the primary grades and both benefited. Parental education and child study were often considered in meetings of the organized kindergarten teachers.

2. CHILD STUDY

Child study like the kindergarten began in Europe and in part through the kindergarten effort. Froebel collected "mother plays and nursery songs" in his native Thuringia, and one could have predicted that the new institution would further the study of children's interests. But the ideas are older than Froebel. Rousseau had urged teachers to study their pupils for, as he said, it was clear that they knew nothing about them. Comenius' little book on infancy revealed his kindly attention to child traits and activities. Pestalozzi for a short time kept a diary of his small son's development. This biographical method was also followed by H. A. Taine in France and Charles Darwin in England. Many later students followed this plan.

A teachers' society in Berlin about 1872 investigated school children's knowledge of their surroundings. It was found that children had not observed the most familiar objects, had not visited the monuments of the city, and thought a forest would be like a park. Boys were compared with girls, city children with those from the suburbs and the country. It was found that those who had attended the kindergarten made the highest scores.

The Berlin report stimulated G. Stanley Hall to probe the *Contents of Children's Minds upon Entering School*. The study was made in September of 1880 by four trained kindergarten teachers who asked the children for their understanding of about one hundred terms ranging from the names of common objects and animals to moral and religious words. A little later J. M. Greenwood, superintendent of Kansas City, made a similar study. Hall discussed the scores, referring to sex and social group differences. He also found kindergarten children "knowing" more than others. He explained that one sees not what is presented but only what is attended to; and he remarked upon the high ratio of ignorance, tradition, superstition, and emotion in the minds of children entering school. Country life seemed to him to have great educational value. He had been a country boy. And, no doubt, country life does educate for country living.

The report of Hall's investigation was published in the *Princeton Review* (1883), in the *Pedagogical Seminary* (1891), in Hall's book, *Aspects of Child Life and Education* (1907), and elsewhere. In old age, Hall wrote of it: "'The Contents of Children's Minds' attracted more comment, was translated into more languages and set the pattern for more similar studies than anything else that I have written." The study has been called the beginning of the child study movement. This, Hall considered an error. But associations for child study were founded in several states and the National Education Association formed a special department for it. Much of the early work was done by Hall's graduate students including Earl Barnes, Henry H. Goddard, J. E. Wallace Wallin, Arnold Gesell, Lewis M. Terman, and other now well-known psychologists. The investigation of 1880 was not made by paper questionnaire, as some books say, but by direct questioning.

The Clark University group in many studies did employ the paper questionnaire and has been severely criticized for it. The editor of the *Educational Review* (November, 1896) spoke of "the silly question-papers sent out at haphazard to be answered by persons of little scientific training or none." This "raking together of an undigested mass of alleged facts" should not, he said, be called research. In his *Life and Confessions of a Psychologist,* Hall admitted grave faults of method in some of the studies, but claimed that many of his students had done good work. There is truth in each of the statements. The field of the questionnaire as a scientific instrument is a limited one.

Since Hall's time the methods of child study have changed. A meeting of those interested in the field was held at the Columbian Exposition in Chicago in 1893. Hall was a participant and urged the importance of the study as an aid to education. This meeting seems to have stimulated James Sully in England and Alfred Binet in France, both of whom made important contributions. In Germany, Ernst Meumann developed an experimental type of child study and educational psychology. This is an example of the way in which different countries contribute to the promotion of a common interest. Twenty years after the Chicago meeting, Edward Lee Thorndike published his *Educational Psychology.* It is evidence of the changes that had taken place since the work of Bain and Hall.

Even when Hall was beginning his work, studies of a wholly different kind were being conducted and he rejected the title of "father of child study" which has been applied to him. He considered H. P. Bowditch as the pioneer. In 1879 Bowditch began the measurement of the height and weight of the Boston school children. Large numbers of such measures were reported in the following decades, and a bibliography of 1920 listed more than 900 of these anthropological studies. The physical measurement of college students was begun by Hitchcock of Amherst in that period. The mental inventory and physical measurement which may be taken as the two poles of child study thus appeared about the same time (1880). The mental inventory has developed into a study of behavior and achievement development, "child growth and development." The anthropologists gradually devised standard procedures, such as the measuring of many dimensions, the use of X-ray pictures to determine skeletal development, and the construction of tables and curves of growth.

A most important phase of child study was developed in connection with the education of mentally deficient children. This was the invention by Simon and Binet in Paris of the intelligence test, its translation by one of Hall's students, H. H. Goddard, and its revision and improvement by another, Lewis Terman. Terman has used the tests in the study of superior children. In World War I, group tests were developed and used to classify recruits. Mental or intelligence tests have proved of great use in educational and vocational guidance, particularly since their capabilities have been more fully understood and when they have been used by trained psychologists. Recently they have led to the better, but still far from complete, understanding of the nature of intelligence. It appears that it consists of a number of special factors or aptitudes such as the verbal, numerical, and others; or of several special factors and a general one. The first of these views is L. L. Thurstone's and the second is that of the English psychologist, Charles Spearman. It is not a unitary aptitude as Binet was inclined to believe.

Many biographical studies of children were made before and soon after the end of the century. These often had the same defects that also vitiated the questionnaire results. Some were made by doting relatives and the several studies followed no common system. Children's speech and drawings were frequent topics. Studies have been made of learning and reasoning ability in relation to age; of the sequence, development, and permanence of child interests; and of the growth of moral and social concepts. When early in the present century children's drawings were studied, it appeared that they tended to parallel language development.

Many students hold that physical and mental child growth follows a general pattern; and their purpose is to draw a complete map of the process. It is also obvious that the environment influences development and that one must not expect such a map to consist of precise outlines. Indeed, the environment is often so powerful that we may have to draw special maps for children of different classes or in different locations. One incidental illustration of environmental influence comes from studies of language development. No sure way has been found of correcting speech errors if the child constantly hears "incorrect" speech. This shows that the out-of-school experience may be more effective than the school; and that it not only directs but thwarts and limits the child's language development. It dooms him, if he is a Milton, to remain "a mute inglorious Milton."

3. ELEMENTARY HANDWORK

The kindergarten paved the way for handwork in the primary grades and thereby helped the children to go beyond the three R's. This connection was noticed by a New York City curriculum committee in 1887. Perhaps they did not know that, long before, Froebel had made the same comment and had indeed used simple activities like stick-laying, less simple ones like gardening, and exacting work with tools. The superintendent of Jamestown, New York, was a pioneer in the introduction of activities into each of the grades. The Society for Ethical Culture in both its kindergarten and its school for workingmen's children developed a continuous course of graded activities with vocational elements in the upper grades.

Felix Adler (1851–1933), who was the founder of the Ethical Culture Society and the director of its schools, had been educated in Germany. He returned during the depression of the 1870's, able, learned, and filled with a reforming zeal that found much work to do in the slums of his native New York. He was an exponent of education by activities and work; and he drew a parallel between experiments in the sciences and invention and creativeness in the arts and industry. "As experiment conjoined with observation is necessary to the discovery of truth," he wrote, "so object-creating must supplement object-teaching in the rediscovery of truth which it is the purpose of all education to facilitate." We shall repeat what was said above. He held that activities are not something added to regular instruction but are an organic part of it. He meant that a course of study which does not develop "a wise and cunning hand" as well as a clear brain is an incomplete course. In his report for 1882, Adler told of inquiries which he was receiving. State and city superintendents were seeking information about the Workingmen's Kindergarten and School because they hoped to introduce similar programs in their home cities. Some had already done so. This was shown by a children's industrial exhibition that was held in New York a few years later. Exhibits were shown from midwestern as well as eastern cities; and they contained work by children of all the grades.

Many of the teachers of those children may have had little specific preparation for their work. At any rate the need for a teachers' school or college to prepare for such work was becoming clear. In the East also, as well as in the Middle West, the professional preparation of high school teachers, for work in all fields, was coming under consideration. The subject had been raised at Columbia University as early as 1858. In 1881 President F. A. P. Barnard devoted a section of his report to the presentation of a strong argument for action. But what he recommended was a series of evening lectures on the history, philosophy, science, and art of education. This was to be especially addressed to the teachers of the city. In the course of his argument, Barnard revealed that although he knew that two educational professorships had been created in Scotland and that work was to start at Cambridge University in England, he did not know that W. H. Payne was occupying such a chair, about 500 miles away, in the University of Michigan. His views were not to be speedily accepted in such an old-line and provincial institution as Columbia College then was. Progress was to come in another way.

An Industrial Education Association was formed in New York in 1884. Its purpose was "to study and devise methods and systems of industrial education and to secure their introduction into schools." They were especially concerned for New York City, which had no public high schools until almost the end of the century, about sixty years after Philadelphia and seventy-five after Boston had developed these institutions. The association became active in the preparation of teachers of industrial arts. It was the active power in the creation of the New York College for the Training of Teachers. With the prodding of Nicholas Murray Butler (1862–1947), this modest school for the preparation of home economics and industrial arts teachers developed into the Teachers College of Columbia University, and began to prepare teachers and educational workers in all fields. It was almost twenty years after President Barnard's proposal when Teachers College became affiliated with Columbia.

Closely connected with the industrial arts and the sciences is the art of drawing. As a language it has many uses, and like other languages all normal people can acquire the essentials of it. The smallest child above infancy can begin, but practice and maturity are needed to perfect it. Drawing was one of the educational skills which Horace Mann wished all teachers to learn; but economic and industrial purposes were more effective than Mann in introducing drawing instruction into the schools.

For artistic, economic, and educational reasons, drawing was introduced into some schools about the middle of the nineteenth century. In Cleveland an enthusiast, John Brainerd, guided and supervised the classroom teachers in teaching drawing. In Syracuse, New York the schools became known in this field about 1858. The state of New York in 1875 made the teaching of drawing compulsory in state normal schools. But Massachusetts had already in 1870 introduced drawing into the common schools and required the large towns to provide free instruction in drawing to adults. The national expositions in Philadelphia in 1876 and Chicago in 1892–1893 gave evidence of national progress in drawing, design, and all graphic and plastic arts. Progress in elementary drawing was important in the teaching of handwork, nature study, geography, and other subjects.

4. THE SPREADING NORMAL SCHOOLS

Twenty years after the state normal schools had been founded in Massachusetts, schools of this kind were still few in number, small and weak, but were beginning to multiply and grow. In 1860 there were twelve state normal schools, one city normal school, and an indefinite number of normal classes or departments in high schools, state universities, and other institutions. Before long the school at Oswego, New York, was to be opened. It began in 1860 as a city school but was adopted by the state. In five years the number of state normal schools almost doubled. There were twenty-two in operation by 1865. They were thinly scattered through half the northern states from Massachusetts to Kansas. They were able to prepare only an insignificant fraction of the teachers for a nation of 35,000,000 people.

There was little that the earliest normal schools could teach beyond the reviews of the common branches and practice teaching. There were no specialized books on school administration or on the psychology, the philosophy, or the history of education. The not uncommon belief that the history of education occupied a large place in early teacher education is a mistake. The two best books, Potter and Emerson's *The School and the Schoolmaster* and Page's *Theory and Practice*, were comprehensive and general treatments of the whole subject of education within the compass of a few hundred pages. But 1860 was the hour before the dawn of 1865.

The rapid increase in the number of state normal schools began before 1865 and continued at the rate of about twenty-five new schools each decade to the end of the century and after. The institution was adopted in the Southern states. A specialized literature on education developed. Curricula were extended from one to two, three, and four years. But in the main, the state normal school continued its close connection with rural education, receiving its pupils from and returning its graduates to the country schools. This connection caused the low entrance requirements. In the cities the high schools maintained pedagogical classes and prepared elementary teachers. Some cities began to establish their own normal schools. St. Louis had taken this step in 1857, creating a school that was later named after her famous superintendent, W. T. Harris, the Harris Teachers' College.

To its formal inquiry in 1871, the United States Bureau of Education received official replies from 114 schools for teachers. These had an average enrollment of less than 100 students in each. Only fifty-one of the schools were state institutions and the rest were a mixed group of county, city, and private normal schools and normal departments in colleges and universities. By 1900 there was a threefold increase of state normal schools over the number of 1871. But meanwhile the population had doubled; and compulsory attendance laws had further multiplied the enrollments. The result was that the state normal schools were no nearer their goal, that of providing rural teachers with an adequate preparation for their extremely difficult and lonely task. All the books point to the rapid expansion of the normal schools after the Civil War, but actually they had to multiply rapidly in order to maintain their position. At the end of the century, most rural teachers still obtained their licenses upon examination after attending a school for teachers for a short time or even without any professional training.

The early state normal schools in many cases lacked the facilities and the qualities which such an institution should have. Their equipment was often meager; they were badly located and received insufficient support; their loyal staffs were overworked and underpaid, and many of their staff members were insufficiently prepared. From the first there were exceptional teachers and exceptional schools. Among the latter one would place the schools of Normal, Illinois; Ypsilanti, Michigan; Bridgewater, Massachusetts; Albany and Oswego, New York; and doubtless others.

5. OSWEGO

The Oswego Normal School became famous for its system of object-teaching. Object-teaching as practiced at Oswego was the stepchild of the Pestalozzian movement, which had been precariously maintaining itself

in the United States for half a century. We have noted the work of Joseph
Neef, the arithmetic text of Warren Colburn, the doctrines of Horace
Mann, the normal schools of Massachusetts, and other traces of Pestalozzi's
influence. Object-teaching came to Oswego not from Switzerland directly
but by way of England. It was presented in a highly formal manner that
made it easy to transmit, and its spread was further aided by a strong
personality, Edward Sheldon.

Edward Austin Sheldon (1823–1897), the leader in organizing the
public schools of Oswego and the state normal school and of object-teaching
in both, had some of the qualities of Pestalozzi himself. Sheldon, like Pestalozzi, was a man of self-denying spirit which did not exclude a keen
desire for recognition; like Pestalozzi he revealed great sympathy for the
poor and the power to enlist the assistance of the rich and to hold the attention and interest of the young. Like Pestalozzi he conducted a "ragged
school." But unlike him, Sheldon was a country boy with an almost fanati-
cal love of fine trees. When a workman contrary to instructions cut down
a great elm at Sheldon's home, "Shady Shore," he "mourned as for the loss
of a friend."

At mid-century the city of Oswego had 12,000 people, several private
schools, the ragged school which Sheldon directed, but no public schools.
A public school party was forming in the town, and of this Sheldon became
the spearhead. When the party became a majority he became, in effect,
superintendent of schools. In this position he revealed organizing skill of a
high order, and in the history of the years following 1853 we find one
example of the ways in which public education came into existence in many
places.

In his own life-story he has told how, closing the ragged school, he
created a graded system of schools offering thirteen years of schooling to
rich and poor. There were three divisions in the lower schools, called primary, junior, and senior, and each had a three-year course. Above these
he provided and opened a four-year high school. Attendance laws were
lacking, and with twelve primary schools only two senior schools were
needed. He also found that many boys and young men between the ages
of eleven and twenty-one who were employed needed and desired further
education. For these he opened an evening school; and for children moving
into Oswego from the ungraded country schools, he organized an unclassi-
fied school to fit these newcomers for the regular classes. For the teachers
he held weekly staff conferences lasting three hours on Saturday mornings.
The school day was fully and strictly laid out, and frequent factual examinations of the pupils were demanded and the results reported to the board

of education. Although Sheldon had attended Hamilton College, he did not finish and had no professional preparation. Of Pestalozzi he had never heard. But whatever one may think of his solutions, it is clear that he did not need to have the educational problems pointed out to him.

Good members of the school board he considered next in importance to good teachers. It was for this reason, he wrote, in the *Autobiography*, edited by Mary Sheldon Barnes, that "I felt it incumbent upon me as far as possible to run the elections. . . . Sometime before an election I was on the alert, picked out a good man and spoke to my friends about him. . . . On election day I was not idle but went the rounds to see that they did their duty. . . . By this eternal vigilance we succeeded in keeping a good board. Occasionally, the opposition was too strong for us and a 'kicker' would be elected. In such a case I was careful to give him every possible attention, taking him around from building to building, showing him conditions and pointing out needs. As a result he sometimes became the most liberal man on the board and moved to advance the budget beyond what the board were willing to approve." It was in such ways that he "gained the reputation of winning over to the interest of the schools every man, however serious his opposition when elected . . . 'they gave me *carte blanche* . . . I got the title of 'Pope Sheldon.'" This was written long after, when the memory of his difficulties had grown dim but that of his success, as is the way with memories, was still bright.

Our brief narrative indicates how a small city system was started a century ago. The mechanical arrangements and the exacting discipline of teachers and pupils would not be approved now and indeed Sheldon himself later disapproved of them. "My tendency was," he wrote in 1897, "to restrain the activities and impulses of children, while now I would encourage and cultivate them by giving them proper direction." He should have applied to pupils and teachers some of the clever "management" which he bestowed upon board members. Some of his teachers must have lacked experience. Sheldon kept the schools under his constant surveillance. He felt that he had "to be everywhere." The lessons, it is no wonder, seemed dull and lifeless. It was these conditions which led to the Oswego object-teaching system.

In a Toronto museum, not in use in the schools of Toronto, Sheldon found a collection of pictures, color charts, and other visual materials. These had been acquired by Egerton Ryerson (1803–1882), chief school official for the province of Ontario, Canada, on his educational tour of England and Europe, and he now sold them for $300 to Sheldon, who was making an educational tour of Canada. Sheldon put the "objects" to work. The materials had come from the stock of an English Pestalozzian group, the

Home and Colonial School Society. From them he also obtained a teacher, Margaret Jones, who came for one year to introduce the new methods; and when her term expired he was able to engage Hermann Krüsi, Jr., the son of Pestalozzi's first assistant. Krüsi, however, voiced some criticism of the formalized type of object-teaching which had been developed in England and which was now applied in Oswego. Before we consider the criticisms we shall examine a sample lesson.

A "lesson on plants" from Sheldon's manuscript has been published. In Dearborn's *The Oswego Movement* it reads, in part, as follows: "1. Require the children to look at some flowers and say in what they are alike. (They all have leaves; they all have stems; nearly all have the *outer leaves* [calix] of a *green* color.) Let the children smell the flowers—they all have some kind of smell. Ask how they are produced (from slips or seeds). If a slip or seed be put into the ground and gets proper nourishment, what takes place? (They grow *[sic.]*) All flowers are grown. . . . Who made the flowers?

"2. Having found out in what flowers are alike, lead the children to discover in what they differ. . . .

"3. Let the children say of whom we should think when we *look at flowers?* . . . Why flowers are made of different colors? . . . Whom they should thank when they gather flowers?"

From this incomplete sample one infers that cut flowers were used and were passed from pupil to pupil. But flowering plants have roots and these have important functions which were neglected. On the other hand, such a lesson may go in any direction, ending up not in science but in religion as this one did. It was standard practice to have the pupils name the qualities of objects. "This apple is large, firm, red, wholesome," and so on. But the discussion might wander off into horticulture or history. Apples have, according to tradition, played various parts as, for example, in the dramas of William Tell, and of Newton, and of a notable couple in an ancient garden. All this raises the vital question of the purpose of object-teaching.

The usual answer to this question was based upon the faculty psychology. This does not call for special remark because the faculty psychology was so generally accepted. Using its terms we may say that object-teaching was intended to develop accuracy of observation and perception, to lead pupils to form correct concepts, and to grow in reasoning power. The Pestalozzian principle was accepted that the materials and lessons were to be adapted to the stages of the children's mental development. And also following Pestalozzi, the lessons were to promote vocabulary growth and skill in describing objects both orally and in writing. There was an alphabet of observation. This was an expansion of Pestalozzi's number, form, and language, and it included also size, sound, odor, color, and ideas of relation such as part and whole.

The true idea of school education, said Sheldon, is not so much to impart knowledge as to prepare the mind to acquire knowledge and to convey it to others. The teacher, he said, must be ready in speech and skilled in drawing so that he will be able to supplement real objects or in their absence to use sketches in place of things. He must be on easy footing with children and have the power to hold their interest and direct it. To this set of teaching qualifications we may add a sentence from Hermann Krüsi, Jr., one of Sheldon's able and loyal assistants. He said: "In the acquisition, or teaching of any branch of study, I have always tried to penetrate to the principle, in order to render the subject clear to myself before presenting it to others," which is a most commendable practice for teachers to follow.

Object-teaching had to face hostile criticism. It will be fairest to begin with the "wounds of a friend." Krüsi thought the lessons often had no connection with each other, followed no over-all plan. There seemed to be too much crude analysis, children being asked to name the parts of the human body, the parts of a plant, as in the above example, or of an animal, perhaps the horse. In the third place, too many unfamiliar words were taught, such words as "fetlock," "pastern," and "withers," or, in other connections, used to name qualities such as "porous," "transparent," and "opaque." An outside critic listed "chalybeate," "imbricated," "amorphous," and many more. Thus the object lesson became a senseless vocabulary lesson. The teachers' questions did not stimulate but instead, as Krüsi said, restricted the pupils' responses. Good answers might be considered wrong because they were not the ones demanded by the lesson plan. Lastly, there was often only one object, an apple or a cube, held up before the class who thus found "observation" difficult. Krüsi thought the best examples of object-teaching were found not in the lessons from which the name was derived but in arithmetic or drawing where pupils were encouraged to develop their own ideas, illustrations, and experiments. All sciences are based upon realities which have to be observed before symbols and abstractions can be useful; but he recognized also that nature studies should lead to ideas and principles which are indeed "real" and "clear" or "true" but not "concrete." He was pleased when H. H. Straight introduced into Oswego a more flexible and intellectual course of nature study that by no means neglected contact with things. But there were difficulties, for some teachers in the normal school were wedded to object lessons and opposed nature study just as their predecessors had opposed object lessons because they were wedded to the book.

The most sensational criticisms of Oswego object-teaching came from outside the school and were made by Dr. H. B. Wilbur of Syracuse. His attacks, called "vindictive" by some, were made first before the state and later before the national educational associations. Replies were made by Sheldon, by committees appointed to investigate, and even by some English Pestalozzians who were drawn into the debate. This became one of the long drawn-out (1862–1865) controversies of American educational history.

Controversy broke out on the home front as well as abroad. In 1872 the school board of Oswego discontinued object-teaching in all grades above the three primary years. But there had been trouble earlier, and when Sheldon wrote his autobiography in 1897 he had forgotten his long-past difficulties. With all his management and his political activities in school board elections, he was not always the master of events. It was partly for this reason that in 1863 he sought and secured state aid for the normal school, which had been a local institution. In 1867 it became a state normal school, and two years later Sheldon gave up his position in the city schools to devote all his time to the preparation of teachers. The teaching profession had in the main supported his program and the publicity was of the greatest service to the school.

If one may judge the influence of the Oswego normal school by the distribution of its graduates, it must have been far-reaching. In the first twenty-five years there had been in attendance between five and six thousand students of whom more than two thousand graduated. The graduates were to be found teaching in the schools of nearly all the states and territories and in several foreign countries. The largest numbers were employed in New York and adjoining states and in the old Northwest Territory states. Such facts do not, however, tell us much because there is no way of telling how well the Oswego methods were received. The greatest deficiency of the teachers lay in the lack of a thorough scientific education. "It is a great mistake," said Agassiz, "to suppose that just any one can teach even the simple elements of science. To have a smattering of something is one of the great fallacies of our time."

6. Spotlight on Quincy

Almost as soon as Oswego had reached the height of its celebrity, the crowds of educators began to turn toward Quincy, Massachusetts. Superintendents, teachers, and reporters came and also some who were intent merely "either to tell or to hear some new thing." They came to see the change which had been worked in a sleepy school system by a new superintendent, Francis Wayland Parker, who had in earlier positions experimented with Sheldon's object lessons. Another part of this book tells more about him; but here we shall deal mainly with the "New Departure," the "New Education," or the "Quincy Methods," as the change was variously called. Colonel Parker always denied that there was in the Quincy methods anything that was entirely new. After we see what there was we may perhaps judge whether any of it was new.

Both the Oswego and the Quincy methods were applied only in the elementary school and mostly in the primary grades. They were alike in the use of concrete materials. To observation both added forms of expression and reporting, such as language, drawing, and modeling in clay. The best-known report on the Quincy methods even calls these activities "object lessons," but there is in them a clear approach to what we shall in the next section call nature study. Some of the lessons were carefully prepared and others were called impromptu exercises. There was an impromptu lesson on the horse, "the beginning of zoology." In Quincy in 1880 all pupils had seen horses, and except for the drawing of a horse by the teacher on the board this was simply a conversation lesson. It was an object lesson; but at Oswego the range of the lesson subject would have been out of the ordinary.

There was a plant lesson, an "introduction to botany," in which the children planted seeds in a box filled with earth brought in by a pupil. There was some conversation on what will grow and what will not. A lesson upon hills was to introduce the pupils to the study of geography. After making hills in the sandbox a pupil poured water on them. This illustrated erosion, but the teachers at Quincy resisted the tendency to use big words. As the lesson ended, the children were told to notice the shapes of the hills on their way home and to prepare to model them in school the following day. This, said the reporter, "may be made the first step to that grandest of all sciences, Geography."

In the primary school years covered by Miss Patridge in her report on the Quincy methods, there are lessons on form, color, number, language, and all the school rudiments. One reporter declared that the children of Quincy wrote English earlier and better than anywhere else. The compositions reprinted by Miss Patridge and the pupils' drawings which she presented in her book are excellent. According to a third commentator, the work was a "tremendous success" so that "a surplus of volunteers" offered to teach in the schools without compensation in order that they might thoroughly learn the Quincy methods.

At Quincy there was an effort to combine subjects. Every lesson was to be made a lesson in the language arts of speech and writing. The spelling book was wholly discarded and spelling was taught in writing and reading. Parker favored the use of many reading books in each grade, not just one. Every language lesson could also be the beginning of science instruction. Lessons on color involved form. Number work could use both form and color. All lessons were to teach good manners and morals. History and geography were to be combined quite after the manner of Herbart; and Parker in some passages seems to hold that history is determined by geography.

All the accounts declare that at Quincy teachers and pupils worked together joyously and harmoniously. From Charles Francis Adams, Jr., who was most responsible for bringing Parker to Quincy, comes the testimony that in both primary and grammar grades the new superintendent created a new spirit. "It was certainly most pleasant to go into the rooms," wrote Adams, "and feel the atmosphere of cheerfulness, activity, and interest which pervaded them."

Three related attempts to improve the quality of elementary education were made in the nineteenth century. Each effort was based upon the improved preparation of teachers. The three leaders were Horace Mann, who led in the creation of state systems of schools and the founding of state normal schools; Edward Sheldon, who spread object-teaching and founded the Oswego State Normal School; and Francis Parker, who made of Quincy an object lesson in good teaching and became head of the Cook County Normal School in Illinois. Thus the professional preparation of teachers was a leading interest of each of these.

All of these efforts were based upon the principle that the elementary school should provide a broad, general education, a truly liberating experience. Such a program, reaching far beyond the three R's and also beyond the so-called professional areas, required teachers who were themselves educated persons, knowing what and why as well as how. Nature study was to be a contribution to this program, but such teachers were not easy to develop in the normal schools.

7 . NATURE STUDY

To tell when nature study began in the schools we should know what it is—a question that presents some difficulty. If it is merely a variety of object-teaching, or if, on the other hand, it is science, we had better call it by the appropriate one of these names. The *Nature Study Review,* which began publication in 1905 when the movement was well advanced, defined it as the simple observational study of common natural objects just because they are interesting. Simple observation is here contrasted with the processes of technical science, such as analysis, dissection, quantitative work, and the search for scientific laws. The phrase "common natural objects" is not entirely fitting. The objects of object lessons were often colors, an egg, a piece of glass, and similarly unrelated things. But the usual objects of nature study are plants and animals and these are observed in their natural habitat. This study of life histories, adaptation, and distribution includes the observation of such matters as soils, weather, bird migration, animal cover, hibernation, and other surroundings and habits of living things. This kind of study comes under what the scientist calls ecology. Nature study is different in matter and method from both object lessons and science. It resembles the activities and interests of the old-fashioned naturalists. The words themselves may have been taken, as has been supposed, from the German *Naturkunde,* which is literally nature knowledge rather than the study of nature. It is certain that the phrase quickly came into wide use about 1889.

Within the field thus indicated there were several kinds of interests. Some naturalists and nature study exponents tend to gush over the "dear" things which they find in the woods or garden, or they sermonize on the "spirit of nature" that to them "seems to hover like a fairy around the waterfalls." At a great distance from this is the nature study which prepares for the study of agriculture, hygiene, or botany and zoology. And to be found between these extremes is the custom of correlating nature study with geography, or drawing, or composition, and sometimes with local history. The latter practices do not necessarily indicate that the observation of nature is lacking in intrinsic interest; but they do tend to affect the materials selected and the methods. With these reservations and illustrations the *Review's* definition may be accepted. Little equipment is needed. Except for a simple microscope and a field glass, the needed apparatus can be made in the school shop or by the pupils at home.

Like other such movements, nature study did not have a noticeable beginning. Here and there in academies and normal schools and even in the common schools, there were teachers who taught children about trees and animals, who took them on trips or brought nature into the schoolroom. The majority did none of these things, but there was an increase in the number of helpful books and materials for those who wished to introduce the study of nature.

In his annual report for 1871 William T. Harris published *A Syllabus in Nature Study* for the schools of St. Louis. He gave economic reasons for this step. Science, he said, explains the processes of nature and thus enables industry to create the products which improve the living conditions of the people. This is evidently not the voice of a mere theoretician. Natural science was recommended because it is an instrument of civilization. The syllabus gave advice on teaching. The lessons were to be largely oral, and experiments and demonstrations were recommended as well as books. The material reached beyond biology and included some physical geography, meteorology, and astronomy, and touched the "human sciences" of economics and pedagogy. The program, which was to occupy one hour a week, did not have the rich variety of organisms and phenomena which later courses introduced; but it was an improvement over object-teaching.

Within a year after coming to Boston, Agassiz was to be found lecturing to teachers in their institutes in Massachusetts. These meetings were held in late summer, and the lecturer appeared with a jar of live grasshoppers. It was one of his devices to have nature herself lecture for him. Each teacher had to hold a grasshopper while Agassiz explained its structure and habits. When his wife opened her school of sixty or more girls, he helped out with daily lectures on natural history illustrated with specimens, models, and drawings. It has been said that he never had a more responsive audience, and it was usually augmented by some of the mothers of the pupils. Although he had the expert's dislike of books by amateurs, he helped his wife, Elizabeth Cary Agassiz, prepare *A First Lesson in Natural History* (1859), a little book for children somewhat in the tradition of Mrs. Marcet. It soon attained a second edition and was also revised for a third.

Agassiz and his students had to do with the creation of many natural history museums. One of his students, Albert Smith Bickmore, "created the design" for the American Museum of Natural History established in New York, known around the world, and in later years long presided over by Henry Fairfield Osborn. Bickmore was one of the pioneers in the movement to bring schools and museums together for nature study. Osborn has told how Bickmore in 1880 started lectures at the museum for teachers; in 1904 for children; in 1902 began to lend nature study collections to schools; and in 1914 sent the museum lecturers with the collections out into the schools. All this began with Agassiz. No one can say how much would have happened without him or how soon. To secure nature's help in teaching was not new when Agassiz used it, but his charm, his scientific reputation, his theism, even his anti-Darwinism, and the intellectual and economic conditions of the nineteenth century increased his influence in the United States. But he was not the father of nature study; its original ancestor may have been Pestalozzi, or Aristotle, or even before these two men

That shepherd who first taught the chosen seed
In the beginning how the heavens and earth
Rose out of Chaos;

and in fact N. S. Shaler's *Autobiography* (p. 298) suggests that this latter
farspun guess may have had the support of Agassiz himself.

On the list of Agassiz's students at Penikese the name of H. H. Straight
(1846–1886) stood first; and this, although accidental, is symbolic of his
rank as "probably the oustanding elementary science teacher" of the group.
That he who made his own way and wrote nothing should by the age of
forty acquire such a reputation is astonishing. Straight early became an
orphan, worked on farms in western New York, and began teaching in his
middle teens. His salary was thirteen dollars a month for a three-months'
term. He entered the preparatory department of Oberlin College, hoping to
find a way to go to Germany to study languages. To earn the means for this,
he again turned to teaching, and at Galena, Ohio, he introduced some
object lessons into the work of his classes. Whatever the effect of this upon
his pupils, it changed his own life. Instead of Germany he studied at Cornell
and Harvard, assisted Shaler in his geological surveys in Kentucky and
neighboring states (1875), and the following year was appointed by Sheldon to teach science at Oswego.

We have seen that Straight was not fully understood at Oswego. He
was repelled by the formality of the object lessons, their pretentious vocabulary, the lack of connection between lessons and the failure to relate them
to the rest of the work of the school. To Straight, Parker gave the credit for
his own interest in the correlation of studies; but it is hard to believe that
after his years in Europe Parker had to come back home to learn about that
Herbartian idea.

At Oswego, Straight taught from living plants and animals in their
natural environment. He had learned from Agassiz and Shaler and at
Cornell from Burt G. Wilder to stress the unity of nature. He took his
classes to the shore of Lake Ontario and to swamp, forest, and field. There
they learned by direct observation and inference how living things depend
upon natural conditions. In 1882 he taught in the summer school at
Martha's Vineyard, and Hermann Krüsi, visiting the school, found that
Straight's "educational wisdom" was receiving greater recognition there
than at home. The following year he joined Parker in the Cook County
Normal School for the last few years of his short life.

The work which Straight was compelled to lay down was taken up
and more fully developed by Wilbur S. Jackman (1855–1907). He was ap-

pointed to the science department of the Cook County Normal School in 1889. When Parker joined the University of Chicago, Jackman accompanied him. He also had been a farm boy with few early opportunities, but he managed to complete a normal school course and at the age of twenty-nine graduated from Harvard College. His sound preparation in science kept him from diluting nature study with romantic sentiment, and his practical administrative skill enabled him to develop a course that carried the students regularly through the seasons. His *Nature Study for the Common Schools* (1894) and his book on field work followed the succession of nature phenomena through "the rolling year." His teaching and writings helped to give nature study an assured place in the elementary grades. When the normal school was united with the University of Chicago he also served as principal of the University Elementary School. In later years Elliot Rowland Downing and other scientists continued to maintain the position of Chicago as a nature study center.

The two decades from 1890 to 1910 and the two states, Massachusetts and New York, were pre-eminent for their contributions to the nature study movement at the height of its influence. Massachusetts was at that time still reaping its harvest from the work of Horace Mann and the normal schools and of Agassiz and his disciples. Penikese and the Martha's Vineyard Summer School have been mentioned. In New York the agricultural depression of the nineties brought together at Cornell University a number of prominent nature study leaders; and the teaching and publication which were begun at that time have been continued by their successors.

In Massachusetts the teachers' association of Plymouth County in 1890 prepared for the schools a series of nature observations and asked the members to report on the work at the following meeting of the association. Observations on plants, animals, and minerals were proposed, and the following year the outline was expanded. This is the county in which the Bridgewater Normal School was located, and the former students of this school had long been given an introduction to science. Many of these responded eagerly to the suggestion of their association and reported the adoption of supplementary reading books in natural history or the correlation of nature study with drawing and language lessons.

In New York the movement had a less academic beginning. In the agricultural depression of the early 1890's, many rural people flocked into New York City and the relief agencies began to ask why the land should have become unable to sustain its people. This question led naturally to an inquiry into the condition of agriculture and the formation of a citizens' committee for its improvement. It was proposed to interest country children in farming by teaching them about nature; and the legislature was induced to make an appropriation for this purpose. The money was made available to the college of agriculture at Cornell University, and the work was directed at first by Professor Isaac Roberts (1833–1928) and then by Liberty Hyde Bailey (1858–   ).

Bailey became an eminent writer, editor, and teacher of agriculture and horticulture and the founder of the Bailey Hortorium at Cornell. He was also an effective promoter of nature study. In this he was putting to use the lessons he had learned from a rural teacher in Michigan. After graduating from the Agricultural College of his state, he became an assistant to the great botanist, Asa Gray. His numerous publications include both technical and inspirational books, elementary textbooks on botany, and a famous essay which he called *The Nature-Study Idea* (1903). This sensible and charming little book was written for teachers, but it does not, as the title might suggest, deal mainly with the philosophy of nature study. It answers many practical questions such as, "How shall I start in teaching nature?" or, "Is nature study thorough?" It has a chapter on the school garden with an account of the gardens at the Hampton Institute, and another chapter on the agricultural phase of nature study. From the way the Cornell movement was initiated one would expect a strong emphasis upon agriculture, but this was not Bailey's idea. He had been a farm boy; and he believed that a flower garden would do more than a bumper wheat crop to keep a boy on the farm. And it is a fact that the Cornell nature study publications did not greatly stress the economics of agriculture.

There is in *The Nature-Study Idea* this discouraging interpretation of educational history, as follows: "We have failed to reach the farmer effectively because we still persist in employing old-time and academic methods. Historically the elementary public school is a product of the university and the college. 'The greatest achievement of modern education,' writes W. H. Payne, 'is the gradation and correlation of schools, whereby the ladder of learning is let down from the university to secondary schools, and from these to the schools of the people.' This origin of 'the schools of the people' from the university explains why it is that these schools are so unrelated to the life of the pupil, and so unreal; they are exotic and unnatural. If any man were to find himself in a country wholly devoid of schools and were set the task of originating and organizing a school system, he would almost unconsciously introduce some subjects that would be related to the habits of the people and to the welfare of the community. Being freed from traditions, he would teach something of the plants and animals and fields and people. Yet, as a matter of fact, what do our rural schools teach? Nothing of this kind." Some of the facts in this useful lesson, as Bailey attempted to teach it, require correction. The elementary school, independent at first, was drawn into the secondary school and university orbit. More recently this trend has been reversed.

To increase the vitality of rural education by bringing it into close connection with farm life, Cornell University used a part of its special appropriation to promote nature study in the schools. In this work Mrs. Anna Botsford Comstock had already shown expertness. She and Bailey visited many rural schools to learn what human and material resources were available. They found that the object and nature teaching of the Oswego Normal School graduates formed a good beginning. Others of the group that collected around Bailey were George T. Powell, director of farmers' institutes, and John W. Spencer, a fruit-grower from Chautauqua County. The New York Experiment Station gave aid. Lecturers were sent into the rural schools to give illustrative lessons and to aid teachers in forming study programs.

Rural school leaflets written by the above-named staff were distributed in hundreds of thousands of copies to the schools. Mrs. Comstock, who was an entomologist and artist, wrote many of them. Out of these and her experience and that of her colleagues she wrote her *Handbook of Nature-Study*. Her preface written in 1911 contains an account of the Cornell movement. Professor E. Laurence Palmer, who has succeeded to the leadership of nature study at Cornell, has prepared many of the later leaflets. In one for September, 1944, he has listed the subjects of nearly 100 such pamphlets beginning with one of January, 1920, on "small winter mammals." Each year there is one intended for teachers. Several of these deal with elementary science books.

There has been an opinion in some quarters that the multitude of nature books has been harmful to nature study. Some schools have made nature study a literary pursuit. Having pupils read about "wild folk at the pond" or about "nature hobbies" is not nature study. But the observational study of nature was not crushed by the mounting pile of publications that have come from the presses yearly since about 1900 or 1910; and wisely used, the better books can be stepping stones to better observation and wider knowledge of nature than the unaided pupil could attain. Some of the opposition to nature study came from those who wished to replace it with vocational agriculture. Others, supplementing Liberty H. Bailey's opinion, thought nature study could be made practical. But it must be admitted that most work in nature study has been and is general and liberal, not really vocational in nature. The study has held its place in some school systems but not in all, not in any large proportion in fact. From two postcard investigations it appears that in the schools of half a dozen states there was no trace of nature study, and in each of such large and populous states as California, Illinois, New York, and Pennsylvania, only twenty-five or thirty cities and school systems reported nature study courses. Some of the actual work may not have been reported, some may have been done under another name, perhaps in connection with geography. But this, or something like this, is the outcome of the work of scientists, institute lecturers, normal schools, and authors over a period of three-quarters of a century.

8. Science-Teaching Trends

The greatest difficulty in improving nature study and in even maintaining it in the schools is to be found in the inadequate scientific education of the elementary teachers; and no curriculum can be effective without knowledge, intelligence, and enthusiasm in those who administer it. The second difficulty grows out of heavy schedules, large classes, and lack of administrative support with which elementary teachers must somehow cope.

With the rise of the junior high school and the development of general science about the same time, there has been a tendency to make the nature study of the fifth and sixth grades more systematic than nature study has sometimes been. The elementary teacher seeking help from the teachers in the junior high school has tended to follow their ideas and methods. This is merely a single example of a two-way movement between lower and higher schools that has always been in existence. Not only have the high school and the college been mutually influencing each other but this is also true of the elementary and the high school. Subjects, methods, and purposes have moved up and down on the ladder as need arose. And the junior high school, partaking of the nature of the school below and the one above, became an easy pathway for ideas. In this interchange there is danger as well as benefit. The danger to elementary school science is that it will become too systematic and logical and that there will be presented generalizations which the elementary school child can not grasp.

The great benefit that may come to elementary science from the junior high school is in the emphasis that will be placed upon the solving of problems. But the problems must be easy enough and not too easy; and this point cannot be readily determined. They should also lead to further questions and to useful applications. How to find a supply of such tasks and to provide the background and materials to set the inquiry in motion is one of the urgent and largely unsolved problems of elementary education. For help we are entitled to look to the specialists in elementary education and elementary school science teaching.

The main current trend in the field is one in the direction of elementary science. If this seems to take us back to William T. Harris and the seventies of the last century, we shall be only partly correct. The new elementary science movement is much richer in ideas and better adapted to the children's interests than the St. Louis efforts of long ago. Teachers and teaching have improved in this area, and the nature study movement deserves much of the credit for the change. But problems may be too easy as well as too hard. In teaching children to think by means of science, we should, indeed we unavoidably must, teach science.

A major trend in elementary education has favored the enrichment of the course of study or, in the current speech, of the experiences of children. A great many activities have been introduced as well as much new knowledge and many kinds of problems. The school has gone beyond the three R's.

After the Civil War a movement developed to enrich the elementary school program and to extend and improve the preparation of the elementary teachers. The kindergarten with its play activities and games, its group exercises and informal manner, became an object lesson to the elementary school and especially so when it became a part of the public school system. Both the discovery that children learn through inventive and creative work and that activities could be educative without being based upon books and formal lessons were of the greatest importance in the reform of elementary education.

The liberal wing of the kindergarten movement did not continue Froebel's "gifts" and exercises or accept his symbolism; but other American kindergartners, under the influence of German fundamentalist trainers, continued the strictly Froebelian practices and theories. The struggle between the two parties continued into the twentieth century. John Dewey after 1896 did not want to admit that the University School had a kindergarten.

Child study was closely related to the kindergarten movement. Froebel himself had carried out studies of the play, games, songs, and constructions of children. The psychologists took up the study of children's growth and development and introduced new methods involving questionnaires, continuous records, physical measurements, mental tests, and controlled experiments. Information was gathered on language development, drawing, reasoning, skills, interests, and other phases in the effort to learn how children mature and what influences affect their development.

Educational and industrial influences led to the introduction of handwork and drawing into the elementary schools. Felix Adler was an eloquent and distinguished spokesman for the education of the hand. He urged that school activities and handwork served a purpose in learning analogous to that of experiment in science. This Froebelian doctrine has had great influence upon child psychology and curriculum practice and theory.

The spread of the normal schools was a major feature of the development of elementary education after 1860. They increased in numbers and also in facilities and power, yet they were hardly able to keep pace with the increasing numbers of teachers and the demands made upon them. Oswego was one normal school that made a definite impression upon American education. But the sort of impression it made was not wholly favorable to progress. Its formalized methods were not adapted to develop the initiative, originality, and self-education of the pupils. The Quincy schools took a step in this direction, and nature study when well directed followed what was later to be known as the Progressive tradition.

QUESTIONS

1. What do children learn by doing—to do, to know, to reason, or to invent and create? What apparently are the educational values to be derived from these several outcomes?

2. What are the positive values and what the limitations of the concept that the teacher is to be merely a child-gardener rather than one who instructs, warns, and controls his pupils?

3. Froebel, it is known, thought that democratic America would be highly favorable to the kindergarten and so it proved. Why, then, in adopting it was it changed?

4. Why was it necessary to create a new separate institution, the state normal school, to prepare teachers when there already were many colleges with capable faculties and not too many students? Find other examples illustrating the same principle.

5. If we truly observe only that to which we actively attend, what success in forming able observers was to be expected from object lessons?

6. Why is the organization of ideas and of knowledge important?

7. Would scientists approve the definition of nature study given by the *Nature Study Review*? Ask several. What do scientists think of "nature study"?

8. What evidence may show that Straight independently discovered correlation of studies? What is the probability that Parker learned it from Straight and not in Germany?

9. Is the account by Payne a true account of the origin of "the schools for the people"?

10. Why has nature study as a separate discipline declined while "nature books" remain popular, for example, Rachel Carson's *The Sea Around Us* (1951)?

11. Why, in the expansion of elementary education, was more attention devoted to knowledge than to activities?

BOOKS AND PAPERS

Each of the chief subjects in this chapter has an independent literature of its own, and some had the support of special magazines such as G. Stanley Hall's *Pedagogical Seminary* for child study and the *Nature Study Review* for the subject indicated. On safeguards to be observed in questionnaire studies, see an article by G. M. Whipple in *School and Society*, August 27, 1927. There were numerous books, historical, expository, and critical, on these subjects. Professor W. H. Kilpatrick's criticism of Froebel is listed below. Agassiz, for all his reputation as a teacher and teacher of teachers, became a controversial figure, the occasion as well as the author of many books and papers.

Bailey, Liberty H., *The Nature-Study Idea*, New York, 1904.

Barnard, Henry, *Papers on Froebel's Kindergarten*, Hartford, 1890, being selections from the *Journal*. The date of the first issue of the *Papers* is in doubt. This revised edition has a critical paper by I. H. Fichte (1797–1879), who, like his more famous father, was a philosopher.

Boyden, A. C., *History of the Bridgewater Normal School*, Bridgewater, 1933.

Comstock, Anna B., *Handbook of Nature Study,* Ithaca, New York, 1941, being a printing of the twenty-fourth edition, revised in 1939.

Dearborn, Ned H., *Oswego Movement*, New York, Teachers College, Columbia University, 1925.

Downing, E. R., *Our Living World, A Source-Book of Biological Nature-Study*, University of Chicago Press, 1919.

Foster, Josephine C., and N. E. Headley, *Education in the Kindergarten,* New York, 1948.

Gordon, Eva L., "Elementary Science Library," *Cornell Rural School Leaflet*, Vol. 43, No. 1, Ithaca, New York, September, 1949.

Hall, G. Stanley, *Life and Confessions of a Psychologist*, New York, 1923.

Harris, W. T., "Relations of the Kindergarten to the School," NEA *Proceedings*, *1879*, pp. 142–158; and *How To Teach Natural Science in Public Schools*, Syracuse, New York, 1895.

Kilpatrick, W. H., *Froebel's Kindergarten Principles Critically Examined*, New York, 1916.

Kraus, John, "The Kindergarten; its Use and Abuse in America," NEA *Proceedings, 1877*, pp. 186–207, an accusatory address.

Palmer, E. L., "The Cornell Nature Study Philosophy," *Cornell Rural School Leaflet*, Vol. 38, No. 1, Ithaca, New York, September, 1944.

Patridge, Lelia E., *Quincy Methods Illustrated*, New York, 1886.

Russell, James E., "Organization and Administration of Teachers College," *Teachers College Record,* January, 1900.

Sheldon, E. A., *Autobiography of Edward Austin Sheldon,* New York, 1911. Edited by a daughter, Mary Sheldon Barnes, teacher and writer, with an introduction by Andrew Sloan Draper.

Teller, James D., *Louis Agassiz, Scientist and Teacher,* Columbus, the Ohio State University Press, 1947, a dissertation, with bibliography.

Underhill, Orra F., *Origins and Development of Elementary School Science,* Chicago, 1941, with bibliography.

Chapter VIII

RISE OF THE HIGH SCHOOL

THE high school, although it is far younger than the English, French, and other great secondary schools of western Europe, has undergone much greater changes than they. It began as a school for boys but soon admitted girls also. It began as a specialized and has become a comprehensive school. It began as a terminal school similar to the realist academy, early assumed classical college-preparatory functions, in mid-career undertook to give vocational education, and should now, in the opinion of some, become a universal school for all American youth.

The greater part of this revolution has occurred since the closing decades of the nineteenth century, when it was transformed into a higher common school whose chief task is not the preparation of selected young people for college studies but the preparation of young people for "the real business of living." It is significant that the quoted words are taken from the early documents of one of the earliest academies, Phillips Andover. But the real business of living and the means of preparing for it have changed since 1787; and the high school has contracted its classical and expanded its realist studies and added the vocations and activities to its program. It has become the center of community activity and the pride of its community. Of many a town and city it can be said that the high school building is the finest building in it. It has spread from the cities to the country districts and is coming to be within reach of all the children.

1. THE MEANING OF SECONDARY EDUCATION

The public high school is not the only American secondary school. Secondary education is a broad term covering private as well as public schools for adolescents. Among these are military academies, expensive and exclusive preparatory schools, and the numerous church-controlled academies and high schools. In earlier times, and in many countries even now, only the preparatory schools, which generally are for a selected portion of the upper classes only, were and are called secondary. In France, for example, the high school would be considered a mixed secondary and higher primary school, secondary in so far as it is preparatory, and higher primary in so far as it continues the work of the elementary school.

An informative passage in Alexander Dallas Bache's *Report* (1839, p. 450) reveals his own liberal American position on this definition and thus shows disagreement between leading French educators. Bache wrote as follows: "It is usual to confine the title of secondary schools to those which prepare for the learned professions, and in this view the only secondary instruction in Prussia is given in the gymnasia," in which the ancient classics received the main emphasis. But Bache, disagreeing with this view, held that the "Real Schools *(Realschulen)*" were equally entitled to be called secondary because the ages of the pupils and the level of their attainment were the same as those of the gymnasial pupils. The objection to the *Realschulen* by some educators was based upon their exclusion of the classics and their stress instead upon modern languages, mathematics, and sciences. They arose in Germany in the eighteenth century, and the English and American academies had much in common with them.

The graduates of the *Realschulen,* Bache said, go to schools of architecture, engineering, and manufactures, and these professional schools maintain as high a standard as the universities. For this reason Bache regarded the *Realschulen* as secondary schools even though many of their pupils did not attend any higher schools but went directly into the business of life. He even included the higher trade schools in the secondary class because they had a standard comparable to that of the classical gymnasium. Bache reported that F. P. G. Guizot, French historian and educator, agreed with him but that Victor Cousin did not. French officials and administrators certainly did not. Perhaps Bache came to his liberal conclusions because he was educated at West Point, not at an old-line classical college. The well-developed American high school came fully within Bache's conception of secondary schools.

The high school had many characteristics which distinguished it from the secondary schools of Europe. Chief of these was its relation to the common schools. The common, normal, and high schools developed together and were intimately related; but the common school was basic to the other two because it furnished them their pupils. The high school was from the first a higher common school, but as time passed it came to a considerable extent under the control of the colleges. Sometimes only those high schools which had the approval of the colleges were considered worthy of the name "high school." It was resistance to this trend, the expansion of its program,

the re-establishment of its earlier alliance with the elementary schools, that
has made it the unique American institution that it has become.

About 1890, which might be taken to divide the early period from the
later, the average enrollment was less than one hundred pupils to a school;
and only three per thousand of the whole people were attending high
schools. The movement to consolidate rural schools gained strength at the
turn of the century, and many rural high schools were established. This
tended to keep down the average enrollment because the rural schools were
often very small. But in the cities attendance rose higher and higher, often
creating the necessity for several schools in a city; and by 1930 not three but
more than forty per thousand of the population were in attendance. This
prodigious growth, more fully indicated in the table given later in this chapter, has been a surprise to professional and lay people alike. It must be due
to strong educational and economic forces.

2. ANOTHER DOOR IS OPENED

Until recent times, in many parts of the civilized world, secondary
schools were for boys alone and for those boys only who belonged to the
wealthy, genteel, professional, or official classes. These privileged children
were separated from the offspring of workingmen and peasants and were
kept separate through the remainder of their schooling and throughout
life. In this way the secondary schools, in the older sense of that term,
shutting the door against the common people, helped to maintain the class
structure of society of which they were an expression.

American society has also had and still has its classes, but these have
been less permanent and less widely separated from one another than those
of older countries. Wealth has been easy to acquire but, without the ancient
law of transmission to the eldest son, hard to hold in the family. The changing economic currents have created many new fortunes and dissipated the
old. And on the other hand, there have been many opportunities to acquire
a competence. Such have been the results of inventions, of the exploitation
of natural resources in land, coal, oil, and the like, and of the competition in
an expanding domestic market. The number of families who could do without the labor of their children increased in the nineteenth century; and
many of these children attended the new high schools.

There were other reasons for the extension of education. Such were
universal suffrage and the spread of the elementary schools. The high
schools prepared teachers, and as the schools were better articulated with the

elementary schools they opened new vistas to the pupils of the upper grades. In many instances, not in all, the press favored the high school. There is an obvious reason why publishers should favor the spread of education. Organized labor had good reasons to favor not only the common but also the high school. The growth of equality between the sexes and the Christian and democratic emphasis upon the dignity of the human being favored universal educational opportunity.

The year 1890, which has been named as the time when the great expansion of the high school began, should not be taken in an absolute sense. The school has always been in transition; but 1890 is near the half-way mark of its entire history, and in the latter half the changes were greater and followed each other more rapidly than in the early years. Take numbers alone. There are ten times as many high schools today as there were then and thirty times as many pupils. The high school door has been opened wide.

The year 1890 curiously synchronizes with the closing of the frontier. The most valuable public lands had been taken up by that time. Farm machinery and farm chemistry were coming into use. The agricultural revolution had begun. Farmers produced a succession of increasing crops with a diminishing labor force. The rural high school soon arrived to prepare rural youth for better farming and better living on the farm; but it also prepared the oversupply of farm youth for careers in the city. In the city, also, jobs for teen-age children were becoming fewer. And an extraordinary rise in high school attendance occurred in the depression of the thirties when there were hardly any jobs. To get children off the streets in that period, legislatures passed more stringent school attendance laws and raised the attendance ages.

From this it might seem that the increased enrollments were due wholly to unusual conditions. But this would be a wrong conclusion. Attendance had been growing ever since 1890 and except during the war period it has continued high. For this there are underlying social reasons, some of which have been mentioned. One of these should be especially remembered. It is the fact that the high school is a continuation of the elementary school. Its main task is to educate more completely the citizens of a free society. It accepts the challenge of Lincoln at Gettysburg to prove that Americans are capable of living as free men, and it hopes to educate all American youth so that they will scorn to become slaves.

We are to review the beginning and early history of the high school in this chapter. To do this it will be necessary to keep in mind that from the beginning the high school was dependent upon the common school. In many cases the high schools grew directly out of common schools; and in all cases high schools could become mature only as the common schools nourished them.

3. High School Origins

The early high schools arose in three or more ways: by establishment according to a definite plan; by the transformation of an academy into a public high school; and by the gradual development of advanced work in an elementary school until a separate organization was formed. The last-named, evolutionary process appears to have been a common and natural development. An ambitious teacher with eager pupils would introduce advanced classes into the program of his school. This frequently occurred even in ungraded schools, in which cases perhaps nothing further happened. In larger schools such an effort might be the beginning of a complete high school. Algebra, natural philosophy, and Latin were favored subjects. They were taught in most academies and many teachers had studied them. Additional subjects could be added until a year of high school work was offered; then two years in a separate room occupying one teacher's whole time, and finally a full course would be given.

Official reports by state superintendents of schools show this process taking place, but in many cases the movement began before the state offices were established. Two superintendents who made such reports were Henry Barnard in Connecticut and Thomas Burrowes in Pennsylvania. Both gave accounts of the teaching of secondary subjects in common schools. The same facts were also noticed in Iowa and California and such conditions must have existed in many other states.

An example of the process in San Bernardino, California, was described by Porter Sargent (1872–1951) in his *The Handbook of Private Schools*. As quoted in the volume for 1951–1952, he wrote as follows:

My only secondary schooling was seven months with six other pupils in a room of an eight-room grammar school in a California town in 1887. It was the first year of a new high school, which was a not too welcome innovation due to the initiative of the principal of the grammar school. He was a rather crude Kansan, with normal school training, but he was alert, lithe, Lincolnesque, with a sparkle in his eye and tremendous energy.

We read Shakespeare aloud, which was all new to him, and he got a tremendous kick out of it. "By golly! That *is* good stuff!" As we went through geometry he kept about two lessons ahead. It was undiscovered territory, so he imparted his interest to us. He knew no science, but he was hungry for it, and with enthusiasm we went through Steele's "Fourteen Weeks in Geology," "in Zoology," in "Chemistry," with a box of apparatus in a little side room. He would stamp his foot in exultation and delight. It was contagious. He was the best kind of a teacher because he was teaching himself and carrying us along on the wave of his enthusiasm.

In Pennsylvania and Ohio special laws were passed to permit particular towns to establish high schools. About 1850 a large number of states were enacting legislation to allow the formation of union districts and union schools or to allow the teaching of advanced branches. Precise information is often lacking but in some of these cases high school work had been started before the permissive legislation was adopted. In Ohio evidence shows that a score of high schools had been started before the Akron law of 1847. Massachusetts took the unusual step (1827) of requiring towns of a certain size to teach secondary school subjects. The law did not mention the high school but its intent was to provide high school instruction including, in the largest towns, college-preparatory work.

The most complete and best-equipped high schools were formed according to plans worked out in advance. The best examples were found in such cities as Boston (1821), Philadelphia (1838), and Chicago (1856). As the movement developed and as the high schools became more standardized, outright establishment became common.

4. English High School of Boston

Boston, as the custom was, distinguished between boys' and girls' education and also between education for boys who were going to college and for those other boys who were not going to college. For boys who were to receive a college education, the city had almost from the beginning maintained a public Latin school. Both the boys who were not going to college and, after 1789, girls received an elementary education in reading and writing schools where the instruction included English grammar, arithmetic, and bookkeeping. Because they were not intended for college and the professions, secondary education was not called for or considered appropriate for them. This was the old idea. In addition to the public schools there were numerous private schools in the city. Some were dame schools teaching reading, for no boy or girl could be admitted to the public reading schools until after he or she had attained the age of seven years and had learned to read, not before. Some of the private schools were high-class schools for girls. Many Boston children also did not attend any school. Educationally speaking we have here four groups of children; those, less than 200 in number, who were in the Latin school, the 2,300 pupils in the public reading and writing schools, the 4,100 attending private schools, and not less than 500 who were not in any school.

This was the situation about 1818 when the story of the first public high school in the United States may be said to begin. At that time after considerable agitation, Boston created a system of public primary schools to teach reading to children under seven. Having thus extended the system downward, the question arose whether it should not be extended upward as well. A committee was formed to consider this question and they reported that boys could finish the elementary school course in five years instead of the seven allowed them. Not only loss of time but also, they said, loss of training in application and industry were the results. And in the second place, they reported that the elementary course did not give a sufficient preparation for their future responsibilities in either mercantile or mechanical pursuits. Many who pay taxes for the support of the existing schools, they said, have to send their sons out of the city to academies in order to prepare them for their lifework. The committee, therefore, recommended "the founding of a seminary to be called the English Classical School."

They proposed a three-year course of study to be normally completed between the ages of twelve and fifteen. Pupils were to be admitted only once a year and upon "strict examination" in reading, writing, English grammar in all its branches, and in arithmetic as far as simple proportion. The teachers were to be university graduates. The course which was proposed included the study of English, mathematics, social studies, and science and was, therefore, a liberal rather than a vocational course. No foreign languages were included and it did not prepare for the colleges of that day. The weight of emphasis fell upon English, especially composition, and mathematics including trigonometry, navigation, and surveying. Both English and mathematics were studied throughout the three years. It is easy to see a resemblance between this course and that of the Philadelphia Academy founded seventy years earlier.

In accordance with this plan the school was opened in 1821. The first name chosen for the school is confusing. It was called the English Classical School. Perhaps this was to convey the idea that instead of the ancient classics this school would stress the great English writers. Actually the school placed far more emphasis upon writing and speaking than upon literature. Perhaps the word was used in the sense of "excellent" and the purpose was to show that the school was of a higher order than the common schools. Whatever the intention the name was soon changed to English High

School. It is claimed that John Pierpont, the secretary of the Boston school committee or board, proposed the new name, perhaps in imitation of the well-known high schools of Scotland. From Boston, as we know, the name was carried to every city, town, and large village and community in America. Few chance ventures in nomenclature have been equally successful.

The first principal was George B. Emerson, who became a noted educator but was in 1821 a very young man for so responsible a place. He personally examined the applicants, admitted 100 boys, and organized the school, not along departmental lines but according to year-classes and rooms as shown in the diagram below. All subjects were required. Each class worked as a unit for a whole year. There were two sections for each of the two lower classes and one section for the third or highest class. Each pupil was assigned to a particular teacher from whom he received all his instruction for that year. The principal had charge of the room for seniors. It was evidently supposed that many entering boys would not remain to complete the course; and the curriculum was so arranged that those who had to leave early would be able to gain as much as possible from their interrupted studies. This was an idea that might have important effects upon curriculum-making.

ENGLISH CLASSICAL SCHOOL PLAN

Principal's Room for senior boys.	
1. Usher's Room for second-year boys. Section I.	2. Usher's Room for second-year boys. Section II.
1. Sub-usher's Room for first-year boys. Section I.	2. Sub-usher's Room for first-year boys. Section II.

Since this is considered to be the first American high school, we shall recapitulate several of the important differences between it and the usual high school of the present time. The Boston school of 1821 was not co-educational and the ages of the boys, twelve to fifteen years, corresponded to the ages of present junior high school pupils. Admission was by examination. The school was organized by grade-rooms like a present-day elementary school. This plan had been in use also in the early colleges. As in the colleges, any given teacher had a fixed group of pupils. Although the school was to prepare the pupils for "mercantile and mechanical employments," the subjects were of the kind now called academic, and not vocational. There was only one curriculum without electives or foreign languages and, therefore, it did not prepare for college. It was a terminal school, not, like the present high school, a middle school between common school and college. It corresponded to the free academy of the time.

Why the committee decided upon a three-year school is not clear; nor do we know why the later high schools adopted a four-year course. The Boston Latin School had a five-year course at that time and European secondary schools longer ones. American boys were apprenticed at fourteen or earlier and it was probably thought that few middle-class boys would remain at school after fifteen. The colleges had adopted a four-year course which normally took in the ages between fourteen and eighteen. And since the more elaborate of the early high schools aspired to become people's colleges, and actually attained a standard equal to the colleges, it is possible that the four-year high school was formed by imitating the colleges. Such conventions once accepted tend to become fixed for long periods. It is certainly not clear that all high school curricula should be just four years or just six years long.

Another development of that time will further illustrate the state of opinion in a city known for its progress in education. In 1826 Boston established a girls' high school under a noted teacher, Ebenezer Bailey. In two years the school became so popular and so many applied for admission that the city refused to vote the funds needed for its maintenance and it had to be closed. The mayor, Josiah Quincy, later to become president of Harvard, was hostile to the school and declared it a failure; but many people did not share this opinion. Not until 1855 did the city again provide secondary education for girls. At that time a "high and normal school" was opened.

5. High Schools in Massachusetts

The industrial revolution, by increasing the number of positions in management and in office work, must have had a great influence upon the rising high school movement. That there was such a movement is shown by the figures. Six towns besides Boston established high schools in the 1820's and about sixteen others in the thirties. By the close of the Civil War there were slightly more than 100 high schools in Massachusetts. The second such school in the state was a high school for girls established by Worcester in 1824. The mill town of Lowell made two innovations. In 1831 that city established (1) a coeducational high school that (2) offered both an English and a classical course. Lowell is an excellent example of the influence of the new social and economic forces. Not all of the 100 high schools of Massachusetts were full-course schools, and almost forty towns which should have had high schools according to the law of 1827 were delinquent.

In the early nineteenth century, New England, and especially Massachusetts, were entering upon a great period of textile manufactures and railroad development. The growth of cities and taxable wealth provided the pupils and the dollars for advanced education and employment for the graduates. The population of Massachusetts increased from slightly over 500,000 in 1820 to 1,250,000 in 1860. The first factories were established along the fall line of the rapid New England streams, but the high-compression steam engine designed by Oliver Evans in 1802 enabled the new industrial capitalists to establish their mills in cities without water power.

By the end of the War of 1812 there were 75,000 industrial workers in the cotton factories of New England and the numbers grew steadily. The war had been so extremely unpopular in that section that secession was advocated and nullification practiced. The "free, sovereign and independent state" of Connecticut refused to honor the nation's call for troops. But in the end the section benefited from the war. By preventing the importation of British goods it gave the American manufacturer a time advantage that the tariff of 1816 was designed to hold for him.

Many of the early high schools taught the subjects of an English education that were supposed to have some use in business. In this group were included bookkeeping, composition, public speaking, drawing, and mathematics including surveying. The aims, topics, and ground to be covered in these and other fields were indicated only by specifying the number of years, or terms, or quarters to be devoted to each or by naming the textbooks to be used. There were no real courses of study. As late as 1890 the president of Harvard University declared that a large proportion of the 230 so-called high schools in Massachusetts were not secondary schools in fact. He certainly meant that they were not effective college-preparatory schools. And in small towns the high school was often a department of an elementary school. In larger centers separate Latin and English high schools were maintained for a time, but eventually the two curricula were almost everywhere united in a single school.

Of the 160 or more high schools in New England by 1865 slightly more than 100 were, as we have seen, in Massachusetts. It was to be a long time before any other state had so many. The movement gradually spread to other sections, but some of the schools in the middle and western states followed an independent course. One of these, the Central High School of Philadelphia, was for many years an outstanding institution known for the breadth of its curriculum and the wealth of its equipment.

6. The Central High School of Philadelphia

Pennsylvania had no long tradition of public education such as characterized the eastern states and for a time adopted no general high school law like that of Massachusetts. For these reasons the state's legal battles over the high school question resemble those of Michigan and other western states. The Pennsylvania litigation has not received the attention given the Kalamazoo case, but because it came early it possesses a particular interest.

By special legislation, Philadelphia was in 1818 made "the first school district" of the state. It will also be recalled that a state system was created by the laws of 1834 and 1836. The right to establish high schools was implicit in these acts, but the school board of Philadelphia felt the need for an explicit grant of power to establish a "central high school" for the city. This was granted in a special act of 1836. The general elementary school law remained permissive until 1849 when public education became mandatory, but by that time all but a small minority of the townships had already established it. This act of 1849 was contested and in 1851 the supreme court of the state passed upon a suit to outlaw the schools. In that decision (*Commonwealth* v. *Hartman*, 17 Pa., 118) the court ruled, as other courts have done, that the state constitution and the school laws fix only the minimum provision which districts must provide and not the maximum which they may establish. But in 1887 Pennsylvania, after all, passed a general high school law.

A windfall from the federal government gave Philadelphia the means to provide its new high school with a building that was luxurious for that time. The windfall was the surplus revenue distribution of 1837. A small part of the state's share was applied on the building of the new Philadelphia Central High School. This building cost $72,000 at a time when city school buildings were constructed for a third of this amount or less. "Imposing in appearance, convenient in its location, and equipped with all the devices that an acute and interested Board could secure, it was one of the prominent buildings of Philadelphia." The most conspicuous of its "devices" was the astronomical observatory with a telescope by a famous German firm, made to specifications prepared by a committee of the American Philosophical Society. This was the fourth observatory to be erected in the United States and perhaps the only one ever erected for the use of a high school. W. H. Wells, superintendent of the schools of Chicago, admitted that the Philadelphia Central High School was without a rival "in the completeness of its appointments and the extent of its course of instruction."

The school was fortunate in securing the help of Alexander Dallas Bache to develop a complete and logical system. Bache, a great-grandson of Franklin was, as stated above, a graduate of West Point. In 1836 he became president of Girard College and spent two years in an examination of European education. This study resulted in his *Report on Education in Europe to the Trustees of Girard College for Orphans*. It is the most extensive of the well-known reports on European education; and a noteworthy feature is the attempt to use the comparative method. Bache's hope that he might find the time to extend the comparisons to all the countries which he had visited was not fulfilled.

Bache was impressed by the thorough work of the Prussian classical and realist schools. The latter prepared some boys for the higher engineering schools and others for immediate entrance upon practical life. Upon his return the Philadelphia board elected him principal of its new high school to serve until the opening of Girard College. At the high school he organized three courses. A "principal course" of four years included studies in English, French, geography, history, mathematics through trigonometry and descriptive geometry, mechanical and natural philosophy, natural history, morals and evidences of Christianity, writing, and drawing. This course resembled that of the German *Realschulen*, but these had a much longer course and included both chemistry and Latin which Bache omitted. His omission of chemistry from a realist course is conspicuous and hard to explain.

In the four-year classical course, Latin and Greek replaced the French and the amount of required mathematics was substantially less than in the principal course. For the remaining subjects the two courses were practically identical. The third course omitted all foreign languages but included English and the other subjects of the courses described above. It was a short course, occupying only two years, and it never became popular. The classical course was taken by those who were preparing for college, but the largest numbers enrolled in the principal or modern language-mathematics-science course.

Admission to the school was by examination as at Boston. The year was divided into semesters and new students were admitted at the beginning and in the middle of each year. The discipline was based upon the West Point system with its demerit marks. Included in the first graduating class (1842) there was one, L. Hall Grandgent, who was to be for many years a teacher in the English High School of Boston.

The new school with its fine building and high standards pleased many Philadelphians; but there were also dissenting voices. The period beginning about 1840 formed a critical time in education when it was difficult to hold the gains of the previous decade. The awakening had aroused the enemies as well as the friends of public education. Of this we have already seen evidence in Ohio and Massachusetts. By 1842 Philadelphia had spent her share of the surplus revenue distribution, the country had not entirely recovered from the crisis of 1837, and there was mounting opposition to the school from some of the taxpayers. Some objected to the nature of the courses. They wanted the school to teach applied chemistry, surveying, bookkeeping and other "practical" courses. Others complained that the school in the center of the city was inaccessible from the outlying sections. Apparently no one objected to the entrance examinations or the exclusion of girls. Philadelphia continued for a century to build separate high schools for boys and for girls as did many other eastern cities.

7. OTHER PENNSYLVANIA HIGH SCHOOLS

Public high schools began to appear in Pennsylvania in the middle thirties and there is evidence that the developments in New England had been observed. The name was, however, sometimes applied to private institutions such as the High School of the Franklin Institute, which was carried on in Philadelphia from about 1824. Priority among the public high schools of the state would not be easy to establish. Each of the three cities, Honesdale, Carlisle, and Norristown, claims to have had a high school by 1836. More complete institutions, it seems, were organized within a few years of that date by Harrisburg, Lancaster, and York. In large towns it was the custom, as in New England, to set up separate schools for boys and for girls.

There were many cases of academies in both regions that deeded their property to the public school board. Many Pennsylvania academies served a whole county and had received state aid upon the condition of admitting all the eligible children of the county. Pennsylvania law provided that a local high school which accepted an academy's property must also assume its educational obligations, a requirement that must have prompted many school trustees to look into the mouth of any such gift horse that was offered to it. There were cases in which the law placed an excessive financial burden upon local districts.

There were over 100 high schools in the state by the end of the century, most of them in larger towns. But by that time the day of the rural township and centralized high school was dawning. A law of 1901 authorized the creation of township and union high schools. Such schools had already been organized by friendly agreement. But there are even now rural and mountain sections in Pennsylvania where neither the law nor public sentiment has been effective in providing high school accommodations.

8. AN EARLY CONNECTICUT HIGH SCHOOL

Middletown in the south-central part of Connecticut was a town of about 3,500 people in 1840 when its high school was started. The schools of the town were still ungraded. Henry Barnard, recently appointed chief state school official, had declared in 1838 that there were hardly any graded schools in the whole state. Ambitious teachers introduced advanced subjects to the detriment of the younger pupils. Barnard urged the towns to grade their schools and to found high schools for pupils who wanted to study algebra, physics, or Latin. This would allow the teacher in the lower school to give proper attention to reading, writing, and spelling.

A special law of 1839 gave Middletown permission to grade her schools. A high school was voted but it was at first more elementary than high. There was no entrance examination, and all of the 252 children in the schools of the city who were between the ages of nine and sixteen were assigned to the high school. The census of 1840 shows that there were about 500 children between these two ages. This indicates that half of the children above the age of nine years were in private schools, at work, or on the street. Middletown was not unique in this respect.

The new high school was conducted in a church basement. There was a department for boys and another for girls. The school charged a fee of four dollars a year. It became free in 1861, twenty-one years after the founding. There was no fixed curriculum at first but the school aimed to prepare some pupils for college and others for practical life. In a period of about ten years, three curricula were organized, an English, a classical, and a mathematical curriculum. Later a normal curriculum was added, with practice teaching, professional subjects, and reviews of the common school branches. For lack of sufficient staff, some use was made of pupil-monitors.

Courses varied from one year to five years but the school eventually adopted the standard four-year course. Evidently this small-town school without adequate resources had to experiment and to some extent to improvise its organization, curriculum, and methods. It illustrates unusually well the experimental and tentative nature of the first high schools. One certain fact about the high school is this, that it is largely a native growth.

9. HIGH SCHOOLS IN THE MIDDLE WEST

In the West as in the East the high school was at first a city institution that was instituted when the schools were graded. In Ohio, as we have seen, a number of high schools were opened before 1850. Both Cleveland and Columbus began high school work about 1846. The Cleveland school was notable for early work in the teaching of science. The first high school in Columbus was opened in a church basement by Dr. Asa D. Lord, who had been for a decade the head of a private normal school at Kirtland, Ohio, called the Western Reserve Teachers' Seminary. Meanwhile, he had become prominent in school affairs in the state and was elected the first superintendent of the Columbus city schools. The establishment of the high school followed almost at once. We now move to Illinois.

The first public elementary school in Chicago was opened in 1834, and for ten years the schools were conducted in rented quarters. In 1844 the city built its first schoolhouse and in 1854 appointed its first superintendent. Meanwhile, a period of astonishing growth had begun. The city which in 1840 had less than 5,000 people had well over 100,000 by 1860. A public high school in a "spacious and elegant" building was established in 1856 under William Harvey Wells, who came from the principalship of a Massachusetts normal school to serve as Chicago's superintendent of schools.

This first high school of the city may have been in part modeled upon the Central High School of Philadelphia. The obvious differences were that the Chicago school was coeducational and offered a normal course. There were three courses in the beginning, classical, English, and normal. Having been engaged in teacher preparation with Henry Barnard and at the Westfield Normal School in Massachusetts, Superintendent Wells placed great emphasis upon professional training including in-service work. In this he was following a current trend of that period. Many city high schools offered a normal course.

Admission to the high school was by examination; and of almost 400 applicants during the first year only 176 passed and were admitted. The school offered them high academic fare in languages, mathematics, and the sciences. There were no laboratories before 1874. But in most respects and for its time this was a well-equipped school.

A collection has been published of the programs offered at different times between 1856 and 1906 by some of the high schools of Iowa. These show some variations from school to school and some changes from time to time during that half-century, but the outstanding facts are that the offerings were generally similar and the changes slight. From time to time more languages, sciences, mathematical branches, and additional kinds of history were offered; but there was no change of type. Like the country academies, they devoted a large part of their energies to reviews of the common branches. One school in 1856 taught reading, spelling, mental and written arithmetic, geography, and physiology. Several of the early Iowa high schools watered their curricula in this way but not always to the same extent. And Iowa was not unique in this respect. Many New England high schools and Ohio high schools in the same period followed the same practice.

Material facilities and teaching aids were also wanting. Textbooks were the only tools. Many of the early schools were begun in rented rooms, church basements, or public halls. The first high school in Burlington occupied a church building for ten years. The one in Dubuque was opened in 1856, closed because of financial distress in 1860, and again opened in a rented room in 1866. These pioneer conditions have long since been overcome in the rich and populous states; but there still are many small and poorly equipped high schools in isolated rural sections of the country.

As the high schools in Iowa became larger, it became possible to offer two or more parallel curricula and to allow some electives. But in this great agricultural state there was not a trace of agricultural instruction in the forty selected curricula which are exhibited in Aurner's history. The preparation of teachers was, however, stressed. The historian of the Iowa schools asserted that in the beginning the preparation of teachers for the common schools was the primary purpose of the high schools. As late as 1900 two-fifths of the Iowa high schools were preparing teachers.

This development was perhaps general, and it certainly was not peculiar to Iowa. In Cincinnati educational subjects were included in a regular high school course. In Chicago, it has been indicated, the high school offered a normal curriculum. In Boston a "high and normal" school for girls was established soon after the middle of the century. The Central High School of Philadelphia in 1896 extended its "course in Pedagogy" to two years and made it a regular department of the school. This became a post-high school department, called the School of Pedagogy, for young men who were preparing themselves for service in the city schools. While the state normal schools prepared rural teachers, many cities prepared their own staffs in the local high schools.

10. SECONDARY EDUCATION IN THE SOUTH

Education in the South may be interpreted in its own terms by comparing its present condition and recent past with the situation which existed at some earlier time such as 1870 or 1900. In such a study we should consider also the resources that were at different times available to promote education and what hostilities and perversities worked against it. Studied and judged in this way, the progress has been great, especially during the last half-century. But it is customary to compare the South with more highly industrialized and more densely populated sections. This also is allowable if the student will keep in mind the differences between the sections, differences which are never merely economic but also social and which may cause the people of one region to desire educational outcomes quite different from those approved elsewhere.

The latter of these two methods will yield almost a complete contrast with northern conditions if we consider public high schools in the South before 1900 as the base of the comparison. There were few high schools in the section at that time and some of these were incomplete. The upper social class preferred the private school; the lower did not expect secondary schooling for their children. At a much earlier period the North had been of the same mind. Since then the urban high school had spread and grown in the North; but in 1900 neither section had many rural high schools.

The South still had many private schools and academies where boys prepared for college and girls finished their school education. In this assortment of private schools one finds a main reason for the slow development of the public high school. There were enough schools of several kinds to satisfy the existing demand for secondary education and to block any decided efforts under the hard economic conditions to foster new public high schools. This balance between supply and demand was broken by a new force, the campaigns of the Southern Education Board, which began to raise the demand far above the available means of satisfying it.

The South was not entirely without public secondary schools before the twentieth century, although some states were almost in that condition. In 1887 Tennessee had only four public high schools that were recognized as competent to prepare students for the state university. The complementary fact is that the state at that time had enough private schools to warrant the closing of the university's preparatory department. Twenty years later in 1906 the state of Virginia had about seventy incomplete high schools but only ten free public high schools that offered four years of work. In that year (1906) the state university had only eight students who had been prepared at these ten schools. This may be a comment on the policy of the University of Virginia at that time as well as a reflection upon the standards of the high schools. Their graduates may have preferred to attend other colleges. About the same time there were only seven accredited high schools in Georgia; and in South Carolina two and one-half times as many pupils prepared for college in private as in public schools. About 1900 Alabama had a considerable number of high schools but many must have been incomplete schools.

In the first decade of the new century the rapid expansion of the high schools in the South began. Several of the state universities were becoming interested in the public high schools as a source of students, especially of those who could not afford to attend private schools. Administrators realized that more students would require bigger budgets but also that larger enrollments would help to persuade the legislatures to increase their appropriations. While Illinois and other northern agricultural states had thousands of boys and girls preparing for college, those in Georgia or Alabama could be counted in hundreds. The difference lay in part in the greater encouragement given the free public high schools in the northern states. In those states the public elementary and secondary schools and the state university, land-grant colleges, and teachers' colleges formed a single system, a highway from the lowest grade to the professional school.

In the South, Georgia led out. In 1904 the University of Georgia appointed a professor of secondary education and assigned to him the task of encouraging the establishment of high schools with local support, aiding them to become efficient preparatory schools, and relating them to the schools below and the university above. By a law of 1906 Georgia provided for agricultural high schools and South Carolina and Virginia soon passed similar laws. Agricultural high schools had been created in Alabama even earlier but they did not become effective vocational schools until the early years of the present century. Boys' and girls' clubs began in the South in the same decade and spread rapidly. The Smith-Hughes Act and the organization of the "Future Farmers of America" began to put new life and spirit into the teaching of vocational agriculture in all parts of the country, and in the South they have been particularly effective. Finally, the consolidation movement has not only multiplied the rural high schools but has promoted better rural elementary schools and helped to secure better-prepared teachers for rural schools of every grade. The average term of the rural schools began to lengthen with the campaigns of the Southern Education Board. The General Education Board aided with funds and skilled advisers in the fight against poor schools, poor farming, and poor health among rural people.

While a main aim of the early high schools in the South and North alike was to prepare the pupils for college, the Southern schools developed farm-life and rural vocation and home-making curricula very early. The work of Seaman A. Knapp was first accepted in the South and marked progress was made in adapting the high school to the practical needs of the people. The land-grant colleges and experiment stations were making themselves felt. Appropriations were made by state legislatures for state normal schools and for departments of education in the state colleges and state universities. In all this the high school was a key institution. If this summary seems to resemble the account of the advances made in the North at an earlier time, the simplest explanation is that the educational awakening had now come to the South.

11. The Worth of the High School

The Kalamazoo case, already mentioned, was a friendly suit at law, brought to determine whether the city had the legal right to establish a high school, to employ a superintendent of schools, and to collect taxes to support these services. Other such suits were brought in other states and, like this one, were carried up to the state supreme courts for determination. The Kalamazoo case has become historic, perhaps chiefly because of the eloquence of the decision pronounced in 1874 by Chief Justice Thomas M. Cooley. The decision (30 Mich. 69) agreed with that in Pennsylvania in 1851 and in every other state where the matter has come up. It was to the effect that the legislators in establishing a system of public or common schools did not set any limit to the number of years that were to be embraced by it or restrict the offices and officers that might be necessary to its proper functioning. But Cooley went into an account of the history of public education and argued that the legislature in establishing the common schools and a state university must have intended thereby to create a complete system of schools, hence the necessity for a high school to complete the path to the university. This argument has always had a special appeal for educational historians. In Illinois and at least seven other states, similar cases were decided in the same way; but perhaps in none of them by an equally eloquent jurist.

It was doubtless no accident that the Kalamazoo litigation occurred in a time of financial scandals and stringency. Few people bothered about the high school as long as it was small and confined to opulent cities, and for a long time it was, as stated before, mainly a city school. Poor roads and the thin population long tended to keep it out of the rural sections. Missouri, the twenty-fourth state, and the first American high school were born in the same year, 1821. Half of the United States was Indian country. Entrance examinations, academic studies, and high standards kept many children away from the schools that existed. The district system impeded the establishment of the high school. It was true as charged that all the people paid for the public secondary schooling of a few. Was the high school worth what it cost; and who received the benefits it conferred? This question is often asked in times of business recession when dollars are scarce. The 1890's, just when pupils began to flock to the schools, were such a time. High school attendance doubled during that decade, and staffs had to be increased at a time when boards of education were in financial straits. Several large city boards dismissed their principals, and proposed a shorter school year and the dropping of the more expensive studies. The old charges were renewed: the high school is not necessary, is undemocratic, and, most important, is too expensive. Europe began to say that the American public could not continue to meet the mounting costs of its broadening program of secondary education.

The 1930's also, the period of the great depression, were such a time. Between 1910 and 1930 the high school enrollment doubled and then doubled again. And in the course of the depression it increased by another 50 per cent. The irony of the situation lay in the fact that financially the schools became most burdensome in the slack times when they were most needed. At such times the young people who cannot find work remain in school in addition to those who would normally be there.

In the history books, the great depression has overshadowed the crises of the nineties. But in the nineties, Coxey's tattered army of the unemployed marched on Washington and Bryan campaigned for free silver. The high school was attacked as it had been in the populist eighties. Again it was affirmed that the high school had been no part of the original plan for public education and this in spite of the fact that there had been no original plan. The high school was becoming expensive because it was reaching larger numbers of pupils; but even then it was argued that the public should not be asked to pay for a school that reached only a minority. In some cities the newspaper press aided in protecting the schools from unjustified retrenchment.

TOTAL PUBLIC AND NONPUBLIC SECONDARY SCHOOL ENROLLMENT

Year	Enrollment Grades 9–12 and Postgraduate	Population 14–17 Years of Age	Number Enrolled per 100 of Population 14–17 Years of Age
1889–1890	359,949	5,354,653	6.7
1899–1900	699,403	6,152,231	11.4
1909–1910	1,115,398	7,220,298	15.4
1919–1920	2,500,176	7,735,841	32.3
1929–1930	4,804,255	9,341,221	51.4
1939–1940	7,123,009	9,720,419	73.3
1941–1942	6,933,265	9,547,713	72.6
1943–1944	6,030,617	9,280,273	65.0
1945–1946	6,237,133	8,903,078	70.1
1947–1948	6,305,168	8,567,971	73.6
1949–1950	6,427,042	8,404,757	76.5

From the *Biennial Survey of Education in the United States, 1948–1950*, by the United States Office of Education, Table 16, page 19.

It was in this period that the state of Massachusetts raised its high school requirements. Dissatisfaction with this policy led Frank A. Hill, the secretary of the state board, to express (1898) his conviction that the high school returned to the public all that it cost. The state had in 1891 taken certain important legal steps. A new law of that year made every high school tuition-free to the children of its town; it required every town which did not have a high school to pay the tuition of any of its children attending the high school of another town; and it abolished the category of second-class or incomplete high schools. Another law passed in 1896 made graduation from high school or its equivalent a condition for admission to a state normal school. These laws placed the high schools of Massachusetts in a more advanced position than they had occupied under the law of 1827.

Secretary Hill stressed the stimulation which a high school gives to the elementary school and its pupils. By the mere presence of the advanced school the elementary pupils, he said, gain a more elevated conception of education and begin to work toward these higher ideals. The high school in 1896 became a factor in the preparation of elementary teachers. Until that time they came to the professional school with only an elementary school preparation, knowing only what the schools in which they were to teach had taught them. The secretary was certain that the elementary schools would benefit from the advanced preparation and the pupils would profit. Henry Barnard had expressed the same view.

To those who attended the high school it offered a choice of studies. Thereby, Hill pointed out, each pupil was able to gain a better understanding of his own capacities as well as a somewhat specialized training. He declared that the high school was offering a better preparation for life than ever before. And yet he proposed further improvement. He said the worth of the high school could be increased by closing the gap between it and the elementary school. Better preparation for life and greater continuity between the primary and secondary stages of that preparation were to become leading themes in the years which followed. Secretary Hill had skilfully selected two critical problems to bring before the people.

Better preparation for the real business of living was to be furthered by the new subjects that were being introduced. Manual training was brought into view by the Russian exhibit at the Centennial Exposition of 1876 in Philadelphia; and manual training high schools were opened in Baltimore (1883) and in a hundred cities by 1900. An agricultural high school was opened in connection with the University of Minnesota in 1888. Others were established in the North but they spread much faster in the Southern states. Drawing and other plastic arts, music, and home-making courses were added in many places. High school commercial courses had to meet the severe competition of the private business colleges, which were often better equipped and had the motive of large profits to urge them forward. It was in the period after the Civil War when the Bryant and Stratton chain of business colleges attempted to gain a monopoly of commercial education. The war with Spain, the resulting introduction of Spanish into the high school ostensibly to prepare for business with Latin America, and the introduction of business administration departments into universities, all furthered the development of commercial courses in high schools. By 1900 the public high school was gaining on the private business schools. All these are examples of the effort to develop what may be considered better preparation for expanding occupations. These changes and the junior high school, which was intended to provide the second of the proposed improvements, will be treated in Chapter XV.

12. STANDARD HIGH SCHOOLS

No other country has so many secondary schools as the United States. The comparison, if it is to be valid, must take into account that European schools are standardized by officials who enforce national laws. In the United States the state requirements have been lenient and many incomplete and substandard high schools have been established. Such schools may give a wide variety of courses, many of them elementary and vocational, in commerce, agriculture, industrial skills, music, fine and practical arts. These may be of real value to the children of a community, but the colleges of the later nineteenth and early twentieth centuries refused to give entrance credit for them.

In most communities some of the young people want to prepare for college, and the local high school is expected to offer the required courses. This the substandard high school was often unable to do. In these circumstances a widespread demand for standard high schools arose, schools whose graduates would be accepted by the colleges without examination or who, if examinations were required, would be prepared to pass them with creditable marks. People wanted an answer to the question: What is a standard high school? That answer can be found only in the history of the school.

Colleges have tried to answer this question by emphasizing the schools' preparatory functions. Now college requirements have always weighed more heavily upon the small high schools which could offer only a few courses and perhaps only one curriculum. Small schools were compelled by public sentiment to make provision for college entrance work and could do little more. As a result the small school has often been prevented from serving the youth of the village community. It had to prepare a few boys and girls for college, even though in consequence many were denied a high school education.

One of the early ways in which colleges determined the real meaning of the term "high school" was that of the accrediting system. The University of Michigan in 1871 began the practice of sending committees of professors to visit high schools, and the graduates of those which they approved were then admitted to the university without examination. Other universities began to accept the accreditation of state education departments. This plan quickly spread because it lifted the entrance examination burden from the backs of the faculties, and the college was not risking very much because the students could be received on probation. Successful high schools considered it an honor to have their names on the list of accredited schools. At the same time accreditation was usually recognized only within a given state and it did not remove the necessity of preparing pupils in the particular studies required by the colleges of their choice. It was declared in the *School Review* for October, 1898, that a tabulation of the entrance requirements of almost 500 colleges showed that the demands of no two were identical.

An effort to promote greater uniformity and to improve secondary education in general was made by the regional standardizing associations. These are voluntary unions of colleges and secondary schools holding meetings for the consideration of common problems and making rules for the guidance of their member institutions. The New England Association was founded in 1885, that of the Middle States and Maryland in 1892, and others as follows: North Central, 1894; Southern states, 1895; Northwest, 1918; and West, 1930. Schools which upon inspection met the standards of their own regional associations were accredited and the colleges of the association accepted their graduates. The standards vary from region to region and there is no complete cooperation between the associations. Further, by far the larger proportion of high schools in the country are not accredited by an association.

A third way of determing the effectiveness of the high schools in preparing pupils for college was developed by the College Entrance Examination Board founded in 1899 by the Middle States Association. A suggestion of this kind had been made by George B. Emerson in 1842 and more recently by President Barnard of Columbia University and by others. The board soon became an independent organization; and it has long conducted subject examinations for college admission in all parts of the United States and in foreign countries. Pupils from both public and independent secondary schools take the examinations.

The National Education Association also took an interest in the relations of the secondary schools to the colleges and in 1892 appointed the Committee of Ten with President Charles William Eliot of Harvard as chairman. Since the committee and its subcommittees were heavily staffed with college presidents and professors, private school teachers, and no women, it is surprising to find that they concluded that it is not the chief business of secondary schools to prepare pupils for college, but to prepare them for life whether they go or do not go to college. They agreed to this because they believed in formal discipline and the general transfer of training. They believed that the same subjects taught in the same way provide the best preparation for both college and life. It is not surprising, therefore, that these academic people stressed academic subjects. The report was too narrow in its outlook for some members of the committee, and President James H. Baker of the University of Colorado wrote a dissenting minority report. The main report received great acclaim and was the subject of much discussion, but it seems to have had little practical effect. The schools continued to expand their programs, increase their electives, and make very decided differences in their treatment of college and non-college youth.

13. The Extended Secondary School

A movement to reorganize large areas of the educational system gave a new answer to the question about the nature of the secondary school. The movement to standardize the high school was a step in this reorganization and the next one was the effort to define the relations between the elementary, secondary, and higher schools and, as one might say, to tighten the joints between them. The desire to produce this closer articulation was one of the reasons for the junior high school and the junior college.

A few illustrations will indicate what the problem was. In earlier times many academies were doing elementary work, many elementary schools had several advanced pupils studying algebra, geology, or Latin. Many high schools were not capable of preparing pupils for college or for a vocation, nor even of providing a good English education; and others were equal to the colleges of that day. At the same time some colleges were academies or high schools in all but name, while others maintained high standards. Such conditions existed as late as 1900 and even later.

When the cities had developed a standard elementary school, when the associations of secondary schools and colleges had defined the nature of the high school, and when the Association of American Universities after 1900 had produced a list of approved colleges, the stakes were set. It could no longer be said that the basic terms of American education were undefined. The meaning of the words "secondary school" and "secondary education" was becoming clearer.

The definitions brought into sharp relief the differences between the education of children, of youth, and of mature men and women. Evidently in a sequence of three schools the gaps would appear at the bottom and the top of the second member. A bridge to make the transition easier was needed between the elementary school and the high school. The junior high school was created for this purpose. By that time, in 1910 or 1920, it had come to be believed that as many children as possible should attend the high school, hence the need for the bridge.

At the upper limit of the high school, a different solution was proposed. It was believed that many high school graduates should not attempt a four-year college course but would benefit from two years of college work. At that point, therefore, a spur was needed to prepare young people for an occupation or to complete two further years of liberal studies. This indicated the need of a junior college.

Many leaders in universities considered the end of the sophomore year as the point of greatest difference in advanced work. These regarded the first two years of college as secondary school work. Only men and women who were able to proceed under their own power, without close supervision, should on this view be encouraged to proceed into the upper division of the college. The junior college, like the junior high school, would be a bridge; and like the junior high school, it would be a secondary education unit. Secondary education would in this case continue from the ages of twelve to twenty years. In connection with a study of "late pattern high schools" in Chapter XV, we shall return to the junior high school and junior college movements.

The high school is a secondary school but it is also, in contrast with European secondary schools, a common school, not the school of any privileged classes. The history of the high school may be treated in two periods, with the year 1890 as the dividing point. In the earlier period those schools which had the means to do so tended to overstress college-preparatory work or themselves tried to become people's colleges.

The high school has been preserved as a common school because the great middle class supports it and there is no sufficiently powerful and permanent class of wealth and privilege to pre-empt it. The school, Antaeus-like, has renewed its strength by contact with the common people. Early high schools were often outgrowths of the common schools, or were academies made over, or in a few striking cases were deliberately planned. In 1827 Massachusetts passed a law compelling certain towns to teach secondary subjects and by 1850 many states had enacted laws that could be applied in favor of high school establishment.

A study of the formation of several of the early high schools illustrates the above statements and reveals the great diversity of standards and means. Two purposes were recognized almost everywhere, preparation for college and for life; and to these, a third, preparation for teaching, was included. The study of cases also shows that early high schools were improvised and that standardization came about slowly and is even now incomplete. The urban and industrial revolution had a powerful effect upon the movement and upon the nature of the schools. Later high schools have been modeled upon the earlier ones.

A new period opened about 1890 or earlier. The program of studies began to expand and the old academic barriers were broken and so were all enrollment records. Each of these is both cause and effect. Vocational education became common, but it is curious that in an agricultural nation, agriculture was late in making its appearance.

The high school had to meet great opposition; and it conquered its enemies by meeting the needs of their children. This may be called the Great Change. Opposition still flares up now and then especially in times of financial stringency.

High school standardization was attempted by the colleges in the 1870's. Later the colleges and secondary schools combined to form regional standards and these have had some success, but it is still true that only a minority of the high schools are able to meet the standards. Committees of the National Education Association tried to define the purpose and function of the high school. The Commission on the Reorganization of Secondary Education (1918) had great influence. But the actual reorganization of secondary educational institutions into the junior and senior high schools and the junior college has had the greatest effect in redefining secondary education in those parts of the country where these institutions have been successfully introduced. The total effect has not been to make secondary education more uniform. Rather it has accentuated the differences which have been from the beginning inherent in the process of free development.

QUESTIONS

1. Why did early secondary education have greater prestige than elementary or common school education? Was this partly or entirely justified?

2. What evidence goes to show that the formation of the high school was the unforced and unpremeditated expression of the common people's desires?

3. Why did the high school movement begin with apparent suddenness in the second decade of the nineteenth century? Will the same factors explain the even greater burst of speed after 1890?

4. Why did academic subjects carry greater prestige than vocational ones? Compare the older emphasis upon Latin, Greek, and mathematics with the current demand for more general and humanistic education?

5. Why did (and do) girls attend high schools in such large numbers? Compare the numbers of boys and girls in attendance and the numbers of each sex graduating in some high schools that you know.

6. People were long opposed to public education, to compulsory attendance, to high schools? Why has this opposition declined? Because of custom, propaganda, experience and conviction, or other reasons?

7. Why would it be fortunate (or unfortunate) if high schools were rigidly standardized by regional associations (or by the state) and after some years all nonstandard schools closed?

8. Why would you favor (or oppose) the extension of the public junior college?

9. What is a high school?

BOOKS AND PAPERS

The history of the high school has yet to be written. Brown's *Making of Our Middle Schools* did not bring the story down to the date of its publication, fifty years ago. Kandel wrote on a vast subject, the *History of Secondary Education,* and could devote only a hundred pages to that of the high school. There are some good monographs and state histories by Gifford, Grizzell, Hertzler, Inglis, and Mulhern. Barnard's *American Journal of Education,* histories of education in particular states, histories of individual high schools, doctor's dissertations, and articles in magazines such as the *School Review* contain material that should be assembled and critically treated. The bibliography of Chapter X contains two further references on high schools.

Aurner, C. R., *History of Education in Iowa,* Iowa City, 1920.

Boynton, F. D., "High School Attendance," *School Review,* September, 1922.

Briggs, Thomas H., *Junior High School,* Boston, 1920; *Curriculum Problems,* New York, 1926; *The Great Investment,* Cambridge, Massachusetts, 1930.

Broome, E. C., *Historical and Critical Discussion of College Admission Requirements,* New York, 1902.

Brown, E. E., *Making of Our Middle Schools,* New York, 1902.

Burrell, B. Jeannette, and R. H. Eckelberry, "The American High School Question before the Courts in the Post-Civil War Period," *School Review,* April and May, 1934; "The Free Public High School in the Post-Civil War Period," *School Review,* October and November, 1934, with bibliography for each topic.

Cornog, William H., *School of the Republic, 1893–1943, A Half Century of the Central High School of Philadelphia,* Philadelphia, 1952.

Dexter, E. G., "Ten Years Influence of the Report of the Committee of Ten," *School Review,* April, 1906.

Editorial, "The College Entrance Examination Board," *School Review,* November, 1902, an account of the first two years of the board.

Edmonds, F. S., *History of the Central High School of Philadelphia,* Philadelphia, 1902.

Gifford, W. J., *Historical Development of the New York State High School System,* Albany, 1922.

Griffin, O. B., *Evolution of the Connecticut State School System with Special*

Reference to the High School, New York, Teachers College, Columbia University, 1928.

Grizzell, E. D., *Origin and Development of the High School in New England before 1865,* New York, 1923.

Hertzler, Silas, *Rise of the Public High School in Connecticut,* Baltimore, 1930.

Hill, Frank A., "How Far the High School a Just Charge upon the Public Treasury," *School Review,* December, 1898.

Inglis, Alexander, *Rise of the High School in Massachusetts,* New York, Teachers College, Columbia University, 1911.

Kandel, I. L., *History of Secondary Education, A Study in the Development of Liberal Education,* Boston, 1930.

Mulhern, James, *History of Secondary Education in Pennsylvania,* Philadelphia, 1933.

Sargent, Porter, Editor, *A Handbook of Private Schools, an Annual Survey,* Boston, 1942, has the passage quoted, by permission of Mr. F. Porter Sargent, in Section 3 above, at p. 82 f. The number issued in 1952 has a portrait and other biographical material on the founder and editor.

[Scheffy, C. C.], *One Hundred Years of the English High School of Boston,* Boston, 1924.

Spaulding, F. T., and Others, *Reorganization of Secondary Education,* Washington, U. S. Government Printing Office, being Monograph No. 5 of the National Survey of Secondary Education, and Bureau of Education Bulletin, 1932, No. 17.

Stout, J. E., *High School Curricula in the North Central States, 1860–1918,* University of Chicago Press, 1921.

Stuart, Milo H., *Organization of a Comprehensive High School,* New York, 1926.

Chapter IX

THE OLD AND THE
NEW SOUTH

THE new government of the United States came into operation in 1789 under a Constitution based upon compromise. There was reasonable doubt about the nature of the Union. Was it now indissoluble or was it still a federation of states as it had been under the Articles of Confederation? Able men disagreed. During the intersectional struggle later, compromise also followed compromise until by 1860 the issue had acquired so keen an edge that further union seemed impossible to many.

Dissension over the nature of the government had arisen early. Even among the founders there was speculation about the permanence of the Union. Some of their successors from time to time suggested, proposed, or defended the idea of secession. There were the Virginia and Kentucky Resolutions, the Hartford Convention, nullification in South Carolina, and the agitation of radical abolitionists who denounced the union of free and slave states with all the violence that language can convey.

None of these attacks resulted in a decisive test, but Calhoun taught that a sovereign state, such as he conceived South Carolina to be, had the right to forbid the enforcement of federal law within its territory. By threat and bargain, Jackson stilled the controversy of 1832. A group of resolute Southern states at that time or later might have broken up the Union. By 1861 the North had become too strong. Her population was four times that of the white people of the South, her industry, railroads, and shipyards were too fully developed, and Lincoln was president. The preservation of the Union was the principle to which Lincoln was most completely dedicated.

The South was not without advantages. She was the invaded section and her people were fighting for their own institutions, their way of life, and their homes. She had the inner lines of movement. Her armies were well led and many of her soldiers were accustomed to the use of horse and gun. Each of the combatants underestimated the resources and the determination of the other. The Northern soldiers had more schooling than the Southern but it was of a sort not directly useful in war. We no longer believe that Waterloo was won on the playing fields of Eton or that the schoolmaster decided the Franco-Prussian War in 1870. Neither section had much formal training in engineering except that of the military schools.

By 1863 it seemed to many observers, foreign and American, that the question how long the Union would last was about to be answered; but in the middle of that year, Gettysburg and Vicksburg showed that the question was to remain open. The war ended in 1865 and after a harsh "reconstruction" the South first acquiesced in the result and then after bitter years learned to welcome the reunion. Rarely after such a war have the opposing sides, even after fifty years, been able to unite in applauding the outcome. Educational philanthropy, extended by the North, was at least of some help in the achievement of this result.

Before the war, Southern senators and congressmen generally opposed federal activity in education. The states' rights argument delayed the creation of the land-grant colleges, and the Morrill Act was adopted in 1862 while the South was not represented in Congress. The Federal Department of Agriculture was voted in the same year. The Bureau for Refugees, Freedmen, and Abandoned Lands was created in 1865. Two years later the United States Department, later Bureau, of Education was formed. The Hoar Bill, a punitive measure intended to impose a federally controlled system of education upon the South, was introduced in 1870 but fortunately it did not pass. The conciliatory Blair Bill to provide federal funds for education to be carried out by the states was also lost but it is significant that many Southerners favored it. Most of such measures, including the two just mentioned, are treated later in this or in the following chapter. The list will serve to suggest the trend which came with the war and reconstruction. Even education became somewhat more national in outlook.

As the country was recovering from the war, the vast plains, mountains, and valleys of the great West called for settlers and the enterprising young men responded. Cities and towns grew up and schools were needed. The war had increased the proportion of young women in the teaching force and this was especially true in the towns. Salaries were higher in the West and there teaching also acquired a distinct glamor. The heroine of more than one Western novel and picture was a young schoolmistress who could choose her man in that man's country.

In the North the graded school, high school, normal school, and college became widely distributed and firmly established. Public education far outdistanced the private school. Enrollments and attendance in the primary schools were stabilized by the attendance laws. City systems developed, with superintendents, increased support, trained teachers, and regular courses of study. The country was in the process of making education universal in fact.

Public education was much less fully developed in the South than in the most advanced states of the North. Some Southern states which had paper systems had few schools, especially in the country districts; and the South was largely rural. The war and the waste and corruption of the reconstruction governments further depleted the material and moral resources of the people. And yet new beginnings were made, laws passed, and public school systems established. There was a great lack of means and the Negro schools did not receive their proportionate share of the funds. Help was given by the Peabody donation and other gifts, but full educational awakening did not come to the South until the end of the century.

1. Opinions and Arguments

Educational opinion in the South resembled that held farther north at an earlier time. What was believed in New York or New Jersey in 1790 was still affirmed in many parts of the South in 1860. In both places and times education was considered a valuable attainment for those who could get it; but like health or fortune its acquisition was a personal and private matter. This was not mere theory. The sparsity of the population, slavery and the unproductiveness of slave labor, the depletion of the soil, the poverty of the small farmers, and the destitution of the poor whites formed a condition in which public education could not thrive. Even the planters were not as prosperous as they seemed. In the cities free schools were possible and some cities were actually engaged in promoting public schools.

There was great opposition to the principle of taxation for public education, and other means of support were diligently sought. Such means were the state school funds, land grants, and the surplus revenue distribution. Special imposts were levied on institutions that were unpopular with many people. Banks and theaters often came within this class, and therefore bank taxes and licenses to operate theaters were approved. Lotteries were a frequent source, as they had been in all parts of the country in earlier times. The use of such sources shows that the people's representatives hesitated or refused to vote a school tax.

Behind the financial difficulty there was the deeper reason that many, poor as well as rich, were opposed to universal public education. In this respect, also, the South held the views that had been held in the North only one or two generations earlier when many of the "best people" preferred and supported private schools. Some families wished to select their school instead of having it provided for them. Many preferred a church school to a secular or a religiously neutral one. Many of the planters did not want their children to associate with those whom they considered trash. Many of the upper classes did not see why the poor should have an education and many of the poor agreed with them. Those in the mountains and the back-woods who had little or no education were not easily convinced of the need for it. Colyer Meriwether reported that there was opposition to public schools "in retired places" and there were many such places in the old South. All this goes to show that the thoughts of the prewar South, although affected by its social and economic system, differed from those of the North mainly in timing.

After the war Southern opposition to public education continued and it did not come mainly from the cabins of the poor. It came instead from former slaveowners, business and professional men, politicians, and professors in colleges and theological seminaries. Some of these, adhering to a *laissez-faire* theory of government, expressed a genuine dread of state paternalism. They professed to believe that public schools might become the means of the absolute control of the thoughts and opinions of the people. Who would now say, after looking about the world, that their fears were wholly groundless? But neither was there safety in the policy which they approved. Popular ignorance would have given false prophets an equal chance with those whom they regarded as the true ones. Looking ahead, they argued that free schooling would be followed by compulsory schooling. And this was hardly a prediction at a time when state after state was enacting compulsory attendance laws.

Some of these opponents insisted that universal education was both impracticable and undesirable. That it was in operation a few hundred miles away did not deter them. They simply denied that it was successful or could be made to succeed. They argued that the greater part of mankind must work for bread and denied that "real mental culture" can coexist with daily labor. They held that state education would be mere smattering, mere reading and writing, which would soon be lost by the laboring class through disuse. But to their minds the worst of the matter was that those who did retain these arts would be likely to become dangerous agitators turning every factory into a debating society.

The opponents of public education did not fail to propose a solution of the educational question. It was to continue the existing practices without change. They claimed that the truly kindly and philanthropic way to serve the genuine interests of the working people was to educate, not the workers themselves, but the higher classes who would then in turn lift the submerged multitudes. By this procedure, it was claimed, all portions of the social organism would be raised together, the true relations of class to class would be preserved, and the lower class would receive by association with its superiors the only real education possible to it.

This might appear to be a parody; but it is a summary of the views of Robert L. Dabney, clergyman and seminary professor, expressed in a newspaper debate in 1876 with William H. Ruffner, the superintendent of public instruction of Virginia, and it is taken from a work by Dabney's son, Charles William Dabney (*Universal Education in the South*, I, 154 ff.). And this line of reasoning was not unique. It was used in other aristocratic societies. But in 1876 in a state which revered the memory of Thomas Jefferson and in a country which had not formally repudiated the principles of the Declaration of Independence it was an anachronism. One is bound also to reflect that under slavery the education of the superior class did not raise the submerged classes, Negro or white, to any dangerous elevation.

The times were, however, out of joint. In the opposing camp were the Republican politicians and their partisans, former abolitionists, soldiers of the Union armies, and all who wanted to be assured that having won the war they would not lose its fruits. As early as 1863 Lincoln had written to General Banks that "some provision should be made for the education of the blacks." The radical section of Northern opinion was determined to secure not only some but equal provision for the education of Negroes. In 1874 General Butler's Civil Rights Bill in its early form included a compulsory demand for mixed schools. But before the bill came up in the Senate, its sponsors became convinced that if adopted in that form it would destroy the newborn public schools of the South because nearly all the white children would be withdrawn from them. All public schools, it was said, would then be attended only by Negroes and the white people would refuse to support them. This would leave many white children without schools of any kind, while the rich would establish and patronize private schools as they had done before the war. The racial coeducation clause was therefore stricken from the bill. But the fight which it had occasioned may be a partial explanation for some of the reactionary theories of the time. Nor is this even now merely ancient history, as all those know who have read of the present state of educational opinion in parts of the South.

2. Progress to 1860

No close comparison is needed to show the difference in the stages of educational progress that had been reached by the two sections before the war. The North had accepted the school tax and demanded the public elementary school, but it was not yet free everywhere. Many of the Northern public schools were graded and the public high school had been established in cities and many small towns. State appropriations allotted by the chief school official enabled the Northern states to enforce regulations on the qualifications of teachers, course of study, length of term, and other items. Rural schools were less efficient than those in the cities but these also were improving, and the principle that they must be regularly maintained was accepted.

The Southern states before 1860 had made only a slender beginning upon such a program. Some states had a body of school law but few good schools. The want of a dependable source of sufficient funds was the primary want. In a number of states the distribution of the surplus revenue aroused great hopes of educational improvement. In some states it was thought that by adding the federal money to the common school fund a system of public schools could be supported without a special tax. It was this idea which led the legislature of Georgia to send a committee to the North to investigate school arrangements and to report a plan for a school system for that state. But it became clear that the available income would be insufficient and the economic recession of 1837 made an end of the proposed plan. The financial distress had a bad effect upon the program of other states also.

One Southern state, North Carolina, was an exception to the general rule. This state, which in 1789 had chartered a state university, also organized a public school system long before her neighbors and about the same time as many of the Northern states. The first effort did not succeed. A legislative committee in 1817 studied the schools of New England but the plan which resulted could not be put into effect. More than twenty years later a second effort was more successful. Until that time the suffrage in North Carolina was limited to landowners, but a new and more liberal constitution extended the right to the ballot. About the same time the state's share of the surplus revenue was added to the school fund. But the main reason for the favorable attitude on public education is to be found in the people.

The western portion of the state lies in the hills and valleys of the Blue Ridge Mountains and is suited to a diversified agriculture on farms of small or moderate size. As this section filled up with independent farmers, the population of the central and western parts of the state began to over-balance that of the eastern part where the plantation economy limited the landowners to comparatively small numbers. These wealthy planters were defeated by the western democratic elements in the election of the legislature and the constitutional convention of 1835. The "back country" won over the seaboard region; and the new constitution laid a broader base for suffrage, provided for equal representation, and required the election of the governor and other state executives by the direct vote of the people, not as formerly by the legislature.

The second event was the receipt by the state of almost $1,500,000 from the surplus revenue. This was applied to education and to internal improvements which, by increasing the state's taxable wealth, later also benefited education. The state now became one of the group of common-wealths which were enacting comprehensive school laws: Pennsylvania, Ohio, Massachusetts, Michigan, and in 1839, North Carolina.

The North Carolina statute was a county-option law; but after a vigorous campaign all but seven counties accepted its provisions. It provided for county boards and the districting of the counties. Each district had a local board, not elected by the people but appointed by the county court. For the support of the schools the law reqired the county tax in the amount of twenty dollars per district and the appropriation by the state of double this amount. Free Negroes were not taxed and their children were excluded from the schools. That the schools were needed is made clear by the returns from the census of 1840 when one-third of the adult white population admitted that they were unable to read or write.

There was no effective state agency to promote, unify, and report upon the local efforts, but in 1853 the state superintendency was instituted. Calvin H. Wiley became the devoted and efficient incumbent and remained in office until 1866. The period, 1853–1860, is known as the educational awakening under Wiley. His methods and achievements resembled closely those of the best mid-century promoters in other states.

Wiley made his last report, the seventh, for the year 1860. It gave the returns from eighty-one of the eighty-six counties. It showed that about 70 per cent of the children of school age were enrolled, that 90 per cent of the teachers were licensed, that the schools averaged about fifty pupils, that the average term was four months, and that more than $100,000 had been paid in school taxes. This with the "two for one" appropriation from the state fund provided about one hundred dollars for each of the 3,000 schools and an average monthly salary of about twenty-five dollars. If this wage was actually received, the North Carolina teachers of 1860 were somewhat better paid than those of most Northern states. However that may be, the school system of North Carolina was the best in the South.

With North Carolina we may compare her neighbor, Virginia. The legislature of the Old Dominion passed "an act to establish public schools" in the early year of 1796. This act, based upon Thomas Jefferson's bill of 1779, was an optional law; and this feature nullified the law. A literary fund, the usual resource of a people not ready to consent to a school tax, was established in 1810 and was increased by large sums owed the state by the national government. By 1816 it amounted to $1,000,000, and the next legislature passed Virginia's second school law. This was a charity school measure, hardly intended as a step toward free public education.

Nor was the literary fund reserved for the benefit of the children and protected against encroachment. Even the Visitors of the University of Virginia with Thomas Jefferson at the head borrowed for the use of the university from the literary fund which had been formed for the support of elementary schools. After thirty years (1820) the fund was providing some schooling for only half of the indigent children of the state. The governor said the law should be repealed and a better one enacted in its place. Unfortunately, the new law, Virginia's third, adopted in 1846 and intended to provide free education for all white children in schools to be supported from the literary fund and a county tax, was another optional law. Only nine counties accepted it. And this was the extent of Virginia's efforts for universal public education before 1860.

Little progress was made in the other states of the section. South Carolina adopted a free school law in 1811 but it was for orphans and poor children only. The schools served a useful purpose in Charleston, but over the state they reached only a small fraction of the children. County systems of free schools without taxation or state supervision were established, more in law than in fact, in Maryland, Tennessee, and Kentucky. The recent history of education in Kentucky by Frank L. McVey places "the real beginning of public education in Kentucky" in the year 1870, "when an act was passed by the legislature implementing the paper system set up by the legislature of 1838." A similar statement would apply to most of the South and even the dates would need little adjustment.

The educational awakening of the thirties which roused the Northern states merely caused those of the South to stir in their slumbers. They would not vote the school tax and effective state supervision. Texas, Mississippi, and Florida made little progress. Of all the states in the deep South, Louisiana came the nearest to a working system. As in the North, some of the Southern cities, New Orleans, Mobile, and Atlanta, were ahead of their states. Also in the later prewar years some progress was made in Georgia and Alabama. It is possible to believe that if the economic, social, and religious facts were available in sufficient detail, the educational differences between the sections could be fully explained. One fact which includes a good many others is this, that an efficient common school system because of its power to dissolve social caste would not have been in harmony with the planters' way of life.

3. POSTWAR DILEMMA

In absolute numbers of men killed and dollars spent, the cost of the war weighed more heavily upon the victors than the vanquished. One hundred thousand more Union than Confederate soldiers lost their lives. The North expended two billion dollars more upon the conflict than the Confederacy. Yet the South suffered more from its smaller losses because it had fewer men and dollars upon which to draw. And while shiploads of immigrants came into the North to work in mine and field and factory and the Northern bondholder got his money back, the South, instead of immigrants, had only carpetbaggers, and the debts of the Confederate state and central governments were never paid. The state school funds disappeared with the rest of the resources. The paper money of the South depreciated until it became worthless.

The destruction of property by the Northern armies was a serious loss for a nonmanufacturing region. In Atlanta, which did have some factories and was a railroad center, Sherman destroyed or carried off everything of any value. The burning of Columbia, applauded by the North, was condemned by the South as the act of barbarians; and accusations and recriminations on account of it continued for decades. The march to the sea had laid waste a belt across Georgia "sixty miles wide." The Shenandoah Valley was devastated by contending armies and finally swept clean by Sheridan. The Union armies marched through the South, camped in it, and foraged on it, while only one great battle was fought on Northern soil.

Such facts have an abstract meaning for those of a later day but to the people of that time they translated themselves into present sorrow and suffering. Grant at Appomattox, at one of the high moments of an uneven career, permitted Lee's soldiers to keep their horses because they would be needed in the spring plowing. But when they arrived at their homes some found that there was no plow, that missing or worn parts could not be replaced, or that seed corn was lacking. The labor system was ruined. Manufactures, banks, railroads, and the state governments were prostrate. A fresh beginning had to be undertaken.

The educational problem was as difficult as any that faced the South during the reconstruction. The upper classes had to develop respect for a more democratic society and for the educational institutions that would help to maintain it. The rural South had few good schools and in many places no schools at all. The poor whites in the pine barrens were isolated from many civilizing influences and suffered from endemic disease. Four million Negroes, more than 90 per cent illiterate, were now free and were to be prepared for the responsibilities of citizenship decreed by the new amendments to the Constitution. As slaves they had been kept in ignorance on principle by laws with severe penalties.

Every meeting to teach Negroes to read and write was, in prewar Virginia, "an unlawful assembly." Participants if they were Negroes were flogged. For the same offense, whites were given a jail sentence and were also compelled to pay a fine. Every Southern state had a law of this type. Teaching slaves to write was especially obnoxious because it might aid them in forming combinations and conspiracies.

Oral religious instruction of slaves was approved as favorable to morals and good order. Southern churches spent considerable sums to Christianize the Negroes and their efforts were effective. Free Negroes sometimes acquired financial means and were able to send their children to the North for schooling. They were a frequent reminder that the race did not lack capacity, as the slavocracy preferred to claim. One objection to the presence of free Negroes near the plantations arose from the likelihood that they would present ideas of freedom to the slaves.

After the war the white people had to be convinced that the education of the Negroes was possible, desirable, and indeed necessary. Before the war the white South had not succeeded in providing schools for all its own children. Military rule, the conflicting activities of the Freedman's Bureau, and corruption in the handling of funds did not simplify matters. Almost a hundred years have elapsed and the problem is still occupying the attention of the section and the nation. This is evidence of the difficulty of the social problem that faced the South. But we must also say that great progress has been made and much of that progress has been due to the colored people themselves.

4. RECONSTRUCTION

Peace did not return at once when the fighting stopped on the battlefields. Reconstruction had to begin in an era of mutual hatred and suspicion and continual recrimination, and it is not surprising that some of its measures were considered vindictive. Besides, there was not a single accepted and well-planned reconstruction policy, but two, the Presidential and the Congressional, neither fully developed.

The Presidential policy begun by Lincoln and, with important changes, followed by Johnson was conciliatory; and by the end of 1865 all the seceded states had formed governments acceptable to the President, had renewed their allegiance to the Union, and had ratified the Thirteenth Amendment abolishing slavery. Presumably they had now again become full members of the Union.

There were, however, many unresolved difficulties. Now that the Negroes were free they became competitors of the poorer whites for work and land and a hot wave of racial antagonism flared up. The great landowners had no money to pay wages and could offer the ex-slaves only sharecropping opportunities. Often the agreements seemed to institute a new form of slavery worse than the old because the white owner now had no responsibility for feeding, clothing, or housing his workers. And the new freedom went to the heads of some of the Negroes and they loafed and wandered about without working. These became a disturbing element of society. Southern legislatures thereupon began to adopt "black codes" designed to compel the Negroes to work and restricting their freedom of movement and contract. To many in the North this seemed intolerable. The idea grew that the South was trying to re-enslave the freedmen.

Congress had never conceded to the President the right to set the terms of reconstruction. The elections of 1866 gave the Radicals, led by Thaddeus Stevens in the House and Charles Sumner in the Senate, the power to undo Johnson's work. They proceeded to secure the passage of laws to enforce their own terms. The laws of 1867 re-established army rule in the South, set up five military districts, and provided for universal Negro suffrage. From that time the reconstruction of the seceded states was in the hands of Congress.

Under Presidential reconstruction, attempts had been made to establish public schools but without providing for the education of Negroes. This last, we know, was contrary to Lincoln's instruction. It is doubtless pertinent to remember that Andrew Johnson had been a slaveholder. The case of Arkansas may illustrate the policy. It will at least show that those are mistaken who teach that Presidential reconstruction made no contribution to education.

In Arkansas the Union armies driving the Confederates before them were able by 1863 to occupy the northern half of the state, including the capital, Little Rock. By Presidential proclamation the citizens were permitted to form a new government. The elected governor had once been a teacher, and in the state convention of 1861 had been the only man to vote against secession. On his recommendation the legislature, composed mainly of former Confederates, voted a tax for free schools and a full complement of state, county, and local school offices. They opened the schools to all white children but made no provision for the education of Negroes.

Military rule and Congressional reconstruction annulled the Arkansas school law before it became effective. A new constitution with a long section on education was adopted and a new school law was enacted. This provided for separate schools for the children of the two races. An outburst of extravagance from which the reconstructionists themselves recoiled exhausted the limited funds and teachers were paid in scrip. A third constitution and school law were adopted in 1874 and new officers did much to moderate the prejudice against the education of Negroes in this border state. The new law was an excellent one but factors which the law could not reach held back progress.

When it became clear that progress would come very slowly, if at all, some in the ruling party decided upon radical measures. Representative George F. Hoar of Massachusetts in his bill of 1870 provided for the appointment by the President of a superintendent of schools for each delinquent state, the appointment by the Secretary of the Interior of division and local school superintendents for each such state, the prescription by federal officers of all textbooks, and the collection by federal agents of an annual direct tax for schools. The measure was contrary to all American educational history and the Hoar Bill never came to a vote in Congress.

The introduction of the Hoar Bill may have had one important result. Argument over the bill directed the minds of many in Congress and in the country to the subject of federal aid for education. Bills were introduced into Congress to create a national school fund from the sale of public lands. When these failed to pass, Senator Henry W. Blair of New Hampshire in 1881 introduced a federal aid bill that provided for the distribution of $77,000,000 to the states in the proportion of the number of illiterates in each state. The money was to be appropriated in specified annual amounts over a period of years. The Senate repeatedly passed the Blair Bill, but every time it failed in the House. The last defeat occurred in 1890, the year which saw the passage of the second Morrill Act for agricultural and engineering education in land-grant colleges.

After World War I there was a great revival of interest in federal aid; and these efforts became prominent again after World War II. The National Education Association has worked for such legislation. Congress, the parties, and the sections have been divided. There has been opposition from some Catholic organizations and from the Chamber of Commerce of the United States. Educators and businessmen have not been united in favor of the policy or have opposed particular features of the several bills. These have in very few instances reached the floor of either House. Meanwhile the heavy burden which school support places upon the poorer states and the disparity in educational provisions that obtains among the states seem to many to provide a sound argument for federal aid.

Under Congressional reconstruction all of the Southern states established public schools not only for whites but also for Negroes, and this has been a permanent gain. It is possible that the fear that the army would order the establishment of mixed schools was one of the reasons for the alacrity with which the South accepted the segregated public school for Negroes. The Negro schools were not given proper financial support, but under Presidential reconstruction the states did not even propose to educate the former slaves. The new state constitutions included mandatory educational provisions and the laws provided for a school tax, state supervision, and universal education. In time, teacher preparation, certification, minimum terms, and expanded curricula were demanded. Compulsory attendance was long delayed.

5. SCHOOLS FOR FREEDMEN

When schools were opened for Negroes, the young and many adults came to learn. For this there were all the usual reasons but also an unusual one. Knowledge may be both pleasant and valuable, but to the ex-slave it was also a symbol of his new status, a privilege formerly monopolized by his masters. But it was soon discovered that getting an education is a long, laborious process, however great the interest may be. Meanwhile, the learners had to live, which was sufficiently difficult for many. They lacked understanding of the best line to take and, without guidance, frequently aimed at impossible goals. Probably their teachers, often Northern idealists, did not provide proper guidance. Many became discouraged and gave up.

From the early months of the war, efforts were made to teach the Negroes who were within the Union lines. The American Missionary Association, formed by the Methodist and other Northern churches, gave aid to a free Negro, Mary L. Peake, who began to teach refugees at Fortress Monroe in 1861. This little school is claimed as the seed-grain from which Hampton Institute grew. And Hampton, under Samuel Chapman Armstrong, did not make the mistake of offering a purely literary education to those who would have to live by manual work. The American Missionary Association also supported schools in cities along the coast, and these were later absorbed by the school systems of Norfolk and other towns. Other organized groups engaged in the support of schools in Southern localities.

Some thousands of teachers and more than $1,000,000 were contributed by the North to aid in such programs. Many teachers came from the old abolition centers and way-stations such as Oberlin on the Underground Railroad. The white people of the South were frequently hostile to this new invasion and refused to rent living quarters or furnish board to teachers whom they regarded as their enemies. Schoolhouses were burned down and malicious reports were circulated in the effort to drive out the Yankee educators.

The army and the federal government undertook to teach as well as protect the freedmen. General Grant in 1862 appointed Colonel John Eaton, later a general and in peacetime the second United States Commissioner of Education, to act as commissioner for freedmen in Arkansas. In 1864 General Banks from the New Orleans headquarters of his military district laid down a detailed educational directive. This was to provide for the "rudimental instruction of the freedmen" under his protection. The directive, really a military order, provided for a board of education with power to tax and in fact to requisition, to build, to hire, and to regulate and discipline. The army supplied books, set up courses of study, and set the school hours. The teachers had to make returns and reports on all these matters. This was a form of compulsory education previously unknown in the United States.

The government also created a special agency to care for the interests of the Negroes, the Bureau for Refugees, Freedmen, and Abandond Lands, always known as the Freedmen's Bureau. It became a government within the government and served as legislature, court, tax collector, and executive, ranging through the whole extent of civil organization and control. It had a superintendent of freedmen's schools who took over and extended the work begun by Eaton. Grants were made to the missionary societies especially for schoolhouses. There was an educational supervisor for each state. In the five years of its existence it gave some elementary education to almost 250,000 pupils. Many now well-known Negro colleges were aided by it, among them Morehouse, Fisk, and Howard. Berea received aid from the bureau and taught the two races in the same classes until Kentucky forbade this by a law of 1904. The bureau was abolished in 1870, many of the Northern teachers went home, and the obligation to Negroes in the South became the obligation of the states where they lived.

In carrying on its work, the bureau disbursed millions of dollars and exercised extralegal controls. Its agents were accused of graft and of devious political activity to promote the Radical scheme of reconstruction. The bureau was an arm of the United States government, controlled by the Radicals. Its head, General O. O. Howard, was honest, but no administrator or judge of men. There were several official investigations of his military and official conduct but he was "exonerated."

6. The Peabody and Other Funds

George Peabody was a pathmaker for the great American educational philanthropists such as Andrew Carnegie, John D. Rockefeller, and the Henry Ford family. Stephen Girard, founder of the Girard College for Orphans, was almost the only predecessor who could be ranked with him. He provided for others what he had failed to get for himself, the chance to go to school. His formal education was all obtained in four terms in a village school. When his birthplace celebrated its bicentennial, he sent as his toast: "Education: a debt from the present to future generations." This sentiment was chosen by the Peabody Education Board for its seal. This board was chartered in 1867 by the State of New York and received from Peabody more than $2,000,000 to be applied in aid of the education of "the entire population" of the South. The board's first general agent was Barnas Sears, who had followed Horace Mann as Secretary of the state board of education in Massachusetts.

The major policy of the board, apparently the work of Sears, was to give substantial aid to a few well-located schools that would serve as examples and models instead of spreading the money in small amounts over a large number without much benefit to any. The aim was to stimulate permanent improvement, not to give relief. A few well-placed, efficient, permanent schools seemed to be stronger arguments for an improved public education than the slight and temporary improvement of many. This principle proposed by Sears has had great influence and has been given extended application by the numerous educational foundations which have followed and imitated the Peabody Fund and Board.

Sears also advised giving aid for the better preparation of teachers. Some subsidy to girls' normal schools was proposed, and scholarships for young men who would agree to teach in the public schools. He thought teacher's associations and educational journals should receive aid as being means toward better public relations. He advised that all of the board's contributions should be distributed through the offices of the state school officers or other public officials, for a main purpose of the board was to stimulate state activity in public education. Considering that the money was to be applied in a dozen states, the income from the fund was not large; but by following the policies indicated, its publicity value was far greater than its purchasing power.

The Peabody Board in forty-six years disbursed about $3,500,000 in twelve states. The general principle was followed that the board would not underwrite more than about one-fourth of the cost of a particular operation. Every Peabody dollar thus attracted three extra dollars from taxation or philanthropy. After 1880 the general agent of the fund was J. L. M. Curry, a Southern planter, legislator, and gospel minister. One of his achievements was the development of the Peabody College for Teachers. Sears had succeeded in opening a normal school in connection with the old University of Nashville. After some years and much effort the state began to make small appropriations, and almost a generation later the Peabody Board appropriated to its endowment $1,500,000 of the fund principal. The school was chartered in 1909 and opened in new buildings in 1914.

The experience of the Peabody Board in the application of its policies was of the utmost value to the Southern Education Board and the General Education Board when at the turn of the century these bodies came to the aid of the educational movement in the South. Earlier and smaller agencies also gained from that effort. A second trust for education in the South was established in 1882 by John F. Slater of Norwich, Connecticut. He gave $1,000,000 for the education of freedmen and their descendants and especially for the preparation of Negro teachers. The Slater trustees conferred with Curry in making their plans and eventually what was left of the Peabody Fund was united with the Slater Fund.

The policies of these early boards tended to concentrate their aid upon the larger schools in the cities where they would be seen; and as a result the smallest, most isolated, and destitute schools for Negroes in the rural South failed to get the needed stimulus. A Philadelphia Friend, Miss Anna T. Jeanes, in 1907 created a fund of $1,000,000 to help these forgotten people. The managers of the fund introduced a new force, the Jeanes teacher. They selected the most successful Negro teachers of a community to spend a part of their time in helping other teachers to improve their work and their schoolhouses and particularly in introducing industrial and domestic education. This scheme of the Jeanes supervisors was suggested by Virginia Randolph, a Negro teacher in Henrico County, Virginia, and the Jeanes teacher idea spread not only in the South but also to the schools of several sections of Africa.

All of these funds later cooperated with the General Education Board. They accomplished much in starting and establishing public education in the South, but the income from a million or even a hundred million dollars was not sufficient to educate the children of twelve states. Those states reaching from Virginia to Texas had 17,000,000 people in 1890 and twice as many fifty years later. Only an efficient tax system together with the help of the federal government could have provided the funds that would have been needed and are needed to educate all the children of this large section.

7. TOWARD UNIVERSAL EDUCATION

The school laws of reconstruction days demanded equal school opportunities for white and black alike, but this promise faded early. For a time after the war the white farmers and the Negroes cooperated in politics in opposition to the planters, but economic competition soon broke up the union. Many whites thought the Negroes should pay for their own schools. The Negroes were more and more deprived of political power; and the tax receipts from the property of Negroes were so low that they also lost whatever chance they may have had for equal school opportunity. Without help from the white people, the Negroes in large areas would have had no schools whatever.

The question of mixed schools for the two races, if it were pressed, was recognized as an insuperable difficulty. But Barnas Sears unaccountably considered this an unrealistic issue. He reported a case in which Negroes admitted, or perhaps he should have said "claimed," that they were demanding mixed schools merely to secure equal, not common, facilities. This may well have been the fact in a given instance, but it is hard to believe that Sears could have taken this as a typical case. Negro leaders knew that separate facilities for a poor, ignorant, and until recently enslaved people, to be paid for by the money of a dominant class, would not be equal. Some of the Northern reconstructionists clearly intended to force mixed schools upon the South, perhaps rather to chastise "the rebels" than to aid the freedmen. After the Southern white people regained control of their state governments, they established separate public schools for the two races but until recent times there was no real attempt to make the Negro schools "equal" to the white schools.

And even equal opportunity would not have been any great opportunity. Ten years after the end of reconstruction, North Carolina had a shorter school term and a higher illiteracy rate than before the war. For a generation the white public schools, although helped by some Northern funds, made little progress. Every state had created a public school system, but the schools themselves, especially in the country, were not well attended, well housed, or well taught. Reports show that in some of the Southern states more than half of the children were not enrolled in the public schools. How many were in private schools is not known. Most of the progress had been in the cities. Lack of money was one great difficulty and the separate schools for the two races made education expensive, especially in the country where enrollments were small.

For a time in the 1880's it appeared that the federal government might help in the support of public schools. The Blair Bill, mentioned above, was introduced for this purpose in 1881 and passed by the Senate of three successive Congresses, but each time it was rejected by the House. By 1890 the South had become convinced that there was no prospect of early national aid. They had also seen the educational progress of the North and, at home, the influence of the Peabody and other funds in selected areas. Unfortunately, the latter had not spread as far and as rapidly as had been expected. The South was beginning to look more to her own resources. The closing decade of the century was one of financial stringency, but in 1898 the first of a series of annual conferences on education in the South was called at Capon Springs, West Virginia.

This may be taken as the beginning of a new educational awakening. It was, however, different from the awakening which had come to the industrial North long before. That was a movement to establish state school systems. The South in 1900 had long had the basic laws, officers, and machinery of public education, and this was an effort to provide the machine with fuel and lubricants and to get it to run.

The original idea of the meetings had come from a Northerner, Edward Abbott, the son of the Jacob Abbott mentioned in an earlier chapter. Abbott's interest, like that of many Northerners, was a philanthropic and missionary interest in the education of the Negroes and mountain whites; and the first conference was called to promote Christian education. Later meetings broadened this reference to stress the general literary education of both Negroes and whites and, one may safely say, of white people especially.

The public response to the discussions revealed people who saw little good in any kind of education for Negroes except industrial education. Booker Washington had succeeded only too well in teaching his lesson that the Negro must literally work his way upward. There were many, also, who believed that if the whites were educated first, the education of the Negroes would follow almost automatically. This was an alluring but untenable idea. Although they received much help from their white neighbors, not always cheerfully given, the fact is that the Negroes to a great extent educated themselves, as all people must do if they are to be educated.

The meetings soon came to be known as the Conference for Education in the South, and they were largely in the hands of the Southern people. The programs glow with the names of Southern men who already were or were to become famous, men such as Curry, C. W. Dabney, C. B. Aycock, Edwin Alderman, Charles D. McIver, and many others. To effect a more permanent organization, the Southern Education Board was formed in 1901. An agent was employed to work during the year in the intervals between the meetings. But the conference and the board had no great amount of money to use and none to distribute. Two years later John D. Rockefeller was brought into the movement and the General Education Board was organized and received national incorporation. This body still further expanded the scope of the work. It was to promote the education of all the people not only in the South but in the United States. The South, however, shared extensively in its benefactions.

The chief value of the whole movement to the South was the arousal of interest in education. Educational campaigns were organized in state after state and some were continued for several years. Every phase of public education was discussed—support, longer terms, illiteracy, teacher preparation, buildings, libraries, rural consolidation, high schools, and a great many phases now included under the recent term, "fundamental education." Among these later activities there were the farm demonstration work of Seaman A. Knapp, club work by boys and girls, sanitation and health work, and the campaign against the hookworm and malaria. The various funds, Peabody, Slater, Jeanes, Phelps-Stokes, and Rosenwald, cooperated with the Southern and General Education Boards.

The interest aroused by this movement also increased the amount and the proportion of public money for education. But as a Southern leader pointed out at the beginning, the wealth to support universal education must be produced before it can be used. The rural South has not had the wealth to provide the schools which its children deserve. Philanthropy, even the philanthropy of the largest fortunes and the richest foundations, it may be repeated, will not educate all the children. And ways must be found to increase the prosperity of the South, to keep at home the wealth that is now siphoned off by the great Northern corporations, and to secure federal aid. Only by such means can the children of the rural South be given the opportunities provided for children in New York or California.

8. EDUCATING NEGRO LEADERS

The various funds, Peabody and others, aided both Negroes and whites or, in several cases, Negroes only. But with the whites in undisturbed

A New England dame school in old colonial times, 1713. Engraving. (*Bettmann Archive.*)

A country school, 1890.

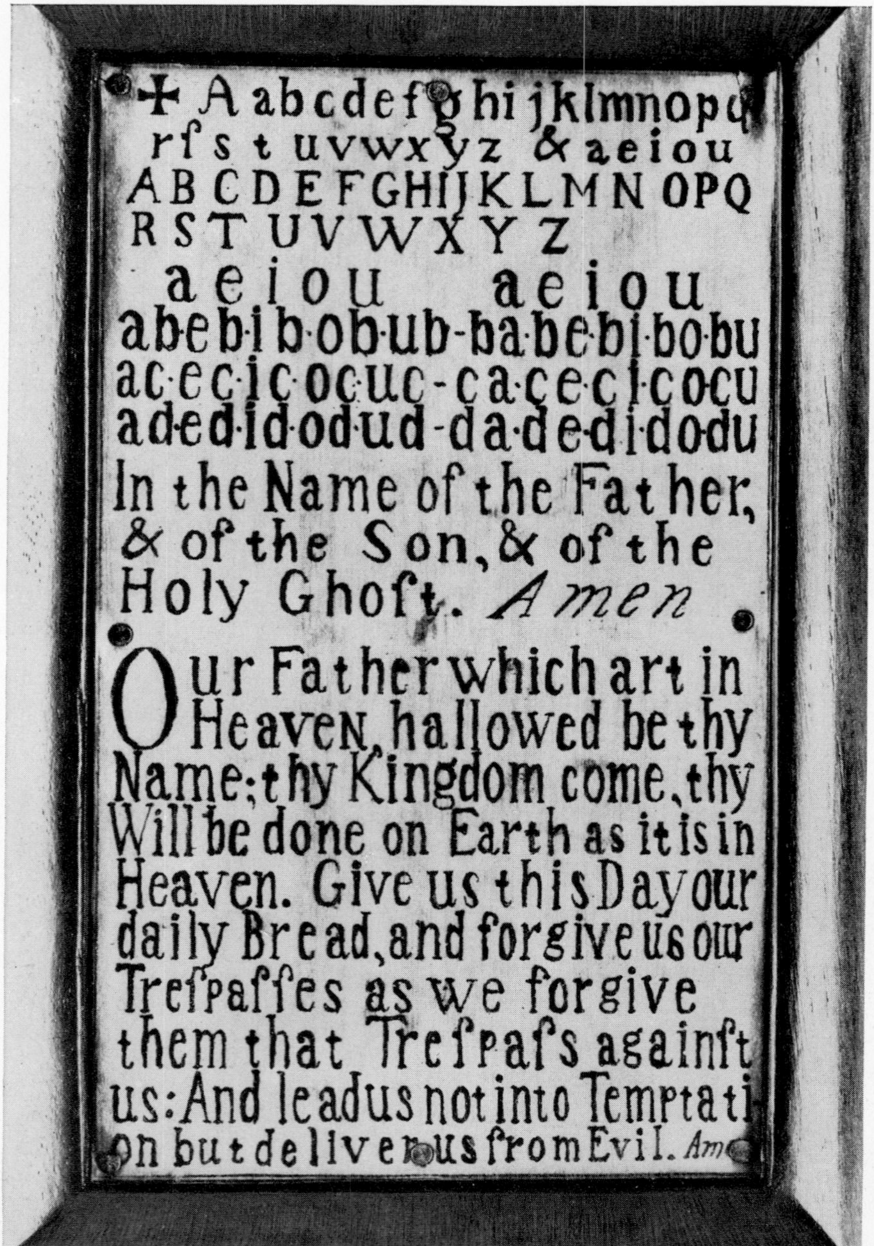

✠ A abcdefghijklmnopq
rſstuvwxyz &aeiou
ABCDEFGHIJKLMNOPQ
RSTUVWXYZ
aeiou aeiou
ab eb ib ob ub - ba be bi bo bu
ac ec ic oc uc - ca ce ci co cu
ad ed id od ud - da de di do du
In the Name of the Father,
& of the Son, & of the
Holy Ghoſt. *Amen*

Our Father which art in
Heaven, hallowed be thy
Name; thy Kingdom come, thy
Will be done on Earth as it is in
Heaven. Give us this Day our
daily Bread, and forgive us our
Treſpaſſes as we forgive
them that Treſpaſs againſt
us: And lead us not into Temptati
on but deliver us from Evil. *Am*

Hornbook.

James Johonnot (1823–1888).

Thomas Hopkins Gallaudet (1787–1851).

Hermann Krüsi, Jr. (1817–1902).

David Perkins Page (1810–1849).

Horace Mann (1796–1859). After a photograph
taken in Boston *ca.* 1850. (*Bettmann Archive.*)

Noah Webster, schoolmaster of the republic. (*Bettmann Archive.*)

Award of Merit, *ca.* 1865.

Louis Agassiz (1807–1873). (*Reproduced by permission of the Smithsonian Institution.*)

WOODWARD HIGH SCHOOL.

Daniel C. Hubbell

Abstract of credit marks for the three months ending *Jan. 21* 1837

Class		Maximum MARK.	Number attained.	Class		Maximum MARK.	Number attained.
	Reading	130	139	"	Mensuration		
"	Definitions,			"	Navigation		
"	Penmanship	20	40	"	Nautical Astronomy		
"	Arithmetic	91	139	"	Analytic plane Trigonometry		
"	Geography	100	137	"	" spheric Trigonometry		
"	English Grammar	136	159	"	Analytical Geometry, including Conic Sections		
"	U. S. History	60	139	"			
"	General History	100	71	"	Differential Calculus		
"	Book keeping			"	Integral do.		
"	Elocution	36	40	"	Chemistry		
"	Composition	86	130	"	Mechanical Philosophy		
"	Latin Language			"	Astronomy		
"	Greek do.			"	Mental Philosophy		
"	French do.			"	Moral do.		
"	Spanish do.			"	Political do.		
"	German do.			"	Rhetoric		
"	Algebra			"	Logic		
"	Plane Geometry			"	Political Economy		
"	" Trigonometry						
"	Surveying						

General Deportment *Good*

No. of half days absent

No. of times late A.M. & P.M.

No. of times absent from Prayers *5*

Parents or Guardians are requested to endorse this Ticket, as evidence that they have examined it, and to add such remarks as they may think proper.

B. P. Aydelott, President.

Report of the Woodward High School of Cincinnati, 1837.

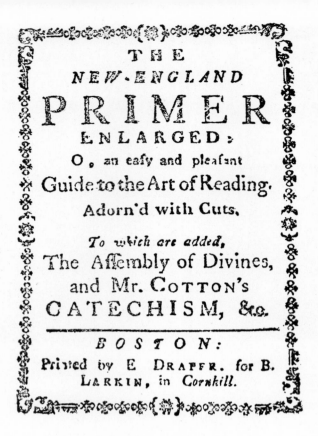

THE
NEW-ENGLAND
PRIMER
ENLARGED:

O, an easy and pleasant
Guide to the Art of Reading.
Adorn'd with Cuts.

To which are added,
The Assembly of Divines,
and Mr. COTTON's
CATECHISM, &c.

BOSTON:
Printed by E. DRAPER, for B.
LARKIN, in Cornhill.

In Adam's Fall
We sinned all.

Thy Life to mend,
This Book attend.

The Cat doth play,
And after slay.

A Dog will bite
A Thief at Night.

An Eagle' flight
Is out of sight.

The idle Fool
Is whipt at School.

As runs the Glass,
Man's life doth pass.

My Book and Heart
Shall never part.

Job feels the rod,
Yet blesses God.

Kings should be good
No men of blood.

The Lion bold
The Lamb doth hold

The Moon gives light
In time of night.

New England Primer from a facsimile reprint.
(Reproduced by permission of Ginn and Company.)

Charles De Garmo (1849–1934).

Dr. Joseph Mayer Rice (1857–1934).
(Courtesy of Mr. Lawrence J. M. Rice.)

Preston Willis Search (1853–1936).
(Courtesy of Frederick Preston Search.)

William Torrey Harris (1835–1909).   Henry Barnard (1811–1900).

Mary Lyon, founder of Mt. Holyoke College. From
a miniature painted in 1832. (*Culver Service.*)

Charles W. Eliot

2 June, 1924.

From a copy of a portrait autographed for the author by President Eliot. (*Reproduced by permission of the magazine* PROGRESSIVE EDUCATION *which used it as the frontispiece of its first issue.*)

Painting of John Dewey (1859–1952) by Edwin B. Child. (*Columbia University.*)

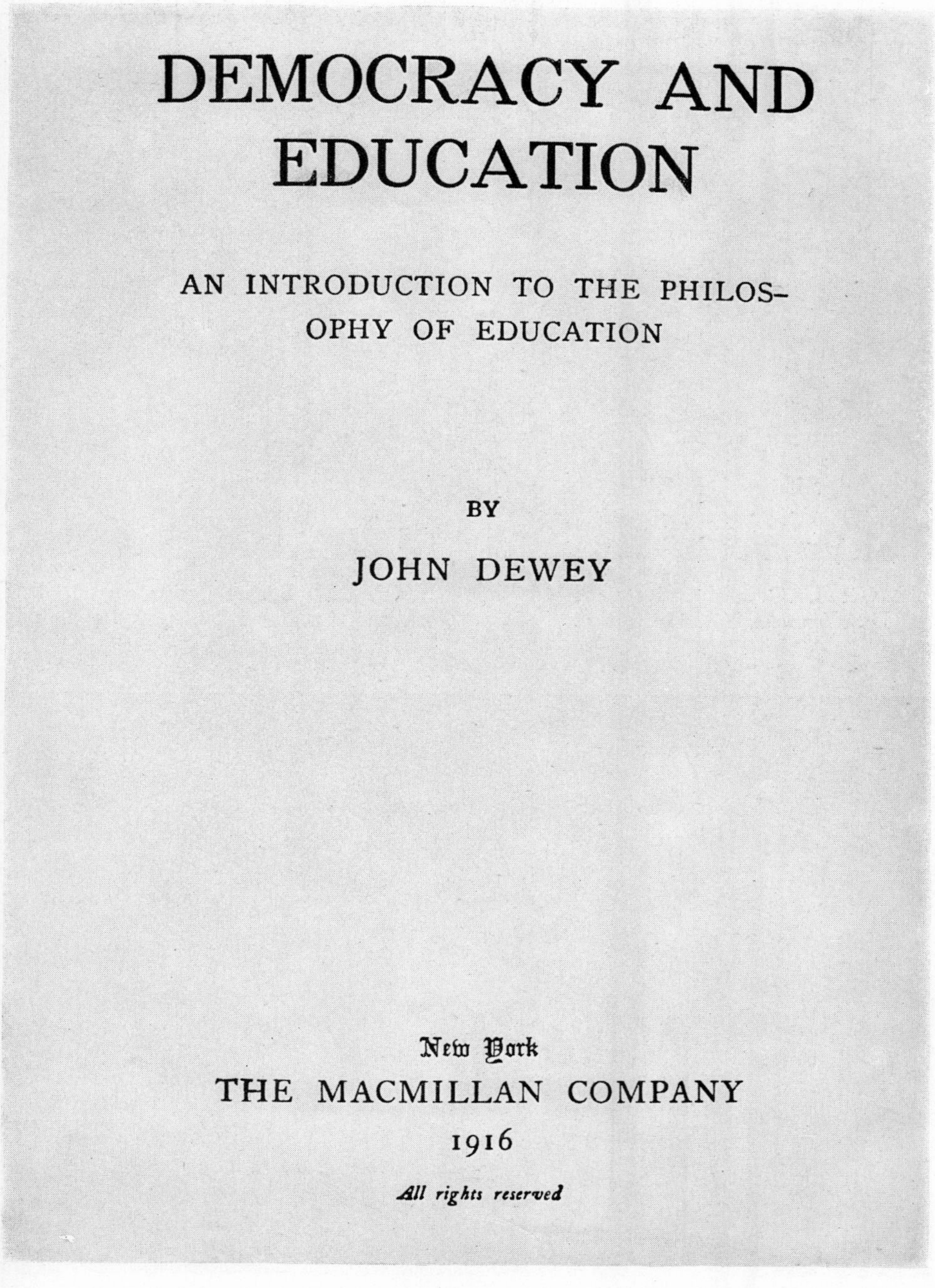

DEMOCRACY AND EDUCATION

AN INTRODUCTION TO THE PHILOS-OPHY OF EDUCATION

BY

JOHN DEWEY

New York

THE MACMILLAN COMPANY

1916

Title page of the most influential American book on the philosophy of education. (*Copyright 1916 by the Macmillan Company.*)

Arnold Gesell. Gesell Institute of Child Development, Yale University.

William C. Bagley (1874–1946). Teacher College, Columbia University. (*Wide Worl Photos.*)

The Cresbard, South Dakota, high school band as they practiced for the seventh annual Mid-West national band clinic appearance. (*Wide World Photos.*)

Ephrata (Pa.) Academy. Founded A.D. 1837.

Ulloa Elementary School in San Francisco. (*Wide World Photos.*)

Academic procession at Swarthmore College commencement, 1933, led by Lady Wylie and President Frank Aydelotte. (*Reproduced by permission of Dr. Aydelotte and the Princeton University Press.*)

control of public education, the Negro schools were even less adequately supported than those for white children. Statistics reported in percentage gains show that Negro education made rapid progress, but the figures will be deceiving unless it is remembered that slaves had received no education. Thus the original base was close to zero and the total enrollment at any time was also the increase in enrollment since 1865.

There were some special schools for Negroes, such as the Hampton Normal and Agricultural Institute, the Tuskegee Normal and Industrial Institution, Fisk and other smaller colleges and universities, and after the second Morrill Act (1890), the seventeen land-grant colleges. All of these have prepared teachers, journalists, bankers, farmers, and leaders in many lines among the colored people. Some of these constitute other cases of philanthropic aid for Negro education.

The founder and first head of the Hampton Institute was Samuel Chapman Armstrong (1839–1893). He was the son of American missionaries in Hawaii and early learned the methods of industrial and intellectual education used at the Hilo Manual Labor School in Honolulu. He graduated from Williams College in 1862, commanded a Negro regiment in the Civil War, worked in Virginia under the Freedmen's Bureau, and in 1868 founded Hampton Institute for Negroes. Later, Indians also were admitted.

It is sometimes said that Armstrong's Hawaiian upbringing fitted him in a special manner to deal with primitive people, but the American Negro of 1868 was not primitive. He had had a long apprenticeship of labor for others. Social conditions and prejudices and the short time the Negro could remain in school made it advisable to teach him to use his hands. He had to work to survive and working skills were likely to be useful. The idea of industrial education for the young Negroes and Indians appealed to employers and men of wealth and both Hampton and Tuskegee received contributions from such sources. Hampton Institute, as the school is now called, has over 2,000 men and women students and is recognized by the Southern Association as a Grade A college. Without question its most famous graduate is Booker T. Washington (1858–1915), the founder of Tuskegee.

Tuskegee was founded in 1881, and Washington always ascribed much of its and his success to the education he had received at Hampton. But great as that contribution may have been, his rise "up from slavery" was due in large part to qualities that schools cannot teach, intelligence and a remarkable warmth of personality. His power of effective public speech and his social and political wisdom may have been increased by his education. Much of his philosophy of education was developed by his experience at

Hampton. His political wisdom is shown in his policy expressed in his famous speech at the Atlanta Exposition in 1895. He said: "In all things that are purely social we [of the two races] can be as separate as the fingers, yet one as the hand in all things essential to mutual progress." This pleased white people as did the policy of Tuskegee in teaching industrial and trade arts and skills, thrift, and honesty, and in campaigning against the one-room cabins in which, Washington said, 6,000,000 Negroes were living. These were Washington's ways of elevating the Negro.

White people did not all press for much Negro elevation but they wanted capable workers. And Northern capitalists were willing to contribute to their training. The capitalists were a major source of the support needed by Tuskegee. Some Negroes attacked the vocationalism of Washington. W. E. B. DuBois, a graduate of Fisk University with a Ph.D. degree from Harvard, was one of these critics. He said the Negro race could be elevated only by its exceptional men, leaders trained not in manual vocations but in intellectual and liberal arts. He thought the Tuskegee work-education was unduly restrictive, tending to keep the Negro in a servile position.

The issue thus joined had already been decided not by theory alone but by the force of broad educational trends. The period when Hampton and Tuskegee were developing was the era of the new land-grant colleges, of the introduction of manual training, and of the spread of the normal schools. Their success in teaching trades and vocations was reinforced by the ongoing work of American industry in the postwar period. But trade training was not as permanently successful as it seemed to be at the time. Mass production by the great manufacturing corporations and the rise of the labor unions were changing the world's work and the social relations of the workers. These trends were not foreseen, and in view of the industrialists' opposition to the unions it is doubtful that Washington would have been willing to introduce special courses for labor leaders into Tuskegee.

Tuskegee has developed into a college of about 3,000 men and women. It started as an elementary and high school and became a college after Washington's time. One of its great teachers and scientists of recent times was George Washington Carver. It offers a great variety of courses in agriculture, education, home economics, institutional management, nurses' training, and others. There are cooperative work-study courses and many of the students earn all or part of their expenses.

In the seventeen states of the South which have traditionally separated the two races in schools, there are seventeen Negro land-grant colleges of "agriculture and the mechanic arts," although in many cases they do not use these words in the title. In the same states there are about fifty other

Negro colleges including Howard University, Fisk University, Morehouse College, and the two, Hampton Institute and Tuskegee Institute, already described. There are also hundreds of small struggling colleges and schools. The land-grant colleges for Negroes now enroll about 25,000 students; but for a long time they were treated in stepmotherly fashion by the states and the quality of their work was poor. All of these public and private institutions together with some normal schools prepare the teachers of the Negro elementary and high schools of the South. This whole phase of educational development will be changed by the Supreme Court decision against segregation.

The cold war between the sections began with the founding of the Republic; and when compromise was no longer possible and war broke out, each side could honestly claim that it was fighting for the right, and could believe that it, being in the right, would be victorious. And great as was the loss of life and material possessions in the debacle of the South, it did not, perhaps, exceed the moral and spiritual damage which she suffered. To this the horrors of reconstruction must be added.

There were causes in nature and society for the slender developments in public education before the war. Included among the latter were the class structure of Southern society, the depressed condition of the lowest classes, and the lack of wealth to pay a school tax. Also family and church control of education was strongly rooted. For these reasons public education made little progress before 1860. A few states and a number of cities had, however, made a beginning; but it does not seem likely, as has been claimed, that an effective system would have developed quickly if the war had not come.

The war left the South prostrate; the planters continued in opposition to public education; there was now a Negro problem; and there was also a drastic reconstruction policy. All these hindered educational efforts. Presidential reconstruction under Johnson might not have done much for the Negro. The Congressional plan, though harsh and vindictive, did at least make some attempt to start the education of the freedmen. Many of the efforts by the missionary societies, military agencies, and the Freedmen's Bureau had only moderate success.

After reconstruction the states took up what was their proper task, the developing of effective state systems. They were greatly aided in the effort to provide for universal and improved education by the boards and funds created by Northern philanthropists. Beginning about 1900 the Southern Education Board initiated campaigns in state after state to inform and arouse the citizens. The work was really done by the Southern people themselves. In regard to education this was the beginning of the new South.

As will be shown in a later chapter, the public high school in the South is also a result of the awakening in the present century. There were few high schools in the section before 1900 and practically none outside the cities. While the first effort was an attempt to develop standard college-preparatory schools, the South became the pioneer in the development of agricultural high schools teaching also home economics, health, and housing.

Teachers for the elementary and high schools are prepared in public and private colleges. A special feature of Southern education is the large number of Negro colleges, great private universities and small substandard colleges, and the Negro land-grant institutions, only now beginning to go forward.

QUESTIONS

1. What would have been the effect of the enactment of the Blair Bill? Was its failure fortunate or unfortunate for the United States? For the children of the South?

2. Evaluate the Southern arguments against public education. We may assume that public education is not perfect.

3. How may we account for the shortcomings of the prewar school law and educational efforts in North Carolina?

4. Compare the Northern postwar educational efforts in the South with those of the United States in Germany after World War II.

5. Why do you agree (or disagree) with the view that the educational differences between North and South had little influence upon the Civil War?

6. What may be learned from the Southern experience concerning educational promotion?

7. Would Booker Washington have been more successful if he could have foreseen the present labor organizations, the status of the leading trades, and other conditions bearing on Negro education? Why or why not?

8. What conclusions useful in American education can be drawn from a comparison of Negro education and race relations in the American South and South Africa?

BOOKS AND PAPERS

Some of the shorter papers by Edgar W. Knight of the University of North Carolina may be located through the *Education Index*. He was a leading student of the educational history of his section, and his *Documentary History* contains many of the sources for a study of the earlier developments in the South. Eleven or more of the Circulars of Information published by the Bureau of Education deal with the Southern states and cover education in the reconstruction period. A list of the Circulars may be conveniently found in Tewksbury's *Founding of the American Colleges,* p. 253. The reports of the General Education Board deal with a later period.

Alderman, E. A., and A. C. Gordon, *J. L. M. Curry, A Biography,* New York, 1911; and Jessie Pearl Rice, *J. L. M. Curry, Southerner, Statesman, and Educator,* New York, 1949.

Bond, Horace Mann, *The Education of the Negro in the American Social Order,* New York, 1934.

Boyd, W. K., "The Antecedents of the North Carolina Convention of 1835," *South Atlantic Quarterly,* January and April, 1910.

Buck, Paul H., "The Poor Whites of the Ante-Bellum South," *American Historical Review,* October, 1945.

Curry, J. L. M., *George Peabody and a History of the Peabody Fund Through Thirty Years,* Cambridge University Press, 1898.

Dabney, C. W., *Universal Education in the South,* University of North Carolina Press, 1926, two volumes.

Knight, E. W., *Influence of Reconstruction on Education in the South,* New York, Teachers College, Columbia University, 1913; *Public Education in North Carolina,* Boston, 1916.

Konkle, B. A., *John Motley Morehead and the Development of North Carolina, 1796–1866,* Philadelphia, 1922, with specially drawn maps to show political history.

Lee, Gordon C., *The Struggle for Federal Aid: First Phase,* New York, 1949.

McVey, Frank L., *The Gates Open Slowly, A History of Education in Kentucky,* University of Kentucky Press, 1949.

Ryan, W. Carson, and Others, *Secondary Education in the South,* University of North Carolina Press, 1946, being a collection of papers by several authors.

Swint, Henry L., *The Northern Teacher in the South, 1862–1870,* Vanderbilt University Press, 1941.

Walker, N. W., "Joseph Spencer Stewart: an Appreciation," *The High School Journal,* January, 1935.

Washington, Booker T., *Up From Slavery, an Autobiography,* New York, 1900.

Chapter X

COLLEGES FOR THE PEOPLE

THE new college of agriculture and the mechanic arts was proposed for the people of the farm and shop who had small interest in purely academic education. Although it was not a wholly unique institution, it was modeled upon no other particular one and it is native to the United States. Efforts to establish similar schools had been carried on for two generations, at least ever since Thomas Jefferson had attempted to include agriculture among the studies of his university; but they had not succeeded for lack of a definite plan, financial support, and the interest of those who were to be benefited.

Undergraduate colleges of agriculture were not unknown in other countries. It was in 1856 that McGill University in Montreal created a faculty or school of agriculture and later one of engineering. Similar provisions were made in Australia and other British dominions which have an undergraduate college. Europe, lacking such an institution, has created separate specialized schools of agriculture, engineering, and other vocations. Latin America combines the technical and higher vocational faculties in its universities, but these are specialized divisions, not providing a general education. It is in educational systems which stem from the British schools that one finds the combination of general or liberal and special vocational studies in the same curricula.

This characteristic also marks the American high school, with which, as we shall show, the new colleges were to be closely connected. The high school also is different from the schools of its type in other countries. The difference is found particularly in its comprehensiveness. Proposing to enroll "all American youth," it attempts to provide a program of courses that will serve every large interest group. The new college was a similarly liberal-vocational school that combined many of the functions of the old college and the technical school; and it has prospered because it has succeeded in opening new doors to youth.

The original name was fairly descriptive. It was a college of agriculture and mechanic arts. Neither of these subjects was well developed in 1860, and the term "engineering" was not much used in early days. More recently the name "land-grant college" has gained in favor, but its brevity is its only recommendation, for it does not indicate the nature or the functions of the school. In view of the prodigality of the government of post-Civil War times, one might with equal appropriateness speak of land-grant railroads. Still later the schools have in many cases adopted the name "state college," which at least indicates that they are public institutions. We shall use these titles interchangeably.

Both the high school and the new college had from the first, or they have developed, a decidedly vocational purpose. Education in the United States became pragmatic long before the word was chosen as "a new name for an old way of thinking." The philosopher merely tried to justify a program that had already commended itself to the active portion of the community. The pragmatic, vocational purpose provided a powerful drive for educational experiment. From ancient times to modern, vocations had been acquired by the conventional, unimaginative method of apprenticeship. The development of schools which joined science and practice marked a new educational epoch. In the nineteenth century such schools were still new, and the land-grant college, especially, was founded upon the view that science could become useful in agriculture and industry.

It was not a doctrine that could be easily made acceptable to the working farmers and mechanics. We shall trace several of the efforts to develop schools of agriculture and engineering prior to the Morrill (land-grant) Act of 1862. Private schools and academies in the colonies and the young nation, as we have shown, taught surveying, navigation, bookkeeping, and other vocational activities. Such training, with some practical experience added, prepared young men to build roads and canals, to lay out towns, and to perform other construction work. Fairfield Academy in New York was known for its elementary engineering courses. The Erie Canal, which was opened in 1825, was built by young men whose schooling was obtained in an academy. Here we have a beginning in the teaching of one of the main fields of the land-grant college, namely, what the Morrill Act called the mechanic arts.

1. SCHOOLS OF A NEW ERA

The opening of the Erie Canal may be taken to mark a new epoch in the life of the United States, the beginning of the age of the canals, railroads, and mass transportation inland. At that time there were no schools of civil engineering in the United States; but the national Military Academy at West Point, which had been established in 1802 and reformed in 1815, prepared military engineers. In times of peace some of these young lieutenants, having resigned their commissions, turned their training to the building of railroads and public works, and some to the teaching of engineering in colleges and academies. Joseph G. Swift, the first West Point graduate, taught such courses at Hobart College. Captain Alden Partridge, when he was dismissed from his position as superintendent of the Military Academy, established Norwich University, where he developed an engineering course. At the old Cincinnati College another West Point graduate began a course in civil engineering in 1836. He was Ormsby M. Mitchel, who made a fortune not by teaching engineering but by practicing it and investing in the railroads which he built.

The supply of engineers from the Military Academy was, however, limited and the demand was increasing. With the growth of cities and the large factories, needing streets, water, power, and other facilities, with the westward expansion of the nation redoubling the need for transportation, with the Civil War and the economic expansion which followed, the demand for engineers increased in a geometrical ratio. And this is where the land-grant colleges came in.

Experiments in the teaching of agriculture proceeded in step with the first attempts to teach engineering. There was no logical necessity for the union, and today, when the two are taught in the same institution as they are in the land-grant college, they are administered in completely separate departments. The reason for their more intimate union in early days is the historical one that the farmer in earlier times had to be a jack-of-all-trades. This may account also for the early designation of the land-grant institutions as colleges of agriculture and mechanic arts.

The idea of a school of agriculture and related skills had occurred to several men, including Thomas Jefferson, before 1800. Further interest in the matter may have been created by the introduction of the Fellenberg manual labor education, but this proved to be an unfortunate effort, partly because it favored practice without science. Several academic colleges undertook to teach agriculture and failed for the opposite reason. They were unable to apply their sciences to practical life. And experience seems to indicate that new kinds of instruction to serve a new clientele are more successful in specially designed schools. A radically new departure is apt to be emasculated if it is made a part of an old school with a successful tradition. To receive fair treatment it must be put into the care of its friends. This is part of the reason why the land-grant colleges succeeded after much travail when other attempts had failed.

Two specially designed schools that were as successful as their resources permitted were the Gardiner Lyceum of Maine and the Rensselaer School of New York. Robert Hallowell Gardiner owned large tracts of land on the Kennebec River. These he donated about 1820 to found a school "to prepare youth by a scientific education to become skilful farmers and mechanics." He had found surveyors and millwrights working by rule-of-thumb, wholly ignorant of the principles underlying their work. "Our farmers were still less intelligent," he wrote. The school was incorporated with six trustees in 1822, received aid from the two-year-old state of Maine, and prospered through the ministrations of a succession of remarkable teachers. Three of these, Benjamin Hale, John H. Lathrop, and Ezekiel Holmes, left their mark on education in several states. The program of studies in 1824 included English but no foreign language, chemistry, agri-cultural chemistry, physics, mathematics, and navigation; but the courses were largely individual and elective, the students working on experiments and special topics. This highly flexible plan and the fact that the school had a system of student self-government, already mentioned in an earlier chap-ter, raises the question whether its founder and teachers were acquainted with the work of the Hill family at Hazelwood School in England. The Gardiner Lyceum has been called "America's first agricultural school"; but after it lost its state subsidy, about 1831, it became under uninspired teachers a humdrum New England academy.

The second specially designed and temporarily successful school of applied science, noticed above, was founded in 1825 at Troy, New York, by Stephen Van Rensselaer and named for him, Rensselaer School. The founder was one of the feudal landlords, deriving from the Dutch patroon system of the early settlements. Since he collected rents from vast estates, one reason for his interest in agricultural prosperity is obvious. The Rens-selaer School used laboratory and field-experience methods in teaching chemistry, physics, geology, natural history, and other sciences useful to farmers. The purpose was the indirect one of preparing teachers "to instruct rural youth in the application of science to the common purposes of life." The school educated many men who became eminent as college professors, state geologists and entomologists, or consulting chemists, but, as in the case of the early land-grant colleges, few of the graduates became teachers of farm children. In 1835 a brief course in civil engineering was offered and became so popular that the school quickly became a technological institu-tion. It is now called the Rensselaer Polytechnic Institute.

A number of other agricultural schools were projected or established. The Cream Hill School in Connecticut and the Farmer's College near Cincinnati were actually opened and maintained for some years. In New

York Simeon DeWitt's plan for an agricultural college and the People's College proposed by Harrison Howard and in Virginia the farm school proposed by Richard Kidder Meade were unrealized projects. With a little more skill and management the People's College might have succeeded. There were also efforts to establish state colleges. It was the failure of the New York legislature to follow the lead of Jesse Buel about 1823 which caused Van Rensselaer to create his private school. The Massachusetts legislature debated the question of a state school about the same time but also refused to act. With all this interest and these "near misses" it was clear that some state would soon hit the target at which so many had aimed. And this actually happened. Michigan, Maryland, and Pennsylvania almost simultaneously about 1857 established state schools or colleges of agriculture that proved to be permanent institutions. The movement had been growing for several decades, and Justin S. Morrill, who had such a large part in furthering it, became a congressman just in time to capitalize upon the interest created by the propaganda.

2. FIRST MORRILL BILL

Morrill was the author of the land-grant bill. This is not denied. But after the colleges had become successful and the original moves had been forgotten, a debate arose over the origin of the idea. There were many direct anticipations of the land-grant act. A call for a federal land endowment for state schools of science, agriculture, engineering, and business was contained in a memorial to Congress submitted by Alden Partridge in 1841. He had even proposed that the proceeds should be distributed to the states in proportion to their representation in Congress. It is possible that Partridge was Morrill's prompter in regard to these ideas. It is even probable, for they lived in the same part of Vermont, and Morrill's business partner was a trustee of Partridge's school, Norwich University. Indeed, Morrill himself had been proposed for a place on the board but refused the invitation. It is known that the two men met and Partridge was not one to conceal his ideas; but yet actual demonstration of Morrill's debt to Partridge is lacking.

The attempt to link Morrill with Professor Jonathan B. Turner of Illinois College at Jacksonville ends in a similarly indefinite conclusion. A number of farmers and industrialists in Illinois attempted to obtain federal aid for vocational education. This so-called "Turner Movement" persuaded the Illinois legislature in 1853 to adopt a resolution asking Congress for a donation to each state of half a million acres of public land for a state industrial university. Turner proposed to have these institutions formed to prepare teachers of agriculture and industrial subjects in high schools and lyceums. It was Turner's view that the higher institutions would reform the lower, making them practically useful to farmers, mechanics, and the working people in general. But as in the case of Partridge, the debt of Morrill to Turner has not been proved. There has been some tendency to minimize Turner's ability and to consider him a blunderhead; but his idea that the colleges should prepare teachers of agriculture and engineering has proved sounder than Morrill's program.

One may believe that Morrill must have learned about the proposals for agricultural schools that were so widely published. Many men for many years had been trying to devise a workable scheme. Yet Morrill claimed that the ideas in his bills were his own; but he freely admitted that some of his colleagues in Congress helped him in getting the legislative approval which gave the ideas all their importance. Some present-day students have concluded that the exact opposite was the fact, that the basic ideas of the legislation were gathered from various sources, but that it was Morrill's parliamentary skill and his persuasive advocacy of the proposals that secured the passage of both the agricultural education bills introduced by him.

The first of these bills was passed by Congress in 1859. It provided for the appropriation to each state of 20,000 acres of public land for each of a state's members in Congress. This endowment was to support colleges of agriculture and the mechanic arts. The bill permitted the teaching of the usual academic subjects but the vocational branches were to be especially emphasized. In the debate Morrill declared that his purpose was simply "to do something for the farmer"; but it has been conjectured that his original idea, not publicly acknowledged, was to attach the farmers and industrial workers to the new Republican party. The debates and the voting on the bill were strongly partisan in complexion, the Whigs and Republicans generally voting for it and the Democrats against it, Northerners generally favoring and Southerners opposing it. It was the time of the Kansas-Nebraska Act, the Dred Scott decision, and the John Brown raid. Instead of considering the educational purpose and probable effect of the law, the debate ranged over questions of states' rights and constitutionality and the probable effect of the dispersal of a quantity of public lands, which was, however, a mere trifle compared to the vast empire donated to the railroads.

According to the bill the land was to be unequally distributed, the largest amounts going to the most populous states. Some argued that this was, on a per capita basis, an equal distribution. These ignored the fact that certain basic expenditures may be just as great for a small as for a larger college. This same question of what constitutes a just and equal distribution was to reappear again and again in the consideration of subsequent educational legislation. The members from the large and rich states are usually reluctant to share their funds with the poorer states. The same broad, humanly selfish attitude which troubled the Constitutional Convention in 1787 frequently appears in educational administration. It was this trait that was revealed in the claim that the state has no right to tax a man for the education of another man's children. Cities do not willingly help in the support of rural schools. Federal aid bills have a difficult time in Congress for several reasons, but one of them is that rich states want to reserve all their wealth for their own use. The author of the land-grant bill certainly saw that it would be difficult to secure its passage unless the states with many votes were given the greater prizes. He reported that his colleagues to whom he appealed for advice applauded the purpose of the measure but doubted that it had any chance of adoption. The bill was passed in February, 1859.

The debate had provided the chief topics for the veto message which President Buchanan sent to Congress. The President said that the bill showed disregard of the financial needs of the government in a time of stringency. This was a reference to the economic distress of 1857. The land market would be glutted by the offer of so many million acres for sale at one time and the government would lose millions. He predicted that the states would soon ask for further aid from the Treasury and this prophecy did indeed come true. He thought the government had "no power and should have no power" to follow the donation into the states to make sure that it would be applied to its intended object. This statement incidentally reveals that there was no real substance to the argument that this law would infringe upon the rights of the states. If the government was helpless in the case it could not at the same time interfere with "state sovereignty." But what the President seemed to imply was that the states could not be trusted. Measures have since been taken to guarantee that federal funds granted to the states for education will be properly applied. The laws which serve this purpose would not have been approved by extreme advocates of states' rights.

The President also held that the law would injure the existing colleges, many of which, he incorrectly believed, were already teaching agriculture. There were only a few efforts in that direction and these were feeble. Without federal aid it is unlikely that they would have soon succeeded. The argument of the message may be largely specious, but as it restated the proclaimed views of almost half of the members of Congress, the supporters of the bill did not have the power to override the veto. The

Civil War and the political and economic forces of later times completely changed the opinion of the country in this matter. Congress has passed several bills providing federal aid to the states for vocational education. Beginning with Lincoln, half a dozen Presidents of both major parties have signed these acts without vetoing or probably even contemplating the veto of any one of them. One cannot miss the significance of this centralizing and nationalizing trend. We shall take up the first and most fundamental of these federal laws, fundamental because it created the institution through which the later laws are administered.

3. MORRILL ACT OF 1862

Outside of Congress the agitation for a land-grant college law continued after the veto as before. In Congress Morrill made what he later acknowledged to have been a rather fretful speech; but in December, 1861, he gave notice to the House that he intended to introduce a bill similar to the previous one. This new bill, after a debate that dealt mainly with public land questions and, as in the former case, hardly at all with educational objectives, was passed and became law through the signature of Lincoln in July, 1862. Two months earlier the Congress had enacted another law that was to have the most far-reaching influence upon the real purposes of the Morrill Act. By that earlier law the Congress had created the United States Department of Agriculture.

In his new bill Morrill had made two major changes from the earlier version. The law as enacted raised the amount of land per member of Congress from 20,000 to 30,000 acres; and it provided that the new colleges were to teach military tactics. According to the new multiplier, New York, with thirty-three members in both Houses, would and did receive eleven times as much free land as Kansas, a new state, with its two senators and a single representative. There were several states that received the smallest possible amount, but we may continue our comparison between New York and Kansas. New York obtained 990,000 acres, or forty-three townships, and Kansas was to have 90,000 acres. The amount actually bestowed was about 97,000 acres. There was no discrimination. The comparison only shows the inequality resulting from the fair application of a bad principle.

The total amount of the grants to all the states under the Morrill Act was 16,000 square miles. This seems like a large amount when one compares it with the areas of the smaller states. There are eight states each with an area of less than 16,000 square miles. But the public lands at one time and another held in trust by the nation comprised about two-thirds of its whole area. Of this vast expanse the agricultural college grant was a small fraction. It is still a small fraction when the comparison is made only with the lands that were granted to various railroads. The government made its first grant of public lands to encourage railroad building in 1850. But in 1862 Congress chartered the Union Pacific Railroad and in less than a decade it chartered, and out of the public lands endowed with more than royal munificence, a whole group of great railroad corporations. Also in 1862 Lincoln signed the Homestead Act which gave a quarter-section of land without cost to any citizen who would improve it and live on it for five years. These and other historical facts are pertinent to any consideration of the grants for education by the Congress of 1862.

The other change made by Morrill in his second bill, the military training requirement, has sometimes been taken to mean that while the colleges are enjoined to teach military tactics, this training may be made optional to the students. Some of the colleges have at times followed this course. But it may be doubted that this was the intent of the framer of the law or of the Congress. We were at war when the bill was passed. Morrill, arguing for the clause, said that the training would improve our preparation against possible foreign enemies. It may be noticed also that Morrill and his colleagues could have known little by report and less by experience of elective systems and optional exercises in college. Such practices were still rare in 1862. In practice, as indicated, some of the colleges have at some time made military training optional with the students. But in nearly all, state law or college regulation has made it a requirement for graduation. Conscientious objectors have in some cases been excused.

According to the Morrill Act each state which accepted the grant was required to apply the proceeds "to the endowment, support, and maintenance of, at least, one college, where the leading object shall be, without excluding other scientific and classical studies, and including military tactics, to teach such branches of learning as are related to agriculture and the mechanic arts, in such manner as the legislatures of the States may respectively prescribe, in order to promote the liberal and practical education of the industrial classes in the several pursuits and professions in life." This language may upon a first reading seem clear; but it proved puzzling to the founders of the colleges, who attempted to use the wording as a guide in developing new institutions. The extreme positions were occupied by opposing groups: those who preferred a broad, inclusive construction of the sentence and those who insisted in placing a narrow and strict limitation upon the studies that could be considered as related to agriculture and the mechanic arts.

The broad constructionists argued for the study of the necessary mathematics, science, and language which would enable the student to understand the principles of his business. The strict constructionists took a "practical" and at the extreme a trade-school view. In the end the broad constructionists won the argument, but since their plan required thorough preparation for entrance and the early students were not well prepared, the victory was delayed for many years. At last it became clear that without a sound scientific and scholarly foundation there can be no collegiate teaching of agriculture or engineering.

4. Organization of the Colleges

Many of the states hesitated to accept the grant. Each had the right to decide upon the location and, within the terms of the act, upon the character of the college. Broad and narrow construction were both within its terms. State legislatures normally set up committees or outside boards to solve these critical questions, and these bodies sometimes split into warring factions. Existing colleges also, without ever having thought about the matter before, suddenly discovered their fitness and asserted their eagerness to serve as land-grant colleges. Not only sectarian colleges or struggling little schools but proud state universities entered into the contest for the federal funds. Evan Pugh of Pennsylvania, who was an able promoter of this type of "new education," referred to the undignified haste of the literary colleges to grasp for resources to which they had no legitimate claim. In Michigan, Maryland, and Pennsylvania the grant was given to the state schools of agriculture which had recently been founded. In Ohio a college of agriculture and mechanic arts and in Illinois an industrial university were created, but these within a few years were transformed into state universities which included the teaching of agriculture and the mechanic arts.

In fifteen states, where the state university had become well established, the land-grant institution was made a part of it, while in twenty-eight others it was established as a separate "A. and M." college. Later other states accepted the former of these two plans. In Morrill's home state of Vermont, when an effort was made to separate the land-grant college from the state university, he opposed the proposal. Massachusetts founded a separate college of agriculture over the opposition of Harvard, Amherst, Williams, and other colleges. This has now become the University of Massachusetts, but it still devotes most of its strength to agriculture, horticulture, and home economics. In this state, however, one-third of the Morrill Act grant was assigned to a private school, the Massachusetts Institute of Technology, for engineering education.

In several other states the grant was assigned to private institutions with results that were not always happy. In four of these the federal grant was afterwards withdrawn from the private institution and applied to a newly organized land-grant college. One of the cases occurred in Connecticut, where the Sheffield Scientific School of Yale University was at first selected to receive the grant. To many this seemed an admirable choice, because Yale had an excellent record in science instruction dating from the early years of the century when Benjamin Silliman joined her faculty. More recently a school of applied chemistry had been developed. And the Yale authorities took special care to assure themselves that they had the facilities needed to meet the demands of the law. They invited its author to a conference at the Sheffield School and Morrill informed them that a farm was not absolutely necessary to fulfill the law's requirements. It had been his purpose, he said, to establish schools of science rather than agricultural schools. The title of the bill, Morrill declared, was not his but was assigned to it by a clerk and was not altogether appropriate. This is one more example of Morrill's vacillation when dealing with educational questions. It is hardly profitable to argue about the source of his ideas when he could not remember what they were.

The farmers of Connecticut had other and more settled ideas. They thought Yale treated agriculture as a secondary interest. They objected to the high admission requirements and the theoretical nature of the teaching. The Grange began to agitate for the removal of the grant to a school that would be closer to the soil. In the Cream Hill School of Agriculture they thought they had an example of what was needed. The Storrs Agricultural School was founded in 1881. It became the Storrs Agricultural College in 1893, and the federal funds were transferred to it after the state had indemnified Yale for their loss. The Storrs School was renamed Connecticut State College in 1933 and the University of Connecticut in 1939. It seems probable that this title will still be in use when the centennial year rolls around in 1981. Other unfortunate unions that ended in divorce occurred at Transylvania University in Kentucky and at Dartmouth College. In a few cases, as at Cornell and Rutgers Universities, the affiliation with a private institution became a permanent arrangement.

The colleges did not find it easy to live within their means. Their lands were mismanaged in some cases or sold at bargain prices. More than half of the states sold them at less than the customary $1.25 per acre, and three states received less than fifty cents per acre. The funds were not always safely invested. The same political and financial irregularities which had led to the dissipation of the federal grants for common schools reappeared in the management of the college. To this there were exceptions. The Cornell lands, for example, were selected and managed by Ezra Cornell, and the university realized an average of just over $5.50 per acre on its almost 1,000,000 acres.

Some clear conclusions may be drawn from this history. Because most American colleges were financially poor they grasped for the "new money" of the federal grant without considering how well they were qualified to carry out the program. But also there was no definite understanding of the program. Even Morrill had no developed plan. Local and state pressure groups exerted undue influence in locating and organizing the schools. And the states failed to secure the services of experts on the conservation and management of their lands and trust funds.

5. COLLEGE PROBLEMS

Other perplexing discoveries came to light. One was that the much advertised demand for the colleges did not come from working farmers. This is shown by the epithets they used and the scorn they heaped upon the schools. After all the clamor about the urgent need for agricultural education, it was found that the men who followed the plow and fed the cattle had little respect for the "book farming" taught in the "cow colleges." And what was worse, there was little scientific agriculture to be taught because the science was in its infancy. Partly for this reason the long exploded manual labor scheme was tried and rejected again. At the Michigan State Agricultural College the students were required to work three hours a day doing ordinary farm work and chores. And this was not unusual. Manual labor, after it was given up in the arts colleges and theological seminaries, was revived in the colleges of agriculture and in time again discarded.

It was found that the young people from the country schools could not read, write, and figure well enough for the work the colleges attempted to do. One-fourth of the students who applied for admission did not have "a good common school education" and the colleges found it necessary to establish preparatory departments. And this was true in Massachusetts as well as in Iowa and Kansas. This evidence in regard to the state of common school education in the country districts is supported by the fact that it was the universal practice of normal schools to review the common branches in regular classes. It also has bearing upon the present controversy over the past and present effectiveness of the schools in teaching the three R's.

In technical matters the early professors were not well prepared. They were, without question, educated men, but educated in classics, theology or, best of all, in medicine. One early professor, whose later success and reputation permitted him to be candid, has described his own beginning practice. He said: "I began to tell the students what I knew about farming. It did not take me long to run short of materials." There was nothing in the library to help him. "One might as well have looked for cranberries in the Rocky Mountains." And "thus fortunately," he concluded, "I was driven to take the class to the field and farm. . . ." This was the tactic of Isaac Roberts, later professor at Cornell University, who obtained practical teaching materials by having students collect weeds from the near-by farms. In other classes the pupils had to recite not merely the ideas but even the words of the textbook.

Every new curriculum departure raises a similar problem: Where to find those who can teach what they have not been taught? On the nonsensical theory that everyone has to be taught everything that he will be called upon to do, there could be no progress whatever. The answer is that a few men of talent will invent new methods, organize materials, and devise equipment. When the new schools become better established, they can supply each other with capable teachers; and this is what the land-grant colleges did. They were aided by the experiment stations, as we shall see.

Step by step the schools developed new policies. Women were admitted almost from the first at several colleges, and at Kansas State College from the very beginning. At Iowa State College about one-third of the students in the first quarter-century were women. Michigan and Illinois admitted women in 1870, Nebraska in 1871. They were not better prepared than the men and many were placed in the preparatory departments. Kansas established a "kitchen laboratory" in 1874, and early forms of home economics teaching were introduced in a number of the colleges. Manual training was taught to men. Winter short courses on the campus and farmers' institutes off the campus were undertaken. The long vacation was placed in mid-winter to permit students to earn money teaching country schools. Some schools attempted to arrange their courses so that those who would not graduate could obtain the greatest practical value from their studies.

Everything possible was done to attract students, but to little avail. Enrollments remained low until about 1900. In the early decades engineering attracted more students and proved itself more teachable and more useful when acquired than agriculture. Only one-third of the early graduates had been enrolled in agriculture, and most of these did not engage in farming, but entered government service, or became scientists or teachers.

This condition changed as the applications of science to agriculture became better developed and the colleges became able to offer more useful and specialized courses in agronomy, animal husbandry, horticulture, and other fields.

Among the several agencies for the creation of a scientific agriculture, the experiment stations had a leading role. Such institutions were well known in Europe and their value was demonstrated before they were introduced into America. Evan Pugh, the first head of the Pennsylvania State University, after obtaining a doctor's degree in chemistry in a German university, undertook a research project in plant physiology at the famed experimental farms at Rothamsted in England. After or even before the land-grant colleges were established, provision for experimental farms was generally made. At least seventeen states had created such farms or stations before federal assistance was given. But in 1887 Congress passed the Hatch Act appropriating $15,000 annually to each state for agricultural research. This amount was increased by the Adams Act of 1906 and the Purnell Act of 1925. These laws recognized that the improvement of teaching in the colleges waited upon the advancement of knowledge. The experiment station became the research arm, coordinate with the teaching function of each land-grant college.

6. Second Morrill Act

The colleges had early learned that they could not thrive on their endowments. Much of the land, as we have seen, had been sold at low prices, the proceeds had not always been well invested, and as a result the annual income was often small and uncertain. One state reported an annual income of less than $7,000. The institutions, mindful that they were to be the institutions of the poor, had a tender conscience and also a sober wisdom that restrained them from setting high rates of tuition or piling fees upon fees. But they needed money. Within a decade after 1862 they were back, as President Buchanan had foreseen, knocking upon the door of the Treasury.

Morrill, whose interest in the schools never flagged, initiated a campaign for an annual money grant to colleges that had been "permanently endowed" by a land grant. This bill proposed to provide equal amounts to the small and the large states. It was repeatedly introduced into Congress in 1872, 1873, 1875, 1879, and so on until 1890, when it finally overcame the long-continued opposition. With the signature of President Harrison the second Morrill Act became law.

During the years while the bill had been under consideration, several states had come to understand that their state universities could not prosper without regular support. The land-grant colleges, on the same ground, appealed to the Congress. The second Morrill Act provided for an annual appropriation from the national Treasury to each land-grant college of $15,000 for the first year, the amount to rise by $1,000 each year to a maximum of $25,000 a year. This maximum was to become the regular and permanent contribution of the government to the current expense of each college.

The law had another provision. It required that the annual appropriation of the act should be withheld from states which required the segregation of the races unless they provided agricultural and mechanical colleges for Negroes. Thus the law in effect required the establishment of the seventeen such institutions which are now in operation in the Southern states. These have been noticed in the preceding chapter.

In the debates on the bill some echoes of old disputes were heard and early experiences of the college recited. It was reported that speculators had resold college lands purchased at a fraction of the government price for a hundred times the amount paid for them. At one time Morrill had proposed joining his forces with the supporters of the Blair Bill, mentioned in Chapter IX; but when he discovered that this bill would not pass, he concentrated upon his own objective and succeeded. The old confusion between broad and narrow education plagued the debates. Really there still were three main views: that the colleges should teach rule-of-thumb farming and shopwork; or that they should teach the application of science to agricultural, engineering, and related interests; or that they should aid the poor, the children of farmers and industrial workers, to obtain a college education. Morrill himself said in 1890 that the colleges should teach "all the learning demanded by any portion of the American people." With this somewhat ambitious phrase we may compare Ezra Cornell's desire to "found an institution where anyone may study anything."

The land-grant institutions may not be able to meet such inclusive demands; but, in competition and cooperation with state and independent universities, they have themselves become universities. With a vocational emphasis that is wanting in some other higher educational institutions, they have developed their own programs without much regard for the abstract ideas of legislators and philosophers. And in the process they have not only met the demands of the technological callings but have helped to develop new vocations that were not anticipated by the founders.

Never in any of the debates on the bills introduced by Morrill was it proposed that the land-grant colleges should prepare teachers. But by 1890 and 1900 several state and independent universities had begun to establish departments or schools of education. Many high schools were teaching manual training and shopwork, home economics, and agriculture, the very subjects in which the land-grant colleges were supposed to be expert and for which they might well have been commissioned to prepare teachers. Yet they did not actively enter upon this work until the twentieth century.

A slight beginning was made through the effort to secure increased income for their rapidly expanding work. The Nelson Amendment to provide further support was added to the 1907 appropriation bill of the Department of Agriculture. A proviso was inserted to permit a part of the money to be used for the preparation of teachers of agriculture and the mechanic arts. The effect of this would have been to draw the high schools into closer relations with the colleges. Actually not much of the new money was applied in preparing teachers. But a decade later the foundation was laid for a nationwide system of vocational education and the preparation of high school vocational teachers. Thus the land-grant colleges came to prepare teachers on a great scale. But before this came about the Congress developed a nationwide system of extension teaching. This action was directly influenced by the boys' and girls' club work.

7. Rural Club Work

Many parents knew long ago that young people on the farm take more interest in their work if they are given a calf, or colt, to raise as their own property; and it helps to make the youngsters not only better farmers but also better people. Parents often acted upon this principle, which involves some of the elements of club work.

Not only parents but also editors, railroad presidents, agricultural fair executives, superintendents of schools, and other community leaders sometimes acted upon the same principle. They may have been idealists or their aid to the youth may have been a skilful form of advertising. In either case the results were the same. Horace Greeley of the New York Tribune paid a prize of fifty dollars to the teen-age winner of a New York corn growing contest. This was in 1856 and the yield of the measured acre was seventy-six bushels of shelled corn—very good for 1856. Similar contests were held in other states. Although these events lacked the scientific basis and the professional guidance of present-day club work, they grew from the grass-roots and were publicly and genuinely competitive.

A high proportion of the leaders of these competitions were rural school officers, and many of the activities were connected with the schools. We have seen that Arbor Day, school gardens, and the nature study movement all began in the latter half of the century. Liberty H. Bailey and his Cornell University associates were among the leaders. We shall mention a few of the school people who led in club work. A township superintendent, A. B. Graham, in Clark County, Ohio, organized a boys' farm club in 1902. Many people had similar ideas, but he was certainly among the early ones. A rural county superintendent, O. G. Kern, was forming similar groups in Illinois. Both men secured help from their state universities and experiment stations. These institutions had a particular interest in the matter because they wanted to get plain dirt farmers to try fertilizers, seeds, kinds of tillage, and other experiments. Kern seems to have been more concerned to develop the interest of parents and children in the schools than he was in growing bigger crops. He tried to connect farm and school by drawing upon the farm work for problems in arithmetic and other school subjects. Kern also organized girls' clubs and campaigned for school gardens.

The true club requires the members to follow the most scientific procedure that can be applied and demands of every member a full account of all expenses, materials used, work done, and every pertinent feature. Everything is measured and stated in quantitative terms. The work is supervised by a competent leader. Prizes and recognition are given to the most successful. This club idea for farm boys and girls spread incredibly fast from state to state and took in more and more activities. In the South it was connected with Seaman A. Knapp's farm demonstrations; and it spread over the country with the county-agent idea.

As superintendent of schools of a Minnesota county, T. A. Erickson developed a program of educational and agricultural improvement similar to that of O. J. Kern in Illinois. In 1905 he used his own money to provide a number of boys with seed corn, the next year he added potatoes, and then settings of eggs. J. J. Hill of the Great Northern Railroad gave him a very modest sum for a prize. Erickson became rural school specialist of the state university and was commissioned to give aid to teachers in working out their agricultural problems.

In Georgia Joseph Stewart, professor of secondary education at the state university, in 1906 developed a system of corn and cotton growing contests. Those teen-age growers who won in their counties qualified to compete in the state contest. Stewart persuaded the State Fair Association to put up $500 for prizes. Georgia was the first state to declare a state corn champion. All this was a part of Stewart's work, which has already been mentioned, of developing high schools.

A similar kind of promotion was carried on by a county superintendent of schools in Oregon. In 1905 Louis R. Alderman organized a county children's fair. There were contests in gardening, cooking, woodworking, raising farm animals, and other activities. Alderman persuaded the Union Stockyards of Portland to provide a full-time man to travel over the state organizing these county children's fairs. This has been claimed as the origin of the 4-H Club movement in the Northwest.

The Department of Agriculture began to cooperate with the movement first in Iowa in 1912 and in half of the states by 1916. The land-grant colleges have also developed close relations with the 4-H Clubs, cultivating hand, head, heart, and health.

Farm demonstration work and the 4-H Clubs developed at the same time and there is work for both. Knapp found that lectures and bulletins are not enough and that farmers pay little attention even to demonstrations that are provided for them. They have to participate and risk their own land, time, and money in a project and then they do pay attention. Out of Knapp's work in fighting the boll weevil and doubling the Southern farmers' corn crop, there grew the work of the county agents. The first county agent was appointed in 1906 and the plan spread in the South and then in the North and West. The federal government began to aid this plan by making special appropriations for the purpose to the Department of Agriculture.

8. FEDERAL-STATE COOPERATION; SMITH-LEVER ACT

The idea of taking useful knowledge directly to the people was discussed in the meetings of the Association of Land-Grant Colleges in 1885, almost thirty years before the Smith-Lever Act was passed in 1914. When the time came to ask the government for regular and permanent support for extension teaching, Woodrow Wilson had just been elected President. He had never been identified with rural life and it fell to Walter Hines Page to explain to the President-elect the great value of farm demonstration work. Page's success was complete and agriculture was further reassured when David F. Houston became the new Secretary of Agriculture. In a period of three years Wilson approved three of the most important farm and agricultural education bills in the nation's history, the Smith-Lever Act (1914), the Federal Farm Loan Act (1916), and the Smith-Hughes Act (1917).

The Smith-Lever Act at last enabled the agricultural colleges to reach the working farmer and to help him directly with his problems. President Wilson called the law "one of the most significant and far-reaching measures for the education of adults ever adopted by any Government." The act was passed "to aid in diffusing among the people of the United States useful and practical information on subjects relating to agriculture and home economics, and to encourage the application of the same."

The cost of the program is shared almost equally between the federal government and the states. There is, however, for the first time, an element of federal control in a federal bill granting aid to education. The state program must meet standards set up by the Department of Agriculture; and the state director of agricultural extension represents both that department and the land-grant college. The element of federal-state cooperation and federal supervision was a departure from the *laissez-faire* policy of the Morrill Acts and its significance in this respect must not be overlooked. The county agent, who is usually a land-grant college graduate, and who reports to the director at the state college, has been called "the key-teacher" of the extension program. He diffuses the knowledge which works, if any does work.

A few years fortunately were given the new extension service before the United States entered World War I. The difficulties and conflicts which arose between federal and state agencies were adjusted in a conference in 1916. In the war the service aided in producing, conserving, and distributing food, feeds, fertilizer, and seed, in the wise use of clothing and fuel, and in the preservation of health. The home demonstration agents were helpful in the 1918–1919 influenza epidemic. But military demands made it difficult to maintain the extension service and the losses had to be restored again after 1918.

9. COOPERATION, SECOND PHASE; SMITH-HUGHES ACT

The Smith-Hughes Act of 1917 was passed to foster the vocational education of youth aged fourteen or over, chiefly in high schools. The land-grant colleges were to prepare vocational teachers for the high schools; and these in turn broadened the vocational content of the high school program. The bill was intended to provide direction and financial aid for this expensive type of education.

The act called for a Federal Board for Vocational Education with the duty of annually apportioning to the states the federally provided funds. Each state was required to form or designate a state board of vocational education. The states accepted the plan with alacrity. Each state board submits its plan for vocational education to the federal board for approval. The power to approve or disapprove is obviously the power to exercise control. A similar scheme of national and local cooperation is used in England to maintain general education in primary and secondary schools. There the local education authorities submit development schemes to the office of the Ministry of Education in London. Whether such plans result in excessive centralization depends more upon the will of the people and the spirit of the administration than it does upon the letter of the law. Such a plan could be adapted to American needs if there is ever to be federal aid to general education.

The Smith-Hughes Act requires each state to provide for vocational education a sum equal to the amount which it receives for the same purpose from Washington. The money is to be used (1) to pay the salaries of teachers, supervisors, and directors of agricultural subjects; (2) to pay the salaries of teachers of trades, home economics, and industrial subjects; (3) to prepare teachers of all these subjects; (4) to study problems connected with the teaching of the same; (5) to pay for the administration of the law. The act includes a simple formula for determining each state's share of the annual appropriation. This formula is based upon the population census returns, and the rapid shifts from state to state and country to city which are taking place within the ten-year periods tend to create inequities that were not foreseen when the law was framed.

The table below shows the yearly amounts appropriated for each of the first four purposes which the law seeks to achieve. The total amount to be appropriated annually was to be $7,200,000; but this was raised in 1932–1933 to $9,800,000.

FEDERAL FUNDS APPORTIONED UNDER THE SMITH-HUGHES LAW

	Agric. Educa.	Home Ec. and T. and I.	Preparing Teachers of Agric., Home Ec., T. and I.	Research	Total Annual Federal Aid	Annual Increases
1917–1918	$ 500,000	$ 500,000	$ 500,000	$200,000	$1,700,000	
1918–	750,000	750,000	700,000	200,000	2,400,000	$ 700,000
1919–	1,000,000	1,000,000	900,000	200,000	3,100,000	700,000
1920–	1,250,000	1,250,000	1,000,000	200,000	3,700,000	600,000
1921–	1,500,000	1,500,000	1,000,000	200,000	4,200,000	500,000
1922–	1,750,000	1,750,000	1,000,000	200,000	4,700,000	500,000
1923–	2,000,000	2,000,000	1,000,000	200,000	5,200,000	500,000
1924–	2,500,000	2,500,000	1,000,000	200,000	6,200,000	1,000,000
1925–	3,000,000	3,000,000	1,000,000	200,000	7,200,000	1,000,000
The maxima were raised in 1932 to the following amounts:						
1932–1933	4,250,000	4,250,000	1,000,000	300,000	9,800,000	2,600,000

The teaching for which the law provides must be on the secondary, not the college level. The pupils must be fourteen years of age or over. The courses may be provided for full-time or part-time pupils and they must be given in public schools. The Smith-Hughes teachers are attached to high schools and the law may be regarded as a high school law. From this standpoint its purpose is to expand the program of the public secondary school. The instruction is intended to prepare youth for agricultural, industrial, and home occupations of an immediately productive kind, and therefore the act is a vocational education law. While the agitation for such an act was in progress, there was a danger that a separate vocational education system would be established. Fortunately, this division of public education into competing systems was averted, but there are also difficulties in the administration of general and vocational education in the same school. There is a third consideration. The Smith-Hughes Act is a high school law and a vocational education law, but it is also a means of national preparedness. Food and technical skill are essential to national welfare under all conditions of peace or war.

10. College Growth

Men have written of "the original conception" of the land-grant colleges as though these words could be made to stand for a clear and settled idea upon which people were agreed. But this is contrary to the facts. The founders and early promoters of the institutions did not agree upon any general plan, nor did their notions of means and ends remain unchanged through the years. The founders should be regarded as a quite miscellaneous group of politicians and creative social reformers trying to give expression to a set of abstract and only partially developed ideas. They were limited, as all reformers are, by the materials that were available for use. The materials with whom and with which they had to work were classically educated professors, poorly prepared students, inadequate funds, undeveloped sciences and methods, and an unresponsive public. Their "original conceptions" were indistinct and unstable and they tried to make them clear and permanent by giving them expression in new institutions. And it was just this which favored the evolution of a new kind of college. The new institutions had to adapt themselves to a society already well supplied with colleges of older types. They had to be different.

One of the early and widely approved ideas was that the colleges were to be inexpensive, for otherwise farmers' and workingmen's children could not afford to attend. It was an "original conception" that the colleges should be free or low-cost schools. The lower schools and high schools which were in some states still collecting rates or tuition were made free in the period when the colleges were forming. The low fees of this new type of public schools, the land-grant colleges, were in harmony with the general trend of the time in public education.

In time in the administration of the colleges, this policy has been so modified or wholly abandoned that many people today do not know that it ever existed. The payments demanded of students grew slowly at first, reached fairly large annual amounts in the early years of the present century, and were doubled between World War I and the great depression. With the rise in operating costs have come both an increase in the number of fees and the requirement for students in public institutions to pay a rising proportion of the costs. The method by which these unjustifiable demands have been built up would often be the indirect one of piling one fee upon another in a series that might include matriculation, tuition, incidental, special, library, laboratory, athletic, health service, nonresident, and other fees. In one of the large state universities which contains the land-grant college, the students were asked to vote on the addition to their term-bills of a five dollar fee to build a new student union. For obvious reasons, one being that most of the voters would not be payers very long, the measure was carried and the building is now in use; and this case was not unique. The state should erect and pay for state college and university buildings on state property. In some schools, professors have collected a book fee in their classes, and other abuses have grown up in connection with the student expenses in the public land-grant colleges. All this has a direct bearing upon the condition that for every student who is able to attend college there is another equally qualified prospective student who is kept away by the expense. It is hardly a sufficient answer to reply that the fees form only a fraction of the cost of a college education.

The growing college enrollment is a major reason for the increases in the fees. In a single year before the outbreak of World War II there were 20,000 students of home economics and 30,000 in agriculture. Although the numbers in veterinary medicine, forestry, and architecture were small, those in engineering and education were each over 100,000. The increasing size of the universities and colleges, especially of the public ones, is one of the phenomena of our time. And since every student costs the college several times as much as he pays, the larger the student body, the greater the funds that must be obtained from outside sources. The hard-pressed colleges do not wish to neglect any source of aid in balancing their budgets, such as the yield from new fees or of an increased tariff upon the old ones. But this is not in the interest of the student or of society if the social worth of a college education is what is claimed for it.

Many causes have promoted the increases in college attendance. Among these must be listed the development of new professions and callings, the acceptance of college-trained personnel in many business fields, the growth of cities which has drawn a larger proportion of the population to the vicinity of some college, the general prosperity, the very great changes that have occurred within the colleges themselves, and government aid for the education of veterans. All of these causes have affected enrollment in the land-grant colleges, but the internal development in these schools deserves special notice.

There has been a fundamental change in the general aims of the colleges. It is true that the sixty-nine institutions do not agree upon any single or closely similar statement of their aims, yet broad generalization from most of them is possible. The early colleges attempted to teach farming, housekeeping, and shop and trade practice to future practitioners. This is what the extension workers under the Smith-Lever Act and the Smith-Hughes teachers in the high schools, not the colleges, are doing now. The present colleges give more attention than they gave in early days to the basic sciences. Each student is usually asked also to choose a special field, such as dairy technology or clothing and textiles, and to study the applications of the sciences to it. The present-day colleges also give more attention than they formerly did to English, economics, sociology, and other humanistic and social subjects; in none do the curricula consist wholly of vocational subjects; in many the aim is to give a broad scientific and humanistic education with varied opportunities to acquire preparation in special fields.

The graduates become county agents, extension workers, teachers in high schools and in agricultural colleges. They engage in government service and in scientific research. Rural banking, the improvement, appraisal, and sale of land, the marketing of farm products, the management of estates, and farm journalism become the occupations of others. They build roads, design and manufacture machinery, and serve as operating and consulting engineers. They preside over good homes. All this is to say that the chief work of the land-grant colleges is not to prepare for general farming but rather to provide an education both cultural and useful. The broad aims and varied offerings of the colleges may be the most important of the reasons for the increased enrollments. This conclusion is supported by the fact that in the land-grant colleges, established to teach "agriculture and the mechanic arts," about one-third of all the students are in the divi-

sion of arts and sciences. More are enrolled in the arts and sciences than
in agriculture, or education, or home economics, and about as many as are
in engineering. The colleges have become or are becoming universities.
They are in more and more instances taking the name of university or
state college.

The preparation of teachers has become one of the leading activities
of the colleges. Instead of teaching the farmers themselves, as the founders
had intended, they prepare teachers and county agents and through these
they reach thousands of present and future farmers and homemakers where
the colleges could directly touch but a few. The close connection which
has developed between the public schools and the colleges is significant.
Pupils from the high schools go up to the state college and return to the
high schools as superintendents, principals, teachers, board members,
patrons, and taxpayers. The state college and the high school exert a mutual
influence, each upon the other. And as a result the land-grant colleges have
helped to enrich and diversify the program of public education of which
they form an important part.

The broad constructionists of the original Morrill Act have gained a
complete victory. The early effort to establish narrow trade schools never
had any marked success, but the colleges began with directly practical
goals. The act had, however, left a wide opening for the introduction of
"other scientific" and even classical studies. This was a fortunate concession
because the colleges discovered that scientific agriculture and engineering
demand a sound general education as a prerequisite and foundation. The
scientific vocations cannot be effectively taught to any who do not have a
knowledge of English, mathematics, science, the use of books, and the art of
study. Outside the colleges a vast urbanizing and technological change
called for the broad, general education of millions who were no longer
needed on the farm and of city-bred youth who were entering new vocations. As a result not only had the broad constructionists won, but the colleges were on the way to fulfill Morrill's dream, that of providing "all the
learning demanded by any portion of the American people"; or, since the
land-grant colleges do not teach law or medicine, it had better be said that
the colleges and the universities together try to come as close to this vision
as the realities of life permit.

The land-grant college is a new type of institution, a vocational higher
institution for the "industrial classes." The active period of its development may
be dated from the opening of the Erie Canal in 1825 and the beginning of the
railroads. The new transportation required more engineers, and the wasteful

practices and isolation of the farmers required a new agriculture. There were many unsuccessful or temporarily successful attempts to establish schools of agriculture. From these efforts and a memorial to Congress in 1841, it seems probable, came the ideas of Morrill's Bill adopted in 1859 but vetoed by the president. The opposition to the bill was political, constitutional, and financial, and not to any great degree educational. Indeed, no one seems to have known just what educational results were intended. In 1862 a similar bill carrying a larger endowment and requiring military training in the projected colleges was enacted. And a supplementary bill to provide for current support, the second Morrill Act of 1890, required the establishment in the South of similar colleges for Negroes. From these two measures sixty-nine land-grant colleges have resulted.

Several problems arose as a result of this legislation. First was the choice of a model for the organization of the colleges, and the choice fell out in favor of scientific rather than trade schools. The problem of regular support has been implied above; and relief was obtained through the second Morrill Act supplemented by increasing appropriations by the states. The lack of scientific knowledge of agriculture was gradually overcome by the experiment stations which were aided by the Hatch Act. The failure to reach the working farmer and housewife was solved (1) by farm demonstrations, club work, county agents, and other extension work in the main brought under the terms of the Smith-Lever Act of 1914; and (2) by the teaching of agriculture, home economics, and trades and industries in the high schools under the Smith-Hughes Act of 1917.

The land-grant colleges have apparently been influenced by the state universities, which are older and reached relative maturity earlier. This is an excellent example of the "capture" of a groping institution by a more powerful one in the same "field"; and it was made easier by the union in many states of the state university and land-grant college. The land-grant college is less vocational and more general than it was. It offers an education that is both cultural and useful; and it prepares many teachers for the public schools.

QUESTIONS

1. Why did the land-grant colleges succeed although other attempts in the same field had failed? Discover reasons not mentioned in the chapter.

2. Compare the work of Hampton and Tuskegee with the early stages of the land-grant colleges.

3. In what ways did the earlier Rensselaer School anticipate land-grant college activities and problems?

4. Would an equal distribution of the public lands, in the same amount to each state, for the new colleges have served education more effectively than the method actually used? Why or why not?

5. What are the advantages and disadvantages of the separate land-grant college as compared with its union with the state university?

6. Consider the value of the land-grant colleges as cause and means for the development of the high schools. And compare this effect with the influence of the high schools upon the elementary schools.

7. How may one account for the difference between the present work and status of the colleges and the early ideas of what they should become?

8. What new activities should the colleges undertake?

BOOKS AND PAPERS

The magazine *Agricultural History*, the *Cyclopedia of Agriculture*, edited by Liberty Hyde Bailey, and the *Encyclopedia of Educational Research* have accounts of agricultural and vocational education, with bibliographies. The following list contains only a few of a large number of histories of individual land-grant colleges. On the plan of Mr. Meade of Virginia, which was to combine the ideas of Fellenberg and Amos Eaton, see the *American Farmer*, May 26, July 21, 1826, October 24, 1828, and October 1, 1830; and the *National Intelligencer*, September 29, 1830. Unfortunately, the plan was not put into effect.

Bailey, J. C., *Seaman A. Knapp, Schoolmaster of American Agriculture*, Columbia University Press, 1945.

Blackmar, F. W., *History of Federal and State Aid to Higher Education*, Washington, U. S. Government Printing Office, Bureau of Education, Circular of Information, No. 1, 1890.

Blauch, Lloyd E., *Federal Cooperation in Agricultural Extension Work, Vocational Education, and Vocational Rehabilitation*, Washington, U. S. Government Printing Office, Office of Education Bulletin, 1935, No. 15, with bibliography.

Eliot, Charles W., "The Achievements of the Democratic Party and its Leader since March 4, 1913," *Atlantic Monthly*, October, 1916.

Kandel, I. L., *Federal Aid for Vocational Education*, A report to the Carnegie Foundation for the Advancement of Teaching, Bulletin, No. 10, New York, 1917.

Klein, A. J., Director, *Survey of Land-Grant Colleges and Universities*, Washington, U. S. Government Printing Office, Office of Education Bulletin, 1930, No. 9.

Powell, B. E., *Industrial Education and the Establishment of the University [of Illinois]*, *1840–1870*, University of Illinois, 1918.

Price, R. R., *Financial Support of State Universities in the Old Northwest Territory*, Harvard University Press, 1924.

Reck, F. M., *History of 4-H Club Work*, Iowa State College Press, 1951.

Ross, Earle D., *Democracy's College, the Land-Grant Movement in the Formative Stage*, Iowa State College Press, 1942; *History of Iowa State College*, ibid., 1942.

Smith, C. B., and M. C. Wilson, *Agricultural Extension System of the United States,* New York, 1930.

Stemmons, Walter, *Connecticut Agricultural College, A History,* The College, 1931.

Stevens, Neil E., "America's First Agricultural School," *Scientific Monthly,* December, 1921. This excellent paper was mentioned in Chapter V. The claim in the title may be arguable.

True, A. C., *History of Agricultural Extension Work, 1785–1923,* Washington, U. S. Government Printing Office, 1928; *History of Agricultural Education, 1785–1925, ibid.,* 1929; *History of Agricultural Experimentation and Research, 1607–1925, Including a History of the United States Department of Agriculture, ibid.,* 1937.

Willard, J. T., *History of the Kansas State College of Agriculture and Applied Science,* Kansas State College Press, 1940.

Woodward, Carl R., "Woodrow Wilson's Agricultural Philosophy," *Agricultural History,* October, 1940.

Chapter XI

EDUCATION AS A PROFESSION

WHETHER there is a profession of education depends in part upon whether there is a science of education: the two questions thus connected are also partly distinct and independent of each other. There are no universally accepted answers. We shall examine the questions separately, considering first the existence of a science of education.

If there is such a science, it must deal with the nature of learning, the capacities and interests of pupils, the curricula, methods, administration and finances of schools, the educational needs of communities, and many other questions not unrelated to these. No one doubts that there is knowledge and intelligent opinion about these matters nor that teachers and administrators find this knowledge and instructed opinion useful and indeed necessary. Later chapters will provide a few illustrations of the development of such knowledge.

But is it science? The answer will depend upon the meaning given to science, a word of several meanings. There is a tendency, not the oldest tendency, to restrict the word to those branches which deal with matter and physical bodies. If we do this, we can distinguish the physical sciences, such as astronomy, physics, and chemistry, and the biological and medical sciences which are less exact but which can make probable predictions.

Education does not belong to either of these classes, but it uses some of the results of biological and medical studies; and it has a close dependence upon psychology, which is partly a biological and partly a social study. This brings us to a tendency, more recent than the one mentioned above and contrary to it, namely, the tendency to stretch the word "science" to cover economics, sociology, politics, and anthropology, the social sciences. Many scholars resist this custom, but it seems to be growing. Education is certainly a social as well as a psychological study. If we are to recognize social sciences, education might well claim admittance into their circle.

There is, however, a special obstacle to this claim: education must take account not only of body and mind, biology and psychology, but also of spirit and purpose. The teacher dare not use pupils as means. The physicist can do as he pleases with his material; the plant or animal breeder does not consult the welfare of his organisms; but the teacher cannot do as he pleases with his pupils and dare not for a moment disregard their welfare. Education is based upon ethics, as well as psychology and biology. It makes use of statistics, of history, of logic, and of general philosophy. It is, therefore, a practical study which draws upon all available knowledge that will promote the welfare of the pupils.

The oldest meaning of the word "science" has not been mentioned. In early times it meant nothing more than organized knowledge; and the root of the word signifies to know or to understand. Educators use a number of sciences, some highly developed, others largely empirical; and this composite may be called the science of education in the same way that we speak of the science of language, or the historical sciences. Like medicine, but to a less degree, education is a science; and to a greater degree it is an art. In speaking of the science of education, the qualifications mentioned in the preceding paragraphs should be remembered.

The educational calling includes many kinds of workers, from classroom teachers to superintendents of schools. When fully prepared they have the special knowledge and skill and the personal character and tact which the professions require. But many are not fully prepared, or remain in the work only temporarily. In public education they are government employees and lack the independence of the physician or lawyer; and there is little more freedom in private schools. The fact that many teachers are supervised and directed by a hierarchy of officials militates against their professional standing. The public also, which assesses the expertness of the physician and lawyer, does not consider the teacher as equally expert in his field. To the question whether there is an educational profession only a qualified affirmative can be given. But teaching is not a trade, and not a business. It is more nearly a profession.

1. Education as a Science

The claim that education is a science was made by Johann Friedrich Herbart (1776–1841), but he spoke of it as a *Wissenschaft*, a broader term than the English word "science," as this is now commonly used. As a realist, Herbart intended, at least, to develop both psychology and education into positive sciences. There is a connection between this purpose and his denial of the freedom of the will. The Scotsman, Alexander Bain (1818–1903), a psychologist of the school of James Mill, chose as the title for a book the words, *Education as a Science* (1878). It has been claimed that William James drew heavily upon this book for his famous chapter on habit. *Education as a Science* presents a philosophical psychology and its bearings upon education, as well as some sections on educational values and methods of teaching. Despite its title it is not very scientific.

In the United States also the claim was made that education is a science. In 1885 William H. Payne published some of his papers under the title of *Contributions to the Science of Education;* but what he labeled science was humanistic and idealistic criticism. He translated Rousseau's *Emile,* Compayré's *Histoire de la Pédagogie,* and other works. For his basic philosophy he went farther back into the past to the great systems of Plato and Aristotle, but what he presented, although stimulating. was neither science nor systematic philosophy, but criticism.

While Payne's book was still new, Wilhelm Dilthey (1833–1911), speaking before the Berlin Academy of Sciences, denied the possibility of a general science of education. He said the claims of Herbart and his contemporaries were an echo of the rationalism of their age when all institutions were to be explained by reason. But much had been learned since the eighteenth century, said Dilthey, namely, that institutions are historical. They are not planned; they grow, adapting themselves to time, and place, and people. Pedagogy alone, he claimed, is still in the arrested state in which it was left by the rationalists. Our system-makers still set up what they consider universal aims-according-to-nature. But no system of ethics has ever won universal acceptance; human nature has never been fully understood; and therefore, because education must be based upon ethics and psychology, it has to be tentative. Education must take account of its own past, out of which its present is growing, must take account also of the history of man and of the biology of the human organism. If the term "science" is to be applied to it we must understand that it has to be an inductive, exploratory, and tentative science, not a universal and dogmatic one.

Strange to say, these relativist views pleased the idealist philosopher, Josiah Royce (1855–1916). He declared against the possibility of a real science of education. Although he cautioned the teacher against the danger of following fads, he recommended child study, object-teaching, and the appeal to children's interests. He thought the chief value of psychology lay in the guidance which it may offer to the teacher in the observation of her pupils. And even though education cannot become an exact science, the study of education is necessary.

As it happened, the study of education was pursued. Its students invented intelligence tests and devised educational measurements. Statistical methods were applied in some fields of educational interest. Even educational and, more frequently, psychological experiments were carried out. This further history suggests that the question raised by Dilthey and Royce had itself become antiquated. There is no universally valid system of government or medicine. We do not greatly miss the lack of such a system of education.

2. EDUCATION AS A BRANCH OF STUDY

The foundations of education as a separate study had been laid by Barnard, Mann, and their contemporaries. Further contributions were made in normal schools and universities, and by that new type of officer, the city superintendent of schools who conducted in-service training courses for his teachers. Of the latter group Edward A. Sheldon at Oswego was an active member. Much of the professional training of the time after the Civil War was still philosophical, but observation and experience also made their contributions. The work of Sheldon and G. Stanley Hall, the early stages of educational psychology, experience with the kindergarten, the industrial arts, and nature study, all made a contribution to the training of teachers and the practical study of education.

The topics to be considered in the present chapter are both theoretical and practical and they will provide direct preparation for the "new era" which is the subject of the next chapter to follow. Among those who had a part in developing the preparation for teaching as a profession were William H. Payne (1836–1907), a pioneer professor of education in a university, and William T. Harris (1835–1909), a pioneer among superintendents of city schools. They represent the theoretical and the practical elements of the new study and may typify the large group of contributors who cannot be brought into one small book.

It was a feature of the time that the main trunk of education as a professional study was dividing into special branches such as school management, methods of teaching, supervision, school law, educational psychology, and the history and philosophy of education. The universities began to offer different courses and sequences for academic teachers and school administrators and still others for teachers of such subjects as home economics, industrial arts, and agriculture. For a time it was possible for a single professor to teach all the education courses that a university offered, but these soon became more specialized. It is this early specialization which we are to consider. The specialization has gone to great lengths. The catalogue of a particular state college in 1955 listed fifty-nine education instructors and 127 courses, and this is, unfortunately, not a limiting case.

We may briefly return to the questions with which this chapter opens. Only qualified answers can be given. It will be admitted that some parts of the teaching vocation are professional. To answer the other question we inquired into the meaning of the word "science." Like *Wissenschaft* today, it formerly meant knowledge, especially organized knowledge such as that of the "science of English grammar." It has been gradually restricted to the study of nature, especially inorganic nature. Psychology hardly passes for a science, and ethics and sociology, all important building blocks of education, are merely "social sciences." To the biological, psychological, and social sciences education belongs.

3. FACULTY PSYCHOLOGY

The system of ideas which forms what is called the faculty psychology is a philosophy of education, not a psychology only, although it employs psychological language. This philosophy was long dominant in America and Europe and maintained itself until 1900 and after. The concept of mental faculties is not, however, an American or a recent idea. It may be traced through the Scotch, the Germans, and in the Middle Ages through the Scholastics back to the founders of philosophy. Scotch immigrants, including John Witherspoon and many less known persons from various countries, brought it with them to America. It is not in good repute today, but it will be well not to speak too scornfully of it until we understand the nature of organism, mind, faculties, and training more fully than we do at present.

Mental faculties are supposed to be such capacities as the power to remember or to think or "to see a point." The notion has had a curious and disconcerting history. Whenever the science of psychology has expelled the faculties from its house, they have slipped in again and have become servants if not regular members of the family. Herbart, the arch-opponent of faculties, admitted that the words for them are very useful. The intelligence tests measure verbal, arithmetical, reasoning, and other abilities, and these are capacities, that is, faculties.

Some psychologists, after denying the existence of a faculty of memory, will assert that we have many memories. This is a way of getting rid of faculties by increasing their number. Others are willing to assume the existence of faculties if they are not regarded as sharply limited and separate. The matter of training is likewise troublesome. One must not speak of memory-training but of learning to remember by organizing materials serially or logically or otherwise into a system.

This account is not an argument for a return to the "faculty" psychology; and this is not the place to deal with these matters. They are considered in the books on psychology. We are here reporting the fact that the faculty psychology was the dominant philosophy of education in the middle of the last century and after. Francis Wayland (1796–1865) was an adherent of this school and he concluded his review of 1854 before the American Institute of Instruction with an outline of his views. Our faculties are, on the one hand, he declared, objective, giving us knowledge of the world around us, and on the other hand, are subjective, telling us of the energies and relations of the world within us. This is Locke's view. The object of education, Wayland continued, is to improve both classes of faculties, in a word, every power of the soul. So also said Pestalozzi and this aim was generally accepted. To improve the faculties was to train, discipline, or strengthen them; and in this process knowledge was to be acquired.

A Yale committee of 1828 had declared that "the two great points to be gained in intellectual education are discipline and the furniture of the mind; expanding its powers and storing it with knowledge." The faculties, so Wayland taught, can be strengthened only by exercise. All our studies should both increase our knowledge and improve our mental powers. We do not study one thing to strengthen the mind and another to increase our knowledge. Herbert Spencer agreed and called this an example of "the beautiful economy of Nature."

The next question concerns the order of the budding and flowering of the faculties. It was claimed that observation shows that the child does not have all the adult faculties; and the question was whether one, such as perception, develops before another, say, memory, or whether imagination becomes full-grown before the judgment. Wayland and his contemporaries were convinced that there is a serial development of the faculties; and that our systems of education must recognize and follow that order. He wrote: "If there is an established succession in the development of the faculties, and if no faculty can be improved but by use, and if we can never use any faculty successfully until it has arrived at some degree of maturity, it will surely follow that the order of our studies must be arranged in conformity to the successive development of our faculties." We would do well to compare with this the principles of readiness of which we hear so much today.

Of the order in which our faculties develop, Wayland thought there could not be much doubt. The objective powers are the first to unfold. Hence the insatiable curiosity of little children about living and moving things and all that can be seen or heard. The powers of forming images and building an inner world develop somewhat later. And not until we approach maturity are we able to deal with higher generalizations and abstract truths and to observe our own nature and the nature of others. The memory accommodates itself to this development of the observing powers. At first it most easily retains the remembrance of sensory experience and of bare facts. "Hence the great power in youth of acquiring languages." As our capacity to deal with principles increases, that for acquiring languages declines.

The order of our studies, he continued, should obviously agree with the order in which our faculties appear and develop. Geography and many phases of natural science as well as languages should be taught early. Drawing is a great help in training the perceptive powers. If we should teach children to observe accurately we might, he believed, increase the number of able scientists, an idea that Charles W. Eliot was, much later, to dwell upon. Not until the third stage can we successfully introduce abstract subjects, such as logic, and subjects demanding taste, such as the books of the great creative authors. How shall we know when a pupil reaches the successive stages? There is an easy rule. It is to teach only what he understands. Wayland was doubtless correct in believing that lack of comprehension is a major reason for lack of interest in studies.

An early book that may be classed as an old-fashioned educational psychology is Wayland's *The Elements of Intellectual Philosophy* (1854). As in the address which has been reviewed, one of the chief themes is the order of the appearance and the growth of the faculties; but it also deals with their cultivation and improvement. Among the conditions of attention we must count health and hygiene. Proper diet, sufficient sleep, a moderate room temperature, and a reasonable limit to the time devoted to study, all will aid in maintaining one's attention. It will be aided also by the use of the pen, making analyses of books read, and writing on the subjects studied.

The book also treats the laws of association in the cultivation of the memory. The memory, we are told, may be improved more, and more quickly, than any other faculty. But Wayland did not distinguish between "strengthening" the memory and the judicious use of devices to aid retention and recall. Precise and definite ideas and information when organized into a system are easily remembered, as the book clearly explains, but we are told by present-day science that, contrary to Wayland's view, this leaves the native tenacity of the mind unchanged. It is important to notice that this "native tenacity" of the psychologists, like their "native intelligence," is a theoretical construct like the "substance" of the philosophers.

Pages were given to the cultivation of the imagination and the reason, but Wayland took a moderate position on transfer of training. He favored the study of many varied subjects under an elective system, a most liberal and original policy in 1850. This view can be harmonized with transfer doctrines if it is supposed that the training effect is very general so that the serious study of any worthy subject will discipline the mind. This was what President Eliot of Harvard, a generation later, maintained, and it was what the Committee of Ten (1894) over the objections of a minority of its members taught.

The Herbartians, as will be shown in the following chapter, made a direct attack about 1890 upon the transfer doctrine. Burke Aaron Hinsdale read a notable paper on "The Dogma of Formal Discipline" before the National Council of Education in 1894. This was still mere philosophy; but William James had made a rather amateurish experiment in memory-training before 1890. Although the subjects in the experiment made a little improvement, the amount was so slight that some began to doubt the importance of transfer effects. This doubt was increased and spread by the slight transfer from specific habits in the more extended experiments of Thorndike and Woodworth (1901). In the last half-century a thousand or more transfer experiments have been carried out, and it has been indicated that the transfer may be very substantial if the learner realizes the similarity of the new situation to the one that has been practiced. Pupils who are ingenious, observant, and able to generalize from cases derive considerable benefits. It is to be feared that too many teachers and teachers of teachers are unaware of the present state of the old transfer controversy. This is unfortunate, for as Hinsdale saw, "the question is absolutely fundamental to the science of education." If there were no transfer, learning would be of little use because situations are rarely quite the same. Before we turn away from this topic we may recall that philosophers have declared that there is some truth in all the greater systems of philosophy.

4. General Principles of Teaching

By general principles of teaching are meant those guiding ideas which apply to all, or to many, or at least to several subjects or situations. Special principles or methods apply to only one subject, such as arithmetic, or to a few related ones, say, arithmetic and algebra. The general principles which were considered in normal schools in the last century may be found in the textbooks on methods.

Between about 1840 and 1860 the nature of these books changed from the moralizing works of such writers as S. R. Hall and Jacob Abbott to the more empirical books such as Potter and Emerson's *The School and the Schoolmaster,* a work which may be considered to mark the first stage of the transition. Later and more advanced examples of the change are the psychological and practical books of Wayland, David P. Page, William H. Payne, and E. E. White. All these are still deductive and philosophical in nature. Among these books is the *Intellectual Philosophy* of Wayland, which has been analyzed.

A contemporary but more influential work than Wayland's was the *Theory and Practice of Teaching* (1847) by David P. Page, the first principal of the state normal school at Albany, New York. This book was in use by classes and reading circles of teachers for half a century. In 1885, forty years after publication, it was revised by the professor of education at the University of Michigan, W. H. Payne, who did not change a word of the text but added a number of passages. These serve a useful purpose today by indicating changes in opinion and practice which had taken place since 1847.

Fitness to teach, Page wrote, involves three kinds of qualifications: scholarship, skill and method in teaching, and understanding of the science of teaching. This science is based upon the principles of psychology, physiology, and ethics. To teach must be the teacher's primary purpose, not money, reputation, or preparation for another profession. The teacher is responsible partly or mainly for the morals, health, intellectual growth, and study habits of his pupils. He must teach pupils how to study intelligently, how to master the principles of a science instead of merely preparing for a recitation or covering a book.

The work contains skilfully illustrated chapters on "right modes of teaching," on ways "to wake up mind," and on school government. Page did not favor the use of corporal punishment, "the discussion of which in all our educational gatherings takes up so much time"; but he did not pronounce against all use of it. He considered the practical problems of school management, the daily time-table, the teacher's care of his own health, and his relations to the community, including those cases when "one part of the district is arrayed against the other." It is a historical fact of interest today that he thought there would be no objection to the teaching in public schools of the generally accepted Christian doctrines; but he did not indicate which doctrines he would include. Sectarian issues were to be referred to the family and the pulpit. Page was mistaken in thinking that there would be no objection to the direct teaching of religion.

In comparison with the brief vogue of most books on education, the Page text had a surprising career. This was due to its clear, practical instruction. It is readable today and those who discover it do, in fact, still read it. It is best read in the Payne edition of 1885; but it was revised several times by a number of editors.

5. METHODS AND MANAGEMENT

Many authors after 1860 prepared works on special phases of education in place of the comprehensive books which Page and his predecessors had produced. The day of the professional specialist was beginning. School management, methods of teaching, supervision, and educational psychology were now to be separately treated. The several phases of education could no longer be confined within the covers of one small book. Topics were treated that had not been thought of before. Such general titles as "theory and practice" or "the school and the schoolmaster" could no longer indicate the contents of the new books.

Specialized books to aid rural teachers in practical ways were written for use in normal schools. Resisting the temptation to write a general book that could be used in all professional courses, James P. Wickersham (1825–1891) prepared a special work on *School Economy* (1864). It contained nearly 400 pages and treated the organization, grading, and government of schools. In a second, somewhat larger book on *Methods of Instruction* (1865) he dealt with the nature of the school subjects and "the methods of teaching them according to that nature."

Wickersham later became state superintendent of Pennsylvania and wrote a history of education in his state, published in 1885. It was one of the early books in the field and is still one of the better ones. Through his writing and speaking and his activity in the National Education Association, he acquired a very considerable reputation. At the time when he prepared his textbooks he was the principal of the newly opened normal school at Millersville.

In the *School Economy* he described the several kinds of graded schools and the effect of the numbers of the pupils upon the organization. This was a subject of current interest because in most states the grading of the schools was in its early stages. The evidence seems to indicate that the graded system was a native development and not copied from Germany, as has been claimed. Wickersham discussed the school plant including the playground and its equipment and urged the esthetic improvement of the schoolroom and the schoolyard. But for the most part the *School Economy* dealt with school routine. It was a conservative book but the author reported that it was used in nearly all the normal schools of its time, about a dozen in number.

The *Methods of Instruction* is mainly psychological. Reference is made to earlier and contemporary writers including Pestalozzi and Spencer. The usual order in which the faculties were supposed to develop was indicated, but Wickersham held that this was not entirely fixed. He held that perception, memory, recollection, imagination, understanding, and reason develop together but come to maturity in the order named. The suggestion is that the faculties are less distinct than had been claimed. This was a slight change in the old psychology.

Method is determined by the maturity of the faculties but also by the stage of the pupil's development, whether that of infancy, childhood, or youth, and by the nature of the branches of instruction. Wickersham in common with other writers of the 1860's dealt with object lessons. He was sufficiently Pestalozzian to propose the use of pictures, toys, puzzles, and other constructions in addition to the usual objects from nature. He was sufficiently critical to condemn the random selection of "unworthy objects" when "all Nature" was available. And he deplored the verbalism which sometimes was the chief outcome of object lessons.

Numerous special books on object-teaching appeared. One of the early ones, *Object Teaching and Oral Lessons* (1860) by Henry Barnard, was composed of materials from his *Journal*. Edward A. Sheldon, the leader of the Oswego movement, wrote another. And a third was by Norman A. Calkins, the assistant superintendent in charge of primary schools in New York City. The office held by him is further evidence of the increasing specialization in education. His book was called *Primary Object Lessons, for Training the Senses and Developing the Faculties*. Published in 1870 it was in its fortieth edition in 1888. Included in the topics of this widely used book were form, color, number, drawing, and human anatomy, "the bones of the body." With "all Nature" before them, the educators of that period chose for little children isolated objects that could be used to represent abstract ideas. With the opportunity to introduce the children to an interesting natural world, they chose to train their faculties.

The *Normal Methods of Teaching* (1879) by Edward Brooks (1831–1912) was an exposition of special methods of teaching each of the common branches. The principles of arithmetic-teaching were illustrated by "model lessons." This was an addition to the pedagogical writing of the period. Brooks also included historical notes on the development of the school subjects, an idea frequently approved in later times. Other writers were also dealing with special methods.

A widely used series of books on education was prepared by Emerson E. White (1829–1902), at one time president of Purdue University. These were *The Elements of Pedagogy* (1886), which was the basic book; *School*

Management; and *The Art of Teaching,* dealing with methods. White was highly critical of the extensive use of written examinations, not only the use made of them in the promotion of pupils but especially of their use as a basis for the comparison of schools and teachers. One may see here the faint beginnings of the survey idea already employed in Boston in 1845. Instead of giving heed to White's strictures, the profession went on to develop more effective instruments and to establish general norms.

The interest in the construction of school buildings was one of the earliest among the special interests which we are tracing. Horace Mann gave attention to the problem in his earliest reports; but the writings of Henry Barnard on this subject were more extensive and exerted a great influence that was long maintained. There were no professional school architects in those days and a book such as Barnard's *School Architecture* was needed.

A volume on *Country School-Houses* was prepared by James Johonnot (1823–1888). The author had some experience as a teacher of rural schools in his native Vermont and he wrote for those who had to build one-room schools and those who had to live and work in them. He treated every phase of the construction and use of such a school plant, the location and grounds, main and accessory buildings, their plan, cost, and construction, and the furniture and teaching apparatus. He gave special attention to the contribution which the physical conditions can make to the health, the moral conduct, and the aesthetic cultivation of the pupils.

Aesthetic cultivation is given a chapter in another book by Johonnot, his *Principles and Practice of Teaching.* This attention to proportion, unity, harmony, symmetry, and other aesthetic elements in education was an unusual emphasis in elementary education, but the topic had been introduced by Wickersham. Johonnot was interested most in the plastic arts but he stressed the importance of music also. He showed great interest in scientific subjects; and the educational reformers whom he admired most were Pestalozzi, Froebel, and Agassiz, especially the last. The sciences, he said, should be taught, as Huxley pointed out, because of their utility; and they should be studied by the direct observation of nature. The simplest equipment is often the best and may be borrowed from any farmer. Johonnot was a graduate of Page's old school, the state normal school at Albany, and the section of Page's book which Johonnot admired most was a lesson on an ear of corn, called "Waking Up Mind." Object lessons, he insisted, should be the gateways to science. Thomas E. Finegan of the New York State Department, who knew him well and admired his devotion to any cause which he advocated, called Johonnot a "radical," but he was merely a "progressive" born a little too early.

6. Broader Specialties

A marked case of growing specialization is provided by a small book on the superintendency of schools. This work added a new province to the educational kingdom. Where separate one-teacher schools under the district system were visited by the minister or were managed by small committees of farmers, there was little practice and no theory of supervision; but education in the cities set new problems.

Several cities established the superintendent's office before 1840: Buffalo in 1837, Louisville and Providence in 1838, St. Louis in 1839. About twenty-five city school superintendencies had been created by 1860. The priorities are, as usual, debatable. The movement spread and by 1870 and 1880 even small towns had begun to employ a chief school officer. According to the small book mentioned above, this was incidental to the grading of the schools and welding them into a system. The book bore the modest title of *Chapters on School Supervision* (1875) and was written by W. H. Payne, who at that time had the direction of the schools of Adrian, Michigan.

The subject of supervision occupied only a part of the space. Three chapters were devoted to the powers and general duties of the superintendent, "who is rather an officer of the Board than a member of the corps of teachers." Other chapters dealt with the admission and grading of the pupils, the organization of the schools, the examination and appointment of teachers, the curriculum, the schedule of classes, records, and matters of personnel management. It is, therefore, a work on school administration; and the author was not aware that any work of this special character had been published before.

This treatise of little more than 200 pages laid a foundation for a new professional study. Judged by present doctrine its errors were few and its sensible answers to real problems were numerous. As we shall see, the author was a conservative critic of education, but in this book, which was based upon practical field experience, he made a positive contribution to what he considered the science of education.

How Sheldon managed and developed the small city superintendency of Oswego, we have seen; and we shall soon note the theory and practice of W. T. Harris in St. Louis. These men and their contemporaries were developing the office as it has come to be. As Burke Aaron Hinsdale explained in a report to the National Council of Education (1888), the American city school superintendency is an office not found elsewhere. The nearest analogy is with the inspectors of schools in Europe; but these are national rather than local officers.

The superintendent's duties were not defined by law, and this Hinsdale considered evidence that the office was not created but had evolved. After a term as superintendent of Cleveland, Hinsdale was somewhat pessimistic about the further development of the office. The big city superintendent would necessarily become a business manager, he thought, and only in smaller places could he remain an educator. Yet he also proposed to confine the work of the board to policy matters and to make the superintendent the executive agent of the board. Like Sheldon and Harris, he was concerned with the problem of securing good members of school boards, and he proposed their appointment for long terms by the mayor or the court. In this as in some other matters, history has not approved his insights.

Further knowledge of the state of education may be obtained from Payne's *School Supervision,* to which we return. He referred to "a graded-school of a thousand pupils and twenty teachers." This would not now be considered adequate staffing; but in the early 1950's enrollments increased so rapidly and teachers were so hard to secure in sufficient numbers that this ratio was no longer as unrealistic as it had seemed earlier.

The local high school seemed to Payne the best source of a supply of teachers. He thought every high school should have a normal class unless there was a municipal normal school such as the large cities maintained. A high school class "composed of pupils who proposed to teach, reciting twice a week and observing good models, using such a book as Page's *Theory and Practice,* may learn much about the art of teaching." In this way the superintendent could prepare his own staff. But times change. And at present, irrespective of the evils of "inbreeding" and meager preparation, this plan is no longer as effective as it was, for this supply of teachers has dried up at the source. In times of full employment at high wages, comparatively few city high school pupils are willing to consider teaching as an occupation. Greatly increased salaries and greatly improved working conditions in the city schools would increase the number of applicants.

The increasing proportion of women in the teaching force was for Payne a disturbing trend and he related it to the "emancipation of women," which was then agitating the public. He thought men were needed to render the staff more permanent, to make the science-teaching more effective, and to assure a "healthy discipline," and he did not mean corporal punishment. He referred to the idea of a single salary schedule but was not in favor of it. These ideas can be seen in their proper chronology and context if we remember that the states had only recently begun to pass laws giving women the right to own property, that they were still wives, mothers, and schoolteachers rather than persons, and that teaching was one of the very few professions open to them.

Boards should change textbooks only when this is in the interest of the pupils. Payne did not suggest that members might line their pockets at such times; but Hinsdale did not hesitate to consider this as a possibility. There is money in books, Hinsdale wrote. Publishers have done much good and some harm. They sometimes enter the political field to influence elections and corrupt the moral sense of teachers and superintendents through "largesses of various kinds." And then he unaccountably adds that the superintendent should have nothing to do with the selection of textbooks "unless he can be protected against foreign interference" (*Studies in Education*, pp. 286 f.). Payne merely warned superintendents and teachers against selling to pupils any materials used in the schools.

The present good opinion of the quality of American schoolbooks was held, as we learn from Payne, as early as 1875. He said: "The American school-book has no superior. No class of books is subject to such vigorous and decisive criticism as this." And he praised the publishers for these conditions because they "have fostered and almost created the authorship of textbooks which are a credit to our age and country."

School administration and educational psychology became special branches of education at the same time. School administration was a broadened and more reasoned school management, a subject that had been touched upon by every writer since Christopher Dock. Educational psychology was cabined and confined by the doctrine of the faculties and the lack of experimentation and fresh observation. Book after book repeated the old formulas, and this in turn affected other branches, especially methods of teaching. A long step toward a new psychology and method was taken by G. Stanley Hall in 1880 when he studied, not faculties, but the "contents" of children's minds. Child study in taking this step achieved more than one value. Child study brought out the differences between the child and the adult, differences in bodily proportions, growth, play interest, dependence, lack of vocational drives, activity, and adolescent changes. Hall thought the principal use of child study was in directing the student to individual differences and personal traits rather than group averages and uniformities. All of these ideas had been considered by Locke and Rousseau, but few had seen very clearly what they implied for the work of the school. Study was required and several generations passed by before this knowledge was applied in the school, if it has been fully applied even now.

Ten years after Hall made his study, William James published his

Principles of Psychology (1890) and almost a decade later his *Talks to Teachers* (1899). James took care to assure the reader that he did not volunteer but was asked to give the *Talks* and he did not place a high value for teachers upon a knowledge of his science. He wrote Hanus that he did not know "just what pedagogic psychology means except the habit, association, apperception, and attention chapters of common psychology." The *Talks* became an interesting book that may not have had much influence upon anyone's teaching. Another literary psychology whose style hardly needs to fear comparison with James was *Psychology and Psychic Culture* (1895) by Reuben Post Halleck. It was written for high school pupils and combines popular psychology with advice on mind-training. Concreteness and thoughtful self-study were the aims of E. A. Kirkpatrick's *Inductive Psychology* (1895). The same author also prepared a widely used *Fundamentals of Child Study* (1903). These are only a few of the many attempts to make a knowledge of psychology valuable to teachers.

Those efforts met with only indifferent success. The results and values of child study did not immediately appear in the normal school classes. Pupils and teachers often felt that the psychology that was taught to prospective teachers had little bearing upon their future work. As late as 1911 Guy M. Whipple reported that teachers of psychology considered normal school students unable to profit from the usual textbooks in their field. The books were technical and lacked practical applications. The result was that the students memorized the words of the book without understanding. It was suggested that the students should carry on simple exercises—one would not call them experiments—in learning and teaching and should report the experiences in class discussion. Such a method would join educational psychology or child study with observation of children and practice teaching, a good idea.

It is appropriate to compare the difficulty of the psychology teachers mentioned above with comparable episodes in the progress of education. The teachers of health and physical education have had to solve problems of selection of materials, clarity of presentation, and practical application and habit-building. A similar difficulty that was not solved in less than fifty years confronted the early teachers of agriculture. There would seem to be an obvious and important conclusion to be drawn from these and similar experiences: knowledge of the subject is not enough.

The work of Hall and his pupils in establishing psychological laboratories (the first at Johns Hopkins) and psychological journals, the child study movement, the *Principles* of James, and the Herbartian pedagogy made the nineties an active period in psychology. Educational psychology was the oldest form of applied psychology, but its most useful applications were the products, not of its earliest period, but of the twentieth century. Among these are the study of the changes in interests with age, readiness investigations, the search for the causes of failures in school, an understanding of the effect of knowledge of performance upon improvement, and tests of intelligence, performance, and aptitude.

A variety of other pedagogical branches gives further evidence of advancing specialization. Textbooks on school law began to appear before 1880. The opening volume of the International Education Series—a series that was edited by William T. Harris—was a translation by Anna C. Brackett of Karl Rosenkranz's *Philosophy of Education,* a Hegelian work. A one-volume general history of education (1886) by F. V. N. Painter and a volume on the history of education in the United States (1889) by Richard G. Boone were included in the same series. Payne translated the general history of education by Gabriel Compayré. Henry Barnard in 1855 began his monumental *American Journal of Education.* An excellent one-volume encyclopedia of education, edited by Henry Kiddle and Alexander J. Schem, had appeared in 1876. Nicholas Murray Butler established and for many years edited an important monthly educational periodical, the *Educational Review* (1891–1928).

The books and papers which have been mentioned here are only a small selection from the mass of educational publications, but they will serve the purpose of revealing some of the major specializations that were taking place. They show that education was more lively and active than it had ever been. They are evidence of the growth of a profession.

7. University Courses in Education

There is further evidence. Early in the 1800's colleges had begun to contemplate offering courses in education, but not many did so until near the century's end. In some cases the marginal colleges made the first efforts. The faculty of Amherst, then small and in a thinly populated section, proposed such courses in 1826, but nothing came of this. Jefferson College at Washington in the mountains of southwestern Pennsylvania showed some interest. The infant New York University in 1831 even chose a professor, T. H. Gallaudet (1787–1851), but it is doubtful that he ever lectured. Brown University announced courses in the art of teaching in 1850.

The sparsely attended and precariously financed state universities of the Middle West began before, and continued for some time after, the middle of the century to offer normal courses for elementary teachers.

Several of these universities had been set down in small country towns like Bloomington, Indiana, and Columbia, Missouri. The growth of the towns and the invention of the automobile have changed matters, but in 1850 these isolated institutions had few students and these were poorly prepared for university studies. What was more natural than that such universities should offer to prepare teachers? This they did, maintaining both preparatory and normal departments.

When the high schools and normal schools became numerous, the state universities gave up the preparation of elementary teachers only to return after a generation to the preparation of secondary teachers. The State University of Iowa was something of an exception. From 1873 it had maintained a tripartite department of mental and moral science and didactics. Didactics was a weak member and there were years when no work in that field was given. A separate "department of pedagogy" was organized in 1890 and a School of Education in 1907. Many universities in these years began to offer work for secondary teachers and administrators. The normal schools prepared elementary teachers. This arrangement tended to maintain the old separation between the schools for the common people and the secondary schools and universities—the schools for the directive and professional classes. In Chapter VI it was explained that the elementary school and normal school tended to become a separate system, divided from the high school and university, which formed the other system. After 1900, when universities again undertook the preparation of elementary teachers and when from two to four years of college work became standard preparation for elementary teachers, the normal schools were driven to raise their standards and to become teachers' colleges. When this was achieved in fact, it helped to make the educational ladder a reality.

The University of Michigan in 1879 created a separate chair of the Art and Science of Teaching. The title is not definitive. The department was to help high school teachers, principals, and school superintendents, both prospective and those already holding positions. The action may be interpreted as a further measure to strengthen the alliance between the university and the high schools of the state, an alliance that had been forged by the university's accreditation policy and the decision in the Kalamazoo case. This was the interpretation placed upon the action by President James B. Angell, who had twice recommended it.

He pointed out to the Regents that many young graduates were at once appointed as principals of large schools or to superintendences of city schools. Before they went to their new duties, he thought they should have been taught something of the work of organizing, managing, teaching, and governing a school. "Experience alone can thoroughly train them. But some familiar lectures on these topics would be of essential service to them." It has been conjectured that President Angell's attention was directed to this matter through an address by Superintendent William H. Payne, and he was appointed to the new chair. The university gave as one of the uses of the new department that it would bring the secondary schools into closer relations with the university. The University of Michigan was thus becoming the head of the public school system of the state.

Other state and endowed universities and colleges followed the example of the University of Michigan. Columbia University and New York University became important centers. President Barnard of Columbia in 1881 produced an extended and able argument for professional instruction for teachers without knowing that Michigan had anticipated him in deeds, not words. Even then Columbia was not ready to follow his lead, but in 1889 a private institution, the New York College for Teachers, secured a charter. This school was rechartered as Teachers College in 1892, and affiliated with Columbia University in 1898. The chief leader in this movement was the young Nicholas Murray Butler, who was to become the twelfth president of Columbia University an office which he held for almost fifty years. Teachers College has had great influence upon all institutions and phases of teacher education.

At Cornell University in 1886, at the University of Chicago in 1901, and elsewhere before and after the turn of the century scores of schools and departments of education and soon after bureaus of educational research were established. R. G. Boone reported that in 1904, 250 colleges and universities out of 480 or 52 per cent offered courses in education. Although, as President Eliot said about 1890, the Harvard faculty had neither interest nor confidence in pedagogy, yet a department was established in 1891 at that oldest American college and thirty years later this was elevated into a Graduate School of Education in order, as one of its high officers reported, "to get our courses out of the control of a hostile faculty." This hostility was not confined to Harvard or to times long past. Instead it has shown itself with considerable virulence in recent times in several parts of the country including the Midwest.

The growth of a profession of teaching was furthered by the work of the universities but also by the leadership of the state and national organizations of teachers and superintendents. Ten state associations sent out a call in 1857 which led to the formation of the National Teachers' Association in that year at Philadelphia. This became the National Educational Association in 1870 and gradually grew into a large and effective organization that currently has over half a million members. Charles W. Eliot, Nicholas Murray Butler, and William Torrey Harris, as well as other distinguished men, became early presidents of the association, and the annual proceedings and addresses became a record of the thought and action of the educational leaders in the entire nation.

8. City Supervision

The reputation of the schools of St. Louis for high achievement reached all parts of the United States at an early period in the growth of that city. This was owing in large part to the enterprise and administrative skill of Superintendent William Torrey Harris (1835–1909). The foundations had, however, been laid earlier. And the rapid growth of the city to which he had come by mere accident contributed to his opportunity. In little more than a decade from his arrival as a half-educated young man with empty pockets and a head filled with impossible projects, he became the city superintendent of schools (1868). At this time he was thirty-three years old. Eventually he was to be acclaimed as one of the most distinguished educators of his time and country.

St. Louis was a border city. The people had come from the North and the South; and, to the number of many thousands, also from Europe. Germans, numbering 60,000 or more, made up more than half of the European immigrants; and as always they were hard to assimilate. They wanted to have the schools conducted in their language; they opposed the use of textbooks; and the Catholics among them wanted to have a share of the public funds for their own church schools. The city was also on the border between the East and the West and a main depot for the westward-bound trains of emigrants, traders, and adventurers. Many of the people were therefore transients. The Civil War brought its own problems; and though the war was over before Harris became superintendent, some of the war problems remained.

Ten years before he was to become superintendent, Harris had begun to teach in the school system. This was still in its formative stages. Less than a decade had passed since Missouri had established the state school fund and since the city had levied its first school tax and opened a high school. The Lancasterian plan was still in use in the elementary schools, but the change to the graded system was accomplished before Harris took charge. School attendance long remained irregular. Missouri delayed to pass a compulsory attendance law until 1905. Children came and went and came back again at will. Many did not come back but left permanently when they reached the fourth or fifth grade. A great many did not come at all but spent their time on the streets until they were old enough to go to work.

The way had been well prepared for Harris. The graded system had been introduced, as has been indicated. The board of education was independent of the city council. Separate tax levies were voted by the citizens, and the board controlled its corporate funds and property without interference. Several capable superintendents had preceded Harris, who thus took over a healthy although immature system. One innovation which has been generally accredited to Harris, the practice of flexible and frequent promotion in the grades, had been introduced by his predecessor, Superintendent Ira Divoll. The irregular attendance of the pupils may have suggested this practice. While Harris was serving (1858–1868) as elementary teacher, principal of an elementary school, and assistant superintendent, he maintained close and friendly relations with pupils, teachers, parents, and the superintendent. The retirement of Divoll was due partly to ill health, partly to his desire to run for the state superintendency. Harris was his natural successor, had his active support, and succeeded to the place without competition. There were no wounds to be tended.

The practice of flexible promotion was continued, and Harris in his annual report for 1873 gave a detailed explanation and defense of it. The school year was divided into four quarters of about ten weeks each. Promotion and reclassification were carried out at the end of each quarter, and an effort was made to form sections of good, average, and slow pupils. This ability grouping was at one time regarded as a great discovery, but it has been practically abandoned in St. Louis; and the report of the St. Louis school survey of 1939 implied that it was based upon unsound assumptions. Others say that the results of the numerous scientific studies of homogeneous grouping are inconclusive.

The new administration did not lack for innovations. To make the system more compact, not to say rigorous, Harris early introduced a scheme of district supervision. Under the plan each of the principals of upper-grade schools served as the supervisor of those primary schools from which his pupils were drawn. Each supervising principal was to visit every school of his district once a week to consult with teachers and principals, observe the work, and report to the superintendent. The supervising principals were not to be entirely relieved from teaching in their own schools. Harris thought a principal should not allow himself to lose direct contact with pupils and classwork. Meanwhile, he did not spare himself. Even as the city grew, he continued to visit schools. When the board received his accounts of expenses for transportation, they decided to furnish him with what Americans of that day called a "rig." His organizing skill and the ability to secure the cooperation of those who worked with him were leading factors in the success of his administration.

The kindergarten was introduced in 1873, but Harris had been planning this step earlier. He had the help of Miss Susan Blow, an able young woman of means and social position. They moved slowly at first, but before Harris left St. Louis the city was supporting more than fifty public kindergartens. At that time (1880) only a very few cities had adopted the institution.

Other institutions were introduced during his administration. Schools with kindergartens for Negro children were added. Evening schools with vocational classes were formed. The city normal school, later to be named for Harris, was separated from the high school. Harris effected a closer grading of the children. Large building programs were completed to keep up with the growing population. Music, drawing, and gymnastics were added to the studies taught.

St. Louis, as we have seen, prepared her own teachers at first in the high school, then in the city normal school, later to be called the Harris Teachers College. But Harris also searched for special talent outside. For this he was criticized because St. Louisans, like others elsewhere, considered their own people the equal of any and also entitled to special consideration in their home town. Harris had set up a graded salary schedule, but when he found Anna C. Brackett teaching in South Carolina for less than $1,000 he paid her $2,000 to take charge of the St. Louis normal school.

There were some persistent problems and some new ones that arose from time to time. Classes in their own language were provided for the Germans but many parents were dissatisfied. They pressed for schools in which German should be the sole language of instruction. Harris reminded them that they had been admitted as citizens of a country of which English was the official and national language. Some took their children out of the public schools and entered them at private German schools. On the opposite side were many Americans who opposed the teaching of any foreign language in a public elementary school and agitated for the removal of all such instruction.

Religious issues in the St. Louis schools attracted widespread attention. There were many Catholic citizens and some, including priests and the supporters of a Catholic religious paper, demanded a share of the school tax dollar for the parochial schools. Attempts were made to effect changes in the Constitution of Missouri that would have allowed this division of the funds. In that city, political efforts were made by a Catholic faction to gain control of the board of education. Other religious factions on the Protestant side wanted to have the Bible in the King James version taught in the public schools. Harris took his stand upon the principle of the separation of state and church. He was in favor of maintaining the public school "as a purely secular institution without any religious instruction." These and other difficulties may have had some influence in leading Harris to resign in 1880 after a highly successful administration of twelve years. But it may be that he left the superintendency to pursue other interests. Some of these he had long been promoting along with his work for the schools; and some new activities were developing only in his last years in St. Louis. One of the latter was the compilation of a set of school readers for D. Appleton and Company, a task which in the course of years netted him a large amount in royalties.

The superintendency in America, as Harris explained, was undergoing a process of evolution. The early city superintendents had not been placed in charge of the education of children but only of the mechanics of a system. They were custodians of school property, they allocated supplies, kept records, and supervised building construction. Gradually they became educators and undertook to deal with the course of study and the methods of instruction. Some, such as Harris himself, thought it part of their function to inspire teachers with the spirit of self-culture, to counsel and advise the members of the board, and even to help in shaping the educational thought of the country.

The superintendent dare not neglect his historically earliest duties, so Harris believed. He must have at least "directive oversight" of the mechanics of the system. No merely theoretical superintendent can succeed. He must be informed concerning apparatus, salaries, finances, and legislation, and must devise and follow a policy in such practical matters. But these, he declared, are merely means to greater ends. His main function is to direct the education of children and youth for active participation in a democracy.

There are important duties contributory to the superintendent's main function. He must educate the members of the board and he must educate himself. One of Harris's own numerous ways of furthering his education was to visit city school systems. In 1872 he with F. Louis Soldan visited Cincinnati, Chicago, Cleveland, Oswego, New York City, and Boston.

In his own mind Harris divided board members into three classes, business and professional men, reformers, and politicians. It may be observed that these classes are not mutually exclusive. The superintendent, he said, must listen patiently and critically to the reformers and to parents, especially when they come with disciplinary problems. He must keep in close touch with the general public. And he must have genuine political skill or the reformers and politicians will combine against him and against the honest and conservative elements on the board.

In his efforts to educate the members of his board, Harris used the board meetings, private discussions with members, and his reports. Some of the topics in his reports were specific, such as grading, salaries, building plans, or German instruction in the schools; but he did not hesitate to consider the broadest topics of educational theory. He discussed the Pestalozzian system in comparison with the methods in common use in the schools; the relations of the public schools to the community and the nation under a democratic system; the teaching of science in elementary schools; and, becoming more practical, the evil tendency of boards of education in times of financial stress to cut and trim the educational budget and program. He thought both "the bulls and the bears" in education should be held in leash and not allowed to run wild.

During his connection with the St. Louis schools he edited the *Journal of Speculative Philosophy,* which he had founded in 1867 while he was a classroom teacher. During this period he was the pivot of the St. Louis movement in philosophy. Among the contributors to the *Journal* were such leading thinkers as William James, Josiah Royce, Charles Peirce, John Dewey, and G. H. Howison. During all these years and afterward, Harris developed his Hegelian standpoint, wrote books including *Hegel's Logic* (1890), and delivered many addresses. He and Francis W. Parker were for more than two decades nationally known educators and among the most eminent members of the National Education Association.

The Hegelian philosophy led Harris to emphasize man's cultural heritage and to consider its transmission as the main task of education. He would not have said that "the culture," in the present-day cant phrase, is more important than the child, but rather that only in a civilized society can the child grow mentally and become a moral person. Harris was not a "naturalist." His view that civilization is a primary fact for education led him to his figure of the five windows through which the child may look out upon the world and may also communicate with its human and subhuman denizens. The use of the word "windows" may tend to show that Harris held what Dewey was to consider a spectator theory of knowledge. Harris, however, was no mere spectator.

The five windows were (1) reading and writing, which by extension lead to communication and literature; (2) arithmetic, number, quantity, geometry, and the higher analysis; (3) geography, science; (4) history, society, government; and (5) grammar, languages, logic, and mental philosophy. These subjects show that Harris wanted to guard against any tendency to overemphasize a merely sensory and scientific education. Science is a field of mental activity, he said, perhaps following Bacon, so easy that all people may enter it successfully; and so practically useful that too many will want to do so. It does not follow that science should be permitted to usurp the place of the humane studies. The school must not reduce all people to a level.

The school must be a community. Harris opposed the Herbartians because their system did not allow for the freedom of the will. Only free and independent persons can form a community. He quoted, with approval, Dewey's statement that "an interest is primarily a form of self-expressive activity"; but the later Dewey did not concede the transcendental freedom which Harris demanded. The fundamental difference between the two men lies in the fact that Harris sought to conserve and transmit, to conserve by transmitting, the achievements of the race. Dewey sought to use those attainments as instruments with which to investigate, discover, and apply ideas. Nicholas Murray Butler in *The Meaning of Education* (1902) said that education is "the gradual adjustment to the spiritual possessions of the race with a view of realizing one's own potentialities." This statement is in harmony with the general view of Harris.

After he resigned from the superintendency in St. Louis, he took part in the Concord School of Philosophy which Emerson had proposed and Amos Bronson Alcott had founded. He served as editor-in-chief of Webster's *New International Dictionary*. He became the general editor of Appleton's International Education Series and wrote the prefaces of more than fifty of those volumes. And for seventeen years (1889–1906) he rendered distinguished service as the United States Commissioner of Education.

Henry Barnard was the only predecessor (1867–1870) in that office whose attainments and contributions invite comparison with those of Harris. Barnard in his *American Journal of Education* and Harris in his official reports published extensive materials for the practical, comparative, and historical study of education. Neither Harris nor Barnard was successful as a politician in Washington. Even his long experience as a city superintendent had not fitted Harris to gain the attention of the Congress; but all educators except the promoters of vocational and agricultural education have had the same difficulty. We have the grateful testimony of Michael Sadler (later Sir Michael) that Harris's educational influence extended across the ocean. The Office of Special Inquiries and Reports, set up in

England, was in part modeled upon the United States Bureau; and Sadler reported that upon application to Washington, Dr. Harris "gave full details on the working of the Bureau and other details of inestimable value."

In the first volume of the Special Reports this help was acknowledged in these friendly words: "Every student of education," wrote Sir Robert Morant, "is under a debt of gratitude to the United States Government for the work of the National Bureau of Education of the United States. Its volumes, published under the direction of Commissioner W. T. Harris, have probably done more than any other single agency to encourage a comparative study of the science and art of education, and of the various systems of educational administration now in force in different countries of the world."

If the number and quality of its professional publications were the sole criteria for the existence of a profession, then it could be pronounced that teaching had reached that status by 1900. Unfortunately, other criteria were not so favorable; and the shifting personnel of the lower and especially of the rural schools, as well as the low level of the general and special education of many teachers, deter one from calling them members of a profession. Many elementary and high school teachers, especially in the cities, deserved that classification. And to a lesser extent the same conditions obtain today and have even been aggravated by the upsurge in attendance and the forced employment of insufficiently prepared teachers. How to adjust the supply of professional teachers to the shifting demands of an unstable society is an unsolved problem. And this is unfortunate if good teaching is as important to the individual and the society as it is claimed to be.

Upon applying the usual criteria to teaching, one may infer that this occupation became more professional after 1860 than it had been. The increasing proportion of women who then came to fill teaching posts may not have had much effect upon this tendency toward professional status. It is probable, however, that salaries were kept low or that in some cases they declined as a result of the employment of a larger number of women. There was no thought of a single salary schedule at that time.

Special preparation for an occupation is one of the criteria of its status as a profession. The increased opportunity to secure this preparation is the chief subject of this chapter. Normal schools, universities, and superintendents were the chief agencies for direct teaching of educational branches. Most of the material was philosophical or at least theoretical. It gave opportunity for the disagreement which philosophical systems seem to invite. The present chapter is therefore a preparation for the following one.

The faculty psychology was the leading philosophy of education when the period began. The faculties were supposed to be separate from each other, to develop in a certain order, and to be improvable through training. Transfer of training meant that training of a faculty in one kind of material improved its performance when dealing with different material. There was also a belief in general mental improvement as a result of vigorous mental activity.

General principles of teaching dealt with teacher preparation and competencies, methods, curriculum theory, and similar broad topics. Early in the period books began to appear which dealt with specialized divisions of the general principles, such as teaching methods and school management. The subject of methods was also divided further into the methods of teaching particular branches, such as reading or object lessons. The planning and furnishing of school buildings became a division of school management. School management was also developed in the opposite direction to become school supervision and administration. Other specialties which developed in the 1870's and later were educational psychology, the philosophy and history of education, and comparative education.

The latter half of the century produced many writers on special educational topics and the rise of ideas that are still of practical importance. One of the hopes, not at once fulfilled, was that education would become scientific in the manner of medicine or agriculture. Criticism was also a leading task of the specialist writers. City school administration was one of the first areas of the whole field of education to become to a marked extent professional and in some measure scientific.

QUESTIONS

1. Why is transfer of training a matter of importance in educational theory and practice? Why did the older views upon the topic come under criticism from several quarters about the same time?

2. Why is it of interest today that some well-informed people in 1885 thought there would be no objection to the teaching in public schools of "the generally accepted principles of Christianity"?

3. Why, in the development of the literature on education, were the books at first general and only later became more highly specialized? Would the reverse of this process have been more logical?

4. Collect evidence on the question whether the city superintendency is a native or imported office.

5. What are the several reasons for the care and expense devoted to the production of schoolbooks in the United States?

6. Collect the evidence for the early beginning of what was later called Progressive education?

7. According to Spencer, is the worth of knowledge intrinsic (valuable in

itself) or extrinsic (valuable for what it will do or produce)? Was Spencer a pragmatist?

8. Why did the St. Louis schools acquire a great reputation under Harris? Was this reputation in your opinion fully deserved? Why or why not?

9. What were the historically earliest duties of the city superintendents in the United States? Compare with their duties and responsibilities today.

BOOKS AND PAPERS

The problems and the views of teachers at any given period may be studied in the addresses, periodicals, and books of the time. The proceedings of the Western Literary Institute and of the American Institute of Instruction and many of the addresses and discussions of national, state, and special subject teachers' associations have been published. Professional periodicals began to appear not far from 150 years ago and have been greatly improved in the latter half of this period. The *American School Board Journal, Educational Review, Pedagogical Seminary, Kindergarten Review, School Review,* and *Primary Education* were among those founded before 1900, and continuing at least to World War I.

Andress, J. Mace, "Aims, Values and Methods of Teaching Psychology in a Normal School," *Journal of Educational Psychology,* Vol. 1 (1911), pp. 541–654.

Boone, R. G., *Science of Education,* New York, 1904. This was written when the measurement movement had barely begun.

Byerly, C. L., *Contributions of William Torrey Harris to Public School Administration,* University of Chicago, 1946, with a bibliography that includes a list of sixty papers and addresses by Harris.

Dilthey, Wilhelm, "On the Possibility of a General Science of Education," an address before the Berlin Academy of Sciences, *Transactions,* 1888, pp. 807–832.

Halleck, R. P., *Psychology and Psychic Culture,* New York, 1895, very popular with teachers although disowned by "real" psychologists.

Harris, W. T., "Elementary School Education," *Journal of Speculative Philosophy,* Vol. 3 (1869), pp. 181–190, a reply to E. L. Youmans' *The Culture Demanded by Modern Life* (New York, 1867). Harris took a social and idealistic view as opposed to the scientific-practical one urged by Youmans. "Division of School Funds for Religious Purposes," *Atlantic Monthly,* August, 1876; "City School Supervision," *Educational Review,* February, 1892.

James, William, *Talks to Teachers on Psychology: and to Students on Some of Life's Ideals,* New York, 1899. Reissued, New York, 1939, with an introduction by John Dewey and William H. Kilpatrick.

Johonnot, James, *Country School-Houses,* New York, 1858; *Principles and Practice of Teaching,* New York, 1878.
Leidecker, K. F., *Yankee Teacher, The Life of William Torrey Harris,* New York, 1946.
Lewis, F. C., "A Study in Formal Discipline," *School Review,* April, 1905.
Logsdon, J. D., *Development of Public School Administration in St. Louis, Missouri,* Chicago, 1946, a University of Chicago dissertation.
Page, David Perkins, *Theory and Practice of Teaching,* edited by W. H. Payne, New York, 1885.
Patrick, George T. W., *An Autobiography,* University of Iowa Press, 1947.
Payne, W. H., *Chapters on School Supervision,* Cincinnati, 1875; *Contributions to the Science of Education,* New York, 1886. Payne was also the translator and editor of Rousseau's *Emile* and other works.
Poret, George C., *Contributions of William Harold Payne to Public Education,* George Peabody College for Teachers, 1930, a dissertation.
Roberts, John S., *William T. Harris, A Critical Study of His Educational and Related Philosophical Views,* Washington, 1924.
Royce, Josiah, "Is There a Science of Education?" *Educational Review,* January and February, 1891.
Whitney, Allen S., "The First Chair of Education in an American University," *School and Society,* March 1, 1941.

PART IV

Chapter XII

OPENING A NEW ERA

THE new era which opened about 1890 was concerned with the change of the high school and even the college into continuations of the elementary school. Not only did they follow the elementary school but they also began to adopt its social views and educational outlook. The three types were being more closely integrated into a single system and their union was not only formal but also spiritual. The old exclusiveness and abstract intellectualism of the upper schools were becoming less pronounced. The curricula were adapted to prepare for the work of the world and the ordinary business of living in it. The colleges were beginning to accommodate future business people, homemakers, and others not destined to the old professions or to public life.

The subject content and the selective character of the high school and college had come from the Renaissance. Pestalozzi led a revolt against Renaissance principles by holding up the ideal of an elementary school that would provide a liberal education. Instead of drawing so heavily upon the "sere remains"—Emerson's words—of ancient and foreign cultures, each nation was to incorporate into its own life-stream the quintessence of living experience.

Several mechanical means had already been used before 1890 to bring the elementary and advanced schools into a single system but without changing their old and differing goals. The importance of entrance examinations had been reduced by the colleges, and the examinations for admission to the high schools were disappearing if they had not everywhere done so. Schools had begun to expand their programs and to allow substitutions for the usually designated subjects; and in this the needs of everyday commercial, industrial, and domestic life were recognized. The colleges which were securing their students from the high schools had begun to prepare teachers for the lower schools. Efforts to standardize the secondary schools were increasing. The Committee of Ten of the National Education Association, which made a major effort to standardize secondary education, was formed in 1892.

There were many participants in the debates of the new era, but four were pre-eminent. Of these Harris and Parker have already been introduced. The others were Charles William Eliot (1834–1926) and John Dewey (1859–1952). Considerable stimulation came from the introduction of the teaching of Herbart on such topics as the mental faculties, pupil interest, and the processes of thinking.

These debates also promoted a closer integration of the advanced with the elementary schools. They showed that all the schools were closely related to the community. The curricula at all levels were broadened to serve wider constituencies. Efforts were made in college and high school as well as in the grades to cultivate student interest. And the relations between teachers and students became more friendly. In several ways the advanced schools became more like the elementary schools.

1. Herbart in America

The new era was shaped as much by its reaction against J. F. Herbart as it was by its agreement with him. Americans knew little of Herbart's philosophy before 1890 and the slight knowledge which was possessed by a few had been supplied by German-Americans employed in the schools. A brief notice of Herbart was included in some lectures to the teachers of Cincinnati, delivered by W. N. Hailmann in 1873. The next year the *Journal of Speculative Philosophy*, directed by W. T. Harris, presented some fragments of his psychology. F. Louis Soldan, also of St. Louis, at a meeting of the National Education Association, read a paper that was based upon the ideas of Herbart. This paper did not do much to enlighten Americans, for the name of Herbart was not mentioned in it. But an intelligently written account of his life and work, two columns in length, appeared in the Kiddle and Schem *Cyclopedia of Education* (1876).

Before 1880 G. Stanley Hall and Francis W. Parker had been exposed to the currents of educational theory in the German universities. At that time Herbart was in great favor there. In 1876 the city of Oldenburg where Herbart was born held a centennial celebration of that event and dedicated a monument in his honor. But it was not Herbart's philosophy that attracted disciples. Philosophers were generally cool toward his metaphysics and critical of his ethical system. It was the educators and psychologists of Germany and Austria who became the professed Herbartians; and this was also the case in the United States.

In the ways indicated, some Americans became aware of the educational movements in Europe and entered German universities for the declared purpose of studying the Herbartian educational doctrines. Charles De Garmo, Charles and Frank McMurry, and C. C. Van Liew were among the early ones, and these, with some who did not closely adhere to the true faith, formed the Herbart Club in 1892. This became the National Herbart Society and later the National Society for the Study of Education. The last-named body quickly forgot its parentage, but in attempting to found a science of education it followed closely what was indeed the central purpose of Herbart. If in his professional life he can be said to have held more firmly to one purpose than to any other it was this one, to make education a science based upon ethics and psychology, just what Dilthey was to declare impossible.

The effect of the introduction of Herbartian doctrine was extraordinary. No previous ideas had stimulated such a volume of educational discussion. This was the opinion of Francis W. Parker. B. A. Hinsdale also thought Herbartianism the most powerful stimulus that had ever acted upon educational thought in the United States. Similar testimony by others could be collected. There was an extrinsic reason for this. There were more teachers, schools, institutes, educational journals, and normal schools in 1890 than ever before. And all were eager to hear and publish the new ideas. More significant was the fact that in the controversial features and even more in the real merits of Herbart's thought there were intrinsic reasons for a discussion that was continued for many years. The ancient arguments on mental discipline served to start this discussion. To this subject, already mentioned, we must now return.

2. Education as Discipline

When it is reported that the study of arithmetic has led to greater skill in dealing with numbers, discipline is affirmed. This kind of discipline is simple learning. Arithmetic, for example, disciplines the pupil in the use of numbers. One who has been thus disciplined shows the results in the performance of such skills as addition and subtraction. No one doubts the reality or the importance of discipline in this sense. But Plato in the *Republic* claimed that the study of arithmetic produces "quickness of apprehension." In this claim he was asserting what is now called transfer of training or formal discipline. For our purpose we may take these two phrases as synonymous. Formal discipline is the doctrine that the study of arithmetic, for example, makes the pupil expert not only in arithmetic but also in other abilities that may be only distantly related to arithmetic.

The speculative belief that the mind is made up of faculties was usually assumed as the basis of the doctrine of formal discipline. Scholars were not always certain about the number, scope, or order of development of the faculties. We have briefly reviewed one such scheme, that of Francis Wayland; and that was a fairly widely accepted one. But there were others.

A different scheme was prepared by the phrenologists Franz Joseph Gall (1758–1828) and Johann Kaspar Spurzheim (1776–1832), both contemporaries of Herbart. Spurzheim lectured in America; but a Scotsman, George Combe (1788–1858), who had Horace Mann for a friend and convert, was much more successful in spreading phrenological lore. Phrenology held not only that the mind is composed of faculties but also that these are correlated with specific parts of the brain which can be studied in the shape of the skull. Phrenology had a great vogue for at least a century in Europe, in Britain, and in America, but it was never accepted as science. Phrenology recognized two kinds of faculties: affective faculties including destructiveness, self-esteem, benevolence, and reverence; and intellectual faculties including calculation, order, language, and comparison. It was not difficult to combine parts of several schemes of faculties—and this was done by Mann and others.

In the faculty psychology it was thought that selected branches of study were especially useful for training particular faculties, mathematics for reasoning, and classics for judgment. In the nineteenth century, when the sciences and other new branches were introduced, the teachers of the older studies had to relinquish a part of their ancient monopoly. Being unwilling to do this, they developed added arguments for their favorite studies. Bain declared that the disciplinary values of the classics were not emphasized while the ancient languages were necessary. In that period their practical value attracted the students; but when the modern languages took their place, the claim was made and redoubled that the classics gave their devotees a uniquely valuable formal discipline, and in fact, a complete education.

A wholly new turn was given to the question by the Herbartians. Herbart taught that the mind acts as a unitary organism, one without any separate faculties. This doctrine where it was accepted destroyed the faculty psychology and the formal discipline of the nonexistent faculties at one stroke. The Committee of Ten reported in 1893 when little was yet known of Herbartian theory, and in its report accepted formal discipline as a fact. Thus they held that ability acquired in one field, such as Latin, could be directly applied to some other, such as English composition.

This view was attacked. President J. G. Schurman of Cornell University insisted upon the value of knowledge; and he thought it likely that in educational theory training was overvalued. Hinsdale stressed specific learning and declared that many and varied activities were necessary in anyone's education. Charles De Garmo said the committee had tried to correct an erroneous theory, the training of the faculties, by making it universal, training without faculties. The answer to this discussion was given, as we have seen in the preceding chapter, by the experimental psychologists. Meanwhile, the denial of formal discipline tended to promote the broadening of the curricula.

3. College Electives

The chairman was the most important member of the Committee of Ten. He was Charles William Eliot, for forty years president of Harvard University. He appears to have been the promulgator of the principle that all studies are of equal value when they are pursued for equal periods of time. This principle can be used to support the elective system, of which Eliot was the chief promoter. He applied the principle only in college. Languages, mathematics, science were still to be required for admission. But in college no study was considered necessary for everyone. In fact when the system was fully developed, the only study which Harvard College required everyone to take was English composition. So that honored course still had some peculiar virtues not found in any other.

The special advantage of an elective curriculum was that it could most easily be adapted to the differing capacities, interests, and future plans of the students. Every kind of talent could be cultivated under this plan, and this seemed essential in a democracy. In Eliot's view only the student knew enough about himself and his plans to select the courses which would suit his special needs. Although not raised by Eliot, there was some question whether the student knew enough about the courses before he had taken them. Incidentally, this self-administering plan saved administrative expense and faculty time.

There were other advantages, some of them educationally significant. By permitting boys to follow their bent it changed many from unwilling to eager students. It led to a great increase in the number of courses because an elective system implies the existence of courses among which to choose. The college was now required to offer advanced and specialized courses for upper-class students. This became expensive. Critics thought it led to overspecialization. They also said that the dull and indifferent were able to graduate, having had only easy introductory work. Eliot replied that under the old plan all courses had to be easy because they were required of all.

By the end of Eliot's administration in 1909 the opposition to the elective system had gained control. Under his successor a new system of concentration and distribution of courses was substituted. Each student then had to take a number of courses in one field and to distribute the rest over several fields. This allowed a considerable degree of choice but also demanded a certain coherence. The elective system, which was really quite unsystematic, was curbed but the old rigid requirements were not reinstated.

4. ECONOMY OF TIME

The National Education Association appointed committees to report on economy of time, the Committee of Ten was interested in the subject, and Eliot and other leaders wrote on it. We should notice that the phrase has two or more meanings. It may mean the better use of a certain period, such as the years of the elementary-secondary school course. By improved methods, revised curricula, and the junior-senior high school reorganization, the twelve or more years of schooling which close with graduation from high school were more effectively used than they had been. The pupils received a better education for the time spent. This was an economy of time in the same sense in which a good investment is an economical use of money.

Economy of time may also mean the shortening of the period devoted to education. In recent times brilliant students have sometimes been allowed to take extra work, pressure has been put upon them, and they have completed a standard amount of work in less than the standard period. This practice has been called acceleration. But the economy of time in which the National Education Association committees were interested was the reduction of the time required by average students to complete a given course. Graduation at an earlier age was the objective.

There were special reasons for this. The age at which students normally finished college had risen by four years in the middle quarters of the nineteenth century. And in the second place, the graduate and professional schools of the universities had begun to demand a bachelor's degree or at least two years of college work for admission. Thus a college teacher or a physician might easily be twenty-five or twenty-seven years old before he could enter upon his lifework. The country had not yet become accustomed to such a situation. Within memory, men, or rather boys, had graduated from college at eighteen, and a century before at an even younger age.

Eliot proposed to reduce the college course to three years. His opponents showed from the college records that the best students, entering with some advanced credit, were already graduating in three years. And they calculated that, if the course were reduced to three years for the average, the brightest students would finish in two years and two months. Eliot, firm as always in his views, could not win over his faculty. But in many colleges students finished in less than four years by carrying extra work.

The junior high school was also supposed to save time by moving high school studies down into the grades. The idea was, however, proposed long before the junior high school movement began. But it has not worked in either case. It was argued that the four high school years were insufficient for adequate preparation for college. And it was held that by omitting "memory studies" such as political geography, reducing the time devoted to arithmetic, estimated at 20 per cent of the elementary school time, and also reducing the English language work, supposed to occupy 40 per cent, time could be saved for algebra, physical geography, and a foreign language.

Algebra and geometry, said Eliot, provide a review and continuation of arithmetic and are far more illuminating than drill in arithmetic. He thought a foreign language would put new life and meaning into English. And every child should have an opportunity to study a foreign language in the elementary school years when he is at the proper age. These ideas were supported by the Committee of Ten, but Eliot had urged them earlier, and he tried to refute all criticism.

That such a program would break up the existing classes of children seemed to him no objection at all. The grades ought to be broken up and the gifted child, although too poor to attend a private school, should have a chance to rise to high position. A democratic school must give appropriate education to all but not the same education.

Are there doubts regarding the children's ability to master the new subjects? How can we know, said Eliot, until we try? Pupils should be given new subjects as soon as they are capable of understanding them. Curiously at variance with this was Eliot's other demand that "the sole ground of promotion should be reasonable fidelity." Harvard did not admit students on fidelity but only upon mastery as shown in an examination.

A city superintendent, Edward Brooks of Philadelphia, who has been named above, answered Eliot. He said the elementary school program had already been shortened from nine or ten grades to eight; the combination of subjects, such as geography and history, or arithmetic and geometry, was already very common in the schools; and capable children were already promoted more rapidly than slower ones. He implied that Eliot was not well informed about public elementary schools. This was hardly warranted.

Brooks favored the enrichment of the course but not by adding college-preparatory subjects. He proposed the addition of vocal music, morals, literature, and mental arithmetic. He said, "No one sells by algebra," and quadratic equations will not help the housewife. He said Eliot's comparison between the selective secondary schools of Europe and the universal elementary schools of America could lead only to wrong conclusions. The difference between the two men was fundamental; but Brooks did not urge the colleges to liberalize their entrance requirements. Eliot, who had made the college course itself liberal, wanted to retain the old preparatory studies intact.

5. Interest and Effort

The doctrine of interest upon which Herbart had laid extraordinary stress became a controversial topic as soon as it came to public notice. One writer, W. E. Wilson, declared that until the Herbartians called attention to it, interest was a neglected subject even among the psychologists. If so, John Dewey, for one, expiated his error by dealing repeatedly and extensively with it. One of his papers, *Interest in Relation to Training of the Will* (1895), was the basis for discussion by a group of the most distinguished educators meeting as a Herbart Round Table. It may well be that the place given to interest in such meetings is the best criterion by which to identify the new era.

In his paper Dewey accepted Herbart's positive claims, that interest is a "stirring up" of the self, a vigorous mental activity; that it involves the absorption of the self in the object; and that it can so reinforce ideas that they will have practical effects upon conduct. Interest is the means to increased effort. This, Dewey said, is sound educational sense; and it evidently provides a means of will-training. But Herbart had claimed that conduct is determined by the ideas which the individual has accepted. The self has in this theory no originating or controlling power. In taking these positions, Herbart was opposing the ethics of Kant. In his ethics Kant had rejected all empirical influence. The agent who did right because it was beneficial, whether to himself or to others, would not, in Kant's view, be moral at all. Herbart postulated a will that would act in accordance with the acquired ideas. This made the self a pawn in the hands of the teacher, parents, anybody who could get him to accept their ideas. The will postulated by Kant, on the other hand, could not be influenced at all by teachers or parents. Dewey insisted that, psychologically and biologically, interest is a means of furthering the life process, of promoting growth, in those directions which reason and experience approve. This is to be moral and to have a trained will.

Herbartian psychology seemed to Dewey to be essentially a schoolmaster's psychology, not the psychology of a growing, inquiring, experimenting child, but the expression of a nation laying great emphasis upon authority and subordination, both in war and in civil life. He said it was not the psychology of a nation believing that every individual has the principle of authority within himself. We are not compelled, he declared, to follow either Kant or Herbart. We may instead either go back to Plato and Aristotle or forward to Hegel.

This conclusion doubtless pleased William T. Harris, who was in the group which discussed the paper for an hour and a half. Harris was the leader of the numerous educators who insisted upon the freedom of the will. And while the Round Table discussion was inadequately reported, the argument on the training of the will and moral education in relation to interest can be followed in the educational journals of the time. Several of the articles are listed below. De Garmo and other leading Herbartians, who at first supported Herbart's determinism, soon retreated, giving up his basic philosophy and declaring that his educational doctrine was sound and could stand alone; or perhaps they meant that it could claim the support of some other philosophy. This is in effect what Dewey claimed in his paper; and Christian Ufer wrote that in Europe the pedagogy of Herbart was widely, even generally, accepted. His psychology and metaphysics were rejected.

6. New Word, New Goal

A word introduced occasionally by Eliot, frequently by Parker—the word "democracy"—was new. For well-known reasons none of the early fathers proposed to educate youth for democracy. From Thomas Jefferson the young nation heard of an education to maintain liberty and civil rights. Washington spoke of the need in a republic of an enlightened public opinion. Emerson, the unpolitical man, thought Americans too vain of their civil institutions, as they indeed may be; but he considered that society has a duty to educate everyone for himself. Whether this could be done without political institutions or best done with some other kind than the American, he did not say. Horace Mann wanted to educate for morality and economic efficiency. And William Torrey Harris desired the school to transmit the fruits of civilization that were gathered up in the great institutions. But Francis Wayland Parker and John Dewey gave universal currency to a new word, "democracy," and a new goal of education, a democratic society. The schools were to be democratic and to produce a democratic social order.

There is some difficulty in determining what Parker meant by democracy. Several of his statements which bear upon this question follow. He professed an "immense faith" in the possibilities of human growth and in man's capacity for self-government; but it is clear that with him democracy is no longer a merely political word. He asserted with Rousseau that children are "born good" but also that "the child is a born savage," evidently a good savage. When children grow up under conditions of freedom, their originally good natures will assure a democratic society. But to freedom he added responsibility and this constitutes a problem: How much freedom, for whom, and when?

Class education and social classes based upon family or property were heavily scored and held up for censure. Class education is linked with charity schools. He thought there was a trend in cities to make pauper schools out of the public schools. It was in this connection that he gave the definition of democracy upon which he meant to stand. He said that democracy means living for others, the strong serving the weak. At this point he approaches John Dewey's idea that sharing is the essence of democracy.

Democracy in education as Parker interpreted it demands the joining of the school and the community. And he considered the home as the natural link between the school and the public which sustains the school financially and morally. He encouraged parents' meetings and the use by teachers of home and community resources.

Teachers should understand the history of the common school. This school is the newest of all the great institutions that make for righteousness and it is a mere babe. But its past growth and work show its capacity for growth and will encourage teachers to strive for the much finer school of the future. He saw mighty forces working for that school of the future, the kindergarten mightiest of all. Others were the education of women, the normal schools, and the study of education in college. But the true history of the common school must show the dark thread as well as the bright one in its past. The common school has often been in a deplorable state. In the country districts the object has often been to provide schooling at the lowest cost without any regard to its quality. Of such conditions he had personal experience.

The charge has been made that Parker did not understand the economic and political forces of his day, gravely underestimated their strength, and consequently overestimated the power of the schools. It was his optimism, devotion to a cause, and strength of character that secured for him fame and an influence that few teachers who were young at that time wholly escaped.

7. Growth of a Philosophy

The circumstances of John Dewey's youth form a middle term between those of two of his intellectual forerunners. Young Dewey was not subjected to the pinching poverty of Emerson's boyhood, nor did he enjoy the easy circumstances of William James. Like them he was a townsman who saw just enough of the farm to acquire an idealized notion of its life. He grew up on the frontier edge of New England; and the careless freedom and "make-do" of a still pioneer community affected his thought to its foundations. He attended public schools and a small undeveloped state university, and like some other educational reformers he was not in his boyhood a notably good student. From the outside and at this distance of time, it seems that any little occasion or vocational opportunity might have diverted him entirely from the intellectual life. There is nothing worth mentioning about his few years as a high school teacher. He had joined the Congregational Church, but the study of physiology and an "experience" converted him to naturalism. In his last year at college two remarkable teachers introduced him to psychology and political science. Biology, psychology, and politics supplied the fuel which, lighted by intellectual sparks at Johns Hopkins, burst into flame and made him a philosopher.

Dewey's first book was his *Psychology* (1886). He had come under the influence of G. Stanley Hall. There is no indication that he worked in the psychological laboratory which Hall had established, but he read diligently and became conversant with the state of the science at that time. His major interest was in philosophy; and it is an example of the integrating trend in his thinking, then and always, that one of the first journal papers was on "Psychology as Philosophic Method" (*Mind,* 1886). In a companion piece in the same year and journal, he declared that all objects of philosophical inquiry must be studied as they are in "experience."

Ten years later he published "The Reflex Arc in Psychology," in which he declared that stimulus and response are not separate events but form a single psychological unit; that each has psychological existence only in connection with the other; and that the arc, or total act, is itself incomplete, being only one term of a series as in walking, or rowing, or cutting down a tree with the ax. At that time, it has been said, "he was half a psychologist." This was the remark of an experimenter. Only a few years later his colleagues considered him enough of a psychologist to make him president of the American Psychological Association. He chose as the subject of his address the topic, "Psychology and Social Practice." This contained an implication that all psychology is social psychology, and a plan for a psychology of education. In *Democracy and Education* he wrote that whenever philosophy has been a serious pursuit it has aspired to "a wisdom which will influence the conduct of life," and that from this standpoint philosophy itself may "be defined *as the general theory of education*."

The history of philosophy presents a long line of technically competent thinkers who have considered the nature of reality, the theories of logic, ethics, and other speculative issues. The history of education presents a parallel line of writers who have worked upon the problems of education. One of the most striking facts of intellectual history is the fact that the two lines have usually been parallel but have rarely come together. To find a philosopher with the technical equipment of Dewey combined with a deep and continuing interest in the problems of education one has to go back more than two thousand years to the ancient Greek thinkers, Plato and Aristotle. This may be one, although not the only, reason why Dewey continued to find Plato the most stimulating of "the bearers of the ceaseless enterprise which is philosophy."

After a period of teaching at the University of Michigan, a year on the staff of the University of Minnesota, and the return to Michigan, Dewey was called to the new University of Chicago. This move and his reading of James's *Principles of Psychology* were important influences upon the development of his pragmatic philosophy of education. The University Elementary School at the University of Chicago was opened in 1896, and the little book describing it, *The School and Society*, was the first of Dewey's publications to reach the great body of American teachers. In time it reached the teachers of much of the world, for it was translated into a dozen languages. Simple and concrete in statement and warm in tone, it deals with two of the topics which Dewey made peculiarly his own: the school in the social order and the active and inquiring nature of the child. During these middle years of his career he wrote several short

books on educational topics. The longest and most important was *How
We Think* (1910). He was fifty-seven years old when his rounded treatment of his educational philosophy, *Democracy and Education,* came out
in 1916.

8. DEMOCRACY DEFINED

The title of *Democracy and Education* announced that the author was
taking up a theme which Parker had laid down, the meaning of democracy
as an educational concept; and a chapter on "the democratic conception of
education" contains the key ideas which the rest of the book amplifies.
Dewey, like Parker, expanded the meaning of democracy far beyond that
of a form of government, which it had borne since ancient Greek times.
He used the word for an associated form of living in which the individual
is respected, men are equal, and the goods of life are freely shared.

The argument runs as follows: Democracy provides the best way of
living, but it is not adapted to raw human nature. It must be consciously
promoted and transmitted to each new generation. The democratic way
of living is best because it provides for the continuing growth of the individual. This means the growth of all individuals. In a democracy all individuals are precious; in an aristocracy, only those of the upper classes. No
controlling instincts, no fixed habits, nothing should be allowed to interfere with growth. In school education this opposition is directed against
imitation, drill, and the training which, one may assert in opposition to
Dewey, are necessary if a complex skill is to be mastered.

Education as a social function depends upon the society which con-
ducts it. There are good societies and bad ones; and the nature of a society
determines the kind of education which it will have. But this doctrine
must not be interpreted in so strict a sense that a vicious circle would be
formed. The freedom of a democratic society enables the school to promote
greater democracy and the society to improve education. This reciprocal
action is one of Dewey's constant themes.

Sharing is the test of a good society. A good society is one in which
the members share their interests and cultural goods. Free communication
between members is therefore necessary. If taken strictly this would rule
out social classes. Dewey evidently does not support so thorough-going
an interpretation. The same test is applied to the relations between groups.
That is a good society which has many wholesome connections, free trade
in both material and mental concerns, with other societies. Again the
emphasis is upon intercommunication and sharing. This rules out the isola-

tionism of all narrow, self-contained nationalism and is pertinent to present world conditions. The reference of the sharing criterion is both political and in a broad sense social. We shall take up the social meaning first.

Repeatedly Dewey chose the family as the example of a good society. Sometimes he chose a criminal band as an example of a bad one. Such a group is criminal because an individual interest in plunder is its main inner connection and because, in regard to those outside, the band in secrecy and isolation takes away the sharable goods of others. In *The School and Society* Dewey praised the educational values that characterized the family on the old farm, still carrying on in the Vermont of his boyhood in a fashion resembling that of colonial times—little machinery and what there was, horse-drawn; domestic industries; closely knit family and closely knit community. Such an old farm family, he believed, mediated educational values which the urban family had lost.

The old farm and the old school were not closely joined together. Each remained separate and only loosely related to the other. The purpose of the old school was to drill the young in reading, writing, and arithmetic and "to train each child as an individual by demanding the recitation of assigned lessons individually prepared." But then the children obtained their real education outside. The constricted and formal process of the school was supplemented among farm children by communion with nature and by a work experience that involved adjustment and experiment. Plants and animals were a part of the daily life and care. The essentials of social living in the family and the local community included an introduction to primitive occupations, the simple technologies of spinning, soap-making, the processing of foods, and many others. Children learned how to live by daily participation in the responsibilities of life, and in the process gained moral experience and discipline. Most of this has disappeared in urban life, which has few occupations, responsibilities, and processes demanding participation by children, and lacks the old neighborliness and cooperation.

This illustration, which has been used by Dewey and his disciples until it has come to be a part of the folklore of American education, invites the comment that the old farm was not an intellectual or artistic center. Parker, in speaking on this topic before the National Education Association in 1889, seems to have read back into his boyhood the ideas and feelings of his maturity. Emerson, too, idealized life on the farm; but in reality that life was hard and offered little incentive or opportunity for investigation. That life demanded the constant labor of children and elders to keep ahead of the weeds—and the sheriff. Most of those who grew up on the old farm had to escape from it if they were to achieve an intellectual outlook. To be good, a society must possess goods; and the range of these on the old farm was narrow. Discipline and character, no mean values, rather than the open and inquiring mind were the outcomes of that manner of life. But the open, inquiring, reflective mind was the chief goal of Dewey's educational program. Even character was based upon that.

And it may be that as Parker and Dewey glorified the old farm so they denigrated the old school. Some great men in our history came out of that little institution, including the two men under present consideration. But the truth would seem to be that there never was an old farm in general or an old school in general but only individual old farms and schools that differed widely among themselves, but were generally poor in both material goods and ideas.

The school, Dewey argued, must now provide what the industrial revolution has placed beyond the ordinary experience of children. The school must become a community and it must have the materials and resources that will enlist the interest, stimulate the minds, and employ the hands of the children. Schools cannot serve as socializing agencies unless the children engage in shared, cooperative activities. If the children cook a meal and serve it, make things out of wood, wire, or other materials, write and put on a play, then a community, a little society, will form itself naturally. The absence of shared activities, Dewey said, marked the tragic weakness of the old school on the ethical side. Children do not become moral, that is, social, without a society. The school must be a society, since the children no longer live in a natural society with the interdependence of the rural community.

Teachers should take a hint, Dewey said, from the playground, where children spontaneously organize themselves into teams and play groups. The schoolroom must follow this example. Cooperative and active occupations will renew the entire spirit of the school, and will reform the discipline and the moral and intellectual teaching as well. With studio, workshop, kitchen, and laboratory as centers and occupations carried on in them, the school will become a real society in miniature.

The school will also use the real society outside as an educational resource. The public services, the problems of the city council and executive offices, the factories and professions, all should contribute to the education of the children. And yet Dewey hesitates to bring life as it is into the school. "Real life" is complex, often crude and immoral, and too intricate for direct study. Education must be based upon life, but upon a simplified, purified, and organized version of life.

Some years before the University Elementary School was opened, Cecil Reddie in England had begun his "New School Abbotsholme" (1889). This became the ancestor of a flock of "new schools" in England, France, and Germany. Reddie's basic principle was that the school must be "a larger home and a smaller state." His school was a boys' residential institution with manual, artistic, and social-moral as well as intellectual activities. As in Dewey's school, the emphasis was upon activities. Much of the work of the farm on which the school was placed, the care of pets and farm animals, the planting and harvesting, and building and repair work, was done by the boys. They organized and operated a self-government association. Boys were admitted at an early age and remained until they were sixteen or eighteen. Although Dewey and Reddie began their work quite independently, both were aware of the existing and impending social changes and knew the philosophies of Pestalozzi, Froebel, and Herbart. The idea of the "new education" was widely current.

In such a school as Dewey desired, the children would work with hand and brain. Such a school would provide materials and teacher-guidance that would enlist the children's fourfold interests in communication, inquiry, construction, and artistic expression. One does not need "to draw out" the children's interests. They are not by nature the restrained beings that one finds in the old school, but are "spilling over with activities." Only when they can talk, work, explore, make things, can they truly live and grow. And only under such conditions would the school be a community in which children, living as responsible and cooperating members, could grow intellectually and morally. Such a change, he thought, would amount to an educational revolution not unlike the Copernican in astronomy. The child would become the sun; the school would be child-centered. Whether the child-centered school would also be a community is a question that merits consideration. Perhaps only a community-centered school could overcome the selfish tendencies of individual children.

So far we have considered the concept of the school as a community in which pupils share and participate freely. Such is the nature of a school democracy. But any definition of democracy must, as Dewey says, have reference to facts, all the facts. In a world in which most schools are sustained and controlled by governments, educational democracy must be a political concept as well as a broad social one. It must come to terms with nationalism.

Writing in the early years of World War I, Dewey criticized the "accentuated idea of national sovereignty" which afflicted the world, the "suppressed hostility and incipient war" between neighboring countries.

He attacked the prevailing assumption that a nation's interests are exclusively its own, that its sovereignty can be absolute in an interdependent world. The League of Nations, the United Nations, and UNESCO are among the agencies that have been created to reduce the exacerbated nationalism which Dewey condemned.

Political democracy, like social democracy, means sharing, associated living, conjoint communicated experience. These are Dewey's words. It means the breaking down of personal, local, racial, economic, and national barriers. Education is necessary for the development of such unity even more than for the success of popular suffrage and the equal administration of the laws. Social democracy is the foundation of political democracy. And Dewey claims that democracy is especially devoted to education. He calls this "a familiar fact." But is it? It is perhaps clear that democracy should especially cherish education. But does it do this? It does not seem so. Hitler gave more attention to education than the democracies, and Russia devotes a larger share of her national income to education than any democracy ever did. Nor can it be claimed that their measures were or are ineffective. Their type of education is narrowly nationalistic, inflammatory, and undemocratic, but unfortunately powerful for the "reconstruction of experience."

There is a difficulty at this point in Dewey's philosophy. Democracy implies sharing among the members of a group or nation and also among groups. The groups are an essential feature in the structure of society; but as long as there are groups the sharing cannot be complete. We may take an example. Dewey did not propose a sharing of all the wealth, for example, and if the wealth is unequally distributed there will be economic classes. As Madison wrote in the Federalist, "the most common and durable source of factions has been the various and unequal distribution of property." But economic interests or "factions" will interfere with free communication, the equal spread of knowledge, opportunity for medical service, and good housing as well as other good things. It was not Dewey but Lenin who proposed to go all the way. But Russia has not followed this path and today her economic class differences are as wide as those of capitalist countries, and the barriers separating occupational classes are harder to cross than they are in the free world. Education and industry are hitched to the star of empire.

It is significant that Dewey used the family rather than the nation or the business corporation or even the college faculty to illustrate democratic sharing. But even in the family there are barriers to complete agreement and harmony, as, for example, between parents and children and between the sexes. We must in general accept Dewey's dictum that good education is that which leads toward the democratic ideal; but the situation and the mood of the world today are not those of 1900. It seems that Dewey may have repeated Parker's error in expecting too easy a victory over man's animal will to power.

9. GROWTH AS THE END

In considering children in the family and especially in the family on the farm in the midst of all growing things, it was natural to hit upon growth as the end of education. Growth seemed like beauty, "its own excuse for being." As beyond space there is nothing but more space, so beyond present growth there seemed to be nothing but more growth, a true absolute in a relativist world. Growth needs no end beyond itself and could not have any, for it is itself to be endless.

Again, it is not strange that in Dewey's thinking about education the idea of growth should become an important concept, because he was greatly influenced by biological studies and the work of Charles Darwin. His emphasis upon movement, transition, continuity, and interaction between organism and environment are biological ideas. These were not recent notions. Aristotle, along with assimilation, reproduction, and the connection of function with structure, had made growth one of the leading principles of biological science. Among them he had also included the fixity of species.

Darwin released the objects of biology from the last-named of these principles and substituted for it the all-dissolving principle of an evolution based upon minute variations and the struggle for survival. This "law" enables us to view the growth of animal forms, from amoeba to man, as one continuous process. We shall not dwell upon the fact that experimental biology now considers the process to be less continuous than Darwin thought. But there is yet another obstacle in the way of using the word "growth" for the lifelong process of education. It is the fact that organisms reach maturity early and then they stop growing. Dewey referred to John Fiske's *Meaning of Infancy,* which taught that man is able to progress and build up a civilization because, compared with other animals, he has a proportionately and also an absolutely long period of immaturity and plasticity. But this was not enough for Dewey. He demanded continuing growth that would prepare for more growth. Upon consideration Fiske's whole argument may seem to be self-defeating. One might have pointed out that if a long infancy promotes a more complex civilization, this will in turn require a still longer infancy for the mastering of it.

It was Rousseau, whom Dewey criticized, who introduced the idea that education should be a natural process of growth. But, as Dewey said, too great a dependence upon nature may tend to make foresight and insight seem unnecessary. This remark was not explicitly directed against Rousseau and does not altogether apply to him. Rousseau emphasized activity, contrivance, and discovery in education more than his predecessors and in a manner similar to that of Dewey himself. Both writers regarded the child as naturally curious, inquiring, exploring, and given to making things.

The identification or at least the comparison of education with the process of growth had been repeatedly made before Dewey adopted it. Such famous writers as Comenius, Rousseau, and Froebel had employed it; and actually the concept was a natural product of the speculation which accompanied the rise of science. One could find it even in Bacon, who praised the schools of the Jesuits. This would mean merely that Bacon was not consistent.

Those who adopted this naturalistic theory did not put their full weight upon such a teetering plank. Rousseau and Froebel, after claiming that education should be a natural process, also suggested a multitude of artificial exercises to promote the work of nature. The arrays of carefully contrived problems and exercises in *Emile* and in *The Education of Man* are too long to quote.

Dewey also pointed out, as we have said, that too great a dependence upon nature may tend to make foresight and insight seem unnecessary. And this, as with the principle of sharing, again brings up the question of how much of each. The simple truth is that education as growth, education according to nature, is only a figure of speech, a bit of persuasive rhetoric. If education is growth and the end of growth is more growth, then it follows that the end of education is more education. But this, which might suit an idealist seeking a liberal education, is such another schoolmaster's philosophy as Dewey detested when he had it from the mouth of Herbart. We might do better to go back, not to Dewey or Rousseau, but to John Locke, who said that the aims of education are character, practical judgment, polite manners, knowledge, industry, and some skills and arts, including those skills and arts which will enable us to entertain ourselves in a leisure hour without resort to a juke-box.

In *Experience and Education*, Dewey considered that growth may take different directions. A burglar may grow to be a better burglar, a direction of growth that accomplices, "fences," and makers of burglars' tools may approve. Here the objector will insist that growth is not a sufficient aim; we must also specify its direction and end. But Dewey disagreed. He said the question is whether the form of growth provides opportunities and stimuli for growth in other directions. He thought growth in the burglar's art probably would not. Society will stamp out unsocial conduct. But the historical and contemporary facts are that democratic society has not been noticeably successful in doing this.

When Dewey on occasion became dissatisfied with growth as the aim of education, he substituted for it the continuous reconstruction of experience. But this is similarly neutral in its bearing. Only if the reconstructed experience is better than the old can this formulation of the aim win approval. Such a statement, that any act or state is better than another, must be based upon a system of ethics. And in his ethics Dewey attempted to substitute statements of fact for statements of value. In the opinion of some he was unsuccessful. And further, possibly both of the efforts to propose a general aim of education were inconsistent with his instrumentalism. It might have been better if he had remained true to another of his insights, namely, that no aim is suitable for all persons, at all times, and everywhere.

When Dewey came to deal with the means of promoting growth, he showed that he had not rejected the teaching of Herbart that ethics or, following Dewey, the principles of the good society will prescribe the direction that growth is to follow, but that psychology will have to supply the means. He repeated this view in *The Sources of a Science of Education* (1929), claiming that there is agreement that the social sciences reveal what pupils are to learn; and that psychology deals with means and how they do and should learn. By learning he doubtless meant experiencing, acting, creating, and thinking. Thinking was for Dewey the primary means of growth and of the reconstruction of experience as well. He was generally opposed to emphasis upon fixed instincts, rigid habits, imitation, and he had little use for external standards or objective tests and measurements. He believed that the environment is the main source of problems and that in thinking the pupil should deal with a total situation. Thus he in a measure anticipated the "field theory" of problem-solving.

1.0. How We Think

Dewey held that we think when we must, that thinking originates in a perplexity, an obstacle, or a doubt. Some have regarded this as a great discovery but it is in fact only a truism. If thinking is defined as the effort to find the answer to a problem or to resolve a perplexity, then, naturally, it cannot occur except in the presence of some difficulty. Like other truisms, however, this one is worth stating. It says that situations can be set up to stimulate thinking.

The sources and varied nature of pupils' problems are themselves problems that closely concern the teacher. Children are active by nature, "spill-ing over with activities," and from these practical concerns many problems arise. How to get out of his play-pen is for the small child a problem that is about on a par with the problem of the cat in a cage. Rousseau and Froebel suggested many children's activities that involve problems, but they did not, like Dewey, consider the detailed ways in which the problems are solved by the children. Dewey suggests a few somewhat more intellectual but still simple problems. From *How We Think* everyone will remember the cases of the ferryboat with a white pole projecting from the front of the pilot-house, the soapy tumblers, and the problem in transportation.

Such examples are altogether appropriate as types of work for children; but they may lead the student to the notion that problems usually or always arise from external conditions. This is not true. Philosophers including Dewey have often gone out in search of problems because they enjoyed thinking. Problems do not always arise from circumstances nor do they have to be assigned by a teacher. It is a fact of history that science has been created largely by pure scientists, Galileo, Newton, Faraday, Darwin, and a host of others who went out to look for problems and investigated them for the love of it.

Dewey was, of course, well aware of this and on some occasions took it into account. He did so in explaining the history and usefulness of pure geometry (*The Quest for Certainty*, p. 150). Symbols for geometric objects and operations, he wrote, could "in no disrespectful sense be played with" and "treated from the standpoint of a fine art," and in this process geometry was developed as a science of ideas, not merely of particular things. But he retains his suspicion of all systems of ideas that cannot be concretely in-terpreted at once. He added that "scientific conceptions are not a revelation of prior and independent reality." But scientists, Dewey should have re-flected, do predict occurrences which they do not control. The astronomer who correctly foretells that future observation will verify his present calcula-tion is not the superintendent of a celestial planetarium.

Dewey, as we have seen, had faith in the capacity of pupils to learn to think. But he insisted that they must be taught. He held that thought results from "impeded habit," that is, from a difficulty; but the interest in solving problems must be nurtured lest it die. There are several ways of reacting to a problem. One may act impulsively, smashing the machine that does not work. One may turn away and take up something else. Mankind has shelved many unsolved problems, although one cannot know that the neglect will be permanent. But experience shows that in teaching it is wiser to deal with problems that can be solved or that can be clearly analyzed at least. This may be the reason why Dewey uses simple mechanical and scientific problems to illustrate the process of thinking. The great social goals of democracy which Dewey has most at heart would pose very difficult problems.

In schools we must select problems which pupils will desire to solve and we must encourage promising methods of attack. Dewey named three essentials of good method (*How We Think*, 1910, p. 30): a certain fund and store of experience and facts; ideas, insights, theories; and consistent and orderly work upon the problem. The first of these, especially the body of facts, has a strange look in the context of Dewey's philosophy and in the second edition it was left out.

Some philosophers and some educators would have retained it. As early as 1885 W. H. Payne and B. A. Hinsdale had noticed "the degradation of the memory" in schools. An experimental scientist, James B. Conant, in *Science and Common Sense* (1951), has recently joined them. He showed that scientific experiment originates from a conceptual scheme or system of ideas. The scientist has to frame or master a system of ideas or theory before he can propose an experiment to test it. This evidently involves logical memory. Conant would call Dewey's examples and problems for pupils to solve instances of common sense, not science; and he indicated his general view by devoting a chapter to "the alleged" scientific method.

Eliot also included memory in his formulation of the steps in scientific discovery. In the most elaborate of his analyses there are five steps, as follows: accurate observation, correct recording and remembering, comparison and true inference, precise expression, and adherence to high ideals of truth and right. He added that these processes may occur almost simultaneously. They are Eliot's version of a complete act of thought and may be compared with Dewey's list in the next paragraph.

The last of the three essentials, "consistent and orderly work upon a problem," is the one upon which Dewey lays the greatest stress. To this he comes back repeatedly, perhaps because teaching can be most helpful at this point. And this leads him to his famous analysis of a complete act of thought. He said that each unit of thinking begins in a perplexity and when completed ends in a solution. Reflection begins only as the problem emerges. Between the two limits, he distinguished five steps or stages, as follows: (1) suggestions in which may lie a possible solution; (2) explicit formulation or reformulation of the problem; (3) exploration by means of tentative hypotheses; (4) selection of the most plausible theory; and (5) testing of the theory by action, either overt or imaginative. In the common shorthand version of this analysis, the first and second steps are usually interchanged;

and Dewey explained that the order of the steps may vary, that the problem may change as thought upon it proceeds, that two of the steps may be merged into one, and, in short, that the thinker should be ingenious. The analysis is a description, not a rule. Dewey offers numerous illustrations of the processes. He omits what Conant considers essential, namely, the system of ideas from which any scientific investigation must start.

This analysis of thinking was regarded by Dewey as a tool provided by psychology to aid the teacher. Psychology cannot do everything. It cannot provide the goals of education but it can often show the best way to the goals adopted. In Dewey's view the true goals are democracy and growth. Each requires thinking for its progressive attainment. And the problem of the teacher is to find ways of training pupils to think "instead of following their instincts and impulses, or relying upon habits or imitation."

In the first edition (1910) of *How We Think* there was a section on "the formal steps of the recitation." There Dewey indicated his debt to Herbart for the idea of the analysis of thinking. He said that little had been done to formulate a general method of conducting the recitation but that "one of these is of great importance and has probably had more and better influence upon the 'hearing of lessons' than all others put together," namely, the Herbartian five steps. He thought the Herbartian analysis was more useful to the teacher in preparing to teach a lesson than it was to the pupils. And it was a stroke of genius to turn the idea of the analysis endwise, as Dewey did, making it an analysis of the pupil's task rather than the teacher's. When the second edition of the book came out in 1933, the Herbartian movement had receded and the reference to it was omitted.

11. Use of Philosophy

Philosophy, it has been said, bakes no bread, but it was Dewey's firm conviction that it should. He believed that it has a practical mission in the world and that those philosophers who make it a serious pursuit must intend to change the world by means of it. Philosophy is, from one standpoint, a sustained effort to make our general ideas clear. But the pragmatist thinks ideas do not become really clear until they are put to work, applied. As long as ideas merely float in the mind they are shadows, mere wraiths of their real selves. They become complete and living ideas when they are embodied in deeds and things.

Education is the process of developing good thinkers having clear ideas; and certainly its purpose is to bake bread and, indeed, to change the world. It undertakes to do this by helping students find the significant problems and to make their ideas clear. And the general theory of how this may be done is, again, philosophy. As we have seen, one of Dewey's definitions of philosophy was that it is the general theory of education. From another standpoint he defined it as "inherently criticism having its distinctive position among various modes of criticism by its generality." Any temptation to think here of criticism as mainly negative must be resisted.

There was, however, also in Dewey a spirit of destructive criticism to clear the ground. He sometimes appeared somewhat disillusioned. He raised his voice against the "lunatic fringe" in education. As early as 1910 in *How We Think,* he spoke deprecatingly of some people's "enthusiastic belief in the almost magical efficacy of any kind of activity." In the second edition he added with apparent sarcasm that "experimental activity in education should be directed by ideas pertaining to a problem." He criticized schools which, after they had introduced a new curriculum, achieved only a pleasant hour with the children instead of an educational experience. Orally and in print he insisted that freedom for the child implied freedom for the teacher, who should not be a mere bystander, "a negligible factor, almost an evil." He should be the intellectual leader of the group. To suppose that the teacher is to be an onlooker while children's chance wishes prevail "is merely silly."

But Dewey's philosophy as criticism was more useful when he led the regiment than when he was fighting with stragglers. As a constructive thinker he impressed upon many the conviction that the world or at least important parts of it are within the power of man's control. The success of the natural sciences and the growth of the social sciences inspired him with the conviction that intelligence can modify human nature and social action. As a practical achievement this is, even with respect to the natural sciences and technology, a recent outcome. Natural science had little practical influence upon the lives of men before 1800. But the expansive days in which Dewey grew up after the Civil War, the developments in biology, psychology, and education, and the Hegelian philosophy conspired to make him an optimist; and this optimism he was able to communicate.

Intelligence and constant planning have enabled man to build machines and conquer diseases. Problems of government, economics, population, conservation, and war, however, are both more threatening and more baffling. Drift will be fatal. In a democracy, general intelligence offers the only effective means of dealing with them. Society must find ways, especially through education, to plan its own future. Such planning cannot deal with the indefinite future but must depend upon constant study. Because of the central place occupied by education in this process, philosophy, or "the general theory of education," holds the key to destiny. This seems to be Dewey's estimate of the use of philosophy.

What use has been made of Dewey's own philosophy, how far and deeply his influence has penetrated, is another question. Our chapter bibliography shows that the question has been studied. But the least insight suggests that there is no simple answer. His books are known in every part of the civilized and literate world. This means that they are known to philosophers, educators, and some teachers. In Great Britain and Germany and in certain countries of Latin America they have found many readers. In his own country he has become the subject of a new branch of study in teachers' colleges, the study of the Dewey, or perhaps of the Progressive, philosophy. Dewey was also known as a liberal and a devoted and courageous supporter of efforts, however unpopular, to promote the public welfare or to relieve social ills.

Naturally, not all of Dewey's ideas have been equally well received. Each of his views, as far as it is controversial, appeals to a somewhat different public. The need for activities and concrete materials in education has had a general welcome if not a universal adoption. In America everybody pays lip-service to educational democracy also. Certain of his views have had especial exponents. Among these ideas are the project method stressed by W. H. Kilpatrick, training in reflective thinking by B. H. Bode, and organized social planning by John L. Childs and Theodore Brameld. Dewey's naturalism has met resistance from many rank and file American teachers and even more from the general public when it is understood. Many philosophers do not accept pragmatism or instrumentalism. It is, however, noteworthy that Dewey was far less eager to assume such labels than others were to clap them on him.

The subject of Dewey's influence further involves the question of his originality. Most students of history accept a principle also accepted by Dewey, the principle of continuity. They would call attention to the early influence of Hegel and the later influence of William James, to the Froebelian and Herbartian strains in his thought, to child study, manual training, and to the social democracy of his Vermont community. Certainly many strains in his educational thought antedate 1859; and Dewey had his bit of fun with the young men who claimed to find "a certain Hegelian deposit" in his thinking.

The opinion that education could become a science grew with the development of experimental psychology. This view was reinforced by Bain and Herbart. But against it was the argument that the bases of education, ethics, and psychology were unscientific and that no science could be built upon such foundations. This did not keep writers from continuing to assume its possibility. Scientific methods came to the aid of education but none of the proposed goals could be described in exact terms. This applied also to Dewey's aim of growth or of the reconstruction of experience.

The Herbartian doctrines led to the almost complete abandonment of formal discipline; but experiment has shown that transfer does occur often in significant amounts. The elective system of Eliot, however, was based upon an unfounded belief in very general transfer. The practical results of free election proved to be unsatisfactory, and at Harvard a system of concentration upon a field and distribution among studies outside the main field was substituted. The time required to complete a full course of studies grew longer as standards were raised. College graduation came at twenty-two instead of eighteen. In order to save time a three-year college was proposed but not adopted. Instead, beginning foreign languages, algebra, and some elementary science were, in a few schools, moved down into the grades. The result was the "enrichment" of the elementary school course rather than a decrease in the amount of time. This trend toward the junior high school was resisted by some of the leaders in public education.

The insistence upon better methods of teaching led to the search for means to increase the pupils' interest. Dewey argued that interest was the great means to increased effort. At this point the debate also led to a dispute over the freedom of the will.

The idea of a democratic school to educate youth for democracy was a relatively new idea when it was taken up by Parker and Dewey. The word "democracy," which had referred to a political system, was now extended to include social and moral relations. Dewey made "sharing" the test of democracy and this pointed toward a one-class society. The pioneer community in which Dewey grew up may have influenced his philosophy more than he was aware or than his disciples recognize. Other influences were the evolutionary doctrine, the psychology of William James, and the Hegelian philosophy.

The practical purpose of Dewey's theory is expressed in his definition, which says that philosophy is the general theory of education. This implies that the purpose of life and of education is human development or growth. And even if action, conduct, or practical application are to be the ends, thinking is the means to these ends. One of Dewey's main educational concerns was the teaching of thinking. Now thought, when it becomes general, becomes abstract; but it begins with concrete experiences and simple problems. This led Dewey to emphasize the experiences of the old farm and the self-sufficient family. These are also prime examples of the quality of the democracy which he praised and wished to see developed. Next to the farm as a stimulus to thoughtfulness were the beginnings of industry. This idea, in which Dewey follows Eliot and Emerson, had received extended treatment in Froebel's Education of Man.

Thinking was for Dewey the primary means of growth. Thinking can be learned. It begins with a problem and problem-situations can be set up. Dewey tended to select problems that lead to immediate action, but he was well aware that problem-situations may lead to play with ideas without reference to concrete application. Yet he retained his suspicion of truths that cannot be concretely interpreted at once. Whether Dewey's emphasis upon practical results will best promote the sciences is very much in doubt. Science seems to depend upon fundamental discoveries, the practical use of which may not become apparent for centuries. But the science which interested Dewey most was that which applied to the "real business of living" by making life safe, healthful, intelligent, active, and friendly.

QUESTIONS

1. Why is the notion of mental faculties so persistent in education? Just what do you understand from the words "mental faculties"?

2. How may the notion that all studies are equally educative be used to support the elective system? Might this notion be used in support of a narrow curriculum?

3. Why do students often work harder on work which they have selected?

4. Why did colleges in the nineteenth century raise both their entrance requirements and their demands upon the students during the college period?

5. Why was Eliot considered a Progressive educator? Was this title warranted?

6. How does it happen that people cooperate, form institutions, follow the leader, if "every individual has the principle of authority within himself"?

7. Do you accept Parker's definition of democracy? Why or why not? How does his democracy differ, if it does, from Christian charity? From Dewey's definition?

8. What philosophers, if any, form exceptions to the statement that not since Plato and Aristotle has a well-equipped philosopher maintained a deep and continuing interest in the problems of education? Consider John Locke, Immanuel Kant, G. W. F. Hegel, and perhaps others, presenting the evidence.

9. How thoroughly did Dewey understand children? Consider whether he underestimated their ability to look to the future, to deal with abstractions, and to accept authority cheerfully from those with wider experience than their own?

10. Try to work out in detail what Dewey seems to have meant by growth.

11. Can education become a science if it is based upon the shifting interests of those who are to be educated? Present evidence and arguments.

12. What evidence, if any, does this chapter offer in support of the thesis stated in the first sentence of the chapter? This question may be considered also in connection with later chapters.

BOOKS AND PAPERS

Things worthy to be remembered and appreciations of Parker were published by W. T. Harris under the title, "Francis W. Parker and His Work for Education," in the *Report* of the Commissioner of Education, 1902, Vol. 1, pp. 231–284. Parker's wide influence was largely personal. He wrote little besides *How To Study Geography*. His *Talks on Pedagogics* (title varies) and his addresses were reported. Some of his addresses may be found in the *Proceedings* of the National Education Association.

The German encyclopedias of education have extensive bibliographies on Herbart. Most of the works mentioned in De Garmo's monograph, *Herbart and the Herbartians*, are in German; but there are also a few in English and more in Frank P. Graves, *Great Educators of Three Centuries*, and S. C. Parker, *History of Modern Elementary Education*. The professional magazines, especially *Education* and the *Educational Review*, have many important papers for and against Herbartian doctrines. Most of Dewey's titles are given in Schilpp and in M. H. Thomas, *Bibliography of John Dewey, 1882–1939*, Columbia University Press, 1939.

Boring, Edwin G., *History of Experimental Psychology*, New York, 1950, has an account of Herbart's psychology.

Brickman, W. W., "John Dewey's Foreign Reputation as an Educator," *School and Society*, October 22, 1949, with extensive documentation.

De Garmo, Charles, *Interest and Education*, New York, 1904; *Herbart and the Herbartians*, New York, 1912.

Dewey, John, *School and Society*, University of Chicago Press, 1900; *Moral Principles in Education*, Boston, 1909; *How We Think*, Boston, 1910, and the second edition, *How We Think, A Restatement of the Relation of Reflective Thinking to the Educative Process*, Boston, 1933; *Influence of Darwin on Philosophy*, New York, 1910; *Democracy and Education, An Introduction to the Philosophy of Education*, New York, 1916; *Experience and Education*, New York, 1938.

Eliot, Charles W., *Educational Reform*, New York, 1898; *More Money for Public Schools*, New York, 1903; *University Administration*, Boston, 1908; *A Late Harvest*, Boston, 1924, with a bibliography of nearly 200 articles by Eliot.

Feldman, W. T., *Philosophy of John Dewey, A Critical Analysis*, Johns Hopkins University Press, 1934.

Hinsdale, B. A., *Studies in Education*, Chicago, 1896.

Horne, H. H., *The Democratic Philosophy of Education*, New York, 1932.

McMurry, Dorothy, *Herbartian Contributions to History Instruction in American Elementary Schools*, New York, Teachers College, Columbia University, 1946, with bibliography.

Mayhew, Katherine Camp, and Anne Camp Edwards, *The Dewey School, The Laboratory School of the University of Chicago, 1896–1903,* New York, 1936.

Mulliner, Beatrice C., Translator, *Application of Psychology to the Science of Education by Herbart,* New York, 1898.

Patridge, Lelia, *Notes of Talks on Teaching by Francis W. Parker,* New York, 1885; *Quincy Methods Illustrated,* New York, 1886.

Schilpp, Paul Arthur, Editor, *The Philosophy of John Dewey,* New York, 1951.

White, Morton G., *Origin of Dewey's Instrumentalism,* Columbia University Press, 1943.

Wilson, W. E., "The Doctrine of Interest," *Educational Review,* March, 1896; and see many other articles in this decade in the *Educational Review,* in *Education,* and other journals on this general topic, in particular one by W. T. Harris on Dewey's doctrine of interest in the *Educational Review* for May, 1896.

Chapter XIII

PRACTICE VERSUS THEORY

FROM the time of the founding fathers it has been thought that in a free nation with a popular government, everyone should be educated. But before 1900, and while 25,000,000 immigrants were streaming into the country, no effective means were used to put this theory into practice. Many of the immigrants did not for several generations learn to use the English language. And many of the native-born cannot even now read and write their mother tongue effectively.

Universal literacy was until yesterday largely theory. Child labor was favored by parents, condoned by the public, and welcomed by business and agriculture. Many children did not get to attend the schools for the short terms during which they were open. They did not have the opportunity to learn the simple literacy which to many of the founding fathers seemed sufficient. If this seems a harsh indictment, it is truth which makes it so.

With the passing of time more was demanded and this greater demand is a mark of the progress of elementary education. It is also a negative sort of index of the new burdens which the courts, the church, and the family have shifted to the school. Today, as formerly, the school teaches the three R's, perhaps better than ever before. But this is only a part of a larger assignment which has been growing for a long time. Included in the task is the teaching of health, cleanliness, and grooming; the cultivation and control of the emotions; the expressive arts and social experience; the principles of morals and manners; science; and the facts and forces of society and its institutions.

From so brief an outline it will be apparent that the few and short terms of the common schools of Madison's century are now insufficient. A long school year, a full day, and regular attendance at good schools are necessary. The enrollment of all the children is required because, if a democracy is to maintain its freedoms, all must be educated. The United States has made great progress but it has not fully met this challenge. The charge has been made that the country has some of the best and some of the worst schools in the world; and this has led a foreign observer to speak of "the paradoxical United States."

Several other countries, in contrast, have better enrollment and attendance records, less illiteracy, more permanent teaching staffs, and schools more uniformly good. Most of those countries are small and densely populated in comparison with the large area and unequal conditions of America. Climate, soil, and people divide the United States into sections differing in wealth, culture, and racial composition. Despite strict immigration laws, foreigners without schooling cross the borders into the country. An eighteenth century Constitution has left education to the states, and for a long time the states left it to the local communities. As a principle of educational development and administration, localism has some virtues and also some serious defects.

If we agree with Madison's opinion that ignorance is a national evil, we must attempt to bring all of the children into good schools. The following sections treat the ways in which schooling was made more nearly universal and the obstacles that had to be overcome. The section on literacy offers a partial index of the effectiveness of the measures taken. The remainder of the chapter deals with improvements in the schools which children must attend. A passage on fundamental education shows how the concept of common school education has been expanded beyond the simple literacy which was its original content. The concept is further amplified by treating of special education for those who deviate from the average in important ways, and by reviewing the history of Progressive education and of scientific research in education.

1. Early Attendance Laws

In both Europe and America there was resistance to compulsory attendance requirements. France and England passed such laws only late in the nineteenth century, that is, between 1880 and 1891. Massachusetts had passed a weak law in 1852 but actual enforcement did not begin at that time.

Two periods may be marked out in the evolution of compulsory school attendance in the United States, and 1900 may be taken as the dividing point. The enactment of a law in each state marks the first period. By 1900 such laws had been adopted in thirty-two states and by 1920 in all states. More than sixty years elapsed between the beginning and the completion of this series of adoptions.

The sectional difference in the timing of these laws is very clear from the table below. Most of the states of the South are grouped together at the end of the list. There are other significant comparisons. Three New England states and Michigan head the list, but Washington, Nevada, California, and Wyoming have places in the first column. Some of the newer states and territories preceded many old and populous ones. The territories of Arizona, Idaho, Montana, New Mexico, Dakota (later split into two states), Utah, Washington, and Wyoming adopted compulsory attendance laws before they were admitted to statehood.

The second period began about 1900, although signs of new trends overlapped the latter half of the first period and continue down to the present. In this period the attendance laws have been made stronger and more detailed; and enforcement has been made more effective and has also been more intelligently carried out. The period has been marked by an increase in the number of the years of required attendance and a decrease in the number of exemptions.

TABLE OF INITIAL COMPULSORY ATTENDANCE LAWS

Mass.	1852	Ill.	1883	Iowa	1902
Vt.	1867	Dak., No.	1883	Md.	1902
N. H.	1871	" So.		Mo.	1905
Mich.	1871	Mont.	1883	Del.	1907
Wash.	1871	Minn.	1885	No. Car.	1907
Conn.	1872	Neb.	1887	Okla.	1907
Nev.	1873	Idaho	1887	Va.	1908
N. Y.	1874	Colo.	1889	Ark.	1909
Kan.	1874	Ore.	1889	La.	1910
Calif.	1874	Utah	1890	Tenn.	1913
Maine	1875	N. Mex.	1891	Ala.	1915
N. J.	1875	Pa.	1895	Fla.	1915
Wyo.	1876	Ky.	1896	So. Car.	1915
Ohio	1877	Ind.	1897	Texas	1915
Wisc.	1879	W. Va.	1897	Ga.	1916
R. Is.	1883	Ariz.	1899	Miss.	1918

The Massachusetts law of 1852 set the original pattern. It specified an age range, some types of exemptions, and penalties. It required school attendance between the ages of eight and fourteen years for a period of twelve weeks in each year, and attendance was to be continuous for six weeks. The rest of the time could be made up at the convenience of the child or the family by dropping in at school perhaps one day in one week and three days the next. If the parents were poor, if the child was being otherwise educated, or if it suffered from ill-health, it was to be exempted from the requirements of the law. It is easy to see that it would have been difficult to secure a conviction under this law because each of the exemptions was a matter for interpretation and discretion. But if convicted, the offending parent was to pay a fine. There is a curious provision in this law. The child was required to attend school for twelve weeks only if the public schools of his town remained open that long. This indicates an educational drouth in some parts of the state as late as 1852.

The history of this law and its earliest successors shows that their practical effect was negligible, but it was the sign and the beginning of a trend. The failure of the law was due to nonenforcement which, as we have seen, had also vitiated the colony's education laws. The law of 1852 was not mentioned in the state reports before 1860; and the secretary of the state board favored Horace Mann's advice to exclude pupils who were irregular in attendance. Such approval of "compulsory absence" shows small regard for the law. A new law to deal with "habitual truants," passed in 1862, was also ineffective.

Massachusetts in 1873 passed her third compulsory attendance law in twenty-one years. This act was somewhat more successful. It placed the responsibility for enforcement upon the local school committees or boards. Connecticut had passed her first law in the preceding year. The United States Commissioner of Education preferred the somewhat more centralized power of this Connecticut statute to the local enforcement of Massachusetts. The superintendent of the schools of Boston, John D. Philbrick, pointed out that for the effective administration of any attendance law, a new instrument was needed, especially in cities. He showed that, without a school census, the board and its agents could not know what children ought to be in the schools.

Confirmation of Philbrick's view could be found, if it were needed, in many recent school surveys. They declare that full enforcement of a compulsory attendance law must be based upon full registration of all the children that come under the law. If the schools are also to provide adequately for the handicapped, the appropriate facts must be contained in the school census report. When the proceeds of state school funds are distributed according to the number of children of given ages in each recipient district, a school census is necessary; and the earliest school census laws were passed to provide a basis for the distribution of state aid. By 1945 three-fourths of the states were using the school census to promote universal schooling, to locate children needing special education, and to predict future staff and building needs.

2. OPPOSITION TO COMPULSORY ATTENDANCE

The weak attendance laws in many states were due to various causes including inertia, the desire to profit from the labor of children, and reluctance to interfere in domestic affairs. The experience of Massachusetts was repeated elsewhere. The Kansas attendance law of 1874 was a near-duplicate of the Michigan law of 1871; and it, in turn, served as the model for the laws of Minnesota and Montana. Not all the early attendance laws remained in force. Some were allowed to lapse, or were repealed.

There were some peculiar reasons for such consequences. The second unit to require all children to attend school was not a state but the District of Columbia. Its ordinance of 1864 could not be enforced because the capital city of the nation did not have schools enough to house its school children. And twenty-two years later the District still had 12,000 of its 32,000 children on a half-time schedule. The Ohio legislature, before it passed the attendance law of 1877, struck out the passage which provided for the prosecution of offenders. Thirteen states passed attendance laws in the 1870's but few of these were effective. The Illinois law of 1883 also was a failure but six years later a stronger law for the first time brought many of the Chicago children into the schools.

The real reason for such fumbling and failure was not inexperience and political ineptness but rather the unwillingness of the people to accept the principle that the state should be given the right to interfere with the traditional authority of parents. "Public education is in the public interest." This was the answer given those who urged that an attendance law would create a new crime, would interfere with the liberty of parents, and would increase the powers of government. The answer was that the law ought to do each of these things. Bringing up children in ignorance should be treated as a crime. There is a law against cruelty to animals and parents should have even less liberty to mistreat children than animals. This was the opinion of B. G. Northrop, secretary of the Connecticut Board of Education, in 1872. And government should have the power, he said, not only to punish juvenile criminals but also to correct tendencies to criminal acts by giving the children a good education.

Good laws and enforcement developed about 1890 or 1900. The courts have affirmed the right of the states to pass and enforce compulsory attendance laws. In a case arising under the Ohio law of 1877, the court held that while parents have rights in respect to their children they do not have sole authority over them. It declared that "the welfare of the minor" is of "paramount importance" and that the state may interfere with the liberty of the parent for the good of the child. This case, decided in 1891, raised the question of the constitutionality of the law and the court affirmed it as have all other courts where this question has been raised. This case attracted attention, and reference to it is found in the educational journals of the time, for example, in the *Educational Review* (June, 1892). Other courts have not always followed the argument in this opinion on the essential basis for compulsory attendance legislation. They have more generally and properly held that the state demands schooling not mainly to confer a benefit upon the child but rather to safeguard the welfare of the community and the safety of the state.

Legislatures have now extended the attendance period beyond the traditional age of fourteen to the age of sixteen and in a number of states to eighteen. This is far beyond the period required for the acquisition of the tools of knowledge and beyond the limits of an elementary education. Some of the smaller rural sects such as the Amish have opposed laws that in effect require their children to attend the high school; and in Ohio and Pennsylvania some parents and ministers have gone to prison for their faith.

The law's interference with the liberty of parents to direct the complete and especially the religious education of their children has been resented by Catholics and others. An answer has been found in parochial and other church schools. In the Oregon case decided in 1925 the Supreme Court declared in effect that no state may require all children to attend public schools. This decision will help to protect the interests of the parochial and other nonpublic schools, which enroll about 10 per cent of the school children of the United States. As another result both of the Oregon decision and of the religious renaissance of the last decade, a number of Protestant denominations have built private elementary and high schools; but these have not yet become numerous enough to have any great effect upon public education.

Whether in private or public schools, children must attend for a number of years set by the laws of their states. The upward climb of the attendance ages from twelve or fourteen years to sixteen or eighteen has been, at least temporarily, halted at the latter figure. If eighteen years should be made the voting age, as the President recommended in 1954, the courts might call a permanent halt to compulsory attendance at that point, holding that it would be an unreasonable interference with personal liberty to compel a person to attend school after he is politically mature. But this is pure speculation at the present time.

There are also economic factors. It was one of the early arguments against compulsory attendance that the child's help was needed for the support of the family. A fine line was sometimes drawn in this issue. Some states exempted boys aged thirteen if their services were needed by "a widowed mother." Courts might feel constrained to speak on the reasonableness of keeping youth from work beyond the age of eighteen. Much would depend upon the chance of getting work. Many states now permit the issuing of work-permits at the age of sixteen. Questions of part-time continuation schools and adult education would also be involved. But when all is said the legislature has the power to set any age limit and might set any that the community will support.

The increasing length of the school year has a direct relation to the need for a longer compulsory attendance period. In 1890 and for many years afterward, a number of states would have been happy to secure universal schooling for three months in the year. Many schools were open for three months or less. At present the school year is almost nine months long and in nearly all the states the children are required to attend the entire session. Instead of receiving three months of schooling for six years, children now attend from seven to nine months a year for eight years or more. No high degree of accuracy can be claimed for these figures, but a larger proportion of children are in school than formerly and those who are enrolled receive from three to five times as many days of instruction as they did sixty years ago.

3. Child Labor and the Schools

Child labor is an ambiguous term, for it is often intended to cover only work that is injurious to children. Children may learn much from reasonable and well-distributed tasks. All children should be taught to work. But unsuitable work may damage their health or morals and it may prevent or interfere with their education and with the recreation and associations needed for complete development.

Child labor and the schools are interconnected. When children work for wages they may be unable to attend school or may be too tired to benefit from attendance. Child labor laws and school attendance laws complement each other and the framers of either type of legislation should take cognizance of the status of the complementary laws. Child labor laws frequently demand a certain level of educational attainment before children are to be permitted to work for wages; and the school authorities must certify that this requirement has been met.

In still another respect child labor is intimately related to education. For a long time under rural conditions of work and living and even in industry, children were an economic asset to the family. Parents tended to resist the effort of society to take them away from the farm or factory where they were helping to support the family. From the earliest times, also, parents or guardians were the chief protectors of their wards and it was thought that only the most extraordinary circumstances could justify any outside interference. It is for these reasons that an understanding of the state of child labor is essential in considering the opposition to compulsory school attendance.

In the eighteenth century men constantly appealed to the natural rights of man to justify their own freedoms and privileges; but these rights were not extended to children. It was the factory system which finally caused a revulsion against child labor. By employing children at the youngest possible ages for the longest endurable hours, the factory awakened the conscience and the pity of the public. No such circumstance helped the little ones who were compelled to string beads and make paper flowers in tenements; and some of this is continuing today. Factory work took children out of the home and exposed their sufferings and privations to public view.

Horace Mann saw the frightful effects of factory work upon the children of England, and upon his return home set up warnings against the danger. But it was a later generation that took effective action. Progress was slow. After Lincoln had proclaimed the freedom of the Negro it was the working children who were declared the only slaves remaining in Christendom. Child labor continued to increase until about 1910 but during the preceding four decades a vigorous attack against it was begun. This is continuing.

The most effective opposition to the misemployment of children was offered by organized labor. Both the economic interest and the humane feelings of workingmen favored the cause of the children. They were against child labor because children competed with adults for jobs but also because the treatment of working minors was often harsh and harmful. Labor shared in the humanitarian trend of the time which included also the movement to safeguard children against parental mistreatment and cruelty. The Society for the Prevention of Cruelty to Children was founded near the end of the century and secured for them the protection of the courts. As industry became more highly mechanized, management often joined in opposition to child labor as uneconomical and socially undesirable. Both sides became more favorable to increased schooling. Thus three interrelated movements of the period may be noted: the restriction of child labor; the elimination of cruel treatment of children; and the longer period of school attendance.

These gains have not been so pronounced in rural as in urban life. Agriculture now employs more than 60 per cent of all children who work for wages. Much of this is monotonous and backbreaking work in beet, onion, tobacco, and cotton fields for long hours at low wages. Some of it is migrant labor, ill-fed and ill-housed. Many of the children are "wet-back" children from Mexico, poor white children from the mountain counties of Kentucky and near-by states, and Negro children from the South. Contrary to common opinion, agricultural child labor constitutes a serious problem, including in its wider reach the problem of reduced and irregular attendance at school. In the cities, where the laws on school attendance are enforced, many children work early in the mornings, late in the afternoons and evenings, and over the week-ends; and this also may have bad effects upon schooling.

Paralleling the changes outside the schools and better attendance, there have been some significant attempts to provide useful activities in the schools to take the place of those eliminated on the outside. If children are spared injurious work outside they should do more wholesome work in school. Such opportunities have been provided by the introduction of manual training, industrial arts, household arts, school gardens, 4-H Clubs, pretrade and trade training, and the cooperative plans under which the pupil works in industry for a short period and then devotes an equal period to his studies in the school. Great progress has been made along these lines. Much still remains to be done.

Progress in curtailing child labor and securing attendance at school, both of which are fundamental, has been made mainly by means of state law. Back of this was the favorable opinion of the public; but public opinion became effective through law. Each of the states has long since had a child labor law. The first laws of this kind were as weak as were the early school attendance laws. Enforcement was and is unequal.

Because the laws of the states are unequal and enforcement is often poor, efforts were at one time made to secure national legislation and enforcement. National attention was drawn to the problem by the political parties. The Prohibition party included a plank against child labor in its platform as early as 1872. In the second Cleveland campaign the Democrats, still true to their Jeffersonian principles, simply urged the states to pass laws prohibiting the employment of children under the age of fifteen years. In Congress, Republicans, led by Senator Beveridge of Indiana, began the effort to enact a federal child labor law in 1906. Gradually the Republicans, the Progressives, and the Democrats, now becoming both nationalist and progressive, all became united upon the necessity of a federal law.

In 1912 Woodrow Wilson at a great turning point in educational history was elected President. The bill creating a Children's Bureau in the Department of Labor had just been signed by President Taft. Wilson was to have the opportunity to attach his name to the Smith-Lever or federal farm demonstration act and the Smith-Hughes Act for vocational and agricultural education. Between these two acts, on September 1, 1916, the President signed the Keating-Owen Bill, which made it a misdemeanor to employ children under the age of fourteen in factories and under sixteen in mines and quarries producing goods for interstate commerce. This law was declared unconstitutional. Another law based upon the Congressional taxing power met the same fate. Thereupon the supporters of federal regulation secured the submission of a child labor amendment of the Constitution to the states; but the necessary number of states has not yet adopted it. For the present the regulation of child labor, like the promotion of public education, remains in the hands of the states.

4. LITERACY

At the suggestion of Henry Barnard, the federal government in taking the census of 1840 included a question on the ability of each person to read and write. The resulting report created a sensation. More than 50,000 white illiterates were found in each of several states. An educational convention was held in Richmond, Virginia, to consider the bad plight of the Old Dominion. Over the country, newspapers commented upon the admission by 500,000 white Americans that they were unable to read and write. Similar revelations in the 1850 and later census returns did not call out any comment.

The meaning of any return obviously depends upon the meaning of the words used. Illiteracy may be total; but literacy exists in many degrees. The early United States census definition of literacy was the ability to read and write, ever so little, in any language. On this basis there may be perhaps 4,000,000 illiterate adults in the United States at present.

The census question was changed in 1940 to ask for the number of years of schooling completed by the respondent. The theory is that nearly all persons with five years of schooling are literate. But schools and school years are not uniform; and, more important, the definition of literacy has been changed to mean that the respondent can read a newspaper and write a letter, that he is functionally literate. This is different from saying that he can barely read and write; but no accurate comparison between the old and the new returns on literacy is possible.

The median number of years of schooling completed by adult American citizens was six years in the first World War and over nine years in the second, a great improvement. But this added schooling was not equally distributed. Illiteracy persisted. The improvement was largely due to increased attendance at postelementary schools, such as high schools and colleges, by people of the classes that were literate in 1917 or earlier. The reports tend to obscure the significance of the fact that 2,250,000 Americans have no record of school attendance at any time.

Present-day illiteracy is not wholly racial or sectional. Some illiteracy is to be found among the people of all races and regions. The most highly literate states are Idaho, Iowa, Nebraska, Oregon, and Utah, all largely rural, midwestern, or western. The rate in Iowa is less than 4 per cent, that is, over 96 per cent of the people have had at least five years of schooling. The rate in Alabama, Georgia, Louisiana, Mississippi, and the two Carolinas is more than 20 per cent. In more than half of the states it is between 5 and 10 per cent. And in populous states, where the rate is relatively low, the actual number of illiterates may be considerable. New York, with a rate slightly below the median, has 1,000,000 adults with less than five years of schooling, and Illinois and California each have almost 500,000.

In the South, where in some places the laws have not kept children in school, where terms may be short and schools poor, the rate is naturally highest. In four Southern states one-fourth of the people are illiterate—a lamentable showing. But it will not do to allow this to divert attention from the deficiencies of other sections. One specialist in this field of study has written that "with one exception, all the states with an illiteracy rate of ten per cent and over are in the South." This is a fact but it is a misleading fact. It is misleading because many states in the urban and industrial North, including Connecticut, New Jersey, New York, Pennsylvania, and Rhode Island, have illiteracy rates that hover close to 10 per cent. And the same writer, Ambrose Caliver of the Office of Education, has said that illiteracy is not the problem of a single section or race. This is also true, although illiteracy is unequally concentrated among sections, races, and ages; and the present distribution has been affected by migrations due to twentieth century wars and defense industries.

5. FUNDAMENTAL EDUCATION

Illiteracy is known by the company it keeps; and it is in part its evil associations which make it so great a private misfortune and public menace.

It is usually found among backward peoples and it is both a cause and a result of their undeveloped state. Low standards of living, disease, infant mortality, the wasteful use of resources, general ignorance, and superstition are frequently associated with illiteracy. Low intelligence becomes a major cause of illiteracy only when it is associated with other deficiencies, such as the lack of good schools and the lack of a community opinion favorable to schooling. Literacy may be acquired by all except those of very limited gifts, and it is certainly useful to all as a means to the communication of knowledge and ideas that can raise the learner's standard of living. Attention is here called to the connection which often exists between literacy and other elements of a good life.

This concept under the name of "fundamental" or "basic" education has been adopted by the United Nations Educational, Scientific, and Cultural Organization; but the idea was in the mind of Pestalozzi, and became a part of the new education of the nineteenth century and of Progressive education in the twentieth. Fundamental education is that education which is necessary for all simply as persons without regard to race, social rank, religion, or any other specialized grouping. Under UNESCO, fundamental education is directed against any system that will promote privilege and is directed toward social unity and equal opportunity for all.

This has also been an aim of public elementary education in the United States, but it is an aim that has sometimes been forgotten and has clearly not been achieved everywhere. Fundamental education adds to the three R's sanitation and health teaching, family and homemaking instruction, education in land use, in manual skills, and in wholesome community relations and recreation. The cultural missions of Mexico, Cuba, and other Latin American countries approach this composite scheme of education. The Sloan, Carnegie, and other foundations have done and subsidized the doing of work of this kind in the Southern states. UNESCO has worked in the South and also in many foreign countries. Some of the educational effort of this type is addressed to adults, including women and girls. Education in reading, writing, and arithmetic is an essential element in fundamental education because people can keep up with changing needs only if they are able to read and write and actually use these formal skills.

Of the 18,000,000 men who were called up in World War II, 5,000,-000 were rejected for physical, mental, and educational reasons, one-seventh or 700,000 for "mental deficiency," which was largely educational deficiency. The full strength of the nation could not be mobilized for war because of illiteracy, and the same remark will apply to the nation's industrial potential. As individuals, also, these undereducated persons, even those not called to the colors, were prevented from attaining full stature.

The term "fundamental" might well be applied to the new conception of elementary education in general and not only, as at present, to the education of backward peoples. All good elementary education teaches the fundamentals of the good life, not merely school skills like reading. And as indicated in the Introduction, this is a sign of the progress of elementary education. Educators have outlined the goals of fundamental education somewhat as follows.

The school has always had some responsibility for conduct and has usually enforced a set of rules. The present assignment is that the school shall teach the principles of moral and social living and shall also provide for practice therein. Moral and social living, we are told, is connected with religious and political faith and a philosophy of life growing out of a considered view of nature, man, and God. A school which is charged to remain neutral on such issues may have some difficulty in teaching the principles of ethics. To avoid making a commitment in these matters is to make a commitment.

Children need social experience and the practice of proper social relations. The school can satisfy this need through clubs, plays, student government, musical organizations, and similar groups and activities. The children need guidance and supervision, but not too much because they are learning to direct themselves. Closely connected with ethical and social experience is aesthetic culture, another problem for the school.

There are the rapidly growing bodies of knowledge of nature and human nature. The school must introduce the children to these great fields. This is a scientific age, and schools have not been altogether successful in interesting children in science. That the cultivation of a knowledge of nature and human nature is a proper goal will be admitted.

In each of these fields the school is to stress knowledge and intelligence, use and application, interest and enthusiasm. It is not enough to learn about health and sanitation. One must also act, intelligently and habitually, on this knowledge; and action depends upon interest and enthusiasm. This is fundamental education. It is a conception that may have been implied in the work of some early teachers; it may have developed in the nineteenth century; but it has become explicit in the twentieth century.

6. Education of Gifted Children

The question whether the special preparation of experts and leaders is more necessary than the fundamental education of all, has not always received the same answer. In early historical times the preparation of leaders received all the attention, and for long ages there were no schools for the masses. In modern times this position was modified and two kinds of schools were maintained, one kind with a long course of special knowledge for the leaders and another kind with a short course of common knowledge for the common people. The United States about a century ago developed a system that was to be open to all throughout its full extent from the primary grades through the technical and professional schools; and only lack of ability or enthusiasm was to hinder any from reaching the topmost rung of their ambition.

That this is an ideal not yet attained is recognized; but the mere entertaining of the ideal raised another question, such as this: Should the gifted children be selected and given special education or is the wide-open door sufficient and, indeed, best? This question also has received more than one answer. We may consider a few of these.

If gifted children are to have special consideration, ways must be found of choosing the children. The measures to be applied may include intelligence test results, school marks, activities records, teachers' judgments, reports of social and emotional balance and maturity, types and strength of interests, and family and personal history. As none of these is completely objective or of a determined value, the selecting committee will have to use its best judgment; but an IQ of 140 or above, high marks, and a favorable history will in the absence of negative evidence convince most judges that the pupil belongs to the gifted class. Students have frequently found that gifted children have developed special talents and aptitudes at an early age.

Both acceleration and enrichment have been tried and are favored by different investigators. They are not mutually exclusive plans. The former is administratively simpler and a number of universities have accepted gifted youths at the completion of the tenth school year, that is, at the age of sixteen or earlier. Time has been gained also by proficiency examinations. It was devices like these that President Eliot favored long ago. It has been claimed by psychologists, for example by Leta S. Hollingworth, that acceleration works to the detriment of the normal development of children along both social and physical lines. Professor S. L. Pressey of the Ohio State University has proposed a plan which includes some acceleration and much enrichment.

The enrichment of the course by the introduction of special units and projects and otherwise is a second way of improving the education of gifted children. There are some administrative problems in this plan because it involves increased individual instruction and guidance and, if the group is numerous, the formation of special classes. It also demands additional library, laboratory, and classroom equipment, appropriate methods, and superior teachers who will stimulate and guide, without cramping the initiative of the pupils.

A special direction was given to the argument in 1932 by Edward L. Thorndike. In favoring more as well as better schooling for gifted than for mediocre children, he argued that the public good rather than private advancement or pleasure would be and ought to be served by such opportunities. He deprecated the continuing tendency to raise the compulsory attendance ages for all to higher and higher levels, holding that the effort and money spent in producing a very slight improvement in masses of dull pupils should be devoted to producing the phenomenal advancement of which a small number of the brightest children are capable.

Thorndike asked for a better distribution of education. He recognized the evils of continued illiteracy and proposed that everyone should be given at least one thousand days of schooling. This amounts to about five years of ten months each or seven years of seven months each; and if the compulsory attendance period begins at seven, this would set the end at the age of twelve or fourteen. The equalization of opportunity he considered "noble" as long as some are unable to read, but in higher education he judged it "ridiculous."

In reply to Thorndike several things have been said. It is not necessary to tie the question which he was discussing to the question of compulsory attendance policy. Thorndike wrote before the extraordinary rise in high school enrollment during the great depression had occurred. To provide further education is not the only reason why children are kept in school. Even without a depression there are few jobs for teen-agers in the great industries, and the school is asked to keep them off the streets and out of trouble.

This situation requires a greater variety in curricula and better ways of discovering the special aptitudes of children. Thorndike apparently placed too great faith in the intelligence tests as the main instruments to be used in selecting the gifted. As shown above, other means are now used but the problem is not solved. But these other means are for the most part highly subjective, and psychologists, notably J. L. Stenquist who was for many years director of the bureau of educational research in the public school system of Baltimore, have pointed out that the conventional tests do not measure the special aptitudes of gifted children and the conventional schools do not develop those gifts whose full use would bring distinction to their possessors and benefit to mankind. Stenquist in 1953 set down a list of great scientists, inventors, entertainers, and authors who had been near-failures at school. The implication is that, if the school had been able to discover the real aptitudes of these men when they were children, both they and society would have reaped great benefits. The Westinghouse Science Talent Search is a specialized program of this kind. A general solution of the problem, how to discover and develop unusual talent, would be an achievement comparable to that of Binet or perhaps of an even higher order.

7. EDUCATION OF THE HANDICAPPED

The handicapped as well as the gifted should receive schooling appropriate to their capacities and needs. The physically handicapped do in fact receive more attention than the gifted. Teachers and doctors can materially help them. The problems of the mentally retarded and the socially maladjusted are difficult, but these also can often be resolved.

Gifted and handicapped classes overlap. The same person may be both gifted and crippled, or deaf or even deaf and blind, like Helen Keller. Charles Steinmetz was one of many examples of persons with a crippled body and great mental gifts. There have been composers who continued working after they became deaf, blind musicians, and blind poets. Parkman, although nearly blind, became one of the greatest of American historians.

A census and estimate made some years ago revealed in the national school-age population of 33,000,000 over 4,000,000 exceptional children including 600,000 gifted and 3,500,000 handicapped. There were three groups of about 500,000 each. These were the deaf and hard of hearing, those with speech defects, and those with low vitality and certain illnesses.

A school for the deaf was opened in Hartford in 1817 by Thomas H. Gallaudet. He taught the sign language and the manual alphabet. Later, methods of lip reading and voice production were introduced. All four skills were imported from Europe. Samuel Gridley Howe opened a school for the blind in Boston in 1832. Other schools for the deaf and the blind quickly sprang up in other states. Howe did a great deal of promotional work. His most spectacular achievement, however, was the education of Laura Bridgman, a little girl who was both deaf and blind. This seeming miracle was accomplished by very simple, but not the best, means. The education of Helen Keller is a more extraordinary case. Her teacher, Anne Sullivan, herself partially blind, was educated at Howe's school, but after his day. She became a teacher of the highest genius and in Helen Keller she had a similarly gifted pupil.

It has been said that "Miss Sullivan began where Dr. Howe left off. . . . By experiment, by studying other children, Miss Sullivan came upon the practical way of teaching language by the natural method. It was for this 'natural method' that Dr. Howe was groping, but he never got to this idea, that a deaf child should not be taught each word separately by definition, but should be given language by endless repetition of language which it does not understand. And this is Miss Sullivan's great discovery." These are the opinions of John Macy and they were published (1903) in a book edited by him, *The Story of My Life by Helen Keller,* which also contains some of Helen Keller's letters, reports by Anne Mansfield Sullivan, and a short account by the editor. The book is an educational classic, one of very few so far written in the United States.

State schools and some private schools for the deaf, blind, and feeble-minded were opened before 1850 by Gallaudet, Howe, Walter E. Fernald, and others. All had gained inspiration and had imported techniques from Paris. From the same center came Edouard Seguin to introduce muscular, sensory, and objective methods into American schools for the mentally retarded. The Binet intelligence test, another French contribution translated into English about 1908 by H. H. Goddard, aided schools in classifying children according to educability.

In the public schools the education of the handicapped had hardly begun before the present century. The general purpose of this work is to fit as many as possible to enter the regular classes and to become independent, emotionally stable, and self-supporting persons.

City schools teach lip reading and speech to the hard of hearing. Sight-saving measures aim to protect children with low vision from excessive and harmful use of the eyes, and to use touch and other senses as substitutes for sight. The deaf and blind must be taught in special schools or classes. Before World War I only a few of the largest cities had provided corrective measures for stammering, lisping, nasality, and other speech disorders. In the next decade such teaching was rapidly extended and its spread has continued along with a great development in normal speech education. Crippled children often need expensive treatment and artificial limbs, braces, or other equipment. Rotary International, Kiwanis, and other service clubs have aided many of these. Tubercular children need open-air schools and these are now common in large cities.

The largest group, over 800,000 were the socially handicapped, those with behavior problems. It is feared and believed that many of these are likely to become delinquent. Juvenile delinquency has been a serious problem for many years. After declining during the depression, it has been increasing since World War II; but caution in dealing with these reports is advisable. Delinquency and social maladjustment are highly subjective terms. Misconduct at school, for example, is differently evaluated by pupils, teachers, and parents; and this holds for all infractions of moral and legal codes.

The socially maladjusted are a challenge to education, but the school cannot alone be held responsible. Cities are responsible when they permit slums, neglect proper street and area lighting, and refuse to maintain good school and recreation services. The public is responsible when they leave the keys in their cars. Parents are responsible when they do not keep in touch with their children's activities and friends. The schools could, however, do a great deal if they had sufficient staffs of qualified teachers, advisers, recreation and activity leaders, and equipment to provide both a daytime and an evening program. If young people are respected and wanted, if the school prepares them for a future that they find desirable and provides directed leisure-time activities, many will be preserved from evils that might otherwise overtake them. If juvenile courts, correctional agencies, and probationary officers had more time and were fully prepared for their duties, more young offenders could be reclaimed. The prevention and cure of social maladjustment is one of the urgent tasks of society today.

8. PROGRESSIVE EDUCATION IN REVIEW

Every unusual situation tends to call out new ideas and actions in order to deal with it. So the education of deaf children, and blind children, and very young children set new problems for their teachers. The ordinary school practices were inadequate in these cases, the usual means of communication did not work well, the academic routine was ineffective. Therefore, the teachers of the deaf devised the manual alphabet, lip reading or, as Alexander Graham Bell called it, "visible speech," and voice production. The teachers of the blind, after a long series of efforts and many conflicts, evolved the Braille alphabet and Braille slate and acquired the use of phonograph and radio. For very young children, Froebel invented the kindergarten. These illustrations could be continued to include such deviates as delinquents, slow learners, rapid learners, and crippled children. The enrollment of pupils with special abilities or disabilities sets new problems for the school; and the problems must be recognized and understood before they can be solved. This is the area of special or differential education.

This is the truth to which Stenquist called attention: gifted children with peculiar aptitudes presumably need special treatment. But since no one yet knows what treatment would be best for superior pupils—or for mediocre ones either—it has been easy to conclude that it would be best to extend to all pupils the freedom to choose for themselves. But unless there were materials and problems from which to choose, this would be an empty liberty. To make real the opportunity for self-education, it was considered best to give to the pupils, teachers to counsel with and things to work with, such as shops, kitchens, gardens, studios, gymnasiums, and libraries. Under expert guidance and favorable conditions the pupils were to educate themselves.

And this was the basis of the original principles of *Progressive Education*. In the first number of the magazine of that name (April, 1924) there is a statement of those principles under seven heads. It took the group weeks of labor to draw up the one-page program. The first topic was "freedom to develop naturally" and under it we read that the pupil should govern himself instead of being governed by arbitrary law; that he should have the free use of an environment rich in material things and full opportunity for initiative and self-expression.

Other principles follow. Interest should be the motive of all work. The teacher should be a guide, not a taskmaster. Progressive teachers will encourage the use of all the senses and the study of life activities as well as books. They will promote the use of information to draw correct conclusions and to express them forcefully and logically. The scientific study of child development, greater attention to health and growth, improved reporting upon schoolwork, and cooperation between school and home in the interest of the children were demanded. The school was to be a laboratory, not controlled by "tradition alone," where new ideas "if worthy" were to be encouraged. This last sentence and the reference to the scientific study of child development should be noted.

This editorial statement, which now seems almost timid, was meant as a definition of Progressive—the capital P is significant—education. The most provocative sentence is the first one, on the pupil's choosing his own conduct. That might raise some questions about ages and the meaning of terms. But there is no Supreme Court to decide what the true sense of these principles is; and later Progressives both reinterpreted them and added others. Of this more will be said in a moment.

Most of the ideas in the preceding analysis were the ideas of John Dewey, Francis Parker, and Charles William Eliot. The portrait of Eliot formed the frontispiece of the first number of *Progressive Education,* and he was the honorary president of the Progressive Education Association which had been formed in 1918 after consultation with him. In his letter congratulating the editor on the contents of the first number of the magazine, he remarked upon the rapidly growing numbers of the Progressive schools and predicted that they would be the "schools of the future in both America and Europe." This prediction has not yet been fully verified but the future is still ahead of us.

One wing of the Progressives of that time, more than thirty years ago, was not recognized in the principles summarized above but was fully represented in the magazine. The leader of this wing was Preston W. Search (1853–1932). While serving as a small-town superintendent of public schools, he had begun before 1880 to experiment with individual instruction. These methods were fully developed at Pueblo, Colorado, and became widely known as the Pueblo Plan. Search was not a man with just one idea. He was a many-sided educational liberal, as his book, *An Ideal School* (1901), proves, but he is remembered for the Pueblo Plan. That individual instruction was considered an element in Progressive education is shown by the space given to it in the new magazine. Among the contributors to the first number were Frederic Burk (1862–1924), Carleton W. Washburne, Helen Parkhurst (all three influenced by Search), John Eades, who described an English version of the Dalton School, and the famous Belgian educator, Ovide Decroly, all exponents of individual instruction.

At any time in the late Victorian period it would not have been hazardous to predict the Progressive education movement. It had been implied by Rousseau, Pestalozzi, and Froebel, and before 1900 their general outlook had become familiar. Child study, the kindergarten, and manual training were spreading. Wealth, or at least economic well-being, and leisure were brought within the reach of a growing class by the urban and industrial revolution. Educational experiments were being tried. The humanitarian movement was freeing the last slave in Christendom, the child.

Several Progressive schools were named in 1901 in *An Ideal School,* but the author did not mention all the existing ones nor go back into history to recall the schools of Alcott or of the Englishman, Rowland Hill. Even a quarter-century later the Progressive Education Association claimed only about forty American schools as embodying its teachings. Nearly all of these were private schools.

The period of most rapid expansion was just ahead, in the twenties. After World War I a number of Country Day Schools were founded in the environs of the large cities and most of them claimed the Progressive title. Being dependent upon fees for support and therefore upon good business conditions, many of them were closed in the depression. Some of the early Progressive schools were connected with universities. Such were the Laboratory School founded by John Dewey and briefly connected with the University of Chicago, the Lincoln School of Teachers College, and the school conducted by J. L. Meriam at the University of Missouri.

Through the teaching of Progressive ideas in the preparation of teachers in universities, and by means of books and lectures, the public schools of many cities were drawn into the movement. Few large school systems became entirely Progressive, but there also were few city systems that remained wholly uninfluenced. Among the general signs of this influence are the greater consideration given to the individual pupil's interests and aptitudes, greater flexibility of requirements, pupil activities usually including the school council or some form of self-government and participation in the management of school affairs, the use of community resources, and cooperation between school and home.

As Progressive education spread, it took on new and varied qualities until it became hard to describe or define. Charles William Eliot, for example, was one kind of Progressive. He is known for his use of the elective system, his emphasis upon science and the cultivation of the senses, and his insistence upon good, even high, academic standards. It is to be noted that he seemed to sanction the dichotomy between knowledge and power to think; and this is one of the marks of his Progressivism or the limitations of it. His relation to the developing movement has been indicated.

At the opposite extreme of the movement a philosophy developed, or rather it was a compliant disposition, that called out a protest from Dewey because it pressed restraints upon the teacher's plans and gave free rein to the desires and even the whims of the pupils. This was a form of the elective system that carried freedom of choice to an extreme. The little poem "Days" by Emerson might be taken for pertinent comment upon this hedonistic position. The "hypocritic Days" in the poem felt only scorn for one who was satisfied with the pebbles at his feet when he might have had diamonds by digging for them.

The question, then, arises whether children have the experience, wisdom, and self-control needed to choose wisely and to persevere in the chosen way. At what age do they acquire these abilities? Now it happens that Progressive, private schools are expensive and patronized by people with good incomes who want to send their children to college. The second question must then be asked. Will Progressive methods prepare these children for the colleges which they wish to attend? A negative answer was given to this question by Ernest Cobb in a book *One Foot on the*

Ground (1932). It was approximately this question that was investigated in the Eight-Year Study.

The Eight-Year Study (1933–1941), which was one of the most considerable achievements by the Progressive Education Association under its original name, gave a different answer. The study was organized to determine whether the customary college entrance requirements were essential to college success or whether pupils from a broader course in a Progressive school could succeed as well in college as the pupils from the college-preparatory course in the ordinary high school.

For the purpose of the study a large number of colleges agreed to waive their regular entrance requirements, and to admit students from the participating schools without inquiring into the details of their preparation. In the evaluation the work of each college student from a participating school was compared with that of a matched student from a nonparticipating school. Two major facts emerged from the comparison. There was no highly significant difference in the academic records of the two groups. And secondly, the students from the participating schools were superior to those in the control group in their extracurricular activities. Questions have been raised about the way the matching was done. The participating schools were not equally Progressive and some even rejected that label. No check was made of the methods used in the nonparticipating schools. But both groups, those who had fulfilled the usual entrance requirements and those who had not, did well, and about equally well, in the college courses.

In the depression of the thirties, Progressive schools lost some of their patrons. Opposition to the more extreme wing of the movement increased. Educators became critical of the extremist views and loose practices of some Progressives and of their failure to demand serious intellectual work and approved conduct from their pupils. This critical group was known as the Essentialists. The general public became concerned about the teaching of the fundamentals of reading, writing, and arithmetic, which they considered insufficient. They thought there should be more drill. They wanted a stricter, more evident, discipline.

The Essentialists, led by William C. Bagley, emphasized these views and some even saw a connection between Progressive education and juvenile delinquency. One heard again the charge which was leveled against Hazelwood School in England a century before. The children, it was said, were arrogant and conceited and had been led to believe that hard-won principles of government and ethics were outmoded, that whatever is, is wrong, and that they could set it right at once by "the method of intelligence." Boyd H. Bode said that "the more prosperous element in society" who were the patrons of the Progressive schools would go with intelligence only a little way. They would not let it interfere with business. It was said the Progressives favored both freedom and guidance, individualism and social cooperation; and critics wanted to know how much of one and how much of the other. In 1944 the Progressive Education Association changed its name to the American Education Fellowship, but not that of the magazine, *Progressive Education*. Later the Association restored its old name, but in 1955 it was dissolved because the dues-paying members had become too few to maintain the organization. The magazine was adopted by the John Dewey Society and continued publication under the old name, *Progressive Education*.

Lack of direction and a frequent tendency to run to extremes have been charged against Progressive education. But although many absurdities have clung to the movement, like barnacles to a ship, and have impeded true progress, a great deal of good has been accomplished. The old mechanical school is not extinct even now, but many people have learned that it should be. The America of many automobiles, once ridiculed by H. G. Wells because of its "immature, undertrained, cheap teachers" who belong to the era of "the one-horse shay," has had a vision of what Progressive education might be and some day may be.

9. THE RISE OF RESEARCH

The scientific and progressive movements in education developed together and each influenced the other. There is no necessity for conflict between them. Some of the investigations of Mann and Henry Barnard were positive and factual studies. The Boston school examination of 1845, which was devised by Mann and S. G. Howe, was an attempt to measure educational products. Child study held some of the purposes of scientific work, although its methods were often entirely unscientific. In the seventies and eighties the requirement of written work, and written examinations in the elementary schools reached a height that some considered absurd, almost a craze. The attempt to improve school buildings and to make schools more healthful goes back to William A. Alcott, Horace Mann, and Henry Barnard. These men were both progressive and scientific.

The Progressive movement has emphasized selected lines of educational research. Its principles of 1924 called upon the schools to become educational laboratories for the study of pupil development. But there is no line separating studies of the pupil from studies of his environment. Statistics are used in the investigating of growth or learning but also in studies of salaries, building costs, or playground space. Historical research is a recognized pursuit in the study of education and it deals with many varied topics. Logical and social considerations apply to philosophies of education. Experimentation is a highly important method of investigation. These few examples illustrate the fact that the field of educational research is a broad one and is not exhausted by psychological studies.

The occasional gathering of objective information for use in education, we have seen, was not new in 1890; but a more investigative era began at that time. The well-known experiment by William Lowe Bryan and Noble Harter on the learning of telegraphy, published in 1897, was as much educational as it was psychological. The construction of scales to measure educational products and mental capacity began about 1900. The Binet-Simon test of intelligence was completed about 1905 and, as noted above, was brought to America a few years later in a translation by Henry H. Goddard. Studies in human capacity had been made earlier by Sir Francis Galton and James McKeen Cattell (1860–1944). J. M. Rice took a first step toward the construction of an achievement scale, or rather a scheme of measurement, in 1894. His spelling investigation followed; and the results were published in 1897. This is often considered to be the beginning of the educational measurement movement in America.

The way in which Rice became both an educational scientist and a progressive educator forms the matter of a surprising story. Joseph Mayer Rice (1857–1934) was educated as a physician and began to practice medicine in 1881. Seven years later, undertaking a new career, he went to Germany to study psychology and education just as De Garmo and other early Herbartians were returning. Like them, Rice went to Jena and Leipsic, learned about Froebel, Herbart, and older writers, but did not become a pure disciple. Perhaps it was his medical education that led him to study European education directly by visiting schools.

When he came home he visited American classrooms and observed the work of 1,200 teachers in thirty-six cities from Boston to Minneapolis and from New York to Baltimore. The results were published in a series of articles in *The Forum* and then in a book, *The Public-School System of the United States* (1893). His report was not entirely pessimistic but he found the teaching mechanical in most schools, the curriculum narrow and based upon textbooks alone, and the discipline repressive. One of his main theses was that when teachers are properly prepared for their work, the curriculum can be indefinitely broadened without detriment to the three

R's. Perhaps Rice had not read Comenius but he agreed with him that the school should be a pleasant place. Teachers and children should be friends. To improve the city schools of the United States three things were necessary: To drive out the politicians, to train the teachers and keep training them in service, and to provide competent supervisors in sufficient numbers. Some of these things he had clearly seen and learned in Germany.

The criticism did not make Rice popular. He was only thirty-five years old and unknown. And as Butler of Columbia said, school people "are to the last degree impatient of criticism and suggestion. They resent them as a reflection on their personal character. As one man, they rush to the defense. The better among them excuse the worse and the worse grow abusive." Horace Mann had experienced just such treatment upon returning from Europe fifty years earlier. Rice did not reply. Butler, with some reservations, endorsed Rice's criticism and said it was needed; and a few years later he took part in reforming the structure of the New York City school system.

The preceding portion of Rice's life-story is not often told. Most writers leave this part of the origin of the testing movement unexplained. It seems that Rice was led to the measurement of educational results through his medical education, study in Germany, and the visiting of schools. He saw that opinions about schools and teaching were only opinions, and that schoolmen had few hard facts to support their judgments. The method which he had used in his tour to test the ability of children in reading at sight shows that he was trying to get objective evidence. One day in October, 1894, the idea came to him that the results of the teaching of spelling could be determined with mathematical accuracy. The same day he selected fifty words and ultimately secured test results on 30,000 children who were being taught in different ways. By giving the same test to all he was able to make comparisons. Although his method was not perfect, this was a fruitful experiment.

The spelling investigation marked the second period of Rice's educational activity. He made extensive tests also of the results of the teaching of arithmetic and language. It has been explained that in the nineties and later, educators were much exercised over the question of "economy of time" in education. This was one of Eliot's themes; and a committee of the NEA worked on the matter. Rice, too, wanted to discover whether the great amount of time spent on spelling was well spent and necessary. He found that children's spelling ability was more closely connected with the quality of the teaching and the maturity of the pupils than it was with the time spent in spelling classes; and this gave him the title of his report, "The

Futility of the Spelling-Grind." His methods of investigation have been exhaustively reviewed and his results have been superseded, as may be conveniently learned from the article on "Spelling" in the *Encyclopedia of Educational Research*. Rice's importance is the importance of a pioneer and it was his fate to be attacked and ridiculed by those leaders who "knew" that educational results could not be measured.

This testing venture changed one of Rice's opinions about education. From his study of city systems he had concluded that local politics was the great evil in the schools, and he proposed to cure or relieve this condition with state control. But he now came to believe that the chief difficulty was the inability to measure results. How is one to choose among such factors as different methods, topics, or time allotments without knowing which is better and how much better? This change of mind began the third period in Rice's work.

Always practical in his aim, he now undertook to interest the profession in the measurement of educational results. Whether preceding or parallel activities in educational and psychological measurement had much effect upon him is an unanswered question. But he must have known that Herbart had attempted to introduce mathematics into psychological explanation and had introduced the idea of the threshold of consciousness, the idea that a stimulus may be just barely strong enough to be noticeable. The Weber-Fechner law was based upon this concept, and Ernst H. Weber's contribution had been made in 1834, Gustav Theodor Fechner's in 1860. Wundt's psychological laboratory had been opened in 1879. In America the professor of physical education at Amherst College, Dr. Edward Hitchcock, began in 1860 to take physical measurements of his students. Experiments in transfer of training were begun by James before 1890. Cattell in 1892 was trying to apply the doctrine of just observable differences to mental conditions. In France, Binet and Simon were at work upon the same problem when Rice was making his spelling investigation. He was not as original as has been claimed, but this is what he did. In 1902 Rice proposed that cities should appoint research assistants to the superintendent of schools; and in 1903, together with twenty-four superintendents and others, he founded a Society of Educational Research. At that point the matter was taken out of his hands.

10. THE SCIENCE OF EDUCATION

The science of education, as it was understood by Alexander Bain and William H. Payne, employed little induction and no mathematics.

Rice, although his methods were defective, introduced the quantitative idea into educational research. Others carried on. C. W. Stone produced a standardized achievement test in arithmetic in 1908 and S. A. Courtis another one the following year. E. L. Thorndike's handwriting scale appeared in 1910. It was based upon the equal difference theorem of Weber and Fechner. Ayres constructed a handwriting scale in which legibility was measured by the rate at which the samples could be read. Scales in other subjects, spelling, composition, language, quickly followed. While the testing movement attracted the greatest attention, other studies were carried forward. There were publications on school law, taxation, and finance, studies of school buildings and building programs, and consideration of children's progress through the grades.

Investigation of this latter topic attracted wide attention and finally gained results. P. W. Search in 1901 presented statistical data on individual differences in growth, school abilities and performance, physical defects including defects in vision, and in a chapter on "the losses of the school," an age-grade table. The superintendent of New York City in his report for 1904 published a similar table and called attention to the number of "repeaters" in the schools. Retardation and elimination from school became, if not household, at least schoolhouse words. Studies of this maladjustment of the curriculum to the children were reported by E. L. Thorndike (1907), Leonard P. Ayres (1909), and George D. Strayer (1911). Search, like Rice, was forgotten. In 1913 Ayres published *Laggards in Our Schools,* a widely discussed book.

About this time the school survey movement began. The studies of the schools of Montclair by Paul H. Hanus in 1911 and of those of East Orange by E. C. Moore in 1912 formed a beginning. The New York School Inquiry of 1911-1912 was the first large city survey and the first to make extensive use of an achievement test. S. A. Courtis gave his arithmetic test to about 30,000 children in this survey, which was conducted by Paul H. Hanus, one of the few educators of standing who had publicly commended the work of Rice.

The school survey movement spread so rapidly that it might be said to have swept the country. The schools of eleven cities and two whole states were surveyed between 1910 and 1913. This was only the beginning. Surveys were usually made by teams of professional educators who were brought in for the purpose. There have been many kinds of surveys. The United States Office of Education conducted a national survey of secondary education (1932). Some cities or single institutions conduct self-surveys or maintain a continuous survey of their operations.

Old-timers met the survey movement with derision, dismay, sometimes with angry denunciation. Some of these reactions were justified in special cases. Surveys have been instituted to discredit a school administration. This was a factor in the New York School Inquiry; and Hanus, who has told the story in his autobiography, had difficulty in securing the publication of his report without having it mutilated; and in fact one section was privately printed, another not at all. It is an obvious principle of school surveying that no part of the report may be garbled or suppressed, and such a requirement is now written into the usual survey contract.

This New York survey should not be dismissed without mention of the city's chief school officer, William H. Maxwell (1852–1920), whose name has been bracketed with those of William T. Harris, Andrew S. Draper, and other notable school administrators. Maxwell was a North of Ireland boy who received a thorough education, taught briefly in his native land and came to New York to follow the same vocation. Finding no opening because he was a foreigner, he engaged in newspaper work and in a few years became the managing editor of a Brooklyn daily paper. When he was twenty-nine he was at last accepted to teach history in the evening schools, and almost at once became assistant superintendent and then superintendent of the schools of Brooklyn. When the boroughs were consolidated in 1898, he became the first superintendent of Greater New York and held the office for twenty years.

Educational organization in the metropolis was almost unbelievably undeveloped at the close of the nineteenth century. Manhattan had only a seven-year, but the other boroughs an eight-year, elementary school. There were local school boards, some controlling only a single one-room school, and borough boards as well as the city board of education. Classes in the primary grades were huge, numbering seventy or more children. Many children were on part-time schedules or did not attend at all. Public kindergartens and high schools were just beginning, twenty-five years after St. Louis had introduced them. The whole system was befogged by personal, religious, and partisan politics. Rice's first opinion that politics is the chief obstruction to good education was correct so far as New York was concerned.

Four years after Maxwell became superintendent, the city charter was revised, the school administration was consolidated, and the superintendent was given power over education, not merely over property. The School Inquiry of 1911–1912 was intended to upset the Maxwell regime but it misfired. In 1912 a great meeting in recognition of the superintendent's twenty-five years in Brooklyn and New York was held in Carnegie Hall.

Maxwell promoted junior high schools, trade schools, industrial and physical education. He needed his great energy merely to keep up with the demands of the rapidly growing city. In his views on the preparation of teachers, which he favored, and on some other professional matters, he belonged to the nineteenth century. But he was a courageous, sufficiently combative, and generally wise administrator.

Surveys have a practical purpose, the improvement of educational practice. The method of the survey and of educational measurement is in the main a comparative one. It seeks to determine, for example, whether the children of the fourth grade are able to spell as well as the fourth-grade children in other cities. Standards are derived from the better schools among those which have been tested. But sometimes there is little effort to apply the knowledge gained from a survey, so that the word itself has come to mean a mere gathering of information. Survey courses in college as, for example, "a survey of English literature," have acquired this same innocuous character.

Surveys are, however, intended to improve education, not to promote research, although they have done this incidentally. The desire to improve education leads to a philosophical question. This question asks what values the community cherishes. Do the people, for example, want their children to spend so much time in becoming very rapid calculators and in gaining ability to spell hundreds of unusual words that they may not have time for current problems and controversy? Rice saw this point. He wanted to save time on the formal studies in order to enrich the curriculum. What use is made of educational science is determined by the philosophy of the people.

The early surveyors had few tools with which to do their work, the New York Inquiry only a single achievement test. But several thousand such tests in many school subjects and skills were developed within two decades after 1910. This was partly owing to the publicity which came from the surveys, partly to the demand which came from teachers, supervisors, and superintendents, and also to competition among the commercial test manufacturers. The resulting tests varied in nature and quality. Some had only a limited application, some were imperfectly standardized, and many were not offered in a sufficient number of comparable forms for use in an effective testing program.

Many of the tests were made in university departments and bureaus of educational research. Such departments were opened at the universities of Oklahoma in 1913, Indiana and Iowa in 1914, and elsewhere in rapid succession after World War I. New methods and courses in educational research were developed in these departments.

The adaptation of statistical methods to educational problems was one of the new lines of work. Thorndike's *Introduction to the Theory of Mental and Social Measurements* appeared in 1904, and Harold O. Rugg's *Statistical Methods Applied to Education* in 1917. Computing correlations became a kind of teachers' busywork at that time, and teachers' marks formed one of the areas where correlation was often applied. Walter Fenno Dearborn (1878–1955) published his study of *School and University Grades* in 1910. Reports on the distribution and on the unreliability of marks attracted wide attention. As in similar cases, the early interpretation of the facts was extreme. Marks can be made more reliable than the first investigators believed.

Another statistical device, the index number, was applied to the comparative study of state and city school systems. Leonard P. Ayres used ten sets of data, half of them financial, to compute educational index numbers for each of the states for the years 1890, 1900, 1910, and 1918. His early work on this problem was done in 1911 and the final results were published in 1920. Others have attempted improvements in the selection and weighting of data. The method has been applied to cities also. The ranking of states or cities according to their educational performance may have some practical value in stimulating rivalry.

Rating scales or score cards for use in judging school buildings were developed early in the century and have been practically useful. A rating method was used also in developing handwriting and other scales. Scales for rating success in teaching have frequently been used. Rating methods, however, are not objective. They do not entirely eliminate the element of personal judgment. Their reliability can be increased by defining what is to be rated, by "educating" the users of the scale, and by pooling the scores of several raters. It is an awkward fact that there is no generally acceptable and exact definition of good teaching, and no accurate measurement of it.

Curriculum investigation will be separately discussed in the following chapter. It has been one of the most popular types of research in education for forty years, but is often criticized for its lack of objectivity. The methods that are employed in curriculum study include job analysis, analysis of social needs, consensus of opinion, study of school practices or previous curricula, of textbooks, and of pupil reaction. Boyd H. Bode was one of the vigorous critics of these highly subjective and generally conservative procedures. He denied the possibility of determining what should be taught from what is taught. It was important to have this said; but the application of the principle of social usefulness has produced important curriculum improvements, as, for example, in arithmetic. Many consider that the resultant pruning of arithmetic was extreme. But most people would agree that curriculum objectives and therefore curriculum content and method ultimately depend upon a philosophy; and this was Bode's main contention.

At the same time science can make important contributions to the curriculum problem. It can, for example, determine the level of intelligence and the time that is required for the comprehension and the learning of common fractions or other topics. It can determine recognized social need as already indicated. It can test the results of teaching to determine when a process has been learned. This kind of knowledge has an obvious use in making a curriculum.

At an early meeting of research people, Thorndike, in striking words, laid down a kind of program for the general movement. He said in effect that whatever exists at all exists in some amount; whatever exists in any amount can be measured; and to know it thoroughly involves knowing its quantity as well as its quality. He hastened to admit that the measurement of some things might be difficult, might require fifty years or more. The movement is now more than fifty years old and a great many educational existents have not yet been accurately measured. One of the difficulties is that they are frequently hard to define. One is convinced that learning is real but just what is it? Another difficulty is that most educational existents cannot be measured directly or at least have not been so measured. But in spite of such difficulties, much progress has been made; and the best evidence of this consists in the radical change in the whole character of educational writing and discussion since the times of W. H. Payne and W. T. Harris.

From the early days of the nation, ignorance has been regarded as a national evil. But when the states began to experiment with compulsory attendance laws as a means of dispelling ignorance, opposition arose. For a long time the laws, although their demands were not great, could not be enforced. The school census came to be recognized as a necessary aid to enforcement.

Industrial conditions have tended to reduce the amount of child labor, but in the country and especially among migrant workers its evils are often extreme. As less work has become available for children to do and as they have been brought into school more continuously, more educative activities have been introduced into the school program. The attempt to provide national control of child labor has not succeeded, and the laws of the states are unequal in their provisions and are not equally well enforced. Effective state laws did not much antedate 1900. They may be satisfied by attendance at private schools.

Literacy for all has become a persistent ideal, but the United States still has several million adult illiterates. These are unevenly distributed, but every state still has an illiteracy problem.

Literacy is an important goal for many reasons and not least because it is a means to the promotion of the fundamental or basic education which makes for health and social efficiency. This is one of the chief objectives of UNESCO and should be stressed in many American communities. The proper education of gifted children is, for very different reasons, perhaps equally or more important to the general welfare.

Since the best means of education are not well understood, many educators have given children freedom to follow their interests in a stimulating environment. They try to encourage the growth of the individual and the promotion of cooperation in forming an ideal society. This is the attitude of Progressive educators who think of themselves as guides and counselors of children. They place great emphasis upon direct experience, problem-solving, and the cultivation of the intelligence. Progressives, however, do not agree in the details of their philosophy. From the beginning, the movement has been under attack from various quarters.

There is no necessary conflict between Progressive education and the scientific movement in education. Educational research has been developing rapidly for more than a half-century and has had a profound influence upon the physical plant, the curriculum, and many other phases of education. The *Encyclopedia of Educational Research* provides material for an estimate of its scope, methods, and results.

QUESTIONS

1. Why does educational progress frequently halt, retreat, and only later again go forward? By what means could steady or at least steadier progress be assured?

2. If the sectional and unequal development of education in various states and regions is undesirable, how could it be made more uniform? The student may wish to argue in favor of state and sectional differences.

3. Which of the arguments in opposition to compulsory school attendance had most, which least, substance? Is not public education at some disadvantage in these arguments since the patron of a private school can choose his school while those who must send their children to a public school have no choice?

4. Why is state regulation of child labor unsatisfactory? Why has it proved so difficult to secure passage of a child labor amendment to the Constitution?

5. How may one account for the mediocre literacy status of the United States as compared with German and Scandinavian countries? This comparison,

in a negative sense in some cases, could be usefully extended to Latin-American and other countries.

6. If the scientific and Progressive movements were opposed to each other, as has been claimed, why did they develop together and often in the same school systems? Is the dispute mainly a jurisdictional one which in a broad view makes little sense?

7. Critics have demanded that Progressive educators should tell how much freedom and how much guidance, how much individualism and how much social cooperation and sharing, they favored. Can this or a similar question be so stated that it can be answered? How, or why not?

8. Why, in your opinion, have the results of the Eight-Year Study had so little effect upon college entrance requirements? Is this owing to the declining prestige of Progressive education? What policies, if followed early, could have moderated the decline in Progressive prestige? The student may wish to reject the opinion that Progressive education has lost prestige.

9. Consider the statement that the early promoters of psychological and educational research were strongly influenced in their work by their past preparation and studies.

10. Select several educational questions that have been at least fairly well answered by the educational researchers and justify your selection.

11. What is the meaning or what are the meanings of the term "Progressive education?"

BOOKS AND PAPERS

Bibliographies on several of the topics of this chapter may be found in the *Encyclopedia of Educational Research.* An early study of the compulsory education laws of the states was included in the *Report* of the Commissioner of Education for 1888–1889, Vol. 1, pp. 470–531; and the progressive passage of additional legislation was shown in the Bureau and Office of Education Bulletins for 1915, No. 2; 1928, No. 20; 1935, No. 4; 1945, No. 1. The adoption of such laws in other nations was indicated in a recent report by UNESCO when, of the forty-eight nations canvassed, only one, Indonesia, had no requirement. The "Anonymous Critic," indicated below, was of the abusive stripe mentioned by President Butler. For Butler's review of J. M. Rice's *Public School System,* in which the words quoted on p. 398 occur, see the *Educational Review,* December, 1893.

Abelow, S. P., *Doctor William H. Maxwell,* Brooklyn, 1932.

[Anonymous Critic], "The Critic at Sea," *Education,* eight instalments, May, 1894, to February, 1895. This is a review of J. M. Rice's *Public School System.* When the journal, *Education,* prepared its index of 1946 these articles were omitted, *spurlos versenkt.*

Brickman, W. W., "Elementary Education," *School and Society*, January 31, 1948; "The Elementary School," December 29, 1951, bibliographical articles.

Caldwell, O. W., and S. A. Courtis, *Then and Now in Education*, Yonkers, New York, 1924.

Caliver, Ambrose, *Literacy Education*, Washington, U. S. Department of Health, Education, and Welfare, June, 1953, Circular 376.

Caswell, Hollis L., *City School Surveys*, New York, Teachers College, Columbia University, 1929; and Caswell with A. W. Foshay, *Education in the Elementary School*, second edition, New York, 1950.

Cobb, Ernest, *One Foot on the Ground*, New York, 1932.

Edwards, Newton, *The Courts and the Public Schools*, University of Chicago Press, 1933.

Ensign, F. C., *Compulsory School Attendance and Child Labor Laws*, Iowa City, Iowa, Athens Press, 1931.

Ginzberg, Eli, and Douglas W. Bray, *The Uneducated*, Columbia University Press, 1953.

Hildreth, Gertrude, *Child Growth Through Education*, New York, 1948.

Kearney, N. C., *Elementary School Objectives*, New York, 1953.

Leigh, Edwin, "Illiteracy in the United States," Barnard's *American Journal of Education*, Vol. 19 (1870), pp. 799–835.

Leonard, J. Paul, and Others, *An Evaluation of Modern Education*, A Report Sponsored by the Society for Curriculum Study [now Development], New York, 1942.

Monroe, Walter S., *Ten Years of Educational Research*, Bureau of Educational Research Bulletin, No. 42, University of Illinois, 1928.

Proffitt, M. M., and D. Segel, *School Census, Compulsory Education, Child Labor, State Laws and Regulations*, Washington, U. S. Government Printing Office, Office of Education Bulletin, 1945, No. 1.

Rice, J. M., The Public School System, New York, 1893; *Scientific Management in Education*, New York, 1913.

Scates, Douglas, "Fifty Years of Objective Measurement and Research in Education," *Journal of Educational Research*, December, 1947, with bibliography.

Sears, Jesse B., *The School Survey*, Boston, 1925.

Stenquist, J. L., "Implications of Intelligence and Cultural Differences," *Teachers College Record*, January, 1953.

Thorndike, E. L., "Distribution of Education," *School Review*, May, 1932.

Tidyman, W. F., "A Critical Investigation of Rice's Investigation of Spelling Efficiency," *Pedagogical Seminary*, September, 1915, with bibliography.

UNESCO, *Fundamental Education, Common Ground for All Peoples*, New York, 1947.

White House Conference on Child Health and Protection, Section III: Education and Training, *Report on Child Labor*, New York, 1932.

Chapter XIV

CURRICULUM TRENDS

CHANGES in the curriculum have occurred in all periods, but the Progressive and the scientific movements transformed both the planning and the execution of the curriculum design. Progressive education demanded that the teachers and even the pupils as well as administrators must be consulted, and that the design must not be rigid or imposed upon all alike. Scientific education broke the content of the curriculum into bits, evaluated the use of each item, studied its difficulty and proper grade placement, and provided achievement tests to gauge the success of the teaching and learning process. Curriculum design belongs to the era of Progressive and scientific education.

Some of the earlier curriculum changes were slight; but others were general shifts, such as those of the Renaissance, the Reformation, and the rise of modern science. All of these affected American education. Educators in these revolutionary periods promulgated novel ideas which in many cases grew from the pressures of the times; but when they got hold of fundamental truths and general principles, their ideas frequently lasted far beyond the period which had inspired them. The humanism of the Renaissance, for example, is still operating, although the ancient classics are no longer its chief instruments.

There are other reasons besides habit, institutions, and conservative human nature, powerful as these are, why the curriculum does not change easily. Even the general curriculum shifts of great movements do not sweep everything off the board. Much of the medieval curriculum remained in the Renaissance; and the ideal of liberal education is effective in the present scientific and pragmatic age. The old professional studies of the Middle Ages and the new humanities flourished side by side in the Renaissance as the old and the new professional studies, the modern humanities, and the sciences do today. The general program of studies is cumulative; and those studies which satisfy the enduring needs of the human spirit are permanent elements of the curriculum.

Curriculum revolutions do not sweep everything before them for the reason that there are constituents which are essential to every curriculum, features that cannot be eliminated because without them there could not be a curriculum. Such are the closely related elements of the medieval trivium, namely, language, logic, and rhetoric, because the need to speak, write, read, and persuade are universal. In the harsh period of the early Middle Ages the curriculum was stripped down to the bone and these arts remained. All curricula and all teaching must use the arts of communication because without them teaching is impossible, and even society would be impossible. Also widely needed are number, order, quantity, and form, the concepts of mathematics; and the ideas of right, good, and expedient and those of organization and administration, which belong to ethics and politics. Arts such as these are indispensable. Greek may not be essential but language is, and so are standards of value, measures of quantity, and forms of organization. They are universal curriculum elements.

The earlier curricula of the schools were not carefully planned and they are not systematic or self-consistent now. They have been formed to meet the local conditions and temporary needs of place and time. Differences exist within the same school and to a degree must be permitted if teachers and pupils are to be allowed any individuality. Although schools, like plants, may be trained, trimmed, and cultivated, they must be allowed to grow. Too much restraint kills.

Under present conditions, a completely stabilized curriculum plan would be undesirable even if it were possible. There are too many genuine and important disagreements within the profession and too many quarrels on the outside to permit a general reconstruction, which would inevitably be an arbitrary one. But improvements have been made and new designs have been tried. Others are possible but a general and final solution of the curriculum problem is not possible. It is one of the persistent problems of education.

Lest anyone should think this unduly pessimistic, he should look at a few facts. The main fact is that the school and school people cannot control the social forces which beat upon them. The community may not allow the consideration of vital controversial questions. Teachers have lost their jobs on such issues. Parents may want their children taught in the good old way; and they vote the bond issues or reject them. Legislation may help or hamstring the school. A better curriculum may, however, in the long run affect community sentiment and turn it in favor of a still better curriculum. The wise course is to make improvements gradually and steadily.

There are special causes for the present wave of interest in the curriculum. The professional preparation of teachers and administrators is one of these. This acquaints those who operate the schools with the philosophy of change and the developments which have come from psychology and educational research. Vocational changes, wars, military recruiting policies, and the present public state of fear have their effects.

Changes in the views on mental discipline have brought about curriculum changes. As long as it was believed that the study of spelling trained the memory and the study of decimals developed reasoning power, it was possible to seem to justify the teaching of the most unfamiliar words and the most abstract topics. Curriculum reform was clearly indicated when the notion of a universal discipline was abandoned. The discovery of the extremely wide ranges of individual differences by the psychologists notified curriculum workers that not all children thrive equally well on the same studies taught in the same way. It was seen that projects, problems, and units dealing with what is worth learning and which is not learned more readily, certainly, and cheaply outside the school should be taught in the school. The pressure for economy of time in schoolwork also made curriculum reform seem urgent. Investigations dealing with the teaching of the common branches have made important contributions. A few of those research findings will now be reviewed before giving attention to the more general history of the curriculum, but first a few definitions of terms.

1. DEFINITIONS

The construction or the improvement of a curriculum is a practical activity. That it will be carried forward by a committee may now be almost taken for granted; but the great difficulty with the committee method is that many members are not able to control their prejudices. Some check upon these may be exercised by an expert presentation of the findings of educational research and some by a review of the new curriculum or revision by an outside board. It is evident that one must distinguish between the practical work of curriculum construction and the scientific task of curriculum research.

The word "curriculum" has taken on a new meaning in latter decades. A curriculum is no longer a group of subjects with some hints regarding methods and expected results. It now is all that a school does which directly contributes to the education of the pupils. In the prevailing professional jargon, it consists of all the "experiences of the pupils" which the school promotes in its effort to educate the pupils. The extracurriculum is not extra to the curriculum but is a genuine part of it. If the definition raises the idea that everything connected with education is covered, this idea must be rejected. The school plant, finances, personnel, and public relations affect the education of the children indirectly and are not regarded as parts of the curriculum. The student may, however, quite properly consider where, exactly, the line is to be drawn and whether the broadening of the older definition is pure gain.

The older tradition emphasized the products of education, increased knowledge, greater skill, a nobler ideal, and so on. The purposes and methods of education were taken as separate from the curriculum. The knowledge was in a book or in the teacher's mind and was to be transferred to the pupil's mind. A skill or an ideal was formed when drill or insight was added to knowledge. The curriculum was composed mainly of the materials or subject-matter which was to be acquired. This subject-matter was considered as a definite body of fact and of explanation that was not much affected by changes in its organization or its applications to actual conditions.

The newer view is that the purpose for which anything is studied, the way in which it is studied or taught, and the content or information are all intimately connected. Arithmetic, for example, when the student is concerned with its logic, its number system, and its techniques, is by no means the same as commercial arithmetic. When a complex skill such as weaving is studied historically it portrays a phase of the development of civilization, but when learned at the loom it becomes a craft. Much depends also upon the extent to which any subject is pursued, and upon the degree to which it is integrated with other studies or is studied as a specialty. And every subject when pursued far enough tends to become both specialized and technical.

In abstraction the elements of a curriculum may be treated separately. Content, method, and purpose are different ideas. But the actual curriculum exists only as an operation and a process in which the elements are fused. The curriculum is what the school does to educate its pupils. It tends to become specialized, and early overspecialization is to be avoided. This is the purpose of the current interest in general education; but general education must be accompanied by specialization if the student is to be prepared for a vocation, a profession, or is to become an investigator.

2. Brief History of Spelling

To illustrate the influence of educational research upon the curriculum, two or three elementary school subjects will be briefly treated and compared. Spelling is to be the first of these. As compared with reading or arithmetic, spelling is a simple skill, not needing the use of the higher mental processes. It depends mainly upon memory and especially upon visual and auditory phases. The auditory sense is not always helpful and may be positively misleading. Examples of words that are often misspelled because they are mispronounced are such, for example, as "athletic," "umbrella," "particular," and "mispronunciation." Others may easily be located in handbooks on composition.

English spelling is extraordinarily irregular and there have been many attempts to simplify it. Benjamin Franklin made such an effort but it was not one of his successful innovations. Noah Webster succeeded in eliminating the "u" in such words as "honour" and "splendour"; and a few other words, of which "programme" and "musick" are examples, have been shortened. But the success of the simplified spelling associations and boards has been very small in comparison with the magnitude of the task. The fault does not lie with the language experts. They favor simple and regular forms but the general public refuses to adopt them. For a time the National Education Association lent its support to the reform cause but without effect. There is no prospect that spelling reform will be achieved at an early date.

The insistence upon the accepted spellings is a late development; and this makes it the more surprising that they cannot be changed. Until the time of Shakespeare, people spelled by ear. About that time a demand for uniformity began to develop. Richard Mulcaster (c. 1530–1611) was a teacher in Shakespeare's London and a writer on elementary education. He included in his book called *Elementarie* a list of 8,000 common words for the purpose of fixing their spellings. This part of the work was a spelling book. A high proportion of these words are still in common use and are included in *The Teacher's Word-Book* (1921) prepared by Thorndike.

3. RESEARCH IN SPELLING INSTRUCTION

Children do not need to spell unless they are writing. This simple truth was hardly recognized by the old spelling book compilers, or at least it was ignored. It was customary to include some of the longest and most infrequently used words of the language in elementary spelling books. It should be remembered that the old spelling bee was a social event and to "spell down" the experts who competed in them some jawbreakers were often needed.

Uniformity of spelling is not as important as many people believe, but this does not make the subject any less important in education. The reason is that business will not tolerate errors in spelling, and it carries the opinion of the general public along with it. The reason is a social one. The school must teach what social use requires.

This principle is applied in selecting the words which are to be taught, namely, the hard words which are frequently written. The selection of these words was a basic step in scientific research in education. Very easy words that are in constant use will be learned without much teaching. Unusual words can be looked up if they should be needed. But between these two groups there are several thousand words that are frequently written and that present spelling difficulties. These words had to be selected and they must be taught.

These words have been identified through word-frequency counts in such materials as personal and business letters, business papers, and school compositions. The extensive count for Thorndike's *Word-Book* was made from printed materials such as newspapers and the Bible. But later lists were drawn from manuscript sources. It has been shown that children at school use a somewhat special vocabulary that is derived from their studies. The word "minuend" from arithmetic is such a word. Each vocation, science, and sport uses a number of special words. "Touchdown" and "scholastic," for example, are not found among Thorndike's 10,000 "most frequently used" words. This indicates that the frequency counts do not reveal all the words that should be learned. A judicious selection also from the somewhat less frequent words should be taught.

The methods of teaching spelling have been studied by investigators. Studies have been made of the relative difficulty of words and of the special points of difficulty in particular words. Attention has been given to the grades in which the selected words can be best taught. This is a comparatively simple problem of curriculum organization because each word presents discrete problems. The problems in arithmetic, science, or history are interrelated and attention has to be given to the logic of the subject.

Should spelling be taught in connection with writing and reading as it may be needed, or systematically in spelling classes? The answer is not clear but there appears to be a place for both methods. Questions of motivation have been examined, and are of great importance to "poor spellers." Much has been learned about the teaching of spelling, but for the details the student must go to special sources. They do not belong here.

The first scientific spelling test was not J. M. Rice's casually chosen list of fifty words but *A Measuring Scale for Ability in Spelling* (1913) prepared by Leonard P. Ayres. Further work was done upon standard spelling scales by B. R. Buckingham and E. J. Ashbaugh. By means of these and later instruments a teacher can judge her success in teaching and can compare her own results with those of other teachers.

Spelling is taught in all elementary schools. It is taught successfully although it is given less time than it received in the old school. Children no longer study spelling in preparation for primary reading, although as shown in Chapter II this was the usual order at an earlier time. No law is needed to require the teaching of reading, writing, spelling, and arithmetic in elementary schools. They are taught in all primary schools and those who complain about the results should not judge from a few chance cases and should also remember that today the laws keep some practically ineducable pupils in school for many years.

4. SCHOOL ARITHMETIC

There is a parallel between the history of spelling and that of arithmetic as school studies. In each case an early period of comparative neglect in the schools was followed by a period of overemphasis and, moreover, of emphasis upon the wrong phases of the subject. Later, common sense and philosophical consideration brought the teaching more into harmony with actual needs and also improved the methods. This third period prepared the way for a fourth, the present era of scientific investigation. It is to be noted that the scientific questions grew out of everyday experience.

In colonial times arithmetic was a vocational subject of commerce and the trades. This commercial arithmetic was also called common or vulgar arithmetic because it pertained to the common affairs of common people. It was taught in special writing and reckoning schools and by special teachers of practical skills.

Before the Revolution, arithmetic was not included in Latin grammar schools curricula. Upon the request of parents the schools excused pupils to take lessons from a writing and reckoning master. The education of Benjamin Rush (1746–1813) was typical. He was educated in a Latin school and graduated from Princeton without receiving any instruction in arithmetic at either place. Until the latter part of the eighteenth century this was hardly unusual.

Many arithmetic textbooks appeared after the Revolution, displacing the English works which had been in use up to that time. One of the new books was by Nicholas Pike. It was published in 1788. A later edition contained a section upon the new decimal coinage which had been recommended by Thomas Jefferson. By 1800 arithmetic had become a frequent subject in common schools, and as public education expanded it came to occupy more and more of the time of the pupils.

The old arithmetic books often contained forty or fifty topics, each with a special rule and with numerous cases under each rule and topic. Six or more ways of calculating interest might be shown, including simple interest, the 6 per cent method, the sixty-day method, the cancellation method, exact interest with four or more cases, interest on promissory notes, annual interest, and partial payments. The subject of weights and measures was also extensive and complicated and much of it useless to most of the pupils.

Arithmetic was often an individual study, the pupil beginning each year at the point reached the year before. When there was no printed textbook available, a manuscript ciphering-book was used. In better schools the classwork consisted in writing solutions of problems on the blackboard and "explaining" them. There was little teaching. The application of common sense to arithmetic instruction was made by Pestalozzi; and Warren Colburn introduced his ideas of arithmetical analysis and primary arithmetic into the United States in 1821. This was the beginning of the third period.

The two movements for economy of time and for the enrichment of the elementary curriculum exerted strong pressure upon the older subjects to gain a reduction in the time allotted to them. The pressure was especially heavy upon arithmetic, which occupied so much of the school day. Topics omitted from many textbooks by 1900 included circulating decimals, equation of payments, partial payments, gauging, tonnage, cube and square root, unusual fractions, greatest common divisor, and least common multiple. The emphasis upon real life problems was growing. A. E. Winship of the *Journal of Education* in 1894 asked, "What can be eliminated from arithmetic?" and Frank M. McMurry in 1904, approaching the problem from the positive side, answered that only what has a clear relation to the needs of life should be included. This is the social use principle. It was to become the guiding principle of numerous investigations.

As in spelling so in arithmetic, scientific research grew out of the practical problems of life and education. It was an effort to test unverified beliefs and to make vague and general statements precise and specific. It is not correct to say that educational reform was begun by the scientific investigators. On the contrary, they continued a trend already set in motion. The student can conveniently verify this statement by examining books on the pedagogy of arithmetic published about 1900 or soon after. David Eugene Smith in *The Teaching of Elementary Mathematics* (1900) and J. W. A.

Young in *The Teaching of Mathematics* (1906) will supply evidence. It is to be understood that these authors were far in advance of the practice of the time.

5. RESEARCH IN ARITHMETIC TEACHING

Ordinary observation indicated that the old arithmetic of many rules, topics, and cases included much useless material. But this knowledge from ordinary observation was not sufficiently precise to guide the curriculum-maker in applying the principle of social use. To do this efficiently, he needed a more exact and detailed knowledge of the arithmetic of daily life. This more accurate knowledge was to be gained by inquiry.

Surveys of the arithmetic concepts and practices needed in occupations appeared as early as 1900. A report to the National Education Association in that year included a digest of 600 replies from businessmen to a questionnaire. Business colleges also gave attention to the problem. Educators were not satisfied, and further surveys of the concepts, skills, and degree of accuracy required were made. The search also became a phase of the job analysis effort of the 1900's, and a chapter in *Curriculum Construction* (1923) by W. W. Charters dealt with the problem.

The general conclusion was that only a small part of the arithmetic found in older textbooks was needed in business; and that the simplification which had been made before 1900 or 1910 had not gone far enough. Everybody agreed that pupils should learn to perform the four fundamental operations with whole numbers and small fractions, confidently, rapidly, and accurately; and that they should be taught to check their results. It was indicated by experiment that checking increased the initial accuracy. Some held out for complete accuracy as the ideal; but perfect agreement was not reached upon this nor upon the degree of speed or skill that would be acceptable. Norms were set, however, when in 1908 and 1913 standard tests began to appear. Some of the later tests were criticized because they included materials not used in business.

The important fractions, it was found, are halves, thirds, and fourths, with occasional use for fifths, eighths, and twelfths, but not for thirteenths, or any of the fractions with large denominators. The role of decimals was discovered to be a small one, confined to statistics and to factories making pistons or other products with tolerances of ten-thousandths of an inch. Also, and as long as fifty years ago, it was pointed out that the use of cash registers, automatic scales, calculating machines, interest and other tables and formulas was narrowing the limits of the pencil-and-paper arithmetic needed in daily life.

This whole simplification process is a part of the movement for economy of time in education. Whatever the purpose of some of the promoters of economy of time, the result of that movement has been to change the content of various parts of the curriculum and not to reduce the number of years that children spend at school. The number of years has been increased, as has been said before, and the years have become much longer. The time that was released by abridging the arithmetic content was promptly given to other materials which were deemed to have greater value.

The psychology of arithmetic has been extensively studied in order to improve the methods of teaching. H. V. Holloway carried out an experiment to determine the relative difficulty of the simple addition and subtraction combinations, $1 + 0$, $1 + 1$, $2 + 1$ . . . and $1 - 0$, $1 - 1$, $2 - 1$ . . . $9 - 9$. His results, published in 1914, interested other investigators and ten years later F. L. Clapp also published lists of the relative difficulty of those combinations. Transfer of training experiments using the same combinations showed that pupils who are taught half of these combinations will complete the others without teaching. The transfer over this very small gap with second-grade pupils ranged from 70 to almost 100 per cent. Helping the pupils to generalize increased the amount of transfer.

Progressive schools frequently select problems and exercises from school and from life situations. Often this social use material generates greater interest. At any rate, pupils seem to learn better with problems that come out of concrete situations, such as industrial arts, cooking, design, and games. From the standpoint of motivation this is not surprising. Incidentally, baseball averages imply a knowledge of decimals in spite of what was said above. It has been found that the homes and the way in which parents were taught influence the success of the school. When parents subtract by borrowing, for example, pupils are less easily trained to use the Austrian or additive method which is universal in "making change." The same sociological factor is evident in the teaching of language, morals, and other fields.

6. STUDIES OF READING

Reading is more widely and frequently practiced than writing, spelling, calculating, drawing, or sewing. Yet many people cannot read and many more cannot read well. It is not surprising, therefore, that great efforts have been made to improve the teaching of this skill. Investigations of reading and of the teaching of reading outnumber those of any other school study; and each year sees the addition of from fifty to one hundred new reports.

Studies of perception in reading were made early; but the first noteworthy results were obtained about 1879 when Professor Emile Javal of the University of Paris made the surprising discovery that the eyes of a reader do not advance smoothly along the line of print but move in sudden short sweeps, alternating with momentary pauses or fixations, that is, the motion is discontinuous. Since then these movements have been extensively studied by various means, but best by means of photography.

We recognize words, it was found, only during the brief pauses while the eyes are at rest; and at such moments we recognize whole phrases and short sentences. William James pointed out that acquaintance with the structure of a language contributes to this ability to recognize large sections of printed matter "at a glance." James was writing of readers who know English grammar. One form of improvement in reading consists in learning to recognize such large sections rather than in attempting to change the eye movements.

Investigators found that the rapid reader is also the one who comprehends best and can report most fully upon what he reads. This is contrary to common opinion, which holds that rapid reading is superficial; and it is true that unfamiliar or technical matter must be read slowly to be comprehended. It was learned that reading such material increases the number of fixations. It leads also to regressive movements of the eyes, showing that parts had been passed over without being sufficiently understood. By practice in increasing the eye-span, sharpening the attention, and other means, efficiency in reading can be so materially increased that business firms are willing to pay for the instruction of their staffs in reading, and colleges carry on remedial reading programs. Investigation has shown that many readers are inefficient because they have fallen into slovenly reading habits.

Other investigations have studied individual differences in reading, changes that come with age, as in the case of changing reading interests, and conditions that facilitate ease of reading or prevent harmful physical effects from reading. Some investigations have dealt with problems of fatigue and eyestrain, illumination, desirable type, near-sightedness, and other problems of the physiology and hygiene of reading. The differences between oral and silent reading have been explored. Francis W. Parker, who took no part in the scientific investigation of reading, nevertheless deplored the exclusive emphasis in schools upon oral reading. Incidentally, the spelling lesson was also an oral exercise at that time.

The first general report on scientific studies of reaching was made by Edmund Huey in 1908; and he proposed that children should learn from the beginning to get the meaning, not mainly to pronounce the words. That was a period when reading was still regarded as elocution. The numerous series of silent reading books which came out in the present century testify to a change in the teaching of reading. The summary by Edmund Burke Huey (1870–1913), entitled *The Psychology and Pedagogy of Reading,* included brief accounts of Huey's own investigations, which had begun about 1898. He was an early but not the first American to work in this field. James McKeen Cattell had considered some of its problems in the 1880's while he was a student in Wundt's laboratory. Huey's interest was started by a question put to him by G. M. Whipple, a young fellow experimenter in the laboratory of Clark University. The question was about the possibility of reading without inner speech.

The book contains a chapter on inner speech, but it deals further with all the current phases of reading research. After more than forty years it still remains a useful résumé. It is divided into four parts. The first part is on the psychology and the last on the hygiene of reading. The intervening two parts treat the history of reading and reading methods, and the pedagogy of reading. The second part is wholly historical and necessarily considers the invention and development of writing and of reading as the two sides of the same coin. The third part is also historical, or since it deals with contemporary practice, some may wish to call it a comparative study. Parts two and three and the rest of the book also are worth the attention of teachers and students of the history of education.

The first steps in learning to read and when they should be taken is one of the topics of the book. Reading readiness was not a new subject in 1908. Many writers, ancient and modern, had treated it; and Rousseau had expressed himself positively on both how and when children should learn to read. Many others had acted as if they believed that whenever the child came to school he should "take up his book," perhaps to read, perhaps "to learn his letters." Rousseau, on the contrary, thought the age of twelve early enough and that children at that age would learn practically without any help from a teacher. Even a little teaching experience should have shown him that this position was absurd. His statement had no influence in America but it has the dramatic value of showing that there is a problem, and one to which science has not yet given an explicit and a complete answer. It may be that teachers currently prepared in colleges of education tend to hold back bright children longer than necessary. Many children have learned to read at very early ages without any apparent bad effects.

Factors that affect progress in reading have been diligently sought. Vocabulary, experience, environmental conditions at home are important. Children from homes in which a foreign language is used exclusively may be hampered in learning English. Teachers may not be able to give them the needed kind of help. Poverty, racial barriers, and isolation are among the reasons for the continuance of much illiteracy. The child's intelligence, while a highly important factor, is not the only one.

7. EVERYBODY'S READING

One part of the "Studies of Reading" which we are considering concerns the extent of people's reading and the influence which that reading exercises upon the state of their information and opinion. This, as the founders of the American government explained, is especially important in a republic. "In a government which gives force to public opinion it is essential that public opinion should be enlightened."

Reading is a phase of communication. The book, magazine, paper, or letter transmits to the reader the thought of the writer. A document is more satisfactory than speech because it can be preserved for study and comparison. It is less satisfactory than speech because, as Plato in the *Phædrus* declared, the author is not available to explain or argue the case. This highly significant statement reflects the place of the conversation in the philosophical method of its author. But modern civilization requires a quantity of information that the ancient world did not have and could not conceive. Modern culture, although it is aided by the radio and television, would disintegrate without printed materials.

Americans read more now than they did in the past. Publications of many kinds are increasing more rapidly than the population and have been doing this for perhaps seventy years. This is because of increased schooling, technical changes, greater leisure, cheap books, wars and rumors of war, and doubtless many other causes. Education and economic causes are of great significance in this change.

An investigation directed by Henry C. Link showed that the amount of reading done by individual persons, like their incomes, intelligence, or education, varies between wide limits. Twenty-one per cent of the people questioned read 70 per cent of the total number of books that were read; and the upper half of those interrogated read 94 per cent of the books. This leaves only 6 per cent of the books which were read for the lower 50 per cent of the readers. About one-third of the homes that were canvassed claimed to have a hundred books or more, a surprising and perhaps incredible result.

Most people, the investigation showed, do not read many books. Efforts were made to learn what else they read. The first answer is that they read newspapers most of all, and many news weeklies, comic books, farm and trade papers, and sensational magazines. The large sale of good titles in paper-back editions may lead some to conclude that the public literary taste has improved. According to reviewers, fiction is less popular than it was but this may be because of the quality of the new fiction. And Link found that three-fifths of the books most recently read were fiction. There have been some successful examples of historical fiction in late years and of fictionized as well as of more trustworthy biography. Some of the most popular novels and biographies have dealt with religion and many books on purely religious subjects have found readers. But during the period of the Link survey "the reading of the Bible was equalled if not surpassed by that of *Forever Amber* and *A Tree Grows in Brooklyn.*" Now if the Bible is read so much one can only express surprise over the ignorance of its contents which every investigator claims to find. Some of these reports must be mistaken; or shall we conclude that people remember almost nothing from their reading?

More books would be read if they were more easily accessible everywhere to those who cannot buy all they wish to read. More libraries in smaller towns and in schools, more bookmobiles, and more imaginative ways of bringing books to the attention of prospective readers are needed. Before taking up the history of the school library, a brief review of the road traversed in the preceding sections will be useful.

8. A Review and Critique

Scientific investigation gained power under the influence of the movement for the economy of time and of the movement to introduce still more subjects into the schools. These pressures fostered the conviction that much of what the schools were doing was wrong or useless, especially the latter. To find out what things were useless a criterion of usefulness had to be found. Social usage was the criterion chosen. The schools were to teach the children to do well all that, and only what, they would need to do in later life. This was the approved principle.

This principle was applied to the selection, for example, of spelling words. Thenceforth pupils were to be taught to spell only those words which they would use in writing, and not such words as "tic-douloureux" or "phthisis," which had actually been included in spelling-books. This excellent principle is excellent only up to a point. There are many words, used by everybody and written by not a few, which are not in the list of the 10,000 most frequently used words. Several examples follow: "arduous," "artery," "beaker," "cession," "clothier," "dexterity," "excise," "intersect," "mascot," "microscope," "opiate," "quorum," "requiem," "velocity," "version," and "whittling." Any of these words might be needed in writing a letter to a friend. They are not technical or "unusual."

The school will not have time, it is true, to dwell upon all of the multitude of less frequently used but still familiar words; but if spelling is as important as society believes, they should be taught as they appear. And the teacher should remember that the extent of the pupil's vocabulary and his familiarity with it are important qualifications of his skill in reading. Further, the school should create a correct-spelling habit and correct-spelling conscience.

The same statement applies to the words that are to be read. The ability to master language is one of the areas in which the intellectual capacity of children is sometimes underestimated. A great deal has been done to bring the language of textbooks down to the children's level. This is useful. The adult and ponderous language of the scholar or specialist is out of place in books for children and often unnecessary in writing for adults. But in the process of simplifying language for children it may lose all sparkle and challenge. The language that is put before children may properly require some use of the dictionary and some attention to the structure of sentences. This is not to be taken as a criticism of studies of readability or of the adaptation of language to grade levels. Those studies have great value. But language can be beneath the level that would be most educative and the trend in this, as in some other areas of American education, seems to be toward oversimplification, mediocrity, and dullness.

The principle of social use as it is commonly interpreted is a double-edged weapon. In cutting away what is relatively less useful, it is apt to cut the nerve of intellectual progress and ambition. Children tend to believe that what the school does not teach is not worth learning. This is more readily illustrated from arithmetic. The application of the criterion of social use eliminated from arithmetic a great mass of useless and time-consuming materials. This was a necessary surgery. But arithmetic is more than sums and practical problems. It is applied logic. The number system is one of the fine and remarkable human achievements, and children who have the capacity should learn to understand it. School arithmetic treats also of quantity and its measurement, and children of capacity should become somewhat familiar with the simplest applications of these ideas in geometry and science. Furthermore, arithmetic is the vestibule to mathematics, and it will not be a service to science or to America if the pupils gather from their schoolwork that its chief uses are found in "playing store," baking a cake, or building a birdhouse. The school has the high duty of paying due respect to the intellectual capacities of children.

Reading may provide another illustration of the misapplication of the principle of social use. This principle tends to reduce the level of the school's reading materials to the interests of children, and of those children who are not the keenest. Juvenile literature, as it is called, tends to be more "juvenile" than "literature." Children of capacity should have the chance to meet Wordsworth, Burke, and Mill, Emerson, Lincoln, and Whitman, before they graduate from high school. Except for their demand for a detailed acquaintance with particular selections, the old college entrance requirements in English literature were on the right track. Schools should teach children not only how to read but also to teach them what is worth reading.

This standpoint implies another curriculum principle which stands in opposition to the principle of social usage. It is that children should be taught to know, to do, and to love those interesting and helpful things which are not met in the ordinary course of work and business but which enrich and ennoble life. Teachers must not balk at this union of opposites. Work and play, the sciences and the humanities, vocational and liberal interests, getting, spending, and sharing, must be combined in every life and in all education. The wise combination of opposites and disparates is one of the main problems of life, philosophy, and education.

The criticism can be stated in another way. The chief difficulty with the social use principle stems from the failure to apply it positively and fully. Great is the social use of a discovery in science, a new insight in philosophy, a better understanding with our neighbors at home and abroad, and in general of the life of reason. But the way to that life is not opened by a negative application of the social use principle.

Scientific investigations in education have dealt with curriculum content but also with methods and with the relative difficulty of items and the grade placement of whatever is to be learned. These studies are an aid to the treatment and organization of the materials. Reading readiness investigations are a special case of such difficulty studies. Intelligence and achievement tests bear on the same problem by enabling the teacher to forecast probable performance on the basis of past results.

The ultimate test of the school and education is found in life after school days. Studies of literacy, of what people read, of their knowledge of public affairs and issues, and of their intellectual capacity and emotional maturity are studies of the effectiveness of the school. Educational science grows out of common sense questions and observations; and it returns to the school and life with practical help for their improvement.

9. School and Library

When the school began to use many books instead of a single textbook, a school library became necessary. The connection of the library with the new curriculum is evident. Frederic Burk recognized this when he cried: "The place to study literature is in a library." So it is, but not literature only, for the library serves the curriculum at all points. Even the work of the laboratory and the shop needs books. School library needs were not often recognized until the time of the educational awakening and they were not effectively met until long after that era.

The library of Harvard College was started with 370 volumes from the bequest of John Harvard. William and Mary College had no important collection for many years, and Yale College began with the few volumes donated by the founding ministers. The other colonial colleges as they developed also slowly collected a few books. But the teaching was carried on by means of textbooks and recitations and by lectures that were usually dictated word for word.

College libraries were not open to the public. And the early conception of the function of a library, even one within the walls, was different from that which is held today. The library was supposed to preserve the books rather than to encourage and facilitate their use. This conception lasted far into the nineteenth century.

The University of Virginia was opened in 1825. Its library management conformed to the usual practice and may serve as an example of it. At first the librarian was required to receive and give out books during only one hour a week. Students were not admitted into the building until the second year, in 1826, when the rule was relaxed and they were admitted by ticket. To consult a reference work they had to secure the written permission of the librarian. Library privileges were withdrawn if they forgot themselves so far as "to violate the rule of silence." A ten-dollar deposit was required to guarantee the payment of library fines. The borrowing of books was hedged about with restrictions. This policy is the more surprising because the University of Virginia was in some ways an original creation. Her library followed the old tradition.

Much later, other colleges were still doing the same thing. Even after

1850 the students of the College of the City of New York could take out only one book at a time. To do that they had to fill out a detailed form and to have it countersigned by three members of the faculty. As in other cases, the library was open infrequently and for a few hours only. Professors were treated more generously. They could take out six books at a time and tutors, three. The current view that the widest use of books is to be encouraged and that the cost of replacements is a normal expense of effective operation is a recent attainment. The holdings of the college libraries were still small in 1850. At that time there were only four such libraries in the country with more than 50,000 volumes and none with as many as 100,000.

Subscription, society, and other semipublic libraries were also started in colonial times. One of the most famous was that of the Library Company of Philadelphia, started by Benjamin Franklin in 1731 when he was twenty-five years old. The Philadelphia Library Company did not conduct a free, but a subscription, library. The cost to subscribers was two pounds entrance money and ten shillings annually, too much for poor people to pay. Merchants' and mechanics' associations, historical and scientific societies, also founded libraries for the use of their members.

National and state libraries were another early species. The Library of Congress, established in 1800, is the most famous of these and has become one of the great libraries of the world. It was formed for the members of Congress, but in the services which it performs it has become a national public library. After the burning of the Capitol in 1814 it acquired the private library of Jefferson by purchase. State libraries were established early by New Hampshire, New Jersey, and Pennsylvania and eventually by each of the states.

About 1850 states began to pass laws permitting towns to create public libraries, but as in the case of public schools many town libraries were created without special legal warrant. In the nineteenth century the public library spread steadily, but the period of its most rapid development began about 1910. The city of Boston was in the field early, and its public library has celebrated the completion of its first century. Among the original promoters were Edward Everett and George Ticknor. Ticknor had the more liberal views. At a time when the future library was still only an idea, he wrote that a free public library "would be the crowning glory of our public schools." School children he wanted admitted upon the recommendation of their teachers. Against the judgment of Everett, he proposed to supply any good popular book in a sufficient number of copies so that many persons could be reading it at the same time. He insisted that the books, although some might be soiled or lost, must be allowed to circulate without cost. Only reference works and rare books were to be reserved for use within the library only. He began the practice of supplying forms upon which the public could enter the titles of books which they desired the library to purchase. Here in the early 1850's we seem to find some of the ideas of modern library management, but none of Ticknor's ideas was more important than that of cooperation with the public schools.

In the last century many of the large cities developed fine public libraries. Edward Everett's hope that they would serve the interests of scholars as well as those of the casual reader have been fulfilled and by none better than by the great New York Public Library. If libraries are educational institutions, and this they certainly are, then the history of the public library is a part of the history of public education. One kind of library, which is public in fact if not in everyday speech, is the library in the public school.

The early school libraries and the early free town libraries were undertaken about the same time, that is, about 1830. These pioneer efforts to provide collections of books for the use of schools were only partially successful. The plan seems to have been to serve the community as well as the school children. They were lending libraries; but from lack of trained librarians and good records, and because the schools were closed during the long vacations, many of the books drawn out were never returned.

The states of New York, Massachusetts, and Michigan began in the 1830's to promote district school libraries. More than a dozen states followed their example. Governors and state school officials favored the plan which seems to have originated with A. C. Flagg, state superintendent of common schools of New York. In 1835 the New York legislature appropriated $55,000 a year for books for district school libraries. The publishers, Harper and Brothers, prepared sets of uniformly bound volumes that were widely sold.

Horace Mann gave his approval to the New York idea and paid tribute to the state "whose enlightened and liberal care of the interests of education" he considered "entitled to the highest praise." Mann was concerned to avoid fiction and other light literature and also all books that might arouse religious controversy. A firm of Boston publishers engaged authors, including Nathaniel Hawthorne, who was to prepare a volume of *New England Historical Sketches;* Jesse Buel, a work on agriculture; and Calvin E. Stowe, a *History of Education both Ancient and Modern,* but this last-named volume was not written.

All three of the states named above required each district to match the money received from the state. This plan produced considerable sums in the aggregate, and New York is supposed to have had 50,000 volumes in its district school libraries. But without state supervision and with a rapidly shifting body of teachers, the books were not easily preserved. The rural schools relapsed into the bookless condition from which governors and educators had tried to rescue them. Cities established their own school libraries, but for the towns help came from the expansion of the public library system.

The American Library Association was founded in 1876 and became the leader in library development and in library and school cooperation. Francis W. Parker had been invited to Quincy, Massachusetts, a year before, and one of his chief sponsors, Charles Francis Adams, Jr., was the head of the town library board. Adams, in a paper prepared for the teachers, proposed that the schools and the town libraries should be joined together into "a people's college." This paper attracted attention, but cooperation between schools and libraries was not new in 1876. Another member of the same family, Brooks Adams, wrote on the introduction into the schools of good literature for free reading. This "new departure," also, was calculated to make the school a vestibule of the public library. To make this possible there must be a public library within reach. In 1955 the then head of the American Library Association, at its seventy-fourth annual meeting, asserted that 27,000,000 Americans "had no access whatever to a local public library."

Public school and public library cooperation was not new in 1876. The new feature was its greater feasibility through the growth and improvement of both institutions. About 1840, when S. S. Greene was superintendent of the schools of Springfield, Massachusetts, he developed a plan of cooperation between the schools and the library of the city. George Ticknor proposed similar relations in Boston at a slightly later time. In 1865 Superintendent Divoll of the St. Louis schools asked W. T. Harris to inquire into and to report upon the administration of the Boston Public Library and its service to the schools. Probably the statements of the two Adamses, especially because they were prominent men, were copied by the newspapers. At least the cities of Chicago and Cincinnati explained that they already had such plans in operation; and there probably were many others. The American Library Association about 1876 devoted whole programs to the subject of books for schools. The importance of such cooperation will appear from the fact that at present school pupils often make up more than half of the users of public libraries.

Schools handle their library problems in various ways. The pupils may go to the central public library or to a branch. The library may place a loan collection in each school. State libraries provide traveling or package libraries and these may be obtained by rural as well as city schools. But these are substitutes for a school library which alone enables the school to teach its pupils how to use a library. The cultivation of this knowledge and skill may easily be one of the more important parts of the whole curriculum.

In some cities there is a general public school library which serves all the schools. In Columbus, Ohio, the public school library was established in 1847 along with the first high school and the office of city superintendent of schools. It served both elementary and high school. In some cities each school has its own library, and collections from its stores may be placed in each room. This plan has evident advantages, but no library, not even the Library of Congress, is complete; and no plan possesses all the advantages without any defects. The school library should, therefore, have the proper connections to secure books that may be needed when these are not in its own collection.

The problem of the bookless schools has been repeatedly studied by the National Education Association and the American Library Association. The Cooperative Study of Secondary School Standards included in its work the study of school libraries and library administration. School surveys, including the New York School Inquiry, have reported on the problems, and so have several state departments of education. Educational foundations have contributed studies and funds. The benefactions of Andrew Carnegie and the Carnegie Corporation to library development in the United States amount to more than $40,000,000. Much of this sum has been spent on buildings. The General Education Board and the Rosenwald Fund have given large amounts to school libraries in aid of Negro schools and the preparation of Negro teachers. But the need is still great in many parts of the country. It may not be extreme to say that one-third of the nation's children are not only "ill-fed, ill-clothed and ill-housed" but also ill-read, in part because they lack the books, magazines, and papers which they need.

10. PLANS AND FADS

The unit plan of teaching, widely used at present and highly praised, correlation, the core curriculum, and the project and other newer methods cannot be as effective as they should be without the use of books, many books. The school library or access to a public library is required for the success of plans in which the pupils carry out investigations.

Some of the earlier special plans were administrative rather than curricular in their nature. Such was the St. Louis plan about 1865 in which pupils were reclassified every six weeks and the brighter ones placed in advanced sections. F. W. Parker at Quincy used a coaching scheme to keep the less able pupils in step with their classes.

At Batavia, New York, a coaching plan was developed which used two teachers in each room, one to help pupils with their lesson difficulties, the other to conduct the class exercises. Apparently there was no connection between the Batavia Plan and the supervised study movement in the high schools early in the 1900's. In this movement the schools used a double period for each class meeting. One period was devoted to aided and supervised preparation and the other to reports, discussions, recitations, and tests of the work done. The supervised study movement declined after about a decade; but schools which have abolished all homework assignments have sometimes set up a substitute. They have introduced additional study hours within a lengthened school day where the teachers can give study guidance.

Some administrators have frankly conceded the impossibility of keeping everybody in step. Some of these vary the amount of material to be studied by the slow, average, and fast groups of pupils. At Cambridge, Massachusetts, this double or triple track plan was in use for a short while. Some private schools and some public school systems have "X, Y, and Z classes."

The preceding plans were introduced into the usual class organization. Another plan, to dispense with classes and group work except in such fields as music and physical education, was promoted by Preston W. Search. Under his individual-study plan, each pupil worked by himself and at his own rate. Search began the plan in the teaching of bookkeeping at West Liberty, Ohio, in 1877, but he developed it more fully at other places including Pueblo, Colorado. His most effective disciple was Frederic Burk, the principal of the San Francisco State Normal School. From there Carleton Washburne carried the ideas to Winnetka, Illinois. Under the Winnetka Plan a large part of the school day was given to group activities, but individual methods were used in the more academic studies. The Dalton Plan, devised by Helen Parkhurst, grew out of the work of Search and Burk; but it was also influenced by Montessori and by Edgar J. Swift, the author of The Mind in the Making (1908).

The essence of the Dalton Plan was in the "job" or individual schoolwork "contracts." Each pupil agreed formally to complete a carefully planned project or unit in a specified time, usually one month. This allowed the pupil to work in his own way and at his preferred rate. Freedom with responsibility was the keynote. There usually was a daily session to plan work and to give counsel concerning difficulties. The Dalton Plan foundered on the difficulty that too many pupils accepted the freedom but neglected their responsibility.

The Dalton Plan spread not only in the country of its origin but also in England, on the continent, and even in Russia in the early years of the Soviet Union when that country seemed to be developing a liberal and popular form of government and education. Experience showed that the Dalton Plan had been praised far beyond its merits and it has been discontinued at home and abroad. It makes a good example of an educational fad, but it is not the only such example among these plans.

A fad is a scheme or device for which magical powers are claimed. Technocracy was a fad in 1932 and 1933. A fad wins a sudden and undeserved popularity because it is not noticed that it lacks the means to produce the promised results. The fashion collapses when men become aware that they have become victims of a delusion. But a fad may sometimes be of use in preparing for a successor of permanent value. It may not be a pure fake like the advertised memory systems or the methods of mastering a foreign language in fifteen lessons.

The Lancasterian monitorial system was a fad. The means it employed were not fitted to achieve what was claimed for it; but it is believed to have promoted public education. Manual training was a fad. It may have aided the rise of industrial arts education but it certainly hampered the movement for vocational education. The calisthenics of Dio Lewis may have contributed to the progress of physical education for women.

Lists of educational fads do not agree in all cases. Jacques W. Redway (1849–1942), a specialist in geography, included the Quincy system, object-teaching, and the Grubé method in arithmetic among the fads. The inclusion of the Quincy system is curious as coming from Redway who, with respect to the teaching of geography, was in the F. W. Parker tradition, and was joint author of a series of textbooks that followed Parker's ideas. Few people and no Progressives would consider the Quincy system a fad. Object lessons, said Redway, "are now [1896] mentioned only in derision." One may agree that object-teaching was a fad; but it must also be admitted that it aided the growth of nature study. Some would also include nature study among the educational fads. The decision would hinge, Redway thought, upon the way it was carried out.

The Grubé method which was named by Redway provides an indisputable case. It was from every point of view a fad. Introduced from Germany and highly recommended by a number of American educators, including Louis Soldan, its wide although temporary popularity justifies a description.

By this method primary arithmetic was taught by using each number to make all the combinations under the four rules, addition, subtraction, multiplication, and division. For example, the exercises on the number 2 were as follows: $2 = 1 + 1$; $2 - 1 = 1$; $2 - 2 = 0$; $2 = 2 \times 1$; $2 = 1 \times 2$; $2 \div 1 = 2$; $2 \div 2 = 1$. On the number 3 there were ten such combinations, and on the number 4, thirteen, and so on. Experienced teachers advised that the exercises up to the number 10 should be completed the first year and to 20 the second year. In some schools the exercises were continued up to the number 144. And still more astonishing, some teachers included the fractional parts of the numbers with the above exercises. This fad was rampant about 1880 but fortunately it disappeared. Such pedagogical excesses teach a lesson that should not be forgotten.

11. Unit Teaching

A coherent portion of the curriculum is currently called a unit, not, as it might be, a chapter, problem, subject, or world of discourse. Like these, a unit is supposed to have a unity which may be logical, historical, psychological, or of some other kind. Psychological unity is that which is developed in the process of an exploration or in the solution of a problem. Any locale such as a city or a valley has a unity which includes the events, people, and institutions that are connected with it.

Well-organized subjects like arithmetic are somewhat intractable from this standpoint. Primary number and counting must precede, and the numerical solution of problems must accompany or follow the fundamental operations. It is, however, possible to have children "discover" the principles of arithmetic and science, and in that case they achieve a psychological unity. With loosely connected materials this is much easier. The problems of democracy, housing, safety education, or conservation have no preordained organization, and units may be formed to suit the purpose of the class or individual. The advantage of the unit in this sense is that it capitalizes upon the pupil's desire to work out things for himself.

Many of the special "plans" and Progressive education have used the term "unit." It was used also by Henry C. Morrison (1871–1945), director of the University of Chicago High School. Morrison held that "assimilating lessons" does not educate. Education means adjustment and this always leads to an either-or situation: the pupil has made the adjustment or he has not. There is no middle ground. Each of the adjustments is achieved in a series of five steps that look and sound like those proposed by Herbart. Morrison began with a goal or desired adjustment that is approved by teacher and pupil and he named the steps as follows: exploration, presentation, assimilation, organization, and adjustment. These are old ghosts brought to life again—or what seemed to be a living state.

The idea for which Morrison is best known was his demand for mastery, thoroughness. Everyone should approve his opposition to slipshod work. There is a great deal of such work and there are many reasons for it. But complete and absolute mastery, thoroughness, and understanding are not within the range of human possibility. All men have their human limitations and no one ever understands anything perfectly. If one picks up a shell or reads a page, questions of meaning and value arise at every turn and line. Aside from the possibility of mastery there is the question of feasibility. The teacher has to see that the studies of the curriculum provide sufficient breadth and variety and this precludes the mastery of one.

The real value of the unit idea is that it tends to break down subject lines. Information is where you find it. Pupils help to plan the units. Individual needs, interests, and differences are considered. A few schools make up the curriculum from day to day. All these processes must be carefully guarded or they become hindrances to education.

12. CORRELATION

Curricula were long made by listing subjects, and perhaps supplying some statements of objectives and methods. This old plan is still the common one of curriculum-making. An investigator who examined 5,000 curricula reported that the overwhelming majority were of this kind.

Subject-matter curricula are criticized because, it is said, they have no plan. The subjects are like bricks lying scattered about. They should be arranged to form a house, a retaining wall, a walk, or some other structure that serves a purpose. Bricks lying scattered about serve no purpose and may be in the way. The analogy is not, however, quite accurate. The subjects, or at least some of them, have an internal organization that is lacking in a brick. Geography, history, and arithmetic are composed of related ideas that form a system.

An early effort to use this internal structure in the organization of a genuinely integrated curriculum was made by Herbart. He proposed to correlate the corresponding parts of two or more subjects; and correlation became an important educational idea even before 1900. S. C. Parker, in his

History of Modern Elementary Education, which came out in 1912, said: "Correlation is now an important factor in the organization of courses of study in many places." He thought the report of the Committee of Fifteen (1895) may have been a cause of its adoption; but Paul Hanus of Harvard correctly pointed out that Harris, the chairman of the Committee of Fifteen, was opposed to Herbart and did not use the word "correlation" in Herbart's sense at all.

As used by Herbart, correlation meant the interlinking of the different parts or ideas of different subjects. Geography, for example, may be taken as dealing with the places, structures, and forces of the crust and surface of the earth; and history as dealing with the purposes, actions, and institutions of men in the geographic environment. But not only can the two subjects be related but they must be if either is to have much meaning. Arithmetic and industrial arts may easily reinforce each other in teaching and learning and so may all the communication skills, such as reading, writing, speaking, and some kinds of drawing and music. Each may be made to support any of the others. A dramatic exercise might easily require the use of all of these.

The worth of correlation is unquestioned and there are constant opportunities and many ways of carrying it out in practice. Ideas in any subject become less inert, to use Whitehead's phrase, or more vital when they are connected with related ideas in another subject. Correlation may enable pupils to transfer their training, unify their experience, and generalize their knowledge and ideas.

13. CORE CURRICULUM

A core curriculum draws together from several subjects materials needed by all pupils. It is an extended and more fully developed form of correlation. Core lessons usually occupy more than one class period. The core is often given a title, such as Democratic Living or Evolution of Civilization. It may be planned and taught by more than one teacher, cooperatively. It is not always easy to distinguish between such forms as General Education, Integrated Program, or Unified Studies and the core curriculum. In all of these, also, the work may be planned by teachers and pupils jointly.

The work of the core curriculum is usually organized in large units or deals with important problems. Each of these may be pursued by a group or committee with provision for integrating the work of the whole class at appropriate points, so that all pupils will benefit from all of it. Activities such as those of the homerooms or community studies or services may be included in the core program. Drills also may be practiced.

The unified studies curriculum may be merely an extended form of correlation and is likely to be the least radical of the core innovations. Other core curricula may be historical in organization. A common example is the development of civilization, which is likely to be a compound of English, history, geography, and the arts and sciences. A third type is called the contemporary problems core, which may have such titles as Our City's Need for Water or Good Neighbors in the Other Americas. Even the contemporary problems course may be largely historical. There was in one school a study of Collective Security which began with the ancient Greek leagues and came by a roundabout way to the United Nations. Some contemporary problems courses stay fairly close to the present; and these sometimes break up into disassociated topics. One such so-called core consisted of a list of thirty separate topics including the following: Preventing accidents; spending money wisely; building a happy home life; and finding the right job. We should note that each ends in "-ing" and is about doing something. This is an example of the life-adjustment education which has been described.

The core curriculum movement is related to several trends which developed a century or more ago. Herbart has been mentioned, and Froebel's emphasis upon pupil activities and child study must be included. The activities of the kindergarten in more mature forms worked their way into all parts of the system. Child study and the work of the child development investigations at such universities as Iowa, Yale, and Michigan have promoted the adaptation of schoolwork to the capacities and needs of the pupils. Handicrafts and industrial arts education, the project methods introduced from agriculture, experimental schools, and new philosophies have together changed the hostility of the nineteenth century to pupil activities.

How deep and wide and permanent the change may be is not yet certain. There is no complete and up-to-date report on the acceptance of the core curriculum. A study published in 1950 showed 15 per cent of all junior high school pupils enrolled in core courses but less than 4 per cent of all high school pupils. The core curriculum is frequently a junior high school feature. It is not equally distributed over the country. The cases where it was in use were concentrated in a few cities in thirty-eight states. But even this gives a too favorable impression. Only in Maryland was the core organization found in any great proportion of the high schools of a whole state; three-fifths of the reported cases were concentrated in seven states; and there were ten states which did not report a single example. These are the reported facts. They have little bearing upon the question of the value of the core organization. They may merely mean that teachers and administrators and the public are too conservative. We may be assured that they are not usually educational radicals.

Curricula have always been changing, usually slowly, but at some periods radically. Yet there are some basic elements which must be included in all curricula. And curricular improvement is also conditioned by the social conservatism which holds the school in its grip.

A curriculum is no longer conceived as a selection of subjects. It includes also the activities, methods, and purposes of the school and indeed all that the school does to educate the children. It has become clear that in practice, the purpose, method, and content cannot be separated. A short review of the treatment of spelling, arithmetic, and reading is included in the chapter and will not be repeated here, except to remark that the principle of social usage or functionalism has important limitations.

The newer school practices require not only space and machinery but also books. Every school should have a library or should have the use of a library with the needed books and trained library workers. One of the chief values of such a library is that it makes it possible to teach children how to use a library. This is an important part of a good school curriculum.

Special teaching plans have been a prominent phase of efforts to improve upon the dreary textbook recitations which so long plagued American education. Two main features of these plans were the attempt to teach children how to read and study a given subject and to encourage children to work upon problems related to a major curriculum topic. Given a skilful teacher, inquiring pupils, and classes that are not too large, the problem method is undoubtedly an admirable plan. These factors are not always present; and the fate of the Dalton and similar plans have suggested that young pupils need supervision and a degree of pressure to produce good results.

Well-informed teachers have always used correlation to some degree, but following the Herbartian influence serious efforts were made to stress and improve it. The core curriculum is a current phase of these efforts and it often stresses investigative methods and functional studies. It is not in general use, and it would be something more than a guess to say that the formal textbook recitation is more frequently used than newer practices.

QUESTIONS

1. Why do primary schools all over the world teach reading, writing, and arithmetic?

2. Compare the kind of influences exerted by Progressive education upon the curriculum with those exerted by the scientific education movement.

3. Why should the curriculum of a school allow considerable freedom to teachers and pupils? How much freedom and in regard to what factors?

4. Why are manuscript sources considered better than printed ones in the determination of the most frequently used words, especially since the printed words were taken from a manuscript? Would you substitute a different word for "used" if you were framing this question?

5. Why do spelling investigations form a good starting-point for a study of the history of the scientific education movement?

6. How did the oral character of schoolwork, that is, the absence of written work, affect the curriculum?

7. What are the fallacies in the claim that the schools should teach only, or mainly, what is widely useful? Explore the uses of the words "useful" and "practical."

8. What correspondences can be traced between the development of schools and libraries? How can one account for them?

9. Which of the plans described in the text were administrative rather than curricular? How does one distinguish between the two?

10. Why should we classify any practices that had useful results as fads? May the use of this word be merely an expression of prejudice?

11. Why and how is a knowledge of curriculum trends useful in developing a new curriculum or changing an old one?

BOOKS AND PAPERS

At frequent intervals the *Review of Educational Research,* since its first volume in 1931, has published curriculum bibliographies. The National Society for the Study of Education in its annual *Yearbooks* has issued several curriculum studies including the following: "Adapting the Schools to Individual Differences" (1924); "Curriculum-Making: Past and Present" (1926); and "The Activity Movement," 1934, this last by Thomas Woody. Almost all educational associations, the National Association of Secondary School Principals, for example, and most subject journals, such as *Industrial Arts and Vocational Education,* deal with curriculum problems.

Adams, Brooks, "New Departure in Public Schools," *Atlantic Monthly,* March, 1880.

Alberty, Harold, *Reorganizing the High-School Curriculum,* New York, 1953.

Cecil, H. L., *School Library Service in the United States,* New York, 1940.

Flanders, J. K., *Legislative Control of the Elementary Curriculum,* New York, Teachers College, Columbia University, 1925.

Funderburk, R. S., *History of Conservation Education in the United States,* George Peabody College for Teachers, 1948.

Holloway, H. V., *Experimental Study of the Elementary Number Combinations in Addition and Multiplication*, Trenton, New Jersey, 1914, a dissertation.

Huey, E. B., *Psychology and Pedagogy of Reading with a Review of the History of Reading and Writing*, New York, 1908.

Lamport, H. B., *A History of Beginning Reading*, University of Chicago, 1935, an unpublished dissertation.

Link, Henry C., and H. A. Hoff, *People and Books, A Study of Reading and Book-Buying Habits*, New York, 1946.

National Education Association, "Report on Relations of Public Libraries to Public Schools," *Report* of the United States Commissioner of Education, 1899–1900, Vol. 1, pp. 663–719.

Peirce, Bessie Louise, *Civic Attitudes in American School Textbooks*, University of Chicago Press, 1930.

Redway, Jacques W., "Psychology of Educational Fads," *Educational Review*, February, 1896; and on the same theme, Louis Soldan, "What is a Fad?" NEA *Proceedings*, 1901, pp. 85–92; William H. Maxwell, "On a Certain Arrogance of Educational Theorists," *Educational Review*, February, 1914.

Reeder, R. R., *Historical Development of School Readers and Methods of Reading*, New York, 1900.

Robinson, R. R., *Two Centuries of Change in the Content of School Readers*, George Peabody College for Teachers, 1930; and on the McGuffey readers, see R. D. Mosier, *Making the American Mind*, King's Crown Press, Columbia University, 1947.

Scott, C. W., and C. M. Hill, *Public Education under Criticism*, New York, 1954, an anthology. On the schools' effectiveness in teaching the common branches see the papers by Archibald W. Anderson, p. 271, and Lowry W. Harding, p. 114.

Search, Preston W., *An Ideal School*, or *Looking Forward*, New York, 1901. The title contains an implicit reference to Edward Bellamy's *Looking Backward* (1888).

Smith, David Eugene, *The Teaching of Elementary Mathematics*, New York, 1913.

Wright, Grace S., *Core Curriculum in Public High Schools, an Inquiry into Practice*, 1949, Washington, U. S. Government Printing Office, Office of Education Bulletin, 1950, No. 5.

Young, J. W. A., *Teaching of Mathematics in the Schools*, New York, 1912.

Chapter XV

LATE PATTERN HIGH SCHOOLS

T HE industrial revolution, which changed many of the ways by which material goods are obtained and the ways in which people lived, also changed the schools. It destroyed old vocations and created new ones. Men traveled faster, transported greater loads farther, and communicated with each other instantaneously over longer distances. New knowledge, and skills so technical that they have to be taught in schools and laboratories, displaced former crafts. On a high level, education prepared the research scientist. Early inventors like Morse, who worked on the telegraph, or like Edison, were amateurs without systematic training. Now pure science has become the foundation of invention and the preparation of research workers has become the task of universities.

On an intermediate level schools may teach expert workmen such as tool-makers, machinists, designers, draftsmen, and pattern-makers. Machinery once installed has to be kept running and this requires the employment of highly skilled repair men. There is also the human side enlisting personnel workers, physicians, nurses, and foremen.

The semiskilled and unskilled workers who operate machines or move goods require, like all others, a general education including moral, civic, and prevocational schooling. Everyone needs training for health, thrift, social cooperation, family life, and all those personal qualities which make life effective and happy.

And in a broader sense, as industry has developed, education has been charged to deal with new social problems of citizenship, public health, labor organization, and recreation. In the small community one knew few people but knew them intimately for a whole lifetime. In the great city one meets hundreds but rarely learns to know them well. Relations in church and school have tended to become similarly impersonal. Family life is changing, often breaking down. Local government is becoming complex, a business for expert public servants. Modern life tends to standardize the individual, to assign him a number, and to employ him in a routine task. Outside of school hours youth is often left to fend for itself, and the juvenile delinquency rate is high and rising. All this indicates that there is work for the school to do; but it is not fair to expect the school alone to do it.

1. Educational Changes

In secondary education as in industry the most readily observed and frequently mentioned changes were physical and quantitative. Compulsory attendance laws which had long been on the books were gradually made effective early in the 1900's. The attendance period was being extended to fifteen or sixteen years of age. A growing middle class was acquiring the resources to send its children to high schools and private schools.

Since 1890 the number of the high schools and the enrollments of the large ones have increased by geometrical ratios. Instead of the 2,800 public high schools of 1890 there are now 25,000 and several thousand private secondary schools, 2,500 of them Roman Catholic. The great number of the schools is due to their spread to the small towns and the country; and the great increase in the size of some is due to their location in large cities. A metropolitan high school may enroll several thousand pupils. The total enrollment in the nation is in the neighborhood of 7,000,000, is growing, and will apparently continue to increase for years. At the same time the average enrollment per school is well below 300 and there are not a few that have less than thirty pupils.

Both the small schools in the country and the large schools in the city are necessary if all American youth are to have the opportunity to attend a high school. The consolidation of schools and the transportation of pupils which began in earnest about 1900 have made the country high school possible. Although a high school education is thus made widely accessible, only 65 to 75 per cent of the youth of high school age are at school. And some educators will not be content until all young people complete a high school curriculum. These educators are advocates of what they call "life adjustment education."

The two decades after 1900 produced many great changes in secondary education. The vocational guidance movement began before 1910, the junior colleges multiplied, and the junior high school is usually dated from that time. Before 1920 the Commission on the Reorganization of Secondary Education made its report, and the Smith-Hughes Act was passed. The Progressive Education Association was organized at the same time. Few periods have seen so many important developments in secondary education.

Complementary to the rapid increase in numbers, and in part a cause of that increase, was the change in the curriculum. During the early years of the present century the high school changed from a school that was mainly academic and preparatory to one that is largely vocational and terminal. The Committee of Ten was formed to resist this change and did resist it but without success. Curricula and activities continued to multiply and methods and standards were adapted to the capacities of the pupils who were flocking to the schools.

The pupils of an earlier day may have suffered from the lack of physical activity and a complete absence of social life. Such defects were corrected. Social clubs now hold initiations and give dances. Other clubs pursue special pupil interests, such as photography or radio. Athletics, debating, and school publications had already been introduced into the early high schools. The vast proliferation of new activities gave teachers new duties or opportunities as advisers, sponsors, and chaperons.

2. BRIDGING THE GAP

The continuity between the elementary and high schools was interrupted by curricular and administrative differences. New subjects, algebra and science, were to be mastered. The pupils were given little help in preparing lessons. They had to satisfy four or five different teachers and preparation had to be made in a study hall or at home. New subjects, strange faces, and the departmental system put fear into young hearts.

High school teachers did not exert themselves enough to bridge the gap between the schools. They were college men, inclined to teach as they had been taught. They complained that the pupils were not well prepared. A writer in the *School Review* in 1902 ascribed the faults of high school teaching to the lack of teacher preparation "in pedagogy and psychology, which are today essential." Another advised high school teachers to give up the proud idea that teaching six declensions and four conjugations is a higher and nobler task than that of the elementary school teacher.

Under the departmental plan the high school pupil, meeting several teachers each day, did not learn to know any of them well nor did he become well known to many of them. He missed the intimacy of the eighth-grade room. There he had been a person of importance, but as a high school freshman he was again on the bottom rung of the ladder. The compulsory attendance period in many states ended at the age of fourteen and this seemed to many to be an invitation to leave school. The gap was to be bridged not by shuffling grades but by having the schools offer better preparation for life. As this was done, the enrollments increased. In the twentieth century the country has turned toward a new policy of offering secondary education to the age of eighteen to everyone. Other countries also have moved toward this goal.

3. RISE OF THE JUNIOR HIGH SCHOOL

The junior high school began to spread after 1910 and it spread rapidly after World War I. The figures which have been compiled by different authors do not agree, but there may have been 2,500 such schools by 1940. Thus the type is far from a universal one. Many 8–4 systems remain and there are other combinations of elementary and high school grades as well. Where reorganization has taken place, the 6–3–3 combination is most frequently found. There is a 6–6 combination which is intended to perform the functions usually proposed for the junior high school but without employing it as a separate unit.

The functions proposed for the junior high school are abstract, armchair statements; but they notify the reader that the school was to be more than an administrative grade reorganization. The junior high school was to bridge the gap between the elementary and high school, making the transition easier. It was to save time. It was to retain pupils in school (1) by offering work that was more interesting and useful than the work of the upper elementary grades and (2) by entering the pupils in a new school before the usual end of the compulsory attendance period at age fourteen. It was to offer some choice of studies, exploratory and orientation courses, individual instruction, and more expert guidance. Some thought the new type of school should be departmentalized, should have a homeroom organization, and should employ homogeneous grouping.

Like the normal school, which was proposed (1789) fifty years before the first state institution was opened in 1839, the junior high school had been anticipated several years before it appeared. The Committee of Ten suggested the teaching of algebra, languages, and science at an earlier age than was customary. A number of other National Education Association committees, including particularly that on economy of time, supported this proposal. But the early beginning of such subjects was not new. Springfield, Massachusetts, had a curriculum that embodied some junior high school principles as early as 1867, but did not have a separate organization for the junior high school period.

And the separate organization of the type was not originally planned. Some cities set up new schools for the upper elementary grades to reduce overcrowding in existing buildings; but if this was all, the name junior high school was not justified. A closer approach to the later ideas was made by Richmond, Indiana, in 1896, when grades seven and eight were formed into a deparmentalized school with some elective subjects, with promotion by subject, and with a homeroom organization. The necessity for the departmental organization is not apparent. This organization was, however, in use in the elementary grades, which had copied it from the regular high school which had copied it from the college. Even in the colleges it was not found in early times when any teacher could gain an adequate acquaintance with the whole program of studies.

The central idea of the junior high school was that at about the age of twelve the child became clearly adolescent, individualistic, and independent, and should no longer be treated as a child. Hence the introduction of exploratory courses, guidance services, and individual instruction. This idea was furthered by the development of a new branch of psychology, adolescent psychology. G. Stanley Hall in 1904 published a work in two volumes entitled *Adolescence;* and he also attempted to outline the educational applications of the new study in his *Educational Problems* (1911). Many books in this general field have now been published, and adolescent psychology is widely studied in universities. The study has given direction to one of the chief functions of the junior high school, which is that of helping the family, church, and community in guiding children through the early adolescent period.

To measure the achievement of the junior high school is difficult. The school program is richer and more diversified than that of the upper grades in most elementary schools and this is an important gain. The pupils have tryout opportunities and receive guidance. There are elective courses and in some degree the school work is adapted to the pupils' individual needs. As a negative outcome, it has been claimed that junior high school pupils do not acquire the fundamental school skills as well as those in the eight grades. But many studies show that there is almost no difference between the two groups in their mastery of reading, writing, spelling, and arithmetic. A comparison between the marks earned in college by those who have graduated from the junior-senior schools with those earned by pupils from the four-year schools again shows no significant difference.

Because the junior high schools are located in many more sections of a city and therefore close to the homes of the children, they draw more pupils and hold them a little better than schools on the 8–4 plan. It does not appear that new studies and better methods have much influence in holding pupils in school. The reasons why pupils leave school early are as complex as society itself and include factors which the school cannot control, such as health, finances, conditions in the family, job opportunities, and many others.

The junior high school attracts more men teachers than the elementary school. This is probably of importance in the education of boys. Salaries fall between those paid in the elementary and the senior high schools. The junior high school costs a little more than the upper elementary grades but not much more. The expectations of those who thought the new school would materially reduce costs have not been met. Nor has the school shortened the time required to complete the full school course. Youth still graduates from the secondary school at the same age as it has been doing for three-quarters of a century.

4. The Junior College

The junior college is most frequently a two-year, freshman-sophomore school, as we saw in an earlier chapter, but there are variants. Four-year junior colleges may include the two upper high school years. Some junior colleges were born such, some grew to this status, and some had it thrust upon them through the decapitation of a four-year college. Some junior colleges choose to remain as they are, but others are biding their time in the hope of becoming four-year schools. A rapid increase in the college-going youth may provide such an opportunity to not a few.

The early origins of schools of this kind are not well understood. About forty junior colleges claim to be 100 or more years old. Some of these are decapitants. The Civil War interrupted the movement, but about sixty were founded between 1870 and 1900 and at least 400 in the present century. How many junior colleges are there? This is more easily asked than answered. A good list of recent issue names 581. Three hundred and seventy of them are in states touching the Mississippi River and states to the west of these. By the list mentioned, California is given sixty-nine, Texas fifty, and ten other states are credited with more than twenty each. There does not seem to be much reason in the distribution. Only two states have no junior colleges at present but some populous states have very few.

Some of the schools are independent but many are public. California has almost seventy, most of them public and controlled by elected school boards. Today many favor the development of junior or senior community colleges. Would this kill off the existing independent colleges in the same way as the high school superseded the academy? Not if we may judge by the conditions in California, which has a full complement of state senior institutions, about twenty-five independent colleges including large ones such as Stanford University and the University of Southern California, teachers' colleges, and junior colleges. For the next few decades the prospect is for large enrollments in all of them.

MAIN TYPES OF SCHOOLS

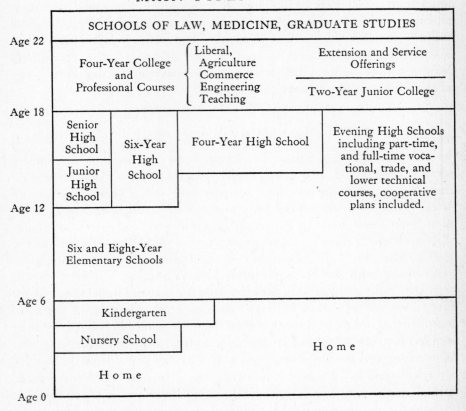

Rising standards of college education and the increase in the usual age of graduation from eighteen to twenty-two years is one reason for the junior college. So many years of life spent in preparation for life, keeping men in school during years that should be productive, has seemed to some to be "too much college." Various palliatives have been proposed. A three-year college is an old idea; introducing preprofessional and professional work into the college course is another; and a third is the admission of bright students by examination before they have completed the high school. None of these has been useful to the great body of college youth.

For those who will not enter a learned profession but who need some

schooling beyond the high school, the junior college may provide a solution. The half-million students who attend such institutions are evidence of their value. Many of these are getting preparation for a vocation. By attending a local institution a great deal of money is saved. If desired, the two-year graduate may later attend a standard college. Junior college work should be different from that of the upper division. Universities claim that they should not be burdened with the heavy weight of freshman and sophomore instruction, which is really a part of secondary education.

This last argument was one of those used by William Rainey Harper (1856–1906), first president of the University of Chicago and sometimes called "the father of the junior college." He wanted to make the university a "real university" on the European pattern. But other early promoters of the junior college, such as Henry P. Tappan of the University of Michigan and W. W. Folwell of the University of Minnesota, had the same view. If this were accepted, then schooling up to the age of twenty would be considered secondary, university work would begin at that point, and the four-year undergraduate college of arts and sciences would disappear from the American educational scene. There is no such prospect at present.

5. GUIDANCE METHODS

Children and youth have always received advice. Guidance may be negative or disciplinary, or it may be merely the expression of a whim rather than of a reasoned judgment. And it may be given only when an error has been committed. Wise counsel and information should look ahead, aiming at improved conduct, partly by preventing bad. Such counsel will attempt to set in motion present changes looking to later results.

Guidance is education as preparation and it is in conflict with the idea of education as merely a full life in the present. In *Democracy and Education* (p. 63), John Dewey said: "To get ready for something, one knows not what or why, is to throw away the leverage that exists, and to seek for motive power in a vague chance." "One knows not what or why" —this is setting up a straw man. Preparation for a future vocation is one of the most powerful of all educational levers, and guidance is to help the pupil to determine for himself both what and why. The guidance movement, including nondirective counseling, would seem to be in conflict with the doctrine that education is to be nonpreparatory.

The regulations and the curricula of a school serve as guides to further education and to life. In a land so devoted to work as the United States is, all education leads ultimately to a life-career objective. Job information is eagerly sought. Several years ago the Bureau of Labor Statistics printed 2,500 copies of a new *Occupational Outlook Handbook*. The edition was sold out in a week, and 40,000 were sold in two years. It was then revised and continued to sell at three dollars per copy.

In the United States vocational guidance is often given by high schools and colleges. This is appropriate, for vocational guidance implies vocational education. In the last half-century guidance has been systematically given. The growth and specialization of industry and the rise of new skilled and technical occupations have increased the need for guidance.

The spirit of vocational guidance is one of its significant characteristics. The counselor does not command the pupil or make decisions for him. He does not determine his future job nor even the curriculum which will prepare him for it. The young person and his family must make the decisions and bear the responsibility. In much of Europe the opposite course is followed. The government in many countries sets up employment bureaus in the department of labor or the interior. The purpose is not to help the individual but to help the nation make the most effective use of its man power. Under dictators no man can leave his job and choose another. It is in the democracies that vocational education and vocational guidance have been linked together to promote individual as well as national welfare.

All seem to agree in ascribing the beginning of the vocational guidance movement to the work of Frank Parsons (1854–1908), who in the last year of his life opened the Boston Vocation Bureau. Others had talked about it; Parsons acted. William Penn had noted the need for care and wisdom in the choice of a vocation, as had others in the seventeenth century. Among these were Comenius and Sir William Petty. But it was the work of Parsons, three centuries later, and the financial aid given by Mrs. Quincy A. Shaw that started the Vocation Bureau.

Events followed rapidly, showing that this had been a timely step. Upon the death of Parsons the direction of the bureau was taken over by Meyer Bloomfield and he was followed by John M. Brewer, who wrote *The Vocational Guidance Movement*, an early account. Vocational guidance was introduced into the schools of Boston (1909) and of Cincinnati (1911). Grand Rapids in 1912 and Des Moines in 1914 created city-wide vocational guidance services in the schools. Helen T. Woolley and Jesse B. Davis were among the new leaders in the Midwest.

World War I had considerable influence upon efforts along these lines. The army's use of intelligence tests and its personnel system stimulated an extraordinary degree of interest and research activity among the country's psychologists. They developed new kinds of group and individual tests. The army also developed occupational specifications and rating scales. These instruments were used by the American Council on Education in cooperative experiments in student personnel work. The Strong Vocational Interest Test and the cumulative record card were developed and a national Vocational Guidance Association was organized in the 1920's.

Knowledge of the individual and of occupations, and wisdom in applying this knowledge to cases, are leading requirements of effective guidance. This knowledge is often hard to obtain and to apply. The instruments are such as (1) the cumulative record of the pupil's interests, attitudes, and achievements in school, home, and social life; (2) batteries of tests of traits and abilities; (3) vocational experiences on the job or in school shops; (4) occupational information; and especially (5) the interview. Teachers who take part in extraclass activities learn a good deal about the pupils in their groups; but studies show that often the regular high school teachers have only a small part of the knowledge needed for effective counseling. Yet the best school guidance systems make use of the regular staff; and it becomes one of the tasks of the school counselor to guide the teachers in obtaining the needed information and developing the skill required for counseling. All this may be regarded as a criticism of the free elective system.

6. THE COMPREHENSIVE HIGH SCHOOL

The comprehensive or general high school is an American development. It comprehends several and often many kinds of curricula, liberal and vocational, preparatory and terminal. It is a school with many purposes. In England schools of this kind are called multilateral or many-sided schools. This name may be a reflection of the phrase "modern side," the name given to the nonclassical curriculum in the nineteenth century grammar schools of England.

The special high school has a narrower field. It may be a commercial, technical, or even, as in the case of the oldest secondary school in America, a classical school. The first high school had a single curriculum which emphasized English and mathematics. The promoters of that school had a practical end in view, namely, to prepare boys for business. In this general sense it was a vocational school but it did not prepare for a definite vocation. A number of cities began to build special schools in the early years of the high school movement, but later they turned to the comprehensive type. When the commercial, manual training, and agricultural curricula were developed, special vocational or prevocational schools were being founded, but in time many of these also became comprehensive. Evidently "there is something that does not love a wall" in American education and that particularly disapproves of the separation of general from special education.

The phrase "vocational education" has been defined in the Smith-Hughes Act. The act calls that education vocational which is of "less than college grade" and which is given to pupils, who are at least fourteen years old, for the purpose of fitting them for "useful employment" or to render them more efficient in it. This language is not entirely precise; but it sets limits and it thereby excludes several kinds of education that might be confused with vocational education. Such are professional education and general industrial arts. It also excludes general education which has only incidental applications to vocations and all merely exploratory courses. On the other hand, the language would cover high school commercial education which fits pupils for useful employment but is not named in the act because it did not provide any funds for this branch of vocational education.

The Smith-Hughes Act and the federal laws that were passed to supplement it provide support for the teaching of agriculture, homemaking, trades and industries, and the distributive vocations. These, together with commerce, may be called the Big Five among the vocations for which the high schools prepare their pupils. But there are many other vocations including journalism and commercial art that do not receive federal aid. Many vocations, also, are taught in evening schools, corporation schools, correspondence courses, and other public and private, part-time and full-time institutions. All these are to be excluded from detailed consideration under the present topic.

The comprehensive high school is the typical American public secondary school, but there are exceptions other than the vocational schools. One exception that is usually omitted because it is not recognized as an exception is the very small school. There are many schools that can offer only one curriculum and very few electives. These are in effect special schools, even though it is their purpose to give a general education.

Much of the remainder of this chapter deals with nonacademic innovations in public high schools and, briefly, with nonpublic secondary schools. The chapter ends with a section on the declining proportion of pupils in public high schools who study academic subjects, such as languages, mathematics, and science. Those high school pupils who do enroll in such courses do well in them. This is shown by a comparison of the scores made by public and nonpublic secondary pupils on the tests given by the College Entrance Examination Board, for "the differences in the mean scores of the two groups are negligible," as the statistical tables show and as the board reports. But it is possible, and it is sometimes claimed, that for every student in college there is another equally competent boy or girl who is not in college. Lack of money is one reason for this condition; and another reason may lie in the weight attached to vocational and other immediately functional courses in the schools.

7. INTRODUCING VOCATIONAL EDUCATION

Before the industrial revolution, skilled workmen were prepared by apprenticeship, but with increasing specialization this system of training declined. Immigration, by bringing in many highly skilled craftsmen, also dealt a severe blow to the apprentice system. Immigration has now been reduced to small proportions, and American industry cannot depend upon Europe to prepare its skilled workers. Many such men are still needed. The machinists in railroad shops and the loom-fixers in textile mills are examples of the many highly skilled and highly paid industrial workers. The low point in apprenticeship training was reached about 1900; and today many industries again train their craftsmen by apprenticeship.

Apprentice standards are set up by industry and labor jointly; but there are also standards set by law and there is a National Association of State Approving Agencies largely composed of representatives of state education departments. There is an old struggle going on between the two. The unions naturally desire to protect the interests of labor, to prevent an oversupply of trained workers, and to maintain high wages. The state departments of education try to inject academic requirements into the training and to reduce the length of the apprenticeship. Thus recently they tried to require that those who supervise apprentice training programs must have bachelor's degrees.

For a century men have also argued over vocational education in the public schools, mostly against it. Common school leaders in vocational education had to walk carefully to secure support for their cause. And free vocational education could easily be made to appear as an offer of special privilege to a few.

There were practical difficulties in the way of vocational education in schools: the high cost, the difficulty of obtaining teachers who were both well educated in school learning and skilled in trades, and the question of what to teach and how to teach it.

There were also theoretical difficulties. The formal discipline philosophy was one of these. It said that the academically well-educated man would easily solve any problem. In that case the man with a good general education should have been an effective vocational teacher; but although it was evident that such men were not capable in that field it was not often noticed that this conflicted with the theory. Another difficulty was the notion of many teachers that the practical and useful skills and knowledge were in some way opposed to the high ideals of truth, goodness, and beauty. Teachers, like others brought up on books and employed in the work of communication, had little first-hand knowledge of industry and felt some antipathy to it. Until 1870 it was widely held that no vocational knowledge should be taught in the schools.

It was in 1878 that Emerson E. White called attention to the growing demand for industrial education. He took what was for the time a liberal position. He proposed to have the elements of vocational knowledge taught in public schools; and he added that the industries should build upon this foundation in their own vocational schools. This was as wise a statement on the subject as had yet been made at that time; and it did not deserve the criticism which he received for it.

The principle of White's solution is accepted today. Schools do in fact teach those features of vocational knowledge and skill that are of general application and usefulness. The employer takes the pupil at that point and completes the training under ordinary operating conditions. Manual training came into the schools soon after White's pronouncement, and was often regarded as a form of vocational education. This mistake was not made by John D. Runkle at the Massachusetts Institute of Technology, for he was not preparing craftsmen but engineers. Manual training gave his students some understanding of tools and materials, which was all that it was intended to provide. But the unfounded faith of others in manual training delayed the introduction of true vocational education into the schools.

General vocational education, such as manual training was supposed to be, has only a limited sphere of applications. Vocations are distinct and have to be learned separately like languages. As in the case of languages, there are common elements. Such topics are shop mathematics, drawing, and science. All of these are useful at least to the machinist, electrician, and others, but have much less relevance to the commercial artist. It was seen also that for many vocations the schools cannot provide complete preparation. Mastery has to be acquired in actual production.

School people hesitated so long before organizing vocational schools that businessmen became impatient. The state of Massachusetts provides an illustration. An investigating commission on the need for vocational education was appointed by Governor Douglas and made its report in 1905. At this time Professor Paul H. Hanus fortunately returned from a sabbatical year in Germany where he had studied Georg Kerschensteiner's system of vocational education in Munich.

When the legislature, upon recommendation of the Douglas commission, created a state commission on industrial education, Hanus was appointed chairman. In 1906 the commission undertook to explain the provision of the legislation for the instituting of vocational education either in separate public vocational schools, or in special departments in regular high schools. Both employers and employees had to be persuaded, one that the education would have practical value, the other that the pupils would not be employed at low wages or serve as strike-breakers. The state board of education was not merely unconvinced but it actively opposed the work of the commission. George H. Martin, who was the secretary, the position first held by Horace Mann, pursued a dog-in-the-manger policy, it has been said, because he thought the state board should have been placed in control. In 1909 both the commission and the state board, all its offices being vacated, were abolished, and a state department of education was established to supervise both general and vocational education under public auspices.

The increased interest in vocational education early in the twentieth century is shown by the numerous studies of the problem made at that time. The New York State Department of Labor made a report on the vocational education needs of that state. The National Education Association had a Committee on the Place of the Industries in Public Education. Under the leadership of Charles F. Richard and David Snedden, the National Society for the Promotion of Industrial Education was formed in 1906. Six years later the society declared itself in favor of a system of public vocational schools separated from the regular high schools. Wisconsin had already passed such a law (1911), creating a state board and local boards of industrial education and a system of vocational schools parallel to the high schools.

A similar movement was progressing in Illinois, where the legislature petitioned Congress for federal aid for vocational training. Chancellor Samuel Avery of the University of Nebraska, President James H. Baker of the University of Colorado, John Dewey, and other prominent educators spoke against separate systems. The author of the Illinois plan was Edwin S. Cooley, former superintendent of schools in Chicago. He replied to Dewey's heated argument that his own plan would not interfere with the regular system but would supplement it by creating a vocational school for youths who would otherwise leave school. The Cooley plan failed; but the framers of the Smith-Hughes Act did not put the vocational system into the hands of the local high schools without some degree of external control over its administration. In the course of time educators and the public have become more interested in vocational education, whether subsidized by the federal government or not; and many vocational high schools have been established.

8. Vocational High Schools

Not all vocational work is done in purely vocational schools. Many comprehensive schools allow a certain number of elective units and some of these may be shop courses; and large comprehensive schools provide complete vocational curricula. Pupils, by making appropriate selections, may graduate in a course in which a vocational certificate may be earned. In order to make the account more concrete, several contemporary schools which are selected merely to serve as illustrations are mentioned by name. These are not necessarily unique in the characteristics which are mentioned, but as examples they will serve as well as any.

The Sacramento Senior High School has no less than a dozen shop courses, including machine shop, mechanical drawing, metal, printing, radio, ceramics, and housecraft. The Senior High School of Springfield, Missouri, is similarly equipped. Both are comprehensive schools; and other comprehensive high schools may offer even more extensive vocational programs. This goes to show that not all vocational education is offered in vocational schools. Practical vocational education under public auspices, however, began most frequently in trade schools.

Private trade schools were opened in New York in 1881 and in several other cities before the end of the century. Cities soon began to open public trade schools. These were usually designed with narrow restrictions, but together with continuation evening schools they were the direct precursors of the vocational high schools of today. The vocational high school is only fifty years old at the earliest and one can hardly speak of a vocational high school movement before 1920.

Since "trade," "vocation," "profession," and "technical activity" are words often confused, a few simple definitions and typical examples will serve a useful purpose. Professional education in such fields as engineering or law is usually distinguished from vocational education, which includes mainly trade or technical preparation. A trade demands skill and special knowledge but usually not much scientific or literary preparation. In addition to skill, a technical occupation involves scientific preparation and nice judgment in applying such knowledge in the arts. Surgery is a profession and also a highly technical occupation, but the latter term is more commonly applied to such work as television mechanics or electronics. Ordinary carpenter work and house painting are trades. Many vocations combine a considerable variety of skills and a considerable range of knowledge. Such vocations as farming and caring for a home and family are partly trades, partly professions, and partly ways to achieve independence. Much depends in all cases upon the level at which the work is performed.

Professional education is carried on in colleges, universities, special institutes, and seminaries. It will not concern us here. Vocational education in many fields is provided in high schools and also in college in many cases. Vocational high schools may be specialized along one or a few lines or they may be almost as comprehensive as the schools which have that title. Thus, as mentioned before, we have here an illustration of the tendency of special schools to become broad and general.

Brief notices of a few schools will illustrate this principle. The Polytechnic High School of San Francisco, with fifteen departments, offers 150 courses with majors in general education, business, numerous shops, mechanical drawing, home economics, and other fields. Although this is a vocational school, it advises its pupils to choose their college early "because each college has its own entrance requirements." Evidently this vocational school also prepares pupils for college.

The Boys' Trade and Technical High School of Milwaukee has three divisions: technical, trade, and "tech-trade." In the first of these, in addition to the shop courses, emphasis is placed upon the English, social studies, mathematics, and science of the comprehensive schools and there is opportunity to elect a modern language. The trade division stresses shops more, academic subjects less, but the latter are not omitted. The school has found that those boys who take a combined technical and trade curriculum succeed best at college and in industry. This school, like the San Francisco Polytechnic, is an example of what Franklin J. Keller has called "a double-purpose high school."

Some high schools are more strictly technical and yet prepare boys for college, chiefly for the engineering colleges. The Buffalo Technical High School may be said to have begun fifty years ago when some boys from the old Central High School were allowed to take manual training at a near-by grammar school. At present it has six technical curricula, and about one-fourth of the student body are preparing to enter an engineering college.

Of the more than thirty vocational high schools in New York City, two will be named as examples, Chelsea and Metropolitan. Many of the New York vocational high schools, including these two, have grown out of former continuation schools and still carry on that work as part of their function. Many also have classes of slow learners which were at one time thought to be a special obligation of the trade schools.

Vocational high schools developed rapidly in New York City after 1933 when the National Recovery Administration of the New Deal raised the legal employment age and the state in consequence raised the compulsory attendance age. The new limit in each case was sixteen years. The Chelsea Vocational High School began to offer a program of four-year terminal courses in 1934 when almost no jobs were open. Later it became a school for boys. The ninth grade is exploratory. Almost 1,000 boys in grades ten to twelve are distributed among seven specialized curricula: electric wiring, sheet metal, machine shop, printing, auto mechanics, radio and television mechanics, and woodworking. The last three are the most popular ones, enrolling almost 70 per cent of all the boys in the school.

The Metropolitan Vocational High School has an unusual curriculum. It is doubtful that there is another public high school of the same kind anywhere. One of its divisions teaches maritime occupations including the services of the deck, engine, radio, electrical equipment, steward, and boatbuilding. A second division as far removed as possible from the first in its repertoire teaches the performing arts including music, drama, and dance arts. Other vocational high schools in other cities, the Arsenal Technical High School of Indianapolis, for example, prepare musical performers; but few prepare actors and dancers for the stage, and maritime courses in public high schools must be even more rare. Only pupils with talent are advised to undertake the performing arts because jobs are scarce and precarious.

A second feature of the school is its practice of preparing its most capable pupils at the same time for college and a vocation. It is, like several others mentioned above, a "double-purpose school" and its graduates enter either liberal or engineering colleges. Not every pupil can do work of this quality. At Metropolitan there are pupils with the low IQ of 60, while those at the other extreme touch 160. It has been estimated that perhaps 10 per cent of the pupils could do both academic and shopwork that would meet the standards both of college admission and of the Smith-Hughes Act.

Vocational education is one of the growing points of the school system. There is no necessary conflict between vocational and liberal education. In a working society, manual, technical, and professional workers are also citizens, neighbors, consumers, and potential leaders, that is, people. All need both a broad and liberal education as people and a specific education as workers. Some of this may be best given in school, some on the job;

and how and when, are matters to be considered by those who are concerned. The prophets of gloom who say that "what should be done about vocational education is to forget it" are both ignorant and prejudiced. They could not be one without being the other also.

9. CATHOLIC HIGH SCHOOLS

The Roman Catholic Church is making great progress in providing secondary schools for youth. There are now 2,500 or more Catholic high schools enrolling over 600,000 young people, and these constitute, perhaps, 60 per cent of the Catholic youth in secondary schools. The rest are chiefly in public high schools. Except for the religious teaching and environment, the Catholic high schools in their curricula, methods, and organization resemble the public schools; and the system has similar financial and personnel problems.

In the past, Catholic schools have depended upon the religious teaching orders, men and women serving with minimum stipends, hardly to be called salaries. But this source of supply is becoming exhausted; and it seems that the schools will be competing with the public schools and with industry for lay personnel to serve in the classroom. This, with the needed building construction, may become extremely burdensome. Incidentally, if the Catholic church should close its schools and send the children to public schools it would create a considerable financial and personnel problem for the states and local school boards.

The earliest Catholic secondary school types were imported from Europe. Schools for girls were finishing schools maintained by the religious sisterhoods; and boys' schools were attached to colleges. Usually the numbers in the schools were much larger than those in the colleges. Many of these preparatory schools have now been separated from the colleges or closed. Another type of secondary school evolved from the parish schools in the way in which public high schools grew out of elementary schools.

The third type is the diocesan or central high school, which draws its pupils from several parishes and is controlled by a board under the bishop as chairman. The first such school was a boys' school opened in Philadelphia in 1890; and in 1912 in the same city a similar school for girls was opened. Both were endowed schools. There are now between 100 and 200 Catholic central high schools enrolling more than 100,000 pupils. The first one, called the Roman Catholic High School of Philadelphia, opened with three curricula, Latin-scientific, commercial, and manual training. These were the most popular curricula in the public schools of that time and this parallelism has been fairly well maintained. The original idea was that the central high schools should include religious training but should provide for the education of Catholic laymen; and that they should be organically connected with the parishes rather than the colleges which were training priests. This is still the plan, yet most of the schools also prepare pupils for college; and many of their graduates attend state and private universities.

Catholic high schools do not share in public funds but are maintained by tuition, assessments on the parishes whose children they educate, and the largely unpaid services of religious teaching communities. As compared with public school costs in an average city, the amount of revenue is low. As a consequence they tend to be conservative in their educational policy and in the shops and laboratories which they provide for their pupils. Some Catholic colleges are curtailing their athletic programs because of the expense. Schools may possibly follow this example.

10. INDEPENDENT SECONDARY SCHOOLS

A second large class of nonpublic schools is formed by the 2,000 or 3,000 institutions which are usually called private secondary schools. These have now chosen to call themselves independent schools, but the old name still clings to them. They are independent of state control but some have close connections with a church, Methodist, Episcopal, Catholic, or some other.

The class of new academies, established in most cases after the Civil War and mentioned in Chapter V, belong to the independent schools. One of these, St. Paul's School of Concord, New Hampshire, was founded in 1855. This Episcopal school has claimed, somewhat too broadly, that "a new trend was given to education in America in the establishment of St. Paul's. It was the first of the church schools to appeal to the new class that was rapidly acquiring wealth from water-power, textile mills, and the exploitation of the continent." It is presently a boarding school of 450 boys, aged twelve to eighteen, and its annual charge for boarding pupils is $1,600 a year.

Some of the independent schools are much older than St. Paul's, and were originally church schools and in fact country academies with low tuition rates. Such was Phillips Exeter, located at Exeter, New Hampshire, and founded in 1783. It is a comparatively large independent school enrolling 700 or 800 boys and possessing an endowment of $18,000,000. The other Phillips academy is at Andover, Massachusetts, and is a little older than Phillips Exeter. Another old Massachusetts school is the Deerfield Academy founded in 1797. It has about 500 boys and collects $2,000 a year from boarding and $200 from day pupils. Like the colleges, the older independent schools often boast about their age. The Governor Dummer Academy, founded in 1761, considers itself "the oldest boarding school for boys in the United States." Recent foundations do not mention the dates of their origin.

Noted independent schools are most numerous in the New England states, especially in Massachusetts, in the states of New York and California, and in the environs of great cities. They are generally expensive, as we have already suggested. What do people get for their money? The most famous ones have small classes and good teachers, although, as in public schools, they are sometimes more highly skilled in Latin than in the teaching of it. Many of these schools have splendid buildings elaborately equipped and appointed. Swimming pools, horseback riding trails, courts and fields for all kinds of games, are provided. Many prepare pupils for college, and in some cases these are pupils whom the public schools might not succeed in entering at college. One thing which parents buy in these schools is "class," prestige. But it is also a fact that some children have educational needs which the local public school cannot satisfy. Schools whose chief merit is their exclusiveness may seem to be undemocratic; but to suppress them would also be undemocratic. The principle is comparable to Voltaire's on free speech: "I detest what you say but I will defend to the death your right to say it."

For some children boarding schools seem to be necessary. There are private schools for slow learners. Military academies and ranch and mountain schools may render necessary services that public schools do not offer. There are schools for homeless children and some for possible or actual delinquents. One of the best known of this latter type is the George Junior Republic, a coeducational school community at Freeville, New York. It has about 125 pupils between the ages of thirteen and twenty-one and a faculty of forty. The school itself reports that it is "for unadjusted or irresponsible youth and prepares them for citizenship through civic, economic, work, and academic experiences." The pupils carry on workshops, farm work, domestic work, operate a bank and stores, and maintain a democratic student-government. "Every function of the American community is duplicated in the George Junior Republic and carried out by its student-citizens." The annual fee in this admirable institution ranges from $1,100 to $2,400. This and the other kinds of schools mentioned in this paragraph are not typical independent schools, most of which stress academic studies. Many are, indeed, educationally conservative, not to say reactionary.

11. LIFE ADJUSTMENT EDUCATION

The high school has made considerable efforts to meet the needs of youth. At any rate, some high schools deal with problems of health, moral conduct, family life, citizenship, consumer education, dating, dress, table manners, and recreation and at the same time offer excellent guidance services; and yet a large proportion of the youth either do not enter high school or drop out during the course. This condition has given rise to the demand that the high school shall provide a program composed entirely of such applied knowledge. Excepting only the "tools of learning," all academic subjects are to be omitted from this "life adjustment education."

The term "life adjustment education" has come into use since World War II and particularly since the adoption of the Prosser Resolution at an educational conference in Chicago in May, 1947. The resolution, offered by Charles Allen Prosser (1871–1952), stated that 60 per cent of American youth are not properly served by the present high schools because the high school does not attract them, or because it does not hold them, or finally, because many who remain have to engage in educational activities so unrelated to the everyday needs of life that when they graduate they are not well adjusted to life. The resolution declared that this large body of boys and girls are entitled to life adjustment training as citizens, and called upon leaders in vocational education and school administration to formulate a plan for educating all American youth in school to the age of eighteen years.

Committees of educators have repeatedly favored this plan as a general policy. But states which have extended their compulsory attendance period to that age grant work-permits at age sixteen. Even so there is complaint about the unwilling pupils in the schools. Would the program of the Prosser Resolution make these more willing? is one question.

There are really two propositions: to extend the compulsory age and to introduce life adjustment education. There is no scientific conclusion in regard to either; and the advisability of either would depend upon many changing social factors. Is it even probable that all children ought to be retained in school to the same chronological age by force of law?

That many children drop out of school at all ages is a present fact that would need to be considered. The figures in the accompanying table are inexact but enlightening. They show that school-leaving is not confined to the high school years. The United States does not provide the opportunity for secondary education to those children who do not complete the elementary course. Some leave and some fail either before they reach the high school or in high school. Life adjustment education is intended not only for those who leave early but also for those who are compelled to take work which the Prosser Resolution describes as "unrelated to the everyday needs of life."

NUMBERS OF PUPILS CONTINUING PER 1,000 IN THE FIFTH GRADE

Elementary School	1925–26	1927–28	1930–31	1933–34	1935–36	1937–38
Fifth Grade	1,000	1,000	1,000	1,000	1,000	1,000
Sixth Grade	911	928	943	944	946	954
Seventh Grade	815	834	872	895	889	901
Eighth Grade	745	799	824	836	839	850
High School						
First Year	642	714	770	792	814	811
Second Year	509	588	652	688	725	679
Third Year	421	485	529	594	587	519
Fourth Year	370	415	463	489	466	428
	1933	1935	1938	1941	1943	1945
High School Graduates	316	355	417	462	439	398
Entering College	112	135	148	142	119	...
	1937	1939	1942	1945	1947	1949
Graduating from College	56	65	69	49	..	..

From Office of Education *Bulletin,* 1951, No. 22, on Life Adjustment Education.

Note: The table shows that pupils leave school at least as early as the sixth grade. If pupils from outside the systems were admitted, then pupils left more rapidly than the table shows. Not all of the pupils in a particular grade in a given year may have been counted in the original thousand. Finally, we have no data on the compulsory attendance laws and their enforcement in these systems.

Some private school teachers have expressed the harshest kind of criticism of the kind of curriculum and standards which life adjustment education implies. Twelve hundred teachers, at the twenty-eighth annual conference of the Secondary Education Board representing several hundred private schools, were, without explicit reference to life adjustment education, told that such courses are "fraudulent" and that in many schools there is discrimination against subject-matter courses in favor of "easy substitutes." As reported in the New York *Times* for March 7, 1954, the speaker charged that guidance officers discourage able pupils from taking mathematics or a language "by telling them that they will never need those things." Another speaker, a college president who is a graduate of a well-known private school, deplored the heavy burden of work placed upon high school teachers, which prevented them from following the intellectual pursuits necessary for effective teaching. Many high school teachers would agree with these views.

At the other extreme of the educational spectrum is the opinion that high schools, as has been said, are not primarily institutions for instruction; that they are "symbols of democracy"; and that they should "admit on as equal terms as possible, all except the outright unteachables." How these latter are to be selected for exclusion and by what method cast out is not indicated.

The question, however, remains whether the high school should not clearly distinguish between its pupils of high talent and ambition and those of average or less than average capacity. To challenge the best pupils to work up to their capacity may be a means to social health today and to national survival tomorrow. The question should also be raised whether such a challenge can be offered in the comprehensive high school. To raise the question is not to prejudge it; but special schools with high standards have not always been considered undemocratic.

12. Academic Studies Less Popular

When many thousands of pupils entered the high schools it became necessary to adjust the program to their various capacities and needs; or, perhaps, as new studies appeared more pupils came. Even the early high schools provided a way of escape from the classical curriculum. They offered mathematics, composition and rhetoric, history, a modern language or two, and sciences which were taught from a textbook in short courses. Besides, there were what may be called fringe courses in civil government, English literature, anatomy and physiology, bookkeeping, drawing, penmanship, and music. These so-called fringe courses varied from school to school, but all of them taken together made up only a part of any curriculum. Many early schools offered two or more curricula, but all were academic, that is, they were mainly constituted of intellectual subjects. This condition obtained as late as 1860 or 1870.

After the Civil War vocational and activity courses were introduced, as has been shown. Manual training evolved into industrial arts education. Commercial courses were aided by the expansion of business and the invention of the typewriter about 1868, and numerous business machines later. There were other courses in agriculture, home economics, fine arts, and music, and a series of new fringe studies and activities. These vocational and activity offerings attracted great numbers of pupils who may have lacked the capacity or the desire to study academic subjects.

As a consequence of the changing character of the school population, enrollments in academic subjects did not keep pace with the increasing high school attendance. Some of the academic subjects have as many enrollees across the country as ever, yet these comprise a much smaller fraction of the total enrollment than they formerly did; and some academic subjects have lost in actual numbers of pupils or have been dropped from the program. This decline, whether relative or absolute, in the popularity of academic subjects is much influenced by the increased offerings of the high school and the mass attendance. When the high school program was almost entirely academic, there was no escape from mathematics, science, and foreign language. When the high school introduced vocational and activity studies and opened its doors to the vast body of the youth of the land, many chose the newer studies in preference to the old. The question whether this flight from academic studies was avoidable and whether the trend can be reduced is one of the momentous questions of present educational policy.

Some of the facts are as follows. Pupils in the ninth grade who do not elect algebra will often be scheduled in general mathematics, a more concrete and for many pupils a more directly useful subject. It is also easier. About 40 per cent of the ninth grade pupils take general mathematics and nine-tenths of these will take no more mathematics, although some will later find themselves in no-credit remedial or refresher courses in college. About half of the pupils who take elementary algebra, making up less than half of the tenth grade, will take plane geometry. Four-fifths of these pupils, having completed elementary algebra and plane geometry, will take no more mathematics after the tenth grade. Few will study solid geometry or trigonometry; and elementary analysis or calculus is rarely offered in high schools. It is not far from the truth to say that mathematics, although it is necessary in much of science and engineering, is a freshman and sophomore study in the high school.

High school science, like mathematics, has developed a standard pattern of courses, and these have a better distribution over the four-year period than the mathematics courses. Several sciences that were taught fifty years ago have small enrollments now, or none. Some have been absorbed and are offered under a new heading. High school science at present comprises general science in the junior high school, biology in the tenth grade, and chemistry and physics in the eleventh and twelfth. Geology, astronomy, botany, zoology, physical geography, and nature study have largely vanished, although topics from these studies are included in general science and biology.

Only two-thirds of the pupils in the tenth grade study biology. Botany, zoology, and physiology are separately offered in some schools, but the whole number of these cases is not large. Slightly less than one-third of the pupils in the upper grades take chemistry and physics. The actual numbers taking these two branches has increased steadily but slowly from 1890 to 1949, while the high school enrollment was growing by geometric ratios. The languages have fared worse.

NUMBER AND PERCENTAGE OF PUPILS ENROLLED IN
SECONDARY DAY SCHOOLS AT CERTAIN

(Adapted from Office of Education Table 18 in Biennial

	1890	%	1900	%	1910	%
Total Enrollment	202,963	%	519,251	%	739,143	%
English	......	...	199,803	38.5	422,051	57.1
Physical Education	......	...	......	...	......	...
Music	......	...	......	...	......	...
Chemistry	20,503	10.1	40,084	7.7	50,923	6.9
Physics	46,184	22.8	98,846	19.0	107,988	14.6
Algebra	92,150	45.4	292,287	56.3	420,207	56.9
General Mathematics	......	...	......	...	......	...
Geometry	43,294	21.3	142,235	27.4	228,170	30.9
Trigonometry	......	...	9,915	1.9	13,812	1.9
Industrial Subjects	......	...	......	...	......	...
Home Economics	......	...	......	...	27,933	3.8
Spanish	......	...	......	...	4,920	.7
Latin	70,411	34.7	262,767	50.6	362,548	49.0
French	11,858	5.8	40,395	7.8	73,161	9.9
German	21,338	10.5	74,408	14.3	175,083	23.7

Although thirteen foreign languages were offered in public high schools in 1949, only four, namely, Spanish, Latin, French, and German, and in this order, were elected with notable frequency. In the last four high school years less than one in four of the pupils was studying a foreign language. The comparative popularity of the four languages in the past and at present may be gathered from the accompanying table. It will be seen that, although there have been some changes up and down, all foreign languages have been declining in popularity. Latin was studied by 50 per cent of all high school students in 1900 and is now in second place with about 8 per cent. Until 1914 German was contending with Latin for first place among the foreign languages; but World War I almost eliminated it, and its gains in the period between the two great wars were again wiped out in 1941. It has been said that since World War II, Americans have been "trying to make friends with a twice-defeated Germany by means of interpreters." A modern language renaissance is, however, beginning in the

SELECTED SUBJECTS IN THE LAST 4 YEARS OF PUBLIC TIMES BETWEEN 1889–1890 AND 1948–1949

Survey of Education in the United States, 1948–1950)

1915		1922		1928		1934		1949	
1,165,495	%	2,155,460	%	2,896,630	%	4,496,514	%	5,399,452	%
680,871	58.4	1,652,232	76.7	2,696,633	93.1	4,071,094	90.5	5,015,890	92.9
......	...	123,568	5.7	435,383	15.0	2,277,775	50.7	3,747,220	69.4
367,188	31.5	544,770	25.3	754,245	26.0	1,148,732	25.5	1,625,235	30.1
86,031	7.4	159,413	7.4	204,694	7.1	339,769	7.6	412,401	7.6
165,854	14.2	192,380	8.9	198,402	6.8	282,896	6.3	291,473	5.4
569,215	48.8	865,515	40.2	1,020,323	35.2	1,367,210	30.4	1,448,966	26.8
......	...	266,918	12.4	228,231	7.9	333,348	7.4	704,742	13.1
309,383	26.5	488,825	22.7	573,668	19.8	767,171	17.1	693,280	12.8
17,220	1.5	32,930	1.5	36,855	1.3	59,858	1.3	108,551	2.0
130,155	11.2	295,905	13.7	391,529	13.5	946,128	21.0	1,434,302	26.6
150,276	12.9	307,553	14.3	477,503	16.5	751,807	16.7	1,304,846	24.2
31,743	2.7	242,715	11.3	273,564	9.4	280,329	6.2	443,995	8.2
434,925	37.3	593,086	27.5	636,952	22.0	721,320	16.0	422,304	7.8
102,516	8.8	333,162	15.5	406,012	14.0	488,710	10.9	255,375	4.7
284,294	24.4	13,918	.6	53,250	1.8	106,672	2.4	43,025	.8

elementary schools. Several hundred elementary schools are teaching foreign language by direct, that is, conversational methods to enthusiastic classes.

The table shows that academic subjects have been losing in popularity in comparison with some of the less academic. Industrial subjects and home economics each enroll about the same number of pupils as algebra, more than all the foreign languages taken together, and twice as many as chemistry and physics. To make the proper comparison, it must be noted that industrial subjects are usually taken by boys and home economics by girls, and that the two studies together enroll 50 per cent of all pupils.

DECLINE OF ENROLLMENT PERCENTAGES
IN CERTAIN SUBJECTS IN 60 YEARS

	1890	1900	1910	1915	1922	1928	1934	1949
Algebra	45.4%	56.3%	56.9%	48.8%	40.2%	35.2%	30.4%	26.8%
Chemistry and Physics	32.9	26.7	21.5	21.6	16.3	13.9	13.9	13.0
Modern Languages	16.3	22.1	34.3	35.9	27.4	25.2	19.5	13.7

Note: Data compiled from preceding table.

The relative decline in the popularity of academic studies is a matter of public moment for several reasons. The maintenance of a complex economic system is directly involved. Agriculture, industry, engineering, business, and the whole American economy depend upon languages including the English language, mathematics, and the sciences. Both practical and research scientists are needed to provide a growing population with the means to maintain an adequate and, if possible, a rising living standard. The whole economy is also the base upon which the nation's system of defense must rest. Furthermore, the United States is committed to a policy of collective security. She needs strategic materials and international markets. In peace and war, for trade and the arts, she must understand her allies and her actual and potential enemies. If ignorance of the languages, the history, the philosophy, and the resources of the countries of the world was ever permissible, that day is past. Isolation is both undesirable and impossible in the present world. High school and college students must study mathematics, sciences, and languages more diligently than they have done in the past, far more diligently than they are doing now.

Chapter Five of the *Biennial Survey,* from which the above figures and tables are derived, is complacent about the matter. The authors seem to think it satisfactory that the actual numbers of pupils in these fields are not declining although the proportions are dropping like a plummet. But this is an error. There is a shortage of diplomats who know Russia and can speak her language, and the same is true of other countries; and a shortage of engineers and first-class physicists. Unless the high schools and colleges can supply many more highly skilled and trained persons in these fields, the country may suffer great harm. There is a further note on this problem in Chapter XVIII.

Psychologists hold that capacities are distributed in the general population according to the normal curve. If so, there must be many pupils now going into minor vocations who could succeed in academic studies. That they do not do so is the result of several conditions, such as lack of money to complete both high school and college courses, a school atmosphere that is unfavorable to serious work, and wrong attitudes on the part of the educational and vocational counselors. The critical shortage of well-trained teachers in these fields is another difficulty and its seriousness is growing. If high school attendance rises to 9,000,000 in 1960, the teaching staff must be increased in the same ratio, that is, by about 50 per cent. At present there are possibly 300,000 high school teachers at work, many ill-paid, ill-trained for the work to which they are assigned, and ill-equipped with the space, time, and materials needed for their work.

The high school is not doing too much for the average and below-average children. They should have every opportunity that they can use to make life fruitful. But so should the presently neglected above-average children; and here an additional argument is pressing—the nation's need for more highly trained men.

The twentieth century, dominated by the complete success of the industrial revolution, has made many great changes in secondary schools and secondary education. More money, more people, and increased demands for skilled and professional services have caused the development of more and larger high schools. The first two decades of the century saw the rise of an even half-dozen movements that were of first-rate significance to secondary education.

People became aware that it was too difficult to get to the city high school and that after the child arrived it was too hard for him to get in and stay in the course. Efforts were made to bridge the gap between elementary and high schools, and the junior high school was created for this purpose. A large number of functions was assigned to the new school, but perhaps the exploratory and orientation courses, attention to the individual, and guidance were the most important. Studies of adolescent development aided in the achievement of these aims. It does not seem that the junior high school was as great an improvement as was predicted; but it has not been abandoned wherever it has been established.

Vocational and educational guidance have had a rapid growth since 1908. Many universities prepare high school counselors, and the larger schools are equipped to provide the kind of education needed to fit pupils for the indicated careers.

The comprehensive high school provides both preparatory and terminal courses, and, using a different classification, both liberal and vocational courses. It is the typical high school but it cannot be maintained in small communities.

Vocational education is still carried on by apprenticeship methods. Educators are attempting to raise the academic standards of the apprentice teacher and supervisor, but they meet some resistance from labor unions. The arguments of both sides may have some merit.

Public school men were lacking in interest in vocational education or were hostile to it. This was partly due to the formal discipline philosophy; and the movement was delayed many years. The federal Smith-Hughes law prevented the establishment of the threatened separate vocational educational system. There are many vocational high schools, some of which are double-purpose schools and may become comprehensive schools. Many of these great schools have grown from very modest trade and continuation schools, a remarkable development of the last thirty years.

The independent schools with a variety of forms, facilities, and functions supplement the public schools at many points, but high fees put their services out of reach of the middle and low income groups. Many of them, like the Catholic high schools tend to be conservative in curriculum policy and keep their standards high. At the opposite extreme in these two respects is the life adjustment education proposed in the Prosser Resolution of 1947. Neither among educators nor in the public mind is there agreement on curricula or standards in secondary education.

Academic subjects have been declining in popularity since World War I and partly for this reason the country is facing a serious shortage of trained man power.

QUESTIONS

1. Why are small high schools relatively ineffective, if they are, as compared with larger ones? In what respects may they be more effective? Is there an ideal size? And could it be realized?

2. Why did so many new departures in secondary education originate about 1900 to 1920?

3. If the junior high school movement be considered as an educational experiment what conclusions can be drawn? What new problems has it raised?

4. Why should the counselor be well educated in several fields, and which ones, outside his specialty?

5. In what ways is the definition of vocational education in the Smith-Hughes Act lacking in precision?

6. Why do state departments and labor unions disagree in matters relating to apprentice-training? What are the underlying factors here? Compare this with the disagreement in 1909 in Massachusetts between the Commission on Industrial Education and the state board.

7. Extend the comparison requested in No. 6 to the struggle between conservative public school leaders and the promoters of vocational education. What conclusions do you draw from the studies suggested in Nos. 6 and 7?

8. Consider the pros and cons of public aid in support of church and independent schools. In dealing with this topic it should be remembered that such aid was traditional in earlier times in America and that England finds no insuperable difficulty in giving such aid.

9. Whether aid is given or not given, should not all schools be inspected by public agencies?

10. Life adjustment education is to include the "tools of learning." What

are these and how are they related to what in the text has been called "applied knowledge"?

11. If further efforts are to be made to provide schooling for the least intellectual, would it not be logical to provide increased incentives and direction to the most intellectual high school pupils? If so, how?

BOOKS AND PAPERS

The *School Review* was founded in 1893 by Jacob Gould Schurman and C. H. Thurber, a university president and a principal of a private secondary school, respectively. There are other secondary school magazines; and some special interest magazines, such as *School Science and Mathematics*, deal largely with problems of secondary education. The articles and bibliographies on secondary education in the *Encyclopedia of Educational Research* cover fifty pages; and the index locates much additional material. Many journals and serials are named in the list of publications used by the *Education Index*. Few of the articles thus found are historical in intention but they become historical as soon as the ink dries on them.

Blauch, Lloyd E., *Federal Cooperation in Agricultural Extension Work, Vocational Education,* and *Vocational Rehabilitation,* Washington, U. S. Government Printing Office, Office of Education Bulletin, 1935, No. 15, with bibliography.

Buck, Paul H., and Others, *General Education in a Free Society,* Harvard University Press, 1945, commonly known as the "Harvard Report."

Burns, J. A., and Others, *History of Catholic Education in the United States,* New York, 1937.

Donahue, J. L., "The Gap between the Secondary and the Elementary School," *School Review,* November, 1902; and a contemporary report of professional opinion on the same subject in E. L. C. Morse, "From Grammar School to High School," *School Review,* October, 1902.

Hanus, Paul H., *Adventuring in Education,* Harvard University Press, 1937. Deals with industrial education in Chapter Eleven.

Hull, J. Dan, and Others, *Offerings and Enrollments in High School Subjects,* being *Chapter Five* of the *Biennial Survey of Education, 1948–1950,* Washington, U. S. Government Printing Office, 1951. Section Twelve of the present chapter is based upon this publication.

Ingalls, Albert, "The Amateur Scientist," *Scientific American,* July, 1954, on training young scientists at Millbrook School, New York State.

Jones, Galen, *Extra-Curricular Activities in Relation to the Curriculum,* New York, Teachers College, Columbia University, 1935.

Keller, Franklin J., *The Double-Purpose High School: Closing the Gap between Vocational and Academic Preparation,* New York, 1953.

Mays, A. B., *Concept of Vocational Education, 1845–1945,* Bureau of Educational Research Bulletin, No. 62, University of Illinois, n. d.; *Essentials of Industrial Education*, New York, 1952.

Parker, W. R., "Foreign Languages and Graduate Study," A paper at the meeting of the Association of American Universities, *Journal of Proceedings*, New York, 1953.

Sargent, F. Porter, Editor, *Handbook of Private Schools*, Boston, 1953, an annual publication.

Simon: Lady Simon of Wythenshawe, *Three Schools or One? Secondary Education in England, Scotland, and the United States*, London, 1943, a pamphlet.

Spiers, E. F., *The Central Catholic High School*, Catholic University of America, 1951, a dissertation.

Tompkins, Ellsworth, *The Activity Period in Public Schools*, Washington, U. S. Government Printing Office, Office of Education, Bulletin, 1951, No. 19.

United States Office of Education, *Life Adjustment Education for Every Youth*, Washington, U. S. Government Printing Office, Office of Education, Bulletin, 1951, No. 22.

Watson, Fletcher G., "Crisis in Science Teaching," *Scientific American*, February, 1954; and with others, *Critical Years Ahead in Science Teaching*, a report of a conference held at Harvard University, 1953.

Chapter XVI

ADVANCES IN HIGHER
EDUCATION

FOR two centuries, America had only one type of institution for higher education, the college. A few medical and law schools were founded, but their standards were such that their work cannot be counted as higher education. After 1825 a few engineering schools began to appear. After the Civil War the state universities at last came to life and the land-grant colleges were established. The latter have been described. Professional schools began to set up significant entrance requirements, first high school graduation, then some college work, and at last a full college course.

Graduate schools, of which Johns Hopkins University was the pace-maker, became the professional schools for college teachers. Universities and colleges began to prepare teachers for the lower schools. Women's colleges and coeducation developed. Teachers' colleges and junior and community colleges, with some notable exceptions, belong to the present century. Diversity among institutions became one of the characteristics of American higher education.

Diversity among functions within many of these diverse institutions became another characteristic. The old college was a simple establishment. It taught several branches but it had no departments, no deans or other personnel officers except the president, little property, and small budgets. It was to higher education what the one-room school was to elementary education. The universities, as they developed, added new colleges to the college of arts: colleges of business, engineering, and others; each college was organized into departments and these into areas. Each area, department, college, division, and the university as a whole acquired an administrative staff. On and off the campus the universities undertook to teach, investigate, advise, and furnish practical services to private individuals, corporations, and to local, state, and national government.

No other institutions of just this scope and kind are found elsewhere.

And a comparable diversity of functions is beginning to develop in teachers' and junior colleges, although it has not yet gone very far. Such diversification seems to be a long-time trend in high schools also. It is a development that is severely criticized, and some of the critics would refuse the title of university to the complex new institutions.

The American university is governed by a board of external trustees, frequently of businessmen. The president is the executive officer of the board rather than a member of the faculty, as the old college president was. The board is a policy-making body and does not normally concern itself with administrative detail. It is more concerned with public opinion, and sensitive to it.

1. BEGINNING OF UNIVERSITIES

A short history of higher education will give a better view of the evolving university of the American type than a general statement could offer. It must be brief. The colonial colleges were described in Chapter III. They were small, their humanism was brittle, the teaching was formal, and although the religious life was often sincere the religious teaching was dogmatic. Divinity was taught from the first; and from the eighteenth century onward, schools of medicine and law were attached to some colleges but not controlled by them. This was, however, the beginning of the university as an assemblage of colleges. The name came into use before 1800. The standards of some of the proprietary medical schools, conducted for the profit of the professors, was at times so low that men who were hardly literate were allowed to matriculate. The reasons are evident.

State legislatures granted college charters freely and without any test of the fitness of the recipient boards to exercise the conferred powers. Although several hundreds of colleges were established and more were projected, less than 200 of those created before 1860 remain today. This indicates that college mortality was high; and it was. Most of the survivors continued in the old ways. But a few older Eastern schools and a few of the state universities had begun to broaden their curricula before 1860.

After the Civil War science instruction was increased and laboratories were established, libraries were enlarged, and the collections were made accessible to the students. The modern languages, which had been introduced earlier, were given a larger place; English, which had been neglected if not excluded, was welcomed into the household; and American history, economics, and political science were taught. As the scope of the instruction was broadened, the number of departments multiplied and specialists were appointed to the faculties. Economics was no longer taught by a historian or sociology by a political scientist. Even these fields were subdivided until the American historian who dealt with the colonial period felt unable to teach a course on the Civil War and reconstruction; and the professor of banking had only general ideas about the tariff or insurance.

In the late nineteenth century, college programs were sometimes expanded too rapidly for college resources. New types of institutions were established, as we have seen, and the standards of professional education were raised, as will be indicated. Preprofessional courses were introduced and thereby the attention given to liberal studies was reduced. Of this also more will be said below. The elective system and the course-credit scheme brought into the college the idea of interchangeable parts which had been so useful in industry. Its use in education has not always been applauded.

The expansion of research and advanced study led to the organization of graduate schools with their deans, secretaries, and committees, a college within the college. The heart of the American university had begun to beat. The graduate school became a professional school, preparing university teachers and research workers. The other professional schools were gradually brought under university control. Students came to the undergraduate departments in growing numbers from private and public high schools; and money, both philanthropic and public, in ever-increasing sums was provided.

When ambitious colleges lacking the library, laboratories, and trained staff for such work began to confer masters' and doctors' degrees, a standardizing agency, the Association of American Universities was formed about the turn of the century to recognize and maintain the quality of graduate work. Only those universities which had an adequate graduate school were admitted. There were fourteen members at the beginning, only three of them state universities. Fifty years later there were thirty-five members, a majority of them state universities.

The training of college and university instructors and investigators has been one of the chief functions of the graduate schools. The doctorate of philosophy was until recently a teaching degree and it still is this to a great extent. This advanced work has done much to raise college scholarship. Whether it has also improved college teaching is more doubtful; and it is claimed that some training in public speech, psychology, and education would help to put the beginner on the road to teaching success. The doctors disagree on this problem, but it may receive more attention as college enrollments swell and the number of young instructors grows.

Higher standards in academic fields made possible the improvement of professional education. The change spread to all professions but it was extraordinary in medical instruction. A whole series of evils had grown from the fact, already noted, that the medical schools were proprietary institutions, that is, they were not controlled by the university boards but by groups of doctors who were teaching in them.

Until 1910, when the Carnegie Foundation for the Advancement of Teaching, in what is called the Flexner Report, published the results of its investigation of medical education, there was a scandalous lack of both facilities and standards in many medical colleges. State laws were lax and there were and are no national laws. As a result of the Flexner Report, the public, led by the American Medical Association and the American Public Health Association, effected the closing of the most inadequate, sometimes even fraudulent, schools of medicine. In twenty years the number of schools was reduced from one hundred and sixty to eighty. Standards were raised, money and clinical means were secured, research was promoted, until American medical education attained high rank in the world. Such rank it holds now. A French authority, for example, has recently called the American schools of medicine "peerless" because they fuse teaching, research, and hospital care and administration instead of "fragmenting" them. He had doubtless seen some of the better examples; but medical education in the United States is generally considered to be in a healthy state. One frequent criticism holds that the number of physicians prepared is inadequate to meet the country's needs. Fifty years ago when the standards were low there was an oversupply, but many were poorly prepared. Thanks largely to the control exercised by the American Medical Association, all three conditions have been reversed; but ways may now have to be found to provide more of these well-trained doctors. The supply of these and of other highly trained professional experts will be further considered below.

2. COEDUCATION

A radical break with academic tradition and one in which the United States was a pioneer and has maintained high rank was the provision of higher education for women, an opportunity that was quickly grasped. One hastens to say that it was not an offer made by men but mainly an achievement by the women themselves. The Middle West opened the first door. The declaration of Theodore Parker (1810–1860) that no New England college had in forty years favored any great reform may have been extreme; but that they long kept their doors closed against women is true.

The way was prepared by the academies; and the normal schools were coeducational. It is, therefore, surprising that the first coeducational colleges should have been severely attacked, as they were, by Mrs. Grundy. This was the penalty inflicted upon Oberlin College, which began as a coeducational school in 1833, admitted women to its degree course in 1838, and graduated four women bachelors of arts in 1842. Antioch in 1853 was opened as a coeducational college under Horace Mann. But it was not mainly the independent colleges but the state universities and the land-grant colleges that most generously opened their doors to women students.

Out on the frontier of that time, the State University of Iowa and the University of Wisconsin admitted women to degree courses in the middle sixties. Wisconsin, under a president who was against coeducation, made some attempt to institute a women's division, but when a new executive came into office the plan was abandoned for coeducation. The University of Michigan, the "down East" University of Maine, and Cornell University, half land-grant college, half endowed university, all became coeducational in the beginning seventies. About that time the other institutions of this class were swept into the same strong current.

State universities and land-grant colleges were young schools in need of students and lacking the large and conservative alumnal bodies of the old colleges of the East. These latter institutions made no concessions. Meanwhile, separate women's colleges, such as Elmira, Wells, Mount Holyoke, Vassar, Smith, Wellesley, and Bryn Mawr, were forming, and they came in time to oppose coeducation as much as Princeton or Yale. Perhaps these are merely examples of a natural conservatism in people or of the reluctance in institutions to change a policy that has been successful.

Some of the men's colleges which refused to adopt coeducation began to create affiliated women's colleges. President Barnard of Columbia College, having discovered that college enrollments were lagging, startled his faculty by proposing to admit women. The college fathers, after a long decade, found a way out of their dilemma. In 1889, Barnard's last year, they created a woman's college with a separate board and an independent budget, made it an affiliate of Columbia, and named it for the retiring president. At Harvard some professors began to give private lectures to women in the year of Barnard's first pronouncement. This became the Harvard Annex and in 1893 was constituted Radcliffe College under a separate board. Tulane, Brown, Western Reserve, and other universities adopted similar plans. Like the land-grant colleges, the early colleges for women conducted preparatory departments because the applicants for admission were not prepared for college work.

The University of Mississippi admitted women in 1882, but in most of the Southern states, including Mississippi, separate state colleges for women were opened in towns remote from the state university. Florida, for example, had a state university for men at Gainesville and a state college for women at Tallahassee. Both have now become coeducational. The former continues to be known as the University of Florida, but the latter in the state capital has been renamed the Florida State University. Confusing nomenclature such as this is unfortunately common in the United States, North and South. The state college for women was a Southern institution.

By slow stages coeducation overtook some of the oldest colleges and universities. The University of Pennsylvania, step by step, admitted women to premedical work, to teachers' courses, to the graduate school (1885), and now to all departments. Many institutions which have kept the arts college as a men's preserve have admitted women to other divisions, especially to the graduate school. The doors of the graduate schools were opened to women in about the following order by New York University, Brown, Yale, Harvard, Columbia, and in 1907 by Johns Hopkins. The medical school of Johns Hopkins University was coeducational from its beginning in 1893. The Woman's Medical College of Pennsylvania had been chartered as early as 1850. Today most medical and dental schools are open to women and men on equal terms and occasionally a woman graduates in veterinary medicine or engineering, and many graduate in law.

The old issues have not all been closed. Some hold that since men and women, boys and girls, mingle in the family and in business, in love and in war, they should be allowed to mingle on the campus. Others argue that just for this reason they should be separated in school. The economic factors favor coeducation; Catholic practice and ancient custom and tradition are against it; but then the most ancient custom is against all education for women. The arguments are no longer heard that study will injure the health and impair the graces of women, or that they will be unable to compete with men for college marks.

What courses are most appropriate for women is still a problem. More than ever before, women are planning twofold careers, in the home and outside of it. For outside occupations they tend to select certain professions and not others. They are active in politics, several have been ambassadors to foreign countries, and perhaps future presidents will not fail to appoint at least one woman to a cabinet position. Men, including university presidents, continue to lecture on the education of women but they do not claim to know the only true and complete answer, nor do the women themselves.

3. UNIVERSITIES BREAKING OLD BONDS

Colleges and universities long confined their efforts to the campus teaching of academic subjects. Now they carry out research, render services to students and to the public, and on and off the campus teach many occupational and welfare subjects as well as academic ones. They have broken many of the old bonds.

Private or independent institutions sometimes anticipated the public ones in breaking the bonds. Schools of business, for example, did not arise in state universities or land-grant colleges. The Wharton School of the University of Pennsylvania, opened in 1881, was the first university school of business. Suggestions along this line had been made earlier by General Robert E. Lee when he was president of the institution now named Washington and Lee University. Engineering was developed at Rensselaer, Yale, and the Massachusetts Institute of Technology before the public institutions became widely active in the field; a little later all the practical studies were much cultivated in the state universities and land-grant colleges. The University of Michigan made an early beginning in engineering. These institutions, because of their close relations to the public elementary and secondary schools, were among the first to prepare teachers for those schools. It was especially in the latter half of the nineteenth century that both the universities and the public high schools broke their bonds. And this coordinate development of secondary and higher public education is a fact that is explained by the connections between them, their common social environment, and their relations to the state.

The idea of extramural teaching came from mid-Victorian England. A group of young women wishing to become teachers asked an Oxford professor for help in acquiring the desired art. Socrates-like, he disclaimed the power to teach this, but offered to give lessons on astronomy. He thought the ladies might by observation learn some pedagogy. History does not say what the outcome was, but the professor's lectures became the starting-point of university extension.

In the United States the movement created great excitement. Melvil Dewey of the New York State Library and Herbert B. Adams, history professor at Johns Hopkins, became leading promoters. An American Society for the Extension of University Teaching was formed (1890). University credit for the courses was arranged. About 1890 and after, lectures were given for some years in a hundred centers, chiefly by professors from Eastern universities. Interest in this, the third notable type of adult education, declined even more rapidly than in the cases of the lyceum and the Chautauqua movement. College instruction in history or science had only a limited and temporary appeal to persons who in many cases had neither the preparation nor the time to pursue them with profit. College lecturers were not always able to gauge the difficulties of their hearers. Every new movement has to catch its second wind before it can become a lasting success. This the early extension movement was not able to do and it practically disappeared soon after 1900.

A new era in university extension, more vocational in nature, began about 1906. One phase was the agricultural extension aided by the Smith-Lever Act (1914). Teachers' classes were also held in towns within the university orbit. Classes in economics and business were taught. And the universities began to take a part in the newly rising movement of adult education. Many administrative questions arose, questions about funds, rates of pay, size of classes, professors' teaching schedules, college credit, and library and field materials.

Summer schools, now almost universal in the large universities, are little older than university extension. Agassiz conducted his session at Penikese in 1873. Chautauqua and Martha's Vineyard followed. Each of these enrolled many teachers. Some universities allowed credit for work done at Chautauqua. Many universities opened their own summer schools before 1900. The University of Chicago was opened in 1892 and adopted an all-year plan in which the summer school occupied one of the four regular quarters. This eliminated the troubles which other universities had with fractional courses, special contracts for instructors, a special administrative staff, and other irregularities. It also disposed of the difficulty found in many institutions where some departments do not open and some courses are not staffed in the summer. The quarter-plan has not been generally adopted; but even where only a part of the university is open, the summer enrollments have become large. There is no longer any question of shutting down huge university plants for one-fourth of the year.

Home study or correspondence departments are maintained by some of the largest universities. From the advertising circulars it is clear that drawing students to the campus is one of the aims of these departments. Some of them offer high school as well as college work. After an examination, usually proctored by someone appointed by the university, credit may be allowed for mail courses; and a certain proportion of such credits may be used to meet entrance or degree requirements. It is true that such courses have certain advantages, but they also have some disadvantages in comparison with courses taken in the classroom. The exclusive dependence upon books and the lack of needed books are such defects. But it is a fault of the whole situation rather than of the individual courses that many students do not complete the correspondence work which they undertake.

Technical services are rendered by state and by private universities. They make building surveys for city school systems, help in city planning, confer and advise with industries and governments, or test the purity of city water or commercial products. Law schools offer certain limited kinds and amounts of legal advice, and accountants interpret income tax laws. Fifty years ago such services were known as the "Wisconsin idea" but they have now been widely spread.

The enlarged scope of its instructional programs is a mark of the difference between the early colleges and the present universities. Some professional instruction, especially in divinity, was given in the first colleges. Before 1850 several schools of science and engineering appeared. From these simple and meager beginnings the numerous and extensive engineering courses of the present evolved. A similar proliferation has occurred in business education.

Schools of social administration prepare those who would help in dealing with poverty and crime and the other diseases of the social order, and in bringing relief to the young who have been deserted and to the aged who have been defeated. There are schools of nursing, hygiene and public health, education, physical education, and general education. The graduate school occupies the topmost floor of the building which has displaced the early college. The old college, like the farmer with his flock of sheep, spinning wheel, and loom, produced excellent products in limited quantities. The same kind of change has overtaken both the college and the domestic industries.

We shall omit the large business and administrative features of the educational leviathan; but one of the further differences is found in the student activities. The college blue-laws have disappeared. Food is plentiful and there are no more diet riots. And organized activities have been developed to fill the vacuum formed by the ending of the old wars.

The new student activities are often educative. Even a century ago some students testified that they learned more from the exercises of the literary societies of those days than from their courses. Some of the current activities have been listed by Stephen Leacock, an unfriendly critic. Concerning the gay collegians, he said: "They sing, they dance, they act, they run mimic newspapers and make-believe elections." The last item should not receive too much stress. American students pay too little rather than too much attention to political issues, and less than the students of many other countries. Yet political education is of primary importance in a democracy. Otherwise, Leacock's list is only the beginning of an index of student activities and leaves out even athletics, the most hotly pursued and most controversial of all.

Football, the national collegiate game, has been especially troublesome. Attacks are directed against the time it consumes, the emotions it arouses, the injuries and even fatalities caused by the competitive fury and physical contacts of the players, and the moral evils which grow out of the public interest in the contests. Many attempts have been made to develop a safer game, but the complaint is heard that if it is made safe it will be tame. Great improvements have, however, been made in the rules.

There was a time when slugging, gouging, and other criminal violence were encouraged, when players had to be "warned" and could not be penalized for a first offense, and when team captains uniformly instructed their men "to take their warning." Conditions were bad in the secondary schools also. Bills to outlaw the game were introduced into state legislatures. College presidents and a President of the United States, the first Roosevelt, took part in the discussion. Roosevelt with his interest in "the strenuous life" wanted the game saved and urged the adoption of uniform eligibility rules to eliminate the "bruisers" who were not genuine students. Physicians, trainers, coaches, and officials who are alert and fearless have done much, but even now, perhaps, no squad goes through a season without serious injuries.

Football was saved to become big business, a multimillion dollar industry. In no other country do universities invite temptation by engaging in a gigantic amusement enterprise. The first stadiums were built in the opening years of the present century, and the big ones, to accommodate 80,000 or more shouting fans, after World War I. To exclude all commercialism and gambling would be difficult; but at the mid-century there were cases of corruption in both football and basketball that shocked the moral sense of the nation. Scandals that will be long remembered occurred at the United States Military Academy, at the College of William and Mary where the athletic authorities were involved, and in several colleges where basketball players were convicted of "throwing" games for money. That public opinion condemned these lapses is also a part of the story.

4. CRITICISM OF UNIVERSITIES

The critics to be considered in this section are not the impartial investigators who usually deal with limited phases of higher education. Examples are E. C. Elliott and M. M. Chambers, who studied the charters, basic laws, and court decisions of the colleges and universities in a series of publications starting two decades ago. The *Encyclopedia of Educational Research* (1950) names many objective studies, some giving only the apparent facts and others containing the writers' interpretation. But the criticisms to be considered here are sweeping indictments based upon personal philosophies and experience, and not upon research.

A prominent example of this kind of writing was furnished by Thorstein Veblen (1857–1929). In his *The Higher Learning in America* (1918) he maintained that a university must be wholly devoted to the satisfaction of intellectual curiosity; and he presupposes a complete, it would seem an impossible, separation of the university from business influence. J. E. Kirkpatrick (1869–1931) in *The American College and Its Rulers* (1926) also proposed to dispense with boards of trustees, usually composed of businessmen, and to have the faculty control the university. There are historical examples of this kind of university government. A later study by H. P. Beck, *Men Who Control Our Universities* (1947), reported the economic composition of the boards of thirty universities and showed the preponderance of businessmen on them. This is a factual study. It may be admitted that boards composed of businessmen may be inclined toward economic and social conservatism, but at least they will not isolate the institution from social reality. The history of such boards and of the politically appointed boards needs thorough study.

We now turn to two critics whom we have accused of composing sweeping indictments based upon personal philosophies. These are Abraham Flexner, whose *Universities, American, English, German* appeared in 1930, and Robert M. Hutchins, who, in numerous addresses, collected and published in *No Friendly Voice* and *The Higher Learning in America*, both in 1936, and in a recent volume, *The Conflict in Education in a Democratic Society* (1953), has dealt with the universities and with education in general.

Some of the criticism of universities lacks a consistent philosophical foundation. This seems to apply to Flexner's strictures particularly. His limits to what a university may do appear to be arbitrary. He rejects some activities because, although proper in themselves, they do not belong to university work, and others because they are worthless or harmful in themselves. But the bases upon which he makes these judgments are obscure. He declares that he will consider whether American universities "now discern and discharge their special functions or whether they meddle with functions which do not constitute their proper business." "Very well," the reader may reply, "but how can he tell? By what principles is this to be determined?"

Flexner, who made the highly effective report on medical education, has no doubt that it is the function of universities to transmit, and by research to increase, the higher learning and to prepare men for the advanced professions. As an undergraduate of the Johns Hopkins University in its early and greatest period, he acquired high respect for science; and when he writes about research he has the laboratory sciences in mind. He also lays great weight upon good teaching and names Paulsen of Berlin and Michael Foster of Cambridge University as pre-eminent professors, although they were not original thinkers. He does not find originality and research in conflict with good teaching.

Although the universities are to renew the higher professions constantly, Flexner doubts that originality, research, and good teaching can develop any of the lower vocations into professions. He opposes vocational education in universities. He would disallow all merely technical, vocational, and popular instruction in the university. There should be no schools of business, journalism, domestic "science," or library "science." He maintains this last-named exclusion in the face of the world's admiration and imitation of American library administration as it is taught in some of the most respected universities. Even engineering is to be barred, apparently because the German universities do not include it.

The school of education barely escapes a similar sentence. Flexner had himself been a successful teacher in Louisville before be became an investigator, and the German universities offered lectures on pedagogy. But he would prune the too luxuriant growths of the school of education—perhaps not a bad idea—and he ridiculed some of the efforts in educational research. The university was not to engage in any secondary school work and this interdict might extend to campus experimental schools. Finally, no home-study or off-campus course or service work was to be offered.

On university athletics, Flexner and Hutchins agree. The position of Hutchins was stated in a sentence: "The social and athletic character that large numbers of students have given the universities has done more than most things to prevent them from being universities and to debase the higher learning in America." Flexner had, in effect, said this earlier and he added that only courage is needed "to place athletics where everyone perfectly well knows they belong." This is too sweeping and too optimistic. Excepting professionals few people seem to know their own minds on this question or remain of the same mind very long.

The Carnegie Foundation for the Advancement of Teaching, as a result of its investigation of college athletics in 1929, favored "not more law but a more genuine regard for existing law," honesty, and better sportsmanship. It did not, as has been thought, propose the abolition of college athletics and it did not justify the sentence quoted from Flexner. It did say that colleges do not make sufficient effort to secure the educational results that could be derived from sports. It severely attacked commercialism and it favored intramural games. The report, which cost a great deal of money and started a nationwide discussion in newspapers and magazines, does not seem to have had any great influence.

The president of the Carnegie Foundation in his foreword to the report on athletics had expressed his private opinion that paid coaches were the cause of the greatest athletic evils. Less responsible critics have used stronger language to the same effect and have called football a farce, have scored the coaches for their eagerness to win, and the university presidents for conniving with those who were defeating the purposes of "genuine education." This is calling for scapegoats and solves no problems. The Educational Policies Commission, in a bulletin on *School Athletics* (1954), quotes many leading educational associations in an effort to show that everybody favors moderation and honesty in athletics. But this also solves no problems for "everybody" includes the frantic "fans" and the "fixers."

Now and then someone not connected with sports comes out in defense of them. In a review of Flexner's book, the historian A. B. Hart declared that "college athletics have gone far in breaking up the student rebellions, the fighting, and the general hell and hullabaloo of three generations ago." There is much truth in this contribution from college history, but Hart concedes that athletics was not the only factor involved in the improvement. Other changes also have aided in civilizing university life. Such are the various student activities, improved teaching and curricula, regard for students as persons, and better living conditions.

In his condemnation of athletics and vocationalism, Hutchins is even more extreme than Flexner; and although he does not define the term he seems to oppose all vocational education. And because of this absolute disapproval, Hutchins seems hardly willing to admit professional schools into the university. It is not surprising, therefore, that he attacks teacher preparation. He wrote: "Vocationalism has suffered no more signal defeat than the abolition of our School of Education [at the University of Chicago] and the creation of the University Committee on the Preparation of Teachers." This is not very different from the Ford Foundation's attempt to turn back the clock of teacher education to prenormal school days.

Hutchins accepts the research function of the university, but he means by this mainly philosophical reflection, with logic as the main instrument. He is lukewarm if not hostile to the gathering of facts. This seems to take him back to the Platonic ideas and intuition. Further, he claims that research and teaching conflict with each other. Such a conflict may exist in some cases, but it is certain that this is not inevitable. Research should serve to improve teaching and often does so.

It was Harry D. Gideonse in his *The Higher Learning in a Democracy* (1937) who claimed that the Hutchins critique is based upon a Platonic scheme of changeless ideas and that an institution constructed upon such a foundation would have no power of further growth. Hutchins rejected this charge; but even in his later volume, *The Conflict in Education in a Democratic Society* (1953), he places the final emphasis upon the "universal ideas." The key question is how "the rational, moral, spiritual values" which he emphasizes are derived. To Gideonse it seemed that the present confusion in education must be tolerated because only in freedom to disagree and to experiment is there a promise of growth.

From preceding pages it appears that there are areas of agreement between Flexner and Hutchins. One could assign labels to their views but it will be more profitable to ask whence they were derived. The early Johns Hopkins and its model, the German university, were influential sources. Now, comparative studies may supply useful suggestions to comparable institutions in comparable circumstances; but they may mislead those who copy practices merely because they succeeded elsewhere. They seem to have misled Flexner.

The American college was based upon an English educational tradition that valued character and administrative ability more highly than technical scholarship. America was a democracy. The high school course was only four years long. The country was engaged in occupying and tapping the resources of a new continent. All these conditions differed from those of Germany, and while the German university system had rendered great services to America, it had been fully studied, applied, and discounted before Flexner wrote.

The conjoint Platonism and Aristotelianism of Hutchins is not that of the originals but the derivative Scholasticism of the Middle Ages. The great Greek thinkers would be surprised that, two thousand years after them, their ideas had become unassailable dogmas. If they are to be our masters we should do better to follow their methods instead of copying their results.

The best reply to the criticism of Flexner and Hutchins is to be found in history rather than in logic. Briefly, the relevant history is as follows: The scientific revolution began to change the American college into a university. The industrial revolution, which resulted from the scientific revolution and in turn also promoted it, caused a further transformation of the infant university. This so-called industrial revolution included a series of constituent revolts in manufacturing, transportation, and communication and likewise in labor organization, government, family life, and many other areas. It is in this new social world that the American university is to function. Like all living institutions, it has been improvised, added to, and subtracted from, and in trying to solve its problems it has become thoroughly American. It must be judged partly by the standards and traditions of the past but not by those alone. It is following an old tradition but also creating a new one; and the new tradition must be judged by its results.

5. DEVELOPING NEGLECTED TALENT

Americans tend to think of schools in terms of opportunities for individual persons. This view conforms to the pioneer spirit but it may become a purely selfish interest. And there is also the complementary idea that the school tax and public education have the general welfare mainly in view. The national defense, public order, economic productiveness, the arts and sciences, morals, piety, and patriotism, all have been considered proper objects of educational promotion. In this process there is a danger that the interests of the individual person may be sacrificed. A good state, by developing the talents of its citizens and binding them together in loyalty to each other, tries to promote the welfare of each and also that of all together.

Such a program implies educational guidance, often a difficult and precarious venture. For illustration, under the high employment conditions of the 1950's there is need for more engineers, physicians, teachers, nurses, scientists, and scholars, especially engineers and teachers. Engineering is now one of the largest professions, exceeded by teaching and nursing only. The great increase in the number of engineers has occurred in the present century through the change from manual and horsepower to mechanical power. Especially since World War II have the industrial and military demands for engineers become far greater than the supply. No one foresaw this.

When the war ended in 1945, the returning veterans chose engineering courses in such numbers that in each of the years 1949 and 1950 the colleges graduated 50,000 engineers. Remembering the great number of

engineers who were unemployed in the depression, educators began to
warn against an impending surplus. The warnings were heeded and there
was an abrupt drop in enrollments for these courses. Then, partly owing
to the Korean War and partly to industrial expansion, a serious shortage
developed. No one knows how long it will last.

Changes in the character of engineering education are doing something to reduce the risks of the profession. Colleges of engineering are
introducing broad courses in English, speech, history, and the sciences.
These liberal elements added to applied mathematics, drawing, design, and
other technical studies provide a training that can be useful in many vocations and stations in life. There are those who think the broadened engineering courses are the best of all college courses.

For reasons similar to those noted in connection with engineering,
there is also a shortage of scientists. The number of scientists employed in
industrial laboratories increased from 36,000 in 1940 to 70,000 in 1950.
There are, further, many pure scientists who are engaged in extending
knowledge without regard to its application. Many basic discoveries which
lead to scientific progress are made by them. Not less important, perhaps,
are the professors of science in universities without whom the supply of
the previous classes would soon dry up. It is to be noted that these classes
overlap. There is no sharp line between pure and applied science, and many
university teachers have made important discoveries.

The research scientist is expected to have a Ph.D. This requires three
or more years of study beyond the bachelor's degree. And it presupposes a
level of intelligence that enables the candidate to complete this advanced
study. The earlier that the pupils with the necessary capacity can be discovered the better. High schools may waste the country's intellectual resources by failing to discover and to encourage talent. Westinghouse Science Talent Search has helped many. The federal government and the
National Science Foundation maintain scholarship programs. The two
critical points come at the times of graduation from high school and from
college. Final success becomes probable if these hurdles are safely passed.

The problem of preparing enough physicians to meet the needs of all
the people is different from the preceding. For years there has been a surplus
of qualified applicants annually seeking admission to the medical schools.
It is asserted by many that too few are admitted, and an increase in the
capacity of the medical schools is demanded. But the schools and the
profession are cautious because they fear overexpansion. There has, however, been some increase in the number of medical graduates, although not
enough by far to meet the demands of the critics. On the other hand, a
decrease in the number of applicants for admission to the medical schools

is now developing. Some schools have nearly as many places as applicants. Deans of medical schools are already (1955) reporting that the quality of the applicants is no longer as high as it was several years ago.

Whether the United States has the intellectual resources to meet all the demands for trained men is a difficult question. The following diagrams show that college graduates are only a fraction of all who are equally

COMPARISON OF DISTRIBUTION OF TEST SCORES OF ARMY PERSONNEL AND COLLEGE GRADUATES.

Figures and data from the Scientific American *for September, 1951, by permission.*

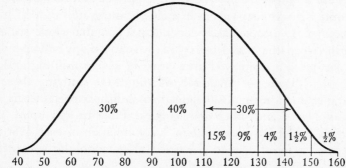

Bell-shaped or normal curve showing that 30 per cent of those taking the Army General Classification Test made scores between 110 and 160.

COMPARISON OF THE NUMBERS OF PEOPLE ABLE TO DO COLLEGE WORK WITH THOSE WHO GRADUATED FROM COLLEGE.

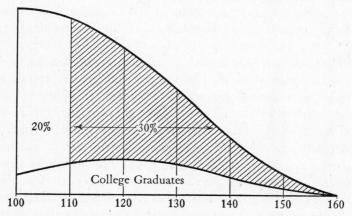

Diagram showing that college graduates are a small proportion of those with scores of 110 or above and able to do college work.

"intelligent." Nearly one-third of those who took the army test made scores of 110 or better. The shaded area of the second diagram represents those in any age group who can make equivalent scores but do not graduate from college. These are potential college graduates, capable of completing more training than they are receiving. Encouraging capable high school graduates to go to college is the first step toward increasing the supply of highly trained men. Intelligence is certainly necessary but not sufficient. Also needed are enthusiasm, industry, persistence, and other character traits. Every teacher of experience has seen bright pupils fail through lack of such qualities.

To secure a proper balance between supply of and demand for highly trained people is a serious problem in a closely integrated society. Increased specialization makes people more dependent upon the whole social order. In Europe between the world wars (1918–1939) many scholars and professional men were unemployed after years of severe training and further years of waiting. Professor Walter Kotschnig after studying these groups concluded that such men, disillusioned and disheartened, easily became the dupes of Hitler and other demagogues. They turned upon a society which, they felt, had misguided them. A combination of early work experience and some general education carried along with the specialty might reduce the danger of frustration.

6. OLD IDEAS RECOVERED

American universities have borrowed ideas from Germany and other countries. The German idea of a university is that of a higher institution of instruction and research in the arts and sciences and the three old professions. Applied sciences are taught in another type of institution called *Hochschulen,* literally High Schools, but actually institutions of university grade.

Freedom of teaching and study was a reigning idea of the German universities at the time when they influenced America. Professors were free to lecture on any subject and generally to say what they thought. There was some ostentatious German boasting about this freedom but it was never absolute. A student also was free to attend any lectures, study any subject, and free also to migrate from one university to another in order to hear the greatest scholars in his special fields. The custom of moving from university to university was one of the admirable gifts from the Middle Ages. This student freedom was sometimes abused, leading to waste of time, but it should not be condemned without consideration of the advantages conferred by it.

A small book on *University Education* by Henry P. Tappan, who later became president of the University of Michigan, was published in 1851. It gave home-staying Americans some account of the European universities; and James Morgan Hart in 1874 in his *German Universities* gave a fuller one. Hart anticipated the major premise of Flexner and Hutchins. He defined "university," as they do, in terms of his own experience and liking. Only the German are real universities, he declared. And although it required a long period of time, he eventually discovered that the German universities did not pretend to give "a so-called general education." Because Oxford and Cambridge do this, neither, Hart declared, "is a university in the true sense of the term." Specialist education is one main characteristic of the German university, he claimed correctly, and freedom is the other. On freedom he wrote this admirable sentence: "The university is a law unto itself, each professor is a law unto himself, each student revolves on his own axis and at his own rate of speed."

Many American students in those universities, beginning with George Ticknor and Edward Everett in the first quarter of the nineteenth century, became professors upon their return to the United States and influenced the institutions where they taught. A few Germans, Charles Beck and Francis Lieber for example, who taught in American colleges may also have had some effect. But when Johns Hopkins University, organized by Daniel Coit Gilman (1831–1908), was opened in 1876, the country was furnished with a living example of a university on the German plan. Thus was introduced and emphasized the idea of research, of discovery, of the advancement of knowledge, not merely its transmission. Research, however, implies specialization. Professor Teufelsdröckh existed only in Carlyle's imagination. There is no research into things-in-general.

Although great administrative changes had occurred in the American college, the English idea of general or liberal education and character formation remained its academic base until the German influence entered. With the development of universities the ideas of academic freedom, research, and specialization became prominent. Now, after a century, the English idea has regained new vigor. There is no intention of neglecting specialized research but there is also an almost universal emphasis upon general education.

John Henry Newman (1801–1890) gave the classic statement of the English *Idea of a University*. According to him, knowledge may be its own end. A university may cultivate all sciences and professions, but it is "formally based" upon the liberal arts, and its primary purpose is to make men rather than scholars, surgeons, or engineers. It is this liberal knowledge that is its own end. The second end of learning should be the training of good members of society, "fit for the world." Both the nearer end of knowledge for its own sake, that is, for the love of it, and the further end of fitness for the world can be best attained in collegial living and the free and intimate conversation of studious youth. Thus Newman wrote.

7. THE RHODES SCHOLARSHIPS

Cecil Rhodes (1853–1902), diamond king, established a series of scholarships at Oxford University for students from the British dominions, Germany, and the United States. Rhodes was an empire-builder, eager to promote the union of the English-speaking peoples, to prepare young men for public service, and to promote international peace. In the nineteenth century England had become, in Bismarck's words, a "satiated nation" with a world-spanning empire. That empire Rhodes wished to preserve but he lived to see the Boer War (1899–1902) foreshadow the growing attack against colonialism. International peace has not been attained. Perhaps the desire to draw the English-speaking peoples together has, of all his aims, had the greatest success.

Whatever influence the scholarships have had in the United States must have been favorable to general education and international education. The scholarships became available early in the present century. The holders have usually been graduates of an American college. The scholars in residence live the collegial life of Oxford, devote the best hours of the day to study and the rest to talk and sports. There are no paid coaches, but everybody plays intensely and without much of a gallery. Talk occurs at breakfasts, lunches, coffee-hours, dinner at High Table. There are club meetings and debates. In all of these and other ways the American student learns what Newman meant when he made conversation between men in the same and in different fields of study a major means of education in a university.

The American student is somewhat disturbed to learn that there are no courses to be taken and that hearing lectures is not thought to be of great value. He has to do the work himself. He is assigned to a tutor who suggests topics to explore, books to read or master as the case may be, and subjects for regular essays. Everything depends upon what in the United States are called final and comprehensive examinations. And these are prepared to test not only his knowledge but also what he can do with it. The aim is to develop power to think, write, and to work independently.

If he is sufficiently well prepared and industrious he can earn a doctorate in three years. The university year is short, twenty-four weeks. The purpose of the long vacations is to allow time in which students may get their work done. They go in small groups to quiet places where there will be no teas, parties, games, or other interruptions. They are not spoon-fed and it is not possible to cram for the examinations.

Vacations leave some time for pleasure, such as travel on the continent or in Scotland. The Rhodes scholar will learn about England and its people. In term-time he will make friends with fellow students, some of whom come from far places in the English-speaking world. It has been said that when he returns to the United States he will be a better internationalist than he was before he left—a result that does not win universal approval in a divided world.

About 1,200 Rhodes scholars have returned home and one-third of them are engaged in educational work, mostly as professors and administrators in colleges and universities. No canvass of their views on general education is available, but some current developments suggest English influence. Such are plans used in many colleges of "reading for honors" and the comprehensive examinations for graduation. The essential elements of an honors system have been set out by Frank Aydelotte, president of the Association of the American Rhodes Scholars, as follows: (1) selection of the best students, (2) provision of a rigorous course of study, and (3) greatest possible freedom of work consistent with adequate supervision; and he reported in 1925 that ninety-three colleges were offering honors work. This number has probably shrunk since then.

Where honors work and comprehensive examinations are used they modify the American course-credit system. Tutorial work has been introduced into many institutions, but it also is hard to combine with course work. Where classes are small the professor can serve as a tutor and combine the two plans as far as a single course is concerned. The scope of the Oxford tutor's work is, however, far wider. Some of the wealthier American universities have built residence halls or "houses" on the English pattern to domicile students in small groups, with a housemaster as guide, counselor, and friend. The purpose is to create the collegial living conditions and to encourage the intellectual conversation of Newman's "Idea." A book on *Comprehensive Examinations in American Colleges* (1933) by Edward S. Jones has a short section summarizing a comparison of the English and American systems by American Rhodes scholars; but apparently the term "general education" does not occur in it.

8. THE HARVARD REPORT

The general education movement was reinforced by the scarcity of jobs and the urgency of many social problems in the great depression, by closer contacts with England, and after World War II by the international outlook of that era. During the war, colleges were trying to foretell the future and to prepare for the "postwar world." The so-called Harvard Report was prepared at that time.

Meanwhile, in 1944 Public Law 346, the GI bill, was adopted and soon the veterans flooded the campuses, almost swamping their facilities. Temporary housing, expanded faculties, and oversize classes resulted. The college enrollment of 1946 was 45 per cent above that of 1944; and in the peak year of 1947 there were more than 1,000,000 veterans in the colleges. The high enrollments continued for several years longer. No such demand upon the colleges had been made in the whole history of the country. These conditions had been only partially foreseen by those who had made plans for postwar education; but as the flood receded and faculties became stabilized, many of the proposed programs were put into effect.

The report which received the greatest attention was *General Education in a Free Society* (1945), the Harvard Report. It was issued after two years of work by an interdepartmental committee of Harvard professors; and it deals with both secondary and college education. As in the case of the Rhodes scholarships, it is impossible to say how much effect the report has had but it has been read. In five years, 50,000 copies were sold. After an experimental period the recommended plan became a permanent program at Harvard in 1949.

The report represents an effort to interpret the word of President James Bryant Conant, that the chief concern of American education is "the infusion of the liberal and humane tradition into our entire educational system." The committee took this to mean the training of men in (1) effective thinking, (2) clear communication, (3) making relevant judgments, and (4) discrimination among values. The courses and methods which they chose will fit only students of high talent with good formal preparation. For this reason the plan has been labeled academic.

Six courses, out of sixteen required for graduation from Harvard College, are to provide general education; but not only these, one hopes. These courses take the place of the old distribution requirement instituted by President Abbott Lawrence Lowell in 1909. Three of the courses are "elementary" and must be taken in the first two years of college, and the other three come in the upper years. Within these limits they may be fitted into any schedule at the student's convenience. This avoids the block programming of most general education schemes and solves a problem to be mentioned again below. In teaching and in evaluating the work of students the plan employs student essays instead of, or in addition to, quizzes and discussion. Possible topics would be: Did Joan of Arc receive a fair trial? or Is Tawney's account of the rise of capitalism acceptable? and similar questions demanding both knowledge and evaluation.

The three elementary courses lie in the areas of the humanities, the social sciences, and the physical and natural sciences. There are several parallel forms of each of the courses. The three areas named are the ones most frequently included in general education in all colleges because they are less technical than statistics, languages, or physics, and because they involve the consideration of questions of values.

To fit abstract physical science into a program of general education presents difficulties that have not been solved. The Harvard science courses in general education seem to be about science rather than ordinary courses in science. There is a course on the principles of physics, one on the evolution of physics, another on the patterns of research; and finally there is one on the influence of technology upon civilization, which should come very close to being a social study.

This kind of solution suggests that even technical subjects may be so taught that they become general. Mathematics, for example is often taught as pure technique but it need not be so treated. The history of mathematics has paralleled the history of civilization. Mathematics has influenced and been influenced by the general culture in which it has developed. Its applications range from the games and puzzles of childhood to the technology of industry and the investigation of nature and society. It is a gateway to profound philosophies and entrancing arts such as music and architecture. There have been those in all ages, including our own, who have believed that God must be a geometer, the Great Mathematician. On these lines the realms of value and general education are soon reached even if not fully occupied. Those who have traveled there sometimes try to describe for others what they have seen. The many recent books on mathematics for nonmathematicians are good examples of such efforts. But unless one has had some acquaintance with the subject, the result may resemble that of travel by guidebook without leaving the fireside. The report admits that general education on the Harvard Plan is not suitable for everyone, student and nonstudent alike. One of its virtues, it must be emphasized, is that it accompanies and is not separate from more detailed college work. This is a vital point to which reference was made on the preceding page. General education should be the opening phase of a lifelong adult education. It is not something to be taken up and finished in a semester.

For contrast we close this section with a paragraph upon a very different plan, one devised by the American Council on Education for the armed services of the United States, and called a Design for General Education. It describes problem-type courses in four areas, as follows: personal and community health, problems of social adjustment, marriage and family adjustment, and vocational orientation. We should never forget that, if they are to be functional, different plans are needed for different people. But these two examples, the Harvard Report and the American Council Design, may be taken to mark the limits at either end of the general education scale.

9. PROGRAMS OF GENERAL EDUCATION

Despite similarities, general education is more than the old liberal education without the old subjects. And the old subjects, the Greek and Latin classics in translation, may be included in substance along with any others that are not by nature specialized and technical. General education is analogous to the core idea in the high schools, and like the core it may be based upon a group of associated subjects or it may try to dispense with all subjects and may try to organize the work under problems.

A main purpose of general education is that of developing a body of common knowledge and understanding to draw people together in devotion to the public welfare. And there is implied an effort to develop college rather than university or specialized education. The movement may be traced from the period of World War I and became full-grown after world War II.

Attempts to define the trend have not been entirely satisfactory. A Columbia University committee declared that all studies which contribute to the art of living, as distinct from direct preparation for making a living, belong to general education. This distinction is certainly not new, but the implied separation of nonvocational from vocational studies would be hard to maintain and would be undesirable. The Harvard University committee held that general education is to prepare people to live as citizens, enjoying, maintaining, and promoting a common culture. The social emphasis of this statement supplements the preceding neutral definition. Both imply the supplementing of specialized and technical education.

Opposition to individualism had been building up for half a century. The introduction of the Hegelian philosophy by Harris is one piece of evidence. Hegel's conservative idealism derived its norms from the institutions and culture of society. Josiah Royce and other authors, such as Edward Caird, continued to support this trend. Arnold Tompkins (1849–1905), who was thoroughly Hegelian, had a loyal following among educators. Even John Dewey from individualistic Vermont, although he discarded his early Hegelianism, maintained a strong social emphasis. From where we stand today it appears that the elective system was the belated expression of a declining individualism.

The social trend has continued. Columbia University in 1919 established a required course in contemporary civilization; and to this beginning two other general courses in the humanities and in science were soon to be added. World War I had only recently ended and perhaps Columbia's measures were war-connected. This was certainly true of the proposal of a Columbia professor, John Erskine, who was moved by his experience in providing educational opportunities at Beaune, France, for American soldiers, and also by his observation of their educational deficiencies. He proposed a system of universal training for peace and war. His system was to be administered by the army and was to prepare men for national service, citizenship, and the art of living, as well as training for making a living. The scheme was pretentious and hardly sufficiently worked out. Few, also, would support Erskine's choice of the army as the educator of a free people. The way the army muffed its educational opportunities in the Civilian Conservation Corps will be told later. Erskine's proposal was immature, and judging from present trends certainly premature.

Erskine had another general education idea, education through "great books." He gave such a course at Columbia and the plan has been followed at St. John's College, Maryland, and elsewhere, including many adult education centers. Some prominent institutions employ the idea but limit the books to be read to a small number. To read books like Plato's *Republic,* Aristotle's *Politics,* or Locke's *Essay* at the rate of one a week results in general distraction rather than general education. A slower pace with the preparation of essays and sufficient discussion may provide one kind of general education.

At the University of Wisconsin a widely discussed Experimental College was in operation between the years 1927 and 1932. The plan was devised by Alexander Meiklejohn, at one time a controversial figure as president of Amherst College. The freshman year of the Experimental College was given over to a study of ancient Greek civilization in all its phases. The sophomores then used their results to compare the Greek with the present American civilization. Only men were enrolled in this college maintained in a coeducational university. They lived in collegiate style in a separate building reserved for them. The plan was expensive. These and other administrative features caused the university to end the experiment after five years.

The present Program of Integrated Studies at the University of Wisconsin was begun only in 1948. It provides courses in the humanities, social studies, natural science, and English composition. The students are not organized into a separate division but remain in the College of Letters and Science. After two years they will choose a major in that college or will transfer to another college of the university.

The University of Minnesota has two separate forms of general education. The General College, opened in 1932, is evidence that colleges and universities, like the high schools earlier, have become concerned about the large proportion of their students—half of those who enter—who do not graduate. At Minnesota the General College offers two years of broad cultural work to students with poor high school records. Those who reveal or develop ability are permitted to take at least one course outside the General College; and eventually those who are most capable, about 20 per cent, may secure a degree. The rest, if they persist, are given an Associate in Arts "degree" at the end of two years.

The General College at Minnesota has served more than one purpose. Other colleges of the University have been enabled to raise their standards, although the University admits all Minnesota high school graduates, as the state law requires. The rise in the standards of the other colleges has had the secondary effect that the General College students find it more difficult to qualify for transfers to the other colleges of the University. The General College has also given help upon a problem of public relations. Formerly numbers of students had to be dismissed during or at the end of the first year. Most of these are now given two years of work; and they can leave feeling that they have completed a program. Another outcome was the establishment about 1945 of a parallel plan, the second form mentioned above, at the same university.

The parallel plan is called the Department of General Studies. It is one of twenty-eight departments of the arts college. At first, students in the regular arts college looked with some disdain upon general education. But the broad, interpretative courses of the General College, the more gradual transition from the high school to the senior college, and the greater attention to the individual student created "an insistent demand that similar opportunities be made available" to those enrolled in the four-year colleges. The Department of General Studies provides these opportunities through courses in communication, family life, humanities, natural science, personal orientation, and social science. It will be understood that communication in this context means mainly the study of English. Several courses are offered in each field. Counselors help in the selections made by students.

The cases described above provide a fair survey of a few of the programs of general education. Although the movement is becoming popular, there are many problems. General education, for example, does not often include mathematics, languages, or the exact sciences, thus revealing a trend also found in the high school. Students with high ability and developed interests may consider general education courses as an interruption of their program. Lack of continuity in American curricula is sharply criticized by foreign observers. General education accentuates this lack. Students with diverse capacities and unequal preparation are put into broad general education courses which cover up these diversities. This may be a way of evading problems instead of solving them. With the introduction of general education courses, numerous administrative problems arise. The large university has to an accented degree the problems that trouble the comprehensive high school; and it has this additional one that high school pupils having begun to specialize are put back into general education when they enter the university.

10. Exchange of Students

In all ages students in pursuit of learning or adventure have traveled from university to university and country to country. Cicero and less famous young Romans studied in Greece; the wandering students of the earlier Middle Ages prepared for the nations or organized groups of students in the universities of a later period; in the Renaissance, all Europe wished to study in Italy and many did; but, with the growth of nationalist feeling, the crossing of frontiers became emotionally and politically more difficult. The Germans continued to circulate among the universities of their own lands, but the English student, once settled at Oxford or Cambridge, remained there.

In England the early Americans could obtain a more advanced education than their country or colony afforded, and this was most especially true of those in the South where schools were few and often poor. Several of those who studied abroad were noticed in Chapter IV. Some of those young Americans attended English public schools or one of the British universities or read law in the Middle Temple or studied in Roman Catholic schools in Belgium or France. But soon patriots, jealous for the success of their experiment in republican government, began to frown upon foreign study. They feared lest the young migrant should become, if not an expatriate, then, at any rate a lukewarm republican. Even in our own time the director of the Institute of International Education "decided that exchanges should be limited to students who had already secured their national education, that is, had their baccalaureate degree."

In the nineteenth century the German universities attracted foreigners, as Athens had once drawn the Romans to itself, or Florence, Padua, and Naples the eager youth from the North. In 1810 the national university, as one may say, of Berlin was opened and other German universities also developed an extraordinary enthusiasm for the advancement of learning. For a brief period it seemed also that Germany might become a democratic country. The doctor's degree from a German university soon became a mark of distinction for the young scholar returning to the United States. This migration continued for almost exactly a century and ended with World War I.

The German were not the only universities that attracted Americans in the nineteenth century. A few studied in Scotland, some in Vienna, and a number in France. Charles Astor Bristed, who wrote a once well-known book, *Five Years at an English University,* is proof that England was not entirely overlooked; but the English universities were expensive and the degrees which they conferred were no different in title, however superior they may have been in quality, from those which could be obtained at home. But many Americans turned to Oxford when the Rhodes scholarships were made available. And hundreds more studied not only in England but in many European countries after Congress in 1944 passed Public Law 584, the Fulbright Act. This provides funds for American students, scientists, and scholars working in foreign lands. A study by the Institute of International Education found that 9,000 students from the United States studied in foreign countries in 1954–1955.

The eastward flow of the student migration was complemented by another moving in the opposite direction, and in the school year of 1915–1916 there were almost 4,000 foreign students in the United States. At that time the largest numbers came from Asia and Europe. Both of these factors have now been changed by the war, the increased national prestige, and advances in American education. There are now more than 33,000 foreign students in the United States, and while more than half of them come from Canada, Latin America, the Near East, and the Islands of the Pacific Ocean, yet every quarter of the globe and a hundred countries are represented.

Upon the signing of the armistice in 1918, ending the fighting of World War I, the Carnegie Endowment for International Peace decided to organize an Institute of International Education. The first director was Professor Stephen P. Duggan (1870–1950), who served for thirty years. His annual reports and a book, *A Professor at Large* (1943), contain accounts of the work of the Institute in supplying information, counsel, and direct help to universities and to exchange students, both those who plan to go abroad and those who hope to come into the United States. International understanding and peace, as well as the dissemination of learning, were the objectives of the Institute under Duggan.

The securing of scholarships for exchange students was one means by which the Institute hoped to promote its aims. In the United States the scholarships for incoming students were supplied from university funds, but in Europe such money was supplied by government.

Early in its history the Institute rendered a special service to students fleeing from the Russian Revolution. A special fund was collected to place 600 of those fugitives in American universities, where they were able to complete their studies. Most of the money has been repaid and the recipients have become American citizens.

Between these "displaced" students from Russia and the ordinary foreign students there are many similarities and also great differences. The most important difference is that normally the students do not remain in America; after one or more years they return home carrying a report upon the treatment they received and the opportunities they enjoyed. They come in many cases to study engineering and other technical and professional subjects, but they do not come for formal education alone. They also want to see the United States and to experience its business, political, and domestic life. Often they come with impressions derived from moving pictures. It is important that they become acquainted with another America.

The distribution of the foreign students has much to do with the achievement of this goal. The 33,000 foreign students are distributed unevenly among 1,400 colleges, universities, and technical and vocational schools. Some of these have only a single foreign student, many have fifty or more, and twelve of the largest together have eight thousand or one-fourth of the whole number. The following table supplies the numbers of foreign students in the United States in certain selected years.

NUMBERS OF STUDENTS IN CERTAIN YEARS

Years	Numbers	Years	Numbers
1916	3,790	1948	19,934
1919	2,109	1950	27,717
1926	1,321	1952	30,844
1937	5,408	1953	33,796

Figures are derived from the *Friendly Ambassadors*.

Universities with large groups of foreign students supply counselors, and provide organizations and plans to welcome, house, and entertain the students and to introduce them to various features of American life. Where the numbers are small, these services are performed more informally, but not all the advantages are with the large institutions. In smaller schools the visitors are almost wholly absorbed in the life around them. In either case they may be made to feel welcome and may be invited to homes, games, meetings, and churches. There is even a national voluntary association, the Committee on Friendly Relations Among Foreign Students, which aids in laying the foundation for real friendship between the students and the American people. It publishes the annual, *Friendly Ambassadors*. The committee was founded by John R. Mott and others and its headquarters are in New York City. Many students need opportunity to improve in their use of English and this can be provided upon either a formal or, without cost, upon an informal basis. Many of the students are poor or at least their funds are limited and to help them to live comfortably at moderate cost is a great service.

Good will and helpfulness form the only solid base of international education. Both the educational and the humane and social aspects of the American residence of these "unofficial ambassadors" depend upon the spirit of their school and community. This is usually admirable but there have been exceptions. The chief criticism of America, and it is often harsh, comes from Asians, Africans, and Islanders, against whom the color bar has been raised. This results in international miseducation. Tolstoi said that "the most important thing in life is for man to unite with man, and the worst thing in life is for men to go apart from one another." For a half-century now, men have been driven apart by wars and hatreds. The exchange of students may do something and should be helped to do all it can do to draw mankind together in peaceful emulation.

The college in the United States offers liberal or general education, and the university is a complex institution with professional and vocational colleges built around the original liberal college. Some of the professional colleges require a bachelor's degree for admission. Universities developed in the last century and especially in the later decades, when the idea of specialization and research was introduced from Germany. State and national governments do little to regulate higher education, and this leaves a wide field for private and church initiative and helps to explain the wide variety and great number of institutions. Progress in higher education has often been made through surveys and reports, and one famous example is the Flexner Report in 1910 on medical education.

Coeducation and women's colleges also developed in the nineteenth century and the former was furthered by the state universities and land-grant colleges. The older schools had grown conservative and their alumni could not allow changes in alma mater. Affiliated colleges and separate colleges for women, and in the South even state colleges for women, were therefore established. Many of the old men's colleges and some of the state colleges for women are becoming coeducational. The "best" education for women, if there is a best one, has not been discovered; and this is a problem that exercises the minds of some educators.

The growth in numbers of students and the need for many kinds of preparation have caused higher education to come down from her ivory tower to the market place. Conservatives hold up their horrified white hands without avail. Courses multiply, courses are given in places remote from the campus, and universities maintain hospitals, experimental farms, and service departments. Summer schools are maintained by all but a few of the large institutions and by many small ones. Student activities and especially athletics have developed to gigantic proportions and various devices are employed to regulate participation.

Just this expansion has been the cause of sharp criticism of universities. Some of the critics seem to favor a return to the past. Others who may admit that there are excesses refuse to accept the past as a criterion for the present. Although all must learn from experience, this latter group insists that universities must deal with present problems. History proves that history alone is not a safe guide. For the present the view that universities and schools should build a new social order is no longer frequently expressed. At least the collectivist social order is not often praised; and one reason may be the assault upon freedom of teaching by legislative investigation. This is politics in education rather than the objective study of education.

There are many reasons for the renewed emphasis upon general education. Some of these are the need for a broader and sounder base for specialization; the desire to provide a greater measure of education common to all students; the effort to stress values and ideals; and the purpose to relieve the overproduction of narrow specialists. England has always placed great emphasis upon general education and may have influenced the new American emphasis which has increased since World War I. The Harvard Report outlines one type of general education but there are many others.

The thousands of students who come to the United States from other parts of the world may be taken as evidence that American universities have won widespread approval. And it is to be noted that many come to study medicine, public health, library administration, agriculture, engineering, and other vocational and technical fields. But they come also because the obstructions and destruction of war have reduced European opportunity, and because they want to see America. Whatever the reason for their coming, American colleges and universities welcome them.

QUESTIONS

1. After examining appropriate yearbooks and guides to gain a view of the many types of colleges and universities in the United States, consider the question: Why does the United States have so many and so great a variety of these institutions in comparison with France or any other selected country?

2. Why, in your opinion, has coeducation been more widely followed in the United States than elsewhere? Look up de Tocqueville for one possible lead on this question.

3. How does the university in its evolution resemble the development of the high school and how do they differ? Is it true that elementary, secondary, and higher schools are developing the same social outlook and comparable purposes?

4. Compare the educational theories implied in the Rhodes scholarships and the research fellowships awarded by the Du Pont Company.

5. Why is it difficult for people to come to universally acceptable conclusions about education, and especially difficult with respect to higher education?

6. What are the chief contributions made by higher education in America?

7. Does the large number of foreigners studying in America prove the excellence of American colleges and universities?

BOOKS AND PAPERS

For current ideas and changes the *Journal of Higher Education,* the *Bulletin* of the American Association of University Professors, *School and Society,* and the Conference *Proceedings* of the Association for Higher Education, NEA, are useful. There are many books on higher education and many histories of individual colleges, but no good general history of higher education in the United States. Of those mentioned below, Thwing devotes too much of his space to the colonial period, and Earnest too much of his to the Ivy League colleges. Wills has prepared a useful outline but it is only that. There is nothing like the work of Paulsen on the German or that of D'Irsay on the French universities.

Boas, Louise S., *Woman's Education Begins,* Norton, Massachusetts, Wheaton College Press, 1935.

Butts, R. Freeman, *The College Charts Its Course,* New York, 1939.

Cole, A. C., *A Hundred Years of Mount Holyoke College,* Yale University Press, 1940.

Duggan, S. P., *Professor at Large,* New York, 1943.

Earnest, Ernest, *Academic Procession, An Informal History of the American College, 1636–1953,* Indianapolis, 1953.

Erskine, John, *My Life as a Teacher,* Philadelphia, 1948.

Flexner, Abraham, *Universities, American, English, German,* Oxford University Press, 1930.

Folwell, W. W., *University Addresses,* Minneapolis, 1909. In this address, President Folwell's inaugural delivered in 1869, the state university is ranked as the highest of the public schools.

Hart, A. B., "New Attack on American Universities," *Current History,* February, 1931.

Havemann, Ernest, and Patricia Salter West, *They Went to College, The College Graduate of Today,* New York, 1952.

Jones, E. S., *Comprehensive Examinations,* New York, 1933.

Kirkpatrick, J. E., *The American College and Its Rulers,* New York, 1926.

Knight, E. W., *Fifty Years of American Education,* New York, 1952.

Kotschnig, Walter, *Unemployment in the Learned Professions,* London, 1937.

Morison, S. E., *Founding of Harvard College,* Harvard University Press, 1935; *Harvard College in the Seventeenth Century, ibid.,* 1936; and Editor, *Development of Harvard University, 1869–1929, ibid.,* 1930.

Norton-Taylor, Duncan, "The Business Schools: Pass or Flunk?" *Fortune,* June, 1954.

Sinclair, Upton, *The Goose-Step,* Pasadena, California, 1923.

Stickler, W. H., Editor, *Organization and Administration of General Education,* Dubuque, Iowa, 1951.

Tappan, H. P., *University Education,* New York, 1851.

Thwing, C. H., *History of Higher Education in America,* New York, 1906; *The American and German University,* New York, 1928.

Wechsler, James, *Revolt on the Campus,* New York, 1935.

Wills, E. V., *Growth of American Higher Education,* Philadelphia, 1936.

Chapter XVII

EDUCATION IN ADVERSITY

T
WO world wars and a deep and prolonged economic depression
have severely shaken and tested civilization within the experience
of many men who are still active. The United States did not enter
World War I until a stalemate or an Allied defeat seemed likely.
Many Americans for a time favored the cause of Germany; and a vast
propaganda effort was undertaken to unify the people on the side of the
Allies. All institutions including the schools were drawn into this effort.
The teaching of German was almost completely discontinued. After the
wars, loyalty and Americanism laws were passed and in the administration
of these the schools were again involved.

Measures to aid the youth who were unemployed and out of school
were taken in the depression. The Civilian Conservation Corps was the
most unusual and, for those who were reached, the most effective measure.
Partly because of the recent introduction of the junior high school and also
because of the phenomenal increase in enrollment, there were several extensive studies of the secondary schools. After World War II great interest
was aroused in international education and in a new agency of this interest,
namely, UNESCO. These are the topics of this chapter.

1. WARTIME PROPAGANDA

In war, men are conscripted for the military services, steel and labor
are allocated, food is rationed, and marginal land is ploughed up to grow
more wheat. Older children leave school for work, attendance declines,
school supplies are hard to get, terms are shortened, and some schools may
be closed. School improvements painstakingly developed are dropped.
Classes and school services are reduced or abolished. Men leave the classrooms for war work or the battlefield. Standards of teacher preparation have
to be lowered because men and women can earn high wages in war industries. Later it may become evident that not all of these acts and incidents
were either necessary or wise. One of the mistakes of the United States in

the world wars was the drafting of advanced students who were on the way to become the scientists, engineers, professional leaders of the future. The mistake was partly corrected in regard to physicians-in-training in World War II and further adjustments were made in the Korean conflict.

In 1917 the German language was the first educational casualty of the war. The United States entered the conflict just when the final examinations were beginning to loom on the school horizon. And as if by prearrangement, the pupils of some of the schools made a bonfire of their German textbooks in the schoolyard; and almost everywhere the study was abruptly dropped. German had been the favored modern language but it has never recovered from the setback which it received in World War I.

Although the children were impulsive, their parents should have known that to understand the language and mind of an enemy may be as necessary as communication with a friend; and that the works of Luther and Goethe still held their former values. The American claim that the war was not directed against the German people but only against the Kaiser and his aggressive government also made the dropping of German studies quite illogical. And the whole action was, in fact, an emotional outburst rather than a reasoned decision. World War II was to deliver another severe blow against the study of German.

Education was affected by the divisions which existed in the country in 1917. President Wilson had only a narrow margin in the Electoral College in 1916, although his popular majority was substantial. A leading argument of his supporters was that he had kept the nation out of war. It was not then known that he had already carried on negotiations that were liable to result in war. Six months after the election, war was declared.

Many people, especially in the Middle West, were opposed to the declaration. Senator LaFollette asserted that in a referendum the vote would have been ten to one against American participation, and he cited the espionage laws, conscription, and other war measures as "complete proof" that Congress knew that the war was unpopular. In these extreme statements there was considerable truth. The Eastern seacoast was war-minded, but the Middle West was not.

It was this division of sentiment which raised the mob spirit of World War I. Families with German names, the so-called "hyphenated Americans," and those who would not buy enough Liberty Bonds to satisfy their vigilante neighbors, were persecuted. Towns and even religious denominations changed their names if they carried any hint of past connection with the enemy people. Even a suspicion of sympathy for Germany was sufficient to draw hostile attention and many secret and illegal attacks were made

upon those believed to be pro-German. There had been enemy agents in
the country and the German Bund had been active before the war. But
the fear that the large population of German descent, estimated at one in
every eight Americans, might resort to violence against the war and the
draft was groundless. If there were saboteurs, there was little sabotage.
There were peace meetings and protests against the war by a farm group in
the Dakotas; and the Industrial Workers of the World were active in the
Northwest; but these were radical associations not mainly composed of
Germans.

In the drive for unity a national Committee of Public Information was
formed, with a journalist, George Creel, as its head. A professor of history
and university administrator, Guy Stanton Ford, was called to serve under
him. The committee would have preferred not to enter the schools at all
but the pressure to have the children thoroughly indoctrinated became ir-
resistible. Business and political organizations, patriotic societies, and the
army were united in this demand. Patriotic speeches by Junior Four Minute
Men, patriotic poems, songs, and flag ceremonies, became prominent parts
of the school program.

Certainly schools should both exemplify and teach love of country.
Children should be patriotic; and if the parents are patriotic there is no
problem. But the furor in 1917–1918 was due to the fear that many parents
were not sufficiently war-minded. The record shows that much of the propaganda was false. But the schools had to yield to the public demand and the
school work was interrupted. In 1950 conditions were reversed when critics
asserted that the schools were giving too much attention to public questions
and neglecting the three R's.

Some educators and some historians were not thrown completely off
balance. In such cases their stand required courage. Charles H. Judd, John
Dewey, and others were critical of the uncritical sentiment that was aroused
in children. The National Education Association passed resolutions favoring the development of "world citizenship" that at a later time would have
called out the charge of "Communism." The Bureau of Education and the
commissioner, P. P. Claxton, worked to prevent use of the schools for war
purposes instead of the education of children.

The change in American opinion of Germany placed some historians
in a false position. One author of a textbook had used a picture of the
Kaiser's family. Another had written of the spread of Christianity among
the Germans, but to many this now seemed questionable or, at best, it was
an unwelcome statement. Other textbook writers had criticized the British
who, after having been fair game since the Stamp Act, were present allies,

helping to guard the sea lanes used by American troopships. More than one scholar changed his text to comply with current prejudices. After World War II other prejudices slipped into the places of these.

The war which began in September, 1914, continued for three and one-half years before the United States entered the conflict. During that time America served as the granary of the combatants. But a critical food problem arose when the army was expanded to 4,000,000 men. The state colleges and the Departments of Agriculture and of Labor worked to enlist school youth for farm work. A few were given preparatory training at state colleges, but most began working without previous knowledge or experience. The program was continued, and in 1918 a quarter-million workers were reported in the United States Boys' Working Reserve.

Where this program was in effect, schoolwork naturally suffered. Schools closed early in the spring and opened late in the autumn. As usual in such cases, it was claimed that farm work had educational value. It no doubt had the moral value of all honest work performed in the public interest. But to give credit in algebra or Spanish for pulling weeds or cutting corn, as was actually done, had no better justification than that others were also doing it. Many states placed limitations on such credits.

War gardens to be worked evenings and Saturdays by school children formed a second phase of the food-raising effort. There was fortunately no question of school credits or shortened terms. The school garden movement had started about 1890. At that time it was to serve educational purposes; but the war gardens were to produce beans and potatoes; and they did. President Wilson spoke in favor of the effort, and it was reported that 1,500-000 children participated. A national director of the United States School Garden Army was appointed. The departments of home economics of the state colleges gave help in conserving the very substantial harvests.

Two professors of the University of Chicago, C. H. Judd and Leon C. Marshall, wrote a series of *Lessons on Community and National Life*. The publication was prepared for the National Food Administration. Professor Judd took the opportunity to assert a principle that would apply also to the next topic, military training in school. The principle is that schools are misused when they are required to serve any end other than the education of children. This was intended as a criticism of war propaganda and activity in school and could also be applied to school military training.

Military training in schools, although not widely practiced, had been fostered long before by Alden Partridge; private military academies were in operation; and some public high schools maintained a voluntary cadet corps. It has been estimated that there were only a few thousand cadets in schools when the war broke out. The preparedness agitation with strong urging by the War Department increased the number to 100,000 in 1918. The National Defense Act of 1916 had provided for a Junior Reserve Officers' Training Corps in high schools; but the regular army officers assigned to train the units were withdrawn when the country entered the war. Some cities and state legislatures encouraged military drill in schools, and New York made it compulsory for boys aged sixteen. In 1919 New York substituted physical education for drill. With the return of peace the interest in military training in secondary schools declined and World War II did not greatly revive it.

School people and especially the directors of physical education have usually been critical of the claim that military drill provides good physical and health education or a discipline appropriate to civilian life. The American Physical Education Association favored athletics, the activities of the Boy Scouts, Girl Scouts, Camp Fire Girls, and similar organizations, but "strongly disapproved" of military drill. The National Education Association called for physical education and opposed military drill in schools.

Within three years after the armistice, half of the states adopted compulsory physical education laws. Behind these remarkable actions there was a remarkable reason. It had been revealed that one-third of the army recruits suffered from physical defects that temporarily or permanently unfitted them for military service. Physical and health education was to prevent many of these disabilities and to teach athletics and recreational skills suitable for the maintenance of health. The efforts were not highly successful. Qualified teachers of physical education were not always available. Public interest declined. The recruits of 1941 had almost as many physical defects as those of 1917.

The United States was in World War I for only nineteen months, but the farms and factories had actually become engaged much earlier and by 1918 a serious shortage of teachers had developed. Four million men were in the army and millions of women were working in factories at jobs that were much easier and paid much better than teaching. Newspapers described a grave situation: discontinued or overcrowded schools in different parts of the country; in New York City 800 classrooms without teachers and the pupils swelling the numbers in other classes; in New England only one-half or fewer of the high school teachers who had served in the spring of 1918 returning to their schools in the autumn. When thousands of teachers were leaving the schools, the press declared that "the public know the reasons perfectly well, namely low salaries, uncertain tenure, and arbitrary administration." This was not a complete analysis. The shortage continued for years and emergency certificates were granted to many who could not meet state requirements. The period after World War II was to see an even worse decline in teaching standards and in school buildings.

The colleges suffered the most complete disorganization in World War I. Colleges for men almost ceased to exist in their usual state. The ill-planned Student Army Training Corps was introduced in the autmun of 1918 to save higher education, but would have injured it almost irreparably if the war had continued. The colleges were turned into armed camps and professors had to carry passes and to take orders from students in uniform. Entrance requirements were reduced and classes were interrupted or can-celed for drill. The severe influenza epidemic also interfered with the suc-cess of the program. The government, however, paid for the use of private property and its money helped colleges over the financial difficulty caused by the loss of student fees. In the official report on SATC, recommendations were made for the collegiate Reserve Officers' Training Corps, which had been started in 1916 but given up for the SATC, and which was now to be permanently established.

World War II affected the high schools in several ways. In the first two years of American participation the enrollment declined by 17 per cent. Many pupils were close to the draft age and others were at or above the employment age. Some enlisted, some engaged in war work, and many who remained were disturbed in mind and unable to concentrate upon their work.

The war also reflected the state of education in high school. The flight from academic and liberal studies which has been described in Chapter XIV was increased by the war. Examinations by the armed services produced results that at least confirmed earlier reports. Two-thirds of the college freshmen in a large number of colleges failed the arithmetic test for admis-sion to the Naval Reserve Officers' Training Corps; and most of the failures were not "near misses," but were far below the passing mark. Only one-fourth of these 4,000 freshmen had taken more than one and one-half years of high school mathematics, and only 400 or 10 per cent had studied trigo-nometry. The best marks in arithmetic in the whole United States were made by students from Troy, Brooklyn, and Buffalo, New York, all school systems under the often-maligned Regents.

To promote the active participation of youth in community war work and to prepare them for induction after graduation, a Victory Corps was set up (1942) in the high schools. The Corps provided a plan to be followed in high schools. All pupils could join. The plan emphasized physical fitness and vocational studies and activities which had a bearing upon the war.

Increased attention was given also to mathematics, science, and English. Social studies were broadened to include the study of foreign countries and areas and thus called attention to the meaning of the struggle to the world as a whole.

The war called attention to many particular weaknesses in secondary education. Some of these have been indicated above. The lack of an accepted philosophy of secondary education was cited by Thomas H. Briggs as a major flaw. The failure to teach languages, mathematics, and sciences effectively and even to maintain enrollments in these courses was another. A third was the failure to realize the American dream of universal secondary education. One-third of the American youth did not enter the high school; and of those who came, only half remained to graduate. It was these latter facts that led to the movement for life adjustment education.

In World War II the armed services profited, although too slowly, from some of the mistakes of 1918. They gradually instituted plans of deferment for college students who were preparing themselves in fields that served the national health and safety. A formula was also worked out which permitted draft boards to grant occupational deferment. Even so, many serious shortages of scientific and technical man power developed. The services in this war also used the specialists on the faculties and the facilities of the universities in training programs. In a global war men who were fluent in Russian, Chinese, Japanese, and other languages were needed. The armed services introduced foreign language classes which worked all day and every day under native speakers together with experts in language analysis. The remarkable success of these classes was due to intensive work and to powerful motivation guided by proper techniques. No lives are wagered upon the success of high school language classes and this is one reason why they are less successful.

Many other defense programs were conducted in the universities. Geographers, meteorologists, and many kinds of engineers taught recruits or rendered direct help to the military forces. The Office of Strategic Services was staffed by men from the universities. Many faculty men also left the campus for work in the armed services or in civilian jobs with the government.

College attendance declined rapidly after the attack on Pearl Harbor on December 7, 1941. Men enlisted or were called into service and both men and women engaged in war industry. Classes dwindled to half or a smaller fraction of their former numbers. Many girls, however, remained and some men's colleges became coeducational in the early years of the war. Colleges that were accepted for one of the specialized training programs profited in their enrollments. Otherwise, the men who remained were 4F's, boys below the draft age, and a few veterans who had been discharged because of wounds or shock. There were also a few hardy souls who were deferred because they were engaged in vital war work and who found time to take college work in addition. All of these together left some colleges, especially the small liberal arts schools, with sharply reduced enrollments and in financial difficulties.

As the end of World War II came into view, the army and navy began to eliminate their specialized training programs. The colleges already in a critical state were hardly in condition to survive a further cut in income. A resolution in the House of Representatives on June 21, 1944, proposed a study of "means by which such effects might be alleviated." That summer, partly to help the colleges but more to help the veterans make up the losses from their interrupted education, Congress passed the GI bill. The happy results which flowed from this legislation were mentioned in the preceding chapter. And we have also noticed the impetus given by the war to general education.

2. WARTIME LEGISLATION

Teachers' loyalty oaths, efforts to enforce "Americanism," to "purify" history textbooks, and to enact laws against the teaching of evolution were among the unsavory products of the propaganda kitchens during and following World War I. Popular passion if balked in one effort will find other victims even though they are innocent. Among the scapegoats in these cases were textbooks writers, teachers, immigrants who had not learned to speak English, and the foreign language press.

In the 1920's some of the censors mentioned above transferred their attention from European to American history texts. They wanted no "nonsense" about the American Revolution, no halting between two opinions, no blemish on any of the heroes. One bill in New York provided that no textbook "shall be used which ignores, omits, discounts, or in any manner belittles, ridicules, distorts, questions, or decries the events leading up to the Declaration of Independence or the American Revolution." Any city using a book in which any of these errors occurred was to be deprived forthwith of all public school support. A New Jersey bill used similar language. Fortunately, neither became law. As the war fever declined, the attacks upon schoolbooks also gradually declined, but from time to time they flared up again. Many of the critics quote sentences out of context, fail to distinguish between liberals, socialists, and Communists, and show ignorance not only of elementary facts but also of the elementary purposes of education.

The emotions of suspicion and fear spread to the supporters and trustees of universities. A banker on the board of Columbia University lamented that it was "very difficult to discharge professors once employed. They make common cause and," he politely added, "howl about academic freedom." Columbia did discharge a number including J. McKeen Cattell who sued and won a judgment of $45,000 for breach of contract. The necessity for academic freedom is not always understood. It is necessary for the integrity of the university and the protection of the public, not primarily of the professors. The American Association of University Professors, founded in 1914, has developed a procedure that has reduced the number of summary dismissals. It has not eliminated them.

Teachers' loyalty oaths had been almost unknown before 1917 but in the next two decades at least twenty states enacted laws demanding them. Half of these states were in the East, but included among the number were Colorado, Texas, Arizona, California, Oregon, and Washington. In some states such laws were passed, repealed, and passed a second time, showing that the public mind was not firmly made up.

The Lusk laws of New York form an example of such vacillation. There were six of them in one package introduced into the state legislature in 1920. Their purpose was to combat a fairly confused set of evil spirits including anarchism and communism but especially socialism, of which there was a trace in New York. Two of the bills had to do with education. One required teachers to pass a loyalty test and the other prohibited all schools not licensed by the Regents. The bills were passed but Governor Alfred E. Smith vetoed them. In the next session they were again adopted and signed by Governor Miller. When Governor Smith returned to Albany for a second term, he called for the repeal of the laws. He said a loyalty test for teachers is wrong in principle, a violation of the spirit of the state constitution and laws, and an unwarranted interference with freedom of opinion. He said the state had enough laws on the licensing and supervising of private schools. The Lusk laws were repealed.

Meanwhile, prominent citizens, including many educators, had pleaded and argued for freedom. The Regents and the commissioner, Frank P. Graves, were reported against the bills from the first. The Teachers' Union was also opposed. Among the educators who were members of the citizens' committee for repeal were Felix Adler, William C. Bagley, Thomas H. Briggs, Morris R. Cohen, John Dewey, and Edward L. Thorndike. They declared that the state could not expect to have intelligent teachers under "conditions of possible terrorism." This phrase was justified by the vague language of the law. Vagueness is, indeed, a frequent characteristic of loyalty legislation; and it gives the demagogue the means to threaten and even to convict innocent persons. The laws were repealed; but in 1934, New York after all decided to have a teachers' oath law, the Ives law, which demanded simply subscription to the constitutions of the state and nation.

New loyalty laws were passed in the great depression and others were adopted as a result of World War II. One widely reprehended law was enacted in 1935 by the Congress of the United States, but it was the administration of the law rather than its text that provoked the sharpest criticism. The law merely said that in the District of Columbia no person "teaching or advocating Communism" should be paid out of federal funds. The school authorities, thereupon, required each teacher every month to take an oath that he had not taught or advocated Communism during the preceding thirty days. This was loyalty on the instalment plan. Newsmen rather than teachers considered the procedure amusing. The law was repealed in 1937.

Laws to Americanize the recent immigrants were sometimes connected with teachers' loyalty laws. Like these, they were intended to repress German Kultur and communism and to promote national unity. The teaching of English and the prohibition of modern foreign languages, particularly German, were chosen as means. Between 1917 and 1921, thirty-one states passed laws that contained one or more of the following propositions: all schools to be conducted in English, certainly a salutary proposal; no German to be taught in public elementary or, in some states, in any elementary schools; no modern foreign languages to be taught in one or either type of elementary schools. After 1921 still other states joined the group.

This type of legislation provoked immediate opposition. Attempts to have the laws declared unconstitutional by state courts met with no success. In 1923 the matter was adjudicated in *Meyer v. Nebraska,* 262 U.S. 390. The Supreme Court held that the Nebraska law, and by extension similar laws, invaded the liberty guaranteed by the Fourteenth Amendment. Mere knowledge of German, the Court said, is not harmful and the right to teach that language is "within the liberty of the Amendment."

An Oregon law of 1922 which was intended to suppress all private elementary schools had been urged by the revived Ku Klux Klan. That body had been relatively inactive until the close of World War I when, within a few years, it gained a reported 4,000,000 members. It was not a fraternal society, as some, perhaps honestly, claimed. Rather it was a conspiracy held together by racial and religious hatreds or in some cases by prejudices merely. Hooded bands threatened, flogged, and even murdered their victims. In less violent but evil ways the Klan interfered in school and college affairs, secured the dismissal of teachers, and in Oregon urged the passage of a law against private, including Catholic, elementary schools. After high officials of the Klan were convicted of heinous crimes, many decent citizens dropped out and by 1930 the organization had largely disintegrated; but there again were some local revivals after World War II, especially in the South.

The Oregon school law of 1922, which the Klan had supported, provided that all children between the ages of eight and sixteen years had to attend the public schools whenever these were in session. The effect would have been to close all private elementary and junior high schools in the state. The Supreme Court in 1925, referring to *Meyer* v. *Nebraska* (1923), declared that "the Act of 1922 unreasonably interferes with the liberty of parents and guardians to direct the upbringing and education of children under their control. . . . The child is not the mere creature of the State. . . ."

The decision in the so-called Oregon case, 268 U.S. 510, denied the right of the states to prohibit, although they might inspect and reasonably regulate, private schools. The famous liberal, Justice Oliver Wendell Holmes, dissented from the majority decisions in both of the cases reviewed here. He believed that in a democracy all children should be educated in public schools, and that the Constitution does not deny the right of a state to order this. It appears that he considered a public school system essential to the republican form of state government which the Constitution guarantees. Heretofore, it should be observed, only autocracies like Nazi Germany and Communist Russia have found it necessary to prohibit private schools.

3. THE GREAT DEPRESSION

Two contrasting periods of prosperity and depression span the twenty years between two world wars. The financial crash of 1929 divides the time into two nearly equal parts. Prosperity was promoted by the automobile business, road building, the electrical and radio industries, and a building boom that created new suburbs and changed the sky line of great cities. The development was not spread evenly. Agriculture, coal, textiles, and some other businesses were less prosperous. Labor and "the little man" did not gain the increased purchasing power needed to maintain the expanded production. High-pressure selling, excessive instalment buying, uninhibited stock speculation, loose banking practices, and market manipulation brought on the crisis. The depression spread over the world because Europe was also in an unhealthy economic condition.

Earlier crises, because they were shorter and less general, had not so seriously hurt the schools. This one was deep and continued so long that it is properly called the depression of the 1930's. A Citizens' Conference on the Crisis in Education was called by President Hoover in January, 1933. One of its resolutions urged the states to reorganize their school districts into larger units that would be sound both economically and educationally. Partly as a result of further investigation by the Office of Education of ten state systems, some reorganizations were effected but not nearly enough. These efforts did not go far in solving depression problems, but the depression called attention to an administrative problem. The solution may come in time as it has in England under the comprehensive education law of 1944.

Each of the early depression years saw a further decline in school efficiency. The chairman of a national commission on the emergency, Professor John K. Norton, of Columbia University, declared in 1935 that the three years immediately preceding had been the most disastrous in educational history. He said the educational opportunities of millions of children had been impaired or denied. Easy solutions there were none, but the commission favored resort to state and federal support instead of the prevalent local and property taxes. Large and well-knit teachers' associations with means to reach the public were needed, it was thought, to counteract the propaganda of selfish interests and the negations and despair of the fainthearted. Unfortunately, the national organizations which were concerned to keep down taxes had many more propaganda dollars than the teachers.

Nearly 5,000 rural schools, it was reported, closed early in 1932 and some had not opened at all. The following year there was an increase of 400,000 pupils in elementary and high schools. To have kept the prevailing teacher-pupil ratio would have required the employment of at least 14,000 new teachers. But there was instead a decrease of about 14,000 teachers from the number previously employed, and therefore a shortage of about 28,000 as compared with the year before.

Teachers' salaries were reduced everywhere and by as much as 25 to 50 per cent. Many were paid in scrip and since teachers have to live from day to day, the scrip was usually cashed at a discount. This amounted to a further cut in salary. Many teachers were unpaid or were paid in part only. Chicago in 1934 obtained a loan of $22,000,000 from the Reconstruction Finance Corporation to pay back salaries; and for the first time in more than three years the teachers of Chicago were paid in full. Three years later the board was again without funds. The case of the second largest city was not unique.

Classrooms were also lacking in many places. Attendance was growing in all sections but there was little construction of new facilities. Many children were housed in buildings that had been condemned as unsafe. Others were put on double-shift schedules.

Cities shortened their school terms and curtailed or abolished many services including night schools, kindergartens, classes for the handicapped, physical education, music supervision, and even home economics and shop-work. Boards of education consoled the public with the hope that the services would soon be restored when the awaited business upturn brought in more revenue. Whether the cuts were made at the right points is a separate question.

4. Youth-Saving Measures

At the beginning of the New Deal, before the new administration had been in office quite a month, Congress authorized a program of emergency conservation work, otherwise called the Unemployment Relief Act of March, 1933. The Civilian Conservation Corps, with 2,600 camps at the peak of its development, was part of this program. The Corps seems to have been the President's own idea, having grown out of his interest in reforestation and land utilization. Suggestions by Louis Howe and Frances Perkins were incorporated; and in the interest of dispatch the latter proposed to put the army in command because it had available tents, cots, blankets, dishes, and cooking facilities. She admitted in the *New Republic,* (June 21, 1954) that this was "a desperate suggestion."

Young men who were in need joined the Corps voluntarily and maintained it at full strength, about 300,000 by filling vacancies as they opened. They enrolled for a six-months' period and were permitted to re-enroll if the need continued. The War Department, aided by other executive branches, was placed in charge of the construction and maintenance of the camps, of the feeding of the men, and of the discipline. The men were well fed and gained in weight and health. But it was mistakenly thought that they would be "tough guys" requiring military discipline.

An incident that is revealing in regard to this evaluation of character has been reported in *The Secret Diary of Harold L. Ickes* (I, 547). After the camps had been in operation almost three years, the question of the compulsory fingerprinting of the enrollees was brought up at a Cabinet meeting. Most of the boys had not taken advantage of the opportunity to be fingerprinted of their own free will, which Ickes facetiously calls "strange" conduct; and he added that the general director of the camps "wants compulsory fingerprinting and so does the Secretary of War and the Department of Justice. The rest of the Cabinet and the President were opposed"; and the matter ended there.

The object of the Corps was to relieve distress by providing jobless and destitute men, aged from eighteen to twenty-five years, with work in improving the national forests and parks and thus promoting both the rehabilitation of men and the conservation of resources. Foresters directed the work of planting trees, removing fire hazards, reducing erosion, and laying out and building paths and roads. The men worked forty hours a week and received in addition to maintenance a small stipend for themselves and their families.

The work was of national importance and was well performed; but the education of the men was to a degree a missed opportunity, and was in fact an afterthought. There were no educational advisers at the camps during the first nine months of operation. And according to Secretary Ickes, when they were added this step was taken "in spite of the Army." It is recorded that the educational advisers in some camps felt that the army officers were opposed to their work. Also, as in other cases when the government has engaged in education, it largely by-passed its own Office of Education. The Commissioner was allowed to appoint the educational advisers but they served under the War Department.

The general director, appointed by the President, was a labor organizer, not a forester. He banned from the camps a pamphlet that contained ideas on labor and industry which he disapproved. The Association of American University Professors protested the ban. But it must be remembered that every phase of the New Deal was under constant criticism by one or another faction of either party. Like other New Deal installations, the plans for the Corps were drafted hurriedly on the theory that the depression would quickly yield to the measures taken. In the short run, education was not considered important.

Under difficult conditions the educational program was gradually expanded. George F. Zook, United States Commissioner of Education, had a better idea of the need than the War Department. He pointed out the opportunity to teach botany and zoology, forestry, surveying, English, and citizenship. Many of the men had had little schooling; others were ready for college and but for the depression would have been in attendance. The courses named by Zook together with certain semivocational ones became popular when introduced.

The classes were relegated to evening and other spare hours when the men were often fatigued. Books were usually scarce or lacking. Some camps had no assembly hall or any good classrooms. One camp in southern Michigan was described by Henry S. Curtis, well-known educator. In 1935 he found that on rainy days the men of this camp had to stay in their bunkhouses. There was no recreational organization. Only one room was set apart as a classroom and it had three tables and ten chairs. Classes met wherever room could be found.

Even under these conditions 60 per cent of the men were enrolled in classes and 50 per cent attended. Perhaps it would be agreed that the camps provided real relief to the men, gave them good food, a wholesome environment, and useful work which they respected and the doing of which gave them self-respect and confidence; but that the educational program was not as good as the work and relief programs.

Outside the camps many kinds of opinions were expressed. Some thought the Corps was a good start for a national system of adult education. Others, perhaps influenced by the theory of William James that "a moral equivalent of war" was needed, thought of the work as a desirable form of national service. This implied that it should be made universal and permanent. On the other hand, Mrs. Agnes E. Meyer, well-known liberal connected with the *Washington Post,* feared just this, that the CCC and similar New Deal agencies might become permanent. She feared it because she thought students and teachers kept on a dole would certainly be regimented. Many condemned the Corps solely on the ground that it was an expensive part of the New Deal. The figures will no longer seem as large as they appeared to be in the depression.

Relief needs declined after the war broke out and the CCC was abolished in 1942. About 2,500,000 young men, or really boys, since most of them were under nineteen, had been furnished work, food, shelter, and some education. The total cost was short of three billion dollars and the value of the work accomplished has been estimated at half of that amount. In addition to its direct benefits the experiment has lessons on conservation and on vocational and adult education that may prove valuable in prosperity as well as in adversity.

The National Youth Administration was a relief agency set up in 1935 under the Works Progress Administration to aid young people of either sex living not in camp but at their homes. To enable young people to stay in school was one of its purposes and it helped millions to do so. The depression was one of the causes of a rapid increase in high school enrollment at that time. And after leaving school it was the young men who felt the deepest discouragement. The numbers of those who could not find employment were far beyond the capacity of the CCC, which was at times unable to accept more than two out of five applicants. The depression was hard upon parents but often harder upon the young; and there were so many of them. One-third of all the unemployed were under the age of twenty-four years. The depression raised in them the soul-destroying feeling that they were not wanted.

The program of student relief was begun by the Federal Emergency Relief Administration, one of the early New Deal agencies. This program was given over to the newly organized National Youth Administration. Together the two administrations gave work relief to more than 1,000,000 young people in school and college. There were three requirements for receiving NYA aid: that the student could not remain in school without financial help; that he must be certified as a person of good character; and that he must have good academic ability. The amount that could be earned was at first limited to fifteen dollars a month. The work might be clerical, bibliographical, research, or other, at the discretion of the instructor in charge.

The NYA aided 125,000 college students in 1936–1937 out of a total enrollment of 1,500,000. But the amount paid to the individual was so small that only those who were almost able to finance themselves could take advantage of the plan. Those who needed help most could not maintain themselves in school with what could be earned.

The plan was not always carried out in good faith. Some of the work was "made-work." Some students interpreted "ability to remain in college" to cover ability to pay sorority or fraternity dues. Some of the work to be done required specialized preparation, such as ability to read Spanish or to give psychological tests, and care was not always taken to make reasonable assignments. Some colleges refused NYA money because acceptance "might be taken to mean approval of New Deal extravagance." A group of professional educators called NYA "just another propaganda mill for the New Deal"; and they added, with reason, that it should have been administered through the Office of Education and the several state departments of education. This has come to be a frequent criticism of several of the educational activities of the federal government. Naturally there was also the argument that there were "too many young people in college anyway" and the fear that the NYA was a step toward federal control of higher education. The NYA, like the CCC, was closed in 1942. A full history with documents of these institutions should be prepared for the guidance of the future.

Other emergency legislation provided funds for school and college buildings and extended relief with employment to teachers, musicians, writers, and artists who had lost their positions. The government, for a short time only, paid for the maintenance of nursery schools, kindergartens, and a variety of adult education classes. Workers' education, vocational education, citizenship classes, the Federal Writers' Project which produced the series of illustrated state travel guides, WPA orchestras, and murals in public buildings are other examples of the effort to help cultural workers through the depression.

5. REPORTS ON SECONDARY SCHOOLS

A National Survey of Secondary Education was authorized by Congress in 1929. The findings were published by the Office of Education in twenty-eight monographs including a summary in *Bulletin, Number 17,* for 1932. This was a comprehensive study but it dealt especially with vocational education, school size, guidance, homogeneous grouping, and the then recent development of the junior high schools.

Secondary education was deeply affected by the depression. Because there were fewer jobs, many young people who would have preferred to work remained in school. The codes of the National Recovery Administration in 1933 set a minimum employment age of sixteen years or higher in some instances. When NRA was declared unconstitutional, child labor increased but it did not reach its former peak. Thus the 1930's became notable for a rapid increase in high school attendance. The increase in numbers and in costs and the financial depletion of those years led to a number of studies.

The American Youth Commission of the American Council on Education began work in 1935. Several motives may have operated in the Council to lead it to create the AYC. The simple desire to alleviate the evils suffered by youth was one. The depression was calling attention to the inadequacies of the schools. But also, many felt that there was danger of the regimentation of youth by national agencies, especially after the government established NYA. A voluntary agency such as the AYC, it was believed, would serve youth without partisanship. How far these opinions were correct is itself a matter of opinion.

Before the AYC could consider solutions, it seemed necessary to secure accurate information on the condition and need of youth. One extended investigation on these lines was reported by Howard M. Bell in *Youth Tell Their Story* (1938); and in more popular form in *How Fare American Youth?* (1937) by the director of the commission, Homer P. Rainey, and others. A scientifically chosen sample of the 250,000 persons between the ages of sixteen and twenty-four years living in Maryland was studied for these reports.

Although the investigation did not reveal many wholly new facts, it provided quantitative and present data. It showed that more than half of the pupils leaving high school left for economic reasons and another fourth left for scholastic or disciplinary reasons. The latter group did not care to learn or were unable to learn what the school was teaching or they did not fit into the routine and regimen of the school. Indirectly the demand for the life adjustment education mentioned in Chapter XIV grew out of such information as this study collected.

The report showed that the pupil with the poorest chance of finishing high school was a Negro boy, one of a large but broken family, with a father who was an unskilled worker. The pupil with the best chance was a white girl from a small family with educated parents in good economic circumstances. It appeared that the children with poor opportunities would in turn have children with a similarly unfavorable outlook. Racial and economic factors were considered very potent.

Although, as we have said, this was not a wholly new discovery, the report put it into concrete terms somewhat as follows. The occupation of a youth's father profoundly affects the amount of the youth's schooling. This in turn affects the kind of job that he will have and the income that he will earn. Further, the youth who leaves school early is likely to marry early and have a large family. This closes the economic-scholastic circle and makes difficult any effort to break up the evil class structure; and the poor and poorly educated will tend to become a permanent mudsill of society.

The report also dealt with youth and the church, youth at work, and youth at play. The investigators seemed surprised to find the church a living influence. Three-fourths of the youth claimed church connections. The investigators proposed the creation of community youth centers and felt that the demand for social recreation was the most significant revelation of their study. They praised the work of the NYA and of the youth-serving agencies.

Teachers may not generally be sufficiently acquainted with the great youth organizations for which America is and deserves to be famous. Many such bodies agree with the schools in some of their aims and principles and the schools should make common cause with them. To do this effectively teachers must know about them and must take an interest in their work.

Such acquaintance could begin with another survey made for the AYC by M. M. Chambers and reported in his *Youth-Serving Organizations*

(1941). This book provides information about more than 300 national but nongovernmental associations that spend all or part of their efforts in advancing the welfare of youth. As examples we name the Junior Red Cross, Boy Scouts, Girl Scouts, Camp Fire Girls, 4-H Clubs, and the American Friends' Service Committee. There are also a great many Catholic, Protestant, and Jewish youth organizations.

Some youth organizations, both secular and religious, are composed of adults who work for youth. Such are the great service clubs and fraternal orders. Some, like the Friends' Service Committee, enlist the services of youth. Others are associations of youths carrying forward their own programs. Many are merely social clubs without any strong welfare purposes, but these may also have their valuable uses.

Some youth organizations, the 4-H Clubs for example, can work directly with the schools. Those with specific religious affiliations may not do this but may work out of school with their own groups of pupils. Physical and health education can be aided by the Scouts and similar groups and all may have a share in social and character education. The United States has not had a national youth movement with political objectives such as existed in Germany when Hitler coordinated all the previous youth groups. The American Youth Congress of the depression years came the nearest to such a youth movement and there have been some Communist groups; but none of these has so far attained great power.

Another publication by the American Youth Commission, written by Dean Harl R. Douglass and entitled *Secondary Education for Youth in Modern America* (1937), set up a list of objectives in the manner of Herbert Spencer. The first five were in fact identical with Spencer's, but to these the commission added (6) education for mental health and (7) education for continued learning. The attention to mental health in such pronouncements is new. Childhood and youth have always suffered from fears, repressions, frustrations, and all sorts of emotional disturbances, but until recently these were not systematically investigated. The strains of the depression, of war, industry, broken families, and the modern city have upset the mental balance of children and teachers. Investigations of mental health in schools appeared in the 1930's and have multiplied since.

A statement with the engrossing title, *Education for All American Youth* (1944), was issued by the Educational Policies Commission. It is not a report but a highly idealized description of two imaginary school systems, one rural and one urban. In the urban system, "the last 'big fight' over a board election had occurred so long ago that only a few people remembered it." Vocational education for the common man is emphasized in this treatment, to the neglect of the preparation of scholars, scientists, creative workers, and abstract thinkers. On the question whether "subjects" are to be completely discarded there is some confusion; but the opposition to "knowledge for its own sake" is pronounced. Although the authors are not isolationists, they find scant space to mention the study of foreign languages; and we are told that in the rural school "one teacher of languages is able to supervise students who are studying Russian, Spanish, French, Italian, German, and Latin." The study of *The Merchant of Venice* has been discontinued for reasons not given; but one can easily guess what they were. The New Deal suggested to the authors that national control of education and state socialism might be imminent; and therefore the main theme of this popular book is that local communities can build ideal schools which pretty well satisfy the needs and wants of everyone.

Some of the assumptions of the book were corrected in the revised edition (1952). Among these were the beliefs that a long period of uninterrupted peace and a business depression would follow close upon the end of World War II. The latter belief closed the eyes of the writers to the teacher and school-building shortages which are repeating the history of the period following World War I. The writers assume that the school should continue to magnify its office and undertake more and more obligations. The opinion that all American youth should remain in full-time attendance at school for the long periods here contemplated should be recognized as the assumption which it is. It is a curious fact that educators who are generally opposed to compulsion in the treatment of youth yet favor a high compulsory school attendance age.

The so-called Thirty Schools Experiment of the Progressive Education Association was begun in 1933 and completed in 1941. It is sometimes called the Eight-Year Study. It was to determine whether the usual college entrance requirements were essential for success in college or whether core and other newer curricula would prepare pupils equally well. The experiment was directed by a commission of the PEA. The results as measured showed only a slight advantage—about 6 points in 250—in favor of the newer curricula and methods. Except in foreign languages, the subject marks of the Progressives were uniformly higher, but the advantage, as indicated above, was so small that it is not considered statistically significant. In outside reading, music, debating, and other extracurricular activities, the records of students from the thirty schools were superior, in some activities much superior. The experiment probably helped the trend toward more liberal requirements for college entrance. Some colleges are tending to place less weight than formerly upon specific books read and courses taken and more upon the student's rank in his high school class, his IQ, his ability to write English, and the recommendation of his high school principal. Other colleges made no changes and there are those which insist upon entrance examinations.

The Cooperative Study of Secondary School Standards by the regional standardizing associations was carried out at the same time as the Thirty Schools Experiment. It undertook to find out what features mark effective secondary schools, and how secondary schools may be improved. The projected standards were to serve the latter of these two purposes. Several hundred secondary schools participated. The work and publications of the study were directed by W. C. Eells as coordinator. Evaluative criteria were formulated provisionally and were improved and refined through repeated trials in the schools. A fairly well-defined plan of evaluation was perfected by 1940. Objective measures, the opinions of teachers, and the judgments of outside specialists were used in carrying out this plan.

A statement of the school's philosophy was usually the first step in an evaluation. Too often this was abstract and general and might have served in another school as well as in the one in question. The further steps included the study of the pupils, community, staff, curriculum, methods of teaching, guidance, administration, equipment, and all other features of a school. This was a qualitative type of survey in place of the older quantitative standards which dealt with teaching loads, number of books in the school library, and similar numerical measures. It also was a self-survey intended to rouse schools to become active in self-improvement. The war disturbed this promising program.

6. INTERNATIONAL EDUCATION

International education may be regarded (1) as the spread of ideas, any ideas, across national frontiers; or (2) as the spread of educational ideas across such boundaries; or (3) as the attempt by educational means to promote peace and mutual cooperation between nations. In the first of these definitions, education is defined as Thorndike defined it: the production of change in people. The content of the ideas which are spread need not come into question. The transmission and borrowing of economic or military ideas would in this primary sense be examples of international education.

International education may also be regarded as the spread of ideas about education and about educational services from nation to nation. This second interpretation of the phrase is the one commonly adopted; and it is the one used by Professor William W. Brickman of New York University, editor of *School and Society,* in an article with the title, "International Education," in the *Encyclopedia of Educational Research* (Macmillan, 1950). So interpreted, the title covers comparative education, teacher and student exchanges, the international influence of the views of John Dewey, for example, and perhaps even the study of foreign languages. Many topics in earlier chapters of this history, including Franklin's plan for an academy with its numerous quotations from European educators, the Lancasterian schools in America, the Rhodes scholarships, and study in German universities by Americans, come under this interpretation.

We should not fail to notice a special type of associations which are covered by this second interpretation. These are the international educational organizations. The "educational commission" proposed in 1817 by Marc-Antoine Jullien (1775–1848) was to be such a body. It was to collect and distribute educational information from and to the nations of Europe. In his draft of a plan, written in 1817, Jullien uses the term "comparative education," and he may have invented this now-familiar phrase. Jullien's proposal was not immediately put into effect, but over the years hundreds of international organizations to promote education have been created. Among these the International Kindergarten Union (1873), the Institute of International Education (1919), and the World Federation of Education Associations (1923) may be named as examples. The International Institute of Teachers College, Columbia University (1923), under the direction of I. L. Kandel, was founded to promote Jullien's idea; and the volumes published by the Institute have been of high interest and great value.

With regard to scope, our three definitions are placed in a descending order. The third is the narrowest. It defines international education as the effort to promote peace and mutual cooperation between nations by educational means. This makes international education a form of propaganda, good propaganda we may hold, but still a proposal to secure agreement upon a policy. It is a policy to prevent wars and to abolish isolationism. This is an effort to initiate a new epoch in history.

The United Nations, in contrast with the League of Nations, has recognized the international functions of education. Thus the United Nations Educational, Scientific and Cultural Organization, or UNESCO, is an agency of the United Nations, as the name "UNESCO" clearly indicates. Both bodies were created in 1945 but not all of the countries in the United Nations are members of UNESCO. The United States adheres to both.

There were two views on the formation of UNESCO. Those who won out created a body to serve, not as an arm of the governments or foreign offices of the member nations, but as representing the educational, scientific, and cultural associations in those nations. In the United States, Congress provided for a National Commission of one hundred, sixty of whom are named by private associations of scholars and educators and forty by the Department of State. The National Commission selects the voting delegates of UNESCO. The first general conference was held at Paris in 1946, with delegates from twenty-eight nations in attendance.

The preamble of the constitution of this unparalleled organization begins with the now-celebrated words that "since wars begin in the minds of men, it is in the minds of men that the defences of peace must be constructed." It rejects the idea that peace can be maintained if it is based exclusively upon political and economic arrangements. Peace, it claims, must be founded "upon the intellectual and moral solidarity of mankind." And this solidarity is to be attained by the "wide diffusion of culture," the universal application of "the democratic principles of the dignity, equality, and mutual respect of men," and education "for justice and liberty and peace." All nations, the preamble declares, have the sacred duty to promote these means to the intellectual and moral solidarity of mankind.

A comparison of these ideas with those expressed at other great moments of history, such as the American and the French Revolutions, would be an educative exercise. That these principles have not always, or perhaps often, been followed and that the peace has not been kept does not condemn the effort. The failures of one period often prepare the way for success in the next. Isaiah, Kant, and many others have had visions of perpetual peace that may and, if the human race is to endure, indeed must become reality.

The United Nations itself began with fifty-one member nations. Others have been added. The largest of these additions, Indonesia, has a population of 70,000,000. Sixteen new members but not including either Japan or Communist China were admitted in December, 1955. The United Nations, contrary to the statements of reactionary newspapers, can show a long line of substantial achievements, in Israel, in Iran, in the repatriation of millions of refugees, in the promotion of the health and welfare of mothers and children through its Children's Fund, and in the work of other subsidiary organizations. Many of the aims of UNESCO are supported also by other United Nations organizations. Isolationists and extreme nationalists are opposed to UNESCO and its work and lose few opportunities to attack it.

UNESCO attempts to promote knowledge and understanding of nations by nations, with special attention to the use of the radio, motion pictures, and textbooks. Textbook revision had been started between the two world wars. UNESCO is particularly interested in the rectification of textbooks in history, the social studies, and literature. These books together with songs, ceremonies, and patriotic ritual have been used in schools over the world to promote chauvinism and the spirit of aggression and revenge. Related to textbook revision are the surveys of national school systems. Fundamental education, the removal of illiteracy—for illiteracy retards progress among half of the people of the world—adult education, and the education of teachers are others among the many interests of UNESCO. To become informed in regard to these matters, far beyond the limits of a short notice such as the present, is the obligation of every prospective teacher of American children.

In wartime, schools suffer from shortages and retrenchment; and the services most recently added are among the first to be discontinued. But in World War I, the study of German, a comparatively old subject, was dropped at once when Congress declared war. This was an emotional reaction rather than a reasoned action.

The schools became involved in the war propaganda, the drives to sell war stamps and Liberty Bonds, and the effort to increase the food supply. Those educators who disagreed and who had the courage to go on record spoke against this diversion of the schools from their normal functions and this integration of children into a war system. The military training which the war brought into the schools disappeared when peace returned. The hastily organized Student Army Training Corps of 1918 also disappeared, fortunately, before it ruined the colleges. World War II led to the permanent establishment of the Reserve Officers Training Corps, and to the passage of the GI bill.

The period of adversity was marked by many attempts in state legislatures to police the minds of teachers. To this both wars and the depression contributed. There were laws against anarchism, socialism, and communism; and laws to promote Americanism without, however, defining it. Related to these laws were the legislative attempts to revise the history textbooks, a task for which legislatures are not well equipped. Many states forbade the teaching of foreign languages in elementary schools. Twenty years later there was a great revival of foreign language instruction in elementary schools. From educational news reports in 1954 came the statement that in 1,000 elementary schools in forty states about 200,000 children were enthusiastically learning to speak Spanish, French, and other foreign languages, and that their teachers were attending night school in order to keep up with them.

The depression had many destructive effects. Salaries were reduced and often remained unpaid for months and even years. Many teachers left the profession. Enrollments rose and there was a building shortage. The curriculum was often emasculated, terms were shortened, and the graduates in great numbers were unable to find work. The public did not realize the depth and severity of the crisis; and they were misled by the past history of business reverses, which had been relatively short. For this reason, among many others, the measures taken to fight the depression were inadequate.

This last fact carries over into the measures taken to aid the destitute and discouraged young people. Although mistakes were made in its organization and administration, the Civilian Conservation Corps did useful work and gave the country experience that may have future application. Other youth-saving organizations, public and private, did important work. Many school men were prejudiced against government activity in this field, regarding it as propaganda for statism. Federal funds for school buildings and for the maintenance of unemployed teachers and other cultural workers were provided. Parallel with these positive efforts there were many surveys of youth problems and secondary education. Along with emergency measures one should also consider the great permanent youth-aiding organizations, such as the YMCA and YWCA, the Scouts, and hundreds of others.

The founding of the United Nations led to the establishment of a new, unprecedented organization to promote international education, UNESCO. It is unprecedented in the scope of its purposes and activities. UNESCO is particularly concerned with the development of international understanding through the promotion throughout the world of education, science, and culture, making them more available to all peoples. It is aided in its purposes by other United Nations subsidiaries. Such are the FAO, or Food and Agriculture Organization, the WHO, or World Health Organization, and many others. The theory seems to be that although "wars begin in the minds of men," their minds are not unresponsive to good physical conditions. Peace depends upon knowledge, wisdom, and good will but also upon relief from oppression, depression, and hunger.

QUESTIONS

1. How did the propaganda effort in World War I affect education? Consider, in this connection, the pro-German accusations and the public dissension of that period and the relation of such social conflict to education.

2. What is the reasonable position in the debate between military training and physical education in the schools? Consider high schools and colleges separately.

3. If "a loyalty test for teachers is wrong in principle," as Governor Alfred E. Smith said, what principle is violated by such a test? Are there any other arguments against such a test?

4. Why, in all probability, did the Klan favor the Oregon law? With this compare the reason why Mr. Justice Holmes dissented from the majority decision of the Supreme Court.

5. If another CCC or similar agency were needed, what modifications of the 1933 plan would you propose?

6. Why did high school attendance increase rapidly in the 1920's? Why in the 1930's?

7. Why do some who oppose compulsion in school insist upon the attendance at school of those who are unwilling?

8. If, instead of NYA, the government had provided funds for the existing private youth organizations to expand their work, would youth have been effectively served? How would such a plan be administered?

9. What was discovered through the Thirty Schools Experiment and how has American education been affected?

10. Why should pupils be taught about the background and origins, the purposes, and the achievements of the United Nations and UNESCO? What obligation is implied in this question?

11. How are comparative education and the studies made by UNESCO related to each other and to the history of education?

BOOKS AND PAPERS

Some of the large city newspapers which reported the events of the wars and the depression as they occurred are indexed. Among the educational journals which gave attention to the adversities of our time may be mentioned *The Nation's Schools, School Life, The American School Board Journal,* and the *School Review.* Perhaps all magazines gave some attention to these calamities.

A *Bibliography on Education in the Depression* (1937) was prepared for the Educational Policies Commission, NEA, by Jesse B. Sears. The Research Division of the NEA was especially concerned with the economic position of the teaching profession.

A sheaf of illustrated articles on UNESCO with facsimile copies of related documents is to be found in the *School Executive* for October, 1946.

Bell, Howard M., *Youth Tell Their Story,* Washington, American Council on Education, 1938.

Brickman, W. W., "UNESCO," *School and Society,* September 24, 1949; "UNESCO Developments and Achievements," *School and Society,* November 29, 1952, both being bibliographies with commentary.

Chambers, M. M., *Youth-serving Organizations, National, Nongovernmental Associations,* Washington, American Council on Education, 1941.

Crowell, Benedict, and R. F. Wilson, *Demobilization, Industrial and Military, 1918–1920,* Yale University Press, 1921.

EPC, *Education for All American Youth,* Washington, Educational Policies Commission, 1944; and a second edition, revised, and subtitled, *A Further Look,* 1952.

Ickes, Harold L., *Secret Diary of Harold L. Ickes, 1933–1936,* New York, 1953. Contains a number of entries with educational interest.

Kandel, I. L., *The Impact of the War Upon American Education,* University of North Carolina Press, 1948.

Lumley, F. E., *Propaganda Menace,* New York, 1933.

Mock, James, and Cedric Larson, *Words that Won the War, The Story of the Committee on Public Information, 1917–1919,* Princeton University Press, 1939.

Pitkin, Stanley Royce, *Public School Support in the United States during Periods of Economic Depression,* Brattleboro, Vermont, Stephen Daye Press, 1933.

Todd, Lewis P., *Wartime Relations of the Federal Government and the Public Schools, 1917–1918,* New York, Teachers College, Columbia University, 1945.

Walworth, Arthur, *School Histories at War,* Harvard University Press, 1938.

Willey, M. M., *Depression, Recovery and Higher Education,* New York, 1937.

Wilson, Howard E., *United States National Commission for UNESCO,* New York, 1948.

Chapter XVIII

UNFINISHED WORK

P ROBLEMS indicate at least the possibility of improvement; and an assurance of it grows with success in overcoming them. The "glory of the imperfect" arises from the incentives and opportunities which it offers to reach for greater perfection. Earlier chapters have shown that the United States has had numerous great educational problems and has resolved many of them; and the future will doubtless see further improvement.

In practical affairs one does not create difficulties merely to have work to do. That is not necessary because the world and human nature are such that the rise of problems is inevitable, and many educational questions are now before the people. The present chapter deals with several of them; but there are others and the ones selected may not be the most important, most difficult, or most urgent. Certainly some of them would rank high in all these respects.

It has been said, even by men who in other respects seem not unwise, that there are few educational problems before the people which money would not solve. This is not true. Money may be necessary, but to be useful it must be applied with intelligence and good will. There is much ignorance, stupidity, and ill will in the world. Starting with conditions and people as they are, it is the task of education to help in overcoming these great evils. If this seems to be like the proverbial pulling ourselves up by our bootstraps, one can say that history supports the hope that this may be achieved. History does not give complete assurance. Therein lies the challenge of the present situation.

1. PEOPLE

Education has to do with people. The people in the United States in 1950 numbered 150,000,000. This is six times the number in the states of 1850 and only two times the population of 1900. The rate of increase was declining. That rate was 3 per cent in the decade from 1840 to 1850 and only three-fourths of 1 per cent in the depression decade, 1930–1940. Before 1930 both laymen and expert students of population were convinced that this continued decline foreshadowed a stationary population by 1960. It is now common knowledge that everyone was mistaken and the mistake has added to the nation's difficulty in providing rooms and teachers for the new and young Americans.

The decade of World War II witnessed a phenomenal rise in the number of births; the population increased by 19,000,000 and by more than 14 per cent. Early marriages and larger families continued into the 1950's, and no one will now make a formal prediction on the permanence of the present remarkably high rate of increase. It is obvious that the country faces an educational emergency that, unless resolute action is taken, will likely become more serious year by year.

The present growth of the population is due not only to the rise of the birth rate but also to the lowering of child mortality and of mortality at all ages. People and especially children live longer because living conditions are improving and medical advice and health knowledge are both growing and spreading to more people. This knowledge is spread by physicians, nurses, magazines, government bulletins prepared under the Children's Bureau—a bulletin on child care is one of the most popular pieces of reading-matter in the United States—and also universally by the schools. The effect of the schools should not be underestimated. Their work is fundamental. They not only teach health directly in classes, in exercises in the gymnasium, and through sports on the playing field, but they also prepare children through instruction in reading and science to understand and to act upon health knowledge.

Among the better educated and fortunate classes no great further reduction in child mortality may be possible. But it will be important throughout following generations to hold the gains that have been attained. In this, education will have a continuous part to play. Ignorant parents will not know how to care for their children or have the means to do it. There are such parents now. Health education needs to be brought more fully to the poor and less educated people who often have large families. Many of these live in blighted sections of the city or the countryside. In these circumstances, it is certain that child mortality could be further reduced by improved sanitation, higher wages, and education in hygiene and child care.

The unexpected and rapid increase in the number of very young Americans soon led to a shortage of elementary schoolrooms and teachers. After World War I there was a similar although less acute problem without an increased birth rate. In both cases the higher wages and easier work of industry had much to do with the teacher shortage which developed. In such times the public is often slow to realize the unfavorable effect upon the morale of teachers that results from overcrowding, evening and weekend duties, lack of discipline and of administrative support, and the long delays in salary adjustments. Such conditions keep many from considering teaching as a vocation. Teachers remember that boards of education were quick in reducing salaries in the depression. It is a more difficult task to persuade them to raise salaries and to restore the staff in time of growing prosperity and inflation.

2. OCCUPATIONS

New inventions and changes in living standards have caused changes in the work that people do. Agriculture, which formerly employed the largest numbers of workers—three in every eight—is now in fourth place, engaging only one out of every eight workers. But agricultural production has not declined; it has increased greatly. Manufacturing, which is now in first place in the number of workers employed, shows a similar increase in efficiency. Improved machines make each worker far more productive than his predecessor, so that to meet the rising standard of consumption it has not been necessary to increase the labor force correspondingly.

In unskilled labor there has been a numerical decline in man power. The change can be expressed in a sentence. Fifty years ago there were 11,000,000 common laborers, pick and shovel men, farm workers, and others who used only their muscles, but at present with double the population there are only half that number, or about 5,500,000. There is, however, another type of unskilled laborers, the workers who tend semiautomatic machines or who work on an assembly line. With shorter hours and powerful unions, these exert an influence that was not given to the pick and shovel men. All these workers present a special problem in civic and cultural education. At the other end of the scale in the managerial field and the number of proprietors there has also been a decrease in numbers. This is due to the concentration of business and industry into larger and fewer units.

What work is left for the rest of the 62,000,000 workers who are actually employed in the middle 1950's? Besides agriculture and manufacturing, there are always extractive, construction, and transportation industries. The armed services engage 3,500,000. The federal, state, and local governments employ several millions. There has been a great expansion of jobs in service occupations such as banking, insurance, hotels, motels, restaurants, entertainment, advertising and promotion, distributive occupations, hospital and psychiatric work, preaching and teaching, and all those occupations in which the practitioner gets paid mainly for his knowledge and skill. There has been a great expansion of the service occupations which now employ one-fifth or even one-fourth of all workers.

3. FINDING NEW FRONTIERS

The school must take account of vocations and of the movement of the population which in many cases is also a change from one job to another. This double shift is providing educational problems of great complexity. The extent of the change from the farm to the village and from both to the city is not apparent; it has to be measured if it is to be realized. In 1850 most of the people lived in the country and country towns; but now 60 per cent of them live in cities where school terms are longer, curricula diversified, and buildings and materials more adequate. The city rather than the open spaces has become the frontier to draw off the surplus population and provide new opportunities in education and occupations.

Change of occupation is only one of many reasons why people move to the city, or across state lines, or to a distant section of the country. Their mobility is one of the great facts about the American people. Construction, repair, and all migrant workers follow their job opportunities. The great corporations transfer their employees from place to place. Large-scale relocations result from industrial expansion and the opening of new plants.

These great voluntary migrations have drawn numbers of Negroes from the South to the industries of the North. New England has lost much of the textile industry. Atomic energy plants are being erected in several parts of the country. A great stream of people has been moving westward. The states of the Rocky Mountains and the Pacific coast, which had barely 4,000,000 people in 1900, have about 20,000,000 now.

Many of these migrations tend to improve the educational opportunities of the children who are moved. But this means that an opposite result follows in the sections to which the less literate people move. For this reason among others, equal educational opportunities in all sections are to be desired. To many this will seem to demand federal aid. The National Education Association has long been agitating and lobbying for such aid. Others, in general the more conservative and traditional ones, think that the states and the localities should reform their tax systems and should themselves provide good schools. High officials of the federal government seem to be using Fabian and temporizing tactics. And leaders of parochial and independent schooling are sometimes opposed to federal aid.

Economic differences separate the people into different groups and levels. In that *Atlantic Monthly* for May, 1940, James B. Conant, then president of Harvard University, expressed his fear that fixed economic classes were forming. Perhaps he had in mind the old saying that in America wealth is accumulated and again dissipated in the space of three generations, the grandfather starting in shirt sleeves and the grandson ending in them. That era, it seemed to President Conant, was passing. America was becoming stratified. He wrote: "We see throughout the country the development of a hereditary aristocracy of wealth." He reported not only the existence of a small privileged class that was exploiting the national and human resources but also the formation of an explosive proletariat at the bottom. In holding this opinion he was not alone.

Some will deny that the unequal distribution of wealth is a recent development. There were many poor in the colonies and in the early Republic, as well as in the more recent past; and not a few rich also. Wealth has always been distributed unequally, but many think the proportion of those who are moderately well-off has been increasing.

Whether the bottom layer, proletariat or not, is explosive is a separate question. The answer at any time will be affected by the contemporary turn of their economic circumstances. Moderate poverty is bearable. It is not so much poverty as the loss or the fear of losing what little one has that rouses resentment, and even this may not set off an explosion. A depression is a severe test and the depression of the thirties gave slight evidence of "explosive material beneath." But this proves little about the future. Conditions may change and another depression might have a different outcome.

There are factors that may prevent the formation of a suppressed and explosive lower class. Organization of labor, the dependence of business upon the purchasing power of the masses, and education are such factors. Education is the means of spreading opportunity, the safety valve to prevent explosions. It increases the number of those who are moderately prosperous. It raises the standards of living and increases the demand for goods and services. Unfortunately, it cannot raise those with little intelligence to any high level; and the decline in the unskilled labor force may make some of these people unemployable. But education is for most an open frontier and safety valve, more accessible than the geographical frontier celebrated by Frederick Jackson Turner.

The people also differ in ethnic characteristics, in what is popularly but inaccurately called race. There are 12,000,000 Negroes. Many Mexicans come across the border for work and some of these remain. There are Puerto Ricans, Japanese, Chinese, American Indians, and others. The Supreme Court is now holding that there is only one class of citizens. The process of educational integration will take time, but that it will be achieved is not to be doubted.

We may gather from this outline that the population of the United States is not yet becoming stationary and that the country will not soon be composed mainly of old people. There are and will continue to be many small children knocking at the schoolhouse door.

Invention and industrial development are changing the occupations of the people and acting to redistribute them among the cities, states, and sections. These shifts raise a national problem and an argument for federal aid and national norms. The demand for vocational skill and knowledge is growing and that for common labor is declining. Education has a part in this continuing adjustment.

Wealth is very unequally distributed in the United States. Some believe that this condition is creating fixed classes of rich and poor and that the poor have or will have no opportunity to improve their condition. There are, however, counteracting factors, of which education is one. And it is to the economic advantage of the rich to support education because it helps to develop the market for goods and services.

We have noticed another cleavage in the American population. The majority are people of European origin with white skins, but there are several groups whose ancestors came from Africa or Asia or who carry the blood of the American Indians and who have pigmented skins. America, which has been notorious for its insistence upon the color bar, is now in process of mending its ways. Segregation in the defense establishment has been officially abolished and the Supreme Court has outlawed it in the schools.

Several other considerations grow out of the outline. Evidently birthrate and future population predictions are rather less scientific than long-range weather-forecasting. Perhaps if every state and district were to study the birth registrations, then the public, the boards, and the schools could prepare buildings and teachers for the increased attendance before the emergency is upon them. Large-scale migrations produce similar problems. Both the school from which the migrants come and those to which they go must make adjustments. Studies of industrial development and population trends should be available to help make the adjustments as satisfactory as possible.

4. ENDING SEGREGATION

In a unanimous decision read by Chief Justice Earl Warren on May 17, 1954, the Supreme Court outlawed racial segregation in public schools and universities. The decision dealt with five suits brought by different states and the District of Columbia but it had the effect of barring segregation in all states, territories, and the federal district. The Court said: "We conclude that in the field of public education the doctrine of 'separate but equal' has no place. Separate educational facilities are inherently unequal . . . the plaintiffs and others similarly situated . . . are . . . deprived of the equal protection of the laws guaranteed by the Fourteenth Amendment."

A legal attack upon segregation in the public schools had been made in Boston in 1849. That case was lost, but six years later Massachusetts became the first of the states to outlaw separate public schools for Negroes. After reconstruction, segregation was required by law in seventeen states stretching from Delaware to Texas and was permitted in Kansas, Wyoming, New Mexico, and Arizona. The other twenty-seven states had either prohibitory laws or none at all. This tabulation clearly exhibits the operation of the well-known principle that education is a function of the states. And this principle has controlled the laws and practice of segregation. The new decision cuts away a part of this long-accepted legal and constitutional dogma. The federal government is undertaking to interfere in the administration of education by and in the states.

The doctrine of "separate and equal" facilities, to which the Supreme Court referred, was implied in the case of *Plessy* v. *Ferguson,* decided in 1896. The case concerned the right of a state to require by law the use of Jim Crow cars on trains; and the Court held that these cars did "not necessarily imply the inferiority of either race" and added that "the most common instance of this is connected with the establishment of separate schools for white and colored children." This somewhat casual illustration originated the "separate but equal" doctrine. In a dissenting opinion, Mr. Justice J. M. Harlan used the prophetic words that "the Constitution is color-blind"; but the doctrine was accepted without question until 1935.

The shock of the depression and World War II against racist enemies raised questions about racism at home and led to a re-examination of the claims of democracy. Japanese propaganda also underlined American discrimination, intending to discredit the United States with all nonwhite peoples. This device became a major weapon in the cold war which began about 1946 but it has backfired. It warned the United States to promote unity at home and to avoid offending actual or possible allies.

Even before American entry into the war, President Roosevelt issued an executive order creating a Fair Employment Practice Committee to reduce discrimination in defense industries. It has been claimed that the need for increased man power was the real incentive. This was clearly one incentive, but the President had also been threatened with a march on Washington by a body of Negroes if he did not find a way to open more jobs to them. Since the war, fair employment policy has been turned back to the states.

By 1947 the issues had been raised to a stage that led President Truman's Committee on Civil Rights to denounce segregation. They held that the separate but equal doctrine branded those to whom it was applied and did not lead to equality. That report fanned the fires of the Dixiecrat rebellion and narrowed the margin of the Democratic victory in 1948, but neither of the major parties has repudiated its principles; and President Eisenhower reaffirmed them in his State of the Union Message in 1953. In recent times a broad front against discrimination has developed. Practice may not indeed equal profession, but the white primary has been abandoned; the armed services have abolished racial segregation; the sign "For Colored" has disappeared from the railroads; and in many other areas discrimination has been reduced or abandoned.

In education the separate but equal doctrine was maintained until 1935 but without the promised equality. In very recent years, the Southern states have tried to provide equal facilities; and while they have made progress in their attempt they have not attained the goal. It is now too late, for the Plessy doctrine has been repudiated by the highest court.

As might have been foreseen, the early court cases arose in higher education and in the border states, the first one in Maryland in 1935. In that case the Maryland Court of Appeals sustained the litigant's plea that a scholarship in a Northern law school was discriminatory because it paid only part of the expense. The court ordered the plaintiff admitted to the Maryland state law school from which he later graduated. In the Gaines case from Missouri (1938) the United States Supreme Court held that a state must provide facilities within its own borders, thus outlawing the out-of-state scholarship device. In later cases from Oklahoma and Texas the Court not only ordered the state universities to admit qualified Negro graduate and professional students but also refused to permit their segregation in classrooms or libraries within the universities. The Court declared that they must be allowed "to engage in discussions and exchange views with other students." Nor could equal facilities be provided by a made-to-order law school, for such a school would lack many of the impalpable but important characteristics of a recognized school, such as the reputation of its faculty, the position of its alumni, or its traditions and prestige. These decisions of 1950 rejected all discrimination between Negro and white students in the highest divisions of the state universities. The cases from 1935 to 1950 were selected and the litigation was directed by attorneys of the National Association for the Advancement of Colored People.

Meanwhile, the undergraduate colleges of the state universities were not yet required to admit colored students. These students were supposed to have "equal" facilities in the Negro land-grant colleges. In 1948 nine states, South Carolina, Georgia, Florida, Alabama, Mississippi, Texas, Arkansas, Tennessee, and Maryland, signed a convention to consider the creation of regional centers for medical, dental, and other professional education. These were to admit both races from the contracting states. More states came into the plan and it was established on a permanent basis under a Southern Regional Education Board. Negro leaders at once denounced the program as a device to keep Negroes, especially undergraduates, out of the state universities. This charge is denied and, in fact, by 1953 there were Negro undergraduates in all Southern state universities except those of South Carolina, Georgia, Florida, Alabama, and Mississippi. The proclaimed purpose is the creation of strong advanced schools at less expense and with less duplication of effort than would be required if every state university were to provide all types of work. It has been pointed out that in the Gaines case the Supreme Court required equal educational opportunity within each state. This regional plan has not yet been before the Supreme Court.

The decision of 1954, as noted above, held that segregation in all public schools of all grades, everywhere, is unconstitutional, and this seems to go to the end of the road. In considering the application of the Fourteenth Amendment, the Court contrasted the status of education in 1868 and that in 1954. When the amendment was adopted, the Court said, free common schools, supported by general taxation, had not yet taken hold in the South. White children attended private schools and education for Negroes was practically nonexistent.

The Court continued: "Today, education is perhaps the most important function of state and local governments. . . . It is required in the performance of our most basic public responsibilities, even service in the armed forces. It is the very foundation of good citizenship." We quote again the conclusion "that in the field of public education the doctrine of 'separate but equal' has no place. Separate educational facilities are inherently unequal."

Because this decision was unanimous, a later one may not tend to cloud the issue as has happened in some decisions upon religion in the schools. The Court granted a grace period to find ways of making an orderly transition. The system for white and the one for Negro children in each of the seventeen states are to be combined. But some states such as South Carolina, Georgia, and Mississippi may attempt to prevent the mingling of the races. Preparations have been made in some states to abolish the public schools. If these proposals are carried out, the Supreme Court may be called upon to apply Article Four, Section Four, of the Constitution which declares that "the United States shall guarantee to every State in this Union a republican form of government."

Except in the deep South and Virginia the Court's decision is being accepted. The separation permitted by the laws of four states will disappear and most of the border states will comply with the national directive. Where all the residents are of one race there will continue to be all-Negro and all-white schools. In some localities prejudice may lead to the gerrymandering of districts to make them racially uniform. But in time all these devices will also disappear.

The argument in the Court's decision has been labeled sociological. Its conclusion grows out of the losses sustained by the nation from defective education. The Court said that education has become the foundation of good citizenship; and therefore, although public education has been a function reserved to the states, the federal government will step in and will outlaw the acts of states when that is considered necessary for the laying of a solid foundation. This decision may have ultimate consequences that will extend far beyond its immediate purpose; but it is clear that not all states will soon honor the Supreme Court's mandate.

5. SUPPORT AND CRITICISM

In the middle fifties the task of providing places and teachers for all the pupils was the most tangible problem before the people and the schools. Enrollments were growing at the rate of 1,000,000 per year. This is a national as well as a local problem because the national welfare hangs upon its solution; but under present laws it must be solved locally, that is, by the states and districts where the shortages exist or threaten. In some cases funds are lacking because of an antiquated tax system or improper districting. In the past the federal government has at times helped in financing school building programs. But the habit of legislatures and boards of neglecting unsolved problems, passing them on to their successors, is one of the reasons for emergencies. And part of this is due to the failure to secure precise and continuing reports on present and future resources and probable needs. These well-known failures are compounded by the apathy which has often defeated bond issues and efforts to raise salaries.

Much has been done to dispel such indifference, at least in some localities, by the National Citizens' Commission for the Public Schools. This layman's group grew out of a meeting called by several educators including President Conant of Harvard University, who impressed upon the meeting the importance of public education for the preservation of democracy and the responsibility of the people for its promotion. The commission was organized in 1949 with Mr. Roy Larsen, president of the corporation which publishes the magazine *Time*, as the head; and all members are laymen, that is, people not professionally connected with education. The services of the commission consist largely in making public the needs of the schools and in arousing the citizens of local communities. They use the press, radio, and public meetings to gain attention; and they answer questions on "how to organize a citizens' committee in our town," "how to raise money for a new school," or "what makes a good board member." But while they have had a large number of local successes, the shortages of buildings and teachers are still growing.

Such help as the National Congress of Parents and Teachers has long given and as is now being extended by the National Citizens' Commission, the General Federation of Women's Clubs, and other groups is much needed. Since 1949 the membership of the National Congress of Parents and Teachers has increased from six to ten millions and the proportion of men has risen by 50 per cent. At the moment the officers of national business organizations, such as the United States Chamber of Commerce and the National Association of Manufacturers, and of giant corporations such as General Electric are urging increased support for schools. This is very different from the language or the silence of some years ago.

Such help is especially needed at present when a great flood of criticism has been sweeping over the schools. Well-informed and well-meant criticism is salutary. But a great deal of the postwar censure was wanting in one or both of these qualities. Some has been directed against the whole idea and practice of public education. Apparent in the motives of several critics has been distrust of democratic government, reactionary economic sentiment, and the real or pretended fear of communism in the schools. Professional agitators entered the fight and a number of front groups were organized to support the attack.

Some of the criticisms tend to cancel each other. It is claimed that education is too general, theoretical, idealistic, and liberal; but also that it is too narrow, practical, and vocational. Doubtless each of these adjectives could find application in some place and time, but until the words are defined and the application is made they do not require much attention.

There are critics who say the schools no longer teach the fundamental or tool subjects as well as they did in former times. This charge is often linked with an attack upon Progressive education. Both of these charges have already been considered in earlier chapters. Probably some schools do not teach these subjects effectively. But tests indicate that, IQ for IQ, the basic skills are taught as well or better than they were in earlier years. But the evidence has not yet convinced all competent people. There are, indeed, pupils who have not learned to add, spell, or read, or to be prompt and dependable. The question is what course is to be followed. It is the duty of citizens to get all the pertinent facts and to provide for any needed improvements. One general fact regarding the American system must be kept in mind: that as people move about, the illiterates in any one area may have come from some other district. This may make it a state problem or a national one.

There is a special reason for the charge that the fundamental school skills are not well taught. This is the desire to cut down the time that might be devoted to public questions and community problems. If more time can be diverted to the teaching of formal subjects and cold facts, if the memory can be exercised almost exclusively, there will be less time for ideas and arguments.

The charge introduces the most alarming of all the criticisms or attacks. It is the charge that many teachers are subversive, slyly introducing Communistic ideas. This the American people do not want and would not permit. But investigation has uncovered only a very few who had Communist leanings or connections. Congressional and state investigating committees have made sensational charges; and the condition of the public mind has been such that many have accepted accusations without asking for evidence. The result has been the suppression of free discussion and of the exchange of opinions in the schools.

The universities have not escaped. Some professors have been dismissed but the evidence has sometimes not been made public. The accused may find it very difficult to obtain counsel because lawyers refuse to undertake their defense. In this connection the student should read an editorial by Norman Cousins in the *Saturday Review,* for May 3, 1952. Even support of the United Nations makes one suspect in some quarters. In the autumn of 1954, teams from West Point and Annapolis were officially forbidden to take part in intercollegiate debates on the question of admitting Communist China to the United Nations.

Textbooks on history, geography, government, and all social topics tend to draw the fire of critics. Even the words "society" and "social" arouse suspicion in the minds of extreme individualists who oppose all forms of socialization and socialism. This makes trouble for all writers and publishers of books on the social studies. Conditions are constantly changing in these fields and textbooks must be frequently revised to keep them up-to-date and acceptable. This gives the unfair critic the opportunity to report an author's former statement as if it were his present position. Thus, to take an example from an earlier chapter, what was said about the Kaiser of Germany in 1913 tended to become less and less acceptable until by 1917 it was likely to support a charge of pro-Germanism. Textbooks are exposed to unfair attack when they have to deal with sensitive topics upon which the public is divided. Among the numerous such topics at present one may name internationalism, the United Nations, UNESCO, public aid, national health laws and now even the teaching of primary reading. But schools are failing in their duty and purpose if they do not at proper levels and at proper times deal forthrightly with controversial subjects.

When textbooks are attacked, boards of education sometimes name a committee of teachers or of teachers and citizens to study and report upon the matter criticized. Teachers should be competent to judge the quality of textbooks and their suitability for a given class or school. This may not always be the case. It is the duty of the board to consider such a report and to act upon it.

6. DIRECT ASSAULT

A guest editorial in the *Saturday Evening Post* (July 14, 1951) contained a broad attack on the public schools including the familiar charge that they are socialistic. The writer, Frank Chorodov, is the author of a pamphlet entitled *Private Schools: The Solution of America's Educational Problems.* The same "solution" is proposed by Robert Cyrus Hoiles, who owns a number of daily papers in Texas, California, and Ohio. Hoiles declares that the school tax is a violation of the Constitution, the Declaration of Independence, and the Ten Commandments. He is for private schools and proposes that the people should "buy education as they buy bread."

If that seems fantastic we should look more closely at the Chorodov pamphlet. It argues against public schools because they can be subverted by dictators who will use them "for ends quite the opposite of freedom." And he illustrates the point by citing Hitler, Mussolini, and Stalin, who did not abolish the public schools but used them for their own ends. This is crooked logic. The fact is that the totalitarians closed the private schools and "coordinated" the public ones. This is an argument against dictators and not against schools, public or private.

The Employers' Association of Chicago, distributed a booklet with the title, *How Red is the Little Red Schoolhouse?* The American Education Association of New York publishes *Signposts* and urges the citizens to keep American schools American. The so-called "Conference of American Small Business Organizations," and other "front" groups with deceptive names are not trying to improve public education. They are opposed to it. To understand why they are opposed one must know who they are and how and where they operate.

The troubles of the age, the experimental efforts to deal with them, and especially the postwar disillusionment and fear of greater evils ahead, all help to open the opportunity for frontal attack. Some of the attackers are professional agitators who live by "sowing distrust" and live very well; but the public does not always know this. Distrust requires a favorable climate. Some of the cities which have been hit by the attackers had difficult problems because the population was increasing rapidly. Some have found their work hampered by old buildings and by the lack of equipment. Bond issues and increased taxation may create opposition. Curriculum revision is a delicate operation, and recently only adroit management by the superintendent of schools kept it from causing trouble in one of the best school systems in a western state. Rezoning a city and transferring pupils from school to school with an unwelcome intermingling of races and classes were factors in the Pasadena explosion. In a time of anxiety and fear, any spark if it is fanned by agitators may become a fire. It is the emotional tension and the threat of a local breakdown that makes agitators dangerous. They have done serious damage in some places, but they have not been as effective as they claim. In comparison with the large number of school systems, few have had any serious disturbance.

Among books and papers the following may be noted: Arthur E. Bestor, *Educational Wasteland*, Urbana, University of Illinois Press, 1953;

Albert Lynd, *Quackery in the Public Schools,* Boston, 1953; Mortimer Smith, *And Madly Teach,* 1949, and *The Diminished Mind: A Study of Planned Mediocrity,* Chicago, 1954. The preceding are critical, in some instances hostile. Both sides are represented in an anthology edited by C. Winfield Scott and Clyde M. Hill, *Public Education under Criticism,* New York, 1954. A case-study is furnished by David Hulburd in *This Happened in Pasadena,* New York, 1951.

Bibliography and comment are furnished by William W. Brickman in articles in *School and Society,* October 27, 1951, and June 20, 1953. See also Frank Buchanan, "Lobbying and its Influence," *The Nation's Schools,* July, 1951; H. Gordon Hullfish, *Keeping Our Schools Free,* New York, Public Affairs Committee, Inc., 1953; and articles in *Saturday Review* for September 8, 1951, March 7, 1953, and September 12, 1953.

7. RELIGION IN PUBLIC EDUCATION

The present revival of interest in religion has increased the interest in religious instruction in school and in the status of religious knowledge among the people. Efforts are made to teach religion in public schools or to use these in some way to further religion and promote religious instruction. Among the ways are teaching about religion in the process of teaching any subject such as history; Bible reading and perhaps the use of religious songs and exercises in the schools; and teaching religion on released time outside the schools.

The attempt to use the public schools to impart religious knowledge and to further religious interests has frequently come into collision with the principle of the separation of church and state. This principle is not stated in these words in the First Amendment to the Constitution but is inferred from it. Some have even declared that there is no such principle. Others have claimed that the separation is absolute. We may provisionally assert that while church and state must be separate there is in law no high and impenetrable wall between them.

The first of the above "ways" is usually accepted. The courts have not yet ruled against an objective consideration of the church and religion in teaching history, literature, art, or morals. And it is impossible to teach the truth in these fields if religion is excluded. Without Erasmus, Luther, Calvin, Loyola, the Society of Jesus, and the Council of Trent, the sixteenth century could hardly be identified. English literature is replete with the ideas, the characters, and the language of the Bible. The history of architecture could not well omit the cathedrals. This objective teaching of religion—or as it is sometimes called, teaching about religion—is recommended by the Educational Policies Commission in its report on *Moral and Spiritual Values in the Public Schools* (1951).

But although the courts have not ruled against it, this way has its dangers. Parents have objected to teachers who tell their children that there are doctrines which conflict with those approved in the home. It is reported in a professional journal that a teacher in a city system was moved to another school because she had explained the difference between Unitarian and Trinitarian views of the nature of Jesus. But at present the public is less sensitive about religion than about free enterprise and socialism. With luck one can teach a great deal about religion and its place in the world. It has, however, been asserted that teaching about religion has no religious value.

Before we take up the history of Bible reading in the schools we shall retrace the steps which have led to the present situation. Colonial schools were Protestant and used the Bible and other religious books. The teaching of sectarian religion created no particular problem because no one was required to send his children to school.

A broader Christianity and toleration became noticeable by 1750. The academies taught many secular subjects; and arithmetic and grammar which lacked religious character were introduced into the common schools. These schools were not much affected by the deistic movement which swept through the colleges after the Revolution, but patriotic and civic materials appeared in the school reading books.

In the new century (1801) there was a return to religion and a revival movement greater in extent than the Great Awakening. Timothy Dwight, Lyman Beecher, and Charles G. Finney were among the leaders. Immigration, meanwhile, brought many Catholics into a country where they had not been numerous. Protestants under nativist and Know-Nothing banners forgot their differences to fight the new religionists. The shameful violence which resulted was in part due to religious differences but also to the low wages resulting from the influx of laborers with a low standard of living.

The nativist influence can also be traced in the public school movement. The public schools were Protestant in spirit and used the King James version of the Bible. The American Education Society and the American Home Missionary Society were organized as instruments of a militant Protestantism trying to preserve the West from both infidelity and Catholicism. The purpose of each society was both educational and religious. Out of this general situation there arose an increasing number of court cases dealing with Bible reading in the public schools.

Legal actions to compel the schools to desist from reading the King James Bible to Catholic children were taken as early as 1854 when the Supreme Court of Maine held that this version was not sectarian. The Supreme Court of Wisconsin came to the opposite conclusion in 1890. The states enacted a few laws on the subject before 1900 but many more since.

People divide over the major questions involved here. Jews object to the New Testament and to Christmas programs and other Christian exercises. Catholics and Protestants disagree upon the versions. Unbelievers object to all religious books. There is wide disagreement over the authority of the Bible, the nature of religion, and the relation between religion and morals.

Three legal positions can be identified. In twelve states and the District of Columbia the reading of the Bible is, without comment in some cases, required. In twenty-five states it is permitted; and in eight it is prohibited, usually on the ground that the Bible is a sectarian book. Three states have no law on the subject. Minnesota is one of the three states, and a Minnesota court decided that the mere reading of the Bible or hearing it read is not a sectarian exercise nor an act of worship. But courts in other states have come to the opposite conclusion, holding that reading the Bible without comment is not teaching and must therefore be considered an act of worship.

The separation of church and state is, as has been indicated, the legal concept which controls most of the decisions in the religious education field; and it is derived from the First Amendment to the federal Constitution which reads in part as follows: "Congress shall make no law respecting an establishment of religion or prohibiting the free exercise thereof." This inhibition of the powers of Congress is applied to the states by the Fourteenth Amendment, which forbids all state laws that would abridge the privileges and immunities of citizens of the United States. Neither the nation nor any state may "establish" any church or interfere with worship or the refusal to worship. This separation is one of the great achievements of the American nation and its people, but it has not prevented litigation over religion.

Two provisions that are intended to support the separation of church and state are included in many state constitutions. These declare that no public funds may be appropriated to sectarian or private school use and that no sectarian religion shall be taught in the public schools. The constitution of Nevada may serve as an example. It provides that "no sectarian instruction shall be imparted or tolerated" in any public school; and that "no public funds of any kind shall be used for sectarian purposes." In earlier times state aid to sectarian schools was so common that it was not often noticed. The present opposition to it is evidence of the outreaching of the public school to gain control of all education.

Constitutions and laws do not prevent churches and church schools from attempting to secure public aid or from the attempt to carry out sectarian purposes through the public schools. These efforts may not arise from any purpose to circumvent the law—although this also has occurred— but merely from the difficulty of determining the intent of the law. Courts also have the greatest difficulty in deciding what is sectarian and what is public.

Illustrations of the questions which come before the courts may be stated: May public school pupils, in a school exercise, for reasons of conscience and religion, refuse to salute the flag? On this question the United States Supreme Court in 1943 reversed the decision which it had reached in 1940. May a public school building be used for sectarian religious services in an emergency, or occasionally, or regularly? May religious apparel or robes be worn by teachers in a public school? Some courts have held that the wearing of a distinctive religious dress is a sectarian act. Some states have passed laws prohibiting the wearing of such garb by public school teachers while engaged in the work of the school. May a state or school district reimburse a private school for teaching pupils placed in the school by the public agency? May public school credit be given for instruction in religion obtained outside the school? Public universities frequently accept such credit. May pupils be released from public school exercises to receive religious instruction from private teachers? And may this instruction be given in the public school building? May free transportation to school, free textbooks, and free lunches be provided for private school pupils by the public authorities? This is a sufficient sample of school problems that arise from the separation of church and state.

Several court decisions in this area have aroused much interest; and none more than those dealing with released time for religious education. This movement has been in existence for a generation. It was sometimes named for Gary, Indiana, where it was developed early. It has now spread to cities and districts located in about forty states. In theory the public school has no obligation except to release the designated pupils at the proper times, usually one or more times a week. In fact some adjustment of the school program and some record-keeping are required, but perhaps no more than when part of a class is excused to practice music or prepare a play.

Serious objections have been charged against the program. It tends to classify the pupils into different faiths and unfaiths and to disturb the harmony of the school. The total number of released time pupils may be about 2,500,000, a small part of the total enrollment; and these are in most cases children who are already receiving religious instruction in church schools. But perhaps the most serious objection comes from those who see in the program an injury to the principle of separation of church and state and religious freedom. Some objectors are opposed to religion itself. It was members of this group who brought the well-known McCollum and Zorach suits.

The McCollum case from Champaign, Illinois, concerned classes in religion on released time which were held in the classrooms of the public schools. The supreme court of the state upheld the practice; but that decision was reversed by the United States Supreme Court (March 8, 1949). The use of rooms in the public school building for religious instruction was especially criticized by the highest court. But its dicta and ruling opinion raised a number of other questions about released time and left the whole issue in such a fog that lawyers and the attorneys general of some of the states were confused. As interpreted by the Champaign county court, it meant that released time programs were to be permitted if the classes did not meet in public school buildings.

The general tenor of the McCollum opinion was against cooperation and for complete *apartheid* or separation between state and church. Yet this opinion cited the Everson School bus case in which the Court had approved a New Jersey law permitting the public buses to transport children to parochial schools. This kind of legislation has been regarded as welfare legislation enacted under the police power of the state to protect children from inclement weather. It could be claimed that the Illinois children should not have been required to go to distant churches in inclement weather when their own classrooms were available and that school buildings are no more the property of the state than school buses.

The somewhat extreme illustration of the preceding paragraph may serve to emphasize the difference in the outlook of the Court in the Zorach from that in the McCollum case. *Zorach* v. *Clauson* on released time was decided by the highest court of New York (July 11, 1951) and on appeal by the United States Supreme Court on April 28, 1952. Both upheld the New York education law of 1940, which permits pupils under proper conditions to absent themselves from public schools for "religious observance and education." The State Commissioner of Education was given the duty of defining the conditions. The New York classes were not held in the school buildings. But it is the apparently wholly new attitude in the

Supreme Court's exposition of the meaning of separation of church and state that is surprising.

The Zorach opinion affirms that the prohibition of the First Amendment of an establishment of religion and of interference with the free exercise of religion is absolute. But the Court continues that this leaves wide areas of friendly cooperation, as when the policeman helps parishioners into their places of worship, when the city protects church property, when prayers are offered in legislative halls, when the President proclaims Thanksgiving Day, or when the Supreme Court itself opens each session with the supplication: "God save the United States and this Honorable Court." But the Court could have mentioned more important items, such as the exemption of church property from taxation and of gospel ministers from military service; the substitution of civilian for military service in the cases of conscientious objectors, the provision of chaplains in the armed forces and in penitentiaries, and the provision of religious education for the nation's wards including Indian children on the reservations. The opinion continues with an illustration of ways in which the public schools normally cooperate with the different faiths; and it adds: "When the State encourages religious instruction it follows the best of our traditions . . . [but] the government must be neutral when it comes to competition between the sects." After all this, it is disconcerting to read that "the government may not give religious instruction or blend sectarian with secular education."

The doctrine of the separation of church and state is one of the most beneficent but also one of the thorniest in American law. It is especially troublesome in its application to schools. Neither in the McCollum and Zorach suits nor in all the cases which have been before the courts has a final interpretation of the doctrine emerged. No one can know how the Supreme Court will decide the next case in which the circumstances will be a little different from any other. And there will be a next case.

Books and papers on this subject follow: Ward W. Keesecker in *School Life* (February, 1949; June, 1952) deals with United States Supreme Court decisions affecting education. There were few such cases before 1910, but an increasing number since that year. Several cases can be located in the following sources.

The Maine and Wisconsin Bible reading cases are in 38 Maine 376 (1854) and 76 Wisconsin 177 (1890); the flag-salute cases in 310 U. S. 586 (1940) and 319 U. S. 624 (1943). Laws forbidding the teaching of a foreign language in private schools were held unconstitutional in *Meyer* v. *Nebraska*, 262 U. S. 390 (1923); and so also a law compelling children between the ages of eight and sixteen years to attend public schools only, in 268 U. S. 510 (1925). A New Jersey law to permit public transportation of parochial children was sustained in the so-called Everson case, 330 U. S. 1 (1947). The McCollum case is in 330 U. S. 203 (1948) and *Zorach* v. *Clauson* in 343 U. S. 306 (1952).

Other authors and publications are the following: William W. Brickman has prepared bibliographies and comment on religion and education and the relations of school, church, and state in *School and Society,* March 27, 1948; May 6, 1950; and October 25, 1952.

Edward A. Fitzpatrick, "Religion in Public Education," *American School Board Journal,* June 1953, and Clarence Linton, "The Function of the Public School in Dealing with Religion," *School Executive,* March, 1954, deal with publications by the American Council on Education, the Educational Policies Commission, and the John Dewey Society on the teaching of religion and social values. Reinhold Niebuhr, "Religion and Education," declares that "objective" teaching of religious history leaves out religion, for this involves commitment. Some other titles are: Ervin L. Shaver, "Three Years after the Champaign Case," *Religious Education,* January–February, 1951; D. W. Tieszen, "Legal Concepts Concerning Religious Influence in Public Education," *Teachers College Record,* November, 1953; Luther A. Weigle, "The Crisis of Religion in Education; Schools Cannot be Neutral as to God," *Vital Speeches,* December 15, 1953; *William* C. Bower, *Church and State in Education,* Chicago, the University of Chicago Press [1940]; R. Freeman Butts, *The American Tradition in Religion and Education,* Boston, 1950; Alvin W. Johnson and F. H. Yost, *Separation of Church and State in the United States,* Minneapolis, the University of Minnesota Press [1948]; F. Ernest Johnson, Editor, *American Education and Religion,* New York, the Institute for Religious and Social Studies [1952]; R. H. Martin, *Our Public Schools—Christian or Secular,* Pittsburgh, Pennsylvania, the National Reform Association [1952]; J. M. O'Neill, *Religion and Education under the Constitution,* New York [1949]; Leo Pfeffer, *Church, State, and Freedom,* Boston, 1953; Vivian T. Thayer, *Religion in Public Education,* New York, 1947; *The Attack upon the American Secular School,* Boston, 1951.

8. FEDERAL AID FOR EDUCATION

The final rejection of the Blair Bill and the adoption of the second Morrill Act (1890) were the actions of the same Congress. This was a strange reversal of the views held by Congress a century earlier. At that time, the Ordinance of 1785 and the sixteenth section grants for common schools, made to Ohio and all later states, declared in effect that the earliest schooling, and not vocational education, was useful and necessary preparation for citizenship and worthy of federal aid.

World War I revealed some of the deficiencies of education. The war excitement and the growth of national administrative agencies, which resulted from the prosecution of the war, caused many to look to the federal government for a remedy. By 1920 Congress had before it seventy education bills and resolutions, many of them involving serious issues of educational administration. One group urged the creation of a Department of Education "with power to shape national educational policy." This language, wholly contrary to history and practice, offended many. But there was a strong demand for the consolidation of the multitude of educational activities that were carried on in thirty or forty federal bureaus, divisions, and departments. Many also urged federal subsidies for general education in elementary and high schools.

The group which sought centralized administration might disagree, it is evident, with those who wanted federal aid, perhaps with little or no federal control. Many questions divided the public, questions of aid to private schools, the division of funds between the races, the matching of federal subsidies, and the educational standards which had to be met by the states.

The Smith-Towner Bill, which took a position on such issues, was introduced into Congress in 1919. This bill had the support of the National Education Association. When it failed to pass, other bills on the same pattern, changed to meet objections and gain support, were introduced in each session of Congress.

The Smith-Towner Bill was designed, first, to create a Department of Education and the office of Secretary of Education in the President's Cabinet; secondly, to provide financial assistance to the states for general education; and thirdly, to erect standards which the states had to meet in order to participate in the financial benefits.

The bill proposed the appropriation of $100,000,000 annually to be spent on five objects: the removal of illiteracy, Americanization, teachers' salaries, physical and health education, and teacher preparation. Definite portions of the whole sum were assigned to each object. Formulas for determining the amount to be given each state were included.

To share in the subsidies, a state would have been compelled to devote equal amounts from its own revenue to the same object. This is the matching principle. A school term of twenty weeks, with compulsory attendance, was demanded. English was to be the language of instruction. Only public schools were to be aided.

This last item was to be the first point of attack upon the provisions. Parochial school interests demanded a fair share of the proceeds and Catholic organizations have persistently fought this and similar bills. Many public school people opposed the control features of the bill and the matching principle, both of which were included in the Smith-Hughes law. The bill was called a war emergency measure put together to gain votes. After 150 years of local and state effort, to turn toward a nationally supported and directed system, exposed to all the storms of national politics, was felt to be a momentous change, indeed a denial of the American past. But those who shuddered at this prospect may not have considered all the personal and local and business politics which normally sway homemade school policies.

Changing conditions, it was declared, may also require the formation of a new tradition. The increasing differences in educational opportunity in different states are such a condition. Some states are rich in children and poor in dollars. The nation drains money from the states and a fair share should be returned to provide education, where it is most needed. The high school enrollment is growing and with this growth a diversified program is demanded. This is too expensive for some states.

Of the organizations supporting the bills, the National Education Association has been the most active. Various Catholic organizations have been opposed. The American Federation of Labor has taken a similar position by declaring for equal distribution of the funds to public and private schools. The Federation has at times favored a minimum foundation program similar to a plan recently proposed by Beardsley Ruml. This new proposal, by the inventor of the "withholding plan" of income tax payment, would have the government make a flat grant annually to every child of school age. This would operate like the foundation program used in many states. It would provide equally for all races and creeds in public and private schools alike. It would be costly; but it would undercut much of the opposition to previous bills. The administration of the Ruml plan would be simple and wholly in the hands of the states. One would hear less of socialism and nationalization from the Chamber of Commerce of the United States and the organized taxpayers but more of the expense of education. In this connection it is well to remember that "the richest country in the world with the highest standard of living" does not devote as large a percentage of its income to education as some other countries.

A high point in the movement to pass a federal aid bill was reached in 1949 when the Senate adopted S.246 by a vote of 58 to 15. This bill provided for a subsidy of $300,000,000; and most of the controls had been eliminated. President Truman had promised to sign the bill but the "delaying tactics" of the chairman of the Committee on Education and Labor kept it from coming up for a vote in the House.

For books and papers see the following: L. A. Beman, *The Towner-Sterling Bill*, New York, 1922, being Volume I, Number 5, of "The Reference Shelf," published by the H. W. Wilson Company. The *Congressional Record* and some of the large city papers are important sources, as are also *School and Society*, the *Educational Review*, the *Catholic Educational Review*, and other educational journals.

Other titles include Frank N. Freeman, "Federal Youth Agencies and the Public Schools," *School and Society*, June 20, 1942; Charles J. Stanley, "Organized Interests and Federal Aid to Education," *School and Society*, January 6, 1951; Edward M. Tuttle, "A New and Different Approach to Federal Aid for Education," *American School Board Journal*, February, 1955.

9. INVENTION AND THE SCHOOL

Spectacular inventions have lately come to the aid of the schools. These include the motion picture, the radio, and television. But indeed the school itself is an aggregate of inventions, among which we must count the arts which the school teaches, writing, arithmetic, drawing, as well as the means with which the school teaches, the blackboard, map, and laboratory. All had to be invented.

Many inventions used by the school were not, like the blackboard, created for the school but were developed outside. Hard roads, the school bus, and the resulting transportation of pupils have transformed the rural school and education. There was some pupil transportation by means of horse-drawn vehicles and the railroad, and Massachusetts had a transportation law in 1869. But the bus has made the great change, substituting the comfortable, well-equipped consolidated schools for the drafty, miserable, one-room cabins which H. G. Wells decried fifty years ago. The process is not complete and some sections may have to be served by the school helicopter.

We have seen how other inventions, the tractor and automatic machinery, are increasing the size of farms and decreasing the number of people who live on them. Those who remain must acquire a science of agriculture that was unknown in 1900, and this is taught in the consolidated school. At present about one child in every five or six rides to school in a public bus. There is a considerable body of laws on the subject and school transportation is a business operation and an administrative problem.

The importance of lighting for learning at school and in the home was noticed in an early chapter. Electricity furnishes both light and power for schools. It is pleasant for teachers to think that an American high school teacher, Elihu Thomson (1853–1937), contributed to the invention of the arc lamp; and that he and a fellow teacher, Edwin J. Houston (1847–1914), formed the Thomson-Houston Company, the forerunner of the General Electric Company. Edison in 1879 produced the incandescent lamp which he and others gradually perfected. Electric power, because it is safe and easy to operate and control, is also of great value to schools. Many school hours are daylight hours and in some cases electric power may be even more useful in schools than electric light. Each now seems indispensable, but until the day before yesterday they were unknown.

Of all inventions, those which aid communication are most useful in teaching, for teaching is communication. Among the recent devices promoting communication are the phonograph, tape-recorder, and the big three, motion pictures, radio, and television. The telegraph and telephone are older and they also had the great educational effect of bringing the world closer to the school; but the big three have brought the world into the classroom.

In the long procession of history all this is contemporary. Edison worked on the phonograph and the motion picture in the eighties and nineties. In 1894 his phonograph had progressed only to the point where with earphones one could hear a thin metallic voice.

Early experiments in the making of motion pictures were directed to the study of animal locomotion. In 1878 Muybridge placed a row of cameras along the old Palo Alto race track in such a way that the horse broke a string and successively snapped his own pictures as he sped along. Eastman's celluloid film and the camera taking instantaneous pictures were great contributions. The principle of the motion picture is illustrated by children's toys consisting of pictures on a rotating wheel or, most simply, by the double-blinker traffic signals in which the light seems to move from one position to the other.

Marconi, with the Hertzian waves as a starting-point, developed radio communication and sent a radiogram across the Atlantic in 1901. Station KDKA broadcast the national election returns in 1920. Photography and radio in combination produced television. In the United States commercial television began in 1941. Educational television is still in its infancy, but a number of stations, about a dozen in 1955, are in operation and others are on the way. It is, in many ways, a new world into which children are being born and a new school is being prepared for them. In our enthusiasm some things are to be remembered. One is that the techniques of using these new instruments in teaching have to be learned. There are books and there are courses in colleges of education that should be diligently studied by teachers. In the second place, the value of any teaching depends upon the content. The radio, motion picture, and television transmit evil and trivial messages as readily as good and important ones. The old problem of the value of what is communicated is still in the center of the philosophy of education. The still picture, blackboard drawing, diagram, map, outline, and other old devices are still useful and may in given circumstances be most effective.

Books which were invented long ago are still the most useful furnishings of the school. They are always accessible, at one's elbow, usable by one person alone. They can be referred to, read, or studied in detail; they do not, like lectures or moving pictures, give only fleeting impressions; and while the author is not at hand to explain what he meant there is no question about what he said.

Textbooks are the most necessary books in schools. The textbook outlines and explains its subject and by means of reading-lists directs the search for further knowledge. It is the "assistant-teacher" and the art of skilfully using and not abusing the textbook is a fine acquirement for any teacher. Its sisters are the handbook, dictionary, and encyclopedia; and this quartette leads the way to the original sources of knowledge.

There is a new school to which the children may go and it is for parents and teachers to make it better than the old. The school is a complex of inventions and some of the teaching aids are so new that their possibilities have not yet been fully explored.

Books on new teaching aids include the following: Edgar Dale, *Audio-Visual Methods in Teaching*, New York, the Dryden Press, 1954; Ellsworth C. Dent, *The Audio-Visual Handbook*, Chicago, Society for Visual Education, Inc., 1942; Anna Verona Dorris, *Visual Instruction in Public Schools*, Boston, 1928. Other books on teaching are: Jacques Barzun, *Teacher in America*, Boston, 1945; Gilbert Highet, *The Art of Teaching*, New York, 1950.

Among books on adult education are: Paul L. Essert, *Creative Leadership of Adult Education*, New York, 1951; Margaret T. Hodgen, *Workers' Education in England and the United States*, New York, 1925; Homer

Kempfer and Grace S. Wright, *One Hundred Evening Schools,* Washington, U. S. Government Printing Office, 1949 (with bibliography), Office of Education Bulletin, 1949, Number 4; Harry A. and Bonaro W. Overstreet, *Leaders for Adult Education,* New York, American Association for Adult Education, 1941; Charles A. Prosser, *Evening Industrial Schools,* Chicago, American Technical Society, 1951 (revised edition); Paul H. Sheats and Others, *Adult Education, the Community Approach,* New York, 1953; Edward L. Thorndike, *Adult Learning,* New York, 1928.

10. ADULT EDUCATION

A list of the forms of adult education has been compiled by UNESCO. It contains twenty-six titles extending alphabetically from "Agricultural Extension" to "Workers' Education." All types together enrolled an estimated 27,000,000 persons or one of every four or five of the adult population. The most important of these types, as judged by the work they do and the numbers whom they serve, are doubtless agricultural extension and the public evening schools.

Adult education in the form of private evening schools began soon after the settlements, but many new beginnings were made in the nineteenth century. One recalls the lyceum and mechanic's institute movements, both of which left a permanent deposit in institutions that are still active. Examples are the Franklin Institute of Philadelphia, the Brooklyn Institute of Arts and Sciences, the Athenaeum of Rochester, and the Lowell Institute of Boston. The Chautauqua developed later, and for a time the Chautauqua Institution (1873) held a university charter.

Cities have long provided adult education through lectures and evening schools. Such public services were in operation in New York, Louisville, Baltimore, and doubtless other cities before 1850. Ohio in 1839 passed a law permitting boards to maintain public evening schools. Cincinnati had an evening high school in 1856 and this example was followed, but at all times evening elementary schools seem to have been more numerous than evening high schools. New York in a recent year had forty-four evening elementary and sixteen evening high schools.

Before the close of the nineteenth century the off-campus teaching of university classes was introduced from England, where it had been started about 1865. Most of the students were not regularly matriculated and were not candidates for a degree. Thus the first university extension teaching was genuine adult education. It was received in the United States with great acclaim and was promoted by a professor of history, Herbert B. Adams

(1850–1901), and a librarian, Melvil Dewey (1851–1931), as shown in Chapter XVII. The universities which first took it up included the University of Pennsylvania, the state universities of Wisconsin, Minnesota, and California, and the new University of Chicago whose president, William Rainey Harper (1856–1906), had long been active in taking learning to the people.

The present period of adult education, it may be considered, took its rise in the early decades of the present century when the Smith-Lever law became effective and when the university extension movement, which had temporarily declined, was revived. The new forms of mass communication developed about the same time and added a new dimension to the movement. The "Wisconsin idea," as it was called, developed in this period. The University of Wisconsin took practical and technical aid of many kinds to the dairymen, gardeners, and other active citizens in every part of the state. It is this kind of service which, as we have seen, has been severely criticized but without greatly affecting the practice. Upwards of seventy institutions are present members of a national University Extension Association.

Correspondence courses are offered by some universities but much oftener by private correspondence schools of varied quality. The numbers of correspondence students in any year runs into the millions. The courses may be excellent or they may be worthless, and the subjects treated run the whole gamut of vocational, technical, liberal, and avocational interests. Before paying the substantial fee for a correspondence course, it is well to be sure that one has the time and will power to pursue it; and it is prudent also to get information about the school's reputation for honesty and competence.

Workers' education is carried on by labor unions and notably by the International Ladies' Garment Workers. Colleges and universities have in the past provided summer schools for union members. Bryn Mawr College near Philadelphia and the University of Wisconsin opened such schools about 1921. Libraries and museums conduct adult education for all classes and ages. Some of these institutions arrange educational exhibits, conduct guided tours, and provide classrooms and even teachers where there is sufficient demand. Some libraries offer the public a skilled reader's adviser to aid those who wish to follow an organized course of reading and study. And they cooperate with all schools, clubs, and other organizations in arranging special collections of source materials for use.

Adult education aids people to prepare for new jobs and, as occupations are constantly changing, to hold the jobs they have. People also need to become better informed and more intelligent about public affairs, domestic politics, and foreign policy. As more people gain more leisure, and perhaps with the use of atomic energy a vast amount of leisure, adult education may help them to use their time constructively. To fulfil these tasks requires improved organization and more effective publicity. At present in any given city few people know where the adult classes are, what they offer and demand, or how to collect enough applicants to form a class in any desired subject.

11. THE WHITE HOUSE CONFERENCE

In his State of the Union Message in January, 1954, President Eisenhower called a White House Conference to study the condition of education in school and college and to report in November, 1955. It was, however, decided to confine attention to elementary and secondary schools. Local and state meetings to consider needs and to formulate plans were held throughout the nation. According to reliable information 500,000 persons participated; and this is an indication of the interest that was shown.

State educational meetings were based upon local investigations and proposals and a distillation of these reports was taken to the national meeting in Washington. Connecticut was one of the first states to report; and her problems were the universal ones, the shortages of teachers, buildings, and finances, and the lack of effective ways and means to gain and hold a lively and well-informed public interest in the schools. These needs were generally known to school administrators, but they had been unable to convince and arouse the people. Among the reasons why the necessary funds could not be obtained were the rapid increase in school attendance, financial inflation, poor districting, obsolete tax laws and restrictions, propaganda against the "tax-spenders," direct and indirect attacks upon public education as noted in Sections 5 and 6 of this chapter, and actual poverty in some states.

The Conference met in Washington during the week of November 28, 1955, with delegates numbering nearly 2,000, in attendance from every state and territory. The chairman was Neil McElroy, a business executive; and two-thirds of the members were not presently engaged in educational work. Besides the delegates chosen by the state conferences, many of them educators, a subcommittee of the Conference worked for several months to select delegates from over 200 business and welfare bodies including the National Grange, the General Federation of Women's Clubs, and the International Association of Machinists. It is true that some of the doctors, housewives, and farmers who were selected had once been teachers; but the Conference was not "stacked" as one large midwestern daily paper charged.

Large claims were made for the Conference. President Eisenhower was to have said that the Conference made "the most thorough, widespread, and concerted study of education" ever made by the American people. The Commissioner of Education, Samuel M. Brownell, said that the program had led to "the greatest amount of activity on behalf of education in history." These statements probably mean that the Conference brought together the knowledge and wisdom of many of those who had studied education long and skilfully and were most concerned for its improvement.

The plan formulated for the state and national conferences was that they should primarily deal with (1) the need for school construction; but they expanded their mandate to include also (2) educational aims or what the schools should accomplish; (3) economical and efficient organization including the proper districting of the states; (4) the recruitment and retention of good teachers; (5) the financing of schools; and (6) the maintenance of public interest in schools. Reports upon each of these topics were prepared in the general conference sessions.

A full account of the conclusions will be found in the printed final report. Little that was new to educators was presented, but at least one surprising vote was taken as we shall see. The stimulation of public interest in schools was an achievement; and if local and state conferences are continued as planned in some areas, the White House Conference will have been a success. But it must be remembered that to enlist the interest of 165,000,000 busy people is a vast undertaking. At present after the longtime efforts of the National Congress of Parents and Teachers, the six years of work by the National Citizens Commission, and two years by the White House Conference, which had a distinctly "good press," it is likely that millions are still uninformed and unconcerned.

To gain and hold good teachers the Conference looked to higher salaries, improved status and better working conditions. An unintended comment on present working conditions may be read into a pronouncement of the New York State Association of Secondary School Principals. At their meeting, held since the Conference adjourned, they declared that discipline is today a major and an increasing problem in schools. Oversize classes and too many of them assigned to the individual teacher is a condition that affects not only the discipline of the school but also the supply of teachers and thus the schools are caught in a vicious circle.

The surprising vote of the Conference mentioned above was the two to one majority in favor of federal aid to the states. The majority was so large because of the urgent need for school buildings; and it does not represent the proportion of the delegates who were in favor of an annual federal appropriation for operating expenses. The present administration has promised to support a plan to aid school construction, a new plan substituted for the unacceptable proposal made earlier. The buildings are needed now. Several years have been wasted in the face of clear knowledge that they would be needed. An informative report on the Conference by a delegate was prepared by Bice Clemow, a newspaper publisher, for the *Saturday Review*, December 21, 1955.

That the Conference could not deal with all the present problems is not surprising. It will, however, be appropriate to name again a few already mentioned in earlier pages. Not included were such topics as the following: (1) the issue of racial integration; (2) the need for more drivers', health, and general safety education; (3) the financial condition of public and private colleges including the teachers colleges; (4) higher standards of academic education for high school teachers; (5) improved science teaching and more effective recruiting of science students.

INDEX

561

Binet, Alfred, 209, 399; use of Binet test, 387
Blackboard introduced, 166, 191
Blair, Henry W., 273; Blair bill, 273, 279, 300
Bloomfield, Meyer, 446
Blow, Susan, kindergarten promoter, 207, 334
Bode, Boyd H., 369, 396, 403
Boone, Richard G., 329, 331
Boston Latin School, 35, 56, 58, 238, 241
Boston Public Library, 425
Boston school examination of 1845, 396
Boston Vocation Bureau, 446
Bowditch, H. P., 210
Brackett, Anna C., 329, 334
Brainard, John, 213
Brameld, Theodore, 369
Brewer, John M., 446
Brickman, William W., 522
Bridgman, Laura, 129
Briggs, Thomas, 510
Brooks, Charles, 166
Brooks, Edward, 35, 161, 323
Brougham, Henry, 178
Brownell, Samuel M., 558
Brown University, 62
Bryan, William Jennings, 109
Bryan, William Lowe, with Noble Harter, a learning experiment, 397
Buchanan, President James, vetoes first Morrill bill, 292, 299
Buckingham, B. R., 413
Buel, Jesse, promoter of agricultural education, 413
Buffalo Technical High School, 453
Bureau for Refugees, Freedmen, and Abandoned Lands, the Freedmen's Bureau, 275 f.
Burk, Frederic, 393, 429
Burlamaqui, J. J., 86
Burrowes, Thomas, 237
Business colleges, 254
Butler, Nicholas Murray, 212, 331, 337, 398; editor Educational Review, 329

California, beginnings of public education, 152–154
Caliver, Ambrose, 384
Calkins, Norman A., 323
Carnegie, Andrew, gifts to libraries, 428
Carnegie Corporation, 428
Carnegie Endowment for International Peace, 496
Carnegie Foundation for the Advancement of Teaching, 472; on college athletics, 481
Carter, James Gordon, educational leader in Massachusetts, 157–158, 177

Carver, George W., Tuskegee scientist and teacher, 282
Catholic high school development, 455 f.
Catholic immigration, 138
Catholic Orphan Asylum, 137
Cattell, James McKeen, psychologist and educational publisher, 397, 399, 419, 510
Census of school children, 377
Chambers, M. M., investigator of legal status of colleges and universities, 474; author Youth-Serving Organizations, 519
Charters, Wallace Werrett, 416
Chautauqua summer school, 476, 555
Cheever, Ezekiel, 44, 54
Chelsea Vocational High School, New York City, 453 f.
Child labor, in colonies, 22–23; general relations with education, 380–383; proposed amendment to Constitution, 383
Child study, 204, 208–211
Children's Bureau, 383, 530
Childs, John L., 369
Chipman, Nathaniel, 93
Chorodov, Frank, 541–542
Cincinnati College, early engineering courses, 288
Civilian Conservation Corps, 493, 502, 514–516; establishment, 514; organization and purpose, 515; education in the camps, 515 f.; accomplishments, 516
Clapp, F. L., 417
Clark University, 209, 419
Claxton, P. P., 504
Clinton, George, 118
Closing of schools in the great depression, 513
Coeducation, 473
Cohen, Morris R., 511
Colburn, Dana R., 175
Colburn, Warren, 176, 415; author, Intellectual Arithmetic, 186
College Entrance Examination Board, 195, 256
Colleges, colonial entrance requirements, 58; list, 59; curriculum, 60; charters, 61–62; relations to churches, 61–62; state, 62–63; student bread riots, 63; opposition to colleges, 95; early national period, 95–97; deism in, 96; states attempting to take over private colleges, 97 f.
Columbia University, 331
Combe, George, 348
Comenius, 65, 66
Committee of Public Information, World War I propaganda agency, 504
Committee of Ten NEA, 256, 345, 349, 350, 440

Keating-Owen child-labor bill, 383
Keller, Franklin, 453
Keller, Helen, 389
Ker, David, 102
Kern, O. G., 302
Kerschensteiner, Georg, 451
Kilpatrick, William H., 369
Kindergarten, American type, 204; criticism
of Froebel's theory, 205–206; introduction,
206–208; developments in St. Louis, 207,
334
Kirkpatrick, Edward A., 328
Kirkpatrick, J. E., critic of college adminis-
tration, 479
Knapp, Seaman A., 251, 302
Knox, Samuel, writer on national education,
81, 94
Kotschnig, Walter, 486
Krüsi, Hermann, Jr., 175, 217, 218 f., 224
Ku Klux Klan, 511

⁓Labor and education, colonial, 29 f.; urban
labor class, 110; labor unions favor public
education, 119; and the high school, 226
LaFollette, Robert M., 503
Lamb, Andrew, 68, 71
Lancaster, Joseph, 136, 139; opinions about,
140
Lancasterian schools, 135; faults, 136, 430;
development in New York City, 137; and
Philadelphia, 138 f.; spread over the na-
tion, 139; in St. Louis, 332
Land-grant colleges, variety of educational
plans, 295 f.; indecision in administration,
297 f.; admission of women, 298; aid from
experiment stations, 299; growth, 306–
309
Larsen, Roy, 539
Lathrop, John H., 289
Latin schools, curriculum, 56–58; origins, 49;
transplanted from England, 51; Locke's
view of, 51; condition in the South, 52; in
New England, 53; in Middle Colonies, 55
Leacock, Stephen, 477
League of Nations, 361
Lee, General Robert E., proposed collegiate
business courses, 475
Lexington, Mass., site of the first state
normal school, 163
Library and school, 424–428; college librar-
ies, 424; semi-public and public libraries,
425; early school libraries, 426
Library of Congress, 94, 425
Liew, C. C., Herbartian educator, 347
Lincoln, Abraham, 109, 381; signed the
Morrill bill, 293
Link, Henry C., psychologist, studied
people's reading habits, 420

Literacy, definitions of literacy and illiteracy,
383; conditions, 384
Locke, John, 31; on Latin grammar schools
in England, 51; theory of government, 86;
the *Essay Concerning Human Under-
standing*, 493
Lord, Asa D., 247
Lowell, Abbott Lawrence, 490
Lowth, Robert, 36
Lyceums, 187

MacClure, William, 128
McElroy, Neil, chairman, White House
Conference on Education, 557
McGill University, 286
McMurry, Charles, 347
McMurry, Frank, 347, 415
Madison, James, 108, 361, 375; favored a
national university, 94
Main types of schools, diagram, 444
Mann, Horace, 11, 124, 127, 129, 134, 140,
225, 276, 348, 354, 377, 426; on education in colonial Mass., 158–159; on contemporary conditions, 159; curriculum
views, 159; created interest in public edu-
cation, 161; founded *Common School
Journal*, 161; controversy with Boston
masters, 164; religious controversy, 164–
165; his influence, 165–167; opinion of
normal schools, 166; recommends teaching
of music, 185; on child labor, 381; president, Antioch College, 473
Manual labor education at land-grant colleges, 297
Marcet, Mrs. Jane Haldemand, author of
popular science books, 188, 223
Marshall, Leon C., 505
Martin, George H., 451
Mason, Lowell, 175; music supervisor in
Boston schools, 185
Massachusetts, school law of 1642, 29–30;
of 1647, 41; copied in Connecticut, 54; of
1789 admitting girls to district schools,
162; establishes state normal schools, 162–
163; attack on state normal schools, 163;
of 1827, prohibiting sectarian teaching,
164
Mather, Cotton, 65
Maxwell, William H., superintendent, 401 f.
Meade, Richard K., 290
Meiklejohn, Alexander, of the Experimental
College, University of Wisconsin, 493
Meriam, J. L., experimental school, Uni-
versity of Missouri, 394
Metropolitan Vocational High School, New
York City, 453 f.
Meumann, Ernst, 209
Michigan, early history of schools, 150–151